J.P. Morgan & Co. and the Crisis of Capitalism

During the interwar period, J.P. Morgan was the most important bank in the world and at the crossroads of US politics, international relations, and finance. In *J.P. Morgan & Co. and the Crisis of Capitalism*, Martin Horn brings us the first in-depth history of how J.P. Morgan responded to the greatest crisis in the history of financial capitalism, shedding new light on the Great Depression, the New Deal, and the coming of World War II. Horn shows how J.P. Morgan & Co. as a business responded to the crash of 1929 and the Depression, including its part in the Wall Street Crash, arguing that the Morgan partners misread the seriousness of the crash. He also offers new insights into the interactions of politics and finance, exploring J.P. Morgan's relationship with the Hoover administration and the bank's clash with Roosevelt over New Deal legislation.

Martin Horn is Associate Dean of Graduate Studies and Research in the Faculty of Humanities at McMaster University. His previous publications include *Britain, France and the Financing of the First World War* (2002) and, with Dr. Talbot Imlay, *The Politics of Industrial Collaboration during World War II: Ford France, Vichy and Nazi Germany* (2014).

J.P. Morgan & Co. and the Crisis of Capitalism

From the Wall Street Crash to World War II

Martin Horn

McMaster University, Ontario

CAMBRIDGE
UNIVERSITY PRESS

CAMBRIDGE
UNIVERSITY PRESS

University Printing House, Cambridge CB2 8BS, United Kingdom

One Liberty Plaza, 20th Floor, New York, NY 10006, USA

477 Williamstown Road, Port Melbourne, VIC 3207, Australia

314–321, 3rd Floor, Plot 3, Splendor Forum, Jasola District Centre, New Delhi – 110025, India

103 Penang Road, #05–06/07, Visioncrest Commercial, Singapore 238467

Cambridge University Press is part of the University of Cambridge.

It furthers the University's mission by disseminating knowledge in the pursuit of education, learning, and research at the highest international levels of excellence.

www.cambridge.org
Information on this title: www.cambridge.org/9781108498371
DOI: 10.1017/9781108653602

© Martin Horn 2022

First published 2022

Printed in the United Kingdom by TJ Books Limited, Padstow Cornwall

A catalogue record for this publication is available from the British Library.

Library of Congress Cataloging-in-Publication Data
Names: Horn, Martin, 1959– author.
Title: J.P. Morgan & Co. and the crisis of capitalism : from the Wall Street crash to World War II / Martin Horn, McMaster University, Ontario.
Description: Cambridge, United Kingdom ; New York, NY : Cambridge University Press, 2022. | Includes bibliographical references and index.
Identifiers: LCCN 2021037842 (print) | LCCN 2021037843 (ebook) | ISBN 9781108498371 (hardback) | ISBN 9781108653602 (ebook)
Subjects: LCSH: J.P. Morgan & Co. | Banks and banking – United States – History – 20th century. | Investment banking – United States – History – 20th century. | Capitalism – United States – History – 20th century. | United States – Economic conditions – 1918–1945. | BISAC: BUSINESS & ECONOMICS / Economic History
Classification: LCC HG2481 .H67 2022 (print) | LCC HG2481 (ebook) | DDC 332.10973–dc23
LC record available at https://lccn.loc.gov/2021037842
LC ebook record available at https://lccn.loc.gov/2021037843

ISBN 978-1-108-49837-1 Hardback

To Lisa, Madelaine, and Miranda

Contents

Figures and Tables

Figures

Tables

Acknowledgements

This is a book about bankers that has been too long in gestation. Less promising opening sentences may be imagined but a search would be needed. There is a view that bankers and banking are grey men (almost always men) conducting a grey business, hardly worth a book. If a book there must be, it, like its subjects, will be dull. I hope that readers will find that this book is not dull, for its subjects and its time are not. One encounter with the J.P. Morgan & Co. partner Russell C. Leffingwell will dispel any notion of the banker as a grey man. If readers do find the book dull, that verdict, like the gestation, should be laid at my feet.

Scholars have generally been uneasy about bankers. Some of this has been due to the abiding strength of Marxist thought in the academy, which, while appreciating that the banker was necessary to move along the dialectic, also regards the banker as emblematic of the persistence of capitalism and its evils. Some of this has been down to a fear that historians who work on banks have been captured either by the bank or by the bankers. Authorized histories – which this is not – are often seen as tainted. Some of this has been a result of the trends that have reshaped history as a discipline. Over time, the fissuring of "That Noble Dream," which has been positive for so many who were ignored or written out of history, has relegated bankers – never a popular field of inquiry even in the days when history was about great white men doing great things –further down the sporting table.

Perhaps this is because one problem encountered in writing about a bank is the archives. Unlike public archives such as The National Archives, UK, at Kew, company archives remain at the disposal of the firm. As J.P. Morgan & Co. was a private partnership until April 1940, where this book leaves off, the records of the firm belonged both to the partners and to the bank. Happily, this has meant the survival of several major collections of archival material, especially concerning the three most important Morgan partners of the 1930s: J.P. Morgan Jr., Thomas W. Lamont, and Leffingwell. Each left copious documentation. In Lamont's case, the finding aid to his papers runs into the hundreds of pages. Less happily, the partnership kept no records of its weekly meetings, and the other Morgan partners' impress is not as detectable in the surviving archival material. Some of this weakness is offset by material held in The Morgan Library in New York. These core collections have been supplemented by research conducted in archives in the United States and in Britain. I would like to thank all of the archives referenced in the bibliography for permission to use their manuscript collections.

I am indebted to various individuals who have helped bring the book to fruition. Archivists are wonderful to deal with; they want scholars to learn from and use their collections. All of those whose assistance I relied on I wish to thank for their generosity of spirit and time. Special thanks go to the staff and personnel at the Baker Library (Harvard), The Morgan Library, and the Herbert Hoover Presidential Library. Karl Taylor, who is not an archivist, deserves particular note. Working on his own history of Nelson Dean Jay, an American partner in Morgan & Cie., in Paris, he brought to my attention the existence of the Jay papers now held at Knox College. To him and to the college, my thanks.

Others have aided by reading what I have written and providing informed, pithy commentary that has improved the book. My sometime collaborator Talbot Imlay and my colleagues Pamela Swett and John Weaver have all read substantial chunks of the manuscript. Their remarks strengthened the book immeasurably. Stephen Schuker kindly gave of his time to share his unrivalled knowledge one night in Charlottesville.

One historian falls into a special category of thanks due. I never met the late Vincent Carosso, the author of the authoritative study of the Morgan bank down to 1913. He had begun work on a successor volume and collected considerable material in the pursuit of this aim, which is now available as the Carosso papers in The Morgan Library; however, he did not get far in writing his sequel. I am quite sure that he would have written a very different study from what readers will find in these pages. I am indebted to his pioneering research.

Stephanie Corazza, Brittany Gataveckas, and Katarina Todić, exemplary graduate students one and all, and now holding well-deserved doctorates, assisted in the research. I am grateful to each of them. Finally, at various times, and in various places, scholarly audiences listened to what I had to say, forcing reflection with their comments and questions, which were always beneficial. To those who participated, my thanks.

Michael Watson, the executive publisher for history and trade, at Cambridge University Press was encouraging in his thoughts about the manuscript and patient as the book moved from idea, to prospectus, to sample chapters, and to submission past the deadline. To him and to his team at Cambridge University Press, my gratitude. To the anonymous reviewers, I am grateful for their positive assessment as well as the directions suggested.

My wife, Lisa Pasternak, was instrumental. She read every word of the manuscript while balancing her busy career as a municipal lawyer. Without her input, the book would be much impoverished.

The book was finished as the COVID-19 pandemic struck. Readers will notice that nothing is said of this crisis and capitalism. As the human tragedy of the coronavirus unfolds, it is too early, too raw, too visceral, to make generalizations about our current crisis and the crisis of the capitalism in the 1930s. More distance is required, not least as we hope that the pandemic will be mastered.

Introduction

Late in February 1930, Owen Young journeyed by private railcar to Arizona. Young was at the height of his fame as a General Electric executive, as the founder of the Radio Corporation of America (RCA), and as an international statesman whose name adorned the just-concluded Young Plan. *Time* magazine named him man of the year in 1929, and he was bruited as a possible presidential candidate in 1932.[1] Discussion with his travelling companion, Everett Case, turned to Young's friend, J.P. Morgan Jr. (Jack Morgan), the senior partner of J.P. Morgan & Co. Young thought that it was a pity that Jack Morgan was so little known to the American public, for J.P. Morgan & Co. was "the most important banking house in the world with the power of affecting the lives of people in this country and throughout the world." A decade later, Morris Ernst, a prominent New York lawyer and the general counsel of the American Civil Liberties Union from 1929 to 1955, wrote another Morgan partner, Russell C. Leffingwell. Ernst mused: "I think your house has a responsibility that is practically superhuman, and assuming complete honesty and ability can never be met to the satisfaction of society."[2] Young was an intimate of the Morgan partners, Ernst a critic who believed that the Morgan part in American life was baleful. Both agreed that J.P. Morgan & Co.'s influence was pervasive. Yet there is no account of the bank during the period, though references to J.P. Morgan & Co., its partners, and its doings populate the pages of many histories.[3] This book corrects that omission.

---

[1] Josephine Young Case and Everett Needham Case, *Owen D. Young and American Enterprise*, Boston: David R. Godine, 1982, is the standard biography.

[2] Everett N. Case, 28 February 1930, St. Lawrence University (SLU), Owen D. Young papers (ODY), Box 976, Folder 2095; Morris Ernst to Leffingwell, 13 February 1940, Yale University Library (YUL), Russell C. Leffingwell MS (RCL), Series I, Box 2, Folder 36.

[3] Ron Chernow's survey, *The House of Morgan*, New York: Atlantic Monthly Press, 1990, devotes several chapters to the bank in the 1930s. Chernow's book is focused on Thomas W. Lamont in these years, a tendency rendered understandable by the poor quality of the one biography of J.P. Morgan Jr. by John Douglas Forbes, *J.P. Morgan, Jr. 1867–1943*, Charlottesville, VA: University of Virginia Press, 1981. Edward Lamont's study of his grandfather, *The Ambassador from Wall Street*, Lanham, MD: Madison Books, 1994, has driven home the impression of a bank that was more Lamont than Morgan in the interwar period.

It has two aims. The first is to assay the history of J.P. Morgan & Co. as a business between 1929 and 1940. There are few book-length studies of banks in the interwar years, though nearly all historians would acknowledge their salience. As 1929 opened, the bank was a partnership in a prosperous United States. There ensued a convulsive decade of Crash, Depression, New Deal, and the coming of a new war. In 1940, the Morgan partners opted to turn their backs on their partnership, choosing to incorporate. Why? Answering this question involves asking others: Who were J.P. Morgan & Co.'s partners and what kinds of business did they carry out? How did the partnership meet and adapt to the challenges it faced from 1929 to 1940 as its business changed? Throughout these years, the Morgan perspective was conditioned by the dilemma of the private merchant banker enduring the crisis of capitalism. There were, the book argues, three different Morgan banks during these years: the J.P. Morgan & Co. of 1929 to mid-1931 when the full effects of the Depression had not yet been felt; the J.P. Morgan & Co. of late 1931 to 1935, battered by Depression and struggling to come to grips with it and with the New Deal; and the J.P. Morgan & Co. of 1936–40, a commercial bank shorn of its investment banking arm that was pondering its future. Navigating the rapids and shoals of the 1930s were the Morgan partners. They helmed the bank and set the Morgan course. For the Morgan partners, the choices of the 1930s were fraught. Events between 1931 and 1933, especially the last quarter of 1931 and the first quarter of 1933, when the bank suffered wrenching losses, scarred, reinforcing the habitual conservatism of these private merchant bankers throughout the remainder of the decade and colouring indelibly how the Morgan partners responded to the challenges that followed. Risk became unthinkable in Morgan banking practice. Forced by the Banking Act of 1933, better known as Glass–Steagall, to make a choice between commercial and investment banking, seeking to cope with an economy that sputtered from 1935, the long-term survival of J.P. Morgan & Co. meant ending their partnership. In this sense, the book is a case study of the response of financial capitalism to the greatest crisis in its history.

The second, wider aim is to integrate the history of J.P. Morgan & Co. with that of the history of capitalism and of the 1930s. While there has been a resurgence of interest among scholars in capitalism, as evidenced in the acclaim for work by historians such as Sven Beckert, there remains much to be done. Linked is another development. Some years ago, Steve Fraser and Gary Gerstle lamented the turn away from the study of elites in American history, seeing in its abandonment by the academy a failing that needed redressing. The Morgan partners were the embodiment of the interwar American elite. If we accept, to borrow the title of a well-known work, that there are "varieties of capitalism," then a study of J.P. Morgan & Co. as a capitalist institution offers insight into the history of capitalism, into the study of elites, and into the varieties of capitalism as the crisis of the 1930s raised questions about its survival.[4] What follows is both granular, in its focus on the bank as a business, and expansive in the sense of the bank as a symbol of American elites and American capitalism.

The Morgan partners were bankers. That reality shaped their responses to the challenges they faced. Yet J.P. Morgan & Co. was not just any bank, as attested to by the testimony of Young and Ernst. From 1918, it was the most important bank in the world. The partners were entangled in domestic politics, international relations, and finance. Ford, Morgan, and Rockefeller were the Olympians of American capitalist gods in the interwar years. As the crises of the 1930s unfolded, J.P. Morgan & Co. were participants in and observers of the tumult. If the overarching story is one of decline – the Morgan bank was less consequential in 1940 than it had been in 1929, Ernst notwithstanding – this arc was less apparent to contemporaries. The Morgan partners were immersed in the New York Stock Exchange Crash of 1929, counselled Herbert Hoover as the Depression progressed, and sparred with Franklin D. Roosevelt during the New Deal. They were pilloried by Father Coughlin and Senator Huey Long, and they were the American bankers to Italy and Japan. Their experience speaks to questions of abiding and enduring interest for economists and historians. How did J.P. Morgan & Co. respond to the Crash and the coming of the Depression? What was the bank's relationship with the Hoover administration? Between 1933 and 1936, Roosevelt's New Deal reshaped American capitalism. How did the Morgan partners react? After Roosevelt's re-election, what part did the Morgan bank play as the sharp downturn of 1937–38 threatened renewed destabilization? As the New Deal's energies flagged, Americans became more preoccupied with the spectre of war. What role did J.P. Morgan & Co. play as the revisionist states of Germany, Japan, and Italy challenged the existing order? What was the relationship between J.P. Morgan & Co. and the foreign policy pursued by the Roosevelt administration?

---

[4] Sven Beckert, *Empire of Cotton: A Global History*, New York: Alfred A. Knopf, 2014. Beckert is also co-chair of Harvard's Program on the Study of Capitalism. Another indication of renewed interest in capitalism was the launch of the journal *Capitalism: A Journal of History and Economics* by the University of Pennsylvania Press in 2020. Steve Fraser and Gary Gerstle, "Introduction," in Steve Fraser and Gary Gerstle, eds., *Ruling America: A History of Wealth and Power in a Democracy*, Cambridge, MA: Harvard University Press, 2005, pp. 1–26. Peter A. Hall and David Soskice, eds., *The Varieties of Capitalism: The Institutional Foundations of Comparative Advantage*, Oxford: Oxford University Press, 2001.

These questions are at the core of the book. The first two chapters address the Morgan bank and its place in the United States and the world before 1929.[5] Background these chapters may be, but they are fundamental in appreciating J.P. Morgan & Co. and the 1930s. If, as the book demonstrates, the crisis years between 1929 and 1940 were far more than a coda to what went before, there is no question of divisibility. Understanding J.P. Morgan & Co., its place in American life and in the world, begins well before 1929. Chapter 1 assesses the firm's antecedents and its connections to Britain and France, as well as setting out the history of the bank to 1918. Within this world, Britain was the lodestone for the Morgan partners, its banking culture and history imparting a permanent stamp on J.P. Morgan & Co. Contrary to what may be thought, the bank of the 1920s was a sober, conservative banking house. Active in a range of areas at home and abroad, delineating these activities – clients, credits, and loans – demystifies what J.P. Morgan & Co. did. An examination of the structure of the bank, with an emphasis on the partners, follows. The senior partners – Jack Morgan, Thomas W. Lamont, Leffingwell, and George Whitney – are analysed to weigh their personalities and beliefs. Their convictions determined the bank's outlook through the 1930s. The second chapter is a consideration of J.P. Morgan & Co. in American life, from the Progressive charge that it epitomized the Money Trust to its status as the bulwark of the established financial order on Wall Street. The American financial system of the 1920s was under duress due to a variety of factors. So too was the Morgan place at the apex of the pyramid of American finance. J.P. Morgan & Co. led Wall Street, but Wall Street was not the sum of American finance, nor was the Morgan supremacy uncontested. There were many voices on Wall Street, not just the stentorian Morgan tone. Much of J.P. Morgan & Co.'s influence arose from its international reach – with its associated firms in London, Morgan Grenfell, and in Paris, Morgan & Cie. – known as the House of Morgan.[6] Chapter 2 suggests that Morgan power was tied intimately to Britain and France as the victors of World War I. When Anglo-French suzerainty over

[5] The history of the bank before 1914 is served by Vincent Carosso, *The Morgans: Private International Bankers 1854–1913*, Cambridge, MA: Harvard University Press, 1987. Pierpont Morgan has been the subject of many studies. The most recent full-length biography is Jean Strouse, *Morgan: American Financier*, New York: Random House, 1999. Susie J. Pak, *Gentleman Bankers: The World of J.P. Morgan*, Cambridge, MA: Harvard University Press, 2013, is a fine study that covers the period 1900–29 in a series of thematic chapters.

[6] J.P. Morgan & Co. was the New York firm. It was also known as the Corner, for its position at the corner of Wall Street and Broad, or as 23 Wall Street, its formal address, or less precisely as the House of Morgan, which included Drexel & Co. in Philadelphia, Morgan Grenfell, and Morgan & Cie. In this book, J.P. Morgan & Co., the Corner, and 23 Wall Street all refer to the New York partnership.

the international system crumbled, so too did Morgan sway erode. J.P. Morgan & Co.'s international orientation meant that its partners, naturally enough, saw the challenges of the 1930s as both international and domestic. The two were interwoven. Chapters 1 and 2 thus contextualize the debates, controversies, and divides of the 1930s in terms of the developments of the decades before 1929.

In October 1929, the New York Stock Market crashed; by 1933, the world was years into the Depression and into the crisis of capitalism. Explaining these events remains a challenge that Chapters 3, 4, and 5 tackle. Division remains in analyses on the origins and course of the Depression. The search for the "Holy Grail" of economics, an explanation that will unite if not all then most scholars in an understanding of what happened, continues. These analyses emphasize systemic failings to understand the Depression.[7] J.P. Morgan & Co. fit uneasily into such explanations. As a private merchant bank, it was not a member of the Federal Reserve and was outside the system in a formal sense. That said, its influence was seen – often negatively – as greater than any other on Wall Street or, in more conspiratorial formulations, than the Federal Reserve itself. The "paranoid-style" is rejected in these pages in favour of a nuanced and, candidly, imprecise formulation of Morgan influence. As for the United States proper, debate about President Herbert Hoover and his administration's response to the onset and deepening of the Depression remains lively. Here, a different perspective is proffered of Hoover.

Chapters 3–5 argue that J.P. Morgan & Co. played a serious, sustained part in the events of 1929–33. The Morgan partners believed in a multilateral liberal capitalist trading order resting on a restored gold standard. They were convinced that American prosperity was connected to European prosperity. J.P. Morgan & Co.'s participation in wartime Allied financing and European reconstruction in the 1920s had solidified this world view. Chapter 3 opens with 1929. As the new year began, the Morgan partners were preoccupied with resolving the last hindrances to a stable, harmonious Europe. Once this was accomplished, they thought a halcyon future beckoned for Europe and for the United States. Creating new financial machinery to accomplish this end, in the form of the Young Plan and the Bank for International Settlements (BIS), drove them in 1929. The Stock Market Crash was of less moment for the Morgan partners. When it came – to their surprise – Morgan efforts were directed at restoring order in the market rather than seeking a resolution to the panic. Nor did the Morgan partners consider the stock market fall

---

[7] Charles R. Morris, *A Rabble of Dead Money: The Great Crash and the Global Depression, 1929–1939*, New York: Public Affairs, 2017, is a recent survey.

a transformative event. For them, it was a fleeting phenomenon betokening no lasting damage. The Morgan partners were, cautiously, optimistic after the Crash, a position that both reflected and fed American opinion. What mattered in the Morgan view was implementing the Young Plan and BIS, a conviction that lasted until the summer of 1930. It was not until the fall that the Morgan partners admitted that a depression was in the offing. This explanation of Morgan actions and outlook in 1929–30 helps us understand why Wall Street was slow to react as the American economy deteriorated. J.P. Morgan & Co., the leader of the Street, was focused on international developments, not domestic considerations.

International turmoil continued in 1931, with shattering consequences, as the fourth chapter discusses. A new Morgan partner, S. Parker Gilbert, the former Agent-General for Reparations, was a notable force in making Morgan policy in 1931–32. Three crises – the collapse of CreditAnstalt in May; turmoil in Germany in June–July; and the Sterling Crisis in Britain in July–September – dominated 1931. The partners took for granted that their advice would be welcomed in Washington, London, and Paris, a reflection both of their importance and of their hubris. J.P. Morgan & Co. counselled that these crises should be met through a reconstitution of the wartime alliance, not just in form but also in deed. This approach, which developed as the crises unfolded, was driven in part by Morgan fear that transmission of the German crisis might destabilize the American banking system. Its implementation depended on cooperation with the Hoover administration, which proved troublesome. The Morgan partners were ambivalent about Hoover, doubted his capacity, lamented his diplomatic skills, and yet needed his support. The British departure from the gold standard in September 1931 was a tremendous blow, confirming to the partners in their view that Franco-American cooperation was necessary if the Depression was to be overcome and raising for the first time the possibility that the Depression threatened capitalism. In the last months of that year, capital fled the United States after sterling's departure from gold, triggering a Federal Reserve rate increase and spurring deflation. The American economy contracted as did global economies. The J.P. Morgan & Co. balance sheet collapsed, with swingeing losses compressed into the last quarter of 1931. The harrowing effects of the latter, financial and psychological, lasted through the remainder of the decade but in the short term catalysed a Morgan reappraisal of what was transpiring. Chapter 4 strengthens the case of scholars who have seen 1931 as the year that transformed a deep recession into a global Depression.[8]

---

[8] Harold James, *The End of Globalization: Lessons from the Great Depression*, Cambridge, MA: Harvard University Press, 2001, is one leading study that has advanced this argument.

The Depression in the United States between 1930 and 1933 is the subject of Chapter 5. Bankers are often seen as missing in action in the Depression in America in these years, conspicuous primarily either by the waves of bankruptcies that whittled their number or through their inertia that contributed to, and was promoted by, economic catastrophe.[9] The argument made in this chapter is for an activist J.P. Morgan & Co. Activism did not mean that the Morgan partners had solutions to the Depression – they did not. Self-appointed as clinicians for ailing private firms, J.P. Morgan & Co. undertook, selectively, to aid New York institutions that found themselves in trouble in 1930–31. The Morgan capacity to perform this role was overwhelmed by the 1931 debacle. Morgan activism of this kind was short-lived. Activism, however, continued albeit in a different form. By the late summer of 1931, Leffingwell and Parker Gilbert were convinced that deflation was cutting into the bone of capitalism. The root cause of the trouble was World War I. Leffingwell and Gilbert argued that 1918 was only a hiatus; economic war had replaced open war, a state of affairs revealed by the Depression, deflation and the British departure from the gold standard. This analysis led the Morgan partners in 1932–33 to urge policymakers to adopt "war-time expedients" to counter deflation. Diluting the force of this argument were various complications. One was the Morgan relationship with Hoover. Superficially the Morgan analysis of the Depression and Hoover's were not dissimilar. Both saw the Depression as an international phenomenon. There similarity ended. Hoover's reluctance to jettison his reliance upon private, associational means to claw the United States out of the Depression meant that his efforts were too tepid for the Morgan partners. They advocated bolder measures to overcome deflation. Hoover resented these efforts, feeding his contempt for Wall Street bankers who he believed were out of touch with America. The Leffingwell–Gilbert prescription to combat deflation called for cuts in government expenditure to bring wages down to world commodity price levels. Somehow equilibrium would result. It was a muddled concoction. Simultaneously they

[9] There is no overarching study of American banking from 1929 to 1933. The most thorough account is Susan Estabrook Kennedy, *The Banking Crisis of 1933*, Lexington, KY: University of Kentucky Press, 1973. Kennedy suggests that: "By protecting themselves rather than by helping others fight the depression, bankers abdicated leadership in their communities and threw away prestige with both hands. The same men who had claimed credit for prosperity refused to accept responsibility for adversity and rejected the opportunity to maintain confidence in themselves and their institutions ... Throughout the 1920s and until 1931, the nation had looked to its bankers first to ensure prosperity and then to lead others out of the depression; thereafter, however, the bankers seemed scarcely able to help themselves. Loss of confidence in the leaders of finance, moreover, made the depression harder to fight and increased the burden on those left in command" (pp. 20–21).

encouraged expanding open-market operations by the Federal Reserve. The Morgan partners remained insistent that the global crisis required international remedies, leading them to fruitless wrangling over war debts and reparation. Any thought that the Morgan partners were Keynesians *avant la lettre* should be discarded. Nevertheless, while the Morgan posture was contorted, it was not idle. Though shackled by what Barry Eichengreen has called "golden fetters," the Morgan partners cast these off before most on Wall Street.[10] Distressed at the savagery of the banking crisis of the opening months of 1933, the Morgan partners abandoned their long-standing belief in the gold standard, having concluded that its preservation was inimical to capitalism's survival. This was a step that a lame-duck Hoover could not countenance. While the Morgan partners were alive from 1931 to the depredations of the Depression and developed a plausible explanation for what underpinned it, they were unable to translate insight into action, contributing to the banking community's ineffectiveness in the face of economic dislocation.

The coming of the New Deal changed the Morgan role in American capitalism. Before March 1933, contemporaries considered J.P. Morgan & Co. as one of the centres of capitalist power in the United States. After 1933, as Chapters 6, 7, and 8 suggest, this assumption was questioned in an America struggling to escape the Depression. J.P. Morgan & Co. still mattered but more as a symbol than as an institution blazing the American capitalist path. In his ringing inaugural peroration in March 1933, one of the most famous of the twentieth century, Roosevelt declaimed that Americans had nothing to fear but fear itself. He told his listeners that "the money changers have fled from their high seats of the temple of our civilization," that there would be "an end to speculation with other people's money," and that there would be no return to the "evils of the old order." This raises the question of the relationship between the Roosevelt administration and J.P. Morgan & Co., which is addressed in the sixth chapter. Generally, historians have portrayed the dealings between the Roosevelt administration and business as adversarial.[11] American business, while welcoming gratefully the energy and purpose of the New Deal in 1933, became progressively disenchanted by it in operation, leading to a wholesale abandonment of the Roosevelt program by 1935. J.P. Morgan & Co.'s relationship with Roosevelt and with the New Deal was complex and not reducible to this familiar narrative. Jack Morgan welcomed Roosevelt's announcement of the American departure from gold with

---

[10] Barry Eichengreen, *Golden Fetters: The Gold Standard and the Great Depression, 1919–1939*, New York: Oxford University Press, 1992.

[11] Patrick Reagan, "Business," in William D. Pederson, ed., *A Companion to Franklin D. Roosevelt*, Oxford: Wiley-Blackwell, 2011, pp. 186–205, is a survey.

a public expression of support in April 1933. The Morgan partners were impressed by the boldness of Roosevelt's actions in 1933. Leffingwell was convinced that the president had saved capitalism. However, the New Deal in action, drawing on its "Money Trust" antecedents, promulgated a package of reform legislation that threatened J.P. Morgan & Co. Glass–Steagall was the most consequential of these measures. Confronted with the legislation, the Morgan partners sought its abolition, delay, or revision. After Glass–Steagall, the chapter argues, the Morgan partners became more insular, more parochial, and less concerned about the crisis of capitalism as they worried about their bank. Despite this, though the Morgan partners were opposed to much of the New Deal legislation, which fractured their initial admiration for the president, the Morgan relationship with the Roosevelt administration did not rupture irretrievably. The firm did not lead or follow much of American business into the camp of the unreconcilables in 1935–36. Contrary to what many Americans suspected, and Father Coughlin and Huey Long proclaimed, J.P. Morgan & Co. was not arrayed with those who preached against Roosevelt. Hatred existed, in the shape of Jack Morgan's bile toward the president and in the utterances of other partners, but there was also Leffingwell and Parker Gilbert, Democrats who continued to champion Roosevelt within Morgan counsels. In 1936, Marquis Childs argued that the animosity of the wealthy toward the Roosevelt administration was such that "they in effect resign-[ed] from the United States."[12] The Morgan partners did not do this, as the book demonstrates. They opposed Roosevelt's domestic agenda, often bitterly, but kept their fidelity to their idea of American democracy, a commitment that meant ongoing engagement with American economics and politics. Paradoxically that commitment helped to maintain the trappings of Morgan power in a New Deal that had hollowed out Morgan consequentiality.

Making this adjustment simpler was foreign policy. If before 1933 J.P. Morgan & Co. influenced American foreign policy, after 1933 the Morgan partners observed rather than made it. The outsized Morgan role in the international relations of the 1920s had rested on the dominance of Britain and France over European international relations, the centrality of economic and financial questions in the processes of reconstruction, the availability of plentiful American capital, and the willingness of the Harding and Coolidge administrations to allow private

---

[12] The article "They Hate Roosevelt" appeared in the May 1936 issue of *Harper's*. In expanded form it was republished as a pamphlet by the Democratic National Committee for use in the 1936 presidential campaign. It is reprinted in Frank Friedel, ed., *The New Deal and the American People*, Englewood Cliffs, NJ: Prentice Hall, 1964, pp. 98–104.

banking interests a substantial role. By the time that the World Economic Conference ended in disarray in the summer of 1933, all of these had disappeared. Chapter 7 considers J.P. Morgan & Co. and Germany, Italy, and Japan. Ominously, all were committed to disrupting the international order in their favour. All three nations were important to the bank in these years: Germany because of its efforts to end servicing of the Dawes and Young Plan loans, Italy and Japan because they were Morgan clients. All three, the chapter argues, were misunderstood by the Morgan partners. This misappraisal speaks to the larger issue of how and why so many in the 1930s misunderstood the imperatives driving Berlin, Rome, and Tokyo. The failure to discern the radical nature of each of these regimes led the Corner to a blinkered, cautious approach that opened J.P. Morgan & Co. to justified criticism. Recourse to such a tack was made easier because it conformed with Washington's foreign policy. Between 1933 and 1937, as Chapter 7 suggests, the foundations for Morgan support of Roosevelt's foreign policy were laid, in part, in shared attitudes toward the revisionist states. Concordance was given a fillip by the lengthening shadow of World War I. From 1934 to 1936, Senator Gerald P. Nye chaired hearings investigating the Munitions Industry. They devolved into a debate on whether the United States had been inveigled into war in 1917. J.P. Morgan & Co. was accused of having bamboozled the Wilson administration into war. The White House could not block Nye, but nor did the Roosevelt administration assist the senator in his exploration of J.P. Morgan & Co.

The last chapter unites the strands of domestic policy, the Morgan bank as a business, and foreign policy. The New Deal was unable to translate its early success in combatting the Depression into a permanent improvement in the American condition. The suddenness of the slump of 1937–38 reawakened worries that the darkest days of 1932–33 might return. Examining the reasons for this state of affairs, scholars have pointed not just to the immaturity of the existing fiscal mechanisms of the American state, Roosevelt's own conservatism, and the implausibility of a massive fiscal stimulus but also to the failings of monetary policy apparent in the reformed Federal Reserve system chaired by Marriner S. Eccles. Almost uniquely, Chapter 8 argues, Leffingwell and Gilbert held that monetary policy was ignoring the ongoing threat of deflation. Consulted by Eccles and by the secretary of the Treasury, Henry Morgenthau Jr., the Morgan partners advised against any measures that might choke the money supply. That counsel was ignored. It should not be construed from this that the Morgan partners were far-sighted. Rather, it was a reflection of their certainty, born in 1931, that deflation was the true enemy. Evidence for this contention is found in the

Morgan palliatives on fiscal policy. They were conventional, differing little from the orthodox nostrums of the day. The severity of the economic contraction in 1937–38 led Roosevelt to sanction publicly and privately Morgan intercession. While this spoke to the White House continuing to believe in Morgan power, the outcome was, as the chapter argues, a hardening of the chasm between the Morgan partners and Roosevelt on domestic policy. At the same time, J.P. Morgan & Co. was struggling as a commercial, deposit bank. Divorced from its investment arm, constituted as Morgan Stanley in September 1935, the partners retreated into a state of near inactivity. Their conservatism in banking practice was so acute by 1938 that they were doing little more than amassing deposits fleeing the fear of war in Europe. The Depression and the New Deal had worked against the partnership, but, as the chapter argues, so too did the decisions by the partners. Hoping for a change of government that would overturn Glass–Steagall, the consequence, when this did not occur, was that the partners were forced in 1939–40 to embrace incorporation in 1940 as the only avenue forward.

Overlapping was the fear of war. Many Americans thought that J.P. Morgan & Co. would drag the United States into a new war. As Chapter 8 shows, this was far from the Morgan desire. Not only were the Morgan partners by the late 1930s bystanders in foreign policy rather than makers of it; they hewed to a cautious course. Wholeheartedly sympathetic to Britain and France, the Morgan partners viewed appeasement as admirable. For them, appeasement offered a solution to European difficulties that would allow for a restoration of a liberal, international trading order and would, with time, promote peace. Making advocacy of this view simpler was Roosevelt's endorsement of appeasement. A great deal has been written about Roosevelt's foreign policy, but the Morgan partners were convinced that he intended to keep the United States neutral come what may, while assisting London and Paris with as much economic aid as could be extracted from Congress. This was a policy that the Morgan partners thought wise. The Morgan partners clung to Roosevelt's foreign policy. They believed in it. As it transpired, the coming of World War II displaced capitalism's crises of the 1930s with a crisis of a different kind – the challenge of survival in a military confrontation.

1 "The Heart of Contemporary Capitalism"
The Partners and Their Bank

The co-partnership notice was sparse and the display advertisement tucked away on page eleven of the *Wall Street Journal* on 1 January 1929 discreet. In fifteen lines, J.P. Morgan & Co. announced that it had admitted five new partners: Henry S. Morgan (Harry Morgan), Thomas S. Lamont, Henry P. Davison Jr., Thomas Newhall, and Edward Hopkinson Jr. All were becoming partners at J.P. Morgan & Co. New York, Morgan Grenfell & Co. London, and Morgan & Cie. Paris.[1] Collectively these firms were known as the House of Morgan. The *New York Times* was less circumspect. Under the banner "Sons of 3 Partners Enter Morgan Firm," the paper informed its readers that Morgan partnerships were "the most coveted posts in Wall Street." "It is doubtful," the article commented, "if in Wall Street equal responsibility has been placed before on three men all under 31." There were compensations, *The Times* hastened to add. Wall Street reckoned that Morgan partners earned a minimum of $1,000,000 per annum.[2]

Serious-minded observers pointed to the attractions beyond lucre. *The Nation*, on the occasion of the announcement of Dwight Morrow's appointment as ambassador to Mexico in 1927, remarked "[h]ardly any post to which the President might appoint him could give Mr. Morrow power comparable to that which he wields as a partner in the greatest international banking firm in the world."[3] Some years later, the writer-cum-historian of contemporary American society Frederick Lewis Allen echoed that verdict. He asserted that becoming a J.P. Morgan & Co. partner was "as high a prize as a financier could hope for ... it was a place on the general staff of what the business world considered the headquarters of financial power."[4] Writing under his adopted name, Lewis Corey, the left-wing intellectual Louis C. Fraina concurred. With

---

[1] The co-partnership notice can be found in the *Wall Street Journal*, 1 January 1929, p. 11.
[2] *New York Times*, 1 January 1929, p. 18.
[3] "From Morgan's Up," *The Nation*, vol. 125, no. 3248, 5 October 1927, p. 327.
[4] Frederick Lewis Allen, *The Lords of Creation*, New York: Harper Brothers, 1935. Reprint: Quandrangle Books 1966, p. 344.

a pedigree honed by experience in the American Communist Party, Corey penned his 1930 study of the House of Morgan under the auspices of the Brookings Institution. Deeply critical of the Morgan influence on American life, he distilled the essence: The House of Morgan was "the heart of contemporary capitalism."[5]

The frisson that rippled through Wall Street in the wake of the co-partnership notice is thus understandable. The admission of new partners to the leading bank on the Street was a notable event. The reaction of the *New York Times* attested to the saying that men scanned their mail anxiously every morning to see if a letter offering them a place at the Morgan bank had arrived. In some Wall Street haunts, envy and irreverence coupled: Jack Morgan and his partners were referred to as "Jesus Christ and the Twelve Apostles."[6]

How had J.P. Morgan & Co. reached this eminence by 1929? How was it organized and what kinds of businesses did it undertake? What of its partners during the interwar years? Who were they, what did they do, and what did they believe? Answers to these questions lay the foundations for understanding the bank and its partners in the crisis years between 1929 and 1940. What follows examines the history of the House of Morgan, its business, and its partners before 1929. The contests of the 1930s did not take place in a void. They were struggles in which the Morgan partners, their friends, and their foes were conditioned by the preceding decades. The debates that swirled in the 1930s – on how to respond to the Depression, on how to reshape American capitalism, on how to deal with the looming threat of war – were inflected by the Morgan rise to prominence well before 1929.

*****

In 1836, when Junius S. Morgan entered into business in a dry goods firm in Hartford, Connecticut, the future eminence of the Morgan firms was remote. Assisted by a bequest from his father, Junius Morgan parlayed his means into a junior partnership with the Boston-based J.M. Beebe in 1851. The firm were traders, financing the flourishing trade between Boston and entrepôts around the world. It was, however, the connection of J.M. Beebe with the London-based merchant bank George Peabody & Co. that proved pivotal. George Peabody, aging, was searching for a dynamic, junior partner. He found Junius Morgan. Junius Morgan moved to London in 1854, bringing his family in tow, including his son,

---

[5] Lewis Corey, *The House of Morgan*, New York: G. Howard Watt, 1930. Reprint: New York: AMS, 1969, p. 449.
[6] W.M. Walker, "J.P. The Younger," *American Mercury*, vol. 40, no. 42, June 1927, p. 133.

Pierpont Morgan. By the time Junius assumed full control of George Peabody & Co. in 1864, renaming it J.S. Morgan & Co. that year, he was established in the City, London's financial marketplace. Pierpont Morgan, after a three-year apprenticeship in London, returned to the United States in 1857, entering Duncan, Sherman & Co., which at the time was the Peabody bank's New York correspondent. A short-lived J.P. Morgan & Co. followed, lasting from 1862 to 1864, before Junius Morgan, uneasy at his son's impulsive risk-taking, insisted on a restructuring, bringing on board a more seasoned banker, Charles H. Dabney. Dabney, Morgan & Co., soldiered on until 1871.[7]

Change arrived with Anthony Drexel. Drexel was the dominant force in Philadelphia banking. His firm, Drexel & Co., had a New York affiliate as well as a Paris house, which from 1868 was styled Drexel, Harjes & Cie., after the managing partner, John H. Harjes. Drexel, who was looking for more effective leadership in New York, had much to offer – a good reputation, a careful hand, and a Paris connection. He also sought stronger links with the City of London. When Drexel, who had done business with Junius Morgan, broached the notion of an arrangement, the latter did not hesitate. The two orchestrated the formation of a new firm in New York, Drexel, Morgan & Co. Pierpont Morgan, who would helm the New York branch, was informed of the plans after the fact.[8] Junius Morgan's death in 1890 left Pierpont Morgan as the senior partner in J.S. Morgan & Co. in London. Soon thereafter, Anthony Drexel died, and his son opted to withdraw from the business. A reorganization and renaming ensued: Pierpont Morgan established J.P. Morgan & Co. in 1895 as the New York partnership. Drexel & Co. continued in Philadelphia as an associated house, with Edward T. Stotesbury as the new senior partner. From this time on, Philadelphia and New York functioned independently. The Paris house was renamed Morgan, Harjes & Cie.

The demands on Pierpont Morgan as the senior partner in New York and in London were formidable, and he was determined to enlist his son and heir Jack Morgan, teaching him the trade of a private merchant banker. From 1891 to 1898, Jack Morgan served an apprenticeship in Boston and then in New York. Upon his father's instructions, Jack Morgan was sent to London in 1898 to be a partner in J.S. Morgan & Co. Jack Morgan was not only to act as Pierpont's lieutenant in London;

---

[7] Carosso, *The Morgans: Private International Bankers*, is authoritative. To this should be added Chernow, *The House of Morgan*, pp. 3–35.

[8] Dan Rottenberg, *The Man Who Made Wall Street: Anthony Drexel and the Rise of Modern Finance*, Philadelphia, PA: University of Pennsylvania Press, 2001, pp. 94–99.

he was directed to recruit new talent to J.S. Morgan & Co.[9] Edward C. Grenfell was duly brought into J.S. Morgan & Co. from Brown Shipley & Co. in 1900, becoming a partner in 1904. In 1910, J.S. Morgan & Co. was renamed Morgan Grenfell & Co. When Pierpont Morgan died in 1913, Jack Morgan succeeded to the leadership of the House of Morgan.[10]

As the foregoing suggests, the connection between the United States and Britain was at the heart of the Morgan identity. All three of the men, the "Seniors" in Morgan parlance, who led the House of Morgan between 1864 and 1941 – Junius Morgan, Pierpont Morgan, and Jack Morgan – lived and worked in London at some point in their careers. From the time that Junius Morgan embarked for the city in 1854, the Morgan firms were linked indissolubly with Britain. Vincent Carosso, who has carried out the closest study of the Morgan banks, observed that "the House of Morgan, like the Barings, Hambros, and Rothschilds, was and remained, both in spirit and in practice, a nineteenth-century merchant bank."[11] More precisely, the model was the nineteenth-century City of London merchant bank. Culturally this meant continuity from father to son of the core values necessary for the merchant bank. The testimonies of Pierpont Morgan in 1912 and of Jack Morgan in 1933 before congressional committees were interchangeable as to what constituted these core values. Both men insisted that trust, character, integrity, and reputation were paramount. There was good reason for merchant bankers to insist on reputation and character. Reputation functioned as a short-cut for assessing risk and overcoming limited information about doing business.[12] Those seeking to borrow always knew more about the state of their business than those lending. This prompted merchant bankers to develop sources of intelligence and to cultivate intimacy with clients that enabled

---

[9] Forbes, *J.P. Morgan, Jr. 1867–1943*, pp. 30–31.

[10] In addition to the works noted thus far, for the early history of the House of Morgan, see Longstreet Hinton, John E. Meyer Jr., and Thomas Rodd, *Some Comments about the Morgan Bank*, New York: Morgan Guaranty Trust Company, 1979, reprinted 1985.

[11] Vincent P. Carosso, "The Morgan Houses: The Seniors, Their Partners, and Their Aides," in Joseph R. Freseand Jacob Judd, eds., *American Industrialization, Economic Expansion and the Law*, Tarrytown, NY: Sleepy Hollow Press, 1981, p. 5. Stanley Chapman, *The Rise of Merchant Banking*, London: George Allen & Unwin, 1984 is a good survey.

[12] Monika Pohle Fraser, "Personal and Impersonal Exchange. The Role of Reputation in Banking: Some Evidence from Nineteenth and Early Twentieth Century Banks' Archives," in Philip L. Cottrell, Evan Lange, and Ulf Olsson, eds., *Centres and Peripheries in Banking: The Historical Development of Financial Markets*, Ashgate: Aldershot, 2007, pp. 177–95.

assessments of character to deputize for informational lacunae. It was a practice that the Corner adhered to religiously. As Arthur M. Schlesinger Jr. put it, "No banking house better represented the cult of character than J.P. Morgan" in the interwar years.[13]

The transmission and inculcation of this ethos were amplified by, and overlapped with, the decades in which the City of London extended and consolidated its sway over international commerce and finance.[14] The Morgan partners identified the extension of the gold standard with prosperity, with the City of London's pre-eminence, and with sterling. Gold and sterling were the foundations of the trade, free movement of capital, and labour that the Morgan partners believed in fervently. Nor was this conviction diminished by the relative decline of Britain as an economic power as the nineteenth century drew to a close. As British industrial supremacy ebbed and then was surrendered to the United States and Germany, London's suzerainty over global commerce and finance was unaffected. The intricate network of accepting houses, bill-brokers, discount houses, jobbers, bankers, and the myriad others that constituted the City was unmatched in its sophistication, making possible the international trade that moved through the medium of the sterling bill of exchange. Powered by international earnings in services and investments, British capital moved abroad in torrential volumes.[15]

The single largest beneficiary of this capital flood was the United States.[16] The House of Morgan was one of the conduits through which British capital sluiced, to the advantage of British investors, American companies, and the Morgan partners. Reinforcing London's importance for J.P. Morgan & Co. was the pre-war sectoral distribution of British capital in the United States. The bulk of British money went into

---

[13] Arthur M. Schlesinger Jr., *The Crisis of the Old Order, 1919–1933*, Boston: Houghton Mifflin Company, 1957, p. 56.

[14] For a sweeping account of the City, see the first two volumes of *The City of London* by David Kynaston: *The City of London, Vol. 1: A World of Its Own 1815–1890* and *The City of London, Vol. 2: Golden Years, 1890–1914*, London: Pimlico, 1995.

[15] Michael Obstfeld and Alan M. Taylor, *Global Capital Markets: Integration, Crisis, and Growth*, Cambridge: Cambridge University Press, 2004, p. 60.

[16] Herbert Feis placed the total British investment in the United States at £754.6 million (approximately $3,720 million) in 1914. Cleona Lewis, working with different data sets, arrived at a figure of $4,250 million in July 1914. Herbert Feis, *Europe: The World's Banker, 1870–1914*, New Haven, CT: Yale University Press, 1930. See the reprint (New York: W. W. Norton, 1965, pp. 23) for the figure of £754.6 million, which I have translated into US dollars based on the EH.Net database exchange rate of $4.93 per pound. For the total British investment in the United States, see Cleona Lewis, *America's Stake in International Investments*, Washington, DC: Brookings Institution, 1938, p. 546.

railroads.[17] Railroads were especially important to the House of Morgan. It was on the back of railroad investment, railroad consolidation, and contests for the control of the railroads that Pierpont Morgan extended Morgan authority.

The asymmetry born of the Anglo-American relationship and the dominance of the City of London in international finance meant that, within the House of Morgan, Morgan Grenfell was more important than the Paris house.[18] Morgan & Cie., as it became in 1927 following the death of Herman Harjes in 1926, was not originally a Morgan firm, nor did successive Morgan seniors ever live and work in Paris, though Pierpont Morgan and Jack Morgan were both fluent in French and German. While France was second only to Britain as a capital exporter before 1914, the direction of those flows was very different. French capital was exported predominantly in Europe, most famously to tsarist Russia.[19] This reality, in conjunction with the fact that American multinationals did not move into the broader European market en masse until after 1918, kept the Paris house firmly behind London in the eyes of the New York partners.[20] The senior partners in Paris after 1927, Bernard S. Carter and Nelson Dean Jay, were American expatriates.[21] In contrast, the named partner in London, Edward C. Grenfell, was British and so too were the other resident partners in Morgan Grenfell. Morgan & Cie. had fewer partners, generated less business, and operated on a smaller scale than Morgan Grenfell.[22] While Dean

---

[17] Feis, *The World's Banker*, pp. 27–28. Lewis, *America's Stake*, p. 546; for her remarks on British investments in US railroads, see pp. 36–41. Ronald Findlay and Kevin O'Rourke, *Power and Plenty: Trade, War, and the World Economy in the Second Millennium*, Princeton, NJ: Princeton University Press, 2007, p. 409.

[18] Youssef Cassis and Eric Bussières, eds., *London and Paris As International Financial Centres in the Twentieth Century*, Oxford: Oxford University Press, 2005, is a comparative study.

[19] The standard works on French capital exports include René Girault, *Emprunts russes et investissements français en Russie 1887–1914*, Paris: Librairie Armand Colin, 1973, to which should be added Jennifer Siegel, *For Peace and Money: French and British Finance in the Service of Tsars and Commissars*, Oxford: Oxford University Press, 2014. See also, Maurice Levy-Leboyer, "La capacité financière de la France au début du vingtième siècle," in Maurice Levy-Leboyer, ed., *La position internationale de la France*, Paris: École des hautes études en sciences sociales, 1977.

[20] Mira Wilkins, *The Maturing of Multinational Enterprise: American Business Abroad, 1914–1970*, Cambridge, MA: Harvard University Press, 1974. Wilkins has contributed a chapter to Hubert Bonin and Ferry de Goey, eds., *American Firms in Europe 1880–1980*, Geneva: Librairie Droz, 2009 that contains several pertinent essays.

[21] There is little on the history of Morgan & Cie. H.O. Loderhose, *A History of Morgan, Harjes et Cie, 1872–1932*, can be found in The Morgan Library (TML), J.P. Morgan Jr. papers (JPM), Box 116. There is also a history of Morgan & Cie. written by Nelson Dean Jay in the 1960s. A copy is held in the Nelson Dean Jay papers (NDJ) at Knox College (KC). The collection is uncatalogued presently.

[22] On Morgan Grenfell and its history, see Kathleen Burk, *Morgan Grenfell 1838–1988*, Oxford: Oxford University Press, 1989.

Jay and "Bunny" Carter were respected in New York, their voices were not as influential as those emanating from London. When the sterling crisis of 1931 transfixed J.P. Morgan & Co., it did so in part because of the centrality of Britain and London within the world view of the Morgan partners. They struggled to imagine a world in which Britain was off gold; it was alien to their thinking. In contrast, when France abandoned the gold standard in 1936, the reaction of the New York partners was muted. It is true that much had changed in the intervening years, but one thing had remained constant: France was less consequential to J.P. Morgan & Co. than Britain.

*****

What kinds of business did J.P. Morgan & Co. do? Under Pierpont Morgan, the bank had floated stock offerings, orchestrated mergers, and participated in high-profile struggles for control of companies. Among the most famous of these were the New York Central and Pennsylvania railroads in the 1880s, the salvation of General Electric in 1893, the formation of U.S. Steel in 1901, and the fight with Edward H. Harriman over the Northern Pacific railroad that same year. "Morganization" became a well-known term, implying financial control with more than a dash of looting. Pierpont Morgan was, in the eyes of critics, the quintessential robber baron.[23] On two occasions, in 1894–95 and again in the panic of 1907, Pierpont Morgan played a significant role in quelling the financial unrest roiling American financial markets. Pierpont Morgan imparted a tincture to J.P. Morgan & Co. that coloured perceptions of the bank well after his death. Greed, imperiousness, ruthlessness, these were the traits that lived in the American public mind as Pierpont Morgan's legacy. Yet, after the war, J.P. Morgan & Co. was not Pierpont Morgan's bank. Directed by Jack Morgan, J.P. Morgan & Co. was less swashbuckling, less rambunctious. Jack Morgan was not inclined to be the promoter. *Fortune* drew the distinction: in Pierpont Morgan's day, the bank was a promotion house; under Jack Morgan, it was a banking house.[24] Between 1913 and 1929, J.P. Morgan & Co. offered no common stocks for sale, handling only bonds and preferred stocks. Bonds were not only safer; they constituted a larger market than equities.

Not all changed. J.P. Morgan & Co. was a partnership from 1895 to 1940. This status conferred cherished privacy, though it imposed limitations. Unlike a limited liability corporation, partners were subject to unlimited personal liability. Consequently, the bank operated with high

---

[23] A classic account is Matthew Josephson, *The Robber Barons*, first published in 1934 and dedicated to Charles and Mary Beard.
[24] "Mister Morgan," *Fortune*, August 1933, vol. 8, p. 84.

levels of liquidity and did not make a practice of retaining securities that it sold.[25] As a firm, J.P. Morgan & Co. did not engage in short-selling. Similarly, the bank did not engage in stock pools. A separate code governed the partners' private business. For their own accounts, the partners could do as they wished, subject to applicable law; and, as the Stock Exchange practices hearings in 1933 (often called the Pecora hearings after the lead counsel, Ferdinand Pecora) revealed, some, though not all, partners sold stocks short and participated in pools. The partners understood that they were merchants – in the business of furnishing credit and buying and selling money. As Lamont told Senator James Watson of Indiana in 1931, "our house, you see, is not a bank in itself; it is really a house of merchants."[26] While J.P. Morgan & Co. accepted deposits, it was barred from advertising for them. This was not deemed an obstacle. An exchange between Pecora and Jack Morgan in 1933 attested to Morgan confidence:

MR. PECORA. Mr. Morgan, is the name of the firm on any outer door of the firm's office?
MR. MORGAN. It is not on the outer door. It is on the inner door.
MR. PECORA. Not visible from the street to the passer-by?
MR. MORGAN. No. Most of them know the address.
MR. PECORA. You do not think the firm suffers any lack of prestige in the banking world because it does not advertise itself to be bankers, do you?
MR. MORGAN. It does not seem to.[27]

The minimum deposit to open an account was $7,500. Prospective account holders required an introduction, restricting further those who banked at the Corner. Governments, corporations, and wealthy individuals had funds on deposit with the firm. The interest rate paid on deposits was that paid by the New York Clearing House. Harry Morgan estimated that J.P. Morgan & Co. had approximately 1,500 accounts in the mid-1920s with deposits totalling roughly $500 million.[28] Deposits stood at slightly more than $562 million on 31 December 1927, before

---

[25] The bank's liquidity ratios stood at 83 per cent in 1927, 82 per cent in 1928, and 76 per cent in 1929. Baker Library (BL), Thomas W. Lamont papers (TWL), Series V, Box 212, Folder 11.

[26] United States Senate Committee on Finance, *Sale of Foreign Bonds or Securities in the United States*, 72nd Congress, 1st session, Part 1, 18 December 1931, Washington, DC: Government Printing Office, 1932, p. 20.

[27] Hearings before the Sub-Committee of the United States Senate Committee on Banking and Currency, *Stock Exchange Practices* (hereafter Pecora Committee), 73rd Congress, 1st session, Part 1, 24 May 1933, United States. Washington, DC: Government Printing Office, 1933, p. 105.

[28] Vincent Carosso interview with Henry (Harry) S. Morgan, 4 December 1975, TML, Carosso Papers (CP), Box 8, Henry S. Morgan (interviews).

declining to $481 million on 31 December 1928.[29] Between 1927 and 1932, thirty-eight corporations kept deposits in excess of $1 million in any year with the bank, with an additional eighty-three companies maintaining more than $100,000 on deposit. Among the companies with more than $1 million on deposit were such well-known firms as General Mills, ITT, Montgomery Ward, and Standard Oil New Jersey. Less is known about governmental and individual deposits, which remain opaque, though it is clear that they were sizeable. Deposits also accrued from the firm's role as a paying agent for the coupons of various securities as well as its function as a custodian overseeing sinking funds.[30]

Contrary to what is often assumed, the J.P. Morgan & Co. of the 1920s was not primarily an investment bank. Rather, it was a general banking house. Though the firm was an underwriter of corporate and governmental bonds, this activity was the smaller part of what the bank did. Setting aside foreign governmental issues, the bank was not a major player in the municipal bond market, offering only a total of $160 million between January 1919 and May 1933.[31] Harry Morgan thought that underwriting in the 1920s represented less than 25 per cent of the firm's earnings. He reckoned that about half of J.P. Morgan & Co.'s business in the 1920s was general banking and foreign exchange, with the residual half being corporate and governmental finance.[32] Questioned in 1933, Jack Morgan told the Pecora Committee that "straight banking" was the larger part of J.P. Morgan & Co. business.[33] Insofar as its general banking functions went, the bank accepted deposits, issued letters of credit, acted as a transfer agent to handle dividends as well as coupon payments, dealt in foreign exchange when clients requested, and, if asked, oversaw trading on the stock exchange for its clients. The latter was described by Whitney as a "very good bread and butter business."[34] For some clients, the bank provided investment counsel. As a partnership, the bank could not act as a corporate trustee, and it was not until late in the 1930s that steps were taken to create an analogue to trust functions within the bank.[35] Finally, the bank did not lend money on real estate, a rule that may have reduced

---

[29] See Appendix 1, J.P. Morgan & Co., Consolidated Statement of Condition, 1927–32.

[30] Pecora Committee, Part 1, 23 May 1933, pp. 5, 20, 49–52.

[31] Pecora Committee, Part 1, 25 May 1933, p. 224.

[32] Vincent Carosso interviews with Harry S. Morgan, 14 May 1974, 4 December 1975, 21 April 1976, TML, CP, Box 8, Henry S. Morgan (interviews). See also a further interview on 9 December 1976 in TML, CP, Box 18, Morgan & Co – Misc. Notes 1920s File 2.

[33] Pecora Committee, Part 1, 24 May 1933, p. 106.   [34] Ibid., p. 124.

[35] See the chapter by Longstreet Hinton, "The Birth of a Trust Department," in Hinton, Meyer Jr. and Rodd, "Some Comments about the Morgan Bank."

profits in the 1920s but sheltered J.P. Morgan & Co. from plunging real estate values after 1929.

On the corporate finance side, the firm was fastidious in selecting its clients. William A. Mitchell, who joined J.P. Morgan & Co. in 1925, eventually becoming a partner in 1939, recalled in his memoirs that: "[w]e had been tossing people down the front steps for years. Mr. Morgan didn't really want to be bothered very much with the commercial banking business."[36] Legacy business in the railroad sector continued, and in the 1920s J.P. Morgan & Co. began a fateful association with the Van Sweringen brothers of Cleveland, who were amassing a railroad empire. At the Pecora hearings in May 1933, Whitney provided a breakdown by category of Morgan offerings between January 1919 and May 1933 (Table 1.1).

Occasionally, the bank engineered mergers or acquisitions. This was the case with Marland Oil, a leading producer whose rapid expansion and consequent money-losing tendencies fuelled a need for capital. Initially J. P. Morgan & Co. loaned money to Marland, before replacing the founder, E.W. Marland, with Daniel Moran as president in 1928. Subsequently, a complex merger involving Marland, Prudential Refining, and Continental Oil was consummated in 1929, the new company taking the name Continental Oil with Moran at its head. Edward Lamont has pointed out that Marland Oil was the first instance in which J. P. Morgan resorted to a practice later to become notorious – the private placement of stock with wealthy investors, a device which was repeated in 1927 with Johns-Manville Corporation.[37] More routinely, J.P. Morgan &

Table 1.1 *Breakdown of Morgan bond and preferred stock offerings between January 1919 and May 1933.*

Railway Company Bonds	$1,845,639,300
Public Utility Bonds (including holding company)	$1,074,750,000
Industrial Company Bonds and Preferred Stock	$578,297,900
Railway Holding Company Bonds	$133,000,000*

Note. * Pecora Committee, Part I, 25 May 1933, pp. 223–25.

[36] I have been unable to locate the Mitchell Memoirs. Vincent Carosso saw a copy and this quotation is from his notes, TML, CP, Box 18, Morgan & Co – Misc. Notes 1920s File 2.
[37] Lamont, *The Ambassador*, p. 252.

Co. issued commercial credits on a considerable scale for its corporate clients. Between 1927 and 1931, these totalled approximately $400 million, funding the export of various American goods, such as fruits, metals, paper, automobiles, and machinery; paying for imports of commodities, like jute, tea, and coffee; and making possible the financing of the storage of American farm products.[38]

Foreign loans took two forms. One was the provision of short-term credits, an example of which was the one-year $20 million revolving credit for the Bank of Spain in August 1928. This particular line of credit was renewed in 1929 but did not run the full term, as the Bank of Spain opted to cancel it in April 1930.[39] More commonly, J.P. Morgan was a wholesaler of bonds, between 1920 and 1931 totalling slightly more than $1.8 billion, for a range of governments, from the state to the municipal level. Slightly more than half of these loans were made to European countries, with Argentina, Chile, Cuba, Japan, Taiwan, Canada and Australia rounding out the picture.[40] Regardless of their geographic dispersion, the ability of J.P. Morgan & Co. to select the loans that they wanted to make ensured that the repayment record was very good.[41] This was a profitable and prestigious business for the firm, though perhaps less remunerative than was believed at the time. Lamont, testifying to the Senate Finance Committee hearings on foreign securities in December 1931, remarked that any calculation of "net profit" on such transactions was impossible as the bank did not break out its costs on a per loan basis. Jack Morgan, in his formal statement to the Pecora Committee on 9 June 1933, was more definitive, suggesting that on foreign and domestic securities the bank had earned a "limited compensation averaging approximately one half of one percent."[42] Using this figure, J.P. Morgan & Co. reaped approximately $90 million between 1920 and 1931 on the $1.8 billion of foreign bonds it issued, though it must be emphasized that this is a crude calculation.

J.P. Morgan & Co. was active in the call money market. Call loans were demand loans made on a short-term basis, usually daily and typically

[38] BL, TWL, Series V, Box 211/20 contains an undated report [Possible Preliminary Report] that includes the $400 million figure. Memorandum to TWL, 17 April 1933, BL, TWL, Series V, Box 211/23 lists the categories of commercial credits without the global $400 million figure.

[39] Pecora Committee, Part 1, 25 May 1933, p. 252.

[40] *Sale of Foreign Bonds or Securities in the United States*, Part 1, 18–21 December 1931, table, J.P. Morgan & Co. sales of foreign government offerings, pp. 159–61.

[41] Marc Flandreau, Norbert J. Gaillard, and Ugo Panizza, "Conflicts of Interest, Reputation and the Interwar Debt Crisis: Banksters or Bad Luck," CEPR Discussion Paper Series, No. 7705, 2010.

[42] *Sale of Foreign Bonds or Securities in the United States*, Part 1, 18–21 December 1931, p. 21; Pecora Committee, J.P. Morgan statement, 9 June 1933, p. 879.

renewable, with the loan being secured by stocks and bonds. The call loan market, as Margaret Myers pointed out long ago, was a "peculiarly American product" that was embedded in the history of the New York money market and distinguished New York from London and Paris where no such market existed.[43] The growth of the call money market, in particular the pumping of funds into speculative investment in the stock market through brokers, was one of the characteristic phenomena of the late 1920s. Call loans were divided into three kinds: loans made by the New York banks for their own account; loans made by the New York banks to non–New York domestic banks; and loans made by the New York banks for the "account of others." Others might be corporations, whether domestic or foreign, investment trusts, individuals, and foreign banks. Analysis of the share of outstanding call loans in the run-up to the Crash indicates that loans made for others, preponderantly corporations, were chiefly responsible for the surge of money into the stock market.[44] While J.P. Morgan & Co. made call loans, they did not lend money for the account of others, believing it unwise – a policy that was to demonstrate its soundness in October 1929. At the end of 1927, J.P. Morgan & Co. had slightly more than $54 million in call loans outstanding. A year later, the figure had reached nearly $110 million. Brokers' loans peaked at 2 per cent of total Morgan loans outstanding in 1929.[45] How much profit such activity yielded the firm is unknown, but the interest rate spread in 1929 was rich.

On the eve of 1929, J.P. Morgan & Co. was in an enviable financial position. The day that the co-partnership notice appeared, the company's net worth was more than $91 million, a considerable jump from the $71 million recorded the year before. The firm was liquid, with more than $259 million available in the form of cash, US government securities, and state and municipal bonds against deposits of slightly more than $481 million.[46] Its principal lines of business were varied and performing well. The bank was not dependent upon any one source of

[43] Margaret Myers, *The New York Money Market*, Vol. 1, ed., Benjamin Haggott Beckhart, New York: Columbia University Press, 1931–32. Reprint: New York: AMS Press, 1971, p. 126.
[44] Benjamin Haggott Beckhart, *The New York Money Market*, Vol. 3., pp. 163–65. See the table on p. 83 breaking down call loans into the three categories.
[45] The 2 per cent figure derives from talking points compiled for Lamont in preparation for his testimony at the Pecora Committee hearings. BL, TWL, V, Box 211/14. National City Bank, a much larger institution, saw its call loans crest at almost $513 million in October 1929. Harold van B. Cleveland and Thomas F. Huertas, *Citibank 1812–1970*, Cambridge, MA: Harvard University Press, 1985, pp. 130–31, table 7.7.
[46] See Appendix 1, Consolidated Statement of Condition of J.P. Morgan & Co.

revenue for its success. Conservatively managed and conservatively run, J.P. Morgan & Co. was flourishing.

*****

In the late 1920s, between 400 and 500 employees worked at the bank, which was organized into departments: Auditing, Bond, Bond Redemption, Bookkeeping, Collection, Coupon, Dividend, Foreign Exchange, Letter of Credit, Library & Files, Loan, Mail, Paying Teller, Receiving Teller, Securities, Statistical, Stock, Syndicate, Stock Transfer, and Vault. These departments were overseen by long-serving staff members, few of whom have left any trace. Their expertise and loyalty were critical to the smooth functioning of the bank. The partners drew heavily upon the staff to compose letters, conduct research, draft position papers, and proffer sage, informed assessments of frequently highly complex questions. Much of what eventually made its way into the public realm as Morgan opinion was the product of hard-working staff. Leonhard Keyes, the chief clerk from 1913 to 1932, before his appointment as general manager in 1932, supervised the departments. During the Pecora hearings in 1933, Keyes emerged from the obscurity that cloaked J.P. Morgan & Co. staff. Other exceptions were Martin Egan, who assisted Lamont in handling public relations, and his successor, R. Gordon Wasson, who had an idiosyncratic career, culminating in his postwar eminence as a leading mycologist.[47] The Morgan partners, as of 31 December 1928, are listed in Table 1.2.

Though nineteen names are listed, the number of active partners was considerably smaller. Stotesbury, Lloyd, Gates, Newhall, and Hopkinson Jr. were Drexel & Co. partners in Philadelphia and played no role in J.P. Morgan & Co. in New York. By 1929, Stotesbury was retired and in 1930 Gates resigned to become President of the University of Pennsylvania. Of the fourteen partners resident in New York, Charles Steele was verging on inactive by 1929. The death of his wife in 1932 was followed by his retirement from the firm in 1934, though he continued to have the largest capital stake in the partnership until his death in 1939. Thomas Cochran experienced health problems beginning in the late 1920s that led to a progressive disengagement from the bank, though he remained a partner until his death in 1936.[48] One notable name is absent – Dwight Morrow. Morrow, who had become a partner on 1 July 1914, withdrew

---

[47] Keyes had joined J.P. Morgan & Co. as an office boy in 1903 and was successively chief clerk, general manager, secretary of J.P. Morgan Inc. in 1940, and vice-president in 1941, before retiring in 1951.

[48] On Charles Steele, a memorial address by Russell C. Leffingwell may be found in YUL, RCL, Series I, Box 9, Folder 184. Cochran's health problems dated from at least 1928. Young to Dwight Morrow, 16 March 1928, SLU, ODY, Box 10, Morrow, Dwight M.,

Table 1.2 *Partners in J.P. Morgan & Co.,*
31 December 1928.

Partner	Date of Entry into Partnership
Jack Morgan	31 December 1894
Edward T. Stotesbury	31 December 1894
Charles Steele	23 March 1900
Thomas W. Lamont	31 December 1910
Horatio G. Lloyd	1 January 1912
Thomas Cochran	31 December 1916
Junius S. Morgan	31 December 1919
George Whitney	31 December 1919
Thomas S. Gates	31 December 1920
Russell C. Leffingwell	30 June 1923
Francis D. Bartow	31 December 1926
Arthur M. Anderson	31 December 1926
William Ewing	31 December 1926
Harold Stanley	31 December 1927
Henry S. Morgan	31 December 1928
Thomas S. Lamont	31 December 1928
Henry P. Davison	31 December 1928
Thomas Newhall	31 December 1928
Edward Hopkinson Jr.	31 December 1928

Note. TML, JPM, Box B.6, Folder 5 contains a chronological list of all of the changes in the partnerships of the Morgan firms down to 1939.

from the firm to become Ambassador to Mexico on 30 September 1927. Morrow's departure was a loss. Along with Lamont, he was the most diplomatically inclined of the Morgan partners, had excellent contacts in Republican circles, especially through his friendship with Calvin Coolidge, and soon demonstrated an independence from his former partners that discomfited and surprised them.[49] Discounting Steele and Cochran, a dozen men constituted the working J.P. Morgan & Co. partners in 1929.

The partners ran the bank. New partners, such as those made on 31 December 1928, were not required to furnish a capital stake when

---

Folder 38. Cochran's health issues related to depression. Thomas W. Lamont to Morgan & Cie, 30 August 1933, TML, Morgan Bank European Papers (MBEP), Box 16, Cables rec'd, 1 June to 31 August 1933.

[49] There is a biography by Harold Nicolson, *Dwight Morrow*, New York: Harcourt, Brace, 1935.

they entered the firm. Their compensation derived from a combination of salary and profit distribution. Salary and profit share were decided by Jack Morgan. In 1931, the individual profit share of partners ranged from slightly less than 1 per cent for the most junior partners to just under 25 per cent for Jack Morgan.[50] Profit distribution was independent of the size of the capital share that an individual partner had in the firm. Through the 1930s, the largest capital shares in the bank were held by Charles Steele and Thomas W. Lamont. Jack Morgan's capital trailed their totals substantially.[51] The partners met daily, typically in the morning, with all those who were present in New York attending. No minutes were kept. Decisions were made on a consensus basis, requiring agreement on a course of action. Any partner could block any piece of business by registering an objection. One vote against meant that the firm did not pursue the matter.[52] The allocation of work followed a straightforward formula – the partner who had raised the business was charged with shepherding it.[53] Among themselves, the partners accepted each other's vouchsafe as binding. Questioned in 1938 in the Securities and Exchange Commission hearings into the bankruptcy of Richard Whitney & Co. occasioned by the fraud of Richard Whitney, the brother of George Whitney, the Morgan partner Francis D. Bartow admitted that he had not questioned extending a loan of $500,000 to Richard Whitney & Co. in the summer of 1931. He testified that he had no idea whether Richard Whitney & Co. had ever been audited, but he believed its affairs were sound, because "I had the best authority in the world when his brother (George Whitney) told me" that they were.[54]

Harry Morgan divided the partners into two categories, those who brought new business into the bank and those who ran the bank. To a point this was a reasonable description. Jack Morgan, Lamont, and Cochran (before his illness) were in the first category. Whitney straddled this division, both bringing in new business and running the bank.

[50] TML, CP, Box 17, Morgan & Co. – JPM & Co., Misc. a/cs 1920s contains a table compiled by Carosso, drawn from J.P. Morgan & Co.'s Private Ledger 5, that lists the partnership percentages from 1925 to 1931.

[51] In September 1935, after Morgan, Stanley was established, Steele's capital stood at $9 million, Lamont's at $8.5 million, and Jack Morgan's at $1.5 million. J.P. Morgan & Co. Capital Account, TML, Ledgers and Journals J.P. Morgan & Co., Private Ledger 7.

[52] *United States of America before the Securities and Exchange Commission in the Matter of Richard Whitney, et al.*, 3 May 1938, United States, Washington, DC: Government Printing Office, 1938, Vol. 2, pp. 851–52.

[53] George Whitney interview, 22 January 1963, Columbia University Library (CUL), Columbia Oral History Collection (COHC), p. 75.

[54] *Securities and Exchange Commission in the Matter of Richard Whitney*, 20 April 1938, Vol. 2, p. 567.

Whitney was the effective head of J.P. Morgan & Co.'s domestic operations after 1929 even if he did not have the title. Bartow fell clearly into Harry Morgan's second category. He was responsible for the Loan Department and functioned as the arbiter within the bank of the credit quality of loans that were made. As he told the Securities Exchange Commission in 1938, he had been given "direct responsibility for the portfolio of the office, including the Loan Department and the management of the internal organization."[55] To Bartow fell the task of economizing expenditures within the bank as the Depression bit. One partner, Leffingwell, was *hors catégorie*, neither a generator of new business nor responsible for running the bank. Leffingwell functioned as J.P. Morgan & Co.'s internal economist and lawyer who also supervised financial analyses of potential loans. Ordinarily he did not participate directly in discussions with clients or governments, though he was an important shaper of opinion outside the bank, notably through his friendship with the journalist Walter Lippmann. Harold Stanley was a generalist. Arthur Anderson (railroads and securities) and William Ewing (securities) had specific expertise, but they were not restricted to those areas.[56] Men such as Anderson, Bartow, and Ewing were respected on the Street but were not seen as front-rank figures. They were younger and in the 1920s newly minted as partners even if they had years of banking experience behind them.

The policy of bringing sons into the firm was mixed in its success. Writing in *The Nation* in 1939, Randolph Phillips identified partner recruitment as one factor in what he argued had been the decline of J.P. Morgan & Co., noting that "[t]he policy of making partners of the sons of partners has brought amiable men but no brilliant minds into the firm."[57] Edward Lamont has suggested that nepotism had its advantages, allowing the bank to make further inroads into well-connected circles, while furnishing individuals who could, by virtue of their socio-economic background, represent J.P. Morgan & Co. on corporate boards with aplomb.[58] Less charitably, neither Junius S. Morgan III (hereafter Junius Morgan) nor Harry P. Davison nor Thomas S. Lamont were as able as their fathers. Harry Morgan was the most competent of the epigone, but he would leave J.P. Morgan & Co. in 1935 to form Morgan, Stanley, taking with him Harold Stanley, arguably the most talented of the younger partners. Beyond the Corner, Wall Street believed with some justification that J.

[55] Ibid., p. 563.   [56] George Whitney interview, 22 January 1963, CUL, COHC, p. 40.
[57] Randolph Phillips, "The House of Morgan: The Price of Its War and Post-War Policies," *The Nation*, vol. 148, no. 24, 10 June 1939, p. 699.
[58] Lamont, *The Ambassador*, pp. 188–89.

Figure 1.1 Jack Morgan on board ship, 1933. Imagno/Hulton Archive/
Getty Images.

P. Morgan & Co.'s strength resided in its senior partners: Jack Morgan,
Lamont, Leffingwell, and Whitney.

Jack Morgan was the undisputed senior (see Figure 1.1). The impression persists that he was an ornamental head, the lesser son of a greater
father, who relied upon the talents of his partners. This view has a long
pedigree. *The Mirrors of Wall Street* noted in 1933 that "many people had
become accustomed to think of [Jack Morgan] as something of
a financial nonentity – living on the family name."[59] Nothing could
have been further from the truth. As a banker, Jack Morgan knew his
craft, having received an excellent training in New York and London.
He cared about the prestige, the reputation, and the integrity of the

[59] Anonymous, *The Mirrors of Wall Street*, New York: G.P. Putnam's & Sons, 1933, p. 45.
The author was Clinton W. Gilbert, who had earlier found success with *The Mirrors of
Washington*.

House of Morgan.[60] B.C. Forbes, the business writer and gadfly, quoted a Wall Street contemporary: "I would trust Jack Morgan behind my back as far as any man living ... I don't think any amount of money, which would be a small consideration, or any amount of prestige, which would be a strong consideration, would for a moment tempt him to do what he knew would be unfair or unjust." A decade later, a jaundiced portrait in the *American Mercury* conceded that Jack Morgan was deemed trustworthy by Wall Street.[61]

Among Jack Morgan's partners, there was never any question of either his probity or his command. Mitchell, after remarking that he never would have left J.P. Morgan & Co. had Jack Morgan lived, said: "He was a most remarkable person in every respect ... he didn't want to be bothered with details at all, but his judgment was unusually good on nearly anything – ethically, particularly. He had the highest ethics." For Whitney, "he was never given credit, because he was shy, but he kept that bunch of primadonnas working ... he was the unquestioned boss and there was never any argument about it ... He wasn't a buccaneer like his father, but he was a hell of a guy."[62] Jack Morgan's authority was buttressed by the J.P. Morgan & Co. partnership agreement, which reserved decisions upon all matters governing the partners, such as the distribution of profits, to his discretion. The partnership agreement was so commanding that John Marrinan, an advisor on Pecora's team investigating J.P. Morgan & Co., advanced the notion that the partners were more akin to employees.[63] Jack Morgan's power, though real, was not exercised in an authoritarian manner. He preferred to operate consensually, sounding his partners on possible courses of action and relying on their skills and knowledge rather than dictating what should be done.

Jack Morgan was reserved, loath to be in the limelight. A nineteenth-century man, believing in the merits of minimal government interference, and imbued with a hierarchical understanding of the world, he lamented the spread of universal suffrage.[64] Deeply religious, and well

---

[60] Jack Morgan to Edward C. Grenfell, 16 January 1925, Deutsche Bank archives (DB), Morgan Grenfell Papers (MGP), Box 50596220, December 1906 to September 1914 JPM.

[61] Bertie C. Forbes, *Men Who Are Making America*, New York: B.C. Forbes Publishing Co., 1917, p. 252; Walker, "J.P. The Younger," p. 134; "Mister Morgan," 86.

[62] TML, CP, Box 2, Folder Morgan, J.P. Jr., File 2, Notes from William A. Mitchell, "Memoir"; George Whitney interview, 22 January 1963, CUL, COHC.

[63] John Marrinan to Senator Fletcher, Senator Costigan, 27 May 1933, Center for Legislative Archives, RG 46, Sen 73A–F3, Box 133, Partnership Agreement – Confidential Memorandum.

[64] Jack Morgan's reply to Helen Harman Brown, the editor of *Reply*, an anti-suffrage magazine, 17 February 1914, TML, JPM, Box 104, Folder 314.

versed in the Bible, he was a major benefactor of American Episcopalianism. His political judgments, despite Mitchell's encomium, were at times sophomoric. Travelling in Italy in 1922, he wrote his classmate Joseph Grew to voice his enthusiasm about the "high-class revolution" fascism represented.[65] In fairness to Jack Morgan, as John Diggins has shown, many Americans were enamoured with Benito Mussolini and his Fascists in the 1920s, among them Lamont.[66]

At greatest ease in Britain, Jack Morgan gravitated naturally to its class-dominated politics, finding close allies and friends. Not enough attention has been paid to Jack Morgan's excellent relationships with the City, the Bank of England, the Conservative party, and the Court in the 1920s and 1930s. Ferdinand Kuhn Jr., writing in the *New York Times* in 1935, recognized this: "There are few Americans whose views carry so much weight in Conservative and business circles here as Mr. Morgan."[67] Throughout the interwar years, Jack Morgan would spend three to four months abroad each year, with a portion of this time, or often all of it, in Britain. While critics might sneer that Jack Morgan still thought that London was the centre of the world, its centrality for J.P. Morgan & Co. was unquestioned. Given that the City of London continued to play a leading role in international finance between 1929 and 1940, the Morgan identification with Britain was understandable.[68]

Jack Morgan was the confidant of Montagu Norman, the governor of the Bank of England from 1920 to 1944, and the Conservative Stanley Baldwin, the leading light in British politics between 1924 and 1937. Lord Revelstoke, the head of Barings, thought Jack Morgan "a great, big,

---

[65] Jack Morgan to Joseph Grew, 6 November 1922, TML, JPM, Box 43, Folder 14.

[66] John P. Diggins, *Mussolini and Fascism: The View from America*, Princeton, NJ: Princeton University Press, 1972.

[67] In the same article, "J.P. Morgan Pays a Call on Baldwin," *New York Times*, 1 August 1935, p. 3, Kuhn Jr. went on: "He had waited patiently at the end of a long line of Dominion High Commissioners and minor officials, who filed quickly past with nothing more than a formal handshake from the King and Queen. But when Mr. Morgan reached the royal stand, according to witnesses, it was as if a long-lost brother had appeared. The King and Queen stood with him fully ten minutes in eager and animated conversation, and hundreds of guests wondered who this portly stranger could be who was so intimate with their royal family. The story is of some interest as showing the unique place Mr. Morgan holds among all the thousands of Americans who visit Britain every summer."

[68] For accounts stressing the resilience of the City, see Peter J. Cain and Anthony G. Hopkins, *British Imperialism, 1688–2000*, 2nd ed., Harlow: Longman, 2001, pp. 406–08 and 464–78; Ranald C. Michie, "The City of London As a Global Financial Centre, 1880–1939: Finance, Foreign Exchange, and the First World War," in Philip L. Cottrell, Evan Lange, and Ulf Olsson, eds., *Centres and Peripheries in Banking: The Historical Development of Financial Markets*, Ashgate: Aldershot, 2007, pp. 73–79.

large-hearted, generous man w/o many personal antipathies, with
a character that is remarkable for straight-dealing," a judgment echoed
by Sir Charles Addis of the Hong Kong and Shanghai Banking
Corporation, who described Jack Morgan as "a great personality and
a big man in outlook as well as in bulk."[69] Grenfell's position as
a member of the Court of Directors of the Bank of England from 1905
to 1940, his standing as the Tory MP for the City of London from 1922 to
1935, and his subsequent elevation to the peerage as Lord St. Just in 1935
cemented Jack Morgan's influence in London. In the crisis years of the
1930s, Jack Morgan, not Lamont, was the first point of call for British
politicians and bankers.

There is a stark contrast between Jack Morgan's integration into the
financial and political circles in Britain and his lack thereof in the United
States. Contemporaries remarked how little known Jack Morgan was on
Wall Street. He was a figure of legend rather than of presence to the
denizens of the financial community. After Benjamin Strong – the governor of the Federal Reserve Bank of New York (FRBNY), the dominant
figure in the post-1918 Federal Reserve system, and a man close to Jack
Morgan – died in the fall of 1928, Jack Morgan's personal tie to the
Federal Reserve system was severed. Politically, Jack Morgan had no
comparable access to or accord with Calvin Coolidge, Herbert Hoover
or Andrew Mellon, let alone Roosevelt, to match his ties in Britain.
Republican reflexively in his domestic politics, Jack Morgan became
more rigid as he aged. Lacking mental flexibility, he was not well-
equipped to navigate the challenges that manifested after 1929. From
the mid-1930s, he was less engaged with J.P. Morgan & Co. Nevertheless,
all major decisions required his sanction throughout the 1930s.

His partner, Thomas W. Lamont, was a man of a different stamp (see
Figure 1.2). Lamont had made his way rapidly from his boyhood in rural
New York to Andover and Harvard. He was industrious, bright, ambi-
tious, and charming.[70] After a stint as a journalist, Lamont revitalized

[69] Revelstoke and Addis quoted in Roberta Allbert Dayer, *Finance and Empire: Sir Charles Addis, 1861–1945*, London: Macmillan, 1988, pp. 189–91.
[70] Beyond the biography by his grandson Edward, Lamont penned three works that shed light on his character: Thomas W. Lamont, *Henry P. Davison: The Record of a Useful Life*, New York: Harper & Brothers, 1933; *My Boyhood in a Parsonage*, New York: Harper Brothers, 1946; and *Across World Frontiers*, New York: Harcourt Brace & Co, 1951. The last was published posthumously. Chernow, *The House of Morgan*, p. 207, has a pithy assessment of Lamont. Robert Freeman Smith, "Thomas Lamont: International Banker As Diplomat," in Thomas J. McCormack and Walter LaFeber, eds., *Behind the Throne: Servants of Power to Imperial Presidents, 1898–1968*, Madison, WI: University of Wisconsin Press, 1993, pp. 101–25, offers a sympathetic portrait of Lamont as a diplomat. For Michael Hogan's argument that Lamont was the exemplar of the private banker as an agent of corporatism, see "Thomas W. Lamont and European Recovery: The Diplomacy

Figure 1.2 Thomas W. Lamont, George Whitney, and Jack Morgan during the Pecora hearings, 1933. Heritage Images/Hulton Archive/ Getty Images.

what became Lamont, Corliss and Company, an advertising firm, before coming to the attention of Henry P. Davison. It was Davison who recruited Lamont to the newly established Bankers Trust and it was Davison who brought Lamont into J.P. Morgan & Co. Widely seen in the interwar years as the real brains within the bank, Lamont, with his fondness for public fora, his love of the social whirl, and his extraordinary facility for making and retaining friends, was the natural spokesman for J. P. Morgan & Co.[71] With his background in the newspaper business, Lamont was attuned to its pulse. Assisted by staff, he devoted astonishing amounts of time and ink to caress, counter, and cultivate reporters and

of Privatism in a Corporatist Age," Kenneth Paul Jones, ed., *U.S. Diplomats in Europe, 1919–1941*, Santa Barbara, CA: ABC-Clio 1983.

[71] A capsule biography in the British Foreign Office files is typical: "Thomas Lamont is a self-made man and very highly regarded in New York. He is always said to be the brains behind J.P. Morgan and Co." The National Archives UK, Foreign Office, 371/17588/ 05265.

Figure 1.3 Junius S. Morgan, Jack Morgan, Harold Stanley, and Russell C. Leffingwell at the Pecora hearings. Charles Hoff/New York Daily News/Getty Images.

newspaper proprietors alike. Lamont's involvement in founding the Council on Foreign Relations, and in supporting financially its journal *Foreign Affairs*, was an example of this imperative and reflected twin aims: his deep-seated interest in international relations and his desire to ensure that J.P. Morgan & Co. was treated fairly. Reading his correspondence, the depth of Lamont's feeling for J.P. Morgan & Co. shines through. He was partisan, fiercely proud of J.P. Morgan & Co., and was unwilling or unable to concede that the bank or its partners had ever transgressed.

Lamont, like Jack Morgan, evinced a "lifelong Anglophilia."[72] He travelled regularly to Britain, though his stays were never as extended as Jack Morgan's. Unlike Morgan, his Anglophilia was qualified. Following his experience at the Paris Peace talks in 1919, Lamont expressed exasperation with the British stance, which he echoed nearly twenty years later in 1936 when he wrote his son Thomas S. Lamont: "With all their delightful qualities, the British are the most go-getting and nationalistic people in the world. They don't grind their own axe half the time, but

[72] The phrase is Lansing Lamont's, *A Life in Letters*, New York: Strawtown Press, 1999, and refers to Lamont and his wife Florence Corliss Lamont, p. 64.

24 hours a day."[73] Asperity aside, Lamont believed in ongoing Anglo-American friendship as axiomatic for global prosperity. He favoured the notion of an Anglo-American alliance in the wake of World War I, as Priscilla Roberts has shown.[74] It was an outlook that married seamlessly with Jack Morgan and the House of Morgan. While Lamont shared Jack Morgan's affinity for Britain, his politics were less defined. His friends in Britain were more varied, less Conservative and less High Church. In the second half of the 1930s, Lamont found common cause with pro-appeasement circles centred around the Cliveden set.

Though Lamont was a Republican, in the eyes of his son, Corliss Lamont, he was a "liberal conservative."[75] He voted Democrat in the 1920 presidential election, animated by his anger at Republican foot-dragging on the issue of the Versailles treaty and membership in the League of Nations. Thereafter his ballot was reliably Republican. Lamont cared more about power and influence and less about ideological identification. This characteristic, coupled with his amiability, allowed Lamont to try to work with Hoover and Roosevelt. *Fortune* described Lamont in 1939 as someone who "[u]nlike many a rich man ... has seen too much and known too much to be shocked by the thought of change."[76] B.C. Forbes, writing in 1930, thought that there were two sides to Lamont – a hard-driving, pragmatic banker that the Street respected but did not love and the private Lamont known to his friends, who was much more sympathetic, generous, and understanding.[77] As Lamont's *New York Times* obituary remarked in 1948, "Mr. Lamont was a man who hated to see a friendship come to an end."[78]

Not all were enamoured. Stuart M. Crocker, a confidant of Owen D. Young, who met Lamont at the Dawes Plan talks in 1924 and saw a great deal of him during the Young Plan negotiations in 1929, was a sceptic, recording in his diary "you have your fingers crossed on him, because he [Lamont] is so damned diplomatic that you never know just where you stand with him." Crocker much preferred Jack Morgan's bluntness. The portrait of Lamont sketched in *The Mirrors of Wall Street*

---

[73] Elisabeth Glaser, "The Making of the Economic Peace," in Manfred F. Boemeke, Gerald D. Feldman, and Elisabeth Glaser, eds., *The Treaty of Versailles: A Reassessment after 75 Years*, Washington, DC: German Historical Institute, 1998, pp. 398–99; Thomas W. Lamont to Thomas S. Lamont, 13 July 1936, in Lamont, *A Life in Letters*, p. 136.

[74] Priscilla Roberts, "The Anglo-American Theme: American Visions of an Atlantic Alliance 1914–1933," *Diplomatic History*, vol. 21, no. 3 (1997), pp. 333–64.

[75] Corliss Lamont interview with Vincent Carosso, TML, CP, Box 8, Folder Thomas W. Lamont.

[76] "East Seventieth Street," *Fortune*, vol. 20, no. 1, July 1939, pp. 82–83.

[77] Bertie C. Forbes, "Tommy Lamont of J.P. Morgan," *Forbes*, 1 August 1930.

[78] Thomas W. Lamont obituary, *New York Times*, 4 February 1948.

(1933) was scathing, decrying him as a man driven by a blind admiration for Pierpont Morgan. Much kinder to Jack Morgan, *The Mirrors* was dyspeptic in its assessment of Lamont, dismissing his activities at home and abroad as froth. Frederick Lewis Allen, who conferred with Lamont while he was writing *The Lords of Creation*, told his sister "[I] would like T. W. Lamont if I really trusted him, which I don't."[79] Arthur M. Schlesinger Jr. believed that Lamont had fallen prey to his own rhetoric, swallowing the line that a New Era had arrived in the 1920s.[80] While this may go too far, Lamont's brilliance was occluded by congenital optimism.

As a banker, Lamont admitted that he was not much of one. Banking was a means to an end. In a 1942 letter, Lamont put it thus, "I have never been greatly interested in banking ... My interests, as you well know, have long been outside the purely routine channels of banking about which I confessedly don't know very much."[81] Caring most about what banking could accomplish, Lamont spent his time primarily on politics, diplomacy, and international relations. His acknowledged banking deficiencies were amplified by an uncertain grasp of economics. This meant that Lamont relied upon the expert counsel of staff and his partners, in particular Leffingwell and, after 1931, Parker Gilbert, for the economic advice that streamed forth in letters and speeches under his name. Though he sought counsel frequently on economic matters, Lamont did not always take it. His habitual optimism could distort the advice that he received, particularly from Leffingwell whose outlook tended to be more pessimistic.

Leffingwell was Lamont's closest friend among the partners (see Figure 1.3). He was by training a lawyer, graduating from Columbia Law School in 1902 whereupon he joined Guthrie, Cravath & Henderson. Made a partner in 1907, he was wooed to the US Treasury as Assistant Secretary in 1917. He served first under William Gibbs McAdoo and then from January 1919 under Carter Glass until 1920, when he left to rejoin his old law firm, which was renamed Cravath, Henderson, Leffingwell & de Gersdorff.[82] Three years later he became

---

[79] Stuart M. Crocker diary, 5 March 1929, SLU, ODY, Stuart M. Crocker diary (SMC), Box 976; Anonymous, *The Mirrors of Wall Street*, pp. 99–112. Frederick Lewis Allen to Hildegard Allen, 10 June 1935, Library of Congress (LC), Frederick Lewis Allen papers (FLA), Box 2, correspondence 1935.

[80] Schlesinger, *The Crisis of the Old Order*, p. 161.

[81] Thomas W. Lamont to Paul G. Hoffmann, 18 September 1942, BL, TWL, Series I, Box 20/16. Hoffmann was in the Department of Commerce. The letter was drafted but not sent.

[82] Ajay K. Mehrotra, "Lawyers, Guns and Public Monies: The U.S. Treasury, World War One, and the Administration of the Modern Fiscal State," *Law and History Review*, vol. 28, no. 1 (2010), pp. 173–225 for Leffingwell's stint at the Treasury.

a partner in J.P. Morgan & Co.[83] In the 1920s, Leffingwell was the paradigm of an orthodox, conservative economic thinker, believing deeply in the gold standard, championing balanced budgets, and disparaging of what he labelled derisively "managed money." His time at the Treasury married with this perspective to inform his understanding of the months following the Crash in 1929. While at the Treasury, the sharp economic contraction in the United States in 1920–21 was occasioned in part by a Treasury effort to stamp out inflation, which had reached more than 18 per cent in 1918 and stood at nearly 14 per cent in 1919. Under Treasury pressure, interest rates were raised markedly, to 7 per cent.[84] Whether or not this prescription was responsible for the recovery that ensued in the United States remains a matter of debate. For Leffingwell, the lesson was clear. Reliving this episode years later, in April 1929, he told Glass that he regarded deflationary Treasury policy as laying the foundations for prosperity after 1921. He concluded robustly, "I apologize for nothing. I am very proud of it all."[85] Given that Leffingwell's economic views infused J.P. Morgan & Co., it is not surprising that the initial reaction from the Corner to the Crash in 1929 was a sense of déjà vu. Short-term deflation, while painful, was a necessary medication that would serve as a palliative corrective. Such views were not unique. Famously, Andrew Mellon thought along similar lines.[86]

Leffingwell was a Democrat amidst a phalanx of Republican Morgan partners. He retained a marked affection and respect for the Democratic Senator Carter Glass, his mentor at the Treasury. Glass, one of the architects of the Federal Reserve system as a congressman, was appointed to the Senate to fill the vacancy left by the death of Virginia's senior senator in 1920. A senator until 1946, he soon became acknowledged by all, including himself, as the leading expert in the Senate on financial and economic matters. Glass and Leffingwell were close, and while the

---

[83] See Stephen Schuker, "Leffingwell, Russell Cornell," in John A. Garraty, ed., *Dictionary of American Biography*, supplement 6, 1956–60, New York: Charles Scribner's & Sons, 1990, 376–78; W. Elliott Brownlee, "Russell Cornell Leffingwell," in Larry Schweikart, ed., *Encyclopedia of American Business History and Biography, Banking and Finance*, New York: Facts on File, 1990, 216–39. Edward Pulling, ed., *Selected Letters of R.C. Leffingwell*, Oyster Bay, NY: Privately Printed, 1979, also contains biographical information. Robert T. Swaine, *The Cravath Firm and Its Predecessors, 1819–1948*, Vol. 2, New York: Private Printed, 1948, pp. 17–18 and 130–32 is insightful on Leffingwell.

[84] Allan H. Meltzer, *A History of the Federal Reserve, Vol. 1: 1913–1951*, Chicago: University of Chicago Press, 2003, pp. 90–109, discusses the move to higher rates and Leffingwell's role therein. The inflation figures may be found on p. 91.

[85] Leffingwell to Carter Glass, 29 April 1929, University of Virginia Library (UV), Carter Glass papers (CG), Series I, Box 14/1929 Banking Correspondence Federal Reserve System.

[86] David Cannadine, *Mellon: An American Life*, New York: Vintage Books, 2008, p. 395.

two men often disagreed, their differences did not affect their friendship. While Glass was an uncertain ally of the New Deal, he proved, as the 1930s wore on, to be reliably hostile to it. More than Glass, Leffingwell was willing to countenance some of what orthodox economists regarded as the New Deal's heresies. As the deflationary grind of the early 1930s milled more finely, Leffingwell began to consider previously unmentionable notions. This shift was to lead him in 1933 to embrace Roosevelt's decision to abandon gold.

Leffingwell's internationalism was less bred in the bone than either Jack Morgan or Lamont. He did not have their experience of travelling and living abroad. During the discussions in 1929 surrounding what would become the Bank for International Settlements, Leffingwell remarked: "What is an international bank? When people talk about us as international bankers we say we are not, that we are American bankers."[87] This distinction hinted at Leffingwell's occasional apostasy as tensions mounted internationally after 1929. Leffingwell periodically voiced anti-French sentiments that were never recanted. His views on Britain were also at times conditional, though never strident enough to challenge Jack Morgan and the dominant ethos of the House of Morgan. He was contemptuous of the League of Nations, seeing in it a body of naïve do-gooders whose activities imperilled peace as much as foolish notions of neutrality did.[88] At the same time, Leffingwell remained committed to an international trading and financial order free of the obstacles imposed by politics.

Leffingwell was a forceful personality. Those who worked with him at the Carnegie Corporation, on whose board Leffingwell sat for decades, make this apparent. Frederick Osborn, a critic of Leffingwell and J.P. Morgan, described Leffingwell as "a man of magnificent character and very charming personal characteristics. He had strong personal views, he was not easily swayed, and he expressed his views very strongly to the board and took it that they were going to be followed by the board." James Perkins echoed Osborn: "He could be a warm man, but he could also be a very ruthless man. He was a tough chairman. He ran it." For Alger Hiss, Leffingwell "was very intellectually impressive. He was an

[87] Leffingwell to Lamont, 16 April 1929, YUL, RCL, Series I, Box 4, Folder 94.
[88] See his exchange with Walter Lippmann in October 1931 at the time of the Japanese invasion of Manchuria, Lippmann to Leffingwell, 22 October 1931, Leffingwell to Lippmann, 23 October 1931, both YUL, RCL, Series 1, Box 5, Folder 108. On neutrality, see Leffingwell to Lamont, 30 November 1935, YUL, RCL, Series I, Box 4, Folder 96.

extraordinary man."[89] Leffingwell was known for writing copiously and speaking likewise, and for being circumspect in his public statements, yet in private he was frequently immoderate and savage. His correspondence with Lamont was frank – startlingly so – biting, and vituperative in condemnation. Like Lamont and Jack Morgan, Leffingwell was animated by a conviction in the fundamental propriety of J.P. Morgan & Co. and its works. Like them, he believed deeply that American liberal democratic capitalism had benefited from the Morgan touch.

Leffingwell shared with Lamont, and to some degree Jack Morgan, an aversion to the "detail of the banking business."[90] Thus lies a paradox: on the eve of 1929, the three most senior partners – Jack Morgan, Lamont, and Leffingwell – were bankers whose interest in banking was qualified. Fortunately, Whitney was a traditional banker (see Figure 1.2). John T. Flynn, a strident critic of J.P. Morgan & Co., considered Whitney to be the ablest of the Morgan partners, its "organizing brains" and a man who was much brighter than his brother, Richard, a leading figure on the New York Stock Exchange (NYSE).[91] Whitney went to Groton and then Harvard where he was a classmate of Franklin D. Roosevelt's. As Whitney recalled, "I never got on with the President." From Harvard, he entered Kidder, Peabody, before moving on to Redman & Co. and Markoe, Morgan & Whitney, firms that specialized in retailing securities. In 1915, he was brought into J.P. Morgan & Co. through the influence of his father-in-law, Robert Bacon, who had been a Morgan partner and remained close to Harry P. Davison. Elevated to partner on 31 December 1919, Whitney was concerned primarily, though not exclusively, with selling securities. It was Whitney who oversaw much of the groundwork of organizing syndicates to distribute the bonds that were the staple of J.P. Morgan's investment work during the 1920s. As he recalled, Whitney had nothing to do with the negotiations that produced the Dawes and later Young Plan loans; what he did was sell the bonds.[92] By the late 1920s, because of Cochran's health problems, Whitney helmed the marketing of securities for J.P. Morgan & Co. Highly regarded on Wall Street, Whitney's Republicanism was not hidden and his

---

[89] All three men worked with Leffingwell at the Carnegie Corporation. The interviews are in CUL, COHC. Osborn was interviewed in 1967; for the remarks on Leffingwell, pp. 15–16; Perkins was also interviewed in 1967, p. 16; Hiss was interviewed in 1968, see pp. 27–28.

[90] TML, CP, Box 2, Folder Morgan, J.P. Jr., File 2, Notes from William A. Mitchell, "Memoir."

[91] John T. Flynn, "Other People's Money," *The New Republic*, vol. 78, no. 1006, 14 March 1934, p. 130.

[92] George Whitney interview, 22 January 1963, CUL, COHC, p. 42.

Figure 1.4 Thomas S. Lamont at the Pecora hearings, 1933. Bettmann/
Getty Images.

combativeness when quizzed by investigators during the 1930s was
marked. Pecora called Whitney the "most mendacious" and "most eva-
sive" of the Morgan partners who appeared before his committee in
1933.[93] Within the bank, the appreciation was quite different. His loyalty
to the firm was unquestioned, and his embrace of its culture whole-
hearted. Whitney was well regarded and deemed sound and capable.

The partners junior to Whitney – Anderson, Bartow, Ewing, Stanley,
and the sons Davison, Thomas S. Lamont, and Junius Morgan– have left
fewer traces (see Figures 1.4–1.6).[94] John Brooks' gibe in *Once in
Golconda*, his lively 1969 account of Wall Street during the interwar
years, that "the partners were extensions of and adornments to J.P.
Morgan's personality," Anglophile, Republican, *Social Register*
Protestants who were "as much a physical as a social type, with
a kinship more primitive than social background or like-mindedness,"

---

[93] TML, CP, Box 6, Folder Ferdinand Pecora.
[94] Harry S. Morgan, interviewed by Carosso in the 1970s on multiple occasions, is an
outlier.

Figure 1.5 Arthur Anderson at the Wheeler Committee hearings, 1936. Harris & Ewing Collection, Library of Congress, Prints & Photographs Division, LC-DIG-hec-21864.

glistens rather than illuminates.[95] A more recent assessment has been provided by Susie J. Pak.[96] While Pak's fine study contextualizes the partners and their networks, there remains a challenge in understanding the dynamics of J.P. Morgan & Co. There was debate, discussion, and difference. Yet internal disputes were never conveyed externally, which masked the extent to which the partners disagreed with the policies pursued by Washington, especially during the Hoover administration.

The Morgan rule never to comment publicly reinforced the outward impression of a cautious, sober conservatism typifying the private merchant bank. Discretion was understandable. Sailing to Europe on the SS *Olympic* in July 1926, Cochran gave an interview to a reporter for the *Wall Street Journal* in which he touted General Motors' prospects. The result,

[95] John Brooks, *Once in Golconda*, New York: Harper & Row, 1969. Reprint: New York: John Wiley & Sons, 1999, pp. 45–46.
[96] Pak, *Gentleman Bankers*.

Figure 1.6 One former J.P. Morgan & Co. partner and two J.P. Morgan & Co. partners at the Temporary National Economic Committee hearings, 1939. Harris & Ewing Collection, Library of Congress, Prints & Photographs Division, LC-DIG-hec-27848.

From left: Harold Stanley, George Whitney, and Russell C. Leffingwell.

as the *Journal* trumpeted on 3 August in its Market Comment column was, "General Motors in High: Stock rushes upward in sensational fashion on Cochran interview – Whole Market Buoyant." Brooks, in *Once in Golconda*, would point to this interview as the catalyst for the subsequent market climb of the late 1920s.[97] While few historians would concur, the reaction to Cochran's off-hand remarks attested to the solemnity with which the financial community treated Morgan utterances, suggesting how weighty the Corner was in the age of Babbitt.

---

[97] "General Motors in High: Stock Rushes Upward in Sensational Fashion on Cochran Interview – Whole Market Buoyant," *Wall Street Journal*, 3 August 1926, p. 16; Brooks, *Once in Golconda*, pp. 87–89.

2   J.P. Morgan & Co. at Home and Abroad in the 1920s

At 12:01 p.m. on 16 September 1920 a horse-drawn wagon pulled up across the street from the Morgan offices in New York. A massive explosion ensued, flinging slugs of cut-up window sash weights into buildings and scything down pedestrians. With dead, dying, and injured victims strewn on the street, the Morgan staff in 23 Wall Street escaped relatively lightly. One employee was killed, and seventeen more were wounded by shards of glass. Among the partners, only Junius Morgan, who sustained a gash to his hand, was injured.[1] Newspapers and journals were quick off the mark to assign blame. The *New York Times*, in one of the many articles that it would run on the bombing, put forward an explanation: "Red Plot seen in Blast: Scenes in Wall Street after the Explosion." The *Wall Street Journal* indulged in conspiratorial speculation:

That the explosion, if part of a plot ... was carefully planned in detail, is the opinion of brokers familiar with the procedure customarily followed by Mr. Morgan on his returns from Europe. On the day of his first return to the office, it is his custom to assemble his chiefs promptly at twelve o'clock for the purpose of lunching together at some place previously decided upon. The fact that the explosion took place practically at noon, gives good basis for the assumption that the perpetrators of the plot were well aware of this custom, and planned to take advantage of it, with the expectation of destroying, at one blow, all the heads of the organization.

For the *Commercial and Financial Chronicle*, the time had come to crack down, to "arouse the American people to the necessity of short, sharp measures and to the folly of temporizing further with insane agitators with an evident mania for indiscriminate homicide of a peculiarly heartless and revolting kind."[2] While there was outrage at the heavy loss of life and breathless wondering whether an "infernal machine" might have been

---

[1] Beverly Gage, *The Day That Wall Street Exploded*, New York: Oxford University Press, 2009, pp. 1–37, is an excellent account of the day, the bombing, and the political violence in American life in the 1920s.

[2] *New York Times*, 17 September 1920, p. 1; "Terrific Explosion Outside Morgan's Office: Explosion at 12:01 P.M.," *Wall Street Journal*, 17 September 1920, p. 3, *Commercial and Financial Chronicle*, vol. 111, no. 2882, 18 September 1920, p. 112.

involved, there was no surprise that J.P. Morgan & Co was bombed. The bank was a logical choice for "Bolsheviki" to attack; after all, was it not the most important financial institution in the United States and the world? How better to strike a blow against capitalism than to assault the Morgan offices?

If the Morgan partners after the explosion deprecated the notion that J. P. Morgan & Co. was the particular aim of the bombers, such protestations only served to reinforce their salience.[3] That the Morgan bank should have been targeted reflected its place in the American imagination and in American life as well as its stature as the standard-bearer of internationalism in the American financial world. London, Paris, and New York – the Morgan trinity – united the old world's pre-eminent financial centres with the rising power of the new world in the wake of war. For those who saw the harbinger of the future in Lenin's Russia, global revolution would sweep aside the entrenched power of capitalism that resided in these financial citadels. For the moment, the Morgan place atop the international financial pantheon was assured, but it was not unchallenged; explosions and the Red Scare aside, structural shifts in American banking were altering the distribution of power in ways that were understood dimly, even on the Street. Paradoxically, while the 1920s were the Morgan heyday, it was also the decade in which Morgan supremacy was under siege on Wall Street.

Morgan pre-eminence in the hard work of postwar reconstruction concealed to some degree this reality. The artificial nature of the postwar system, with a prostrate Germany, a Russian pariah state, a disaffected Italy, a Japan antagonized by the unwillingness to accede to its requests for racial equality, and a League of Nations disfigured by American disavowal, bestowed on Britain and France preponderance. While London and Paris eyed one another with the scepticism born of the reawakening of centuries of great-power animosity, J.P. Morgan & Co. worked to bridge hostility. London and Paris aside, the Corner cultivated strong ties with Rome and Tokyo in the 1920s. Durable peace, in the Morgan view, rested upon an appreciation that politics and economics were indivisible. Multilateral trade, open markets, and a revived gold standard would underpin European revival, or so the partners hoped. Economic prosperity went hand in hand with the development of political goodwill among the former combatants. The willingness of Americans to lend, and foreign longing to borrow, made the agents of transmission powerful. With its unmatched connections to the victors of World War I,

---

[3] Gage, *The Day That Wall Street Exploded*, p. 165.

no American bank was as influential as J.P. Morgan & Co. in the 1920s at home and abroad.

*****

The bombing added to the myth that encrusted the Morgan firm. Much of the Morgan aura derived from Pierpont Morgan whose legacy shaped J. P. Morgan & Co. long after his death. Popularly, Pierpont Morgan was seen as having played the leading role in surmounting the panic of 1907, demonstrating, apparently, the inability of government to resolve such peril without recourse to private bankers. Pierpont Morgan had mastered calamity, in the process saving the American financial system. Without his intercession, the abyss beckoned.[4] Thereafter, J.P. Morgan & Co. was in thrall to a legend of 1907. Should another great crisis occur, in the expectation of many Americans J.P. Morgan & Co. would marshal the response of the financial community. The Morgan partners would come to the rescue as Pierpont had in 1907.

Tangibly, the 1907 panic spurred the creation of the Federal Reserve system.[5] The lack of an American central bank had long been bemoaned as a weakness in the American banking system. The question was, how should a central bank be constructed and what would its powers be? The discussions that produced the Federal Reserve Act in 1913 resulted in the creation of a central bank that did not mimic the European models but instead opted for a dozen regional Federal Reserve banks overseen by a Federal Reserve Board in Washington. Almost immediately the new system was confronted by the outbreak of war. The FRBNY was always likely to wield disproportionate influence within the system given that New York was the nation's financial hub, but Benjamin Strong's intellect and drive amplified this tendency. The Federal Reserve Board in Washington suffered from two notable weaknesses in the 1920s: some of its members were ill-suited to sit on the board and Washington itself was distant from what was transpiring in the financial markets.[6]

As a private bank, J.P. Morgan & Co. was not a member of the Federal Reserve system. Nevertheless, its partners had intimate contacts with

---

[4] See Strouse, *Morgan: American Financier*, pp. 573–96, for Pierpont Morgan during the 1907 crisis. J. Lawrence Broz, *The International Origins of the Federal Reserve System*, Ithaca, NY: Cornell University Press, 1997, offers an alternative assessment.

[5] Elmus Wicker, *The Great Debate on Banking Reform: Nelson Aldrich and the Origins of the Fed*, Columbus, OH: Ohio State University Press, 2005.

[6] Lester V. Chandler, *Benjamin Strong: Central Banker*, Washington: The Brookings Institution, 1958, pp. 256–57. John Kenneth Galbraith, in *The Great Crash 1929*, 3rd ed., Boston: Houghton Mifflin, 1972, p. 32, was scathing, labelling the Federal Reserve Board "a body of startling incompetence."

Strong. These dated from the pre-war period and lasted until Strong's death in October 1928. Strong counted Lamont, Leffingwell, and Morrow among those who mattered to him personally. As Strong told Owen Young in 1927, it had been Jack Morgan, Henry P. Davison, and Morrow who had convinced him to take the job of governor of the FRBNY.[7] The tie between the J.P. Morgan partners and Strong was tightened by the close friendship that sprang up between Strong and Montagu Norman, the governor of the Bank of England. Strong's belief in the necessity of European stabilization and Anglo-American comity mirrored the outlook of the Morgan partners.[8] Jack Morgan furnished Strong with the bank's private statement of financial condition as part of this relationship. In return, J.P. Morgan & Co. paper was discounted by Strong. While the Morgan partners often saw matters similarly to Strong, he was his own man with his own ideas. Critics, however, were inclined to believe that Strong and the Federal Reserve were puppets dancing on Morgan strings.[9]

Fears that J.P. Morgan & Co. dominated American finance, American industry, American railroads, and by extension the American economy took sustenance from 1907, animating the 1912 Investigation of Financial and Monetary Conditions. The investigation, often called the Pujo investigation, after its chair, Congressman Arsène P. Pujo of Louisiana, was a product of the impulses of both Populism and Progressivism. It drew upon agrarian anger at the imposition of the gold standard and upon the oft-recounted stories of the depredations of big-city bankers preying upon farmers. It was given momentum by the desire to reform an America that seemed to be the plaything of ever larger, more sprawling corporations. The rise of these corporations threatened the health of the American body politic in the eyes of many. As discussion swirled about establishing a central bank, the worry was articulated that it would be controlled by the same parochial financial interests whose activities had done so much, in the reform view, to warp American life.

Among the witnesses that testified before the committee was Pierpont Morgan. Sparring with Samuel Untermyer, the chief counsel for the committee, Pierpont Morgan made his famous comment that character was the basis of credit. He denied resolutely that he had any particular control or influence over other financial institutions and did not agree that the presence of Morgan partners on the boards of banks or insurance companies connoted a concentration of wealth and power. Pujo and

---

[7] Strong to Young, 6 March 1927, SLU, ODY papers, Box 303, George Harrison confidential.
[8] Chandler, *Benjamin Strong*. On relations with the Morgan partners, pp. 25–31.
[9] Anonymous, *The Mirrors of Wall Street*, pp. 9–10.

Untermyer sought to demonstrate the contrary. The hearings adumbrated the interlocking directorates of the Morgan partners, tabulated those directorships, and introduced diagrams that pictorially demonstrated these links. When the Pujo Committee report was published in February 1913, its authors professed the conviction that there existed a "Money Trust" in which the concentration of control of money and credit was in the hands of a "few men" who exercised control through interlocking directorships. The Pujo Committee reckoned that banks led by J.P. Morgan & Co. had at their disposal resources of at least $1.3 billion.[10] Later that year a series of articles was published in *Harper's Weekly* by Louis D. Brandeis. Collected, they appeared in book form in 1914 under the title *Other People's Money*. Brandeis built on the work of the Pujo Committee and extended the attack on investment bankers, with J.P. Morgan & Co. as his chief target.

The Morgan partners, whether under Pierpont Morgan or Jack Morgan, scoffed at the "Money Trust" charge. Grenfell, writing to Lamont in 1930 regarding allegations levied by Republican Congressman Louis T. McFadden that hidden Morgan power dictated international finance, commented:

Loose talk of that sort does harm because it is difficult to catch up and deny statements mixing up J.P.M. & Co., Federal Reserve Bank, Ben. Strong, Bank of England and Norman. We all remember before and during the war how any fool could draw up a diagram indicating that J.P.M. & Co. directly controlled all the railways, the banks, Steel and Harvester and Atlantic shipping, whilst through the affiliates of the London partners with the Bank of England it would appear also that all the English industries and shipping companies were in a wicked group.[11]

During the Pecora hearings in 1933, Jack Morgan and Lamont gave different answers to interlocutors on the question of Morgan influence. Queried by Senator William Gibbs McAdoo as to whether Morgan directorships gave them a disproportionate say in the corporations on whose boards the partners served, Jack Morgan replied "We have no more domination than one vote gives us, Senator McAdoo." Two weeks later,

---

[10] *Money Trust Investigation of Financial and Monetary Conditions in the United States* [Pujo Committee], Subcommittee of the Committee on Banking and Currency, Washington, DC: Government Printing Office 1913. Pierpont Morgan's comment regarding character and credit was made on 19 December 1912 and is on p. 1084. *The Report of the Committee to Investigate the Concentration of Control of Money and Credit*, House of Representatives, 62nd Congress, 3rd session, House of Representatives, Washington, DC, Government Printing Office, 1913, may also be found at https://fraser.stlouisfed .org/title/report-committee-appointed-pursuant-house-resolutions-429-504-investi gate-concentration-control-money-credit-1329. See especially pp. 129–31.
[11] Grenfell to Lamont, 27 May 1930, TML, CP, Box 18, Morgan & Co. – Misc. Notes 1930s.

Lamont told Senator Edward P. Costigan that the public grossly over-
estimated Morgan influence. When pressed by Costigan if he would
characterize Morgan influence as slight, Lamont demurred: "We hope
that in sound directions it is much more than slight."[12] If this reply
suggested there was substance to tales of Morgan power, historians are
divided. Forty years after the Pecora hearings, Carosso adjudged that
a "Money Trust" never existed.[13] David Kotz, writing later the same
decade, drew a distinction between two explanatory schools of thought:
the financial control thesis that went back to Brandeis and traced its path
through Corey to Pecora and the managerial control thesis which had
been pioneered by Adolf Berle and Gardner Means, reaching its most
influential statement in Alfred Chandler. If the former championed the
notion of widespread Morgan influence, the latter rejected it on the
grounds that the growth of the modern corporation with its managerial
class was inimical to external control. While Kotz was a partisan of the
financial control thesis, he agreed that between 1930 and 1945 banker
control over large corporations receded.[14]

In truth, it is difficult to gauge the Morgan reach. Evidently the bank
and its partners were integrated into the Atlantic seaboard elite. The
business and personal links with Morgan Grenfell in London and
Morgan & Cie. in Paris afforded the Morgan partners privileged access
to Anglo-French business and political circles. Some observers were
unequivocal about the scope of Morgan influence. The author of *More
Merry-Go-Round*, the sequel to the bestselling *Washington Merry-Go-
Round*, classified Lamont in 1932 as one of the "super-lobbyists" for
whom "[t]he door of the White House, of every Cabinet office, always
is open. They advise, and they are listened to. Many of them have
performed important public service and at some sacrifice. But it is exactly
this that makes their influence so powerful, their position so dangerous."
Frederick Lewis Allen and Elliott V. Bell, the financial beat writer for the
New York Times in the 1930s, two acute contemporary observers who
knew the bank and the financial world well, were less categorical. Both
confessed that Morgan influence was tangible but ineffable, real but
fundamentally mysterious.[15] Others were studiously vague. Benjamin
Beckhart and James G. Smith, in their 1931 volume on the New York

[12] Pecora Committee, 24 May 1933, p. 33; 9 June 1933, pp. 156–57.
[13] Vincent Carosso, "The Wall Street Money Trust from Pujo through Medina," *Business
History Review*, vol. 47, no. 4 (1973), pp. 421–37.
[14] David M. Kotz, *Bank Control of Large Corporations in the United States*, Berkeley, CA:
University of California Press, 1980, chaps. 1–2.
[15] Robert S. Allen, *More Merry-Go-Round, by the Authors of Washington Merry-Go-Round*,
New York: Liveright Press, 1932, p. 458; Allen, *The Lords of Creation*, pp. 345–46; Elliott
V. Bell, "The Decline of the Money Barons," in Hanson W. Baldwin and Shepard Stone,

money market, remarked of the private banks, "their power is not to be measured in terms of their assets alone, but in the prestige of the firms and the personal connections and fortunes of the partners."[16] No bank was as prestigious as the Corner, nor did any private American bank have the contacts that the Morgan partners enjoyed. J.P. Morgan & Co. was a member of various industry groupings or associations, such as the International Chamber of Commerce and the Investment Bankers Association. Yet there is little to demonstrate that the firm took a leadership role in these organizations; when in 1934 Lamont and Parker Gilbert attended the American Bankers Association (ABA) convention, the *Wall Street Journal* observed that, while the firm had been an ABA member for years, it was the first time that Morgan representatives had attended a convention.[17]

Privately the partners evinced an astonishing range of contacts, at least as judged through their memberships in clubs, fraternal bodies, societies, and various other leisure, personal, and professional bodies. Anderson was a member of the Downtown Club and the Century Association and indulged in sport at the Bedford Golf and Tennis Club. Bartow's clubs included India House and the Union League, while he too golfed. Cochran was a trustee of Philips Andover and the Metropolitan Museum of Art (as were Jack Morgan and Lamont), while his clubs were varied – Union League, University, Metropolitan, Yale, Recess, and the Racquet and Tennis Club in Manhattan. Senior partners, such as Jack Morgan and Lamont, belonged to both American and international bodies. A few examples suffice. Jack Morgan was a golf member throughout the 1930s at the Club de Golf de Morfontaine in France (as was Lamont); a member of the Roxburghe Club in London, a selective (forty members) aristocratic group interested in books and manuscripts; the Union Interalliée; and a member of the Société d'histoire générale et d'histoire diplomatique. Lamont's associational activity beggars belief in number and scope.[18] Practically there were limits; even the indefatigable Lamont, who personified the ideal of a well-connected banker, could not possibly have maintained relations suggested by widely publicized spider-web diagrams depicting the Morgan reach, a point that he made during the Pecora hearings in 1933.

---

eds., *We Saw It Happen: The News behind the News That's Fit to Print*, New York: Simon and Schuster 1938, pp. 151–53.

[16] Benjamin Haggott Beckhart and James G. Smith, *The New York Money Market*, vol. 2., p. 5.

[17] "Bankers Ready, A.B.A. Head Says," *Wall Street Journal*, 22 October 1934, p. 1.

[18] Pak, *Gentleman Bankers*, discusses the Morgan networks.

The archives furnish little clarity. While they testify to Morgan contacts with banks, with industry, and with the press and politicians, confirmation that the Morgan partners directed others is harder to discern. In some instances – such as the United States Steel Corporation – engagement is clear. Throughout the 1930s Jack Morgan and Lamont paid careful attention to the affairs of the Steel Corporation, frequently signing off on major policy decisions. The Morgan hand is apparent in other prominent corporations, such as Johns-Manville. Yet the Morgan writ was often overstated. At the behest of Hoover, in 1932 Lamont and Cochran lobbied Sewell Avery, the president of Montgomery Ward, the leading Chicago department store chain, to aid the dissemination of Hoover's message in the Midwest. Although Avery had been appointed by J.P. Morgan & Co. to turn around Montgomery Ward, he rejected Lamont's plea to cooperate with the president's re-election efforts. Lamont confessed to Theodore Joslin, Hoover's press secretary, that "I urged Mr. Avery just as far as I could." This suggested the limitations of Morgan influence even in a firm that was deemed to be a "Morgan" company.[19]

J.P. Morgan & Co., and in particular Lamont, paid careful attention to the press. Partners cultivated Wall Street reporters, editorial writers, owners, and publishers. Advertising was placed where Lamont thought "goodwill" and prestige would accrue, an objective buttressed by having partners write articles and speeches for publication where appropriate. Egan and subsequently Wasson were encouraged to foster a network with as many publicists and figures in the press as feasible, with the intent of demonstrating that "the firm is composed of human beings."[20] At the core was Lamont's practice of writing letters to papers across the country in response to their coverage of J.P. Morgan & Co. While Lamont recognized that he had a tendency to overdo this effort, he thought its value "immeasurable." Penned to columnists, editors, or publishers, labelled "Personal," and never for publication, Lamont's letters argued, challenged, corrected, informed, and redressed stories printed. A sample from 1933 runs the gamut from correspondence to the syndicated columnist Drew Pearson and his daily "Washington Merry Go Round" column to the *Tampa Tribune*, the *Janesville Gazette* of Wisconsin, *the New Orleans Item*, the *Raleigh Times*, the *Denver Post*, the *Seattle Times*, the *Chicago American*, the *Arizona Silver Belt*, the *Ventura Free Press* of California, and the *Minneapolis Tribune*.[21] No publication was too small

---

[19] Lamont to Hoover, 25 March 1932, 31 March 1932, BL, TWL, Series II, Box 98, Folder 21, Hoover, Herbert C., 1932.
[20] Lamont, 1 June 1934, "J.P. Morgan & Co. and Their Relations to the Public," BL, TWL, Series V, Box 214, Folder 13, lays out the Morgan effort.
[21] See Lamont to Drew Pearson, 26 April 1933, BL, TWL, Series II, Box 116, Folder 18.

or too obscure to receive a letter. In 1937 John Franklin Carter, who wrote under the byline Jay Franklin as the "Unofficial Observer," exposed this practice in an open letter in the *New York Post*. Carter asserted that Lamont had been operating a Morgan censoring machine devoted to shaping comment on J.P. Morgan & Co., using his influence in the newspaper and publishing industries to bring recalcitrant journalists, editors, and publishers to heel. In Carter's view Lamont's letters demonstrated anew the power of the "economic royalists" in American life. Humorously, Lamont replied to Carter with a "Personal" not for publication letter.[22]

Certain newspapers and journals were susceptible to Morgan blandishments in the 1930s. Financial vulnerability engendered by declines in advertising and readership meant that some organs sought Morgan goodwill. Throughout the decade the bank maintained a rotational policy with its advertising dollars, distributing its placements among the principal New York papers. Even the *New York American*, a Hearst paper noted for its hostility to J.P. Morgan & Co., was the beneficiary of Morgan spending.[23] As this suggests, it is unwise to assume advertising spending purchased fealty. The financial press, ranging from the *Commercial and Financial Chronicle* to the *Wall Street Journal* and the various magazines that catered to business news, such as *Forbes*, *Barron's*, and *Fortune*, was reliably conservative in its outlook. Their support could be counted on by the Corner in most instances. The mainstream press, whether it was newspapers or magazines, was more diffuse. Western-based papers as well as rural organs were hostile. Much of the coverage in the Midwest, where negative sentiment against J.P. Morgan & Co. was heartfelt, was antipathetic. So too the writings of the Hearst chain, whose proprietor viewed the Corner in dire terms. Magazines of a liberal or progressive persuasion, like *The Nation* or *The New Republic*, ranged against J.P. Morgan & Co., though Lamont's wide-ranging acquaintances, including Ellery Sedgwick, the owner of *The Atlantic*, offset this disposition. *Collier's*, one of the leading weeklies of the decade with a massive circulation, was a special case. Through his interest in the Crowell Publishing Company which controlled *Collier's*, Lamont wielded influence. Gertrude B. Lane, the long-time editor of the *Women's Home*

---

[22] BL, TWL, Series II, Box 86, Folder 13 contains copies of the Open Letter in *The New York Post* of 18 December 1937 and Lamont's response of 3 January 1938.

[23] Wasson to Thomas W. Lamont, Thomas S. Lamont, and Martin Egan, 6 January 1937, JP Morgan Chase Corporate History Collection, JP Morgan collection, J.P. Morgan & Co. Ads 1930s has a breakdown of the 1936 advertising distribution. The JP Morgan Chase Corporate History Collection is closed to outside researchers and consequently is not included in the Bibliography.

Companion, one of the journals in the Crowell stable, told Herbert Hoover in 1935 that a George Creel article assailing Republicans in *Collier's* "caused a tremendous stir in this organization. So much of a stir that we held a meeting at which the officers of the company were present and also some of our important stockholders, including Mr. Thomas W. Lamont." The upshot was that the editorial staff agreed not to run any political articles that had not been vetted beforehand by a committee that had both Democratic and Republican members.[24] *Time* magazine, a *Collier's* rival, was also not immune – Egan, Lamont's right-hand man on public relations, sat on its board of directors from 1926 to 1936.

The partners cared especially about the New York press. The two most important New York dailies in the Morgan view were the *New York Times* and the *New York Herald Tribune*. Relations with the *New York Times* were cordial. Arthur Krock, the Washington bureau chief of the *New York Times*, socialized with Morgan partners. Stronger reasons existed for thinking that the *New York Herald Tribune* was susceptible to Morgan desires. Conservative ideologically, the paper was struggling. Financial data shared with Lamont by Helen and Ogden Reid, the paper's owners, revealed losses of nearly $350,000 in 1931 and slightly more than $500,000 in 1932. The Metropolitan Museum of Art, through the will of Mrs. Whitelaw Reid, was owed payments of $150,000 in 1933, money the Reids did not have. Meeting on 21 April 1933 in the Morgan Library, Lamont, Jack Morgan, and Myron Taylor – all directors of the Metropolitan Museum – gathered with William Sloane Coffin Sr., the president of the board of trustees of the Metropolitan. The Reids had asked for an eighteen-month postponement on repayment of the $150,000 from the Metropolitan while they sought a loan from the Irving Trust company. The request was granted and the loan arranged. Helen Reid, the power at the *Herald Tribune*, understood well that it was Morgan intercession that had staved off disaster. Repeatedly in the years to come she would ask Lamont for assistance in tiding the paper over during its financial troubles.[25]

More problematic was any Morgan means to shape the message imparted on radio, which reached millions weekly. The screeds of Father Coughlin and others who assailed J.P. Morgan & Co. were unanswerable even if the charges made were risible. To this vulnerability needs to be added another: the 1930s were a decade in which Americans flocked

---

[24] Gertrude B. Lane to Hoover, 1 November 1935, Herbert Hoover Presidential Library (HHPL), Post Presidential Individual Correspondence File (PPICF), Box 119, Lane, Gertrude B. 1933–41.
[25] BL, TWL, Series II, Box 120, Folder 10. For Helen Reid's gratitude, see the handwritten letter of 14 March 1936 crediting Lamont with saving the day.

to movie theatres. Weekly attendance in 1930 stood at the astonishing figure of 80 million, roughly 65 per cent of the population. While attendance declined thereafter, tens of millions of Americans still went to the movies every week.[26] Cinema newsreels were a part of daily life. The exposure given to high-profile events such as the Pecora hearings in 1933 conveyed to millions the Morgan name. For such audiences, whether Morgan influence and power were real or not is perhaps immaterial. What mattered was perception, flickering on screens or booming from the radio. Americans believed in Morgan power and this power was all the more fearsome because of uncertainty regarding its immensity. Those who railed against J.P. Morgan & Co. extended the idea of its influence even as they decried the Morgan reach.

The Pujo investigation and *Other People's Money* echoed through the World War I years; *The Great Conspiracy of the House of Morgan and How to Defeat It* remained a staple trope even if the war banked up the fires of Progressivism.[27] Besieged by a government that sought to enforce its vision of unity, Progressivism retreated. The struggle over the Versailles Treaty and the League of Nations marked a setback for reformist hopes in the context of the Red Scare at home. By the mid-1920s, as the economy grew, prosperity took much of the sting out of the critique of the Money Trust.[28] However, the nostrums advanced by Populists and Progressives did not disappear. They remained, albeit largely dormant through the 1920s, subsumed by a politics of prosperity dominated by Republican power, complacency, and a conviction that a New Era had been born.

Symptomatic of the shift in Progressive outlook was George Soule's 1924 article in *The New Republic* entitled "The Myth of Wall Street." Soule, a labour economist noted for his involvement in reform causes, attacked the understanding of Wall Street common in Progressive circles. While the Pujo investigation might have popularized interlocking directorates, Soule was dismissive. The conceit that American life was the product of "secret conferences" held in the J.P. Morgan & Co. offices was absurd. He argued that Wall Street was not monolithic, that there was no singular guiding force, and that the Street's control over big business was minimal. Large corporations did not need the banks. In Soule's view, while there was affiliation between companies and banks, it was not clear

[26] Michelle Pautz, "The Decline in Weekly Cinema Attendance," *Issues in Political Economy*, vol. 11 (2002), p. 1 and appendix.
[27] Henry L. Loucks, *The Great Conspiracy of the House of Morgan and How to Defeat It*, Watertown, SD: n.p., 1916.
[28] Alan Dawley, *Changing the World: American Progressives in War and Revolution*, Princeton, NJ: Princeton University Press, 2003. William Leuchtenberg, *The Perils of Prosperity*, Chicago: University of Chicago Press, 1985, 2nd ed. 1993.

which way control – if there was control – ran: "it is often difficult to say whether the bank controls the manufacturer of the manufacturer controls the bank." In Soule's estimation, small business, through its organized lobbies, such as the Chambers of Commerce and Rotary Clubs, had more power than Wall Street.[29] While Soule's assessment was more intellectual than most, in the context of the 1920s it represented the zeitgeist.[30] After 1929 as economic crisis deepened, the Money Trust discourse re-emerged in a way that drew upon both Soule and the older vision of Pujo and Brandeis. Bankers, large and small, urban and rural, but especially on Wall Street, were to blame for American woes. What this critique overlooked were the deep-seated problems of American banking.

The American banking system in the 1920s was rickety, but its frailties derived from considerations beyond those raised in the Pujo investigation or by Brandeis. The dual banking structure, wherein banks were chartered at either the national or the state level, allowed for a proliferation of institutions, the bulk of which were not members of the Federal Reserve system. Supervision was lax, a problem deriving from and compounded by the fact that there were too many banks.[31] Contraction occurred overwhelmingly among the thousands of small, poorly capitalized rural banks. Afflicted by the travails of the American farmer in the 1920s, whose livelihood was eroded by low commodity prices, sapped by the growing movement of people to the cities that was emptying small towns, and made redundant by the advent of the automobile that encouraged farmers to bank in the nearest sizeable town, rural banks failed in their hundreds every year in the 1920s.[32] Matters were worsened by resistance to branch banking. Although branch banking grew in the 1920s, it was fought bitterly outside large urban centres on the grounds that branch banking permitted large banks to penetrate into the countryside. In eighteen states in 1930 no bank had a branch office. Efforts to reform the banking system foundered, as did attempts to persuade more banks to join the Federal Reserve system.[33] Concurrently, a movement toward

[29] George Soule, "The Myth of Wall Street," *The New Republic*, vol. 39, no. 506, 13 August 1924, pp. 324–25. Soule's name was not on the byline but he was the author of the piece.
[30] This is a theme of Steve Fraser, *Every Man a Speculator: A History of Wall Street in American Life*, New York: Harper Perennial Edition, 2006, pp. 375–85.
[31] On 30 June 1921 there were 29,788 commercial banks. By 31 December 1928 the figure had fallen to 25,579. *Banking and Monetary Statistics, 1914–1941*, New York: Board of Governors of the Federal Reserve System, 1943, part 1, table 1, p. 16, https://fraser.stlouisfed.org/title/banking-monetary-statistics-1914-1941-38?browse=1940s#6408.
[32] *Banking and Monetary Statistics, 1914–1941*, part 1, table 14, p. 52, https://fraser.stlouisfed.org/title/banking-monetary-statistics-1914-1941-38?browse=1940s#6408.
[33] Lester V. Chandler, *America's Greatest Depression, 1929–1941*, New York: Harper & Row, 1970, pp. 78–9; Eugene Nelson White, *The Regulation and Reform of the American Banking System, 1900–1929*, Princeton, NJ: Princeton University Press, 1983.

a concentration of banking resources accelerated. New York and Chicago were the two leading centres, with the former incomparably larger. Huge banks such as National City Bank or Chase National Bank, both of New York, were the behemoths of the day. National City's assets at the end of 1929 had surpassed $2.2 billion, while deposits stood at $1.649 billion. Chase, for its part, following its merger with Equitable Trust in 1930, could command resources of $2.7 billion.[34] The power of the giants within the banking system was growing yearly.

J.P. Morgan & Co.'s means were outstripped substantially by these leviathans. The firm had strong bonds to First National Bank, dominated by George F. Baker senior, and National City Bank. George F. Baker senior was one of Pierpont Morgan's oldest allies. Cooperation between the two banks continued through the 1920s when the leadership of First National passed to George F. Baker junior. Charles E. Mitchell, National City Bank's chief in the 1920s, blazed his own path but worked regularly with the Morgan partners.[35] Two other large New York banks, Bankers Trust and Guaranty Trust, had close Morgan connections. Bankers Trust, created in 1903, owed its existence in large measure to Harry P. Davison, who, supported by Pierpont Morgan, had pioneered its establishment. As for Guaranty Trust, it had long-standing ties with J.P. Morgan & Co. Just after the war, the Morgan partners assisted Guaranty in overcoming difficulties involving its holdings in Mercantile Trust. Through the 1920s the Morgan partners Thomas W. Lamont and George Whitney sat on the Guaranty board which lent credence to those who believed in a "Money Trust." In addition to the great New York banks were the insurance companies, the most important of which had at their disposal significant pools of capital. Here too, J.P. Morgan & Co. had relationships with companies such as Aetna Life Insurance, Metropolitan Life Insurance, and New York Life Insurance Co. These ties benefited the Morgan bank in various ways but did not mean that the partners controlled these institutions. Suggestions to this effect were rebuffed sharply by those who ran them. William C. Potter, the chairman of the board of directors of Guaranty Trust, was peremptory when asked by Senator Burton Wheeler in 1936 whether Guaranty was one of the "Morgan group of banks." Potter told the Senator abruptly "Not by me," pointedly remarking that he took pains to correct the misapprehension that Guaranty was a Morgan bank.[36]

---

[34] Cleveland and Huertas, *Citibank 1812–1970*, p. 134, table 7.8; John Donald Wilson, *The Chase: The Chase Manhattan Bank, 1945–1985*, Cambridge, MA: Harvard Business School Press, 1986, p. 15.

[35] Cleveland and Huertas, *Citibank, 1812–1970*, p. 139.

[36] *Investigation of Railroads, Holding Companies, and Affiliated Companies* (hereafter Wheeler Committee), Subcommittee of the United States Senate Committee on Interstate

Irrespective of the question of Morgan influence, the structural trends in American commercial banking were diluting the importance of private banks. Investment banking, long the special province of the private banker, was changing. While the overall number of American commercial banks fell in the 1920s, in the investment banking field the converse was occurring – more firms were entering it. There were various reasons for this development. One was a shift in the type of securities retailed. Traditionally bonds had been the preferred vehicle for corporations to raise funds. Increasingly large companies did not need recourse to the capital markets as they were generating from internal sources the capital that they required.[37] Despite this, the growth of the American economy in the 1920s was such that the volume of domestic corporate bond issues rose steadily from 1919 to 1927, reaching a total of $4.769 billion. Thereafter they declined. In 1928 and 1929 stock issues outpaced bond issues by dollar value. From $3,491 billion in 1928 corporate stock offerings jumped to a remarkable $6,757 billion in 1929, overshadowing corporate bond placements of $2,620 billion.[38] The seemingly irresistible surge of business on offer enticed new entrants into investment banking. Carosso, in his authoritative study, has observed that the 1920s were a decade of growth in investment bank numbers, with 3,000 extant by 1929, though, as Eugene White has observed, five or six principal players dominated.[39]

Investment banking was alluring because of the prospect of bundling American capital for foreign borrowers. Fundamentally this was driven by the transformation in the American capital position occasioned by the war. In 1914 the United States was a debtor nation; after 1918 it was a creditor, the largest creditor in the world, and New York rivalled London. This reordering did not manifest itself immediately in new, large-scale American lending abroad. In 1919 net new foreign dollar

Commerce, 75th Congress, 1st session, 9 December 1936, United States, Washington, DC: Government Printing Office, 1938, pp. 111–12. See the Hathi Trust: https://babel .hathitrust.org/cgi/pt?id=umn.31951d035053289&view=1up&seq=122&skin=2021.

[37] See two articles by Stuart Chase, "Capital Not Wanted" and "Shadow over Wall Street," in *Harper's Magazine*, February 1940, vol. 180, pp. 228–34 and March 1940, pp. 367–74.

[38] Bureau of the Census, *Historical Statistics of the United States, Vol. 2: Colonial Times to 1970*, United States Bureau of the Census, Series X 510-515, p. 1006, https://fraser .stlouisfed.org/title/historical-statistics-united-states-237/volume-2-5808.

[39] Vincent Carosso, *Investment Banking in America*, Cambridge, MA: Harvard University Press, 1970. Especially chaps. 12–14, pp. 240–99. The figure of 3,000 is on p. 267. Eugene N. White, "Banking and Finance in the Twentieth Century," in Stanley L. Engerman and Robert E. Gallman, eds., *The Cambridge Economic History of the United States, Vol. 3: The Twentieth Century*, Cambridge: Cambridge University Press, 2000, p. 752.

loans amounted to $613.7 million. Not until 1924 was this figure sur-
passed. The boom years of American lending abroad were 1924 through
1928, with the peak reached in 1927 when net new foreign lending
reached $1.081 billion. The fall in foreign lending apparent in 1929 was
driven in part by the greater returns that appeared to be available in the
American domestic market. The year 1930 was the last in which there was
a net new dollar loan surplus.[40] Much has been written about the surge of
American lending abroad in the 1920s. Morrow for one, in a 1927 article
in *Foreign Affairs*, "Who Buys Foreign Bonds," attempted to show that it
was "average" American investors who were driving purchases. His partner, Lamont, in a May 1927 speech to the International Chamber of
Commerce in Washington, was uncharacteristically negative, warning of
competition "on almost a violent scale" among American investment
houses to make loans abroad that watered down the quality of those
offerings.[41]

While J.P. Morgan & Co. could afford to be, and was, selective in its
foreign loans, the Corner had many challengers. National City Bank and
Chase National Bank had moved with alacrity into lending abroad after
1918 and through the 1920s expanded their activities overseas. National
City had ninety-eight offices in twenty-three countries by the end of the
decade.[42] The Morgan partnership was seen as an impediment by an
aggressive cohort of investment banks little inclined to follow 23 Wall
Street docilely.[43] Among these, Harris, Forbes & Co. of New York;
Halsey, Stuart of Chicago; and Blyth & Co. of San Francisco were
notable.[44] It has been suggested that some investment banks, such as
Dillon, Read & Co., existed on the sufferance of J.P. Morgan & Co.[45]
This view overstates the Morgan reach. The Morgan partners were
hostile to Clarence Dillon and he to them. Dillon's wariness of J.P.
Morgan & Co. stamped the reality: J.P. Morgan & Co. was the scion of
an old-line establishment that sought to deter interlopers, often allied

[40] Figures from Lewis, *America's Stake in International Investments*, p. 629. See too Barry
Eichengreen, "U.S. Foreign Financial Relations in the Twentieth Century," in
Engerman and Gallman, *Cambridge Economic History of the United States*, table 8.2,
p. 476.
[41] Dwight Morrow, "Who Buys Foreign Bonds," *Foreign Affairs*, vol. 5, no. 2 (1927), pp.
219–32; Lamont speech 2 May 1927, quoted in Lewis, *America's Stake in International
Investments*, p. 380.
[42] Cleveland and Huertas, *Citibank, 1812–1970*, pp. 123–25. For National City's securities
activities, pp. 135–52.
[43] Emily S. Rosenberg, *Financial Missionaries to the World: The Politics and Culture of Dollar
Diplomacy*, Cambridge, MA: Harvard University Press, 1999, p. 155.
[44] Harris Forbes was acquired by Chase in 1930.
[45] Robert Sobel, *The Big Board: A History of the New York Stock Market*, New York: The
Free Press, 1965, p. 239.

with like-minded firms such as Kuhn, Loeb & Co., Lee, Higginson & Co., and Kidder, Peabody.

New competitors in investment banking, the growth of the major money-centre New York banks, and the existence of the Federal Reserve system were redistributing where power lay in American finance in the 1920s. Popularly 23 Wall Street remained the locus where the conspiratorially minded detected coordination, even if in truth no single institution spoke for the Wall Street financial community, not even J.P. Morgan & Co. A.P. Giannini's Bank of America, often cited for its fractious relationship with J.P. Morgan & Co., was unexceptional in its conviction that the Morgan partners neither spoke for nor represented American banking writ large. Nor, it should be acknowledged, did Jack Morgan or Lamont presume that they led American finance. They were private merchant bankers. This reality was obscured by the prestige of the Corner, which remained towering in 1929. The foundations of that prestige were built upon pillars driven into the Old World, in London and Paris.

*****

When World War I broke out in 1914, J.P. Morgan & Co. was fortunate – London and Paris were ranged together on the Allied side. The firm's partners did not hide their sympathies, either at the time or later. Jack Morgan's candid acknowledgement in 1936 that he, his partners, and his firms were wholeheartedly with the Allies from the beginning of the war was perhaps the most forthright statement to this effect but it only reinforced what had long been recognized.[46] What mattered was not the nature of Morgan sentiments but rather the ramifications of World War I for J.P. Morgan & Co., the United States, and international politics.

J.P. Morgan & Co. fulfilled two principal functions for the Allies between 1914 and 1917. The first was to raise money to meet their expenditures in the United States. Command of the sea meant that the Allies could place orders in the United States and could ship those goods across the Atlantic, provided that they could pay. This task became increasingly difficult as waging the war exacted a heavier toll. London and Paris found themselves pressed to raise funds in the United States to meet their escalating purchases. As the strain mounted, borrowing to obtain dollars became a necessity. Beginning on a small scale, this ramped up quickly. The $500 million Anglo-French loan of 1915, unprecedented

---

[46] *Special Committee Investigating the Munitions Industry* [hereafter Nye Committee], United States Senate, 74th Congress, 2nd session, Part 25, 7 January 1936, Washington, DC: Government Printing Office, 1937.

in its size, was a harbinger of the heavier borrowings to come. The Anglo-French loan proved difficult to market and, consequently, subsequent financial operations moved steadily in the direction of smaller loans, often short-term and, increasingly, backed by collateral to reassure purchasers of their soundness. By April 1917, when the US Treasury assumed the burden of meeting Allied dollar needs, the demand loan that J.P. Morgan & Co. had extended to Britain, the most credit-worthy of the Allies, stood at approximately $400 million.[47]

The other chief function of J.P. Morgan & Co., no less meaningful than the financial, was commercial. It soon became apparent that neither Britain nor France was able to manage its wartime purchasing require-ments efficiently in the United States. A variety of factors were responsi-ble, among which were inter-allied rivalry, the competing demands of ministries, incompetence, gullibility, and greed. Accordingly, in January 1915 the British government named J.P. Morgan & Co. its commercial agent in the United States. France followed suit in May 1915. The arrangement between London and Paris and J.P. Morgan & Co. was not exclusive. Certain goods, notably commodities like flour and wheat, were outside the purview of the agreements. Motor transport and horses were also sourced independently. To coordinate purchases, J.P. Morgan & Co. established an Export Department, headed by Edward R. Stettinius, who subsequently became a Morgan partner. Under Stettinius, thousands of contracts were placed for the British and French governments, with a dollar value of more than $3 billion.[48]

While the entry of the United States into the war as an Associated Power in April 1917 meant a gradual cessation of Morgan activities on behalf of the Allies, the wartime years boosted the fortunes of J.P. Morgan & Co. This was true in a literal sense – Jack Morgan's gross income in 1916 exceeded $9.5 million (equivalent to $233 million in 2020) – but also in other, less tangible ways that in the long run were more consequential.[49] The scope of the financial operations undertaken on

---

[47] Kathleen Burk, *Britain, America and the Sinews of War*, London: Allen & Unwin, 1985 is indispensable; Martin Horn, *Britain, France and the Financing of the First World War*, Montreal: McGill-Queen's University Press, 2002.

[48] Stettinius died in 1925. There were 3,938 contracts placed, with a dollar value of $3,131,014,509. The figures are from F. Carrington Weems, *America and Munitions: The work of Messrs. J.P. Morgan & Co. in the World War*, 2 vols., New York: Privately printed, 1923, vol. 1, p. 222. Kathleen Burk, "A Merchant Bank at War: The House of Morgan 1914–1918," in P.L. Cottrell and D.E. Moggridge, eds., *Money and Power*, London: Macmillan, 1988. For France, Yves-Henri Nouailhat, *France et États-Unis: août 1914–avril 1917*, Paris: Sorbonne, 1979.

[49] Jack Morgan's gross income in 1916 was $9,570,941. Lamont's was $5,334,896 or the equivalent of $130 million in 2020. Figures from the Pecora Committee investigation in 1933. Center for Legislative Archives, RG 46, 74th Congress, Special Committee

behalf of the Allies extended the reach of J.P. Morgan & Co. within the United States. The Anglo-French loan of 1915 required a huge syndicate; 2,200 distributing houses across the United States were involved in placing the bonds, many of them coming into contact with J.P. Morgan & Co. for the first time.[50] Close ties were developed especially with Chicago and Charles G. Dawes.[51]

A second by-product was familiarity in dealing with government, whether in the United States, in Britain, or in France. The wartime experience reshaped both J.P. Morgan & Co. and the governments that they dealt with. As the state burgeoned to meet the needs of prosecuting war, as the financial and commercial requirements became more pressing for the Allies, so too did J.P. Morgan partners become accustomed to dealing with government. Habitually, Morgan partners such as Jack Morgan, Thomas W. Lamont, and Dwight Morrow found themselves meeting with ministers of finance, with secretaries of state, prime ministers, presidents, and central bankers. Postwar, capital-starved European governments looked to J.P. Morgan & Co. for loans, while the questions that arose from the Paris Peace settlements, infused as they were by economic and financial entanglements, ensured that the wartime practice of regular contact between J.P. Morgan & Co. and governments persisted.

In December 1918 J.P. Morgan & Co. gazed upon a vista that looked very different from August 1914. The Tsarist Empire was gone; its replacement uncertain. Whether the Bolsheviks would survive was unknown, though the fear that they inspired was already widespread. The *Kaiserreich*, the German Empire of William I, Bismarck, and William II, had slipped away as the Kaiser headed into exile at Doorn. The third great continental empire, Austria-Hungary, was a casualty too, disappearing suddenly after centuries of dominance in Eastern and Central Europe. The successor states and their boundaries were in flux, awaiting the deliberations at Paris and the abatement of the violence that stalked much of Eastern, Central, and Southern Europe. Liberal Italy had come through on the Allied side, but few rated Rome highly, certainly not when measured against London and Paris. Britain and France were the powers that mattered, and they were indebted to J.P. Morgan & Co. For the Morgan partners, what counted was that the Allies had won World

---

Investigating the Munitions Industry, Box 157, Executive File – Morgan. Conversion on the basis of consumer price index (CPI) increase.

[50] This was the figure agreed to by Lamont in December 1931. *Sale of Foreign Bonds or Securities*, Part 1, 18 December 1931, p. 4.

[51] Annette B. Dunlap, *Charles Gates Dawes: A Life*, Evanston, IL: Northwestern University Press, 2016, pp. 92–96.

Figure 2.1 The Morgan & Cie. partner Nelson Dean Jay as a Lt. Col. in the US Army, c.1918–19. With the permission of Knox College.

War I and the House of Morgan had been, and could expect to be in the years ahead, the private banker to the victors (see Figures 2.1 and 2.2).[52] There was good reason for *Fortune* magazine to write, "In 1907 Morgan's was powerful because J.P. Morgan headed it. In 1920 Morgan's was powerful because it was the banker for England and for France."[53]

In this changed world there were constants: to be a J.P. Morgan & Co. partner was to accept that the United States was part of the international community and could not be divorced from it.[54] The partners were

[52] Kathleen Burk, "The House of Morgan in Financial Diplomacy, 1920–1930," in B.J. C. McKercher, ed., *Anglo-American Relations in the 1920s*, Edmonton: University of Alberta Press, 1990, pp. 125–57, is the best overview.

[53] "Mister Morgan," *Fortune*, vol. 8, August 1933, p. 84.

[54] An overview of American engagement with Europe is George C. Herring, *From Colony to Superpower: U.S. Foreign Relations since 1776*, New York: Oxford University Press, 2008, pp. 378–434. For the debate on the nature of the postwar peace, P.M.H. Bell, *The Origins of the Second World War in Europe*, 2nd ed., Harlow: Longman, 1997, runs through the case for and against the Thirty Years' War thesis in chaps. 2–3, pp. 16–43. Peter Temin,

Figure 2.2 Edward Charles Grenfell of Morgan Grenfell, 1929. The National Portrait Gallery UK.

committed uncompromisingly to a transatlantic axis that ran from New York to London and Paris. There was never any suggestion of severing this link. Throughout the interwar period, worries about British and European stability dominated their thoughts and actions when the old sureties had vanished with the disappeared empires. This focus did not mean the bank ignored the rest of the world. Japan, for much of the interwar period, and in the 1930s China featured. Elsewhere, Mexico and Argentina were important to the partners.[55] Yet always Europe was primary.

Lessons from the Great Depression, Cambridge, MA: MIT Press, 1989, is an influential work by an economist that accepts the notion of a Thirty Years' War. Sally Marks, *The Illusion of Peace: International Relations in Europe*, London: Macmillan Press, 1976 and Patrick Cohrs, *The Unfinished Peace after World War I*, New York: Cambridge University Press, 2006, doubt stability was attained in the second half of the 1920s. Zara Steiner, *The Lights That Failed: European International Relations 1919–1933*, Oxford: Oxford University Press, 2005, is more open-minded.

[55] On Japan see Pak, *Gentlemen Bankers*, chap. 6, pp. 160–91; for Mexico see Smith, "Thomas Lamont: International Banker As Diplomat," pp. 101–25.

Given this, while it has been argued that the Anglo-American financial relationship in the 1920s was conflict-ridden, with the City fending off the global challenge from New York, for the House of Morgan such a depiction lacks credibility.[56] The war had reordered international finance, diminishing Britain and the City of London and correspondingly strengthening the United States and New York. Jack Morgan was devoted to Anglo-American comity. Rivalry existed but was buried by his desire to see J.P. Morgan & Co. and Morgan Grenfell cooperate when possible. His partners were less wedded to his conception of Anglo-American relations. As the cleavages of the 1930s intensified, as the partners in both New York and London with close personal ties aged, there was a fraying of the Anglo-American ideal within the House of Morgan. Nonetheless, this never came to an open caesura while Jack Morgan lived.

A desire to see Britain return to the gold standard preoccupied the Morgan partners in the first half of the 1920s. This objective had been signalled by the 1918 Cunliffe Committee and commanded near unanimous support within the City, if not within British industry.[57] The Morgan partners believed that returning to gold would benefit Britain, pave the way to global prosperity, and hasten a return to political and economic stability. In concert with Strong, J.P. Morgan & Co. made a commitment to provide credits that allowed sterling to return to gold.[58] With this assurance, the chancellor of the exchequer, Winston Churchill, opted to take the step in 1925.

As for "Europe," it is an imprecise term; specifically, the Morgan partners cared most, thought most, and devoted their energies most to Western Europe. Of eighteen European government bond issues floated by the firm between 1920 and 1930, fifteen were to Western European states and one was to a municipality – Rome in 1927. The two loans that were not made within Western Europe were the $25 million Austrian bond issues of 1923 and 1930. Belgium was the recipient of six loans between 1920 and 1926, ranging from $30 million to $50 million. After Belgium, France (three), Italy (three, including Rome), Germany (two), and Switzerland (two) were borrowers. These loans were concentrated temporally. Of the eighteen, fourteen were made between 1920 and 1926.

[56] Michie, "The City of London," pp. 41–79. Some historians have seen the 1920s as dominated by Anglo-American rivalry. Frank C. Costigliola, "Anglo-American Financial Rivalry in the 1920s," *Journal of Economic History*, vol. 37, no. 4 (1977), pp. 911–34. More generally, see the essays in B.J.C. McKercher, ed., *Anglo-American Relations in the 1920s*, Edmonton: University of Alberta Press, 1990.
[57] Robert W.D. Boyce, *British Capitalism at the Crossroads 1919–1932*, Cambridge: Cambridge University Press, 1987, esp. chap. 2, pp. 35–78; for the engagement of Strong and the Morgan partners, pp. 71–72.
[58] Burk, "The House of Morgan," pp. 136–38.

Only four loans, two to Italy (both in 1927), one to Germany (1930), and one to Austria (1930), occurred after 1926, by which time it was thought that Europe had stabilized.[59]

The emphasis on Western Europe was a product of several factors. One was historical – the deep ties to Britain and France, with the existence of Morgan Grenfell in London and Morgan & Cie. in Paris, meant familiarity and comfort. The wartime experience reinforced these pre-existing contacts. It was not happenstance that in the 1920s twelve out of eighteen Morgan loans to governments went to states that were part of the wartime Allied coalition. The Morgan networks were strongest with bankers, businessmen, and politicians in Britain, France, Belgium, the Netherlands, Spain, and Italy. In Italy J.P. Morgan & Co. had a dedicated agent from 1920, Giovanni Fummi (see Figure 2.3).

Fummi filled a unique position in the interwar House of Morgan. He had been recruited by Lamont, who met him at the Paris Peace talks in 1919. A banker, Fummi was a professional business director who had close ties with Giovanni Agnelli of Fiat, on whose board of directors he served. Fummi was also a director of Pirelli and one of a number of bankers who managed the properties and investments of the Vatican. Fummi navigated the passage from Liberal Italy to the Fascism of Mussolini with ease. For J.P. Morgan & Co., Fummi was the intermediary with Italian bankers and with Il Duce, making possible Morgan loans to Italy. Fummi remained the Morgan agent in Italy until 1940, providing information and advice on Italy as Mussolini's course became more bellicose.[60]

The two Austrian loans and the two German loans were, at first glance, inconsistent with the Morgan preference for loans to ex-Allied states. However, the Morgan partners were convinced of the necessity of European reconstruction. Lamont and Whitney had both been present at the Paris Peace talks in 1919. Lamont and another American delegate, Norman Davis, wrote a memorandum in May 1919 that argued that American prosperity had been driven by the European export market. A failure to restore this market would lead to depressed growth in the United States, a prescription that was accepted widely by American

---

[59] A complete list of the Morgan loans from 1920 to 1930 is in *Sale of Foreign Bonds or Securities*, Part 1, 18, 19, and 21 December 1931, pp. 159–61.

[60] Carosso conducted a series of interviews about Fummi with Lewis Harcourt of Morgan Grenfell in 1977, with Pierre Meynial, a member of Morgan & Cie., in 1981, and with Harry Morgan in 1978. Professor Roland Sarti provided Carosso with additional information on Fummi. TML, CP, Box 3, Folder Morgan Grenfell & Co; TML, CP, Box 3, Folder Morgan, Harjes; TML, CP, Fummi, Giovanni. See also Gian Giacomo Migone, *The United States and Fascist Italy: The Rise of American Finance in Europe*, trans. Molly Tambor, New York: Cambridge University Press, 2015.

Figure 2.3 The Morgan representative Giovanni Fummi in Rome, 1919. George Grantham Bain Collection, Library of Congress, Prints & Photographs Division, LC-USZ62-98991.

business in the years to come.[61] Subsequently the Morgan firm had been ranged in the camp of those in the United States who championed the Treaty of Versailles and membership in the League of Nations. American

[61] Michael Hogan, *Informal Entente: The Private Structure of Cooperation in Anglo-American Economic Diplomacy, 1918–1928*, Columbia, MO: University of Missouri Press, 1978, pp. 29–30; Frank Costigliola, *Awkward Dominion: American Political, Economic, and Cultural Relations with Europe, 1919–1933*, Ithaca, NY: Cornell University Press, 1984, p. 33.

rejection of the Treaty of Versailles in 1920 did not mean any renunciation of Morgan effort. In a 1922 speech to the American Bankers Association (ABA) entitled "The American Banker's Responsibility Today," Lamont exhorted his audience to accept the responsibility that came with the power accrued from the war. He urged his audience to forge a peaceful, prosperous Europe for the good of all, concluding his peroration by drawing on scripture to drive home the moral and ethical imperative of doing so.[62] This conformed to the views of Norman who was worried about the struggles of the Austrian state. Austria, as it emerged from the breakup of the Habsburg Empire, was the old imperial capital, Vienna, surrounded by little more than a rump of its hinterland. Financially and economically Austria was a cripple. Norman, animated by worries about the exposure of City banks to Austria, took the lead, pressing Strong and Jack Morgan to consider a loan, while canvassing the French and the League of Nations. After much jockeying, a reconstruction loan was floated in 1923 in which J.P. Morgan & Co. handled the American tranche.[63] The Morgan willingness to accommodate Norman reflected their desire to help the governor as well as a belief that the loan would aid postwar stabilization.

Similarly, the German loan of 1924 was undertaken as part of a broader effort to resolve the financial and economic problems arising from the war. The 1924 Dawes Plan loan was designed to put the German currency on a new footing, while simultaneously seeking to redress reparations. After the failure to agree upon a figure for reparations at the Paris Peace talks in 1919, a sum had been agreed to at London in 1921. The trouble was that successive German governments had no interest in paying. Ministries in Berlin blamed German economic difficulties on reparations, thus making feasible, it was hoped, a revision of reparations and more generally the Treaty of Versailles. These ambitions were less implausible than they appeared because Britain, having done much to make impossible agreement on a figure in 1919, had shifted its position. London was convinced that the struggling postwar British economy needed a German export market. The British thought that the most beneficial step would be the cancellation of war debts and reparations, a prescription that the Balfour Note of August 1922 made plain to the distress of Paris. For the Harding, Coolidge, and Hoover administrations, there was no link between reparations and war debts. Washington's view was that the Allies, having borrowed money from the United States, had

[62] Thomas W. Lamont, 3 October 1922, "The American Bankers Responsibility Today," LC, Ogden Mills papers (OM), Box 71, Reparations and War Debts, 1921–28.
[63] Sir Henry Clay, *Lord Norman*, London: MacMillan & Co., 1957, pp. 179–91.

to repay it, irrespective of what the defeated powers paid the Allies. Matters came to a head in 1923–24 with the French occupation of the Ruhr, provoked by another German failure to meet their reparations obligations.[64]

The ensuing settlement has been ably described by Stephen Schuker in *The End of French Predominance in Europe*, which remains the most persuasive account.[65] J.P. Morgan & Co. found themselves in a difficult situation; while they were reluctant to badger the French government of Édouard Herriot, the Morgan partners were unwilling to contemplate a German loan without surety that Berlin would be relieved of French pressure, whether political or military. The French ability to resist the pressure emanating from London and New York was undercut by the weakness of the franc, which was sagging on international markets. A solution was found in the flotation of a Morgan loan to France, as well as the Dawes Plan loan to Germany. J.P. Morgan & Co. led the American syndicate for both. The German loan was a product of the Morgan desire to see a comprehensive peace fashioned in Europe. It did not mean a change in Morgan policy with regard to lending to Germany.

Prior to 1914 the House of Morgan had had dealings with various German banks, largely through Morgan Grenfell whose contacts extended to Bleichröders, Mendelssohns, Warburgs, Dresdner, and Darmstädter banks. The outbreak of war severed these links. Jack Morgan had never liked Germany, a distaste arising initially from his stay in the country in the 1880s. The wartime experience, when Jack Morgan survived an assassination attempt at home by a German

[64] "Reparation" and "reparations" are used indiscriminately as terms in the literature. I have opted for the plural usage throughout. Selected recent works on the Treaty of Versailles include Manfred F. Boemeke, Gerald D. Feldman, and Elisabeth Glaser, *The Treaty of Versailles: A Reassessment*; Margaret MacMillan, *Paris 1919*, New York: Random House, 2001; Alan Sharp, *The Versailles Settlement: Peacemaking After the First World War*, 2nd ed., London: Palgrave Macmillan, 2008; Sally Marks, "Mistakes and Myths: The Allies, Germany, and the Versailles Treaty, 1918–1921," *Journal of Modern History*, vol. 85, no. 3 (2013), pp. 632–59. On reparations and war debts, Sally Marks, "The Myths of Reparation," *Central European History*, vol. 11, no. 3 (1978), pp. 231–55; Denise Artaud, "Reparations and War Debts: The Restoration of French Financial Power, 1919–1929," in Robert Boyce, ed., *French Foreign and Defence Policy, 1918–1940*, London: Routledge, 1998, pp. 88–105; Robert Self, *Britain, America and the War Debt Controversy: The Economic Diplomacy of an Unspecial Relationship, 1917–1941*, London: Routledge, 1988; the special issue of *Diplomacy and Statecraft*, vol. 16, no. 3 (2005), which includes articles by Gerald D. Feldman, "The Reparations Debate," Conan Fischer, "The Human Price of Reparations," and Patricia Clavin, "Reparations in the Long Run"; and finally, Leonard Gomes, *German Reparations 1919–1932*, London: Palgrave Macmillan, 2010.
[65] Stephen Schuker, *The End of French Predominance in Europe*, Chapel Hill, NC: University of North Carolina Press, 1976.

sympathizer who fired two bullets into his abdomen in 1915, melded with his wholehearted pro-Allied sentiment to solidify his belief in German militarism.[66] He was willing to make an exception for the Dawes Loan in 1924, but in the jostle of American banks striving to lend to Germany after 1924 the Corner was conspicuous through its refusal to join the fray.[67] When in 1928 discussions among the three Morgan firms regarding developing future business in Europe took place, it was agreed that it was worth cultivating Vienna, Prague, and Budapest but not Berlin. Jack Morgan had ruled out the idea of resumption of business with Germany.[68] This reticence, as it transpired, worked in favour of the House of Morgan after 1929. Unlike many in the City and on Wall Street, when the 1931 German crisis struck J.P. Morgan & Co. was less exposed, as, save for the Dawes and Young Plan loans, it had lent nothing to Germany.

The practice of making foreign loans in the 1920s, whether by J.P. Morgan & Co. or any other American financial institution, was subject to the explicit sanction of the State Department and the implicit approval of the departments of the Treasury and of Commerce.[69] Discussions had begun in 1921 between bankers and the Harding administration. Both sides were agreed that having private interests take the lead in lending was

---

[66] Forbes, *J.P. Morgan Jr.*, pp. 27–28 for his pre-war view of Germany. On the assassination attempt, Forbes, *J.P. Morgan Jr.*, pp. 93–94, and Chernow, *The House of Morgan*, pp. 192–95.

[67] Henry M. Robinson, "Are American Loans Abroad Safe?," *Foreign Affairs*, vol. 5, no. 1 (1926), pp. 49–56. Despite the title the emphasis is on loans to Germany. For a scholarly analysis, see Stephen Schuker, *American Reparations to Germany: Implications for the Third-World Debt Crisis*, Princeton, NJ: Princeton University Press, 1988.

[68] Dean Jay to Carter and Joy, 16 March 1928, TML, CP, Box 17, Morgan & Co. – Commercial Credits 1920s; Germany; Credit Anstalt. Benjamin Joy was then a partner in Morgan & Cie. in Paris. This folder contains additional material on how the three firms might develop business in Europe. Whigham to Joy, 21 January 1929, TML, CP, Box 17, Morgan & Co. – Banking Business Germany, where Whigham makes it clear that Jack Morgan is opposed to German business.

[69] Interested readers may consult the following on private and governmental American economic and financial interaction with Europe in the 1920s: William Appleman Williams, *The Tragedy of American Diplomacy*, 1959, reissued and enlarged 1962, New York: Delta, 1962; Carl Parrini, *Heir to Empire: United States Economic Diplomacy 1916–1923*, Pittsburgh, PA: University of Pittsburgh Press, 1969; Hogan, *Informal Entente*; Melvyn P. Leffler, *The Elusive Quest: America's Pursuit of European Stability and French Security, 1919–1933*, Chapel Hill, NC: University of North Carolina Press, 1979; Daniel P. Silverman, *Reconstructing Europe after the Great War*, Cambridge, MA: Harvard University Press, 1982; Costigliola, *Awkward Dominion*; William C. McNeill, *American Money and the Weimar Republic*, New York: Columbia University Press, 1986; Rosenberg, *Financial Missionaries*; Marc Flandreau, ed., *Money Doctors: The Experience of International Financial Advising, 1850–2000*, London: Routledge, 2003; Zoltán Peterecz, *Jeremiah Smith Jr. and Hungary, 1924–1926: The United States, the League of Nations, and the Financial Reconstruction of Hungary*, London: Versita, 2013.

advisable though it was not until March 1922 that the State Department issued a public statement stipulating that banks required permission from Washington before any loan was extended.[70] Benediction was nearly always forthcoming, but the policy allowed Washington to maintain oversight. Banks such as J.P. Morgan & Co. were happy to have the imprimatur of the State Department, suggesting a degree of consanguinity, though Jack Morgan recoiled at the notion that his firm was an unofficial agent of the State Department.[71] Washington had an interest in European recovery, even if the fractious reparations and war debt issues complicated the American posture. The Morgan attitude on war debts was staked out early. In August 1922 Jack Morgan, then in Paris, was asked about the war debts owed by the erstwhile American allies. His response, as the *New York Times* reported, was unequivocal: "Those debts should be cancelled."[72] Thereafter, the attitude of the Morgan partners on this question remained fervent that modification of war debts, either whole or partial, was required. Certitude of this kind was beyond Harding, Coolidge, or Hoover in the 1920s for sound political reasons. If at the official level Washington's freedom of action was subject to constraints, central bankers were less bound, which suited successive Republican administrations.

Central bankers have at the extremes been portrayed either as visionaries whose efforts failed but who paved the way for a more durable international financial order after 1945 or as villains whose well-meaning but maladroit actions brought on and deepened the calamity of the Depression.[73] Strong and Norman, Émile Moreau, governor of the Bank of France from 1926 to 1930, and Hjalmar Schacht, president of the Reichsbank from December 1923 to March 1930, were a quartet who interacted regularly with the Morgan partners. Strong's death in October 1928 removed one friend; Norman remained throughout the 1930s. While the connection with Moreau was never as close as that existing between J.P. Morgan & Co. and Strong and Norman, the partners developed very good relations with Charles Rist, a leading French economist and, in 1927 as Deputy-Governor of the Bank of France, Moreau's representative at the central bankers' talks in New York. As for Schacht, he was to bedevil the Morgan partners from 1929 onward.

---

[70] Hogan, *Informal Entente*, pp. 79–83.

[71] Harold Nicolson to Vita Sackville-West, 1 June 1935, Harold Nicolson, *Diaries and Letters, 1930–1939*, ed. Nigel Nicolson, London: Collins, 1966, p. 203.

[72] "Morgan and Kahn favor cancellation," *New York Times*, 3 August 1922, p. 6.

[73] For a positive appreciation, see Chandler, *Benjamin Strong*, pp. 475–76; for a hostile reading, see Liaquat Ahamed, *Lords of Finance: The Bankers Who Broke the World*, New York: Penguin Press, 2009.

While the partners had no direct hand in the various agreements among the central bankers after Britain's return to gold, indirectly they sympathized with, and encouraged, cooperation as a means to redress economic grievances. In 1927 Bartow's Long Island residence served as the gathering place for perhaps the best-known example of central bank concord when Strong, Norman, Schacht, and Rist met.

*****

On the eve of 1929 J.P. Morgan & Co. operated in a landscape transformed at home and abroad by World War I. Much was familiar – the institutional structure of the House of Morgan was unchanged, the tie to Britain and to the City of London was as strong as it had been before the war, and the core cultural values of the partners in New York had not altered. J.P. Morgan & Co. remained the leader of Wall Street, the most influential voice in a financial community whose counsels were heard across the country. Imprinted by the nineteenth-century merchant bank, the Morgan partners were devoted to the preservation of the existing order. They were the scions of the status quo. Evolution might be countenanced; revolution was beyond the pale. Pursuing stability, the partners believed that their activities were for the betterment of all.

Making such a world view more understandable was the receding of the threats represented by Populism and Progressivism, by Pujo and Brandeis, that had faded with the postwar march of American living standards. While many Americans remained convinced of the malevolent influence of J.P. Morgan & Co., seeing in the House of Morgan international bankers whose aims were unknown but were inimical, voices calling for the breakup of the "Money Trust" were fewer and fainter, while Hoover's triumph in the 1928 presidential election promised a continuation of Republican dominance.[74]

Abroad, though the Europe of 1914 had ceased to exist and war debts and reparations were an ongoing source of acrimony and vexation, it appeared as if the continent was on the mend, economically and politically. The Morgan partners had become accustomed to being consulted in international relations, to participating in putting Humpty-Dumpty back together. Morgan partners shared, imbibed, and articulated an internationalist ethos in which renewed prosperity was attainable through a commitment to multilateralism forged on a restored gold standard. What would happen, however, if the conditions underpinning Morgan influence in international relations – ample American capital seeking

---

[74] Charles R. Geisst, *Undue Influence: How the Wall Street Elite Put the Financial System at Risk*, Hoboken, NJ: John Wiley & Sons, 2005, p. 13.

foreign returns, the dominance of Britain and France in international affairs, the presence of a friendly administration in Washington committed to economic internationalism – should change? These possibilities do not seem to have crossed the minds of the partners. Fortified by the conviction that their world was improving, on 31 December 1928, when the new partners were named, all was well at the Corner. As the calendar turned to 1929, confidence was the watchword.

3   The Young Plan, the Bank for International Settlements, and the Wall Street Crash, 1929–1930

The year 1929 is remembered as the year of the Crash in New York and the beginning of the Depression. This was an unlikely prospect when the year opened. Confidence in the future was most striking in the rise in the NYSE. Whether this upward momentum meant that a crash was inevitable remains debated.[1] The first wave of literature frequently described the Crash as a causal agent in the coming of the Depression. Emphasis upon the psychological shock imparted by the Crash to business confidence was often stressed. Typically, little was said about the international aspects of the Crash and origins of the Depression.[2] More recent analyses have tended to bifurcate the Crash from the Depression, while emphasizing the ways in which international considerations influenced developments in the United States. Peter Temin's essay on the Depression in *The Cambridge Economic History of the United States* may be taken as representative, dismissing the Crash as a factor in the onset of the Depression.[3]

What of J.P. Morgan & Co. and the Crash? Allen wondered in 1935 if the Corner could have stopped the "wild financial proceedings" in 1929 and thus, perhaps, headed off the Crash and, by extension, the Depression.[4] Bell suggested in 1938 that J.P. Morgan & Co. might have

---

[1] The most detailed account is Barry A. Wigmore, *The Crash and Its Aftermath: A History of Securities Markets in the United States, 1929–1933*, Westport, CT: Greenwood Press, 1985. A recent survey has concluded that, after the opening six months of the year, the markets moved decisively upward into unsupportable territory. Morris, *A Rabble of Dead Money*, pp. 110–13.

[2] Two examples that insist on the linkage between the Crash and the Depression are Frederick Lewis Allen's classic, *Only Yesterday*, New York: Harper and Brothers, 1931, pp. 281–85 and J.F.T. O'Connor, *The Banking Crisis and Recovery under the Roosevelt Administration*, Chicago: 1938, Reprint New York: Da Capo 1971, p. 8. O'Connor was Comptroller of the Currency 1933–38 and Vice-Chair of the Federal Deposit Insurance Corporation 1934–38. Galbraith's *The Great Crash*, pp. 192–93 accepts the blow to business confidence; a restatement is Fraser, *Every Man*, pp. 413–14, which argues against the notion of divorcing the Crash from the Depression.

[3] Peter Temin, "The Great Depression," in Engerman and Gallman, *Cambridge Economic History of the United States*, p. 305.

[4] Allen, *The Lords of Creation*, p. 347. Charles R. Geisst, *Wall Street: A History*, New York: Oxford University Press, 1997, p. 187, is insistent that "Wall Street itself was primarily responsible for the crash and the subsequent depression."

forestalled the Crash but did not. Bell identified two factors as responsible for Morgan inaction. The first was that the structure of American finance had changed greatly since 1907. With the Federal Reserve making the Morgan role in combatting crisis ambiguous, J.P. Morgan & Co. expected the Federal Reserve to take the lead. Assuming this, the Morgan partners recused themselves. The second reason Bell advanced was distinct: the Morgan partners, he wrote, realized that the Crash heralded the coming of the Depression. Here lay classic Greek tragedy. "Morally and intellectually ... head and shoulders above the rest of the Street," Morgan far-sightedness availed them little, for they divined their power-lessness in the face of the magnitude of the storm looming.[5]

Closer examination reveals that omniscience without omnipotence, as Bell might have it, is illusory. This chapter examines J.P. Morgan & Co., the Young Plan, the Bank for International Settlements (BIS), the Crash, and its aftermath. For the bulk of 1929 the attention of the two most senior Morgan partners, Jack Morgan and Thomas W. Lamont, was riveted on Europe where they were engaged in negotiating what became the Young Plan and the BIS.[6] They believed that doing so would buttress European recovery and, with it, American fortunes. They were guardedly cheerful – about the Young Plan, about the BIS, about Europe, and about the American economy. Prosperity, at home and abroad, was inter-twined: divisibility between international and domestic considerations was fictional for the Morgan partners. The Morgan partners did not see the Crash coming; but when it came, it did not dispel Morgan certainty that matters were improving. To be sure, there were moments where this was not the case, when gloominess reigned, but on the whole confidence rather than despair pervaded the Corner. At first glance this seems odd, as it clashes with the dominant recollection of 1929–30. In memory, these years unspool a grim montage – the Crash, a dour and feckless President Hoover, the onset of the destruction of the Weimar Republic in Germany. Dearth, depression, and dictatorship flash by.

Economists, historians, and political scientists might point to the fra-gility of the postwar economic and political order, but challenge to the global dominance of liberal democratic capitalist states was limited before 1929. The ensuing years were to manifest confrontation on multiple fronts, economic, intellectual, military, and political. Retrospectively, if

---

[5] Bell, "The Decline of the Money Barons," p. 155.
[6] Jon Jacobson, *Locarno Diplomacy, Germany and the West, 1925–29*, Princeton, NJ: Princeton University Press, 1972, offers a very good assessment of the Young Plan, pp. 239–78. The best account of the creation of the BIS is Giovanni Toniolo, *Central Bank Cooperation at the Bank for International Settlements, 1930–1973*, Cambridge: Cambridge University Press, 2005, pp. 24–60.

scholars have stressed this as a defining arc, it was not apparent to the Morgan partners in 1929–30.

*****

Once it was agreed in September 1928 to convene a second international committee of experts to modify the Dawes Plan, the pressing question was, who would be the American delegates? Young was the Coolidge administration's preference. Young had begun his career as a lawyer before moving into business, where he rapidly made his name as a forward-thinking executive who was unusually broad-minded. Young and General Electric were emblematic of growth and modernity, of the American technocratic miracle.[7] His internationalism was well known, highlighted by involvement in the Dawes Plan talks of 1924. A standard-bearer for all that was brightest about American business in 1929, Young was a natural choice. Despite this, Young was reluctant to commit and through the fall of 1928 refused to make his intentions known. His baulkiness led to other names being suggested, notably Morrow's. At length, Young agreed to serve. He did so with the understanding that he would likely chair the deliberations.[8]

Jack Morgan was chosen as the second American delegate. *The New Republic*, not always a friend of J.P. Morgan & Co., thought that this selection was "an extraordinarily good idea" as his view on reparations "would be virtually final" in financial circles.[9] The *Commercial and Financial Chronicle*, the paper of record for business, was categorical in its endorsement. On 19 January 1929 it commented, "Mr. Morgan belongs in a class all by himself," for "the Morgan firm is a synonym for integrity and a tower of strength," which "commands the confidence not only of the entire banking and financial community of the United States, but that of Europe and the whole world."[10]

Both Jack Morgan and Lamont, who was to be Jack Morgan's alternate, were conflicted about participating.[11] The drawbacks were apparent: each state had its own desires and objectives, which ensured difficulties; it was unclear what support might emanate from Washington given that

---

[7] Stephen Schuker, "American Foreign Policy and the Young Plan, 1929," in Gustav Schmidt ed., *Konstellationen Internationaler Politik 1924–1932*, Bochum: N. Brockmeyer, 1983, p. 126.

[8] Case and Case, *Owen D. Young*, pp. 416–33.

[9] *The New Republic*, vol. 57, no. 738, 23 January 1929, p. 255.

[10] *Commercial and Financial Chronicle*, vol. 128, no. 3317, 19 January 1929, p. 289. The other American alternate was Thomas Nelson Perkins, a lawyer and corporate director who had been a member of the Reparations Commission from 1924 to 1926.

[11] Grenfell to Lamont, 4 February 1929, BL, TWL, Series II, Box 111, Folder 20 Morgan Grenfell & Company 1928–29.

the November 1928 presidential election had been won by Hoover who had not chosen a secretary of state; and reparations were scarified after nearly a decade of lacerations inflicted on all of the participants. Jack Morgan and Lamont did not believe that war debts and reparations could, or should be, separated, a stance at variance with the outgoing Coolidge and incoming Hoover administrations. There was a possibility that no way forward might be found.

Positively, the Morgan partners were encouraged by the active involvement of Parker Gilbert, the Agent-General for Reparations Payments based in Berlin, who was urging their participation. Parker Gilbert had been a protégé of Leffingwell's at the Treasury during the war and was well known to the partners. Parker Gilbert would join J.P. Morgan & Co. as a partner in January 1931 and he may have already had discussions about this prospect with Jack Morgan by the fall of 1928.[12] As for Young, he was a friend, an ally, and someone whose judgement the Morgan partners respected. Given that the Morgan partners, especially Leffingwell, had been part of the effort to persuade Young to take the job, they could hardly deny Young when he asked Jack Morgan to be the second delegate. With Young as chair there was an opportunity to reach a final settlement on reparations that might do much to restore harmony in Europe. If there was to be prosperity in the United States, European political stability and economic well-being was required. With this prospect in the offing, the Morgan partners agreed.[13] Having done so, contrary to what the *Commercial and Financial Chronicle* assured its readers, Jack Morgan was insistent that his role would be as a loyal lieutenant to Young.[14]

Prior to the opening of the talks, Jack Morgan and Leffingwell met in Paris in October 1928. They were joined by Parker Gilbert who had been considering what the upcoming conference might accomplish. Writing to George Harrison of the FRBNY on 11 October, Parker Gilbert enclosed a memorandum that he had composed on 26 September.[15] Asking Harrison to treat it as "strictly confidential," Parker Gilbert made an

---

[12] There were rumours as early as 1927 that Parker Gilbert had been approached about joining J.P. Morgan & Co. Certainly, it was no later than August 1929 when Jack Morgan had talks with Parker Gilbert. Parker Gilbert to Morrow, 25 November 1929, Amherst College (AC), Dwight D. Morrow papers (DM), I, Box 24, Folder 12.

[13] See Jack Morgan's comments to Lord Revelstoke, 18 January 1929, cited in Beth A. Simmons, "Why Innovate? Founding the Bank for International Settlements," *World Politics*, vol. 45, no. 3 (1993), footnote 105, p. 399; Grenfell to Lamont, 4 February 1929, BL, TWL, Box 111, Folder 20 Morgan Grenfell & Company 1928–29.

[14] The Crocker diary makes this clear. For example, Stuart M. Crocker Diary, 11 February 1929, SLU, ODY papers, SMC, Box 976.

[15] Harrison was not yet Governor of the FRBNY. Strong died in October 1928. Harrison was not selected formally until late November 1928. Parker Gilbert to FRBNY, 11 October 1928, CUL, George L. Harrison papers (GH), Box 1, Binder 1.

exception for the Morgan partners. He requested that Harrison pass the memorandum to Lamont and said that he would do likewise in Paris by giving Leffingwell a copy. Parker Gilbert's September memorandum argued that commercializing German reparations bonds was dependent upon reaching a final total that the Germans owed. "Fundamental" to success was mobilization, by which he meant that the bonds should be sold to private investors. Mobilization, which the French promoted, would allow the respective Treasuries to receive funds immediately without the risk associated with retaining the bonds.[16] Allowing for the likely size of the bond issues, Parker Gilbert believed that cooperation was required, especially in the British, French, and American markets. The trouble was that at present bond market sentiment was negative, a reality that had to be faced. The American market in particular would benefit from a reduction in bond issues of all kinds to allow a period of recuperation to make possible the absorption of new issues. In this context Parker Gilbert was insistent that any German reparations bonds offered must be of very high quality. The role of the Expert Committee should be to prepare a plan that would safeguard the success of bond flotations on the markets irrespective of the types of bond. This stipulation required that the Expert Committee membership must be of sufficient stature to reassure the markets. Parker Gilbert confessed to Harrison that he was alarmed at the "pessimistic sentiments" emanating from American banking sources.[17]

Reviewing this document, Morgan and Leffingwell agreed that a German annuity should be fixed in both amount and duration. Neither man was in favour of specifying a total capital debt that the Germans would be obligated to discharge. Morgan and Leffingwell imagined that any bonds issued should come on to the markets at German initiative. They hoped this would alleviate worries about political interference, while commercializing the bonds. The attraction of commercialization was straightforward – it promised a means to remove politics from reparations. Sensitive to the implications for the existing Dawes Plan bonds, the Morgan partners would not support any scheme that might imperil their repayment. Morgan and Leffingwell felt that, if all went well, the proceeds realized would be sufficient to allow the Allies to discharge their war debts to the United States.[18]

---

[16] Simmons, "Why Innovate?," p. 391.
[17] Parker Gilbert to FRBNY, 11 October 1928, CUL, GH, Box 1, Binder 1.
[18] Leffingwell to Lamont, 22 October 1928, BL, TWL, Series II, Box 103, Folder 13. The letter was circulated to all of the New York partners.

Following the conclave in Paris with the Morgan partners, Parker Gilbert went to London where he met Norman and, through the latter, the prime minister, Stanley Baldwin, on 15–16 October. While there, Parker Gilbert canvassed the names of possible delegates with Norman and Baldwin, as he had done with Morgan and Leffingwell. Jack Morgan discussed candidates with Norman on 23 October, as did Leffingwell during his visit to the Bank of England on 12 November. All were agreed that Young was the best American choice, while Norman made it known that he preferred Lord Revelstoke and Sir Josiah Stamp as the British team.[19]

The meetings opened in Paris on 11 February 1929 with Young in the chair. It soon became apparent that neither Morgan nor Young had read the tea leaves correctly. While both men realized that the Germans, led by Schacht, wanted a marked decrease in their reparations payments, and that the French, whose lead delegate was Moreau, would resist reduction on the scale that the Germans hoped to attain, they had failed to appreciate how wide the chasm was between Paris and Berlin. Moreau wanted reparations payments that would be made at a level commensurate with the French commitment to discharging their war debts to the United States. Paris favoured commercialization on the grounds that it would subject the Germans to market discipline. Should the Germans fail to make the payments on commercialized reparations bonds, it would have consequences for German credit on the international capital markets, thus building in an incentive to comply. The looming August 1929 deadline for ratification of the 1926 Mellon–Bérenger Agreement by the National Assembly was also on French minds.[20] Schacht wanted not only a reduction in the Dawes Plan payments but the abolition of the Agent-General's office and completion of the French evacuation from the Rhineland, a list that Paris baulked at.

Two weeks after the meetings began, Young and Morgan were doubting whether any agreement would be possible. As the delegates struggled, Émile Francqui, the principal Belgian envoy, advanced the idea of an international bank to handle reparations. This notion was not new. As far back as the 1880s such schemes had been tendered. At the Genoa economic conference in 1922 the delegates had accepted a suite of ideas

[19] Clay, *Lord Norman*, pp. 267–68.
[20] The Mellon–Bérenger Agreement of 29 April 1926 settled the French war debt owing to the United States. Andrew Mellon was the secretary of the Treasury. Henry Bérenger was the French ambassador at Washington. Under the terms of the arrangement, the French debt to the United States was put at $4.025 billion, which was to be discharged over a 62-year period at an average interest rate of 1.6 per cent. Benjamin D. Rhodes, "Reassessing Uncle Shylock: The United States and the French War Debt, 1917–1929," *The Journal of American History*, vol. 55, no. 4 (1969), p. 799.

that resembled what became the BIS.[21] Schacht seized on Francqui's proposal and repurposed it. Schacht envisaged an international clearing house whose mandate would go well beyond reparations to bolster European trade and economic development through credit creation. Schacht hoped that German exports would benefit from credits granted to developing states by this new institution. Young's reaction was to consider how these separate approaches might be utilized. To do so, he pressed into service Dr. Walter Stewart, then an economic advisor to the Bank of England, Dr. W. Randolph Burgess of the FRBNY and Shepard Morgan of the Agent-General's office to hammer out the details of the proposed international bank.[22]

Over the ensuing days, as Stewart, Burgess, and Shepard Morgan worked on drafts, they consulted with Young who in turn discussed matters with Jack Morgan and Lamont. Meeting on 5 March with Young and the drafting team, Jack Morgan raised three chief points. First, in his view an international bank should be a forum for the resolution of future international disputes. Secondly, with this in mind, Jack Morgan argued that the wording of the draft should refer throughout to the Reichsbank and not to the German government. His third concern was that, as framed, objections might be raised that the proposed bank would be trespassing on the territory of commercial banks.[23] Jack Morgan and Lamont – who shared this last fear – were animated by, and reflecting, the perspective of J.A.M. de Sanchez and Jeremiah Smith Jr.

De Sanchez was a Morgan employee. He had been involved in analysing the Morgan loans to France and Belgium in the mid-1920s, as well as participating as an observer in the Locarno talks. De Sanchez was responsible for generating much of the statistical data utilized by the American delegates during the Young talks. An ardent free-market thinker, De Sanchez had doubts about an international bank. He believed that its proposed functions were already fulfilled adequately by existing commercial banks. Smith, who had been one of the "money doctors" involved in Hungarian financial reconstruction, and was close to Lamont, was also opposed, wondering where the capital required to fund such a bank would come from. Young managed to mollify both Jack Morgan and Lamont on these counts.[24] This was perhaps easier accomplished than

---

[21] Toniolo, *Central Bank Cooperation*, pp. 20–23.

[22] Ibid., pp. 35–36; Stuart M. Crocker Diary, 25 February 1929, SLU, ODY, SMC, Box 976.

[23] Stuart M. Crocker Diary, 5 March 1929, SLU, ODY, Box 976.

[24] On de Sanchez, see TML, CP, Box 30, De Sanchez, J.A.M. with the comment by Harry Morgan; on Smith, a classmate of Lamont's, see Peterecz, *Jeremiah Smith Jr. and Hungary, 1924–1926*; Stuart M. Crocker Diary, 25 February 1929, SLU, ODY, Box 976.

might be thought. Jack Morgan and Lamont were in favour of ending the reparations and war debts imbroglio. What they had not counted upon was opposition in New York.

Cabling their partners on 11 March, Jack Morgan and Lamont touted the plan. There was a pressing need to dispel the "old war atmosphere" and eradicate "the war machinery" so that the German public would appreciate that the page had been turned. The Morgan commitment to European stabilization overrode Jack Morgan's instinctive anti-German posture. The new bank would efface the acrimony of the past by furnishing a venue where issues could be worked out calmly between states. As part of its mandate Jack Morgan and Lamont suggested that the international bank assume the duties of the Dawes Loan Trustees. These ideas were too much for Leffingwell, who worried that the international bank might compromise the autonomy of existing central banks. Jack Morgan and Lamont changed tack, reminding New York that, without a mechanism such as the proposed bank, existing obligations, notably the Dawes Plan bonds, might be endangered by a program of unrestrained issues. This did not soothe. On 14 March, following the publication of an article in the *New York Herald Tribune* that forecast the new bank would have capital of $80–100 million, which would be furnished largely by private sources, Leffingwell, Charles Steele, Junius Morgan, and George Whitney cabled tartly, "If there is any idea of having private banks subscribe, we hope the privilege will not be extended to private bankers."[25]

Work on the BIS ploughed ahead. By 25 March its basic Charter and Statutes were drafted, principally by Sir Charles Addis of the Hong Kong and Shanghai Banking Corporation. A contrite Leffingwell retracted his earlier remarks, telling Lamont "we so stupidly misunderstood your cable about the International Bank." Yet doubts lingered. Visiting Harrison and Burgess in mid-April, Leffingwell aired his concerns. While eliminating the Agent-General's office would reduce animosity, he could not fathom how the BIS would survive. Leffingwell told Harrison and Burgess that foreign exchange operations alone would not suffice to keep the BIS in the black. When Harrison "laughingly" suggested that he and Leffingwell should be the American directors, Leffingwell refused flatly. It was not until May that Leffingwell abandoned his opposition to the BIS.[26]

---

[25] Jack Morgan and Lamont to J.P. Morgan & Co., 11 March 1929, Leffingwell to Jack Morgan & Lamont, 11 March 1929, Jack Morgan and Lamont to J.P. Morgan & Co., 12 March 1929, Leffingwell, Charles Steele, Junius Morgan, and George Whitney to Jack Morgan and Lamont, 14 March 1929, TML, JPM, Box 178/238, J.P. Morgan & Co. Cables concerning Reparations.

[26] Leffingwell to Lamont, 5 April 1929, BL, TWL, Series II, Box 83, Folder 2, Austria 1928–34; Leffingwell to Lamont, 16 April 1929, Leffingwell to Lamont, 9 May 1929, both in YUL, RCL, Series I, Box 4, Folder 94.

Two considerations drove this reversal. Jack Morgan and Lamont had staked their prestige on the BIS. By embracing it, they had identified with it. Leffingwell might not like the BIS but he could not disavow his partners. Connected to this was the second reason: Jack Morgan and Lamont believed in the work of the Young committee and in the BIS. As Lamont wrote to Young on 24 March 1929, the committee had a chance to create a "new era" in international relations, based upon the amicable cooperation of the six powers.[27] Months later, attempting to persuade a reluctant Philip Snowden, then chancellor of the exchequer, of the virtues of the Young Plan and the BIS, Lamont remarked, "[o]ne cannot but help to see the need for new forms of international financial machinery to carry out the vast financial movements of the present day."[28] The Young Plan and the BIS were that machinery.

The struggle over the BIS was interwoven with the tussle inside the Young committee to reach agreement on reparations. After 25 March, discussion returned to the central issue: how much would Germany pay over what period? Young employed Jack Morgan and Lamont to batter Schacht and Moreau. On separate occasions, acting at the behest of Young, Morgan and Lamont prodded Schacht to increase what Germany was willing to pay while extracting from Moreau a commitment to reduce what France was willing to accept. Neither Schacht nor Moreau succumbed.[29] Young attempted to break the stalemate by proposing new figures in a memorandum circulated to the delegates. Predictably, his démarche failed to attract consensus. Damagingly, it sparked open disputation with Washington. Young was aware that any association of reparations with war debts would elicit a powerful reaction from Washington.[30] Over the following days, a series of cables, between the American delegation in Paris on the one hand and the Hoover administration on the other, were exchanged. Young endeavoured to maintain his independence in the face of the evident fear in Washington that he and his colleagues were too compliant. Young threatened to resign on 20 April, after which a modus vivendi was struck. The insistence of the secretary of state, Henry L. Stimson, and Hoover that there be no acknowledged connection

---

[27] Lamont to Young, 24 March 1929, SLU, ODY, Box 801, Folder 1297K11.
[28] Lamont to Snowden, 20 August 1929, TML, Carosso papers, Box 31, Morgan & Co. – Bank for International Settlements.
[29] Young tried to lever the influence of J.P. Morgan & Co. from an early point. See the Crocker diary entries for 19 February 1929, p. 28, and 20–21 February, p. 41. The attempt to coerce Schacht occurred in early March, Stuart M. Crocker Diary, 7 March 1929, SLU, ODY, Box 976. A similar effort was made with Moreau in early May 1929, to no avail. Stuart M. Crocker Diary, 1 May 1929, SLU, ODY, Box 976.
[30] Schuker, "American Foreign Policy and the Young Plan, 1929," p. 128.

Figure 3.1 President Calvin Coolidge, Secretary of the Treasury Andrew Mellon, and Secretary of Commerce Herbert Hoover on the steps of the White House, 1928. Harris & Ewing Collection, Library of Congress, Prints & Photographs Division, LC-DIG-hec-35070.

between war debts and reparations was accepted by Young and in turn he was given the latitude to reach a deal.[31]

For the Morgan partners, this episode contributed to their unease about Hoover, just as it freshened Hoover's apprehension about J.P. Morgan & Co.[32] Prior to Hoover's ascension to the presidency, the Morgan partners had had relatively little to do with him (see Figure 3.1). During Hoover's tenure as secretary of commerce, especially in 1921–22, when American policy vis-à-vis loans to Europe was being fashioned, there had been interaction which petered out. J.P. Morgan & Co. would have preferred

---

[31] SLU, ODY, Box 799, Folder Important Papers 1297K10.

[32] Stuart M. Crocker Diary, 9–10 April 1929, SLU, ODY, Box 976, contains the following: "As a matter of fact, none of the men here have any regard for Hoover, because they think he is too shifty in his affections and moreover because he thinks nobody can do any kind of job as well as he can. The only man here who has always admired Hoover and counted him among his good friends is Mr. Young."

another term for Coolidge, with whom their ex-partner Morrow was a personal friend. This did not mean that the partners were opposed to Hoover, though Leffingwell had a dim view of Hoover dating from his stint in the Treasury. In 1928 a scathing memorandum he had written about Hoover a decade earlier came into the hands of Oswald G. Villard's *The Nation*. Initially, Villard agreed not to publish following a plea from Leffingwell, but months later *The Nation* did so with the *New York Times* picking up the story. In his memorandum Leffingwell had said, "Hoover knows nothing about finance, nothing about exchange and nothing about economics ... Hoover ... has never failed to be wrong when his duties confronted him with problems of that nature." While the *New York Times* accompanied its 1928 article with an apology issued by Leffingwell to Hoover in 1921, the episode was embarrassing but revealing, for Leffingwell never lost his conviction that Hoover was overrated.[33] This said, the partners, save Leffingwell, were Republicans who understood that they had to work with Hoover's administration and could not sever themselves from Washington's wishes, however ill-considered they might deem these wishes. With the new administration only a few months old, an open break was unthinkable. Even in much more dire circumstances, in 1932, amidst the ravages of mass unemployment and economic desolation, the partners could not bring themselves to abandon Hoover.

Nevertheless, Morgan reservations were reciprocated. While it has been suggested that Lamont was Hoover's "chief adviser" on the Street, this overstates the case.[34] Theodore Joslin, Hoover's press secretary, identified Lamont as one of a number of industrialists and bankers whose views Hoover solicited. It would be more accurate to say that Hoover did not have a prominent Wall Street figure as a confidant. Hoover had never found Wall Street congenial. Throughout his presidency he regarded Wall Street with a mixture of contempt, scorn, and mistrust.[35] Hoover preferred the counsel of Henry M. Robinson, of the

---

[33] Stuart M. Crocker Diary, 17 May 1929, SLU, ODY, Box 976 for Jack Morgan's reaction to the Stimson announcement. Oswald G. Villard to Russell C. Leffingwell, 13 March 1928, YUL, RCL, Series I, Box 7, Folder 166. Leffingwell replied to Villard on 16 March 1928. On 24 April Villard told Leffingwell that *The Nation* had opted not to publish. "Socialists Take Up Attack on Hoover," *New York Times*, 1 August 1928, p. 3.

[34] Chernow, *The House of Morgan*, p. 314.

[35] Theodore Joslin, *Hoover off the Record*, Garden City, NY: Doubleday, Doran and Company, 1934. Reprint Freeport: New York, Books for Libraries Press, 1971, pp. 23–24; see the comments by Albert Romasco, *The Poverty of Abundance: Hoover, the Nation and the Great Depression*, New York: Oxford University Press, 1965, pp. 85–89. Herbert Feis, the economic advisor to the State Department in Hoover's administration (and Roosevelt's to follow), told Edward W. Bennett in 1951, "that Hoover was the last man to let himself be dictated to by New York bankers." Edward W. Bennett, *Germany and the Diplomacy of the Financial Crisis, 1931*, Cambridge, MA: Harvard University

First National Bank of Los Angeles, on banking and financial matters. Robinson married extensive international experience with California residency, demarcating a literal distance from New York which appealed to Hoover. It was Robinson who acted as the go-between for Hoover in his dealings with Wall Street. While Hoover might have to deal with J.P. Morgan & Co. as the acknowledged leader of the Street, his attitude toward the Corner was ambivalent. Hoover's doubts about the Corner, about the Young report, and about the BIS were reinforced in late July 1929 by an administration study that warned the BIS might serve as a vehicle for the aggrandizement of Morgan power.[36]

Underpinning these fears was a shift in Hoover's outlook on Europe since his days at the head of Belgian relief. Kendrick Clements, in his excellent biography, has argued persuasively that Hoover's assessment of Europe was an amalgam of conflicting impulses. Hoover understood that the United States needed a stable, prosperous Europe, though he mistrusted European motives and designs. Hoover wanted the United States to be as independent as possible from Europe but favoured American membership in the League of Nations and the World Court. He pursued repayment of war debts, espoused protective tariffs, and championed the expansion of American business at the expense of European interests. Clements concludes: "His extensive international experience, instead of making him more supportive of a policy of cooperation and collaboration to stabilize the international economy, rather reinforced his economic nationalism."[37]

Hoover's peregrination from internationalist to nationalist was not singular. He was symbolic of the transformation of the Republican Party in the 1920s. The Republican Party was a congeries of competing groups, loosely split in economic terms into nationalists and internationalists. From the 1920–21 depression and the Fordney–McCumber Tariff of 1922, the tide within the party inexorably moved toward the nationalists. The reason for this was simple: the domestic manufacturers who benefited from tariffs were more numerous, had a far larger workforce, and in electoral terms were able to mobilize their influence more effectively. Hoover was their champion and his triumph in 1928 reflected their shared victory. The contretemps surrounding war debts did not help the internationalists within the Republican Party, but they were losing ground irrespective of this in the 1920s. The Smoot–Hawley Tariff of

Press, 1962, p. 138. Lewis Strauss of Kuhn, Loeb & Co. was close to Hoover, but his stature on the Street was not of the first rank.

[36] Dayer, *Finance and Empire*, p. 201.

[37] Kendrick A. Clements, *The Life of Herbert Hoover: Imperfect Visionary, 1918–1928*, London: Palgrave Macmillan, 2010, p. 431.

1930, which the Morgan firm opposed, as did nearly all Republican internationalists, stamped the victory of the nationalist camp.[38]

The dispute in April 1929 between Young, Morgan, and Lamont on the one hand and the Hoover administration on the other was camouflaged because they had to maintain a working relationship, made more necessary by Schacht's recklessness and the death of Lord Revelstoke. Schacht, whom the veteran Paris-based journalist Sisley Huddleston described during the talks as "the most tactless, the most aggressive and the most irascible person I have ever seen in public life," alienated his fellow delegates in an ill-conceived statement on 17 April (see Figure 3.2).[39] Earlier, Schacht had indicated to Young and Morgan that he was thinking along the lines of Germany reclaiming some of its former colonies as well as chunks of the Polish Corridor if it had to bear

Figure 3.2 Hjalmar Schacht and Montagu Norman, 1930. Imagno/ Hulton Archive/Getty Images.

[38] Joan Hoff Wilson, *American Business and Foreign Policy 1920–1933*, Lexington, KY: University Press of Kentucky, 1971; Clyde P. Weed, *The Transformation of the Republican Party, 1912–1936: From Reform to Resistance*, Boulder, CO: Lynne Rienner Publishers, 2011, pp. 81–83.

[39] Sisley Huddleston, *In My Time*, New York: E.P. Dutton & Co., 1938, p. 256.

the ongoing burden of what he deemed excessive reparations. When Schacht raised this possibility in conjunction with a stipulation that a payment of 1.65 billion marks annually for 37 years was the maximum that Germany could bear, the uproar that ensued brought the discussions to the brink of dissolution, an outcome that was avoided in part, as Liaquat Ahamed has remarked, by Revelstoke's death on 19 April giving Young the chance to declare a recess.[40] When the conference reconvened, a chastened Schacht, who had been instructed tersely to return to Berlin for consultation, where he received orders to dismiss his fantasies of territorial gain, was more cooperative.[41] Even with Schacht hobbled the delegates struggled to reach a deal. The problem was now not Schacht, for he had signalled his willingness to accept Young's 2.05 billion marks figure, but the recalcitrance of the French and, to a lesser degree, the Belgians. A deal was not reached until 29 May and it was announced to the press on 7 June 1929.

It would be misleading to portray the Morgan reaction to the settlement as unequivocally positive. Weary of the taxing negotiations, Jack Morgan's enthusiasm had flagged. In a jaundiced letter to Bartow he wrote, "When or if ever I get home, it will be a long time before you find me trying to help along the cause of peace in the World. I am fed up on it and it is of no use anyhow." His partners had qualms. Cochran was opposed. Lamont and Leffingwell followed Jack Morgan's lead. Lamont saw the committee report as a means to pacify an unruly continent. As for Leffingwell, he expressed his outlook bluntly: "I defy anybody to detest them [the Germans] more than I do. Just the same I think it is discreditable, after licking them good and thorough ten years ago, to go on kicking them and mauling them about."[42]

There remained the BIS. The Hoover administration was heartened by the knowledge that such a reliably Republican and orthodox forum as the *Commercial and Financial Chronicle* had expressed its worry, lobbying for a prohibition on Federal Reserve system participation in the planned "International super bank." An open expression of disapproval of the BIS by Stimson led Jack Morgan to decry the "fools" in Washington.[43] Following a luncheon at the White House on 25 June, where Young, Jack

---

[40] Ahamed, *Lords of Finance*, p. 335.   [41] Jacobson, *Locarno Diplomacy*, pp. 258–60.

[42] Jack Morgan to Bartow, 29 April 1929, TML, MBEP, Series 5, Bartow, Francis D.; Leffingwell to Lamont, 5 April 1929, BL, TWL papers, Series II, Box 83, Folder 2, Austria 1928–34.

[43] "The Proposed International Bank – the Federal Reserve Should Not Participate," *Commercial and Financial Chronicle*, vol. 128, no. 3326, 23 March 1929, pp. 1781–82; Stimson took the step of issuing a formal statement that the United States would not participate in the BIS on 16 May 1929. "America Rejects Part in World Bank," *New York Times*, 17 May 1929, p. 3; Crocker diary, 17 May 1929, SLU, ODY, Box 976, p. 248.

Figure 3.3 Members of the American Reparations Commission, in conference with the Secretary of State Henry L. Stimson, 1929. Harris & Ewing Collection, Library of Congress, Prints & Photographs Division, LC-DIG-hec-35421 (digital file from original negative).

In the front row, seated left to right: Jack Morgan; Secretary Stimson; and Owen D. Young, chairman. In the back row, left to right: Thomas W. Lamont; Thomas Nelson Perkins; Undersecretary of State Joseph P. Cotton; and Assistant Secretary of State William R. Castle.

Morgan, Lamont, and Nelson Perkins met with Hoover, Stimson, and Mellon to discuss the Young report and the BIS, a thinly veiled *New York Times* article demarcated the divide starkly (see Figure 3.3). The piece remarked that, while "prominent financiers" conceded that perhaps the BIS had been "somewhat overpraised," negative consequences might ensue should the BIS embark upon open-market operations without reference to the Federal Reserve. The article concluded with a blunt statement that Wall Street expected that a J.P. Morgan & Co. partner would join the BIS board.[44] Even the dullest reader could recognize that

---

[44] "Regret Bank on Debt Bank: Bankers Hold Absence of Officials May Embarrass Federal Reserve," *New York Times*, 27 June 1929, p. 12.

J.P. Morgan & Co. and the FRBNY differed with the Hoover administration.

Not all difficulties were found in Washington. Two days before the Young report was announced, a new Labour government took office in Britain. Ramsay MacDonald became prime minister on 5 June 1929 with Snowden at the Exchequer. Labour's stance on the Young report was guarded. Snowden favoured the abolition of reparations but, if this was not forthcoming, he was adamant that Britain's share of reparations should not be diminished. The Young committee report recommended a reduction in the amount that Britain should receive, on the order of £2.4 million per year over a 37-year period. Within Whitehall, senior officials at the Treasury and the Foreign Office favoured accession. One important figure, Sir Frederick Leith-Ross, the Deputy-Controller of Finance in the Treasury, dissented. Leith-Ross shared Snowden's apprehension about the Young Plan and encouraged him to adopt a bellicose stance. Late in July 1929 Snowden informed Parliament that Britain would be seeking changes when a conference convened to discuss the Young Plan opened at The Hague on 6 August. Paris had no such trepidation, viewing the proposed settlement as the most favourable to be obtained in the circumstances. France had ratified the report and signalled a desire to settle the other outstanding issue, the creation of an organizing committee that would frame the structure of the BIS.[45]

It was in this context that Jack Morgan and Lamont returned to Europe. While Grenfell was antipathetic to Labour, as befitted a banker and Tory MP (he referred consistently to Labour as "Reds and Socialists"), he made an exception for MacDonald and Snowden.[46] MacDonald was known to the Morgan partners as an amiable politician whose ideological complexion was less red and more blush with every passing year. Snowden was dour and ascetic. By 1929 any trace of his Fabian Socialism had washed away. Snowden believed in free trade and balanced budgets and after 1925 harboured an "obsession" with keeping Britain on the gold standard. His relations with the financiers of the City of London

---

[45] This paragraph follows the discussion in Robert Boyce, *The Great Interwar Crisis and the Collapse of Globalization*, London: Palgrave Macmillan, 2009, pp. 197–206; Sir Frederick Leith-Ross, *Money Talks: Fifty Years of International Finance*, London: Hutchinson & Co., 1968, p. 103.

[46] Grenfell to Leffingwell, 12 June 1929, TML, CP, Box 18, Morgan & Co. – Misc. General Econ. & Business Conditions.

were, unsurprisingly, excellent.[47] In his economic comportment, Snowden was the ideal Labour chancellor for J.P. Morgan & Co.

Some of Snowden's appeal was offset by his belligerence. Ahead of The Hague conference opening, Lamont and Jack Morgan had discussed with Parker Gilbert the delicate question of the membership of the BIS organization committee. Worryingly, the British were exhibiting the "greatest reserve." Lamont's conversations with Moreau and Pierre Quesnay of the Bank of France later that month demonstrated these concerns.[48] The French feared that Snowden was out to secure changes to the Young Plan. Raymond Poincaré, then premier, believed that the sluice gates of revision would open if Snowden attained his objective.[49] To counter this prospect, Moreau cabled Harrison and Jack Morgan, with the aim of securing American support. On the eve of The Hague Conference, an entente between the French and J.P. Morgan & Co., backed by the FRBNY, had emerged.

There were two principal issues at stake at The Hague: first, ratification of the Young committee report so that the plan could become operational; second, finalizing the organization committee for the BIS. The Morgan partners were aghast at the possibility that Snowden's truculence might doom the Young Plan. They had trouble, as Jack Morgan put it, understanding his "incomprehensible attitude."[50] They shared this worry with France, though French concerns were transcendental. Paris was opposed to Snowden's declared intent to revise the percentages received in German reparations payments. Lamont and Jack Morgan were willing to countenance alteration in the shares allocated, provided doing so did not mean the destruction of the plan.

Morgan efforts were devoted to limiting the damage that Snowden might inflict. A coordinated approach was adopted. Having made common cause with Paris, Jack Morgan and Lamont made sure that Young was kept informed, while simultaneously relying upon Grenfell and their

---

[47] Colin Cross, *Philip Snowden*, London: Barrie and Rockliff, 1966, pp. 202–36; Kenneth Laybourn, *Philip Snowden: A Biography, 1864–1937*, Aldershot: Temple Smith, 1988, p. 96.

[48] Quesnay died in 1937. For his influence, see Olivier Feiertag, "Pierre Quesnay et les réseaux de l'internationisme monétaire en Europe (1919–1937)," in Michel Dumoulin, ed., *Les réseaux économiques de la construction européene au XXᵉ siècle*, Bern: Peter Lang, 2004; Renaud Boulanger, "La question de rapprochement financier et banquier entre la France et les États-Unis a la fin des années 1920. L'entremise de Pierre Quesnay," *Histoire@Politique*, no. 19 (2013).

[49] Lamont to J.P. Morgan & Co., 16 July 1929, KC, NDJ; Lamont to Young, 28 July 1929, SLU, ODY, Box 315, Folder 1297W8. Poincaré's ministry fell on 29 July 1929. Aristide Briand, who succeed Poincaré as premier, was less concerned.

[50] Jack Morgan to Harry Morgan, 10 August 1929, TML, JPM, Box 38A, 35.1 – Cable Book.

excellent relations with Norman to rally him to the cause. On 9 August Jack Morgan, Parker Gilbert, and Norman met. The discussion was fearful rather than productive. As Jack Morgan told his New York partners, "Sorry to be so vague but Snowden's extraordinary methods of negotiation have thrown the whole thing into such confusion that no one can see his way anywhere and the whole thing is clouded by the fear of the complete rupture of the conference before it has fairly begun." Norman's worries arose from a familiar spectre – he was alarmed, as he told Harrison, that Snowden's undiplomatic approach might spark a crisis in Germany, with a threat to the gold standard ensuing. Several days later Norman had regained his equanimity, telling Harrison that matters looked better and that he had kept Jack Morgan apprised of developments.[51]

While Jack Morgan dealt with Norman, Lamont was tackling Ramsay MacDonald and Snowden. Lamont met with both men at the urging of Addis and Stamp in an effort to sway Snowden. Lamont's efforts were unsuccessful as the chancellor made it clear that he was determined to win a larger percentage of reparations for Britain come what may. MacDonald proved of little assistance and indeed may have planted in Snowden's mind the notion that Lamont was angling for an invitation to the conference proper. This was not the case, but Snowden thought it was.[52] Lamont's protestations were unavailing. Quesnay was urging Lamont to go to the conference, but Lamont declined, telling Quesnay that Snowden was already resentful of his efforts and "the less he saw of experts, American and otherwise, the better."[53] This did not prevent Lamont from penning a long personal letter to Snowden on 20 August. Lamont laid out the vision of the BIS that France, J.P. Morgan & Co., and Norman had agreed. He argued that the BIS should be free of political interference, that the role of private banks should be minimal, and that central banks should be at the heart of the BIS. Lamont stressed that the world needed new financial machinery to supplant the "archaic and

---

[51] Jack Morgan to J.P. Morgan & Co., 9 August 1929, TML, CP, Box 17, Folder Morgan & Co. Misc. Priv. Telegs 15 May to 21 November 1929; Jack Morgan to Harry Morgan, 12 August 1929, TML, JPM, Box 38A, 35.1 – Cable Book; Norman to George Harrison, 9 and 13 August 1929, CUL, GH, Box 8, Binder 18.

[52] Dayer, *Finance and Empire*, p. 200, accepts that Lamont was attempting to wangle an invitation. Lamont had told Owen Young on 31 July that he did not want to go to The Hague and this stance was confirmed by Jack Morgan in his cable to Harry Morgan of 9 August 1929. Lamont to J.P. Morgan & Co. for Owen Young, 1 July 1929, TML, CP, Box 17, Folder Morgan & Co. Misc. Priv. Telegs 15 May to 21 November 1929; Jack Morgan to Harry Morgan, 12 August 1929, TML, JPM, Box 38A/35.1 – Cable Book.

[53] Lamont to Snowden, 14 August 1929, TML, CP, Box 17, Folder Morgan & Co. Misc. Priv. Telegs 15 May to 21 November 1929; Lamont to Quesnay, 14 August 1929, TML, CP, Box 17, Folder Morgan & Co. Misc. Priv. Telegs 15 May to 21 November 1929.

casual" practices of the past.[54] It is unlikely that this missive had any meaningful effect upon Snowden, in part because Grenfell vetted the letter with Norman and Jack Morgan before it was despatched to Snowden, by which time the crisis at The Hague Conference had come and gone.[55]

The Morgan partners never appreciated what motivated Snowden in August 1929. They failed to understand that Snowden was interested in securing a domestic political triumph. He ignored Norman throughout August, brushed Lamont aside, and was prevented from forcing a breakdown at the conference only by MacDonald and Arthur Henderson, the foreign secretary, who grew weary of Snowden's intransigence. It was their intervention that secured accommodation. Once a compromise was reached at The Hague and Snowden returned home to the plaudits of the press and public opinion having recouped £2 million more per year, his interest in the BIS, never strong to begin with, lapsed.[56]

After Snowden's theatrics there remained the question of the BIS. Lamont had told Quesnay that J.P. Morgan & Co. was not willing to participate in the BIS if the British Treasury view that greater government control was a *sine qua non* prevailed.[57] Given that the Hoover administration had rejected Federal Reserve involvement, this threat carried weight as only J.P. Morgan & Co. had the necessary stature in the American financial community to sponsor the BIS. Hoover's doubts about the BIS remained strong, though they were mollified somewhat by Robinson, whose name had been floated by Jack Morgan and Lamont as a possible American representative on the BIS. Robinson told Hoover in late October 1929 following a conversation with Young that there were "sound" reasons for creating the bank as it might "stabilize the European position."[58] While this might suggest that Hoover was malleable, his administration's tepid endorsement complicated the search for acceptable American representatives on the organizing committee. Jack Morgan took the lead as Lamont had returned to the United States.

---

[54] Lamont to Snowden, 20 August 1929, TML, CP, Box 31, Morgan & Co. – Bank for International Settlements.

[55] Grenfell to Jack Morgan, 22 August 1929, TML, JPM, Box 179/239.

[56] Clay, *Lord Norman*, p. 270; Boyce, *British Capitalism*, pp. 209–10; Cross, *Philip Snowden*, pp. 237–39.

[57] Lamont to Owen Young 19 August 1929, TML, CP, Box 17, Folder Morgan & Co. Misc. Priv. Telegs 15 May to 21 November 1929.

[58] Garrard Winston to Ogden Mills, 27 August 1929, LC, OLM, Box 8, 1929 Folder. Winston told Mills that Isaac Marcosson, who was writing an article on the Young Plan for the *Saturday Evening Post*, had told him that Hoover viewed the BIS as an "iniquitous institution." Winston was a former undersecretary of the Treasury from 1923 to 1927. Robinson to Hoover, 26 October 1929, HHPL, Herbert Hoover papers (HH), Subject File, Box 183, Financial Matters, Correspondence 1929–30.

Parker Gilbert, Harrison, Young, and the New York partners were can-vassed. At length Jackson Reynolds, the president of the First National Bank of New York and Melvin Traylor, the president of the First National Bank of Chicago, were chosen. As Reynolds later acknowledged, Jack Morgan and Young had picked him.[59] To support Reynolds and Traylor, de Sanchez acted as secretary. The organizing committee met for the first time at Baden-Baden on 3 October 1929.

Over the following weeks, the committee drafted the BIS statues, determining its governance, its capital, and its functions. Jack Morgan directed Morgan participation, counselling Reynolds, who had been elected chair of the committee. Complicating matters were two factors. Schacht, who was not one of the German delegates at Baden-Baden was exploring the possibility of external loans while the Baden-Baden discussions were in progress. Jack Morgan, George Whitney, and the Morgan Grenfell partner Charles F. Whigham met with Schacht early in October about the possibility of a loan for the German railways. These feelers did not yield anything concrete, in part because the Morgan partners were concerned that any operation might jeopardize the anticipated Young Plan bond commercialization.[60] This did not deter Schacht, who con-tinued to search for lenders, contacting Kreuger & Toll about a loan based on the German match monopoly, while also sounding out Dillon, Read & Co. These initiatives soon became known to the Morgan part-ners. Alarmed, Jack Morgan consulted with Norman and Parker Gilbert as to how they might be thwarted.[61] The second consideration clouding the Baden-Baden discussions was the posture of the British Treasury representatives, who were, according to Reynolds and de Sanchez, obstructive and duplicitous. They were failing to keep the Bank of England informed while insisting that the BIS be limited in its scope.

Tensions came to a head in late October and early November. On 25 October an agitated Reynolds informed the heads of delegation at Baden-Baden that, if they wanted American participation in the BIS, there could be no government interference. As Reynolds apprised Jack Morgan, both the British and the Germans were occasioning difficulties. Jack Morgan, after consulting with Norman and confirming that the Treasury representatives were acting independently of the Bank of

[59] Jackson Reynolds, CUL, COHC, pp. 101–02.

[60] Jack Morgan and George Whitney to J.P. Morgan & Co., 7 October 1929, TML, CP, Box 17, Folder Morgan & Co. Misc. Priv. Telegs 15 May to 21 November 1929; CFW to TWL, 26 August 1929, 28 August 1929, TML, CP, Box 17, Folder Morgan & Co. Misc. Priv. Telegs 15 May to 21 November 1929.

[61] Kreuger & Toll loaned the German government $125 million in fifty-year bonds at 6 per cent.

England, wrote Reynolds. Jack Morgan told him that, if the BIS was to work, the cooperation of J.P. Morgan & Co. was essential and laid out eight stipulations: the BIS had to be controlled by its directors; it should be a bank for central banks and only have accounts in the name of central banks and governments; when the BIS wanted to act in the market of any country it must do so through the central bank of the state in question; the BIS must be empowered to deal with the German annuities as well as have the power to act as trustee for bonds of German annuities; it should contract with the governments interested in German annuities and be paid for this service; there should be no government control over the BIS save for the involved central bank heads; the latter should select the directors who would run the BIS; and finally, the directors should have "ample power" to draft the rules and regulations governing the BIS.[62]

At the request of de Sanchez, Jack Morgan lobbied Moreau through Dean Jay, adding Moreau's backing to Norman's.[63] As Harrison was already in agreement and the Hoover administration had de facto left matters in the hands of J.P. Morgan & Co., this had the intended effect of strengthening Reynolds' negotiating stance. When the conference broke on 13 November, the statutes and regulations governing the BIS had been settled on the basis favoured by J.P. Morgan & Co., the FRBNY, the Bank of England, and the Bank of France. Basle was selected as the headquarters of the BIS. It was agreed that the BIS would begin life with capital of $100 million, the American tranche of which would be subscribed to by a consortium of private banks led by J.P. Morgan & Co. Left undecided was the roster of directors and the thorny question of the executive members, the president, the vice-president, and the general manager of the BIS.[64]

*****

While the delegates laboured at Basle, the NYSE crashed. Analysis of the 1929 Crash has languished as economists and historians have focused on a depression causally divorced from the stock market collapse. The line of explanation advanced by Milton Friedman and Anna Schwartz in 1963 in their *Monetary History* paid careful attention to the failures of monetary

---

[62] Jack Morgan to Parker Gilbert, 29 October 1929, Private and Confidential, TML, JPM, Box 179/239; Jack to J.P. Morgan & Co., 31 October 1929, TML, CP, Box 17, Folder Morgan & Co. Misc. Priv. Telegs 15 May to 21 November 1929.
[63] De Sanchez to Jack Morgan, 5 November 1929, Reynolds to Jack Morgan, 2 November 1929, Jack Morgan to Lamont, 6 November 1929, TML, JPM, Box 179/239.
[64] Toniolo, *Central Bank Cooperation*, pp. 39–44. The American consortium was led by J.P. Morgan & Co, First National Bank of New York, and the First National Bank of Chicago.

policy as contributing to the Depression but had little to say about the Crash, an inclination followed in monetarist accounts generally.[65] As has been observed, monetarist explanations are often parochial explanations, mesmerized by monetary policy in the United States.[66] For the Morgan partners, this was nonsensical. The House of Morgan was international, its orientation transatlantic rather than internal. Did this resolutely international culture convey a different appreciation of looming trouble in 1929? Bell thought so, as did Allen. Robert Boyce in his recent major work, *The Great Interwar Crisis*, has suggested that "leading international bankers privately acknowledged as early as July 1927 that the international payments system was severely dislocated." In this reading, the failure of Norman's effort in collaboration with Harrison to convince the Federal Reserve Board in Washington to raise rates in February 1929 was symptomatic of a pre-existing crisis, as money continued to flow to the United States to chase the returns offered by soaring call loan rates. With little recourse, Norman was forced to raise rates at home. Desperate, he told Jack Morgan in March 1929 that the gold standard was threatened, importuning the latter to press the case home with Mellon.[67] The connections – among rising stocks, the gold standard, the ongoing Young committee talks, the adverse UK balance of payments capital account, and the crisis that blossomed in the fall – are apparent.

Less certain is that the Morgan partners were persuaded by Norman's fears. There is evidence of consternation. With Jack Morgan and Lamont in Paris through much of 1929, Leffingwell was best positioned to interpret what was transpiring in the United States. Leffingwell had been following the efforts by Harrison to get the Federal Reserve Board in Washington to change its policy of "direct action." Harrison's endeavours in this regard predated Norman's intervention.[68] "Direct action" was a policy of moral suasion, warning banks of the dangers of overextending credit. Its aim was to check the funds flowing to the call loan market. Harrison believed "direct action" was inadequate, as did Leffingwell. Harrison favoured a rise in rates, a course of action backed by Norman. Rate increases, Harrison averred, would combat the rise in the stock

---

[65] Milton F. Friedman and Anna Jacobson Schwartz, *The Monetary History of the United States 1867–1960*, Princeton, NJ: Princeton University Press, 1963, pp. 305–08. In a 700-page study, the authors devoted three pages to the Crash.

[66] Temin, "The Great Depression," p. 301.

[67] Boyce, *The Great Interwar Crisis*, p. 243 for the 1927 quote; pp. 221–22 for Norman and Jack Morgan. McNeill, *American Money*, remarks on p. 228 that "In 1928–29, many American and British officials believed that the world economy and especially the German economy, was headed for a crash."

[68] Meltzer, *A History of the Federal Reserve*, vol. 1, pp. 234–41, argues that Harrison and Adolph Miller were in favour of raising rates from the fall of 1928.

market and thus reduce the attractiveness of the American market to Europeans. In Leffingwell's assessment Harrison was struggling to do what he could to rectify the errors made by Strong and Norman. The two had been complicit in a policy of easy money that had made it possible for Britain to stay on the gold standard but that had the unfortunate consequence of a flood of cheap money fuelling the speculation in the stock market. Leffingwell predicted, "we are going to have a world credit crisis. If sharp and swift as it should be, then it will be brief and not too serious for business. If long and dreary and protracted . . . then of course business will suffer." Chernow suggested that these remarks are proof that Leffingwell foresaw a looming smash-up but neglects to mention Leffingwell's caveats.[69]

Leffingwell's letter to Lamont closed with a postscript: "This is all my own spleen. I haven't had a chance to show it around the partners here. So don't take it too seriously." Leffingwell confessed he was having one of his "gloomy days." Lamont needed little convincing. He told Leffingwell that he and Jack Morgan had met Norman who had warned them of the threat to the gold standard as Boyce has noted. Lamont, however, found Norman "panicky" and unconvincing. Lamont did not agree that the gold standard was in jeopardy. In his view the stock market was independent of monetary policy. Boosting money market rates would only hurt business and do nothing to stabilize the exchange. This said, Lamont confessed that Jack Morgan did not concur, taking Norman's warning more seriously.[70] Shortly thereafter, Leffingwell confided to Jack Morgan that he was certain that Harrison would win his struggle with a Federal Reserve Board in Washington dominated by Adolph Miller. Leffingwell thought Miller's closeness to Hoover was part of the problem. There was little for Norman to do, Leffingwell advised. Harrison must prevail. On 5 April Jack Morgan replied that he was willing to watch events unfold rather than seeking to intervene.[71]

Two months later, as agreement neared in Paris, Leffingwell returned to monetary policy, the gold standard, and the markets. Writing to

---

[69] Leffingwell to Lamont, 8 March 1929, BL, TWL, Series II, Box 103, Folder 13, Leffingwell, Russell C. 1928–29; Chernow, *The House of Morgan*, p. 313. Chernow's account does not mention the postscript. More generally, on Norman and Harrison and the Federal Reserve Board, Ahamed, *Lords of Finance*, pp. 320–21, is critical of the plan to raise rates, labelling it "completely absurd." Clay, *Lord Norman*, pp. 241–50, argues that Norman's fears dated back to 1928.

[70] Leffingwell to Lamont, 8 March 1929, BL, TWL, Series II, Box 103, Folder 13, Leffingwell, Russell C. 1928–29; Lamont to Leffingwell, 21 March 1929, BL, TWL, Series II, Box 103, Folder 13, Leffingwell, Russell C. 1928–29.

[71] Leffingwell to Jack Morgan, 22 March 1929, Jack Morgan to Leffingwell, 5 April 1929, YUL, RCL, Series I, Box 6, Folder 127.

Grenfell, he observed that while "direct action" should be abandoned in favour of the instruments that the Federal Reserve had at its disposal – manipulating the discount rate and buying and selling bills – he retained faith in Harrison. More generally, he doubted the wisdom of "having Federal Reserve Banks smash our stock market – partly because the darn thing seems to be indestructible and partly because the Federal Reserve Bank's club, though it looks hard and heavy, may be only made of papier mache." For Leffingwell, the strength of the American economy was decisive: "Business here is in fact good; commodity prices are on the whole stable; our own wealth is great; and speculative opportunities here, quite as much as high money rates, attract European capital."[72] Until these conditions changed, there was little to be done. Harrison was already fighting the good fight; there was no need to badger the Hoover administration on Federal Reserve Board policy.

If the Morgan partners were less worried about monetary policy imperilling the course of the American economy and the stock market than has been suggested by historians, what was the Morgan assessment? Two observations may be made. The first is that until October 1929 Morgan business activity was routine; the second is that the Morgan partners were taken by surprise by the Crash. Leaving aside the Young Plan and the BIS, these were quiet months for J.P. Morgan & Co. It is true that the bank ventured into the world of holding companies. United Corporation was created in January 1929 in collaboration with Bonbright & Co. in the public utility field as a competitor to Samuel Insull's Midwestern power-generation empire.[73] The Alleghany Corporation followed closely thereafter for the Van Sweringen railroad empire, though the third Morgan sponsored holding company launched in 1929, Standard Brands, did not appear until September. The three were departures for J.P. Morgan & Co., stamping a return to stock sponsorship in a manner last seen under Pierpont Morgan. Yet it was stock flotation with a twist: J.P. Morgan & Co. did not make a public offering of the stock in these holding companies, leaving that to syndicates headed by others. The Morgan share of the stock was distributed to what became known as "preferred lists" of family, friends, and business and political notables, as had been done in the case of Johns-Manville two years earlier.[74] Neither United nor Alleghany nor

---

[72] Leffingwell to Grenfell, 29 May 1929, YUL, RCL, Series I, Box 3/69.

[73] "High Finance in the 'Twenties: The United Corporation (I)," *Columbia Law Review*, vol. 37, no. 5 (1937), pp. 785–816, is a detailed account of United's formation.

[74] In the case of Alleghany, J.P. Morgan along with Guaranty Company, First National Bank of New York, and National City Company headed a 15-year, $35 million convertible bond offering priced at 100. The stock, preferred ($25 million) and common (offered at $24 per share), was handled by a syndicate led by Guaranty Company, Lee &

Standard Brands made much of a mark on the markets in 1929 – they were among a number of holding company offerings that were dwarfed by the flood of money into the even more attractive investment trusts and did not have any notable effect on the direction of stocks. Their real importance lay in the future when they were featured in the Pecora hearings of 1933, becoming a political issue of the first rank.

Worries were expressed that the competition between United and Insull was consolidating the sector to an unhealthy degree. United sparked a resurgence of Money Trust rhetoric, with, among others, the governor of New York, Franklin D. Roosevelt, asking what the new corporation might mean for the development of hydroelectric power on the St. Lawrence river.[75] Alleghany's formation was accepted as another instance of the ambition of the Van Sweringen brothers. The railroad industry, long a field of intense Morgan activity, was struggling and consolidation was necessary. The critical questions were, how should it proceed and which companies would emerge from consolidation? J.P. Morgan & Co. bet on the Van Sweringens as the answers to these questions. As it turned out, this was a very poor wager.

Morgan investment banking activity in 1929 was steady rather than frenetic. No sovereign loan was floated by the firm. There was only a total of six bond issues led by the bank during the year. Participation in offerings managed by others was more significant. The thirty transactions (not including the two Alleghany offerings) in which J.P. Morgan & Co. made a financial commitment ranged from well-known companies such as Procter & Gamble and Bethlehem Steel, to the fifteen-year bonds offered by the Porto Rican American Tobacco Company, to various railway stocks, to a Chilean bank, and to a share in a bond issue for the state of Minas Gerais in Brazil.[76] Precisely how much of this stayed on the books of the bank is unknown, though it seems little did.[77]

As for the rise in the stock market and the subsequent Crash, in January 1929 Whigham wrote Bartow inquiring whether he could recommend a list of stocks for a friend to invest in. Six months later, in

---

Higginson, Dillon Read, The National City Co., Harris, Forbes, The Union Trust Co. of Cleveland, The Union Trust Co. of Pittsburgh, Hayden, Miller & Co. Cleveland, and Wood, Gundy & Co. *Commercial and Financial Chronicle*, vol. 128, no. 3319, 2 February 1929, pp. 728–29. A second tranche of preferred stock for Alleghany issued on 14 May 1929 conformed to this practice.

[75] Kenneth S. Davis, *FDR: The New York Years 1928–1933*, New York: Random House, 1985, pp. 88–93.

[76] Details may be found in the Pecora Committee hearings, Part I, 25 May 1933, appendix, especially Group 1, A and Group 7, A.

[77] Lamont, *The Ambassador*, p. 268, remarks that the partners had "largely liquidated the firm's stock holdings" by October 1929.

June 1929, the Morgan Grenfell partner Michael Herbert made a similar request. He had, he told Bartow, a "nest egg" on account with J.P. Morgan & Co. in the United States that he wanted to invest in stocks. Herbert added that his brother as well as a close friend also had cash at their disposal that they wished to deploy in the American market.[78] Could Bartow advise which stocks to purchase? Shortly before the market collapse in mid-October, Jack Morgan informed his sons that he wanted to sell 5,000 shares of Johns-Manville at 205 or better and 5,000 shares at 210 or better. After consulting with Bartow, Harry and Junius Morgan advised postponement until the announcement of Johns-Manville earnings. Evidently neither Bartow nor Harry Morgan, nor Junius Morgan, expected the Crash. Subsequently Harry and Junius Morgan cabled their father that, while the market was "weak," they had concluded after reviewing his portfolio that he was better off sitting tight. On 7 November, after the fall, a contrite Junius cabled his father: "Sorry about your Johns-Manville. No doubt in light of recent events my advice was bad. I still have mine too."[79] Lamont's timing was better: he liquidated some of his holdings, but even so, when the Crash came, he suffered heavily.[80] Edward Lamont has stated that the firm, as distinct from the personal holdings of the partners, had sold the bulk of its stocks before the Crash, which seems to have been happenstance rather than prescience.[81]

In the weeks leading to the Crash, the markets yawed. After a sharp drop in the first week of October the NYSE bounded upward before plunging once more between 14 and 18 October. It was in this context that Hoover sounded out Lamont, through Robinson, for counsel. The request provoked discussion among the partners. On 7 October Leffingwell penned a letter suggesting what should be included in a reply. His advice was to be blunt: "The protracted bull market in stocks seems to have passed all bounds. I think it is diverting too much credit from business but above all it is diverting the attention of the people from their work to gambling." Leffingwell attributed some of the responsibility for this state of affairs to the policy of the Federal Reserve Board, commenting that its efforts at moral suasion had substituted political

---

[78] Whigham to Bartow, 22 January 1929, TML, CP, Box 17, Morgan & Co. – MG & Co.'s Client Investments; Michael Herbert to Bartow, 21 June 1929, TML, CP, Box 17, Morgan & Co. – Partners' & Staff's Personal Investments.

[79] Jack Morgan to Harry and Junius Morgan, 14 October 1929, TML, JPM, Box 38A/35.1 – Cable Book; Harry and Junius Morgan to Jack Morgan, 17 October 1929, TML, JPM, Box 37/27; Junius Morgan to Jack Morgan, 7 November 1929, TML, JPM, Box 38A/35.1 – Cable Book.

[80] Florence Corliss Lamont to Austin Lamont, 1 November 1929, Smith College, Lamont-Corliss Family Papers, Box 3, Folder 8.

[81] Lamont, *The Ambassador*, p. 268.

judgement for what properly should be decisions on money rates made by the Federal Reserve Banks. The investment trusts were another factor impelling upward movement in stock prices. Leffingwell argued that the "rapid growth" of trusts boosted stock prices through their investing activities and the concurrent rise in the price of their own stock. While he worried that the trusts might have a baleful effect on corporate governance, he was especially fearful of their influence in the banking sector. Leffingwell warned that the intrusion of investment trusts into the banking sector was "thoroughly bad" as the trusts threatened the fundamental tie between bank and depositor. As a partial solution, Leffingwell recommended prohibiting investment trusts from holding stocks in chains of banks. Beyond this, there needed to be liberalization in the banking laws to allow for expedited growth of branch banking which would both help to stabilize the banking industry and thwart the predations of the investment trusts.[82]

Much of what Leffingwell advocated was challenged by his partners. As was typically the case within the bank for important letters or memoranda for external consumption, drafts were circulated for comment. This practice helped to forge consensus. When Leffingwell's letter was circulated, there was strong disagreement with his characterization that stocks were overvalued or that Americans had succumbed to gambling fever. Nor was there acceptance of his assertion that the stock market was sopping up capital better utilized by business. His partners thought that Leffingwell had overstated the dangers of investment trusts. Tighter regulation of investment trusts was, in their view, unnecessary.[83] The final composition of the letter rested with Lamont. He was responsible for interacting with Washington. Lamont was not the man to douse Hoover with a cold shower of pessimism. His response was not insincere; it reflected the preponderant view within J.P. Morgan & Co.[84]

The letter to Hoover of 19 October 1929 was long (eighteen pages) and on the whole positive. After admitting that there were elements of concern, Lamont remarked "nonetheless, there is nothing in the present situation to suggest that normal economic forces, working to correct excesses and to restore the proper balance of affairs, are not still operative and adequate." He dismissed talk of a speculative boom or of a gambling mentality in sentences that were the antithesis of Leffingwell. According to Lamont, more efficient financial machinery was drawing the savings of

[82] A copy of Leffingwell's suggested letter is in BL, TWL, Series II, Box 98, Folder 15.
[83] Mr. Leffingwell's letter, 11 October 1929, BL, TWL, Series II, Box 98, Folder 15.
[84] In sending Jack Morgan a copy of the letter to Hoover, Lamont remarked "many of the partners had some ideas to contribute." Lamont to Jack Morgan, 22 October 1929, BL, TWL, Series II, Box 108, Folder 14.

Americans into the stock markets. The bull market reflected this efficacy as well as the growing conviction of Americans that stocks were a good long-term investment. Lamont took umbrage with the notion of a speculative bubble, arguing that stock averages were misleading. Companies in areas such as fertilizer, lumber, paper, oil, and cement, had seen their stock prices languish. Where there had been appreciation, it was not excessive when measured in years rather than months. As for the surge in speculative loans in the call money market, Lamont attributed this to the growing number of stock offerings coupled with a shift in corporate financial operations. Companies were increasingly issuing stock, foregoing bonds, and shunning borrowing from banks.

Lamont followed Leffingwell in his remarks about the Federal Reserve Board, observing, in sentences borrowed directly from him, that its policy errors had contributed to price growth on the stock market. On investment trusts Lamont differed from Leffingwell. Lamont agreed that they had proliferated, perhaps too luxuriantly, but he told Hoover that the market for trusts was "sated" and starting to correct its excesses. He conceded that the relationship between investment trusts and banks needed to be watched, but the extension of branch banking was a remedy of greater importance than curtailing the investment trusts.

Lamont's conclusion was rousing: the overall situation of the American economy was favourable, the place of the United States in the world was extraordinarily auspicious – indeed the most fortunate globally – and there was no reason to take any rash steps, legislative or otherwise, to hinder prosperity. For the future, the prospects looked bright, particularly because the administration was taking steps to check the greatest possible threat to American well-being, namely war, through its championing of disarmament talks, a reference to the naval discussions slated for London in the upcoming year.[85] A clearer expression of Morgan optimism could not be found.

In his memoirs Hoover observed sourly that the memorandum makes "curious reading today."[86] Robinson, writing to Hoover on 25 October, after the stock market had fallen precipitously on 23–24 October, judged Lamont's letter "conservative" and deemed its counsel banal, as it was. He advised Hoover, "From my viewpoint, there are greater dangers and greater troubles in the situation than the memorandum would indicate and I am inclined to think that most of the bankers and industrialists

---

[85] Lamont to Hoover, BL, TWL, Series II, Box 98, Folder 16.

[86] Hoover, *Memoirs*, vol. 3, p. 17. Privately he wrote a marginal comment on the memorandum that "this document is fairly annoying in light of two years after." Herbert Hoover, undated, HHPL, HH, Subject files, Box 188, NYSE.

would feel that this is true."[87] Lamont was aware that the letter was bland. He told Jack Morgan, whom he sent a copy, that "almost all that it contains is essentially obvious." Blandness was by design, for Lamont did not want Hoover to act; he had no intention of recommending Leffingwell's bolder prescription. The letter is more indicative of the state of mind of the Morgan partners than of its policy impact. Egan, the Morgan staffer who worked closely with Lamont in handling public relations, met with the president shortly after the letter was sent. Hoover had not yet read it. While he promised to do so, he told Egan that he favoured inaction, a statement that was undoubtedly welcome.[88]

Events overtook the president. On Wednesday 23 October, the NYSE suffered a sharp drop on heavy volume of 6.4 million shares. The Dow Jones Industrial Index fell 20 points, from 325 to 305. The following day, 24 October, was "Black Thursday." The market broke. Waves of selling overwhelmed the NYSE, which found itself incapable of keeping up with the volume of trades. The ensuing chaos, both within and without the NYSE and across the country, has been portrayed vividly in many accounts. Over the following weeks the market recorded a precipitous drop. The Dow Jones Industrial Index bottomed at 198 at the end of trading on 13 November. The date 14 November marked the end of the Crash. Thereafter, the market moved smartly up to 248 on the Dow, where it finished the year.[89]

The Morgan role in the drama is well known. Generally, it has been seen as ineffectual. Worth recalling is the experience of the senior Morgan partners – especially Jack Morgan, Lamont, and Leffingwell – when confronted with panics. They had lived through and participated in confronting the paroxysms of 1907 and 1920–21. Having done so, past trials infused a view that panics, while daunting, were a feature of capitalism, had been mastered, and thus, while to be respected for the damage they could wreak, were not to be feared unduly. Nor did panic necessarily betoken anything more fundamental for the direction of the American economy. The Morgan role was not to restore order – that was the province of the Federal Reserve – but to try to meet the expectations of the Street bestowed by their acknowledged position at the head of the hierarchy of the Wall Street financial community. They had to act, even if privately the partners appreciated that their influence was limited.

---

[87] Robinson to Hoover, 25 October 1929, HHPL, HH, Subject files, Box 183, Financial Matters, Correspondence 1929–30. Lamont to Jack Morgan, 22 October 1929, BL, TWL, Series II, Box 108, Folder 14.

[88] Martin Egan to Lamont, 23 October 1929, BL, TWL, Series II, Box 98/16.

[89] Wigmore, *The Crash*, pp. 6–25.

Consequently, on 24 October, Lamont coordinated a response in keeping with what popular opinion, both on the Street and without, anticipated. Leading bankers met in the Morgan Library, an evocative move recalling 1907. Widespread publicity attended the gathering, as papers across the United States trumpeted the news. Present were Albert Wiggin, the chairman of the Chase National Bank, William Potter, the chairman of the Guaranty Trust Co., Seward Prosser of the Bankers Trust, and Charles Mitchell of the National City Bank. Absent from this initial gathering on 24 October were the Bakers, George Senior and Junior, who controlled the First National Bank. Subsequently the Bakers committed First National to the effort, while some financial luminaries, such as the Guggenheim brothers, contributed funds but did not attend the regular meetings of what became known as the "Bankers' Pool." Still others, such as Young, offered counsel, while later Chellis Austin, the president of the Equitable Trust, a Rockefeller-affiliated institution, became part of the group. The group acted both publicly and privately. The former had its most famous expression on 24 October through Richard Whitney, brother of George Whitney, and the vice-president of the NYSE. In a flamboyant gesture Whitney placed an order for 25,000 shares of U.S. Steel at $205 when the stock price slumped to $195. The gesture, though memorable, was ephemeral. Quietly, the day after Whitney's bravura performance, the group sold 51,000 shares in various stocks that it had amassed.[90] Lamont, supported by George Whitney and Bartow, served as the Morgan representative. Frequently he acted as the public face for the group, holding press conferences. Less openly, Lamont was in regular contact with the governors of the NYSE, the Federal Reserve Board in Washington, and the FRBNY.

The initial Morgan assessment was that irrationality had seized the markets. The fall on 24 October had taken place in a "perfectly wild illogical and uncontrolled manner." Five days later, on "Black Tuesday," 29 October, J.P. Morgan & Co. described the day's "severe decline" as a product of "hysterical selling." On 1 November Florence Lamont, Thomas W. Lamont's wife, wrote her son Austin that "The whole thing was due to a sort of fear hysteria. There was nothing in business conditions to warrant it. But everybody got scared & began selling at once." Given this, the New York partners reported to Jack Morgan, who was still in Britain, "We [the Bankers' Pool] decided to make a sort of faith cure demonstration by purchasing certain pivotal Stocks." Confidence was the only answer to "cure" irrationality. On

[90] J.P. Morgan & Co. to Jack Morgan, 26 October 1929, TML, JPM, Box 37, Folder 27.

24 October the five banks in the Bankers' Pool acted, spending $25 million on the "faith cure" that day. However, there were limits to the dosage: "Certainly we do not intend to attempt to stop a general market decline nor do we intend to organise a pool for the purpose of buying and selling Stocks," his partners told Jack Morgan. He approved: "I realise of course that you do not for a moment think of pegging any prices but only to give people an opportunity to liquidate quietly."[91] The action taken by the Bankers' Pool was haphazard and disjointed in its application, as the group did not proceed in its buying with a clear strategy in mind. Each participant nominated stocks to purchase without consultation with other Pool members, a procedure that suited its limited aim.[92] As the market declined, the Bankers' Pool dipped in and out of the market. It did not meet every day. Cumulatively, the Pool purchased 1,146,609 shares of stocks at a total cost of $137,752,705. On these efforts the participants in the pool split a gross profit of $1,067,355.04 in 1930.[93]

After a steady day on Friday 25 October, during which the Bankers' Pool bought and sold stocks, the markets reopened on Monday 28 October. The NYSE fell heavily, declining from 298 to 260. The Morgan partners had been anticipating weakness in the market, but not on this scale. They confessed to Jack Morgan that the "group has increased its holdings materially." Once more they stressed that they were not trying to prop up the market. "Black Tuesday," 29 October, while troubling, was less upsetting. The cable to Jack Morgan on the day's events opened, "To repeat yesterday's message to you would just about tell the story of today, although it may be said that the feeling at the close of the market, despite the drastic decline, was just a trifle more hopeful."[94] The wellsprings of this faint optimism were several. There had been a hint of positivity, despite the turmoil, in their communications as early as 25 October. There was an inclination to perceive that the worst had passed. In analysing what had occurred on 29 October, the partners indicated that "enlarging" the Bankers' Pool commitments was driven by

[91] J.P. Morgan & Co. to Jack Morgan, 25 October 1929, TML, JPM, Box 37, Folder 27; J. P. Morgan & Co. to Jack Morgan, 29 October 1929, TML, JPM, Box 37, Folder 27; Florence Corliss Lamont to Austin Lamont, 1 November 1929, Smith College, Lamont-Corliss Family Papers, Box 3, Folder 8; J.P. Morgan & Co. to Jack Morgan, 25 October 1929, TML, JPM, Box 37, Folder 27; Jack Morgan to J.P. Morgan & Co., 25 October 1929, TML, JPM, Box 37, Folder 27.
[92] Wigmore, The Crash, p. 10.
[93] George Whitney, Friday 2 June 1933, Pecora Committee, Part 1, 25 May 1933, pp. 536–39.
[94] 29, 30 October 1929, J.P. Morgan & Co. to Jack Morgan, TML, JPM, Box 37/27, Cables received and sent by J.P. Morgan in London.

the conviction that stabilization might take a few days longer. The partners noted that "there has been some first rate investment buying today," a message that was repeated on 30 October, when they lauded "European buying."[95]

Another source of buoyancy was their cooperation with Myron Taylor of U.S. Steel. Steel had announced an extra dividend of $1 on its common shares.[96] Beyond the special dividend, Taylor, in coordination with Lamont, and with the sanction of Jack Morgan, implemented a plan to purchase 50,000 shares of U.S. Steel common for the employees. U.S. Steel's action was not singular – other large companies declared special dividends. Corporate earnings were, on the whole, reasonable. The Morgan partners were encouraged that no brokerage house or bank had succumbed during the panic. Two further steps, which they had championed in the Bankers' Pool meetings, and which they regarded as beneficial, were taken: the decision to renew call loans at 5 per cent and the reduction in margin requirements announced by banks to 25 per cent. Harrison's policy of "heavy buying" of eligible securities had assisted materially in stemming panic. John D. Rockefeller Sr.'s public statement that he was purchasing stock, which J.P. Morgan & Co. was alerted to beforehand, was another positive sign. All told, the Morgan partners informed Jack Morgan, "We are by no means out of the woods but certainly everything looks better." Further signs of hope, such as the decline in the bank rate pushed through by Harrison, and the massive fall in call loans outstanding, on the order of 1 billion dollars, hinted at an end to the drop.[97]

If on 1 November the situation appeared to be improving to the Morgan partners, it was a false dawn. As the reality of ongoing decline sank in, the Morgan analysis of the Crash shifted. The emphasis on irrationality as the driving force in the market's fall was superseded by more searching analysis. Call loans were one area of inquiry. Jack Morgan, in replying to his partners on 24 October, had asked whether J. P. Morgan's calls were being met. The response was reassuring, as New York told him that not only were their calls being filled but queries with other banks yielded the information that leading New York banks

[95] 25 and 29 October 1929, J.P. Morgan & Co. to Jack Morgan, TML, JPM, Box 37/27, Cables received and sent by J.P. Morgan in London.

[96] Jack Morgan was the chairman of the board of U.S. Steel. It had been Jack Morgan and George F. Baker senior who had convinced Taylor to become the chairman of the finance committee of U.S. Steel in 1928. Kenneth Warren, *Big Steel: The First Century of the United States Steel Corporation*, Pittsburgh: University of Pittsburgh Press, 2001, pp. 145–47.

[97] J.P. Morgan & Co. to Jack Morgan, 31 October 1929, TML, JPM, Box 37/27, Cables received and sent by J.P. Morgan in London.

had been sparing in calling loans. Guaranty Trust had called $35 million out of $1 billion in loans, while National City had called $25 million and Bankers Trust had called $50 million. By 31 October the tone of the reports to Jack Morgan altered. Over the week lenders had panicked and called loans, prompting the banks through which the loans had been made to take them over lest greater disruption ensue. The New York partners reckoned that the magnitude was considerable: several leading banks had absorbed $200 million or more each of such loans. This development was a "real difficulty" for the market. It was a conclusion also reached by the *Commercial and Financial Chronicle* which in its issue of 2 November 1929 dismissed "mob psychology" as underpinning the Crash and instead focused on brokers' loans as the true culprit. The *Commercial and Financial Chronicle* minced no words a week later, lambasting Professor Irving Fisher as the high priest of the creed of exuberance, while attacking the "mongrel crowd" of outside lenders who had made matters dramatically worse by calling their loans.[98]

A second reason for ongoing weakness, in the Morgan view, was specific. Prior to the Crash the National City Bank, led by Mitchell, had announced plans to merge with the Corn Exchange Bank Trust Co. The proposed deal had been structured to give Corn Exchange Bank shareholders an option: they could tender their shares in exchange for National City Bank shares or they could receive $360 in cash per share. When the merger was agreed, National City Bank stock was at $550. Mitchell and his board of directors expected that the overwhelming majority of Corn Exchange Bank shareholders would opt for shares rather than cash. The Crash changed this expectation. The rapid fall in National City Bank stock had taken its price to under $400 and thus there was a strong possibility that Corn Exchange Bank shareholders would choose cash for their shares. Facing a potential outlay of $217 million in cash payments should this scenario come to fruition, Mitchell and the National City Bank board withdrew their proxies in favour of the deal, guaranteeing that the two-thirds majority required from National City Bank shareholders was unobtainable. The deal died. Mitchell informed Walter Frew, the head of the Corn Exchange Bank, of this outcome on Monday night, 4 November. The Morgan partners were aghast. They pressed Mitchell for an explanation, having called him to 23 Wall Street. Despite the fact that by this time Mitchell was indebted personally to J.P. Morgan & Co. – the bank had lent him $12 million on 28 October against

---

[98] *Commercial and Financial Chronicle*, vol. 129, no. 3358, 2 November 1929, p. 2727; *Commercial and Financial Chronicle*, vol. 129, no. 3359, 9 November 1929, pp. 2899–900.

Mitchell's own holdings of National City Bank stock – Mitchell refused to change course in the face of warnings about the damage this action would have for National City Bank and for the fragile market. The Bankers' Pool met on 5 November, a holiday, to consider what might be done. Mitchell was absent, but Gates W. McGarrah attended, representing the FRBNY. The conferees were unanimous in condemning Mitchell's action, prompting Lamont, Whitney, and Bartow to speak privately with Mitchell, Percy Rockefeller, and John D. Ryan.[99] The effort was for naught. From the Morgan perspective, the "exceeding weakness" displayed in the markets was due to this "overhanging situation." On 8 November New York cabled Jack Morgan that the market was "very satisfactory to-day . . . While we are still keeping our fingers crossed we are hopeful that with the National City Bank Corn Exchange Bank Trust Co. situation out of the way forced liquidation is pretty well at an end."[100] This was too rosy a prognostication: it was not until 14 November that the market steadied but the Bankers' Pool did not intervene in the markets between 11 and 13 November.[101]

Emerging from the days and weeks of stress, the partners of J.P. Morgan & Co. were in self-congratulatory mood. The bank itself had navigated the Crash with skill. J.P. Morgan & Co. policy had been "to maintain great strength in our depositary institutions, preferring to maintain large balances against emergencies and letting them loan it out on call for their own account rather than lending it ourselves or having it loaned for our account." This stance was made possible in part by the firm's enviable position. Having refrained from making loans for others the bank was protected as these loans were called. As the partners cabled Jack Morgan on 31 October 1929, "We have seldom been so pleased over anything as the justification of our policy not to loan 'for others'."[102] The bank's efforts were applauded within and without. Charles Steele and Leffingwell cabled Jack Morgan praising Lamont, Whitney, and Bartow. Grenfell writing from London conveyed his congratulations, *Time* magazine featured Lamont on its cover as the hero of the hour, while Lamont and Jack Morgan concluded that J.P. Morgan & Co. had emerged from

---

[99] Rockefeller was on the National City Bank board of directors. He had close ties with Ryan, the moving spirit in Anaconda Copper Mining Co., who was also a member of the National City Bank board.
[100] J.P. Morgan & Co to Jack Morgan, 6 November 1929, Jack Morgan to J.P. Morgan & Co., 7 November 1929, J.P. Morgan & Co. to Jack Morgan, 8 November 1929, TML, JPM jr papers, Box 37/27, Cables received and sent by J.P. Morgan in London.
[101] Wigmore, *The Crash*, pp. 24–25.
[102] J.P. Morgan & Co. to Jack Morgan, 31 October 1929, TML, JPM, Box 37/27; J.P. Morgan & Co. to Jack Morgan, 1 November 1929, TML, JPM, Box 37/27.

the Crash with its prestige enhanced on the Street, especially when compared to Mitchell and National City.[103] *Time* misread what had transpired. The "shock troops" of the market, the New York money-centre banks, had, backed by Harrison's FRBNY, absorbed the panicked requests from out-of-town banks, corporations, and individuals for settlement of their call loans.[104] Their willingness to absorb settlements had been decisive. Credit for ensuring that the Crash was not worse was theirs – not J.P. Morgan & Co.'s. The Morgan partners had played only a secondary role in mastering the crisis.

The Crash did not shake the Morgan world view. Rather the partners believed that their stature had been bolstered. As Lamont told Joseph Knapp, the publisher of *Collier's*, early in January 1930: "Now take the recent so-called panic. I have seen awfully few knocks against the firm and, on the contrary, a great many handsome tributes even from remote parts of the county . . . things are going so nicely I hate to stir them up."[105] It might be objected that J.P. Morgan & Co. did not represent all of Wall Street, was far from typical of the American experience, and that the Morgan perspective was myopic and short-sighted. Such objections have merit. Certainly, the Crash inflicted hardship on Americans, American business, and American institutions well beyond the walls of the Corner that the Morgan partners failed to discern. This accepted, appreciating that the most powerful bank in the United States had a different assessment of the ramifications of the Crash helps us understand why Wall Street expected better times in 1930.

*****

"The country seems to be rapidly getting back to a normal basis, at least financially, after the speculative debauch which eventuated in the stock market panic of October and November," opined the *Commercial and Financial Chronicle* in its first issue of 1930.[106] This sentiment was pervasive early in 1930. It ranged from Bernard Baruch to Andrew Mellon to

---

[103] On Morgan satisfaction, Steele and Leffingwell to Jack Morgan, 1 November 1929, TML, JPM jr papers, Box 37/27, Cables received and sent by J.P. Morgan in London Grenfell to Lamont, 19 November 1929; TML, CP, Box 18, Morgan & Co – Misc. Notes 1920s file 2; Florence Corliss Lamont to Austin Lamont, 1 November 1929, Smith College, Lamont-Corliss Family Papers, Box 3, Folder 8; Jack Morgan to J.P. Morgan & Co., 7 November 1929, J.P. Morgan & Co. TML, JPM jr papers, Box 37/27, Cables received and sent by J.P. Morgan in London.

[104] Myers, *The New York Money Market*, vol. 1, p. 270; Beckhart, *The New York Money Market*, vol. 3, p. 83.

[105] Lamont to Joseph P. Knapp, 8 January 1930, BL, TWL, Series II, Box 101, Folder Knapp.

[106] *Commercial and Financial Chronicle*, vol. 130, no. 3367, 4 January 1930, p. 1.

the progressive journalist John T. Flynn. Mellon said, "I see nothing in the present situation that is either menacing or warrants pessimism," while Flynn, soon to begin writing his regular column for *The New Republic*, "Other People's Money," was optimistic that the effects of the Crash would be short-lived.[107] The Harvard Economic Service and the Yale economist Irving Fisher anticipated swift recovery, drawing upon the experience, like Leffingwell, of 1920–21.[108] Jeremy Attack and Peter Passell have noted that "most economists and policy makers" underestimated the severity of developments in 1930.[109]

The year 1930 began promisingly. The Japanese government wanted to return to the gold standard. Discussions had begun in November 1929 and involved banks in New York, London, and Tokyo. Formal announcement that Tokyo would return to the gold standard was delayed until January 1930 when the Japanese government announced that the gold embargo had been lifted.[110] This success was followed by the settling of outstanding issues regarding the BIS and the Young Plan. After the Baden-Baden agreement of November 1929, the question of the executive of the BIS and the composition of the board of directors remained. While the principle of an American president for the BIS was agreed to readily, who this should be was more difficult. Morrow was suggested by Jack Morgan, but this was rejected. There were doubts in New York about Morrow's fitness, some of which may have been grounded in the friction between Morrow and his former partners over Mexico. Though Parker Gilbert made an effort to persuade Morrow to take the position, by the time he did so Morrow had agreed to serve as a delegate to the forthcoming London Naval Conference.[111] At length, Jack Morgan and Young settled on the tandem of McGarrah and Leon Fraser to serve as president and alternate to the president respectively. The Hoover

---

[107] Jordan A. Schwartz, *The Speculator: Bernard M. Baruch in Washington*, Chapel Hill, NC: UNC Press 1981, pp. 258–59; Mellon cited in Schlesinger, *The Crisis of the Old Order*, p. 164; John E. Moser, *Right Turn: John T. Flynn and the Transformation of American Liberalism*, New York: New York University Press, 2005, p. 21–22.

[108] Temin, *Lessons from the Great Depression*, pp. 57–9.

[109] Jeremy Attack and Peter Passell, *A New Economic View of American History*, 2nd ed. New York: W.W. Norton, 1994, p. 565–66; see too the remarks in David Kennedy, *Freedom from Fear: The American People in Depression and War*, New York: Oxford University Press, 1999, pp. 39–40.

[110] The first reference to the discussions is in J.P. Morgan & Co. to Jack Morgan, 7 November 1929, TML, CP, Box 17, Folder Morgan & Co. Misc. Priv. Telges 15 May to 21 November 1929. For context, Toshiki Tomita, "Direct Underwriting of Government Bonds by the Bank of Japan in the 1930s," NRI Research Papers, No. 94, September 2005, pp. 1–2.

[111] Jack Morgan to Lamont, 7 October 1929, Lamont to Jack Morgan 9 October 1929, Jack Morgan to Lamont, 9 October 1929, TML, JPM, Box 37/27; Parker Gilbert to Dwight Morrow, 25 November 1929, AC, DM, Series I, Box 24, Folder 12.

administration agreed with these selections, as did the European central banks. This left the question of who should fill the key position of general manager. The Bank of France was lobbying hard for Quesnay against the opposition of Schacht. Quesnay was highly thought of by the Morgan partners. Lamont commented, "As to Quesnay most of us over here feel that he is the broadest and most internationally minded of all the Frenchmen we know."[112] Supported by Young, Harrison, Moreau, and Jack Morgan, German opposition was overcome, though Quesnay was not appointed general manager until April 1930.

With the BIS executive and board of directors settled, the last spasms of Schacht's efforts to revise the Young Plan quieted in January and February 1930 at the second conference held at The Hague. This gathering ultimately reaffirmed the August agreement, though not before the Morgan partners found themselves having to rebut suggestions that they supported Schacht in his quest for revision of the Young Plan. Parker Gilbert, whose relationship with Schacht had broken down irretrievably, warned the Morgan partners that Schacht was circulating rumours in Germany to the effect that he was backed by J.P. Morgan & Co., that only Schacht's personal relationship with the partners was keeping German credit in the United States respectable, and that Schacht was boasting that he was in possession of a letter from Jack Morgan that attested to his support. Parker Gilbert believed Schacht's pose as the champion of German nationalism was contrived, though Parker Gilbert admitted that "it is difficult to fathom what Schacht really wants." Parker Gilbert worried that Schacht's "pack of lies" was having an effect on Norman, whose sympathies for the Germans Parker Gilbert thought too pronounced.[113] His warnings impressed themselves upon the Morgan partners. Their response, following consultation with Young and Reynolds, was to take up a suggestion made by Parker Gilbert to meet the German ambassador at Washington. Jack Morgan and Lamont did so on 3 February 1930. They told the ambassador, Friedrich Wilhelm von Prittwitz und Gaffron, that Morgan communications were with the

---

[112] Moreau to Young, 29 November 1929, Moreau to Young, 18 February 1930, CUL, GH, Box 13, Binder 28, 29 November 1929; Lamont to Grenfell, 14 February 1930, TML, CP, Box 17, Folder Morgan & Co. Misc. Priv. Telges 21 November 1929 to 3 March 1930.

[113] Parker Gilbert to Pierre Jay, 29 January 1930 and Parker Gilbert to Jay, 31 January 1930, CUL, GH, Box 1, Binder 1. From 1927 to 1930 Jay was a member of the Transfer Commission and Deputy Agent General for Reparations under Parker Gilbert. Jay had been Chairman of the Board and Federal Reserve Agent of the FRBNY from 1914 to 1926. From 1930 to 1945 Jay was Chairman of the Board of Fiduciary Trust Co. NY; Shepard Morgan to Eugene Agger, 21 November 1955, Rutgers Special Collections and University Archives, Eugene E. Agger papers, Box 5, Correspondence 1955–56.

German government and not with Schacht. Contrary to rumour, Jack Morgan had not written any personal letter to Schacht.[114] Jack Morgan and Lamont were careful not to attack Schacht directly. They feared that his threat to withhold the participation of the Reichsbank in the BIS was more than bluster. Schacht's resignation from the Reichsbank in March 1930 cleared away one problem but substituted another, for Schacht continued his campaign against the Young Plan and the BIS, framing the latter as the Reparations Bank.

Schacht was far from the only foe of the Young Plan and the BIS. Louis McFadden, the Republican chair of the House Committee on Banking and Currency, had already begun his trek toward his laager of anti-Semitism, international conspiracy, and paranoia. He retained some credibility by virtue of his chairmanship, his authorship of the McFadden bill of 1927 restricting branch banking, and his small-town banking background. On 27 March 1930, in a radio broadcast sponsored by the Daughters of the American Revolution carried by the National Broadcasting Corporation nationwide, McFadden charged that the Young Plan and the BIS were little more than a scheme to entangle the United States in wider political and economic commitments – the Treaty of Versailles, the League of Nations, and the World Court. He denounced the forthcoming Young Plan loan as illegal. J.P. Morgan & Co., "the most powerful banking force in the world" was diverting American banking resources to sustain a moribund Europe. McFadden indicted J.P. Morgan & Co. for the "orgy of speculation" that had led to the Crash. They dominated the Federal Reserve Board, had pushed its cheap money policy before 1929, and were actively in collusion with central bankers abroad.[115] He repeated these themes in another radio speech two months later. The *New York Times*, in its editorial "Mr. McFadden's Outburst," dismissed McFadden: there was "little danger of Mr. McFadden's incoherent talk being taken seriously." The sentiments expressed by McFadden were out of date and place, the *Times* judged. Their spiritual home was the Populist Party's platform in the 1892 election, which had inveighed against the peril represented by the international banker.[116]

Partly in response to Schacht and McFadden, J.P. Morgan & Co. mounted a counteroffensive lauding the virtues of the Young Plan and the BIS. One prong was to provide journalists with material. Walter

---

[114] Lamont to Parker Gilbert, 3 February 1930, CUL, GH, Box 1, Binder 1.

[115] "Attacks Morgan and World Bank," 30 March 1930, *New York Times*, p. 3. On McFadden, see two books by Charles R. Geisst: *Deals of the Century: Wall Street, Mergers, and the Making of Modern America*, Hoboken, NJ: John Wiley & Sons, 2004, pp. 82–88, and *Undue Influence*, p. 72.

[116] "Mr. McFadden's Outburst," *New York Times*, 29 March 1930, p. 18.

Lippmann, for example, was cultivated carefully by Lamont and Leffingwell. A second approach reassured investors. In April 1930 an article entitled "The Final Reparations Settlement" appeared in *Foreign Affairs* under Lamont's name. After recapitulating the negotiations, Lamont pointed out that German obligations were fewer under the new plan than formerly. The BIS "offers in my opinion greater protection to German economy than the old Transfer Committee ... With the Germans cooperating loyally with the Bank they need have no fear of the future." Though Lamont acknowledged that American governments refused to accept a connection between German reparations payments and Allied war debts to the United States, there was an "economic link." Average German payments under the Young Plan would run at $495 million per year and in turn the Allies would pay to the United States $325 million yearly in discharge of their war debts. Lamont reassured readers, "the adoption of the Young Plan ought to prove an immense stimulus to the European economy ... the fresh methods of cooperation through the International Bank ... should go far to tranquilize Western Europe, and to hasten all the processes of reconstruction."[117] This campaign had success – the flotation of the $98.5 million American tranche of the Young Plan loan in June was oversubscribed, with the lists closing the day of the announcement.

Despite this achievement, the Morgan partners wondered about the direction of the American economy. Surveying matters for Morgan Grenfell they adopted a cautious tone, telling London that "While general business is slow ... We think that there generally exists a feeling of optimism as to the future."[118] Such lukewarm sentiments were outweighed by Hoover's public bravado. In a speech to the United States Chamber of Commerce on 1 May 1930, which he admitted later was a "political mistake," Hoover told his audience that "I am convinced that we have passed the worst and with continued effort we shall rapidly recover."[119] Lamont continued to view matters beatifically. Introducing Sir Josiah Stamp to the members of the Academy of Political Science early in June 1930, Lamont declared that Stamp, American bankers, and the American investing public had made possible "the final liquidation of the War" and the pouring of a "firm foundation for the new epoch of economic and political peace in Europe."[120] This was the last hurrah of uninflected Morgan exuberance.

[117] Lamont, "The Final Reparations Settlement," *Foreign Affairs*, vol. 8, no. 3, April 1930.
[118] J.P. Morgan & Co. to Morgan Grenfell, 1 April 1930, TML, CP, Box 17, Folder Morgan & Co – Misc. Private Telegs 4 March 4 to 29 April 1930.
[119] Hoover, *Memoirs*, vol. 3, p. 58.
[120] Thomas W. Lamont, Academy of Political Science, 2 June 1930, SLU, ODY, Box 802, Folder 1297S11.

From June onward, evidence mounted of a marked downturn. This coincided with the passage of the Smoot–Hawley Tariff. J.P. Morgan & Co., true to its free-trade, internationalist outlook, was opposed to the tariff increases as were many economists, businessmen, and public figures. Lamont made an effort to dissuade Hoover from signing the bill, telling Robinson that passage would be negative for the country and the Republican Party. Hoover, he told Robinson, would benefit politically from vetoing the bill. Lamont sought to push Morrow, now the Republican candidate for Senator for New Jersey in the 1930 election, to intercede with the president.[121] These efforts came to naught, for Hoover signed the bill on 17 June 1930. The nationalist wing of the Republican Party favoured Smoot–Hawley, which was ultimately determinant for Hoover.[122] Following its passage, the *Commercial and Financial Chronicle* described a "very gloomy picture" amid "a renewed violent collapse in the stock market."[123] A month later, Lamont confessed "business here is slower than death," a sentiment he reiterated in mid-September to Jack Morgan.[124] Hoover's address to the American Banking Association convention on 2 October 1930 took place amidst a "feeling of gloom and utter hopelessness."[125] De Sanchez, asked by Lamont to analyse Hoover's speech, was scathing, labelling it a "thoroughly mischievous statement. The President lays bare for all to see the jejune quality of his economic thinking."[126]

Further reflection was prompted by Taylor, who had written Lamont expressing his disquiet at the direction of the economy. On 13–14 August Taylor met twice with Leffingwell. Taylor proposed various remedies: expressions of confidence from leading business and political figures should be made to buoy public opinion; J.P. Morgan & Co. in cooperation with the First National Bank should purchase a substantial amount of U.S. Steel stock which would reassure markets; and business should buy large quantities of raw materials. Leffingwell dismissed these ideas as

[121] Lamont to Morrow, 7 June 1930, BL, TWL, Series II, Box 113, Folder 16; Chernow, *The House of Morgan*, p. 323.
[122] The Smoot–Hawley tariff was not responsible for the Depression. Douglas A. Irwin, "From Smoot-Hawley to Reciprocal Trade Agreements: Changing the Course of U.S. Trade Policy in the 1930s," in Michael D. Bordo, Claudia Goldin, and Eugene N. White, eds., *The Defining Moment: The Great Depression and the American Economy in the Twentieth Century*, Chicago: University of Chicago Press, 1998, pp. 333–37; Barry Eichengreen, "The Political Economy of the Smoot-Hawley Tariff," NBER Working Paper Series, No. 2001, August 1986.
[123] *Commercial and Financial Chronicle*, vol. 131, no. 3391, 21 June 1930, p. 4289.
[124] Lamont to Martin Egan, 10 July 1930, BL, TWL, Series II, Box 92, Folder 24; Lamont to Jack Morgan, 12 September 1930, BL, TWL, Series II, Box 108, Folder 14.
[125] *Commercial and Financial Chronicle*, vol. 131, no. 3406, 4 October 1930, p. 2106.
[126] De Sanchez to Lamont, 21 October 1930, BL, TWL, Series II, Box 91, Folder 17.

impractical. Hoover had already attempted the positive speech route, it had failed, and Leffingwell saw no reason to pursue the "nostrums of Mr. Fixit." Stock purchases or building raw material inventories encountered a basic obstacle: if business was deteriorating, how could you "persuade business men to buy commodities in excess of their requirements, or buy stocks?" While Leffingwell was dismissive, he acknowledged that Taylor was a "very, very able man" and such ideas were circulating widely – they were being discussed by Hoover, Young, Harrison, and Dillon. What mattered, Leffingwell remarked, was "the state of mind about the situation that they [the ideas] reflect in the immensely important people who discuss them seriously."[127]

Taylor's suggestion to purchase raw materials was transformed in September and October into schemes designed to give a fillip to American industry and trade, to support commodities, and to advance international comity. The connection was made by Hoover, whose interest was sparked by Robinson and Young. At dinner on 17 September the president raised with Lamont the notion of a rubber for cotton swap. He told Lamont that Firestone Rubber was willing to buy 100,000 tons of British rubber and in return wanted British companies to purchase an equivalent value of American cotton. Lamont undertook to explore London's attitude through Morgan Grenfell and Norman. His soundings were mixed. While Bank of England officials were "sympathetic" and Norman was willing to entertain the notion, he had his doubts.[128] Harry Davison, in conversation with the management of the United States Rubber Company, informed Lamont that the industry was less keen on the barter plan than Hoover realized. This information, along with the Davison memorandum, Lamont passed on to the secretary of commerce.[129] The latter had, in the interim, been approached by the Japanese government about a silk for cotton swap. Tokyo was willing to purchase 1 million bales of American cotton if the United States bought 200,000 boxes of raw silk. In communicating this information to J.P. Morgan & Co., the secretary of commerce wondered if something might be done. Subsequently Robert P. Lamont asked Lamont whether a scheme involving copper might be feasible.[130] While Lamont was

---

[127] Leffingwell to Lamont, 14 August 1930, BL, TWL, Series II, Box 103, Folder 14.
[128] Lamont to Mellon, 18 September 1930, BL, TWL, Series II, Box 107, Folder 14; J.P. Morgan & Co. to Morgan Grenfell, 19 September 1930, BL, TWL, Series II, Box 98, Folder 17; Lamont to Robert P. Lamont, 25 September 1930, BL, TWL, Series II, Box 98, Folder 17.
[129] Harry P. Davison to Lamont, 19 September 1930, Lamont to Robert P. Lamont, 22 September 1930, BL, TWL, Series II, Box 102, Folder 20.
[130] Robert P. Lamont to Lamont, 18 September 1930, Robert P. Lamont to Lamont, 23 September 1930, BL, TWL, Series II, Box 102, Folder 20.

willing to investigate these ideas, principally because the White House was involved, he thought it remote that anything would transpire.

Lamont's dealings with the White House in the fall of 1930 were shaped by a more parochial concern. The Van Sweringen railroad empire was staggering under the weight of its debt. At the capstone of its pyramidal corporate structure was the Vaness Corporation. Vaness controlled the Alleghany Corporation that J.P. Morgan & Co. had launched in 1929. Alleghany had a dominant interest in the Missouri Pacific Railroad and the Nickel Plate Road and through the Chesapeake Corporation controlled the Chesapeake & Ohio Railway and the Erie Railroad. Of this assemblage, only the Chesapeake & Ohio was profitable and generating the cash flow that the brothers needed to meet the payments on their loans. Guaranty Trust were their principal creditors. It had been evident for months that a crisis was building. In October 1930 the reckoning arrived. Hoover, understanding the importance of the railroad sector, was willing to do what he could to assist.[131] On 22 October Hoover received the Van Sweringen brothers at the White House. Later that day, the brothers met their bankers at Lamont's townhouse in Manhattan (see Figure 3.4).[132] Present were Lamont, Arthur Anderson, and two senior executives of Guaranty Trust, William C. Potter and Joseph Swan.

The brothers knew their empire was destitute and so did the bankers. Neither J.P. Morgan & Co. nor Guaranty Trust wanted to be in the business of running railroads. Well aware of the precarious state of the economy, fearing the ramifications that might flow from bankruptcy for the stock market, and appreciating that Hoover would not welcome this outcome, the bankers hoped that providing more money might allow the brothers to survive. Underlying this gamble was the prospect that, if and when the economy recovered, the railroads would need modernization and re-equipping, a vision that offered the tantalizing notion of future profits. It was, as Whitney later admitted, a "rescue party" though it was not just the Van Sweringen empire that was being saved.[133] On 23 October, having secured agreement from J.P. Morgan & Co. and Guaranty to fresh loans

---

[131] Hoover's calendar indicates that he held multiple meetings in October 1930 with railroad executives and labour leaders. Lamont lobbied Hoover regularly in October and November 1930. See the memo detailing a phone conversation of 31 October 1930, Memo, 31 October 1930, BL, TWL, Series II, Box 98, Folder 17, as well as his letters of 8 and 19 November and his telephone message for Hoover on 25 November.

[132] The Wheeler Committee accepted a date of 23 October for this meeting but Harwood's account, based on material not available to the Wheeler Committee, is convincing that there were two separate meetings, one on the night of 22 October and the second during the day on 23 October. Herbert H. Harwood, *Invisible Giants: The Empires of Cleveland's Van Sweringen Brothers*, Bloomington, IN: Indiana University Press, 2003, pp. 239–40.

[133] See the testimony to the Wheeler Committee; Whitney's "rescue party" remark was made on 4 March 1937.

Figure 3.4 The Van Sweringen brothers, O.P. and M.J., at the Pecora hearings in 1933. Bettmann/Getty Images.

totalling $39.5 million to Vaness Corp and Cleveland Terminals Building Co., O.P. Van Sweringen obtained another $5 million.[134] The bankers certainly understood the riskiness of the loans that they were making. George F. Baker Jr., rather than saddle his First National Bank with such a low-quality loan, absorbed it personally.[135]

*****

On 14 November 1930, two weeks after the "grim anniversary" of the Crash, Lamont admitted that a depression existed in a widely publicized

---

[134] M.J. van Sweringen described how O.P. "pulled his chair over to a window in Lamont's office, propped his feet on the sill, and with his back turned to Lamont, George Whitney, Harold Stanley, Arthur Anderson, and several Morgan lawyers, ignored all their arguments. After a while they capitulated and told my brother they would agree." Harwood, *Invisible Giants*, p. 240.
[135] Ibid., p. 239.

speech. Six causal considerations drew his attention: overproduction of basic commodities; the failure of price-support schemes designed to keep commodity prices high; the drop in silver prices that hurt silver-producing countries but in particular India, China, and Mexico; the movement of gold to France and the United States; widespread political turmoil, with India, China, and South America afflicted severely; and "a spirit of rampant speculation" which had manifested most dramatically in the United States in the run-up to the Crash.[136] Much could be accomplished, Lamont advised, by reforming anti-trust laws that he deemed antiquated and contributory to overproduction through the lowering of entrance barriers to industry. The Smoot–Hawley Tariff should be scrapped, for its provisions impaired trade. Positively, speculation had been broken. Community and business were more sober and stronger. Lamont recalled that there had been many economic crises in the past – he listed thirteen – and that after each one business had recovered. He told his audience that the United States was at the low point of the business cycle but that the Federal Reserve was up to the strain: savings bank deposits had risen; inventories were lean; and corporations were liquid and well capitalized. In a typical flourish, Lamont finished with a scriptural reference: "Be of good courage."[137]

Privately, Leffingwell was alarmed. Commenting on a draft of Lamont's speech, Leffingwell could not contain his astonishment in a bracing commentary distributed to his partners: "I am perplexed by your optimism and wonder on what it is based." He adumbrated the reasons for bleakness, beginning with dropping world prices due to the "restoration of the gold standard and the demonetization of silver." Declines in retail prices and wages had not matched this deflation, while commodity inventories continued to burgeon, a function in part of overproduction that had lasted too long. Wealth had been diminished by the Crash, investors were short of confidence, and cheap money had not

---

[136] Burton Rascoe, "The Grim Anniversary," *The New Republic*, vol. 64, no. 830, 29 October 1930, pp. 285–88. The *New York Times* ran a front-page article as well as reprinting the address in its entirety. The *Wall Street Journal* and *Washington Post* devoted space to his remarks, as did numerous other papers. "T.W. Lamont Says Inopportune Tariff Hurt World Trade," *New York Times*, 15 November 1930, p. 1; p. 13 for the speech; "Lamont hopeful for Prosperity," *Wall Street Journal*, 17 November 1930, p. 8; "What the Bankers Want," *Washington Post*, 16 November 1930, p. S1.

[137] Thomas W. Lamont, "Phases of The World Depression," 14 November 1930, The Academy of Political Science. Many were not convinced. The *Washington Post* dismissed the speech as the desire of "big money" to have the "antitrust laws amended, the protective tariff reduced, and the war debts cancelled." "What the Bankers Want," *Washington Post*, 16 November 1930, p. S1. Dawes voiced his fear that what was in train was an "elemental depression" akin to 1837, 1873, and 1893. Dawes to Young, 13 October 1930, SLU, ODY, Box 17, Dawes, Charles G., Folder 57b.

found enterprises to deploy it. The banks were in trouble, while government at all levels – municipal, state, federal – was afflicted by diminishing revenue and rising expenditure. Politically, the prospect for the next two years was dismal: neither Democrats nor Republicans inspired hope. Abroad, revolution stalked China, Turkey, and South America. India was afflicted by turmoil, while the French were stricken by their fear of war. England and Germany were plagued by a "vicious circle: excessive taxes, unemployment, doles, more taxes." Russia, Leffingwell charged, was "waging economic war on Europe" and was challenging "our civilization ... most effectively." "Drastic modification" of the postwar political and financial order was needed as tariff barriers rose higher, making trade more difficult. The flow of cheap labour, made possible by emigration and immigration, had ceased with negative consequences for the American economy going forward.[138]

Leffingwell offered no solutions, for, though he fretted, there was a strain of moral self-satisfaction that welcomed the downturn. Writing Lamont in August 1930, he remarked, "To me this is a first class deflation after a first class inflation. It is a healthy purge that is being put through the economic body after a seven years' debauch."[139] In the event, Leffingwell's pessimism secured no purchase in Lamont's speech. The divide between the two partners reflected the tensions inherent in Morgan action. Jack Morgan's and Lamont's conviction that progress on European reconstruction was the *sine qua non* to American prosperity dictated what the partners did in 1929–30. The Young Plan and BIS negotiations were fundamental; the Crash, while disturbing, was of lesser moment, for it was a transient phenomenon. In October and November 1929 the Morgan partners demonstrated that they regarded redressing the panic as principally an effort in stabilizing prices. Symbolically this meant the formation of the Bankers' Pool, but the practical work of restoring order fell to the FRBNY and the New York money-centre banks. Leffingwell did not dissent from the priority of European stability, though he rued the direction of American monetary policy and the ills of speculation. In fairness, much of the American business, financial, and political community thought in similar terms about the impact of the Crash.

Optimism, driven by what they regarded as acceptable resolutions to war debts and reparations in the shape of the Young Plan and the BIS, coloured the outlook of the Morgan partners until the summer of 1930. Growing evidence of deeper-seated troubles did not find open expression

[138] Leffingwell to Lamont, 13 November 1930, BL, TWL, Series II, Box 103, Folder 14.
[139] Leffingwell to Lamont, 14 August 1930, BL, TWL, Series II, Box 103, Folder 14.

outside the confines of the bank until Lamont's speech. Even then, his words balanced acceptance of the Depression with a desire to appease the Hoover administration. Pressed to retain good relations with the White House, J.P. Morgan & Co. did not believe that the Depression imperilled their position, Wall Street, the United States, or capitalism. The year 1931 challenged those assumptions.

4   "The End of the World"? The 1931 Crises

Driving on the Columbia Highway through Oregon in 1931 Jackson Reynolds was intercepted on the road by a waiter waving his white apron asking if there was anyone in the car named Reynolds, that he was wanted on the telephone.

> I ... went inside and it was Mr. George Baker on the other end in New York and he told me had just been talking with J.P. Morgan over the Transatlantic Radio Telephone. Mr. Morgan had told Mr. Baker England was going off gold on the following Monday, the 21st ... all my hair stood on end ... when England went off gold it was like the end of the world to financial thinking and it produced a tremendous repercussion all over the world, this country included.[1]

When Britain left the gold standard in September 1931, it "was one of the turning points in the monetary history of the twentieth century."[2] Postwar reconstruction – monetary, economic, and political – tottered. Surveying the damage wrought by a year of crises in November 1931, the Morgan partners were dismayed but not accepting, cabling Morgan Grenfell: "We have worked too hard too long together at rebuilding the world after the War not to want to make every imaginable effort."[3]

The series of events that had led to this remarkable statement mixing defiance and hubris began in the spring of 1931 when the Austrian CreditAnstalt bank collapsed.[4] Though the BIS and the European central banks managed to contain the Austrian crisis, fresh turmoil in Germany

---

[1] Reynolds, CUL, COHC, pp. 150–51.

[2] R.S. Sayers, *The Bank of England 1891–1944*, 3 vols., Cambridge: Cambridge University Press, 1976, vol. 2, p. 387.

[3] J.P. Morgan & Co. to Morgan Grenfell, 30 November 1931, TML, CP, Box 19, Misc Priv Telegs 23 November to 22 March 1932.

[4] Nathan Marcus, *Austrian Reconstruction and the Collapse of Global Finance, 1921–1931*, Cambridge, MA: Harvard University Press, 2018, pp. 298–334. Marcus emphasizes the contained nature of the CreditAnstalt crisis, portraying it as distinct from the ensuing convulsions in Germany and Britain. Following Marcus, see Flora Macher, "The Austrian Banking Crisis of 1931: A Reassessment," *Financial History Review*, vol. 25, no. 3 (2018), pp. 297–321. For a more traditional view, Iago Gil Aguado, "The Creditanstalt Crisis of

drove a speculative attack on the City, whose German commitments were
well known. Under pressure, gold fled London. Sterling sagged, rallied,
and then was ultimately forced off gold. While J.P. Morgan & Co.,
Morgan Grenfell, and Morgan & Cie. were insulated from the effects of
the Austrian and German crises by virtue of their limited exposure to the
area, Morgan involvement built steadily as Britain was affected, reaching
a crescendo in August and September 1931. Throughout the Morgan
partners had one aim: maintaining the gold standard through a revival of
the wartime Allied coalition. If the CreditAnstalt crisis and German
affairs were a crisis of the losing belligerents in World War I, sterling's
abandonment of gold was a crisis of the victors – Britain, France, and the
United States. J.P. Morgan & Co. was identified with the victors. Their
disarray and weakness implied Morgan weakness. Though the September
crisis dealt a blow, the solution was not withdrawing from the field but
accepting that France was now the key to European harmony. Hoover, in
the Morgan estimation, needed to be guided to this conclusion. Hoover,
however, did not wish guidance from the Corner. The events of 1931
were devastating to postwar stability. The view from 23 Wall Street
reinforces those interpretations that have argued that 1931 converted
economic crisis into the Depression.

*****

The crisis that blossomed in Austria in the spring of 1931 caught the
Morgan partners unaware. On 8 May 1931 the CreditAnstalt bank,
associated with the Rothschilds and the dominant bank in Austria,
informed the Austrian government that it was in dire straits. Its losses
were roughly 85 per cent of its equity. Frantic, secret meetings ensued as
the Austrian government attempted to determine what might be done.
The formal public announcement of its losses came on Monday 11 May.[5]
The Bank of England had known for some time of the CreditAnstalt's
vulnerability. Nevertheless, the international markets, including the City
of London, and J.P. Morgan & Co. in New York, were surprised. The
11 May announcement by the Austrian government pledged to backstop
CreditAnstalt, through assistance provided by the Austrian government,
the Austrian National Bank, and the Rothschilds. The remaining outstanding losses would be covered by dipping into the reserves and reca-
pitalizing the bank. This plan failed to reassure investors. Norman had

1931 and the Failure of the Austro-German Customs Union Project," *Historical Journal*,
vol. 44, no. 1 (2001), pp. 199–221.
[5] Aurel Schubert, *The Credit-Anstalt Crisis of 1931*, Cambridge: Cambridge University
Press, 1991, chap. 1 has the background.

suggested to the Austrian government that the BIS was the appropriate vehicle through which assistance could be afforded. This idea was pursued with alacrity by Vienna. McGarrah began to sound out central bankers about extending a loan, soon set at 100 million schillings, to the Austrian National Bank.[6]

Initially, the Morgan partners in New York knew little more than what they read in the New York papers. Cabling Morgan Grenfell on 13 May for more information, they confessed their ignorance, remarking with relief that apparently CreditAnstalt was "now in good standing."[7] Even though J.P. Morgan & Co. had made loans to Austria, it had never been central to Morgan interests, nor did the firm have representation in Vienna. New York relied upon Morgan Grenfell in London, Morgan & Cie. in Paris, and its connections with the BIS to evaluate what was happening. Fummi, in Rome, does not seem to have furnished information. News from London and Paris on 14 and 15 May made it clear that CreditAnstalt was not "in good standing." The Morgan partners were informed by Morgan & Cie. that Fraser had signalled that the Austrian National Bank was seeking to borrow 75 million schillings externally, contrary to the terms of the 1930 Austrian government loan in which J. P. Morgan & Co. had been a participant. Morgan & Cie. cabled that the French government had asked the Banque de Paris et de Pays-Bas (Paribas) to explore a loan to the Austrian government and were hoping that J.P. Morgan & Co. might lead an American group. The Morgan partners, replying, demonstrated both their hesitance and their confusion. They told Morgan & Cie. that they had not been asked to participate in an Austrian loan, but conditions in the United States ruled out any such operation. While they were heartened that French assistance was a possibility, the Morgan partners were mystified as to why aid was needed – had the CreditAnstalt rescue collapsed?[8] As it became apparent that additional capital was required, J.P. Morgan & Co. indicated that, while they were willing to waive the covenant restricting fresh Austrian borrowing in the 1930 loan agreement, they were not prepared to stump up new funds. When CreditAnstalt contacted Morgan Grenfell directly on 19 May asking for a six-month extension of credit lines, the answer was

---

[6] Toniolo, *Central Bank Cooperation*, pp. 90–97 discusses the BIS and the CreditAnstalt crisis, pp. 106–14.

[7] J.P. Morgan & Co. to Morgan Grenfell, 13 May 1931, TML, CP, Box 19, Morgan & Co. Priv. Misc. Telegs 29 April to June 1931.

[8] Morgan Grenfell to J.P. Morgan & Co., 14 May 1931, Morgan Grenfell to J.P. Morgan & Co., 15 May 1931, J.P. Morgan & Co. to Morgan Grenfell, 16 May 1931, all TML, CP, Box 19, Morgan & Co. Priv. Misc. Telegs 29 April to June 1931.

a firm "no" following consultations in the City and with J.P. Morgan & Co.

The BIS struggled to consummate the Austrian central bank credit, which was not finalized until 31 May.[9] Eyeing these troubles, Norman, who had struck a committee of the CreditAnstalt's foreign creditors in late May, asked Morgan Grenfell to join. The latter did so but only after seeking the sanction of the Morgan partners in New York. Reluctantly, J. P. Morgan & Co. agreed, fearing that the committee might end up frightening, rather than reassuring, foreign creditors.[10] In late May J.P. Morgan & Co. took two other steps. One was to confer in New York. The partners discussed matters with Harrison and Paul Warburg of the Bank of Manhattan. The objective was to clarify the attitude of New York bankers to maintaining their credit lines to Austria, while attempting to discern how large those lines were. National City Bank had reduced its credit line to Austria to $1 million from $2 million, while Guaranty Trust had cancelled its credit line of $2 million. Ruefully, J.P. Morgan signalled to Morgan Grenfell that they had not been consulted by either bank before they made their decisions, a confession that suggested the limits of Morgan influence on those institutions. The second step was to inform Dean Jay in Paris, in the "strictest confidence," about Norman's activities in London. For his part, Dean Jay informed his partners in New York that Paribas was doing everything they could to float a loan to Austria and was anxious to bring it to fruition.[11]

Crisis rippled. Berlin and Vienna had announced their intention in March 1931 to explore a customs union, a possibility that alarmed Paris. The initial French reaction was to refrain from deploying French financial power to block the customs union as the price of providing aid to rescue CreditAnstalt.[12] Within Germany there was a growing range of political, economic, and financial strains. The marked gains made by the National Socialists and the German Communist Party (KPD) in the German federal elections of September 1930 had revealed the burgeoning political strength of the extremes. With the centrist parties enfeebled, Heinrich Brüning's government was dependent upon the support of the aged president, Paul von Hindenburg, for its survival. The much-derided Young Plan was a target for Brüning and his foreign minister, Julius

---

[9] Stephen V.O. Clarke, *Central Bank Cooperation 1924–1931*, New York: Federal Reserve Bank of New York, 1967, pp. 185–87; Toniolo, *Central Bank Cooperation*, pp. 90–93.

[10] Clay, *Lord Norman*, pp. 375–77; J.P. Morgan & Co. to Morgan Grenfell, 26 May 1931, TML, CP, Box 19, Morgan & Co. Priv. Misc. Telegs 29 April to June 1931.

[11] J.P. Morgan & Co. to Morgan Grenfell, 27 May 1931, Morgan Grenfell to J.P. Morgan & Co., 27 May 1931, J.P. Morgan & Co. to Morgan Grenfell, 28 May 1931, all in TML, CP, Box 19, Morgan & Co. Priv. Misc. Telegs 29 April to June 1931.

[12] Bennett, *Germany and the Diplomacy of the Financial Crisis*, pp. 100–04.

Curtius. Schacht had shown the way: in October 1930 he had made a lecture tour in the United States where he declaimed openly that Germany should no longer meet its Young Plan obligations. While the Brüning government had not yet taken that step when the CreditAnstalt crisis broke, the temptation to do so was growing.

The American ambassador to Germany, Frederic M. Sackett, had for some time been signalling to Stimson and Hoover that reparations had been made the scapegoat for the worsening economic situation in Germany. Sackett had reached the conclusion that American banks were increasingly leery of throwing good money after bad and were worried about their outstanding short-term credits to Germany. Fixated on the communist threat represented by the KPD, Sackett returned to the United States in the late spring of 1931. Conversing with Hoover on 6 May, Sackett suggested that relief was necessary but that a crisis that might bring the KPD to power was not imminent.[13] There ensued discussions among Hoover, Stimson, and Mellon which were inconclusive. Ogden Mills, the undersecretary of the Treasury, and Eugene Meyer, the governor of the Federal Reserve Board from September 1930 to May 1933, were also apprised. Following a warning from Harrison to Stimson on 27 May that the CreditAnstalt crisis might spread to Germany, Hoover, Stimson, Mellon, Mills, and Meyer were aware that German public finances were deteriorating.[14] Sackett met again with Hoover on 2 and 3 June, this time with his fellow ambassadors, Dawes and Hugh Gibson, to press his assessment.[15] As it happened, these talks took place against the backdrop of a planned visit by Brüning and Curtius to Britain on 5 June to meet with MacDonald and Henderson.

The Morgan partners understood that pressure was mounting. Unlike many New York banks, J.P. Morgan & Co. had no short-term credits outstanding to Germany, while Morgan Grenfell was the least exposed of the leading City of London merchant banks.[16] Yet there was reason for concern: the partners feared what might happen in the event of a unilateral German decision to cease servicing the Dawes and Young Plan loans. On 3 June 1931 Lamont attended a private lunch for Sackett in New York where the guest list was dominated by the heads of the

[13] Ibid., pp. 132–33; Joslin, *Hoover off the Record*, p. 88, traces the Hoover moratorium to this conversation.
[14] Wilson, *American Business and Foreign Policy*, pp. 132–40.
[15] Dawes was the American ambassador at the Court of St. James, while Gibson was the ambassador at Brussels.
[16] Grenfell told Lamont that "the direct advances and acceptance of M&G & Co. for Germany, Austria and Hungary are small as compared with those of any other House of good position in London." Grenfell to Lamont, 18 July 1931, BL, TWL, Series II, Box 111, Folder 23.

New York banks. Trying to reassure the bankers about Germany, and the safety of their short-term loans, Sackett made, in Lamont's words, a "dreadful" speech which inadvertently "scared them to death." Relaying this assessment to Lippmann – the choice of correspondent an indication of how serious Lamont thought the matter – Lamont guessed that short-term credits outstanding in Germany were approximately $2 billion. Much of this total had been extended by American banks. The Chase National had more than $90 million in frozen credits in Germany in July 1931 and National City Bank had more than $87 million. Two banks noted for their Morgan connections, Guaranty Trust and Bankers Trust, had respectively $46 million and nearly $21 million of exposure.[17] There were thus good reasons for Morgan concern. If the Germans opted for a reparations hiatus under the terms of the Young Plan agreement – which they had the right to invoke – Lamont feared that panic would ensue, the mark would fall, and the short-term American credits to Germany would hang in the balance with attendant negative consequences for banking stability in the United States. While economic historians have challenged whether "transmission" of the crisis occurred, there is little question that its possibility preoccupied the Morgan partners.[18]

A lengthy cable despatched by the Morgan partners in New York to Morgan Grenfell the same day was sombre. Its purpose was to distil the American perspective and to ensure that Norman understood matters clearly. J.P. Morgan & Co. argued that any German effort to either impose a moratorium on reparations or call for the convening of a Special Advisory Committee under the Young Plan would be a mistake. A moratorium would be interpreted in the United States as "repudiation," unsettling American holders of German short-term paper, already uneasy given the ongoing CreditAnstalt saga. The risk of capital

[17] Olivier Accominitti, "International Banking and Transmission of the 1931 Financial Crisis," London School of Economics and CEPR, November 2016, table 3, p. 56. https://cepr.org/active/publications/discussion_papers/dp.php?dpno=11651.

[18] Lamont to Lippmann, 4 June 1931, BL, TWL, Series II, Box 104, Folder 28. The debate among economic historians on the issue of transmission of the European financial crisis is discussed by Accominitti as well as in two papers by Gary Richardson and Patrick Van Horn, "When the Music Stopped: Transatlantic Contagion During the Financial Crisis of 1931," NBER Working Paper Series, No. 17437, 2011 and Richardson and Van Horn, "Intensified Regulatory Scrutiny and Bank Distress in New York City During the Great Depression," *Journal of Economic History*, vol. 69, no. 2 (2009), pp. 446–65. In their 2009 article Richardson and Van Horn argued that it was heightened regulatory inspection that drove increased levels of New York City banking failure in July and August 1931 prior to the British leaving gold. In 2011 they suggested that New York money-centre banks were well equipped to deal with the crises of the spring and summer of 1931. Transmission of the crisis was a function of FRBNY action in September and October 1931 to raise interest rates to check the outflow of gold.

flight from Germany was real. The New York partners had refined Lamont's estimate: American banks held about $1 billion in short-term German obligations, including deposits in German banks. While for the moment those banks that they had spoken with were standing firm, anxiety best described their attitude. Should the American banks cancel their lines of credit and withdraw their deposits, "it would be quite impossible for the German banks to meet the enormous volume." If such a scenario manifested, New York warned that counting on the Reichsbank, the BIS, or European central banks to save the day would be foolhardy. Given this, while J.P. Morgan & Co. appreciated the conundrum faced by the Brüning government, the Reichstag was not scheduled to meet until the fall. The Morgan partners counselled that doing nothing was the most sensible course. They confessed that not all in New York concurred – Mortimer L. Schiff of Kuhn, Loeb & Co. and Paul Warburg were two on Wall Street who thought otherwise. Imaginings of a quid pro quo on reparations and war debts were flights of fancy in Morgan eyes. Lamont had told MacDonald in May 1931 that he should disabuse himself of such hopes.[19]

Confronted with this cable, Grenfell met Norman. The latter "had no illusions." He told Grenfell that Austria and the CreditAnstalt remained "in a chaotic state" despite efforts to restore order. Morgan Grenfell warned that if the Germans opted for a moratorium after the upcoming London meeting, "the results would be lamentable and full of danger not only to all Europe but to the other continents." New York was informed that Brüning had suggested to Hindenburg "a very drastic decree ... involving heavy reduction of expenditure, fresh taxes and reductions of salaries. Both extreme wings in German politics are gaining in strength and the proposed program will make the Government increasingly unpopular. We hope however that Hindenburg may be willing to take such strong measures." As for speeches in the United States that advocated cancellation of war debts, Morgan Grenfell recognized that they were not mainstream but were seized on eagerly in Britain.[20]

Such was the situation when Lamont telephoned Hoover on 5 June 1931 with a proposal. Lamont's intervention was designed to find a way out of the impasse – outright cancellation of reparations and war debts was impossible given congressional opinion. Failure to act, however, might imperil American banks. Within J.P. Morgan & Co. Leffingwell drafted a memorandum suggesting a time-limited

---

[19] Grenfell to J.P. Morgan & Co, 5 June 1931, TML, CP, Box 19, Morgan & Co. Priv. Misc. Telegs 29 April to June 1931.
[20] Morgan Grenfell to J.P. Morgan & Co., 4 June 1931, TML, CP, Box 19, Morgan & Co. Priv. Misc. Telegs 29 April to June 1931.

moratorium. The memorandum was given to Lamont, who seized upon it and consulted with Jack Morgan. He was in favour of bringing it to the president's attention. The decision was taken to contact Hoover.[21]

Lamont suggested a holiday on international government debt payments. He informed the president of the J.P. Morgan & Co. cable to Morgan Grenfell on 4 June. A German moratorium, Lamont told Hoover, would be devastating for American banks holding short-term German credits. As the debtor powers were not in a position to suggest a moratorium, only the United States, the chief creditor, could plausibly declare a moratorium without damaging effects. Hoover was unconvinced, remarking that the political obstacles were formidable. The congressional elections of November 1930 had robbed the Republicans of their working majority in both the Senate and the House of Representatives. Congress was anti-cancellation, dismayed at European armament expenditures, and viewed France's growing gold stockpile as a threat. Lamont acknowledged these impediments but worried that, if nothing was done, a European crash would "prolong our agony of business depression by years." If framed properly, with a message that a moratorium would benefit American farmers and workers, Lamont thought that much of the political opposition could be defused. Doing so, he advised Hoover, would not only benefit the country but also end the whispers that had been circulating about denying Hoover the Republican nomination in the 1932 convention. This amalgam of blandishment and menace failed to convince. Hoover told Lamont that he remained "very doubtful." The phone call ended with Hoover inquiring with Lamont whether or not Morrow, now a Republican senator from New Jersey, had been consulted. When Lamont indicated that he had not been, Hoover asked if Lamont would let Morrow know that he would be in contact. Lamont wrapped up the conversation by remarking: "One last thing, Mr. President, that is, that if anything by any chance ever comes out of this suggestion we should wish to be forgotten in the matter. This is your plan and nobody else's."[22]

It has been argued that this phone call establishes that the Hoover moratorium was a Morgan plan.[23] Such an interpretation, while appealing from a perspective that sees Morgan influence as dominant within the

---

[21] Debt Suspension Matter memorandum, Lamont, 5 June 1931, BL, TWL, Series II, Box 98/18. Lamont, *The Ambassador*, pp. 294–99, has excerpts from Lamont's conversations with Hoover on 5, 8, and 29 June.

[22] Ibid.

[23] Thomas Ferguson, "From Normalcy to New Deal," *International Organization*, vol. 38, no. 1 (1984), pp. 41–94. Ferguson attacked the interpretation of this episode proffered by Wilson, in *American Business and Foreign Policy*, pp. 132–40, on the grounds that Wilson had been gulled by a fabricated Hoover diary entry.

Hoover administration, is unconvincing. Prior to the phone call considerations of relief had been in the air for months. The transcript of the conversation makes plain Hoover's hesitancy; he was far from won over. His natural inclination was to question counsel proffered by the Morgan partners.[24] Years later, when Stimson was asked by Allen about the genesis of the Hoover moratorium, Stimson professed that his memory on the matter was "very sketchy" but he was certain on one point: "It was in the minds of all of us. I have never heard from anyone that the plan was originated in Owen Young's mind or that 'continual pressure from Morrow, Mellon, Dawes, and various New York bankers' was exerted." He went on to tell Allen that the plan as it was formulated was "essentially" Hoover's.[25]

Stimson's recollection may have been vague but the thrust of his remembrance is accurate. Following the phone call between Lamont and Hoover, conversations ensued in which Parker Gilbert was the principal Morgan participant. Parker Gilbert had become a Morgan partner on 2 January 1931. With his expertise in reparations and war debts, honed by his years as the Agent-General for Reparations Payments in Berlin, Lippmann judged that Parker Gilbert had "unmatched authority."[26] For an individual whose interwar reputation stood so high that he was nicknamed the "King of the World," Parker Gilbert has vanished into the mists of time (see Figure 4.1). Today only specialists in international relations and finance recognize his name. He once graced the cover of *Time* magazine and was described by Moreau as a "great American." Montagu Norman tried and failed to get him a Nobel prize as well as an honorary doctorate at Oxford.[27] Parker Gilbert differed from his partners

---

[24] This point has been made by Diane B. Kunz, *The Battle for Britain's Gold Standard in 1931*, London: Croom Helm, 1987, p. 55, and by Boyce, *The Great Interwar Crisis*, pp. 312–13.

[25] Stimson to Allen, 6 June 1939, LC, FLA, Box 2, correspondence 1939.

[26] Lippmann to Lamont, 20 July 1932, BL, TWL, Series II, Box 105, Folder 1.

[27] His premature death in 1938 is one reason why Parker Gilbert remains largely unknown today. He left few papers, save for the material generated while he was Agent-General. There is no biography and it is unlikely, given the paucity of archival material, that there ever will be. A retired Rutgers university economist, Eugene E. Agger, began work on a biography in the 1950s before illness forced him to abandon the project. Agger completed a biographical entry of Parker Gilbert for the *American Dictionary of National Biography* that never appeared in print. A copy is available in the Eugene E. Agger papers, Rutgers Special Collections and University Archives, Eugene E. Agger papers, Box 5, Folder 6 Manuscript. The "King of the World" sobriquet is from William Randolph Burgess to Agger, 10 November 1955, Rutgers Special Collections and University Archives, Eugene E. Agger papers, Box 5, Folder 5 Correspondence 1955–56. The same letter remarks on Parker Gilbert's work ethic. For Norman's efforts on Parker Gilbert's behalf, see Bank of England (hereafter BE), G1, 413, 10 January 1957; for his putative appointment to the Federal Reserve, see Leffingwell to Lamont, 13 May 1933,

Figure 4.1   S. Parker Gilbert, Agent-General for Reparations and J.P. Morgan & Co. partner 1931–38. Dephot/ullstein bild/Getty Images.

in his assessment of the overall responsibility of the principal states in the complications arising from the World War I settlements. Parker Gilbert was anti-German, which fit neatly with Morgan culture, but his animosity vis-à-vis the Germans was extraordinary. His time in Berlin had not been a happy one. He emerged from the experience with a visceral distaste for the Germans, with Schacht the chief target of his bile. The latter Parker Gilbert regarded as duplicitous, untrustworthy, and egomaniacal, all of which was accurate but impolitic to display as openly as Parker Gilbert did.[28] More muted, but apparent, was Parker Gilbert's jaundice about the British. Parker Gilbert deemed that behind a mask of pretending to act on behalf of humanity, London was pursuing its "world policy" to the detriment of others. Parker Gilbert had clashed with British Treasury officials, notably Leith-Ross. Contrasting were Parker Gilbert's views on France. As he told Morrow, "France, in my opinion, is as true a friend as we have among the nations, and in all my five years over here there is no country

YUL, RCL, Series I, Box 4, Folder 95 and Marriner S. Eccles to Leffingwell, 24 May 1946, YUL, RCL, Series I, Box 2, Folder 34.

[28] Parker Gilbert made no secret of his view of Schacht. See the devastating portrait that he sketched of Schacht in a cable from Berlin on 12 January 1930 that was circulated to McGarrah, Harrison, Young, Jack Morgan, Lamont, Pierre Jay, and Leon Fraser. Parker Gilbert to FRBNY, 12 January 1930, TML, JPM, Box 179, Folder 239.

that has played as fair and straight with us as she has." In Parker Gilbert's estimation, Paris had been working faithfully and stolidly to maintain European stability.[29]

As the discussions unfolded, Harrison, Mills, Parker Gilbert, Morrow, and Meyer debated, occasionally soliciting advice from Young. There were two questions: first, should the Hoover administration do anything; second, if the answer was yes, how should it be done? Harrison, Mills, Parker Gilbert, and Morrow agreed that the United States should act. Mills duly informed Hoover of this consensus on 9–10 June. His recommendation was that the United States should adopt an active role but that a lack of reliable information was handicapping American decision-making. Accordingly, Mills suggested that Harrison be sent to Europe to report first-hand. Hoover agreed, but when Mills raised the idea with Harrison, he baulked as did Meyer, both of whom thought that it was inadvisable. Sending Harrison meant delay. Other options were then canvassed. Harrison, following consultation with Young, laid out three possibilities: the calling of a general conference on war debt and reparations by Washington which gave rise to the objection that it would not be a swift resolution to the problem; prodding the debtors to submit a request for a postponement; or an American offer to postpone debts for two years. Harrison, Mills, Parker Gilbert, and Young all preferred the third choice.[30] Hoover did not make a decision until sometime thereafter. Hoover departed the capital for Rapidan Camp and then Indiana and did not return to Washington until 18 June. Dawes spoke with the president on 16 June, by which date Hoover had accepted the notion of a moratorium but was unsure as to whether he would opt for a one- or two-year grace period. Hoover settled on a one-year moratorium, largely because it made the task of corralling congressional support simpler.[31]

Morgan doubts about Hoover's ability to juggle successfully the competing interests involved led Leffingwell and Parker Gilbert to urge Lamont to contact the president. Their fear was that Hoover would foreclose French adherence to the moratorium by proposing too rigid a plan. Reading their correspondence, it is plain that the Morgan partners thought that Hoover was not the man to be negotiating with the French. His jagged obstinacy needed smoothing. Lamont's hubris lay in thinking

[29] Parker Gilbert to Morrow, 25 November 1929, AC, DM, Series I, Box 24, Folder 12. The letter was written as Morrow was preparing for the London Naval Conference of 1930.
[30] George L. Harrison memorandum, 11 June 1931, CUL, GH, Box 21, Binder 45.
[31] Jordan Schwartz, *The Interregnum of Despair, Hoover, Congress and the Depression*, Urbana: University of Illinois Press, 1970, pp. 78–80.

that he could accomplish this task. Lamont and Hoover spoke on 19 June and again on 20 June. The conversations revealed the distance between the Morgan partners and Hoover. Lamont's suggestion on 19 June that Hoover frame the proposal as generally as possible to allow for flexibility was rejected unceremoniously by the president who told Lamont that he had made commitments to obtain congressional backing for the plan. The moratorium proposal would be straightforward. "The French," Hoover told Lamont, "can take it or leave it." The next day Hoover rang Lamont in the evening. Because so many congressmen were leaking the plan, the president informed Lamont, he had decided to issue it to the press earlier than planned. Hoover then read the text of his statement to Lamont. Lamont, who had not been informed of its contents, asked Hoover when he intended to release it. Hoover told Lamont that he had already done so, ahead of calling him. Lamont was taken aback, raising with Hoover the likelihood that given the character of the statement, which disavowed any connection between war debts and reparations, and rejected cancellation of war debts in favour of a one-year moratorium on intergovernmental debts that would disadvantage France, there was bound to be a "mess with the French." Hoover understood this; he hoped that Morgan influence in Paris would dispose the French government to react favourably. Lamont was sceptical, telling the president that, while J.P. Morgan & Co. had cordial relations with the Bank of France, "our contacts with the present government in France are very slight."[32]

Lamont's misgivings were borne out. Paris did not greet the Hoover moratorium with approbation. The French had received more warning than J.P. Morgan & Co. of the plan's appearance but not much. Pierre Laval's ministry construed the Hoover moratorium as a return to a policy of bludgeoning France to spare the Germans in the interest of salvaging British and American private finance. The French were aware that both the City of London and New York had substantial short-term commitments to Germany. Paris negotiated, seizing on the moratorium as a means of securing concessions from Germany on issues such as the customs union, naval construction, and a continuance of German payment of unconditional reparations.[33] Lacking immediate French acquiescence, Hoover fumed. In conversation with Lamont on 29 June, Hoover lambasted the French: "Their attitude has been intolerable." Lamont, seeking to redirect Hoover's anger, agreed that the "The French are the most difficult people to deal with in the whole world."

---

[32] Memoranda detailing the Lamont–Hoover conversations of 19 and 20 June 1931 are in BL, TWL, Series II, Box 98/18.

[33] Bennett, *Germany and the Diplomacy of the Financial Crisis*, pp. 169–78.

Having mollified Hoover, Lamont sought to nudge the president toward compromise, observing that, while reaction in the United States to the moratorium had been very positive, if it should fail at the first jump Hoover would be blamed, just as he was blamed for the Depression by the American people. The president was recalcitrant, arguing that "principles" were more important than credit. Lamont was "all wrong" if he believed that Congress would defer without a struggle. His gambit having failed, Lamont reminded the president "that the Germans have been the ones chiefly responsible for bringing this situation on themselves." In this light the French were resistant, naturally, to having to "pull Germany out of the pit which she has dug for herself."[34] Irate, Hoover told Lamont that perhaps the way forward lay in bypassing France. As it happened, despite Hoover's bluster, a Franco-American agreement was reached in the days that followed on 6 July.

Lamont fussed. He worried that his efforts to influence Hoover's approach to the moratorium had been construed by the president as intrusive and unwelcome. Lamont instructed Martin Egan to contact the White House to pledge his loyalty, to impart the message that he had always had Hoover's best interests at heart, that he wanted the moratorium to succeed and desired fervently that Hoover be "renominated and re-elected." J.P. Morgan & Co., Lamont insisted, had endeavoured to persuade the French to accept Hoover's plan. Much of this abnegation was typical of Lamont and may be discounted as the expression of his desire, whenever possible, to remain on good terms with the White House. Underlying the grovelling was a hard kernel – the partners believed in the virtues of the moratorium plan. As Leffingwell put it, "the world is no longer heading for the precipice."[35]

By early July there were signs that the first flush of enthusiasm within the United States for the moratorium was fading. Expectations that an agreement would pave the way for an improvement in the American economy were beginning to look ill-founded. The *American Bankers Association Journal*, in an article and editorial on the moratorium, noted French "hesitancy and inability" as "disconcerting." Any push toward cancellation of war debts by the administration would be unpopular with the American public. This was not simply an abstract calculation:

Today, with several millions of men and women unemployed and with tax burdens increasing, war debts take on a new aspect, because any revision or suspension mean or seem to mean an increase in our tax burden. Taxes are an

---

[34] Memorandum of phone call between Lamont and Hoover, 29 June 1931, BL, TWL, Series II, Box 98, Folder 18.
[35] Leffingwell to de Sanchez, 2 July 1931, YUL, RCL, Series I, Box 1/29.

intimate, personal problem in America, hence our interest in the Hoover proposal.

The ABA warned that there was a danger in heeding the cry again to "save Europe," proponents of assistance would exhaust American goodwill.[36] The *Commercial and Financial Chronicle*, after an editorial on 4 July voiced the conviction that "[a] definite start has now been made towards a better state of things," was a week later acknowledging "disappointing" early returns, remarking that a recovery in trade will be "slow ... and perhaps be quite gradual."[37]

Doubt was furthered by a worsening of the German financial crisis. On 26 June the announcement of a $100 million renewable central bank loan in which the FRBNY, Bank of France, Bank of England, and BIS took equal shares furnished the Reichsbank with some breathing room in the face of heavy losses of its reserves in gold and foreign exchange. The Hoover administration had been wary of American participation, fearing that doing so would remove any leverage on Paris to comply with the Hoover moratorium proposal. As matters transpired, the reprieve was momentary. Pressure mounted on the Reichsbank again, with heavy losses of gold between 30 June and 3 July. By 4 July the entirety of the central bank credit had been exhausted and the Reichsbank was below its legal note cover ratio in gold and foreign exchange. Facing serious domestic financial complications within Germany, in the shape of the failure of a leading woollen textile firm, Nordwolle, and attendant strain upon the Darmstädter und Nationalbank and Dresdner banks, both of whom were owed significant sums by Nordwolle, the Reichsbank governor, Hans Luther, staunched the wound by drawing down the entirety of a $50 million credit that had been arranged through a group of New York banks in the 1920s under the auspices of the International Acceptance Corporation.[38] Luther hoped that he would be able to parlay this credit into a much larger loan from Britain, France, and the United States. He intended to voyage to London to meet Norman ahead of the latter's journey to Basle for BIS meetings. Harrison, who had been canvassing the New York banks to ensure that they were maintaining their outstanding lines of credit with Germany, was informed by Norman on 8 July that the Reichsbank had lost another $10 million in reserves that day. Norman told Harrison that he thought Luther hoped to obtain a loan of somewhere between $500 million and $1 billion to

[36] *American Bankers Association Journal*, vol. 24, July 1931, pp. 17, 19.
[37] *Commercial and Financial Chronicle*, vol. 133, no. 3445, 4 July 1931, p. 1; *Commercial and Financial Chronicle* vol. 133, no. 3446, 11 July 1931, p. 167.
[38] Clarke, *Central Bank Cooperation*, pp. 189–93.

combat the drain. Harrison was blunt, telling Norman that there was no possibility that Luther could find the "huge amount" that he sought in the New York market, a view that was confirmed on 16 July when Harrison met with leading New York bankers, including Wiggin and Mitchell. Their collective assessment was that even $50–75 million might not be attainable, which Harrison duly relayed to Mills.[39]

J.P. Morgan & Co. had been kept informed through Grenfell and Harrison.[40] Norman had authorized Harrison to share information on the talks with only Morgan on Wall Street. The Morgan partners were furious at Luther's manoeuvring. In a cable to Grenfell on 10 July they made known their displeasure. There was no hope of raising the amount that Luther contemplated. The German choice to halt service of the Young Plan loan has "very gravely impaired her own credit." Nor was it apparent why this step was necessary, as the Hoover moratorium granted the German budget substantial relief the coming year, on the order of $400 million. What the Germans were trying was unconscionable: "it seems incomprehensible to us that the responsible authorities in any modern civilized State could even be thinking in such terms." The Morgan partners charged that the Germans were exporting their financial problems to the world, running the risk of a withdrawal of credit and subsequent paralysis of the German economy in the process. They urged that Berlin meet its obligations even if this meant a drop in Reichsbank reserves and a depreciation of the mark. The Reichsbank had shirked its duty; the discount rate must be raised and restrictions imposed to prevent capital flows abroad. The Brüning government was complicit, as it, in common with past German governments, had failed to tackle the financial weakness at home.[41] Striking in its obtuseness regarding political conditions in Germany, Grenfell was asked to show the cable to Norman as soon as possible. Norman was en route to Basle and so Grenfell passed it to the deputy-governor, Sir Ernest Harvey, and requested the Treasury cable Norman in Switzerland with a copy. Jack Morgan, the following day, made sure that McGarrah was circulated the

---

[39] Harrison to Norman, 8 July 1931, CUL, GH, Box 9, Binder 20; Mills had rung Harrison asking what might be done. As it happened Harrison was meeting with the New York bankers at the time. Harrison memorandum, 16 July 1931, CUL, GH, Box 21, Binder 45.

[40] McGarrah cabled Harrison on 9 July inquiring whether American banks were seeking to take advantage of the central banks by withdrawing their funds from Austria and Germany. Harrison, after consulting with Jack Morgan and Owen Young, reassured McGarrah that this was not the case. McGarrah to Harrison, 9 July 1931, Harrison to McGarrah, 10 July 1931, CUL, GH, Columbia, Box 1, Binder 2.

[41] J.P. Morgan & Co. to Grenfell, 10 July 1931, TML, CP, Box 19, Folder Morgan & Co. Misc. Priv. Telegs 1 July to 28 October 1931.

cable as well. Neither the Bank of England nor the BIS could be in doubt of the Morgan position.[42]

Motivating this extraordinary missive was fear – fear that the Germans would no longer service the Dawes and Young Plan loans whose bonds had already fallen markedly in price on US markets, thus damaging Morgan prestige; fear that transmission of the financial crises in Germany and Central Europe to New York would ensue; fear that Berlin was manoeuvring to secure cancellation of reparations with the aim in mind of obtaining revision of the Versailles Treaty; fear that if reparations ended, so too would war debts with the attendant political consequences in the United States; fear that the Morgan efforts to help rehabilitate and stabilize Europe, from Dawes to the Young Plan to the BIS, had been for naught. The strident language deployed comported with the firm's instinctive anti-German posture. Morgan Grenfell, while acknowledging that the cable represented the views of all the Morgan partners, was moved to declare "we thought we traced the hand of Parker Gilbert."[43]

The London partners were correct: Parker Gilbert was the force behind this cable. With the complicity of Morrow, Parker Gilbert was telling Mills and Hoover in mid-July 1931 that reparation was a European problem, not an American one. The solution to the German financial crisis, Parker Gilbert posited, was to accept that no new American loans would go to Germany. American policy should be to tell the Europeans to get their own house in order, given that it had been the Germans who had destroyed their own credit. The appeal of this line of reasoning to Hoover, whose mind was tracking toward the conviction that the Depression had arisen in Europe, was undeniable.[44] While the White House might find a scapegoat in Germany, there were risks for J.P. Morgan & Co. The Morgan partners did not want an embittered Germany to renounce the Dawes and Young Plan loans.

The willingness of the Morgan partners to be swayed by Parker Gilbert owed much to their identification with the wartime triumvirate of Britain, France, and the United States. When Herbert was asked to sit on a committee composed largely of accepting houses and clearing banks in the City with outstanding commitments in Germany, he declined, to

---

[42] Grenfell to J.P. Morgan & Co., 10 July 1931; Jack Morgan to Grenfell, 11 July 1931, both in TML, CP, Box 19, folder Morgan & Co. Misc. Priv. Telegs 1 July to 28 October 1931.

[43] Grenfell to Lamont, 18 July 1931, BL, TWL, Series II, Box 111, Folder 23.

[44] Parker Gilbert to Morrow, 20 July 1931, AC, DM, Series I, Box 24, Folder 12; Parker Gilbert to Morrow memo, 21 July 1931, AC, DM, Series I, Box 24, Folder 12. This memo was sent to Mills. A copy is in LC, OLM, Box 9, 1931 Folder. For the continuing belief of Mills in Parker Gilbert as a counsellor, see Mills to Parker Gilbert, 1 October 1931, LC, OM, Box 9, 1931 Folder.

the relief of the Morgan partners in New York. As Whigham, who was in New York, told Grenfell on 14 July, "They feel strongly that none of the Morgan Houses should be dragged into a position involving responsibility for dealing with the German situation."[45] If the Morgan firms became entangled, there was every chance that J.P. Morgan & Co. would run afoul of one or more of London, Paris, and Washington. The Morgan partners were well aware that the three ex-Allies had differences on the German financial crisis. Too much involvement might result in alienation. J.P. Morgan & Co. policy in the Austrian and German crises was not to offend Britain, France, or the United States, while simultaneously attempting to secure continued compliance by Berlin with the Dawes and Young Plans. Success was unlikely but there was no real choice, for, while German failure to service the Dawes and Young Plan loans would hurt J.P. Morgan & Co., a divorce from Paris, London, or Washington would be unthinkable.

The hardship of the balancing act was demonstrated in mid-July. On Sunday 12 July a conference was held at the FRBNY. Those present – including Mills, Parker Gilbert, Leffingwell, and Burgess – knew that the Darmstädter Bank was not going to open Monday morning. How, if at all, should the United States respond? Meyer, who had not been invited to the meeting and had learned about it inadvertently from Lamont, joined the gathering in progress. Hoover, who was at Rapidan Camp, was consulted by phone. Under consideration was whether Washington should issue a statement expressing sympathy with the German situation. Most present were in favour of expression of support for the Germans. Parker Gilbert, however, was opposed on the grounds that it would represent an open-ended "moral commitment." Meyer agreed with Parker Gilbert. An annoyed Hoover, who had been inclined to side with the majority position, conceded in a huff.[46]

Days later the House of Morgan became enmeshed in a spat within the Hoover administration between Stimson and Hoover and, overlaying it, a dispute with France regarding the German financial crisis.[47] At issue was a hastily scheduled conference in London called to discuss German

---

[45] Whigham to Grenfell, 14 July 1931, TML, CP, Box 19, Folder Morgan & Co. Misc. Priv. Telegs 1 July to 28 October 1931.

[46] Eugene Meyer interview, 10 June 1952, CUL, COHC, Eugene Meyer, pp. 592–97.

[47] Wilson, *American Business*, p. 141, has treated this episode on its face, namely, that Hoover and Stimson were furious with J.P. Morgan & Co. Boyce, *The Great Interwar Crisis*, pp. 312–13, has suggested that not only did it reveal the hostility between Hoover and the Morgan firm but crucially it displayed a schism between Stimson and Hoover. Stimson, in Boyce's view, feared that Morgan action would ruin Franco-German concord, while Hoover worried that Morgan action might promote Franco-German amity and drag Washington into supporting Paris.

financial woes. Stimson and Mellon were in Europe, though it was the
former who took the lead, as Mellon, while still nominally the secretary of
the Treasury, had been supplanted by his undersecretary, Mills. The
Morgan partners in New York were bemused as to the point of the
London conference. They could not see any justification for it should
the aim be to reel American financial institutions into making loans to
Germany. As J.P. Morgan & Co. told Grenfell on 15 July, "our banks are
loaded up with short-term German paper" and "America has done her
bit." Correcting Germany's problems, the Morgan partners said, was
Europe's challenge, views that were reiterated in a subsequent cable to
London on 17 July. For his part, Grenfell agreed; he could not see what
the conference was likely to accomplish. Dashed expectations were the
likely outcome.[48] Lamont met with Hoover on 15 July and it is hard to
believe that he had not made this stance crystal clear. Certainly, if Lamont
did not do so on the 15th, he did on 18 July following a contretemps in
Paris involving Dean Jay of Morgan & Cie., Stimson, the Bank of France,
and Pierre-Étienne Flandin, the minister of finance in Laval's
government.

Dean Jay had been cabled J.P. Morgan & Co.'s assessment that there
was no prospect of raising money for Germany in the United States,
a message that he duly passed on to Governor Clément Moret of the
Bank of France. At dinner on 17 July Flandin asked Dean Jay about the
chances of a German loan, to which query Dean Jay furnished the unvar-
nished opinion of his New York partners – no loan was feasible. Later that
evening, at the residence of the American ambassador, Stimson, Flandin,
and Dean Jay conversed. Flandin told Stimson that there was no reason
for French participation in the upcoming London conference if an
American loan had been ruled out, as any plausible scheme was doomed
without it. Stimson, who had staked his hopes on the success of the
London conference, lambasted Lamont and Leffingwell who had written
the offending cable and dressed down Dean Jay for meddling in "unregu-
lated language." Stimson phoned Hoover and asked him to intercede
with Lamont to undo the damage that Stimson thought had been
wrought.[49] A phone call between Hoover and Lamont ensued, in which

[48] J.P. Morgan & Co. to Grenfell, 15 July 1931, TML, CP, Box 19, Folder Morgan & Co.
Misc. Priv. Telegs 1 July to 28 October 1931; J.P. Morgan & Co. to Morgan Grenfell,
17 July 1931, TML, CP, Box 19, Folder Morgan & Co. Misc. Priv. Telegs 1 July to
28 October 1931.
[49] Stimson's account of this episode may be found in Henry L. Stimson, 17 July 1931,
Memorandum by the Secretary of State of Conversations with M. Flandin and M. Jay,
Foreign Relations of the United States, [FRUS], 1931, General, Volume 1, https://history
.state.gov/historicaldocuments/frus1931v01/d229. Wilson, in *American Business*, p. 141,
argues that the Morgan partners bungled matters.

Lamont told Hoover that, while the bank was wholly behind his moratorium plan, "we ought not to fool ourselves on the investment phase of the situation."[50]

What the conference imbroglio revealed was the growing distance between Hoover and Stimson, the tension between J.P. Morgan & Co. and the Hoover administration, and how complicated reparations and war debts continued to be for Morgan partners desiring not to see friction among Britain, France, and the United States.[51] The London conference itself, held 20–23 July, was a damp squib, as the Morgan partners had forecast, with its only serious steps the renewal of the $100 million central bank credit to the Reichsbank and the sanctioning of what became the Wiggin Committee that was charged to examine the problem of short-term credits to Germany.[52] This outcome owed little to Morgan action, irrespective of what either Stimson or Hoover might have thought.[53] Late in July 1931 Lamont urged Hoover to make another effort to encourage French and German conversations. He told the president that without a European settlement on reparations American prosperity would remain elusive.[54]

Yet, in urging this course, it is apparent that Lamont failed to understand how traumatic the events that had begun with CreditAnstalt were. Young wrote Lamont, "I think your judgment and that of Parker Gilbert that Germany needed to be shaken down to help herself is turning out to be one hundred per cent correct." Frequently the Morgan partners voiced the conviction that a clearer day had dawned; late in June, early in July, and again at the end of July this was apparent. Lamont told Hoover "the storm seems to be dying down" and Grenfell that "the worst of our crises is over for the time being."[55] A more far-sighted assessment was furnished by Rist. Writing Leffingwell early in August, he warned that since

[50] J.P. Morgan & Co. to Morgan & Cie, 17 July 1931, BL, TWL, Series II, Box 110, Folder 12; Lamont to Hoover, 18 July 1931, BL, TWL, Series II, Box 98, Folder 19.
[51] On American diplomacy, see Robert H. Ferrell, *American Diplomacy in the Great Depression: Hoover-Stimson Foreign Policy, 1929–1933*, New Haven, CT: Yale University Press 1957; Margot Louria, *Triumph and Downfall: America's Pursuit of Peace and Prosperity, 1921–1933*, Westport, CT: Greenwood Press, 2001, pp. 172–79, has stressed the discord between Stimson and Hoover in the summer of 1931.
[52] Toniolo, *Central Bank Co-operation*, pp. 123–27. The Wiggin Report formalized the standstill agreements which maintained existing short-term credits to Germany.
[53] Bennett, *Germany and the Diplomacy of the Financial Crisis*, pp. 274–77.
[54] Lamont to Hoover, 27 July 1931, BL, TWL, Series II, Box 98, Folder 19.
[55] ODY to TWL, 3 August 1931, SLU, ODY, Box 28, Lamont, Thomas W., Folder 224. For examples, see Carter to Dean Jay, 26 June 1931, TML, MBEP, Series 5, Carter, Bernard S.; Leffingwell to de Sanchez, 2 July 1931, YUL, RCL, Series I, Box 1/29; Lamont to Hoover, 27 July 1931, BL, TWL, Series II, Box 98, Folder 19; Lamont to Hoover, 27 July 1931, BL, TWL, Series II, Box 98, Folder 19; Lamont to Grenfell, 31 July 1931, BL, TWL, Series II, Box 111, Folder 23. Underlining in the original.

Stresemann's death the "extreme nationalist elements have revived with limitless audacity ... No conciliation is possible with such elements ... which precipitated their own country and all Europe in the 1914 catastrophe." Rist dismissed the Red threat propagated by Sackett: "The Communist peril, about which Germany makes much ado, will always be, in Germany as in France, a mere phantom which the police can quiet whenever they wish. The only real peril to the peace of the world is nationalism, because at heart the majority of the German nation is prepared to follow the Nationalists if they win."[56] Leffingwell, in circulating this letter to his partners, underlined in double the last sentence. Morgan policy, however, insisted on German compliance with the Young and Dawes loans regardless of what the ramifications might be for German politics and for European stability.

*****

The toast by Ambassador Paul Claudel, upon the occasion of the Franco-American agreement on the Hoover moratorium in July, "To the crisis we have just avoided and to the catastrophe which will follow," displayed a surer understanding as German financial crisis was followed by British financial crisis.[57] The events that led to Britain's abandonment of the gold standard have attracted considerable attention. The contemporary legend of a "banker's ramp" attributed a central, villainous role to the Morgan partners who dictated the fate of a hapless, woebegone Labour government. Scholars have interred this myth which no longer commands notice.[58] Historians have depicted the summer of 1931 as either the apex of Morgan influence internationally, in which relations with the British government were especially intimate, or the ending of an interwar period in which private bankers played an unusually prominent part in international affairs.[59] While there is no doubt that the House of Morgan was integral to the unfolding of the sterling crisis, the most striking traits concerning the Morgan posture until the collapse of the Labour

---

[56] Rist to Leffingwell, 8 August 1931, YUL, RCL, Series I, Box 7, Folder 145.
[57] Cited in Bennett, *Germany and the Diplomacy of the Financial Crisis*, p. 177.
[58] A selected list includes Philip Williamson, "'A Banker's Ramp'? Financiers and the British Political Crisis of August 1931," *English Historical Review*, vol. 49 (1984), pp. 770–806; and his *National Crisis and National Government*, Cambridge: Cambridge University Press, 1992, pp. 255–426, which is the outstanding political account; Sayers, *The Bank of England*, vol. 2, pp. 387–415; Alec Cairncross and Barry Eichengreen, *Sterling in Decline*, Oxford: Basil Blackwell, 1983, pp. 27–110; Kunz, *The Battle*; Burk, *Morgan Grenfell*, pp. 146–56.
[59] Kunz, *The Battle*, p. 162; Burk, *Morgan Grenfell*, p. 146. For the argument that 1931 demarcates an end to private banker involvement in interwar international relations, see chap. 6 in Youssef Cassis and P.L. Cottrell eds., *Private Banking in Europe: Rise, Retreat and Resurgence*, Oxford: Oxford University Press, 2015.

government on 23 August are reactivity and an insistence on engaging France. J.P. Morgan & Co. responded to initiatives from London rather than instigated them, while the Morgan partners thought that reconstitution of the victorious wartime alliance would allow for the maintenance of the gold standard by Britain.

As early as mid-July the auguries were worrying. On 23 July Grenfell warned that the Bank of England had lost £20 million in gold "in the last few days." The bank rate had been raised by 1 per cent to 3.5 per cent. Grenfell told Jack Morgan, en route to London, that Norman wanted a long talk as soon as he arrived. The following day Grenfell cabled that the Bank of England had lost another £5 million in gold. The Bank of England gold reserve dropped from £164 million on 15 July to £132 million on 29 July. Upon landing, Jack Morgan met Norman with Grenfell and Whigham.[60] The talks left Jack Morgan feeling uneasy; Norman was not well, had fulminated about the lack of grip of government ministers, and had asked whether J.P. Morgan & Co. might arrange an American loan. Jack Morgan had told Norman that this would only be possible if the Labour government tabled a plan to move to a balanced budget. His New York partners were leery – in their view the timing was not propitious for a British loan. If the groundwork was begun, it might be possible to undertake an operation. Jack Morgan dismissed this idea, instructing his partners that they were not to raise the prospect of a British loan with other banks. While the New York partners restated their commitment to Britain and indicated that they thought the British financial position was "per se impregnable," their tone suggested otherwise.[61] Hesitancy may have been driven by their knowledge that the central bank credit talks were underway. Their conclusion seemed for a fleeting moment to redress British problems.

Expectation of improvement was ill-founded. Norman left the Bank of England at the end of July, having succumbed to the strain, and was replaced by Harvey.[62] This change did not alter the flow of information to Jack Morgan. As he put it, "they have ... taken me into rather secret councils." Jack Morgan was informed in the first week of August that the central bank credit had failed to stem the pressure on sterling. Privy to this

---

[60] Morgan Grenfell to J.P. Morgan & Co., 23 July 1931, Morgan Grenfell to J.P. Morgan & Co., 24 July 1931, Jack Morgan to Grenfell, 24 July 1931, TML, JPM, Box 38A/33, Cables Received and Sent by J.P. Morgan. For the decline in the Bank of England gold reserves, Sayers, *Bank of England*, vol. 3, appendix 37, "Gold and Foreign Exchange holdings, 1925–1931," p. 355.

[61] J.P. Morgan & Co. to Jack Morgan, 29 July 1931, Jack Morgan to J.P. Morgan & Co., 29 July 1931, J.P. Morgan & Co. to Jack Morgan, 30 July 1931, TML, JPM, Box 38 A/34, Cables exchanged while in London and Paris 1931.

[62] Clay, *Lord Norman*, p. 385.

information, Jack Morgan forwarded an analysis of the political and financial situation to his partners. The Labour government, "weak kneed and rather stupid," was handicapped by the inability of Snowden and MacDonald to control the party. To his son Harry, Jack Morgan confided that he thought that confidence could be restored quickly with "strong action" leading to a balanced budget, but "of course no one knows whether they have the guts to take such action." No help could be expected from Lloyd George and the Liberals, for, while Lloyd George grasped matters perfectly, he feared triggering an election that would result in the eradication of his party. With political will lacking, the projections of an increased budget deficit trumpeted in the May report were driving market apprehensions.[63] Undoubtedly there was more than a dash of Grenfell and perhaps a soupçon of Baldwin in this missive, for Jack Morgan had met with the Conservative leader before he went on holiday.

New York responded with two cables on 8 August, telling Jack Morgan that Harrison, on his own volition, but with the blessing of Harvey, had approached them about a British credit in New York. The partners were taken aback – this was scant days after the central bank credit had been opened. New York told Jack Morgan that they had made this point with Harrison, stressing that the chances of a loan were slim. Their advice to Harrison was that the way forward was through closer central bank cooperation. France needed to be consulted. Jack Morgan agreed. He told his partners that Grenfell understood the necessity of working with the Bank of France and the FRBNY, as did the Bank of England.[64]

Jack Morgan departed London for Scotland on 9 August. Between 8 August and 19 August there was no communication between Morgan Grenfell and J.P. Morgan & Co., though Grenfell did communicate with Jack Morgan sporadically. Grenfell continued to be engaged in the London discussions by virtue of his position on the Court of Directors and his standing as a Tory MP, though he did not participate in meetings attended by Cabinet ministers.[65] Harvey at the Bank of England, aided by allies in the City, maintained a steady drumbeat in favour of budget economies lest the gold standard be imperilled. MacDonald and Snowden were receptive, as were Conservative and Liberal politicians.

[63] Jack Morgan to Harry Morgan, 6 August 1931, TML, JPM, Box 38 A/34, Cables exchanged while in London and Paris 1931; Jack Morgan to Lamont, BL, TWL, Series II, Box 108, Folder 15.
[64] J.P. Morgan & Co. to Jack Morgan, 8 August 1931, Jack Morgan to J.P. Morgan & Co., 8 August 1931, TML, JPM, Box 38 A/34, Cables exchanged while in London and Paris 1931.
[65] Burk, *Morgan Grenfell*, p. 149.

Indeed, as Philip Williamson has noted, there was virtually no dissension in such circles with the proposition that being forced off gold would be a debacle.[66]

Correspondence resumed on 18 August when Grenfell wrote Jack Morgan a "Private and Confidential" letter. Grenfell expressed confidence in Harvey and his handling of government ministers. Grenfell stressed that he had been forthright in his talks with Tory ex-cabinet ministers, stipulating that any foreign loan must have a "very comprehensive" plan behind it. This had been transmitted, as anticipated, to MacDonald. The ball was now in his court. The following day, Grenfell cabled Jack Morgan. MacDonald, Grenfell said, had voiced his belief that if the government acted appropriately a loan would follow. Accordingly, Grenfell appended a proposed cable to J.P. Morgan & Co. in New York for Jack Morgan's approval. The cable asked New York whether a five- or ten-year borrowing might be possible if there was a "satisfactory announcement" on the budget. The response from New York demonstrated that caution ruled. Although the partners professed themselves "ready and anxious" to assist the government in any planned operation, the cable cast doubt on the feasibility of any operation until the government could show the market that it was capable of putting its own financial house in order. A long-term loan was dismissed as implausible, though if the government was prepared to wait until after Labour Day such an operation would have a greater chance. Wall Street, the Morgan partners signalled, was captivated by the gossip that the central bank credits were nearly exhausted. Their counsel was that the best means forward for the government was to take decisive action on the budget, let the market digest this news, and wait for sentiment regarding British credit to become more bullish. The partners also advised involving Paris, a theme that had been sounded repeatedly in their missives as the crisis mounted and which New York now pressed with greater urgency.[67]

While the New York partners had not pledged themselves to a short-term credit, they had allowed that they were willing to consider what might be possible. This non-committal sally was seized upon by the Bank of England and communicated to the Cabinet on 21 August in the company of a statement from the bank that its reserves to support sterling would be gone in four days.[68] The Cabinet was still grappling with

---

[66] Williamson, *National Crisis*, pp. 292–94.
[67] Grenfell to Jack Morgan, 18 August 1931, Grenfell to Jack Morgan, 19 August 1931, J.P. Morgan & Co. to Grenfell, 21 August 1931, Grenfell to Jack Morgan (private), 21 August 1931, TML, JPM, Box 38 A/34, Cables exchanged while in London and Paris 1931.
[68] Williamson, *National Crisis*, pp. 318–19.

retrenchment and had not agreed on the scope and scale of budget cuts. Grenfell confided in Jack Morgan that the political situation was becoming acute as the fissures within the Labour Party threatened to split the government. As Cabinet struggled, J.P. Morgan & Co. were informed on 22 August that Britain wanted a major loan next week. The Morgan partners displayed their surprise at the sum Britain hoped to obtain – $500 million. So "stupendous an amount" could only be obtained with the active cooperation of the French. J.P. Morgan & Co. was not sure how much might be raised in New York. They had been operating under the assumption, evidently a misapprehension, that any operation would take place in the fall and for a much lesser amount. Given the size of the contemplated loan, the Morgan partners insisted that "prior Parliamentary action," by which they meant approval of a stringent balanced budget, must be obtained. Agreement among the party leaders would not suffice. The partners warned that there were strong headwinds to be overcome: doubts about Europe in the United States, the Wiggin Committee report, the struggles of Germany, declines in the prices of the two German loans and the Austrian loans, as well as misgivings regarding British handling of the crisis. Reminding Grenfell that they had counselled against precipitate action consistently over the past weeks, the partners concluded "that a certain amount of time is necessary to educate our public and . . . any too urgent operation should be avoided."[69]

Confronted with an urgent plea for counsel, the partners gathered at Bartow's Long Island house on Sunday 23 August. Joined by Harrison for their deliberations, they did not diverge from points that they had been making for weeks: American investor sentiment was unpredictable and not prepared to support blithely a British loan; the chances of success were uncertain; France must participate if there was to be any hope; and the government must display a commitment to a balanced budget. Telephoned by Whitney to Grenfell on 23 August and communicated to the Cabinet, the message was enough to satisfy those Labour ministers who preferred the collapse of their government as an exit from a political cul-de-sac.[70]

The entry into office of the National Government on 24 August, with MacDonald and Snowden retaining their places as prime minister and chancellor of the exchequer respectively, was welcomed by J.P. Morgan & Co. As Jack Morgan told his son Harry Morgan, the formation of the new

[69] J.P. Morgan & Co. to Morgan Grenfell, 22 August 1931, TML, JPM, Box 38 A/34, Cables exchanged while in London and Paris 1931.
[70] Williamson, *National Crisis*, pp. 330–43; see Grenfell to Lamont, 27 August 1931, BL, TWL, Series II, Box 111, Folder 23.

ministry "makes a wonderful difference."[71] With American investor sentiment buoyant, the Morgan partners were anxious to move to market as quickly as possible for a British loan, capitalizing upon the favourable reaction to the change of government. Conducted hurriedly, the negotiations were a matter of triangular discussion among New York, Paris, and London. The structural advantage of the House of Morgan, with Morgan Grenfell in London and Morgan & Cie. in Paris, eased their conclusion. Morgan & Cie. played a notable, albeit understated, role. With Dean Jay absent, Carter coordinated phone calls and cables from Lamont and Whitney in New York, with Whigham in London, while communicating with various parties in Paris. Among them were S.D. Waley and H.A. Siepmann of the Bank of England, Leith-Ross from the Treasury, and on the French side Robert Lacour-Gayet and Moret of the Bank of France, as well as Flandin. Carter, well aware that his function was to act as a "liaison," did so admirably, reassuring his New York partners that the French were committed to aiding Britain and were acting as expeditiously as possible, while concurrently keeping the French informed.[72] Harrison supported the effort to forge a deal, employing Lacour-Gayet as an intermediary with Moret, leading Lamont to praise Harrison's role as "magnificent."[73] Reached on 28 August 1931 the loan took the form of a $200 million one-year credit from J.P. Morgan & Co. and a $200 million loan from France, divided into two $100 million tranches, one tranche furnished by a French banking syndicate, the other tranche a public issue of one-year Treasury bills on the Paris market.[74]

Residual uneasiness was apparent among the Morgan partners. Lamont, always sensitive to public opinion, voiced his uneasiness to Grenfell regarding Labour criticisms that he thought threatened fragile American investor confidence in Britain. Although Leffingwell told de Sanchez on 7 September that England was "strong and sound and rich" and that he "firmly believed" in Franco-American assistance, by mid-September his pessimism had returned with a vengeance. The occasion for its blossoming was the drafting of a memorandum by Parker Gilbert

[71] Jack Morgan to Harry Morgan, 25 August 1931, TML, JPM, Box 38 A/34, Cables exchanged while in London and Paris 1931.

[72] Carter drafted daily memoranda on his activities for his partner Dean Jay, who was holidaying at Cap d'Antibes. These memoranda are in the Dean Jay papers at Knox College.

[73] Lamont to Jack Morgan, 28 August 1931, TML, JPM, Box 38 A/35.1 – Cable book 4 January 1926 to 31 December 1931. Lacour-Gayet was well known in American financial circles, having served as the financial attaché at the French embassy from 1924 to 1930. He was thought of highly by Harrison and Leffingwell, though Grenfell took a dimmer view.

[74] The $100 million Treasury bill issue placed in Paris did not occur until 10 September 1931.

on 14 September that suggested pushing for a reform of British war debts owed to the United States through a revision of the Mellon–Baldwin agreement. Parker Gilbert argued that doing so would not only help relieve the pressure on sterling but might produce a welcome alteration in British policy on reparations. Since the Balfour Note Britain had supported Germany against France, Parker Gilbert claimed, and in so doing had undermined the Dawes and Young Plans. He told Lamont that Mellon would welcome a proposal in this direction. Undoubtedly, Parker Gilbert, Lamont, and Leffingwell were aware that the newly approved British government credit was being drawn down rapidly in defence of sterling.[75] Leffingwell's reply was emphatic. He dismissed war debt relief as likely to lead to "disaster." If Lamont bemoaned the "silly pessimism" engulfing Wall Street, Leffingwell was among these pessimists, and with reason, for the moment of decision had come in London.[76] The Bank of England decided on 18 September that the gold standard must be sacrificed. A public announcement was made on 20 September 1931.

*****

A glum *Commercial and Financial Chronicle* labelled sterling's departure from gold "one of the catastrophic events of the century, sure to be attended by a long train of ill consequences."[77] For the Morgan partners, consequences were apparent immediately. On 21 September the Associated Press published an interview with Jack Morgan in London. Jack Morgan described sterling's departure from gold as "the second necessary stage in the work of the National Government, the first being the balancing of the budget."[78] Chernow has argued that Lamont, angered by the implication that leaving gold was a deliberate policy decision, attacked Jack Morgan for failing to appreciate the damage the affair had inflicted on J.P. Morgan & Co.'s prestige and reputation. According to Chernow, Lamont's letter of 25 September, which was co-signed by Charles Steele, amounted to a "palace revolution" which "marks the moment when the House of Morgan ceased operating as a family bank."[79] This goes too far. Unquestionably there was rancour and recrimination, but the letter did not reach Jack Morgan until

[75] Kunz, *The Battle*, p. 126, notes that as early as 7 September J.P. Morgan & Co. had expressed alarm that 40 per cent of the credit had been drawn down.
[76] Leffingwell to Parker Gilbert, 15 September 1931, YUL, RCL, Series I, Box 3/63; Lamont to de Sanchez, 17 September 1931, BL, TWL, Series II, Box 91, Folder 17.
[77] *Commercial and Financial Chronicle*, vol. 133, no. 3457, 26 September 1931, p. 1961.
[78] "Morgan holds Gold Decision A 'Hopeful Event'; Calls Step a Stage toward revival of Trade," *New York Times*, 22 September 1931, p. 1.
[79] Chernow, *The House of Morgan*, pp. 334–36. For the letter, Lamont to Jack Morgan, 25 September 1931, BL, TWL, Series II, Box 108/15.

sometime after 1 October by which date there had been cables and phone calls that rendered the letter's impact nugatory. It is not clear when Jack Morgan received the letter, nor is it certain that he ever read it.

On 29–30 September 1931 there was an exchange between the Morgan partners in New York and Jack Morgan. The long cable (eight pages) from New York on 29 September was prompted by fears that London was contemplating mobilizing British holdings of American securities, a notion that had been raised prior to 18 September. The prospect frightened New York, who argued it would spark greater flight from sterling while playing into the hands of the "Socialists." The Morgan partners believed that internal speculation against sterling, driven by worries about Labour's policies, had occasioned the abandonment of gold. Policy blunders committed by the Bank of England and the Treasury had exacerbated the problem, resulting in the frittering away of hundreds of millions of dollars in futile defence of sterling. Why, the Morgan partners asked, had London opted to peg sterling? Why was the bank rate not raised to combat speculation?[80] Looking ahead, it was critical to avoid any more mistakes to allow confidence in British financial management to recuperate. The key, the Morgan partners thought, was to restore budgetary and economic equilibrium at home that would allow British industry to be competitive globally. Advancing this counsel, the New York partners stressed that Jack Morgan and the Morgan Grenfell partners should not infer any criticism of their actions. The Morgan partners in New York insisted that they were aware that neither Jack Morgan nor Morgan Grenfell could have "changed the course of past events. We have from start to finish quite realized that the management of the credit lay entirely outside your hands." Jack Morgan's continued presence in London "can be of very great value in presenting a sound and detached judgment as to the kind of policy towards which the British should now be directing themselves."[81]

Jack Morgan responded on 30 September. He dismissed concerns about the mobilization of securities as purely a theoretical exercise engaged in by the Treasury. There was no reason to worry on this count. Reflecting on the choices made by London during the crisis, he confessed, "I am not sure that the time has yet come to discuss the details

[80] An exchange of letters between H.A. Siepmann of the Bank of England and Francis Rodd on 20 October and 23 October 1931 makes it clear that the Bank of England was alive to the criticism lodged against its handling of the sterling crisis. DB, Morgan Grenfell papers, Box 50592324, Correspondence with H.A. Siepmann. Rodd was at this juncture with the BIS. He joined Morgan Grenfell in 1933.

[81] J.P. Morgan & Co. to Jack Morgan and Morgan Grenfell, 29 September 1931, TML, JPM, Box 38 A/34, Cables exchanged while in London and Paris 1931.

of or the reasons for past decisions. They were taken with the best judgment available and have turned out in some glaring instances to have been mistakes which everyone regrets." As for restoring confidence, Jack Morgan thought that the looming British general election would be decisive. The City feared that until it was held on 27 October the government would drift, making planning "impossible." Typically, he encouraged his partners, noting that their suggestions were welcome and that they should continue to make them.[82] The relief in New York was palpable: "We cannot thank you and London Partners sufficiently for your tolerant reception of our cable."[83] That day Lamont telephoned Jack Morgan to press the point home, telling him that the letter of 25 September was not a criticism: "Mr. J.P.M. said he had not as yet received the letter, but that he would understand it in exactly that sense."[84]

After the shockwaves passed, the partners concentrated on assisting the Bank of England and the Treasury until the British general election resolved the political situation. The pressing issue was managing sterling on the foreign exchange markets. Spurred by a complaint from International General Electric in New York that they were having trouble obtaining sterling, the New York partners cabled Jack Morgan that this might be an opportunity for the Treasury to gather dollars and francs which would allow it to "regain its independence in this and Paris market because it would acquire the ammunition with which to set up a future defence of the pound in those two markets." A supplementary cable asked Jack Morgan to push London to be open-minded about intervening in the exchange markets and to give J.P. Morgan & Co. broad discretion to act secretly on Treasury behalf.[85] The Bank of England had already been contemplating what might be done, aware of the dangers of failing to restore equilibrium in foreign exchange markets, not the least of which was inflation. Sir Robert Kindersley's Foreign Exchange Committee, benefiting from Norman's loss of power within the bank, had taken initial steps.[86] Jack Morgan, independent of his New York partners, reached agreement with Kindersley on 3 October. J.P. Morgan & Co. was

---

[82] Jack Morgan to J.P. Morgan & Co., 30 September 1931, TML, JPM, Box 38 A/34, Cables exchanged while in London and Paris 1931.

[83] J.P. Morgan & Co. to Jack Morgan, 1 October 1931, TML, JPM, Box 38 A/34, Cables exchanged while in London and Paris 1931.

[84] Lamont note, 1 October 1931, BL, TWL, Series II, Box 108/15. Lamont's unease about this episode lingered for months. See a memo to Jack Morgan of 30 March 1932, BL, TWL, Series II, Box 108, Folder 15.

[85] Both cables, J.P. Morgan & Co. to Jack Morgan, 2 October 1931, TML, JPM, Box 38 A/34, Cables exchanged while in London and Paris 1931.

[86] Sayers, The Bank of England, vol. 2, pp. 417–20.

authorized to act for either the Bank of England or the Treasury "in connection with sterling exchange in the New York market, with the idea of accumulating a sum of dollars for future use in maintaining an orderly market." Such action was to be at Morgan "discretion" in the forward and spot markets. Kindersley would receive daily reports. The accumulated dollar balances in the United States would be placed on deposit with the FRBNY in credit of the Bank of England. J.P. Morgan & Co. would make payments in London through Morgan Grenfell. The letter stipulated that the Treasury did not want J.P. Morgan to buy below a rate of "about 3.90." Jack Morgan agreed that the bank would do this without commission for three months, when the issue would be revisited.[87] His New York partners protested plaintively, for they had had not been kept abreast by Jack Morgan and had hoped for a broader mandate. New York wanted to act in the Paris and London exchange markets as well, a desire that Jack Morgan, backed by Cochran and Harry Morgan who were also in London, quashed firmly.[88]

Vindication for Jack Morgan came with the general election results on 27 October. The National Government was returned with a commanding majority, holding 554 of the 694 seats in Parliament. Baldwin's Conservatives gained more than 200 seats to boost Tory numbers to 470. Labour was obliterated, falling to forty-six seats under Arthur Henderson. The Morgan Grenfell partners were "dumbfounded." Lavish thanks were bestowed on their New York partners for their help "in all our troubles since 1914." The response from New York a day later was equally magnanimous, insisting that the "laurels" belonged to Morgan Grenfell: "We have never been prouder than now of our association with Great Britain nor prouder of the spirit and work of our London partners these last few months." In the same triumphal, ecstatic vein, Jack Morgan despatched a private cable to his New York partners, lauding the common sense of the British working man. Lamont was jubilant, expressing his delight at the "tremendous step forward" at the demonstration "that Great Britain was right" and "that our faith were justified."[89]

---

[87] Jack Morgan to Sir Robert Kindersley, 3 October 1931, TML, JPM, Box 44, Folder 8.

[88] J.P. Morgan & Co. to Jack Morgan and Thomas Cochran, 7 October 1931, Jack Morgan, Thomas Cochran, and Harry Morgan to J.P. Morgan & Co., 19 October 1931, TML, JPM, Box 38 A/34, Cables exchanged while in London and Paris 1931. J.P. Morgan & Co. proceeded as discussed.

[89] ECG and London Partners to New York partners, 28 October 1931, J.P. Morgan & Co. to Morgan Grenfell, 29 October 1931, TML, CP, Box 19, Folder Morgan & Co. Misc. Priv. Telegs 1 July to 28 October 1931; Jack Morgan to J.P. Morgan & Co., 28 October 1931, TML, JPM, Box 38 A/34, Cables exchanged while in London and Paris 1931; Lamont to Jack Morgan, 30 October 1931, BL, TWL, Series II, Box 10/15.

While the election results eased the minds of the Morgan partners, there was no ignoring that circumstances had changed. Sterling's departure from gold occasioned two developments in the United States: a massive outflow of gold in the six weeks after 21 September, amounting to $730 million of which approximately $350 million was for French account; driven by this, a rise in rates in an effort to stem the outward flow of gold. FRBNY discount rates that stood at 1.5 per cent on 26 September had reached 3.5 per cent on 17 October.[90] Capital flight promoted, and was fuelled by, whispers that the United States might also leave the gold standard as rumours swirled in London and in Paris about the stability of leading American banks. Chase National, National City, and Guaranty Trust were the subject of intense speculation as to their soundness, rumblings that reached Stimson and Mills.[91] A coordinated campaign was orchestrated by Harrison, Lamont, and Jack Morgan to counter these rumours. Harrison spoke directly with Norman and Harvey of the Bank of England and separately with the BIS to reassure them the gossip was baseless. In London Jack Morgan delegated Grenfell to meet with the heads of the major British banks to quell doubts, which occurred on 3 October. Several days later Jack Morgan journeyed to Paris with Cochran and, in the company of Dean Jay, met with Barons Edouard and Robert de Rothschild. Jack Morgan told the French bankers that rumours of vulnerability among the leading American banks were unfounded.[92]

Jack Morgan's trip to Paris had another purpose. Laval was scheduled to visit Washington in October and the Morgan partners were determined that it be successful. Jack Morgan met Laval shortly before the latter left for the United States. Heartened by the news that Rist was accompanying Laval, Jack Morgan suggested that Laval make a brief visit with the Morgan partners in New York. Underlying this invitation were doubts about Hoover, the state of Franco-American relations, and shifting

---

[90] For gold flows, see *Federal Reserve Bulletin*, November 1931, vol. 17, no. 11, p. 603 and p. 609, table "Gold Movements to and From United States," https://fraser.stlouisfed.org/title/federal-reserve-bulletin-62/november-1931-20720. Of this $730 million, $415 million was not exported but earmarked for the account of foreign central banks held in the FRBNY. On interest rate increases, Meltzer, A *History of the Federal Reserve*, p. 346, table 5.14.

[91] Dawes to Stimson, 8 October 1931, CUL, GH, Box 50, Mills, Ogden.

[92] J.P. Morgan & Co. to Jack Morgan, 2 October 1931, TML, JPM, Box 38 A/34, Cables exchanged while in London and Paris 1931; Harrison record of phone conversation with Norman and Harvey, 2 October 1931 HH, HHPL, FRBNY papers, Box 3/3115.2, Norman, Montagu 1931; Harrison to BIS on 2 October 1931, CUL, Harrison papers, Box 1, Binder 2; Jack Morgan to J.P. Morgan & Co., 3 October 1931, TML, JPM, Box 38 A/34, Cables exchanged while in London and Paris 1931; J.P. Morgan & Co to Jack Morgan 8 October 1931, Jack Morgan to J.P. Morgan & Co., 8 October 1931, TML, JPM, Box 38 A/34, Cables exchanged while in London and Paris 1931.

Morgan appreciations about France. The Morgan partners faulted Hoover for his handling of the moratorium vis-à-vis France. They were unconvinced of his fitness as a diplomat. Leffingwell, in characteristic prose, told Lamont in mid-October that "The President's technique of dominating men by exciting their terror and magnifying the disaster which he intends to avert has pretty well undermined the morale of some leaders of finance and politics at home." He worried that Hoover would speak in similar tones to Laval, guaranteeing disaster. Leffingwell suggested that Parker Gilbert talk with Mills, Harrison, and Meyer to get "the leopard to change his spots," though he conceded that it was more likely that "the reign of terror will continue until March 4, 1933."[93] Jack Morgan, in alliance with Robert Masson, the director-general and guiding spirit of the French bank Crédit Lyonnais, proposed through Walter Edge, the American ambassador, that Laval and Hoover issue a joint communiqué pledging France and the United States would uphold the gold standard.[94]

Underpinning these negative assessments of Hoover as diplomat lay a conviction that the balance of power in Western Europe had shifted. Leffingwell stressed by early September "the dominant political and financial position France has re-won in Europe."[95] A month later, he declaimed,

France by accident or design has become the dominant power in Europe, politically, economically, financially, and in a military sense ... Such an immense reversal of fortune in so short a period is bewildering. The English haven't recognized it. The Americans haven't recognized it. The Germans don't want to recognize it. Even the French, far from recognizing it, are still governed by a fear of invasion and a sense of inferiority acquired during their bitter years when their best provinces were occupied by the Germans and the later years when their currency and credit were fading away. If the French will believe in themselves and act boldly, self-confidently, and generously, as befits their immense power of today, all will soon be well. But the possession of over-whelming wealth and power by a nation which is ridden by fear and a sense of inferiority or inadequacy is likely to make trouble.[96]

While Carter in Paris deemed Leffingwell's analysis "exaggerated," it was seized upon by Lamont. Aware through Parker Gilbert that the Jack Morgan and Masson suggestion for a joint declaration on the inviolability of the gold standard had been rejected by the State Department as unwise

[93] Leffingwell to Lamont, 15 October 1931, YUL, RCL, Series I, Box 4, Folder 95.
[94] Walter Edge to Stimson, 19 October 1931, HHPL, HH, Subject Files, Box 186, Financial Matters Gold and Silver Correspondence August to December 1931.
[95] Leffingwell to De Sanchez, 7 September 1931, YUL, RCL, Series I, Box 1/29.
[96] Leffingwell to De Sanchez, 2 October 1931, YUL, RCL, Series I, Box 1/29.

and likely to excite British resentment, Lamont sought to impress upon Hoover the necessity of continued American engagement with France, arguing that only with active French cooperation was it possible to settle European problems.[97] A memorandum drafted by Lamont on 20 October recommended how the president should treat with Laval. Included were Leffingwell's words concerning France's new-found hegemony. Lamont suggested Hoover should give Laval "complete reassurance" that the United States intended to remain on gold because the French had been shocked profoundly by the British decision to leave the gold standard, suffering heavy financial losses as a consequence. Lamont stressed French strength and French fragility; without delicate handling and a thoroughgoing understanding of their situation, progress on issues such as war debts, reparations, and the Polish Corridor would be impossible.[98]

Hoover was disinclined to take lessons in diplomacy from Lamont. The sudden death of Morrow on 5 October had removed an intermediary between the White House and J.P. Morgan & Co. Egan, sent by Lamont to present the memorandum to Hoover, reported that, while Hoover read it carefully, the president's initial concurrence with what Lamont had written had given way rapidly to a darker tone. Hoover told Egan that he had not invited Laval and that the French government through the Bank of France and the French press had connived to attack the American dollar. Hoover agreed that France controlled future developments in Europe, but his own room to manoeuvre was circumscribed tightly by Congress. Egan's sally stressing the importance of common cause on maintaining the gold standard was, discouragingly, rebuffed. Overall, Egan concluded, "[h]e gave me the impression of a terribly tired and terribly harassed man without much patience or tact or finesse."[99] Lippmann, furnished by Lamont with both the memorandum and Egan's report, had a different reaction. Hoover, he told Lamont, following a conversation with Stimson, had been furious at Lamont's unsought advice but had now gotten over his "wrath."[100]

The Hoover–Laval talks, from 22 to 25 October, covered a range of topics, from disarmament, to the Polish Corridor, to Franco-German

[97] Elliot A. Rosen, *Hoover, Roosevelt and the Brains Trust*, New York: Columbia University Press, 1977, pp. 81–84, suggests that the discussions on 19 October set the template for the American posture in discussions on international economic relations through the Lausanne Conference in the summer of 1932.

[98] Lamont to Hoover, 20 October 1931, BL, TWL, Series II, Box 98/19.

[99] Egan to Lamont, 21 October 1931, BL, TWL, Series II, Box 98/19. The Egan visit is not in the Hoover calendar. It took place on either 20 or 21 October.

[100] Lamont to Lippmann, 22 October 1931, Lippmann to Lamont, 23 October 1931, BL, TWL, Series II, Box 104, Folder 29.

relations, to war debts and reparations. While Leffingwell thought that "real progress" was made even if it was regrettable that the French had resorted to the "obsolete Young Plan" and Lamont told Jack Morgan that "the feeling was excellent" between Hoover and Laval, in truth little concrete followed.[101] There remained sharp divergences of opinion on disarmament, with Laval insisting on the continued French need for security from a resurgent Germany, while alteration to the territorial provisions of the Treaty of Versailles was also ruled out. Laval asserted that, while he was open to reparations relief for Germany, it must be undertaken through the Young Plan mechanism. For his part, Hoover was cagy, agreeing to consider the possibility of war debt revision but with the proviso that any movement in this direction was subject to the sanction of Congress, which Hoover knew would not be forthcoming.[102]

The administration's wariness at being identified explicitly with Wall Street was demonstrated anew as Luther manoeuvred to obtain permanent concessions on reparations via the Young Plan mechanism. Fraser cabled Harrison that the BIS wanted him to suggest an American delegate to the Special Advisory committee being constituted in response to the German request. This cable crossed with a telegram from Moret to Harrison. Moret told Harrison that the American delegate chosen needed to be someone familiar with Europe. Parker Gilbert's name had arisen in conversations between Dean Jay and Flandin. Moret was enthusiastic about Parker Gilbert's candidacy, knowing the latter's views on France and Germany. Harrison, who consulted with Stimson, Mellon, and Meyer, was less taken. The conferees agreed that neither J.P. Morgan & Co. nor National City should name the delegate. Following these conversations Stimson briefed Hoover. The president was inclined to leave the decision to Harrison. Hoover and Harrison discussed the matter directly, with Hoover stipulating that no banker favouring cancellation of war debts should be considered, while Harrison thought it advisable that it not be a New York banker. Both provisos ruled out a J.P. Morgan & Co. partner. Parker Gilbert's name was dropped.[103]

[101] Leffingwell to de Sanchez, 28 October 1931, YUL, RCL, Series I, Box 1/29; Lamont to Jack 30 October 1931, BL, TWL, Series II, Box 10/15.

[102] On the talks, see Costigliola, *Awkward Dominion*, pp. 246–48; Henry Blumenthal, *Illusion and Reality in Franco-American Diplomacy 1914–1945*, Baton Rouge, LA: Louisiana State University Press, 1986, pp. 157–58; Rosen, *Hoover, Roosevelt*, pp. 84–86.

[103] Walter W. Stewart was named the American delegate. Stewart was an economist who had advised Coolidge and Hoover along with working with the Bank of England from 1928 to 1930. For the Special Advisory Committee (also known as the Beneduce Committee after its Italian chair), Toniolo, *Central Bank Cooperation*, pp. 127–31; Moret to Harrison, 18 November 1931, CUL, GH, Box 14, Binder 29; for conversations with Stimson, Mellon, Meyer, and Hoover, 18 and 19 November 1931, CUL, GH, Box 21, Binder 45.

As 1931 drew to a close, the interconnections between war debts, the Hoover moratorium, and economic recovery were thrown into stark relief. Late in November 1931 Morgan Grenfell cabled J.P. Morgan & Co. that Norman had raised the prospect of Austria and Hungary defaulting on their public debt. The reaction was horror in New York. Analysing matters, the Morgan partners attributed this possibility to a rigid adherence to the gold standard and to the imposition of severe foreign exchange controls that had choked off the supply of exchange required to meet external obligations. In their view "the gold standard is only a means to an end, the end of making payment in stable money." The contradiction of attempting to stay on gold while declining to meet contracted obligations was apparent. After this missive, which drew a soothing reply from Whigham in London, there followed a longer disquisition from New York.[104]

Its central tenet was straightforward: "These views all concentrate on a single thought namely that all hope for the future depends upon the restoration of faith in paper promises." This faith has been "shaken to its foundations" by fear of defaults. The "policy of a partial moratorium" was "almost equally disastrous." How should confidence be restored? According to the Morgan partners, a series of palliative steps would go far. First, the harm occasioned by the advent of the standstill agreements reached in August 1931 needed undoing, for "[t]his was a blow at the basis of private international credit from which the world will be long in recovering and all the Governments share the blame for it."[105] The Wiggin Committee report had needlessly tied reparations and private debts together, further exacerbating difficulties; while specific failings, such as Baldwin's myopia to French security concerns, and Hoover's bungled handling of his moratorium proposal, had alienated Paris to the detriment of international cooperation. Skilful, patient diplomacy that took in account the critical role of France would pay dividends. With respect to Germany, Austria, and Hungary, J.P. Morgan & Co. was insistent that they must continue to service their loans, the Dawes and Young Plan loans as well as the first and second Austrian and Hungarian loans contracted through the assistance of the League of Nations. They stressed that the Austrian and Hungarian default proposal was

---

[104] Morgan Grenfell to J.P. Morgan & Co., 27 November 1931, J.P. Morgan & Co. to Morgan Grenfell, 28 November 1931, Whigham to J.P. Morgan & Co., 28 November 1931, all TML, CP, Box 19, Misc Priv Telegs 23 November 1931 to 22 March 1932.

[105] The First Standstill agreement was agreed on 19 August 1931. It preserved outstanding acceptances, deposits, and cash advances made by foreign bankers, chief among them American, British, and French institutions, to Germany. See Sayers, *The Bank of England*, vol. 2, pp. 503–12.

"overwhelming in its importance," for "[w]e cannot say with too much emphasis or too often that to our minds the whole business of reconstructing the world again depends upon maintaining what little faith men have left in the promises of Governments made to private lenders."[106]

Grenfell and Whigham, in concert with Norman and Sir Otto Niemeyer, sought to assuage New York's fears. They emphasized that, while they thought it likely that Hungary would default in the coming months, there was a chance that it would not do so on the League-sponsored loan, while the Austrian situation was looking better. The League of Nations and the Bank of England were doing what they could to stave off default. Depression was the chief culprit in fostering tariff wars that had crippled these states. Niemeyer believed that a visceral dread of inflation rooted in the memories of the postwar upheavals was impelling Vienna and Budapest to avoid the social and political trauma associated with those years, which explained their desire to cling to a "crippled and nominal gold standard." As for the standstill agreements and the Wiggin Report, London dismissed them as "matters of history," reassuring New York that through continued application and hard work relief would come. Though the Morgan partners were not wholly calmed by this cable, they were appeased, and while they pressed their message of the inviolability of private credit throughout December, the worry apparent early in the month receded.

In this exchange may be seen the Morgan conception of capitalist prosperity – it rested ultimately on private trust, private obligations, and faith in contracts – which had been strained to the breaking point by the events of 1931. The gold standard was nothing more than the expression of this fundament. From the Morgan perspective the standstill agreements and their ilk, far from fending off crisis, had worsened it. If there was uncertainty at the opening of the year at 23 Wall Street as to whether capitalism was in crisis, by the end of 1931 this was no longer in doubt. Equally, J.P. Morgan & Co. was not prepared to acquiesce meekly in the destruction of a liberal, capitalist multilateral order. Ultimately, as the cable hinted, the gold standard was dispensable if other means could be found to uphold the sanctity of private contracts. Here may be seen the Morgan apostasy on gold that was to lead the partners in 1933 to acknowledge that remaining on gold was inimical to the greater task of saving capitalism from depression.

*****

While the threat of Austrian and Hungarian default transfixed the Morgan partners, in the United States the ongoing political struggle

---

[106] J.P. Morgan & Co. to Morgan Grenfell, 30 November 1931, TML, CP, Box 19, Misc Priv Telegs 23 November 1931 to 22 March 1932.

over the Hoover moratorium was reaching a climax. Since the announcement of the moratorium in June, congressional opposition, especially in
the House of Representatives, had been growing. Laval's visit in October
sparked rumours that a deal linking together reparations and the cancellation of war debts either was in the offing or had been struck. Many
congressmen were suspicious of the administration and disinclined to
sanction passage of the moratorium. Among them was McFadden,
whose rhetoric against Hoover and the moratorium indulged in new
paroxysms. More damagingly, the House Ways and Means Committee,
in approving the moratorium, attached a declaration to its agreement
forbidding the abrogation of Europe's war debts to the United States.
The White House was unable to secure revocation of this amendment.
The House approved the moratorium on the evening of 18 December
with this rider.[107] That day, Lamont testified to the Senate Committee on
Finance.

The Senate Finance Committee hearings on the Sale of Foreign Bonds
or Securities in the United States in December 1931 were instigated by
Senator Hiram Johnson of California. Johnson was not a member of the
committee, but he was an ardent opponent of Hoover and of J.P. Morgan
& Co. Johnson was a cantankerous progressive Republican. His contempt
for "God," as he derisively labelled the president in 1929, devolved
rapidly into assessments of Hoover as "the prince of bunk artists" and
a man who is "inept and untrustworthy and without real capacity."[108] His
views on J.P. Morgan & Co. conformed closely to Money Trust certain-
ties. For Johnson, 23 Wall Street ran American foreign relations and had
done so since the war. In cooperation with the "Hughes family and the
Root office" J.P. Morgan & Co. "govern us in our domestic as well as in
our international policies." For Johnson, the Hoover moratorium, as he
told his sons, was an opportunity to publicize Morgan dominance.
Johnson knew that blocking passage of the moratorium in the Senate
was impossible, but he could prod his Senate colleagues to examine the
role of bankers in American life. If the aim was to discomfit J.P. Morgan &
Co., then it failed, for Lamont's testimony on 18 December was practised
and smooth, as he fielded questions from the committee, including
Johnson, who was afforded the privilege of participating in the questioning, with ease. A distraught Felix Frankfurter raged to Herbert Feis, the
economic advisor to the State Department, "Those poor boobs on the

[107] This paragraph follows the discussion in Schwarz, *The Interregnum*, pp. 81–87.
[108] Hiram Johnson to Jack and Archibald Johnson Jr. (his sons), 26 October 1929; Hiram
Johnson to Jack Johnson, 23 November 1929, Hiram Johnson to his sons,
11 December 1932, all in volume 5 of Robert E. Burk, ed., *The Diary Letters of Hiram
Johnson, 1917–1945*, 7 vols., New York: Garland Publishing, 1983.

Senate Committee don't know enough to examine Tom Lamont and Mitchell. Nothing makes me sicker than that these incompetent leaders of finance should still swagger around as though they were entitled to respect."[109] Frankfurter's ire was mirrored by Johnson, who emerged from the hearings more convinced than ever that leading bankers were corrupt, despoiling the American people, and that his Senate colleagues were terrified of confrontation. "Our people," he wrote, "have been soaked unmercifully for the profit of these international bankers."[110]

The December 1931 hearings, uneventful as they seemed to the Morgan partners, were a harbinger not just of future, more invasive examinations of the bank and its practices but also of the revivifying effect the Depression was having on Progressive courage while simultaneously battering the standing of the Hoover administration and Wall Street. The confidence of the Morgan partners had already been dented badly by the traumas of 1931, with the British abandonment of gold inflicting the most grievous blow. J.P. Morgan & Co. hoped that salvation might be found in a Franco-American entente to restore order, but this was proving difficult to manifest, not least because of Hoover, whose facility frustrated the Morgan partners. This was all the more worrying after September 1931 when acceptance of the Depression was transformed into acceptance of a depression that might threaten capitalism. While 1931 had been dominated by international crises, the congressional debate over the moratorium and the Senate hearings in December 1931 made it clear that international crises could not be isolated from the domestic crisis.

---

[109] Felix Frankfurter to Herbert Feis, 19 December 1931, LC, Herbert Feis papers, General Correspondence Series, Box 16, Frankfurter, Felix.
[110] Johnson's views may be traced in Burk, *The Diary Letters*, to his sons, all in volume 5, on 12 December, 19 December, 27 December 1931, and 9 January 1932. The quotation is from his letter of 9 January 1932.

5 "Witchcraft": J.P. Morgan & Co., Hoover, and the Depression in the United States, 1930–1933

Every year that Herbert Hoover was president the American economy deteriorated. The year 1930 was bleaker than 1929, 1931 more dire than 1930, 1932 grimmer still. By November 1932, when Hoover lost the presidential election to Roosevelt, his political failure was identified indelibly with American economic failure. The long interregnum before Roosevelt took office, lasting until March 1933, prolonged the agony. Millions of Americans were unemployed or underemployed, their lives uprooted, their worlds precarious. Suffering abounded. What had happened? Writing in January 1932 Jack Morgan confessed that "I find it most difficult to explain" the Depression.[1] He was not alone. A mordant American Banking Association editorial entitled "Witchcraft" captured the spirit:

The conclusion is unmistakeable that the depression either was caused or is being prolonged by the shortage of gold, the over-production of everything, the stock market, interallied debts, democracy, the under-consumption of everything, the maldistribution of gold, high wages, low wages, governmental extravagance, timid factory owners, distribution, the railroads, the business cycle, thrifty bank depositors, lack of leadership in high places, concentration of power in high places, silver, the bankers, prohibition, cost of the World War, preparations for the next, the Republican party, the Democratic party, inflation, technological unemployment, deflation, Bolshevism, Fascism, Americanism, reparations, the Federal Reserve System trying to do too much, France, the Reserve System not doing anything, Germany, high tariff, England, low tariff, Mussolini, President Hoover, the failure of the American Government to appropriate several billions and spend them, and vice versa.[2]

Contemporaries, not least of whom was Hoover, were convinced that bankers were among the most blameworthy, a belief that suggests why the ABA was eager to advance a multitude of causes in "Witchcraft." Leaving office, Hoover assailed bankers for sabotaging his efforts, branding them intransigent liars "without ability and without character."[3] Father Coughlin

[1] Jack Morgan to the Marquess of Linlithgow, 4 January 1932, TML, JPM, Box 93.
[2] "Witchcraft," *American Bankers Association Journal*, vol. 24, June 1932.
[3] Agnes Meyer diary, 6 March 1933, Eugene Meyer, CUL, COHC, p. A 94.

railed against the culpability of "international bankers" condemning Hoover as the plaything of Wall Street.[4] A leading figure in the American Federation of Labour charged early in 1933 that bankers had reduced industry to "servitude" with their "control of credit" prohibiting industry from introducing palliative measures. Senator Elbert Thomas of Oklahoma, rueing that Congress was "impotent" and the Hoover administration feckless, confessed in a letter to selected bankers that "I am convinced that our troubles are mainly financial, that you and your associates, control our fiscal policies and legislation, and knowing of your power, I am appealing to you to divert your abilities to the task of providing a program for the consideration of the Congress."[5] Such claims, melding the helplessness of politicians with the omnipotence of the bankers, persisted, hinting at wilder formulations that the Depression was engineered.[6] Randolph Burgess, speaking to the California Bankers Association in 1939, told his audience, "[w]hen nearby Hollywood is writing its scenarios the natural thing is to make the villain of the piece a banker, and if he is to be a particularly villainous villain he should be a New York banker."[7] Though Burgess did not say it, the most nefarious New York banker for many Americans in the Depression decade was a J.P. Morgan & Co. partner.

If economists and historians have been chary of blaming the Depression upon bankers, this has not prevented scholarly judgements that bankers "abdicated leadership," favouring self-interest at the expense of the communal good. Their collective cowardice worsened the Depression, a verdict that has found support in utterances such as that of Agnes Meyer, the well-informed wife of Eugene Meyer, who recorded in her diary, "Certainly the New York bankers have proved that they are no heroes. The wealthy classes as I have learned to know them through the depression are not much to be admired. They are overcome by fear and selfishness." Months later, she expressed similar views more harshly: "If the general public realized the ignorance, smallness, futility and greed

[4] Donald Warren, *Radio Priest: Charles Coughlin, the Father of Hate Radio*, New York: The Free Press, 1996, pp. 39–40.

[5] John P. Frey, secretary-treasurer of the American Federation of Labor (AFL) metal trades department testifying to a Senate Judiciary sub-committee in late January 1933, *New York Times*, 27 January 1933, p. 2. Senator Elmer Thomas to J.P. Morgan & Co., 15 February 1933, TML, JPM, Box 46.

[6] Galbraith noted sardonically, "Moreover, implicit in hue and cry was the notion that somewhere on Wall Street – possibly at Number 23 and possibly on an obscure corridor in one of the high buildings – there was a deus ex machina who somehow engineered the boom and bust." Galbraith, *The Great Crash*, pp. 3–4.

[7] W. Randolph Burgess, "The Banker and His Public," *Banking*, vol. 32, no. 1, July 1939. Burgess was at that time vice-chairman of the board of the National City Bank. *Banking* was the renamed ABA journal.

of the average N.Y. banker, I think they would certainly hang a few of them, beginning I hope with Charlie Mitchell."[8]

The story of bankers and the Depression, of J.P. Morgan & Co. and the Depression, is a complex one. The connections among banking failures, bank weaknesses, and the deepening of crisis remain contested. These years, with their manifold complexities, render explanation challenging, for exposition threatens to rob them of their chaotic dynamism. This is a long chapter in which the wash of crisis lapped over the United States and J.P. Morgan & Co. It begins with the effect of the Depression on the Morgan bank, arguing that the devastating effect of the Depression on the Corner coloured the response to crisis. Evidence of this follows, as the chapter then considers the travails of American banking and the Morgan effort to assist private firms in trouble in 1930–31, a short-lived endeavour abandoned as a consequence of Morgan financial weakness. The railroads in particular were a source of worry for American banks, J.P. Morgan & Co., and the Hoover administration, a theme that the chapter takes up next. As railroad relief was being discussed, Leffingwell became convinced that deflation was emerging as an existential threat to capitalism. Combatting deflation became the Morgan mantra, a stance that led the Morgan partners and the Hoover administration into conflict in 1932. For this reason, Morgan disenchantment with Hoover meant that Roosevelt's victory in November 1932 did not alarm the Corner. The last section explores the implosion of the American economy in the opening months of 1933, Morgan surprise, and the growing isolation of the Morgan partners from both the outgoing and incoming presidents even as they embraced the view that the gold standard must be discarded to allow capitalism to overcome crisis. Throughout, the argument is made that Morgan policy confronting the Depression was activist, if not perhaps in the ways in which the literature has understood it to be.

*****

Early in January 1932 Jack Morgan wrote his friend the Marquess of Linlithgow. Business, he confided, was dreadful. J.P. Morgan & Co.

---

[8] A recent summary is Luca Pensiero and Romain Restout, 3 December 2018, "The Gold Standard and the Great Depression: A Dynamic General Equilibrium Model," Institut de Recherches Économiques et Sociales de l'Université catholique de Louvain, Discussion Paper, pp. 2–4, https://sites.uclouvain.be/econ/DP/IRES/2018016.pdf. For scholarly condemnation, Kennedy, *The Banking Crisis of 1933*, pp. 20–21; Harris Gaylord Warren, *Herbert Hoover and the Great Depression*, New York: Oxford University Press, 1959. Reprint Greenwood Press, 1980, p. 140; Romasco, *The Poverty of Abundance*, pp. 81–85. Agnes Meyer, 29 April 1932, 11 August 1932, A 79, Eugene Meyer, CUL, COHC, p. A 39.

was "having as bad a time here as anyone."[9] Understanding the degeneration of the Morgan balance sheet in these years is critical to appreciating how and why the partners acted as they did. Selected measures of the bank's financial performance between 1929 and March 1933 are summarized in Table 5.1.

Two periods of extraordinary stress stand out: 1931 and the opening quarter of 1933. The contraction in 1930 in net worth of almost $27 million was a blow, though at the end of the year net worth was marginally greater than on 31 December 1928 when it had stood at $91 million. Disquiet among the partners at 1930's results was understandable, but the year was not entirely negative – assets, deposits, and loans outstanding had risen. These rays of sunshine brightened by the early months of 1931 were marked, as had been the case a year earlier, by rallies on the stock market and in bond prices. The Dow Jones index, which had been fluctuating between 165 and 170 in December 1930, moved upward, stabilizing around 185 where it remained until late March 1931. As interest rates declined, bonds rose to levels that had not been attained since the Crash.[10]

The catastrophe came after. If the 1931 calendar year portrait is black – Morgan assets plummeted by more than $271 million, deposits were shorn by more than $184 million, while partnership net worth fell almost $40 million – these declines obscure the concentrated nature of the impact in the last quarter of the year. An internal memorandum written by Leffingwell attributed the fall in the loans and deposits of New York banks to the German standstill agreement of 1931 and the large-scale withdrawals by "French and other foreign deposits" consequent upon sterling leaving gold.[11] Certainly, the firm was not unique in seeing its deposits shrink: deposits in New York City banks fell more than 30 per cent between June 1930 and June 1932, while the pre-eminent rival to J.P. Morgan & Co. in the private banking world, Kuhn, Loeb & Co., saw its deposits plummet from $88.5 million in 1929 to $15.2 million in 1932.[12] Yet J.P. Morgan & Co. had a disproportionately high level of foreign deposits, both governmental and individual. The flood of foreign withdrawals in September and October 1931, principally by the governments of Belgium,

---

[9] Jack Morgan to the Marquess of Linlithgow, 4 January 1932, TML, JPM, Box 93. Linlithgow, Victor Alexander John Hope, the 2nd Marquess of Linlithgow, "Hopie," as Jack Morgan called him, was a Tory grandee, politician, and between 1936 and 1943 the Viceroy of India.

[10] Wigmore, *The Crash*, pp. 235–36, 285–86.

[11] Leffingwell Memorandum, 2 April 1932, YUL, RCL, Series I, Box 8, Folder 174.

[12] Charles W. Calomiris and Barry Wilson, "Bank Capital and Portfolio Management: The 1930s 'Capital Crunch' and the Scramble to Shed Risk'," *The Journal of Business*, vol. 77, no. 3 (2004), p. 435; Carosso, *Investment Banking in America*, p. 408.

Table 5.1 *J.P. Morgan & Co. consolidated statement of condition, in millions of dollars*

	31 December 1929	2 January 1931	2 January 1932	31 December 1932	31 March 1933
Assets	680,381,938.63	703,909,403.69	432,566,788.70	424,708,095.56	317,837,290.44
Cash	59,476,918.24	67,461,469.73	44,531,897.66	33,857,665.95	40,214,732.14
US Govt. Securities	165,667,994.49	190,739,957.32	110,821,189.69	224,580,150.03	146,071,407.50
State & Mun. Bonds	64,577,005.43	82,752,582.41	12,173,741.20	6,745,299.56	1,895,874.95
Call Loans	79,050,000.00	8,425,000.00	21,075,000.00	7,325,000.00	N/A
Loans, Time & Demand	132,325,530.49	158,617,186.91	141,908,803.05	82,705,607.00	73,831,227.52
Deposits	492,292,666.39	503,898,014.82	319,403,848.57	340,047,701.88	238,739,982.08
Net Worth	118,604,183.75	91,843,140.28	52,959,772.70	53,194,076.80	44,862,920.84

Note. The consolidated statement of condition may be found in Appendix 1. The figures include results from J.P. Morgan & Co. and Drexel & Co. but do not include either Morgan Grenfell or Morgan & Cie. They were entered into evidence by the Pecora Committee. The last column, that of 31 March 1933, was published by the Associated Press and printed in the *New York Times* on 10 June 1933, p. 7. It is not included in Appendix 1, but is included in Appendix 2. With regard to the row "Loan Time & Demand" I have combined two originally separate categories.

Britain, and France, struck hard. To meet the outflow the Morgan partners liquidated approximately $150 million of securities, consisting of $80 million of US government securities and $70 million of state and municipal bonds. The balance was made up through reductions of corporate stocks and bonds and cash.[13] It was a hammer blow, crumpling the Morgan balance sheet with devastating force.

If deposit haemorrhaging reduced the room for manoeuvre that J.P. Morgan & Co. enjoyed, capital impairment was a further constraint. For the private banks, what has been deemed the "capital crunch" was acute. J.P. Morgan & Co.'s capital was partner net worth. Banks such as National City or Chase could have recourse to the markets to raise capital even if this was impractical in the Depression. Partnerships such as J.P. Morgan & Co. were dependent upon the financial wherewithal of their partners. National City or Chase could cut dividends when besieged; for J.P. Morgan & Co. the burden in reduced earnings fell directly on the partners. Traditionally private banks could improve their capital position by admitting new partners. The one Morgan partner admitted after 1929 – Parker Gilbert in 1931 – did not bolster net worth, for he contributed no capital when he entered the firm.[14]

The effects of the crisis of 1931 are apparent: the Morgan partners shifted assets to the safest category that they knew, US government securities, which more than doubled in the year from $110 million to $224 million. It was a choice that New York banks adopted widely as they sought refuge in greater liquidity. The nearly complete disappearance of state and municipal, in favour of federal, bonds from the Morgan portfolio attests that the latter two categories were not viewed as offering the same quality harbour. Almost as striking was the sharp drop in loans outstanding. If the Morgan firm had, in the course of 1930, retreated from making call loans in keeping with a general shift away from this type of loan by the Street, this had not been true of time and demand loans.[15] The latter, on 2 January 1932, stood at a level higher than two years earlier. Throughout 1932 J.P. Morgan & Co. whittled their loan

[13] A *New York Times* analysis of 24 May 1933, p. 16, citing "financial circles" attributed the massive drop in deposits to withdrawals by the three governments mentioned. A passage in the testimony of Leonhard Keyes at the Pecora hearings in May 1933 suggests that the firm made profits of $3 million to $4 million in 1931. This must have been in the first half of the year when there was some good news in the markets. Keyes, in response to questioning by Senator James Byrnes, Pecora Committee, 24 May 1933, p. 83.

[14] Charles D. Dickey, formerly of Brown Brothers Harriman, was admitted as a partner in Drexel & Co. in Philadelphia on 2 January 1932. Dickey would eventually move to New York in 1937, see Chapter 8.

[15] Broker's loans, which were call loans, peaked on 4 October 1929 at $8,525 million. At the nadir, on 30 June 1932, broker's loans totalled $335 million. Federal Reserve Board, *Banking and Monetary Statistics, 1919–41*, vol. 1, table 139, p. 494.

portfolio, reducing it by nearly $60 million. Stabilization was the Morgan imperative in 1932. The chaos of the opening quarter of 1933 struck when the partners thought J.P. Morgan & Co. well-fortified. The slump in 1933, though not quite so sharp as 1931, was startling: in a span of three months assets fell by 25 per cent, deposits dropped 30 per cent, and net worth fell 16 per cent. Prestige, it transpired, was not prophylactic.

Investment banking was responsible for much of the pain. The industry felt the brunt of the Depression beginning in the summer of 1931. Membership in the Investment Bankers Association, which had stood at 690 in 1928, fell to 378 in 1933.[16] Total American lending abroad, which had powered earnings for many investment banks in the second half of the 1920s, plunged after a modest rebound in 1930. Repayment of existing loans outpaced new foreign issues in the United States between 1931 and 1933.[17] For J.P. Morgan & Co., the last long-term Morgan-led foreign bond issue was a $22.8 million bond placement for the Electric Power Co. of Taiwan in June 1931. After the short-term British government credit operation of August/September 1931, the firm floated no foreign loans to March 1933. Precisely how much the contraction in foreign lending reduced Morgan revenues is unknown, but there is little doubt that the cessation of fees and commissions hurt.

If foreign borrowing withered, at home matters were gaunt. Corporate borrowing dwindled. New domestic corporate security issues (including bonds and stocks) in the United States slid from more than $8 billion in 1929 to $1.55 billion in 1931 and $325 million in 1932, before reaching the paltry total of $161 million in 1933.[18] Morgan loans outstanding, which were not all corporate, contracted sharply in 1932. The Morgan partners embarked upon a searching examination. In July 1931 Dean Jay told his partner Bernard S. Carter that Morgan & Cie. was battening down the hatches, combing through accounts, sifting through the loan book, reducing some commercial lines of credit, and on some private loans asking for more collateral.[19] New York undertook a similar process. The commercial paper and banker's acceptances markets suffered. In May 1932 J.P. Morgan & Co. cabled Morgan Grenfell that they wanted to reduce their existing acceptances of cotton bills, which "constitute more than half of our present outstanding acceptances," from $6.75 million to $4 million. This desire was driven, the cable acknowledged, by the "natural shrinkage" of the market, but New York was also

---

[16] Carosso, *Investment Banking in America*, pp. 307, 317.
[17] Lewis, *America's Stake*, pp. 392–93.
[18] Federal Reserve Board, *Banking and Monetary Statistics, 1919–41*, vol. 1, table 137, p. 487.
[19] Dean Jay to Carter, 6 July 1931, TML, MBEP, Series 5, Carter.

anxious to rein in its acceptances.[20] This made sense given the trajectory of the acceptance market, which had peaked in December 1929, declined moderately until May 1931, and thereafter tumbled dramatically, reaching a level in August 1932 that was only 40 per cent of the 1929 figure.[21]

Investment banking was not the only culprit. The fall in the volume of NYSE transactions exacted a toll. The Morgan firm had seats on the NYSE through which they earned commissions on orders for clients. Share volume on the NYSE was, by 1932, at roughly one-third the level of 1929.[22] Similarly, the ending of heavy speculation volumes on the Exchange in 1929–30 drove a marked reduction in Morgan call loans. The rich margins extant before the stock market crash in 1929 disappeared. As for the other lines of Morgan banking business, such as foreign exchange, the picture is murky. With trade declining and Americans remaining at home rather than voyaging abroad, the earnings from foreign exchange transactions diminished. The foreign exchange equalization account agreed to by Jack Morgan in October 1931 with the British Treasury constituted the majority of foreign exchange holdings shown on the bank's books. At the beginning of 1931 J.P. Morgan & Co. had slightly more than $40 million of foreign exchange on its books, dropping to $37.5 million in January 1932 before a sharp fall to $18.6 million at the year's end.[23]

To round out the tale of woe, these years saw a spike in bad loans and a buttressing of reserves. Through the 1930s a number of loans, such as those made to Charles Mitchell, or latterly to the Van Sweringen brothers, proved, in the Morgan parlance "slow." A $500,000 loan made to Richard Whitney in the summer of 1931 is a case in point; the loan, originally an unsecured time loan, was converted to a demand loan, and at the end of 1934 J.P. Morgan & Co. set up a reserve of $200,000 on its books against the loan, recognizing its delinquency. Subsequently in 1937 the loan was reclassified as an obligation of Richard Whitney & Co. When this firm failed in 1938, a balance of $474,000 remained outstanding on the principal.[24] Reserves had to be held to cover such defaults. Whitney

---

[20] JPM to MG, 13 May 1932, TML, CP, Box 19, Folder Morgan & Co – MG & Co. Misc. Priv. Telegs 14 April to 13 August 1932. This suggests that J.P. Morgan & Co. acceptances were on the order of $10 million to $15 million.

[21] Federal Reserve Board, *Banking and Monetary Statistics, 1919–41*, vol. 1, table 127, p. 466. In December 1929 acceptances were $1,732 million, $1,413 million in May 1931, and $681 million by August 1932.

[22] In 1929 NYSE share volume was 1.125 billion shares; in 1932, 425 million. *Historical Statistics of the United States from Colonial Times to 1960*, table series X, p. 659.

[23] See Appendix 1.

[24] *United States of America before the Securities and Exchange Commission in the Matter of Richard Whitney et al.*, testimony of Francis D. Bartow, 20 April 1938, vol. 2, pp. 570–71. The complete hearings may be found at *The Hathi Trust*: https://catalog.hathitrust.org/Record/001740544.

told the Pecora hearings that at the end of 1932 the bank's reserves against bad loans stood at $18 million, remarking that Morgan policy was "not to fool ourselves about the goodness of our assets" given that "money and reputation" was at stake.[25]

Before 1931 there does not appear to have been substantive discussion about cost-cutting, strengthening the argument that the Morgan partners did not foresee a protracted Depression. Parker Gilbert's admission to the partnership in January 1931 validates this point, for when he joined J.P. Morgan & Co. his accession increased expenditures in the short term. Partner salaries in 1932 and 1933 were fixed at $150,000 for Jack Morgan and $100,000 for the other partners.[26] Drawings by partners were reduced in 1933 by 50 per cent. Evidence that the junior partners were feeling the strain in these years was furnished later by the Pecora investigation, which noted that a number of the partners were in debt to the firm. Late in September 1931, Jack Morgan agreed with his son Junius that cost-cutting must take place.[27] Discretionary expenditures were scrutinized carefully. Contributions to organizations as diverse as the National Bureau of Economic Research and the International Chamber of Commerce were reduced. The latter, fearing the effect an open acknowledgement that J.P. Morgan & Co. was reducing its dues would have upon other contributors, pleaded with Lamont to maintain the level at $5,000 per year. Reluctantly, Lamont agreed to furnish $4,000.[28] Staff reductions were insignificant, with the bank maintaining employment levels of 400–50 employees throughout the early 1930s, though salaries were cut by 10–20 per cent in 1933.[29]

When Roosevelt entered office in March 1933, J.P. Morgan & Co. was much diminished. Measured by assets, deposits, and net worth, the bank was less than half the size it had been when 1931 dawned. The Morgan partners had not fled the temple as Roosevelt's famous inaugural address charged; it had collapsed with them in it.

*****

[25] Pecora Committee, 24 May 1933, p. 117.

[26] TML, Ledgers and Journals J.P. Morgan & Co., Private Journal 6.

[27] Jack Morgan to Junius Morgan, 29 September 1931, TML, JPM, Box 38 A/34 – Cables exchanged while in London and Paris 1931.

[28] Lamont to Edwin F. Gay, TWL to Edwin F. Gay, 30 June 1931, BL, TWL, Series I, Box 57, Folder 9, National Bureau of Economic Research, rejecting Gay's request for a continuation of the Morgan donation of $1,000. The discussion among Lamont, his secretary E.T. Sanders, and John Gregg of the International Chamber in February–March 1933 may be found in BL, TWL, Series I, Box 18/5, Folder Chamber of Commerce US. After Gregg's plea, it was agreed that the firm would furnish $4,000.

[29] Hinton et al., "Some Comments about the Morgan Bank," p. 35.

Figure 5.1 Depositors outside a Bank of the United States branch, 1930. Bettmann/Getty Images.

When Lamont spoke to the Academy of Political Science on 14 November 1930, this bleak future was undreamt. The day that Lamont delivered his speech marked a step on the road to March 1933, for that day Caldwell and Company, a Nashville bank, failed. A month later, the Bank of the United States, based in New York City, became insolvent (see Figure 5.1). When the Bank of the United States collapsed, its suspension was the largest of any commercial bank in American history. The insolvencies were evidence of the distress within the banking sector. In 1929, 629 commercial banks had failed in the United States. The months of November and December 1930 saw 608 banks close their doors. Another 198 foundered in January 1931.[30] In their *Monetary History*, Friedman and Schwartz argued that four banking crises, the first of which occurred between October 1930 and January 1931, were an important factor in spreading the contagion of the Depression

---

[30] *Banking and Monetary Statistics, 1914–1941*, part I, p. 283 for the 1929 figure; Elmus Wicker, *The Banking Panics of the Great Depression*, New York: Cambridge University Press, 1996, p. 32.

through their constricting effect on the money supply.[31] Debate has swirled since.[32] Insofar as J.P. Morgan & Co.'s role in the collapse of the Bank of the United States is concerned, Friedman asserted subsequently that Morgan anti-Semitism was decisive. J.P. Morgan & Co., animated by anti-Semitism, prodded the New York Clearing House to reject rescuing the Bank of the United States, thus conflating an explanation for the Depression – contagion – with anti-Semitism.[33]

Friedman did not have the benefit of access to the Morgan archives when he made this claim. There is no doubt that J.P. Morgan & Co.'s culture was anti-Semitic. In a cable to Morgan Grenfell on 12 December 1930 disclosing the failure of the Bank of the United States, the partners remarked, "its clientele consisted largely of the lesser Hebrew element … its 450,000 depositors will eventually suffer some loss … But we feel that the situation is less serious financially than if the Bank had a clientele of major importance."[34] Jack Morgan's anti-Semitism was so marked that he commented in 1933 to a British correspondent that he considered Hitler's attitude toward Jews "wholesome."[35] However, Morgan anti-Semitism did not dictate the Morgan attitude vis-à-vis the Bank of the United States. J.P. Morgan & Co. had, and continued to have, cordial business relations with some Jewish New York banks, in particular Kuhn, Loeb & Co, the second most important private banking house on the Street.[36] This

---

[31] Friedman and Schwartz, *Monetary History*, pp. 342–43, 351–57.

[32] For differing recent assessments, Morris, *A Rabble of Dead Money*, pp. 149–51, drawing on the work of Temin, White, and Wicker, among others, accepts the view that the banking crises had little to do with propagating the Depression, save for the 1933 banking crisis. Michael Bordo and John Landon-Lane, "The Banking Panics in the United States in the 1930s: Some Lessons for Today," in Nicholas Crafts and Peter Fearon, eds., *The Great Depression of the 1930s: Lessons for Today*, New York: Oxford University Press, 2013, pp. 188–211, back the Friedman and Schwartz argument.

[33] Joseph L. Lucia, "The Failure of the Bank of the United States: A Reappraisal," *Explorations in Economic History*, vol. 22 (1985), pp. 402–16; Friedman and Schwartz, "The Failure of the Bank of the United States: A Reappraisal. A Reply." *Explorations in Economic History*, vol. 23 (1986), pp. 199–204; Anthony Patrick O'Brien, "The Failure of the Bank of the United States: A Defense of Joseph Lucia," *Journal of Money, Credit, and Banking*, vol. 24, no. 3 (1992), pp. 374–84; Paul B. Trescott, "The Failure of the Bank of the United States, 1930: A Rejoinder to Anthony Patrick O'Brien," *Journal of Money, Credit, and Banking*, vol. 24, no. 3 (1992), pp. 384–99. Friedman's *Newsweek* comment is in vol. 84, 16 November 1974, p. 74. In their reply to Lucia in *Explorations in Economic History*, Friedman and Schwartz, pp. 201–02, amplified the comment about Jack Morgan's anti-Semitism. Chernow concurred with Friedman, *The House of Morgan*, pp. 325–27.

[34] J.P. Morgan & Co. to Morgan Grenfell, 12 December 1930, TML, CP, Box 19, Folder Morgan & Co. Misc. Priv. Telegs 27 October 1930 to 24 April 1931.

[35] Jack Morgan to Countess of Buxton, 23 March 1933, TML, JPM, Box 94, Folder 103. More generally, Chernow, *The House of Morgan*, pp. 214–17.

[36] Pak, *Gentleman Bankers*, chap. 3. Pak has a careful, convincing study of Morgan anti-Semitism.

extended to the Rothschilds. When Baron Edouard de Rothschild asked in 1932 if a place could be found for his only son, Guy de Rothschild, with J.P. Morgan & Co. in the New York office, the Morgan reply was positive despite "the racial objection," because the firm valued the importance of the connection.[37] Writing Grenfell in December 1934 Lamont recounted the visit of a British emissary from Oswald Mosley's Fascist Party of Great Britain who had come to solicit funds from Henry Ford and J.P. Morgan & Co. Lamont was flabbergasted at this "naïve suggestion," telling his visitor "that we had no anti-Jewish complex and were on excellent terms with all the high class Jewish banking houses."[38] If this riposte was inaccurate in its denial of Morgan anti-Semitism, it embodied a reality: the Morgan partners differentiated among the Jewish banks on the same basis as they did with non-Jewish banks. What mattered was the standing of the institution in Morgan eyes.

Following the failure of the Bank of the United States, J.P. Morgan & Co. informed Morgan Grenfell that, contrary to whispers in the City of London, Goldman, Sachs, a Jewish firm, was sound. Thomas S. Lamont attributed these rumblings to "the tremendous deprecation" in the price of the securities that Goldman, Sachs had floated. He told Grenfell that private acceptances, save for J.P. Morgan & Co.'s, had been languishing. Buyers were skittish, unfairly but understandably. To strengthen the market, J.P. Morgan & Co. purchased bills for Morgan Grenfell's account of: Kidder, Peabody; Goldman, Sachs; J. Henry Schroder Banking Corporation; Brown Brothers; Heidelbach, Ickelheimer & Co.; Manufacturers Trust Co.; and Public National Bank & Trust Company.[39] Of these seven firms, four – Goldman, Heidelbach, Manufacturers, and Public National – were Jewish. If anti-Semitism was the determinant factor colouring Morgan praxis, as Friedman suggests, the Morgan partners should have let weakened Jewish houses struggle to place their bills. Instead J.P. Morgan & Co. bought their obligations.

Nor is Friedman correct to interpret J.P. Morgan & Co. as controlling the New York Clearing House. This charge, bruited since the Pujo hearings, resurfaced periodically. Sustenance for it may be drawn from Lamont's remark in a 1934 memorandum to his partners, "The adherence and loyalty of the Clearing House banks undoubtedly grew in these

[37] Carter to Harry S. Morgan, 30 August 1932, J.P. Morgan & Co. to Carter, 2 September 1932, TML, MBEP, Box 15 – Cables sent, 1 July to 30 September 1932.
[38] Lamont to Grenfell, 24 December 1934, BL, TWL, Series II, Box 112, Folder 6.
[39] Thomas S. Lamont to Grenfell, 30 December 1930, TML, CP, Box 9, Morgan & Co. – Banking Situation and Crisis, 1930–33, File 2.

years."[40] Against this, J.P. Morgan & Co. was not a member of the Clearing House, a point which the discussion concerning the failure of the Bank of the United States has neglected. Nineteen banks belonged to the Clearing House when the decision was made not to extend assistance to the Bank of the United States.[41] Four were associated with J.P. Morgan & Co. – Bankers Trust, Guaranty Trust, First National Bank of New York, and New York Trust. Morgan partners were consulted during the Clearing House deliberations. Leffingwell attended at least two meetings concerning the Bank of the United States in mid-November and Lamont was present at the decisive meeting of the Clearing House in December that rejected the plea of Joseph A. Broderick, the New York State Superintendent of Banks, to support the Bank of the United States. As Friedman and Schwartz have admitted, it was Lamont who made it possible for Broderick to be heard.[42] The Morgan partners were listened to, as the Broderick episode showed, but they did not have authority over the Clearing House. Reynolds, the president of the Clearing House, was "adamant" in his reminiscences: the Clearing House declined to support the Bank of the United States because of uncertainty regarding the scale of the latter's liabilities.[43]

There remains the broader question of J.P. Morgan & Co., contagion, and the progress of the Depression. Lamont, writing to Dawes in January 1933, framed Morgan policy in heroic terms: "We have had to run a day and night hospital service for the financially wounded and dying and have had to be quite ruthless regardless of personal interests, in hope some times of salvaging somewhat situations that nobody else apparently could handle but ourselves."[44] While the image is striking – financial triage conducted selflessly – it is overblown. A cold-eyed story emerges from the archives. In keeping with their stance in October and November 1929, when Morgan efforts were directed at minimizing damage arising from the stock market crash, the Morgan partners did not believe that it was their responsibility to rescue the financial system. The Federal Reserve existed to undertake that duty. Fanciful notions of trying

---

[40] Lamont memorandum, 1 June 1934, "J.P. Morgan & Co. and Their Relations to the Public," BL, TWL, Series V, Box 214, Folder 13.

[41] Manufacturer's Trust and Public National Bank & Trust, which had been in discussions with the Bank of the United States, were admitted to membership in the New York Clearing House on 11 December 1930, bringing the total to twenty-one.

[42] Friedman and Schwartz, *Monetary History*, p. 310n9. See Broderick's testimony, 12 May 1932, *New York Times*, p. 15.

[43] Reynolds, CUL, COHC, pp. 145–49. Reynolds claimed that he warned Hoover on 2 December 1931 that the Bank of the United States was going to fail and that at the crucial meeting on 10 December 1930 held at the Federal Reserve he successfully fended off Harrison's desire to rescue the Bank.

[44] Lamont to Dawes, 5 January 1933, BL, TWL, Series II, Box 91/11.

to recreate Pierpont Morgan in 1907 were chimeras. As Leffingwell put it years later:

For J.P.M. [2nd] and his partners to have attempted to stem the tide of deflation let loose by the limitless power of the Federal Reserve System would have been suicide for them, and a suicide in which they would have pulled down with them all banks and bankers, who might, from loyalty, have followed such insane leadership.[45]

Insanity was not the stock and trade of sober merchant bankers, nor was the prospect of a financial Charge of the Light Brigade appealing.

Certainly, the partners were disturbed as suspensions rattled Wall Street late in 1930. At the year's end Thomas S. Lamont told Grenfell that "the closings have had a bad effect upon the whole community. They have added an element of uncertainty to the situation as viewed by the average man in the street and they have hurt his business courage and morale." Early in 1931 Adolph S. Ochs, the publisher of the *New York Times*, lunched with Lamont and Owen Young. Ochs raised the failure of the Chelsea Bank & Trust, a small bank that catered to a Jewish clientele. He asked Lamont whether the New York banks had done enough to forestall its failure. A week later, writing to Ochs, Lamont professed that he thought the Clearing House banks had fulfilled their duties but noted that J.P. Morgan & Co. was only peripherally involved: "As you are aware, our house has had to content itself chiefly with the condition, – good, bad or indifferent, as the case might be, of private banking concerns, whereas the Clearing House banks have properly taken the lead in institutional difficulties."[46] Less formally, Lamont had told his daughter months earlier that "It's been panicky down in Wall Street. I have had to organize sudden rescue parties."[47] This was a reference to the troubles, either real or rumoured, afflicting a number of private firms. Winslow, Lanier & Co; Kissel Kinnicutt & Co.; Brown Brothers & Co.; Lee Higginson; Goldman, Sachs & Co.; and Kidder, Peabody were all roiled and this was the Morgan theatre for action in 1930–31.

---

[45] Leffingwell to Lamont, 5 May 1943, YUL, RCL, 1030, Box 4, Folder 100. It is noteworthy that here Leffingwell laid the blame for the Depression at the feet of the Federal Reserve. During the early 1930s his analysis was different.

[46] Lamont to Ochs, 30 January 1931, BL, TWL, Series II, Box 120, Folder 21. In support of this letter, Lamont included a five-page memorandum written by Bartow who had participated in two meetings regarding the Chelsea Bank. Bartow argued that the Clearing House banks had behaved appropriately, that Chelsea was neither a member of the Clearing House nor of the Federal Reserve system, that there had long been doubts about its management, and that the pressure of time and the unknown risks in extending additional aid were determinant. Ochs was not convinced, as his reply to Lamont of 2 February 1931 showed.

[47] Lamont to Eleanor Lamont, 6 November 1930, in Lamont, *A Life in Letters*, p. 110.

Private firms could not count on backing from the New York Clearing House nor were private banks members of the Federal Reserve system. Yet they were important components of the Wall Street ecosystem. As the strongest of the Wall Street private banks, J.P. Morgan & Co. was looked to for aid when private firms ran into trouble. The Morgan partners made choices about assistance. Approached in October 1930 about rescuing Munroe & Co., the bank declined, on the grounds that it "is not warranted by the character of the business or the importance of the firm." Callousness was apparent. Bell recalled one partner telling him when the brokers Pynchon and Company failed in April 1931, "Too bad, but these ripe apples must fall."[48] When a decision was made to assist, Bartow was the partner who took the lead. This was the case with Winslow, Lanier & Co. An old, established specialist firm in railroad securities, it found itself strapped by the travails of the railroad sector and the overall decline in the stock market. In October 1930 the Morgan firm intervened, with Bartow ushering the firm over the ensuing months into an orderly liquidation. Kidder, Peabody, a much more prestigious Boston firm linked closely to J.P. Morgan & Co., was another instance where the Morgan partners acted. The decision was made to restructure the firm, whose fortunes had declined precipitously. Between November 1930 and March 1931 J.P. Morgan & Co. orchestrated a restructuring of Kidder, Peabody, finding new partners to inject capital and dynamism into the firm, while arranging for a revolving credit of $10 million to buttress the new Kidder, Peabody.[49] This was not, as Carosso has commented, an "altruistic" step. The Morgan partners feared the effects on their prestige if Kidder failed, while they fretted its bankruptcy would have a cascade effect in an already unsettled market.[50]

Brown Brothers & Co. was another old-line firm with established pedigree that found itself struggling. Its salvation was a merger with Harriman Brothers. Here the Morgan partners played no role, other than to welcome the development as positive for the Street.[51] Kissel, Kinnicutt; Goldman, Sachs; and Lee, Higginson were other firms that found themselves under

---

[48] Bell, "The Decline of the Money Barons," p. 154.
[49] Of the $10 million, J.P. Morgan & Co. loaned $2.5 million, Chase National Bank $2.5 million, First National Bank of Boston $1.25 million, Bankers Trust $1 million, Guaranty Trust $1 million, National Shawmut Bank of Boston $750,000, First National Bank of New York $500,000, Merchants National Bank of Boston $250,000, and Second National Bank of Boston $250,000. TML, CP, Box 30, Morgan & Co. – Assistance to KP & Co., 1931.
[50] Carosso, *Investment Banking in America*, pp. 308–17 has a full discussion.
[51] On Brown Brothers, see John A. Kouwenhoven, *Partners in Banking: An Historical Portrait of a Great Private Bank Brown Brothers Harriman & Co. 1818–1968*. New York: Privately Printed, 1968, p. 16.

attack as rumours spread about their soundness. Well aware of the calami-
tous effects that gossip could have, the partners sought to reassure interlocutors that these banks were sound.[52] Noteworthy is the judgement that
both Kissel, Kinnicutt and Lee, Higginson were in good shape, an indication of how difficult it could be for even a bank as well connected as J.P.
Morgan & Co. to discern the financial health of others, given that both
Kissel, Kinnicutt and Lee, Higginson were to fail in the next eighteen
months. Beyond the informational problem discerning the exact state of
affairs of competing firms in a financial community where rumour and
speculation warred with discretion and secrecy, the scope of the catastrophe washing over the Street imposed limits on Morgan effectiveness.
New York City had boasted 233 investment banking houses in 1929. By
1933 that figure had dropped to 145.[53]

The self-appointed Morgan role as the paladin of private firms *in
extremis* ended in 1931. Rescuing private firms was beyond the Morgan
means thereafter, though the extent to which the firm had been battered
by the losses of 1931 was not realized on the Street until the revelations of
the Pecora hearings in 1933. J.P. Morgan & Co. continued to be consulted in a variety of high-profile cases in 1932–33, notably the ongoing
financial difficulties of New York City and the summer 1932 crisis in
Chicago that required the rescue of Charles Dawes' former bank, Central
Republic Bank and Trust, but such instances were collaborative, multi-
party, and did not necessitate the engagement of significant financial
resources by the Corner. There was anxiety in the fall of 1932 about the
financial health of First National Bank, connected closely to J.P.
Morgan & Co. George F. Baker junior asked Lamont and Jack Morgan
whether they would be willing to become directors of First National in
a visible sign of Morgan support for the firm. After discussion, Jack
Morgan and Lamont rejected the idea, fearing the complications that
might arise from the bank's First Security securities arm. Four years later
they parachuted Fraser into First National to strengthen the bank's
executive.[54] The most spectacular failures of 1932 – that of Lee,

---

[52] J.P. Morgan & Co. to Morgan Grenfell, 12 December 1930, TML, CP, Box 19, Folder
Morgan & Co. Misc. Priv. Telegs 27 October 1930 to 24 April 1931; Morgan Grenfell to
J.P. Morgan & Co., 19 December 1930, TML, CP, Box 9, Morgan & Co. – Banking
Situation and Crisis, 1930–1933, File 2, inquiring about Goldman, Sachs; Thomas
S. Lamont to Grenfell, 30 December 1930, TML, CP, Box 9, Morgan & Co. –
Banking Situation and Crisis, 1930–33, File 2.
[53] Carosso, *Investment Banking in America*, p. 320.
[54] Lamont to Jack Morgan, 23 September 1932, Jack Morgan to Lamont, 7 October 1932,
Leonhard Keyes to Jack Morgan, 18 October 1932, Lamont to Jack Morgan,
26 October 1932, BL, TWL, Series II, Box 108, Folder 15; Jack Morgan to Arthur
Curtiss James, 18 December 1936, TML, JPM, Box 44, Folder 6.

Higginson occasioned by the bankruptcy of Kreuger & Toll and the disintegration of Samuel Insull's utility empire – saw J.P. Morgan & Co. involved tangentially rather than directly. Shrunken Morgan means was one reason why, but other considerations were in play. Jack Morgan had declined to become involved with Ivor Kreuger, doubting his veracity, while Insull's Midwestern utilities were a rival to the Morgan-controlled United Corporation. Morgan attention was drawn elsewhere as crises mounted, in the first instance to the railroads.

*****

The railroads were commanding in their economic importance. Sectoral employment, which had peaked in 1920 at more than 2 million, still stood at nearly 1.7 million as the decade ended. On 1 October 1929 the value of all publicly traded stocks on the NYSE was $79.1 billion, of which total $10.1 billion was railway stocks, the single largest component on the exchange. Outside of government bonds – federal, state, and municipal – railway bonds constituted the largest group on the bond market. The FRBNY estimated in December 1931 that railway bonds were more than one-fifth of the bond market.[55] Railroad stocks and bonds were the bedrock of the American investor's portfolio, a staple of bank holdings, and responsible for much of the lifeblood of Wall Street. Yet the railroads, plagued by overcapacity, faced with stiff competition from the trucking industry, and with a history of acrimonious labour relations, were finding survival challenging as the economy shuddered and traffic declined. As an ABA editorial remarked in June 1931, "With practically every bank in the country holding railroad securities, the crisis which appears to be developing in the rails makes the future of the roads a matter of direct banking concern."[56] This was even truer for J.P. Morgan & Co, for whom the railroads had been one of the building blocks in their rise to pre-eminence on Wall Street. Railway bonds had constituted the greatest share of domestic bonds issued by the bank after 1919. Morgan action was expected. The progressive lion Senator George Norris roared in February 1933, "Today if the government wanted to take over the railroads, we would only have to go to one man – just one man – J.P. Morgan."[57]

[55] Employment figures from *Historical Statistics of the United States from Colonial Times to 1957*, table Q 141–152, p. 437; stock total from Wigmore, *The Great Crash*, p. 34; for the FRBNY estimate, Harrison to Hoover, 15 December 1931, HHPL, HH, Subject Files, Box 181, Federal Reserve Board Correspondence 1931, enclosing a memo of 8 December 1931.
[56] *American Bankers Association Journal*, vol. 23, June 1931, p. 968.
[57] "Web of Wall Street Assailed by Norris," *New York Times*, 24 February 1933, C 11.

Such authority may well have been a relief to Jack Morgan had it existed. For the Morgan partners, the Van Sweringen railroad empire was increasingly burdensome. As was discussed, the Morgan partners had been forced to participate in the rescue of the Van Sweringen brothers in October 1930, leaving them, reluctantly, as one of the de facto owners of a sprawling railroad empire. Unfortunately, the injection of capital proved inadequate. A series of additional operations were undertaken to buttress the Van Sweringen moorings.[58] These financial contortions, which weakened a struggling Missouri Pacific Railroad, part of the Van Sweringen agglomeration, were driven by the inescapable reality that the Van Sweringens were unable to service their debts. Demand loans from a J.P. Morgan & Co.–led consortium (the other participants were Guaranty Trust and Kuhn, Loeb & Co.) to the Missouri Pacific were employed to conceal this unpalatable truth. The first such loan was made on 31 March 1931 in the amount of $3 million at 4.5 per cent for thirty days; five further loans at the same interest rate followed at the end of April, July, August, October, and December 1931, taking the total extended to the Missouri Pacific to $11.7 million. The Morgan share was $5.85 million.[59]

The Morgan partners recognized that such efforts were stop-gap. Fundamental reform of the railroads of the kind that the Transportation Act of 1920 had enjoined was needed. Through the 1920s little had been done – but crisis might spur meaningful action. This was the theme of Morgan pressure on Hoover in the fall of 1930 to secure consolidation within the industry. Lamont told Hoover that Jack Morgan had sanctioned any assistance that J.P. Morgan & Co. might tender if the outcome should be restructuring. Pointedly, in November 1930, Lamont blamed General W.W. Atterbury, the president of the Pennsylvania Railroad, for obstructionism, warning that Atterbury's opposition was blocking consolidation. If movement was not forthcoming, Lamont cautioned Hoover, the railroads would find securing the necessary financing for

---

[58] On 1 January 1931 the brothers created Terminal Shares Inc., a company vested with real estate properties in Kansas City and St. Joseph. Terminal Shares then issued five-year, 5.5 per cent bonds secured by its stock. The Missouri Pacific railroad, another Van Sweringen property, was given the option of purchasing the Terminal Shares properties, a right for which it agreed to pay $1.6 million per year in four installments of $400,000. Subsequently, a Morgan-led syndicate offered $61.2 million of fifty-year Missouri Pacific bonds at 5 per cent to the market in January 1931.

[59] The best place to follow what is a complex story lies in the Wheeler Committee Report, Part I & II, December 1936. Part II deals with the Missouri Pacific and Terminal Shares Contracts. A table of the demand loans advanced to the Missouri Pacific as well as the breakdown of the Morgan, Guaranty Trust, and Kuhn, Loeb & Co. participation is in Exhibit 273, pp. 1239–40.

their operations impossible.[60] Late in 1930, prodded by Hoover, the four principal eastern systems agreed to consolidate, informing the Interstate Commerce Commission of this in early January 1931, a triumph that soon proved illusory. Nine months later O.P. Van Sweringen wrote the Morgan partners that if concrete steps were not taken to implement consolidation when Congress reconvened in December, then the impetus to public ownership of the railroads might become irresistible. The threat was enough that Lamont wrote the four railway presidents to urge them to press their case before the Interstate Commerce Commission, despite misgivings on the part of some Commissioners who wanted a five-party railroad system rather than a four. As the *Wall Street Journal* reported on 2 October 1931, the momentum favoured exponents of the four-party plan, "with the pressure of the present economic situation regarded as a powerful influence in this direction."[61]

Lamont wrote Hoover on 8 October, informing him that the Interstate Commerce Commission was struggling not solely with the question of consolidation but also with the issue of railroad rates, telling the president that if this news should leak it would depress the price of railway bonds even more.[62] Lamont had been warning about the dangers in the railroad bond market for some months. Late in August 1931 he had sent the president a personal letter in which he placed the total amount of railroad bonds on the State of New York legal list at $7.7 billion. The legal list consisted of securities that it was permissible for banks and insurance companies to hold on behalf of investors and pension plans. Lamont estimated that $5.44 billion, or 70 per cent, would no longer qualify for legal list status in light of their depreciation in price. Should this occur, Lamont pointed out, banks, insurance companies, and investors would suffer grievously.[63]

Senator Arthur H. Vandenberg of Michigan wrote Hoover twice in September 1931 to warn him of the "unliquidity" of Midwest banks, but Hoover did not need to be prompted by Vandenberg; he had earlier met with Meyer to urge him to persuade the leading New York banks of the virtues of a voluntary banking cooperation scheme that would extend assistance to banks in need. Meyer was dubious, favouring a revival of the wartime War Finance Corporation. Nevertheless, he agreed to try to

[60] Memo, 31 October 1930, BL, TWL, Series II, 98/17; Lamont to Hoover, 8 November 1930, 19 November 1930, and telephone message 25 November 1930, BL, TWL, Series II, Box 98/18.
[61] Lamont to O.P. Van Sweringen, 7 October 1931, BL, TWL, Series II, Box 126, Folder 12; "I.C.C. May Favor Four-Party Plan," *Wall Street Journal*, 2 October 1931, p. 12.
[62] Lamont to Hoover, 8 October 1931, BL, TWL, Series II, Box 98/19.
[63] Lamont to Hoover, 28 August 1931, BL, TWL, Series II, Box 98/19.

cajole the New York bankers into compliance.[64] Banks, the railways, the worsening economy, and the aftershocks of the British decision to leave gold melded when Hoover addressed a meeting of nineteen leading New York bankers at Mellon's apartment on 4 October 1931. Present were Lamont and Whitney.

Hoover called for "concerted action on the part of our leading bankers and strong banks to avert a possible threat to our entire credit structure," asking those present to form a national organization with capital of $500 million. Its stated purpose was to rediscount bank assets that the Federal Reserve System was not allowed to loan on as well as to loan money to closed banks against their assets to relieve pressure on depositors. The Morgan reaction was favourable, though J.P. Morgan & Co. did not participate in the $150 million from the New York Clearing House banks that was pledged to form the National Credit Corporation (NCC). Tellingly, Harrison observed that, while the plan would help banks afflicted with liquidity problems, it would not do anything for institutions whose future had been compromised by solvency worries, driven by the sharp decline in real estate values and the bond portfolios that they held. Harrison cautioned that there were "unavoidable limitations" to what could be done through the NCC and recommended that Hoover explore the possibility of creating a bond pool to support the railroad bond market.[65]

Ongoing lobbying by Lamont and Harrison had an effect. Hoover conceded to Lamont in late November that "[t]he railway situation is indeed the principal impediment to domestic recovery," though he refused to become involved directly in the question of industry wage rates.[66] To drive home the connections between railroad wage rates, the railroad bond market, and the peril facing American banking, Harrison phoned the president on 15 December 1931. Their conversation was preceded by a two-hour-long talk that Harrison had had with Lamont, Leffingwell, and Whitney. Harrison told Hoover that he had warned the

[64] James Stuart Olson, *Herbert Hoover and the Reconstruction Finance Corporation, 1931–1933*, Ames, IA: Iowa State University Press, 1977, p. 24; Arthur H. Vandenberg to Herbert Hoover, 10 and 23 September 1931, HHPL, HH, Box 213, Vandenberg, Senator Arthur H. 1930–33. William Barber, *From New Era to New Deal: Herbert Hoover, the Economists, and American Economic Policy, 1921–1933*, Cambridge: Cambridge University Press, 1985, pp. 125–38, argues that Hoover abandoned voluntarism between October 1931 and early 1932.
[65] A copy of Hoover's statement to the assembled bankers may be found in HHPL, HH, Subject Files, Box 184, Financial Matters Banking and Bankruptcy Correspondence 1931 September–December; Harrison to Hoover, 7 October 1931, CUL, George L. Harrison papers, Box 24, Binder 53; Lamont to Hoover, 7 October 1931, BL, TWL, Series II, Box 98, Folder 19.
[66] Hoover to Lamont, 20 November 1931, BL, TWL, Series II, Box 98, Folder 20.

Morgan partners that banks were facing the wall due to declines in bond prices and that there would be many failures quickly if something were not done. Harrison urged them to form a pool to support the railroad bond market. The Morgan attitude, Harrison informed Hoover, was "generally sympathetic" but they had insisted that no pool would work unless negotiations leading to wage cuts were successful. The Morgan partners wanted assurances that there would be an acceptable deal. Hoover, pressed, told Harrison that he would do his best to ensure that a sectoral wage deal was reached. Harrison followed up the phone conversation with the despatch of a letter and memorandum to Hoover that had been written for Meyer a week earlier. The memorandum, entitled the "Banking Situation in the Second District," put flesh on the bones of a stark warning. According to the FRBNY, nearly 300 banks would show losses due to bond depreciation equal to or close to equal to their capital and another 150–200 banks would have losses that would mean "capital impairment." More than half of the banks in the second district were vulnerable, a condition that the FRBNY thought was mirrored across the country. By the time that Hoover spoke with Harrison, he had acted. Frustrated at the laggardly pace of NCC loans to troubled banks, and alarmed by a renewed move downward in the securities markets, the president had proposed on 7 December legislation that would create the Reconstruction Finance Corporation (RFC), a tacit admission that Meyer's advice in September had been correct.[67]

The RFC was to become a critical vehicle in the reconstruction of American capitalism after its foundation in February 1932.[68] One of the RFC's first loans was to the Missouri Pacific, which allowed the railroad to discharge the demand loan that had been made by the Morgan-led syndicate. Much to Lamont's chagrin, the transaction became public knowledge, prompting Senator James Couzens to assail the loan as well as to introduce a bill to transfer authority from the RFC to the Interstate Commerce Commission overseeing railroad loans. Lamont and Couzens had a testy exchange of letters. Couzens pointed acidly to what he called the lamentable impression made upon public opinion from loans that aided private bankers while there was such "great distress" in the country. Lamont vented his feelings to his partners in a memorandum that chastised the "very stupid blunder" by the Missouri Pacific treasurer that had

[67] Harrison to Hoover, 15 December 1931, HHPL, HH, FRBNY papers, Box 2/2010.1; Memo, Banking Situation in the Second District, HHPL, HH, Subject Files, Box 181/ Federal Reserve Board Correspondence 1931, September–December; Olson, *Herbert Hoover and the Reconstruction Finance Corporation, 1931–1933*, pp. 28–29.
[68] Jesse Jones, *Fifty Billion Dollars: My Thirteen Years with the RFC 1932–1945*, New York: The Chronicle Company, 1951. Reprint New York: De Capo Press, 1975.

left the bank "rather embarrassed."[69] Embarrassment aside, the RFC loan postponed the day of reckoning for the Van Sweringens and for the Morgan bank. RFC assistance propped up the railroads in 1932–33 but did little to reshape an industry in peril. Anderson, the in-house Morgan expert on railroads, ascribed the formation of the RFC to a desire to guide the railroads through difficult times in the expectation that once this was done rail traffic would rebound and so too would profits. However, traffic volumes continued to slide. For Anderson, the basic problem was simple: "Originally – and incorrectly – the authorities at Washington felt that the depression was a temporary affair that could be ameliorated by favorable psychological factors."[70] What he neglected to say was that this too had been the Morgan assessment in 1929–30.

*****

While the railroads were worrisome well before Anderson wrote, Leffingwell had reached a state of near panic about deflation. Since the fall of 1930 Leffingwell's views on the Depression had undergone revision. Speaking to the Academy of Political Science in April 1931 he insisted on the war as the fundament of the evils that had ensued, with war debts, reparations, and tariffs the symptoms. There remained a residue of morality. "We became," Leffingwell told his audience, "a nation of spenders and speculators" for which a curative could be found in "hard work and thrift in our private lives."[71] The crises of the summer made plain that, whatever the attractions of rectitude as an explanation and a solution for American trials, urgency dictated action. As Leffingwell told Parker Gilbert in September 1931, when Morgan nerves were stretched taut by the sterling crisis, now was not the time to worry about revising war debts:

But now I beg you ... to take note of the fact that our civilisation today, at this moment, is in gravest jeopardy and that the question is how to save it. All over the world ruin and starvation are staring men, tens of millions of them, rich and poor, in the face. The infinitely delicate economic machine is breaking down. The problem may be insoluble. But its gravity demands a capital operation. The

---

[69] The RFC lent the Missouri Pacific $12.8 million, $5.8 million of which was transferred to J.P. Morgan & Co. The Couzens–Lamont exchange is in BL, TWL, Series II, Box 125/24, Lamont to Couzens, 31 March 1932, Couzens to Lamont, 2 April 1932, Lamont to Couzens, 6 April 1932. Lamont's memorandum to his partners is 15 April 1932 in the same folder. For the Couzens bill, see "ICC Again Opposes Loans to Pay Banks," *New York Times*, 2 April 1932, p. 3 and the account in Jones, *Fifty Billion Dollars*, pp. 121–24.
[70] Anderson to JAM de Sanchez, 1 June 1932, TML, MBEP, Series 5, Anderson Arthur M.
[71] A copy of the speech, given on 24 April 1931, is in YUL, RCL, Series I, Box 9, Folder 183.

whole building is on fire now. It is too late for dear old Secretary Mellon's pretty little Pyrene Extinguisher.[72]

Though Leffingwell appreciated the peril, there were limits to a "capital operation." He was not prepared to follow John Maynard Keynes, though he conceded that Keynes was the "most brilliant journalistic-economic mind of our time." Keynes had been the intellectual motive force behind the MacMillan Currency Report that was published on 13 July 1931. Struck in 1929 to illuminate the reasons for the sluggishness of British economic performance, the report called for managed money directed by the Bank of England, an effort to restore world price levels to those of 1928, and criticized Britain's return to gold in 1925 as yielding parsimonious dividends at the expense of damage to industry. Two weeks after the appearance of the MacMillan Report, the May Committee Report, forecasting a government budget deficit of £120 million in the 1932–33 financial year, called for sweeping economies. Keynes, in *The New Statesman* on 15 August 1931, attacked the May Report for its failure to appreciate that implementing the economies suggested would boost unemployment rolls.[73] Leffingwell deemed Keynes' ideas a "half-truth." Leffingwell agreed with Keynes that government spending created employment, wages, and tax revenue, but in a wasteful manner. For Leffingwell, "private enterprise tends to be more economical and more productive." Keynes wanted the gold standard abandoned and wanted managed money, which would write the "epitaph of laissez-faire," dooming capitalism.[74] Leffingwell admitted that the problem of deflation and inflation was "infinitely perplexing" but was adamant that Keynes was a false prophet, his acolytes deluded. Keynes and those who thought like him "have not the judgment of practical men ... confidence is based on keeping one's promises. That is something that Keynes will never know." Robustly, Leffingwell insisted that American policy must "walk the straight and narrow path, with our heads set against deflation on the one hand, and paper money inflation on the other."[75]

With this maxim, the Morgan partners crafted a lobby that mixed fidelity to the tenets of orthodox finance – balanced budgets, preservation

[72] Leffingwell to Parker Gilbert, 15 September 1931, YUL, RCL, Series I, Box 3/63.

[73] On Keynes and the MacMillan Report, see Robert Skidelsky, *John Maynard Keynes, Vol. 2: The Economist As Saviour*, London: Macmillan, 1992, pp. 343–62; for Keynes' criticism of the May report, p. 394.

[74] Leffingwell to Lamont, 29 August 1931, YUL, RCL, Series I, Box 4, Folder 95. Leffingwell to Parker Gilbert, 18 November 1931, YUL, RCL, Series I, Box 3, Folder 63. Leffingwell did not always dismiss Keynes. Writing to Lamont in 1932 he commended Keynes' article in the January issue of *Vanity Fair* on bank values and money.

[75] Leffingwell to Lippmann, 30 December 1931, YUL, RCL, Series I, Box 5, Folder 108.

of the gold standard, disdain for managed money – with confronting deflation. Surging numbers of bank failures in the fall of 1931, conjoined with the strain on the Morgan balance sheet occasioned by foreign deposit withdrawals, galvanized the partners.[76] Leffingwell and Lamont led the effort; the former engaging with Lippmann, Harrison, Meyer, and Glass, while Lamont interacted with the president. Given Hoover's move toward greater experimentation with the NCC and RFC, it might be thought that the president would be sympathetic. To a point this was correct, but Hoover's tendency to see Wall Street negatively sat uneasily with Morgan advice.

Leffingwell advanced two propositions in the fall and early winter of 1931–32: the first was an insistence that encouraging American prices and wages to sink to the lower level of world prices would wring out deflation; the second was that credit contraction had to be fought through policy changes implemented by the Federal Reserve as well as remedial legislation supported by the White House. Only then, Leffingwell thought, would recovery begin. Convincing others was necessary, and thus the Morgan partners sought to persuade selected individuals of the wisdom of their views, consistent with their practice as merchant bankers that emphasized personal contact. Lippmann, seen at the Corner as the most consequential figure in shaping informed American opinion, was of especial importance.

Lippmann had long known the Morgan partners, and his admiration for them was undimmed. Writing in December 1930, Lippmann enthused at the "courage and quiet unselfishness of some of the big bankers ... The burden which Tom Lamont, for example, has carried has been immense, not of course personal to himself or his firm, but for the banking community."[77] Leffingwell and Lippmann met on 29 October 1931 to discuss how the United States might extricate itself from the Depression. That week two prominent university-based economists, Yale's Irving Fisher and Princeton's E.W. Kemmerer, had called for an expansion of the money supply, arguing that the gold cover of the Federal Reserve system was more than ample, despite hoarding and the heavy withdrawals to Europe that had characterized the weeks after sterling left gold. Fisher and Kemmerer suggested that an injection of liquidity would help kick-start a rise in prices. Effectively this was a call for inflation – or so Leffingwell interpreted it. Writing Lippmann on 30 October, Leffingwell attached a Federal Reserve statement on its

[76] A total of 1,860 banks containing deposits of $1.449 billion failed between 1 September 1931 and January 1932. Friedman and Schwartz, *Monetary History*, p. 317.
[77] Quoted in Ronald Steel, *Walter Lippmann and the American Century*, New Brunswick, NJ: Transaction Publishers, 1999, p. 289.

balance sheet for the last year, observing that Federal Reserve credit had jumped by $1.5 billion, note circulation was up by $1 billion, the gold reserve had fallen $300 million, and despite these changes prices had continued to fall. Leffingwell drew two conclusions: first, "monetary inflation won't stop the depression"; second, "our resources are insufficient to permit further experimentation along that line anyway" even though he had favoured a cheap money policy until "two or three weeks ago." Rather than trying to raise wholesale prices to 1928 levels, Leffingwell advised that policy should work to "bring rents, wages, rates and retail prices down to the present wholesale price levels." If this happened, "we should be out of the woods in six months." Too high a wage level worked against labour by increasing unemployment and immiserating the working class. It did not affect the middle class, but Leffingwell charged, it is "wicked fraud against the workers. They are being cheated of their means of livelihood by the leaders who pretend to befriend them." Leffingwell's emphasis on wage cuts was not novel. Repeated calls for wage cuts had been made since the spring of 1931 by leading bankers and rebuffed angrily by labour leaders.[78]

Lippmann was not convinced. Uncertain, he inquired how much prices might rise should Leffingwell's counsel be implemented, a query that was followed swiftly by another: Had deflation run its course?[79] While Leffingwell momentarily thought in mid-November 1931, as he told his partners, that the "third panic" of the depression had ended, continued deflationary pressure led him to reverse course, stressing that matters were desperate.[80] Writing to Lippmann on 18 December, Leffingwell insisted that he was pursuing a middle course between inflation and deflation, urging Lippmann to combat "the spirit of defeatism which is sweeping over the country" and to "call upon patriotic people in and out of Congress to rally around our constitutional leader."[81] After a further exchange, a grateful Lippmann sent Leffingwell a short note: "Thanks enormously for your letter which is full of solemn wisdom."[82] Although Leffingwell would tell Grenfell that "nobody on earth can control Walter

---

[78] Romasco, *The Poverty of Abundance*, pp. 79–80; Leffingwell to Lippmann, 30 October 1931, YUL, RCL, Series I, Box 5, Folder 108.

[79] Leffingwell to Lippmann, 6 November 1931, Lippmann to Leffingwell, 10 November 1931, YUL, RCL, Series I, Box 5, Folder 108.

[80] Leffingwell to Lamont, 13 November 1931, BL, TWL, Series II, Box 103, Folder 15.

[81] Leffingwell would elaborate on this notion, stressing that Federal Reserve open-market operations should play a central role in halting the decline in wholesale prices, offsetting contraction in member bank credit through injection of central bank credit. Leffingwell to Lippmann, 18 December 1931, YUL, RCL, Series I, Box 5, Folder 108.

[82] Lippmann to Leffingwell, 31 December 1931, YUL, RCL, Series I, Box 5, Folder 108.

Lippmann," his columns deviated little from the economic panaceas advanced by Leffingwell and Parker Gilbert in 1932–33.[83]

Harrison, Meyer, and Glass, experts, required a different tack than Lippmann. Leffingwell's communications with Harrison and Meyer had an overriding theme: "to stop the contraction of credit which has proceeded for two years and with devastating speed in recent months." Absent was the insistence on letting American prices decline to world levels as a curative. Leffingwell urged Harrison to consider a range of helpful measures from offering bill maturities on a sliding scale, to letting banks lend on a wider range of good collateral, to reducing the Federal Reserve borrowing rate for banks. Leffingwell warned Harrison that there was a "semi-panic in the bond markets" due to the size of the government deficit and the failure of recent bond issues. Raising interest rates to make sure future offerings would be counterproductive, for it would "impair" outstanding issues. Treasury deficit financing, he told Meyer, was making matters worse, as it was "highly deflationary." Leffingwell argued that Federal Reserve member banks, already reeling from deposit losses occasioned by a combination of foreign withdrawals and domestic hoarding, were forced to call loans and sell securities when the Treasury sold bills to them. This reduced deposits, exerted pressure on equities, and shrank bank resources, and "thus the Treasury accelerates the vicious circle of deflation." Leffingwell urged Meyer to encourage the Federal Reserve system to carry larger balances in banks that bought Treasury bills. Federal Reserve banks could help by offering banks a lower borrowing rate on Treasury paper than the paper itself bore. "This," he reminded Meyer, "was the war practice; and this is war."[84] Federal Reserve open-market operations had their place, but Leffingwell believed they should be secondary. Should inflation appear, the Federal Reserve could control it by raising the discount rate. Federal government borrowing, which now dominated the market, had to be managed "in such a way as not to contract credit further."[85]

Neither Harrison nor Meyer could have been startled by what Leffingwell propounded. Writing Leon Fraser, Harrison observed "there is a surprising unanimity of opinion among industrial and banking leaders and our leading economists that liquidation has proceeded beyond the point of whatever benefits it may confer."[86] Meyer had

---

[83] Leffingwell to Lippmann, 8 December 1932, YUL, RCL, Series I, Box 5, Folder 109; Leffingwell to Grenfell, 29 April 1933, YUL, RCL, Series I, Box 3, Folder 69.

[84] For shrewd observations on the frequency of the war metaphor as the Depression tightened, Romasco, *The Poverty of Abundance*, pp. 175–81.

[85] Leffingwell to Harrison, 4 January 1932, Leffingwell to Meyer, 9 January 1932, YUL, RCL, Series I, Box 3, Folder 73. The 9 January letter was shown to Harrison.

[86] Harrison to Leon Fraser, 16 January 1932, George L. Harrison papers, CUL, Box 2, Binder 3.

already shown his willingness to push forward expedients to tackle deflation. Ogden Mills, who succeeded Mellon as secretary of the Treasury in February 1932, accepted that deflation had gone too far, articulating this understanding in a series of speeches early in 1932.[87] Weighing Leffingwell's influence on Harrison and Meyer is thus difficult. Alan Meltzer has argued that in December and January 1931–32 Harrison was resistant to open-market operations, delaying them repeatedly, a stance that Leffingwell favoured.[88] Yet Leffingwell's anti-deflation impulses were more absolutist than Harrison was prepared to allow. If the latter worried that inflation anxiety was ingrained so deeply within the financial community that its mere mention caused trembling, this was not an anxiety shared by Leffingwell. He told Carter, "The last thing I fear is inflation. Still I suppose that there are a certain number of people who in an Arctic winter worry about the heat of the tropics." Leffingwell was more disturbed at the possibility that no "local program here to arrest the deflation can succeed," given deflation's global reach.[89]

Leffingwell's nightmares drove Morgan efforts to pressure Glass into modifying his proposed legislation to reform the Federal Reserve Act. Glass, whose identification with the Federal Reserve system as his personal creation bordered on the obsessive, believed that systemic financial failings had occasioned the Depression. Commercial banking desires, in Glass' view, had warped his system. Their transgressions in security lending, made possible by heavy borrowing from the Federal Reserve banks, had contributed massively to speculation, fomenting the 1929 crash that had spawned deflation. Commercial banks, Glass thought, should be prohibited from securities lending and confined to catering to the needs of agriculture and industry. Beyond the depredations of the commercial banks, too many banks existed, while restrictions on chain and branch banking crimped the establishment of stronger institutions. Glass wanted all banks to be members of the Federal Reserve, a perspective that he urged on Hoover in November 1931. He favoured increasing capital requirements for banks, to help them withstand economic vicissitudes. Greater control over the system should be fostered by reforming the Federal Reserve Board in Washington and freeing it from undue banking industry influence. From the spring of 1931 Glass worked on legislation to remedy these supposed ills.[90]

---

[87] Romasco, *The Poverty of Abundance*, pp. 195–96.

[88] Meltzer, *A History of the Federal Reserve*, p. 354.

[89] Leffingwell to Carter, 30 January 1932, YUL, RCL, Series I, Box 1, Folder 17.

[90] Rixey Smith and Norman Beasley, *Carter Glass: A Biography*, New York: Longmans, Green and Co., 1939, pp. 304–6; George J. Benston, *The Separation of Commercial and Investment Banking: The Glass-Steagall Act Revisited and Reconsidered – A Retrospective of the Pecora Committee*, Oxford: Oxford University Press, 1990, pp. 216–17.

Leffingwell, though he shared some of Glass' outlook, notably that American banking was too fragmented, was opposed to much of what the senator advanced. Taking advantage of their friendship, Leffingwell showered Glass with paper, including an extraordinary letter of 3 February 1932 that ran to thirty pages and that incorporated a detailed examination of every section of Glass' proposed bill, S 3215. Leffingwell worried Glass was attempting to deal with the inflation of 1927–29 when it was halting deflation now that mattered. He laid out a dark scenario, conjuring the prospect that Glass' remedies would worsen deflation, lead to the destruction of sound money, bring an end to the gold standard, and allow the triumph of "the greenbackers and bimetallists and managed-money-men." Leffingwell told Glass that he was "appalled" by the bill, for, should it become law, it would "complete the collapse of our economic system." Leffingwell's objections were rooted in his conviction that the Federal Reserve needed to be given more leeway to inject liquidity by allowing banks to borrow on any good paper, while the gold reserves of the Federal Reserve should form the basis of more courageous lending. Boosting capital requirements and divorcing commercial banks from their security affiliates would only traumatize the banking sector further. While he concurred with Glass that the rural banking lobby had far too much power, Leffingwell abhorred the idea of centralizing authority in Washington, rejecting any notion of inserting political power more directly into the Federal Reserve. Leffingwell chided Glass, suggesting branch banking be allowed on a Federal Reserve district basis rather than state-wide as Glass wanted. Leffingwell told Glass the bill should be withdrawn, emphasizing that Harrison and Meyer shared his fears. Though the two men met for two hours on 2 February and again on the afternoon of 6 February to thrash out their differences, Glass was intractable.[91]

While Leffingwell tackled Glass directly, Lamont was helping to marshal opinion against the proposed bill. Quietly, Lamont spoke with the Republican senator from Connecticut, Frederic Walcott, about the legislation. Walcott, a Hoover ally, agreed with Lamont that the best way to revise the bill was not to pass "anything at all at this time." Harrison, alarmed at the potential infringement upon the FRBNY's autonomy incorporated in the Glass bill, was also amenable.[92] On 1 February

---

[91] Leffingwell to Glass, 8 January 1932, Leffingwell to Glass, 3 February 1932, Leffingwell to Glass 8 February 1932, Glass to Leffingwell, 9 February 1932, YUL, RCL, Series I, Box 3, Folder 66. Leffingwell's fears were heartfelt; Anderson, some months later, remarked that the bill "frightened almost everyone to death." Anderson to de Sanchez, 5 May 1932, TML, MBEP, Series 5/Anderson Arthur M.

[92] Lamont to Leffingwell memo, 27 January 1932, BL, TWL, Series II, Box 103, Folder 15, discussing Walcott and Harrison.

a column distributed by the McClure newspaper syndicate appeared in newspapers across the country. McClure was the largest newspaper syndicate in the United States. The column discussed the views of an anonymous "leading international authority" on the principal economic questions of the day. Lamont was the authority. He had suggested the article, had furnished the questions, and had provided the answers. Unsurprisingly, in discussing the RFC, the railroads, the Mellon tax program, war debts/reparations, and the gold standard, Lamont supported the president's agenda. The RFC was lauded as a means to check deflation through assistance to the banks, while the Mellon tax initiative, with its proposals for raising additional revenue, was described as a "considerable step in the right direction," though Lamont recommended heavier expenditure cuts and possibly higher taxation. As for the gold standard, in a passage borrowed verbatim from Leffingwell, Lamont waxed eloquently about its atavism, claiming that love of gold was intrinsic to human nature.[93] Hoover was undoubtedly pleased, for the column championed faithfully his sheet anchors – a balanced budget, the gold standard – while praising initiatives pioneered by his administration. Conversely, the president was disinclined to find in Glass' nostrums hope for exiting the Depression. White House opposition ensured that S 3215 encountered heavy resistance. What emerged from Congress, the Glass–Steagall Act of 1932, as Anderson commented, "bore about as much resemblance to the original as black does to white."[94] The 1932 act gave the Federal Reserve greater flexibility to lend through loosening the collateral restrictions on both the Federal Reserve and commercial banks. Soon thereafter the Federal Reserve, driven by Harrison, relying on Glass–Steagall, and fearing that Congress might be driven to legislate inflationary measures, embarked upon a program of open-market purchasing. Cautious at first, it gathered pace from April 1932.[95]

*****

Successful passage of Glass–Steagall was not enough for Hoover. While the president could claim that his administration was taking steps to check deflation and spur economic recovery, recovery would not be instantaneous. With the 1932 election on the horizon, Hoover wanted to stake an unassailable claim to re-nomination. If on the one hand the president was persuaded that European dislocation was at the root of American troubles, thus shuffling responsibility for the Depression offshore, on the

[93] Lamont to McMullin, 18 January 1932, BL, TWL, Series II, Box 107, Folder 2.
[94] Anderson to de Sanchez, 5 May 1932, TML, MBEP, Series 5/Anderson Arthur M.
[95] Meltzer, *A History of the Federal Reserve*, pp. 358–63.

other he fastened on a needed villain at home in short-selling. Short-sales involved speculators borrowing stock for a fee from a brokerage or individual and selling the stock on the market, wagering that the stock in question would fall in price. When it did so, the speculator would purchase shares to return to the lender. The difference in price amounted to the speculator's profit. It is easy to see how short-sellers were accused of exacerbating stock market declines. Hoover's antipathy toward short-selling had strengthened in 1931, but it was not until February 1932, when the president was informed of rumblings by Walcott that Democratic short-sellers were preparing fresh sallies, that Hoover pushed the Senate to act by opening an investigation into Stock Exchange practices. Leffingwell thought that attacking short-sellers was a clever choice by Hoover, for it would be popular in the country.[96] The politics of short-selling was to embroil J.P. Morgan & Co. in an unwanted confrontation with Hoover in the spring of 1932.

On 16 March 1932 Lamont met the Republican senators David Reed and George Moses in Washington before seeing Hoover and Stimson. Lamont was planning a European trip in April and May 1932. Two subjects dominated his discussion with the senators: the dependence of American well-being upon European prosperity and short-selling. Meeting with the president and the secretary of state, the three men covered these themes while discussing Hoover's re-election prospects, canvassing as they did a bleak slate of occurrences – the wrangling in Congress over a balanced budget, the suicide of the financier Ivan Krueger and the collapse of his empire, and the Lindbergh kidnapping.[97] The Morgan view of short-selling was clear. The practice was a necessary part of the functioning of the stock market, was not in and of itself evil, and was not contributing to the ongoing weakness in prices apparent on the New York Stock Exchange. Lamont and Hoover had "quite an argument" about short-selling, as Lamont tried, and failed, to convince the president to foreclose the incipient Senate investigation. Two weeks later Lamont sent Hoover a memorandum summarizing a study that J.P. Morgan & Co. had conducted on short-selling in the market over the past nine months. The memorandum argued that short-selling had stabilized stock market prices. Responsibility for falling stock market prices lay with the steady selling of "long" positions. Overall, decline, Lamont suggested, was a barometer of company earnings and future expectations, but it had little to do with banking where the bond

[96] Carosso, *Investment Banking in America*, 322–23; Leffingwell to Lamont, YUL, RCL, Series I, Box 4, Folder 95.
[97] Lamont notes on Washington visit, 16 March 1932, BL, TWL, Series V, Box 211, Folder 6.

market had been more consequential in weakening banks over the preceding year. Lamont pointed out to Hoover that two recent steps imposed by the NYSE, restricting lending of customers' stocks and doubling the stock transfer tax, had curtailed short-selling. There was no need, he counselled, to go any further.[98]

Hoover was unpersuaded. His obstinacy was stiffened by renewed downward movement in the stock market. The Dow Jones Industrial Index (DJII), which had stood at 381 in September 1929, had fallen to 71 in February 1932 before rebounding to 88 early in March. Thereafter, the market's slide resumed, falling uninterruptedly to the end of May when it reached 44.[99] Hoover replied that Lamont was ignoring that stock market prices were the outcome of a concerted "pounding down of prices" through "obvious manipulation of the market and propaganda," betraying the public weal while forcing honest investors from the market. Confidence and recovery were being undermined by unscrupulous men who were "not justified in deliberately making a profit from the losses of other people." Lamont soft-pedalled, telling the president that, though he was impressed by his arguments, the Morgan perspective was that those who needed income were selling their investments because they were not yielding sufficient earnings. Utilizing the metaphor of thin ice bearing too many burdens – the inability to reach a balanced budget, the proposed Glass bill, the soldier's bonus, and the tax hike proposals – Lamont told the president that the ice had cracked, fractured by these developments in conjunction with the Krueger and Toll debacle. This had stalled a nascent bond market recovery. Now in train was liquidation, not short-selling.[100]

The debate was fed by the president's mounting antipathy toward bankers. Late in March 1932 Hoover forwarded Harrison a letter that he had received from "one of the most responsible business men of the country." The letter was a diatribe against bankers in Chicago and in New York, blaming their pessimism for fomenting the Depression. The writer implored the president to order bankers to be more constructive, asserting "they are a most servile class when spoken to from authoritative power above them." A pained Harrison took time to respond. When he did, Harrison admitted that bankers were "cautious and skeptical" but many had been "energetic, courageous, and helpful." He pointed out that the FRBNY had opened the liquidity taps, citing a $148 million jump in loans and investments by New York banks over the previous week as

[98] Memorandum, 1 April 1932, Lamont to Partners, 15 April 1932, BL, TWL, Series II, Box 98, Folder 21.
[99] Wigmore, *The Crash*, pp. 331–32. The record low of 41 was reached on 8 July 1932.
[100] Hoover to Lamont, 2 April 1932, Lamont to Hoover, 8 April 1932, BL, TWL, Series II, Box 116, Folder 7.

a welcome sign. Hoover was unmoved, dismissing Harrison's suggestion that legislative foot-dragging, rather than bankers, was paramount in the country's economic woes.[101] Lamont was doing what he could to appease the president, meeting with Colonel Robert McCormick of the *Chicago Tribune* and William Dewart of the *New York Sun* to persuade them to support Hoover's tax bill. Morgan desire to placate the president was driven by more than a realization of Hoover's hostility. It was framed by worry.

Dean Jay, visiting the United States, wrote Carter in Paris on 1 April 1932, "[t]here is practically no business here ... the earnings of all the industries are bad and the discouraging thing is that no one seems to see any signs of improvement." Jack Morgan found himself having to fend off a suggestion from Allen Forbes, president of the State Street Corporation in Boston, that the time had come to fix prices on the NYSE, as had been done at the outbreak of war in 1914.[102] The journalist, and advisor to U.S. Steel, Samuel Crowther, argued in a memorandum circulated to Leffingwell that, even if the RFC and the Glass–Steagall Bill slowed the progress of deflation it would not end it. Crowther forecast two possible outcomes of the Depression – a general foreclosure and scaling down of all debts or a revolution. He thought the latter more likely. Insufficient work existed for all, "[h]ence discontent will be too widespread for any palliative measures." Federal Reserve action alone would not meet the craving for employment. Crowther's solution was a combination of open-market operations with the creation by a number of "strong corporations" – General Motors, General Electric, and U.S. Steel – of "their own credit money – that is, buying and selling with negotiable instruments, giving and receiving them at cash prices" to increase "the credit volume of the country." Crowther admitted that commercial banks and the Federal Reserve would have to cooperate to make his solution work. Leffingwell, in a commentary circulated to his partners, adjudged the proposal the end of "sound money," dismissing it unequivocally.[103]

Leffingwell's rejection reflected not solely the Morgan commitment to the gold standard but also disdain for the appropriateness of collectivist

[101] Hoover to Harrison, 22 March 1932, Harrison to Hoover, 22 April 1932, Hoover to Harrison, 26 April 1932, Harrison to Hoover, 3 May 1932, CUL, George L. Harrison papers, Box 46, Hoover, Herbert.
[102] Dean Jay to Carter, 1 April 1932, TML, MBEP, Series 5, Carter, Bernard S; Harry S. Morgan to Egan, 2 April 1932, TML, Martin Egan papers, Box 50, Folder Morgan, Henry Sturgis; Allen Forbes to Jack Morgan, 14 April 1932, Jack Morgan to Forbes, 19 April 1932, TML, JPM, Box 49, Folder 9.
[103] Leffingwell to Partners, 9 April 1932, YUL, RCL, Series I, Box 6, Folder 127. Kennedy has observed that docility rather than revolution struck many contemporaries as dominating. Kennedy, *Freedom from Fear*, pp. 89–90.

solutions for a nation that held individualism dear, thus his insistence to Lippmann that both conservatives and progressives shared the same political philosophy, namely wanting "a lot of government," while liberals, which he counted himself as, desired "as little government as possible."[104] Moreover, the Morgan partners had become accustomed to plans to restructure American capitalism. Crowther was not exceptional. Among the most publicized schemes was Gerard Swope's 1931 blueprint to remake American industry on lines akin to cartelization. Sundry ideas were tabled, criticized, and discarded metronomically in the search for solutions among economists, businessmen, and politicians in 1931–32. The *Commercial and Financial Chronicle*, in a caustic editorial, lampooned the vogue for "Master Planning" as the way out of the Depression.[105]

The Morgan partners accepted that when Lawrence Dennis asked *Is Capitalism Doomed?* in 1932 he was posing a pertinent question.[106] Unlike Dennis, whose answer to his own query was yes, and who came to believe that salvation lay in fascism, the Morgan partners did not believe that revolution, either from the Left or from the Right, was desirable or imminent. Neither the Soviet Union nor Fascist Italy were an appealing model. An American future without capitalism was inconceivable. To be American was, in the Morgan view, to accept liberal, democratic capitalism as the ordering political and economic principle. Refuge was taken in the insistence that the United States would muddle through without the need for structural change prescribed by Crowther, Swope, or others.[107]

Nevertheless, Morgan fears about the economy and about Hoover's re-election prospects prodded Lamont to take an extraordinary step. Newly returned from Europe, relying upon material drafted by Leffingwell and Parker Gilbert, he urged Hoover to invoke a Joint Session of Congress to confront the economic emergency in late May 1932. A sixteen-page-long memorandum enjoined the president to cut public spending by $500 million, returning federal expenditures to 1926–27 outlays. Since the "general price level" had fallen 20 per cent since 1929, so too should government spending, which could be accomplished by cutting government wages and salaries and reducing government departments, agencies, and the Veterans Bureau by that percentage. To oversee these cuts,

---

[104] Leffingwell to Lippman, 13 April 1932, YUL, RCL, Series I, Box 5, Folder 109.
[105] Ellis Hawley, *The Great War and the Search for a Modern Order: A History of the American People and Their Institutions, 1917–1933*, New York: St. Martin's Press 1979, pp. 199–201. "Master Planning," *Commercial and Financial Chronicle*, vol. 132, 6 June 1932, pp. 4126–28.
[106] Lawrence Dennis, *Is Capitalism Doomed?*, New York: Harper Brothers, 1932.
[107] Jack Morgan to Morris Whitridge, 19 May 1932, TML, JPM, Box 71, Folder 153/2.

the memorandum recommended bringing Dawes back as head of the Bureau of the Budget. Revenue had to be increased and thus the Morgan partners supported Hoover's efforts to pass the Revenue Bill before Congress. In keeping with their anti-tariff impulses, they advised the president that tariffs on oil, copper, coal, and timber should be dropped as they were harming world trade. Railroads, too, drew Morgan attention. Railroads were hobbled by the restraints imposed by the Interstate Commerce Commission, which should be relaxed. Subsidies extended to road transport and inland waterways that hurt railroads should be reviewed. As for unemployment, private recovery was essential. Until this happened, suffering must be relieved, leading the partners to recommend directing $300 million through the RFC in loans to states or local governments to provide food and shelter to the needy. Echoing Leffingwell's views, the memorandum was against the expansion of public works, complaining that there already had been too much: $1.5 billion from 1 January 1930 to 30 June 1932. This spending hurt efforts, the memorandum asserted, to balance the budget on which business recovery rested. An executive summary made plain where the Morgan partners thought responsibility for mastering the Depression lay: "The demoralization of the bond market and the general worsening of the financial situation are due mainly to the uncertainties arising out of Washington."[108]

Hoover's receptiveness to this plea was influenced by a mix of considerations. Robinson, Hoover's banking confident, had informed the president that Lamont, in cooperation with Otto Kahn, was exploring the idea of persuading Coolidge to run for the Republican nomination. Hoover remarked, "That shows how much of a friend Lamont is. Of course Kahn would do anything, but I didn't think it of Lamont."[109] Pique aside, the stock and bond markets remained depressed, while unemployment was rising. The furore surrounding the thousands of veterans who had marched to Washington, with their dependants, demanding payment of their military service bonus, increased the pressure. As Hoover considered, he was mindful that Lamont and Whitney were working with Young on a Committee on Investment, the latest of the president's forays into

---

[108] Lamont to Herbert Hoover, 25 May 1932, Memorandum, 26 May 1932, HHPL, HH, PPF, Box 168, Lamont, Thomas 1929–32.

[109] This episode is recounted in Glen Jeansonne, *The Life of Herbert Hoover: Fighting Quaker 1928–1933*, New York: Palgrave Macmillan, 2012, p. 407 and Joslin, *Off the Record*, pp. 226–27 as well as the Joslin diary, 1 May 1932, HHPL, Theodore Joslin papers, Box 10, Diary 1932. Whether Lamont was conspiring is an open question. The published accounts imply that Lamont was present at this meeting, but he was in Europe on 30 April 1932. It is possible that Lamont had played a role in arranging the meeting before he left for Europe weeks earlier.

voluntary associationism aimed at alleviating distress.[110] Concurrently, J.P. Morgan & Co. was exploring how the bond market might be supported. Hoover knew that these discussions were occurring. Lamont's memorandum had alluded to the prospect, suggesting that there would be no "organised buying of bonds" without presidential leadership. While he might disparage Lamont's loyalty, Hoover was not prepared to reject openly the Morgan program at the risk of forestalling these endeavours.

Practically, the president shuffled off the memorandum. His true feelings were apparent later, when he damned it as "morally wrong." Joslin, in his *Off the Record* (1934), later referred anonymously and dismissively to Lamont, assailing him as a "thoroughly frightened" and "panic-stricken banker."[111] Joslin's scorn reflected the conviction of Hoover's inner circle. Conspicuous is the language employed to savage Lamont. The Morgan partners were frightened, and justifiably so, given the state of the American economy in May 1932. This did not mean that in their effort to sway Hoover the Morgan partners had the answers to the Depression. The solutions they propounded were unlikely to have improved matters. Staving off deflation through more deflation was not a means to spark recovery. Austerity breeds austerity rather than prosperity. Yet the Morgan partners were correct on a key point – a national emergency existed. Decisive action was needed from Washington, something that Hoover and his advisors failed to grasp.

Passage of the Revenue Bill in Congress on 2 June and the announcement of the formation of the American Securities Investing Corporation (ASIC) by J.P. Morgan & Co. the following day, in tandem with Hoover's re-nomination at the head of the Republican ticket later that month, quieted tensions between the president and the Corner. This had taken effort; the announcement of the ASIC turned on the quelling of the contretemps over short-selling. Hoover and Mills pressed Harrison, Lamont, George Whitney, Young, and Richard Whitney to ban the practice on the grounds that its existence was torpedoing the efforts of the administration. Hoover groused to Mills, "I have hesitated to make any public statement on this matter as it might attract more activities in this direction by people who believe that there are groups in New York who are always right." At length, Harrison convinced Mills and the president that the bond market and the stock market were two different

---

[110] Romasco, *The Poverty of Abundance*, p. 198; Leffingwell to Mills, 25 May 1932, YUL, RCL, Series I, Box 6, Folder 126.

[111] The phrase "morally wrong" that appears in marginalia in Hoover's hand on the executive summary sent by Lamont appears to have been written later. Lamont to Herbert Hoover, 25 May 1932, HHPL, HH, PPF, Box 168, Lamont, Thomas 1929–32; Joslin, *Off the Record*, p. 235.

things. Reviving the former was more consequential. The Morgan partners had made it plain that formation of the ASIC was conditional upon
no action being taken to ban short-selling. While short-selling flared once
more in July 1932, it soon subsided, ending its political ramifications.[112]
As for the ASIC, its $100 million capital was dedicated to purchase
bonds. The New Republic observed caustically that much ado was being
made about nothing. Anderson, reviewing ASIC's operations two months
later, thought that it had made its participants money, broadened the
bond market a bit, injected some stability, and had attracted new buyers
who had been deterred by the chaos and instability before its formation,
a modest accomplishment that suited the Corner.[113]

The economic doldrums of the summer of 1932 were dispelled periodically by brutality, the hard-hearted dispersal of the veterans' encamp-
ment in Washington standing out, a renewed discussion on the running
sore of war debts in the Lausanne Conference occasioned by the expira-
tion of the Hoover moratorium, and from July the gathering force of the
presidential campaign with the selection of Roosevelt as the Democratic
nominee.

Morgan views on war debts had not altered. Lamont, in a speech in
Boston in June 1932, listed the first two causes of the Depression as the
Great War and the economic warfare that had ensued in the shape of
reparations and war debts.[114] American policy on war debts in the spring
and summer of 1932 was complicated by the now distant relationship
between Hoover and Stimson. The former, fearing the political costs of
any arrangement that might be interpreted by American voters as hinting
at the cancellation of war debts, was determined to be steadfast. Stimson,
who voyaged to Europe on the same ship as Lamont in April 1932, was
open to a compromise, but his influence with the president had waned.
Into this void stepped Lamont who convinced Paris and London not to
act until after the elections, while managing to secure acquiescence from
Hoover and Stimson. Lamont favoured a quiet revision of the Young Plan

---

[112] Hoover to Mills, 3 June 1932, Hoover to Young, 3 June 1932, contains the quotation
from Hoover though the letter, which was given to Mills to deliver to Young, was not
forwarded. HHPL, HH, FRBNY papers, Box 2/2012.2 Mills, Ogden, 1932–33;
Harrison memo to files, 3 June 1932; two memos by Harrison recording his conversations with Mills, as well as the record of a gathering attended by Harrison, Lamont,
George Whitney, Richard Whitney, 3 June 1932. Both may be found in HHPL, HH,
Subject Files, Box 189, NYSE Short Selling and Bear 1932 March–December.

[113] J.P. Morgan & Co. to Leffingwell and Morgan Grenfell partners, 4 June 1932, TML,
CP, Box 19, Folder Morgan & Co – MG & Co. Misc. Private Telegs 14 April to
13 August 1932; Anderson to de Sanchez, 2 August 1932, TML, MBEP, Series 5
Anderson Arthur M.; The New Republic, vol. 71, no. 915, 15 June 1932, pp. 109–110.

[114] Lamont speech to the Algonquin Club, Boston, 22 June 1932, BL, TWL, Series II,
Box 98, Folder 22, Hoover, Herbert C.

and an extension of the moratorium to three years, while preservation of reparations payments in reduced form was kept in being, ideas that found expression in the eventual outcome of the Lausanne Conference.[115] Within J.P. Morgan & Co., sentiment in favour of cancellation was growing.

Leffingwell spent June 1932 meeting central bankers, politicians, and businessmen in London and Paris. His mission had two aims: one was to re-establish more cordial relations among central banks; the other was to elicit a better understanding of the British and French perspective on war debts and reparations. Leffingwell conveyed a positive message to the Bank of England and the Bank of France about Federal Reserve open-market operations. Having doubted the latter as a deflation fighting tool earlier in the year, by the spring of 1932 he was praising their efficacy to Norman and Niemeyer at the Bank of England and Moret and Rist at the Bank of France. In his talks Leffingwell stressed Harrison's competence as well as the necessity of central bank cooperation in mastering the Depression.[116] This said, renewed heavy withdrawals of gold from the United States in May and June 1932, especially on French account, had done much to blunt the force of open-market operations, a point that Leffingwell pressed on his trip.

The greater part of Leffingwell's energy was spent informing himself about the British and French perspective on war debts and reparations. What he found was unsettling. Jack Morgan had mused to Grenfell that British attempts to placate the Germans on reparations were doing little more than alienating the French, making Anglo-French concord unlikely. Leffingwell's consultations convinced him that both Paris and London were open to ending reparations, the former preferring a face-saving arrangement to make it possible, while the latter favoured surgical sever-ance. The trouble was the reciprocal step required from Washington – the cessation of war debt payments by Britain and France to the United

---

[115] On the divide between Hoover and Stimson, see Louria, *Triumph and Downfall*, pp. 144–47. Leffler, *The Elusive Quest*, pp. 290–91, is the clearest exposition of the argument for Lamont's guiding influence: "Thereafter, Hoover and Stimson adopted Lamont's approach as official American policy." Wilson is not so categorical, arguing that Lamont sought to forge a compromise deal as an "unofficial liaison" between the Hoover administration and Britain and France. Wilson, *American Business*, pp. 148–49.

[116] Grenfell remarked that Harvey of the Bank of England "admits that communications between the two Banks have been much less frequent and intimate than they were previously." Grenfell to Leffingwell, 13 June 1932, BL, TWL, Series II, Box 112, Folder 1. Anderson thought that open-market operations had been helpful, Anderson to de Sanchez, 2 August 1932, TML, MBEP, Series 5 Anderson Arthur M, AMA. Leffingwell would later tell Lippmann that "I think the open-market policy instantly stopped the deflation," Leffingwell to Lippmann, 8 December 1932, YUL, RCL, Series I, Box 5, Folder 109.

States – was anathema to Hoover. As Leffingwell consulted, the more uneasy he became. Rumours of threats to the continued servicing of the Austrian government loans, of a suspension of the Argentinian sinking fund, intermingled with the war debts and reparations, would lead him to fear the repercussions of failing to act on war debts.[117]

War debts needed to be cancelled, Leffingwell urged. A "clean slate" was the only way forward. Delay could not be brooked "while the disintegration of economic life continues and accelerates." Without cancellation Leffingwell forecast "complete default and or repudiation" on a wide swathe of obligations. The Austrian and Argentinian loans would be the beginning. Lamont and Parker Gilbert were fooling themselves to think any other course was feasible. Leffingwell thought that there was an opportunity for Hoover. Paraphrasing King Henry of Navarre – "I should rather not be King than King of a ruined people" – Leffingwell argued that renouncing war debts would give a fillip to the economy, demonstrate the president's leadership, and do more to accomplish his re-election than any other step he could take.[118] Leffingwell's counsel misread both Hoover and congressional opinion. Hoover was not Henry of Navarre. The latter's apocryphal remark, "Paris is well worth a mass," when he converted to Catholicism from his Huguenot faith, which made possible his later assumption of the throne of France as Henry IV, drives home the point: it was not in Herbert Hoover to convert, nor was Congress inclined to cancellation.[119]

Reinforcing presidential stubbornness was the imminent failure of Dawes' former bank, Central Republic and Trust of Chicago. There was no direct connection between war debts and the troubles of Dawes' bank but the politics of rescuing the bank ruled out concessions on war debts. Money could not be given both to Central Republic and, seemingly, to Britain and France through forgiveness of war debts. Two emergency meetings on 26 June 1932, the second of which Lamont and Parker Gilbert participated in, agreed to an injection of $90 million from the RFC into the Central Republic and Trust to

[117] Jack Morgan to Grenfell, 3 June 1932, TML, JPM, Box 25, Folder ECG; Leffingwell to J.P. Morgan & Co., 6 June 1932, TML, CP, Box 19, Folder Morgan & Co – MG & Co. Misc. Private Telegs 14 April to 13 August 1932; Grenfell to Leffingwell 13 June 1932, Leffingwell to Grenfell, 14 June 1932, BL, TWL, Series II, Box 112, Folder 1; Leffingwell to Lamont, 14 June 1932, BL, TWL, Series II, Box 103, Folder 16; Leffingwell to J.P. Morgan & Co., 17 June 1932, 22 June 1932, TML, MBEP, Box 15, Cables sent, 4 May to 30 June 1932.
[118] Leffingwell to Lamont, 27 June 1932, 28 June 1932, TML, CP, Box 19, Folder Morgan & Co – MG & Co. Misc. Private Telegs 14 April to 13 August 1932.
[119] I am indebted to my colleague, Dr. Megan Armstrong, an expert in early modern French religious history, for the information that Henry's remark was likely apocryphal.

prevent its failure.[120] Given these circumstances, Lamont's effort, prodded by Leffingwell, to shift Hoover's position on war debts was a failure. Lamont had prepared the ground assiduously, delivering a speech in June that analysed the reasons behind the Depression while defending Hoover's record. He listed the administration's accomplishments, ranging from the Hoover moratorium that had saved a "complete collapse in Central Europe," to the NCC that staved off banking failures in the Midwest, to the positive work of the RFC in rescuing banks and railways, to the February 1932 passage of the Glass–Steagall Bill, to the defeat of the Soldier's Bonus and other "inflationary schemes," to congressional passage of the Revenue Bill to help balance the budget. All of these salutary measures, Lamont said to his former Harvard classmates, demonstrated Hoover's leadership.[121] Through Egan, Lamont sent Hoover the speech and asked the president whether he would like it repeated. Hoover was pleased, urging Lamont to give the speech elsewhere though he suggested that Lamont give more emphasis to how his administration had saved the American credit structure. Lamont duly complied, the two men collaborating in September 1932 on a recycled version of the speech to lobby the *New York Sun*. While trumpeting Hoover's accomplishments the text warned of past Democratic failings and Roosevelt's indebtedness to dark forces, addenda requested by Hoover.[122]

Hoover was less welcoming of the other message from Lamont relayed by Egan. Pushed by Leffingwell, Lamont inquired whether means might be found to grant relief to Britain and France on war debts. Hoover was unreceptive. The Lausanne Conference had wrapped up with the effective abolition of the Young Plan and the ending of reparations underwritten by an ostensibly secret Anglo-French understanding not to enforce the agreement until an arrangement could be reached with the United States to terminate war debts.[123] This outcome upset Hoover. His animus vis-à-vis the French, spurred by the grudge that he nursed from the moratorium discussions in 1931, spilled over. He told Egan that the French were to blame for painting the British into a corner. Public anger, he claimed, was tremendous, citing the "hundreds of messages" he had

[120] George Harrison to W. Randolph Burgess, 28 June 1932, HHPL, HH, FRBNY papers, Box 3/2210.2, Meyer, Eugene 1931–33.

[121] A copy of the speech, given on the fortieth anniversary of his 1892 Harvard classmates, on 22 June 1932, is in BL, TWL, Series II, Box 98, Folder 22, Hoover, Herbert C.

[122] Lamont to Egan, 12 July 1932, Egan to Lamont, 14 July 1932, Lamont to Hoover, 21 September 1932, Joslin to Sanders, 24 September 1932, BL, TWL, Series II, Box 98, Folder 22, Hoover, Herbert C.

[123] Zara Steiner, *The Lights That Failed: European International Relations 1919–1933*, Oxford: Oxford University Press, 2005, pp. 685–86.

received against any attempt to "gang us" on war debts. Lamont was out of touch with the temper of the American people.[124] Hoover's reaction demonstrated how far the belief that Morgan advice was being driven by European concerns permeated the White House. Despite this rebuff, Lamont was not prepared to give up. Leffingwell and Parker Gilbert, in an internal memorandum to Jack Morgan in early August, argued that the time had come to settle the inter-allied war debts with Britain and France rather than waiting until after the election. They suggested a lump-sum payment might suffice.[125] Shortly thereafter Lamont tried anew to convince Hoover, telling the president that "[s]ustained business recovery – a refilling of the empty dinner pail – is the essential thing now," which in turn depended on settling war debts. To reinforce this message, Lamont raised the spectre that Roosevelt would act in this direction first and that Al Smith was already planning to: "He is no mean politician and he sees the moving of public opinion."[126] This too failed to sway Hoover.

The presidential campaign found the Morgan partners torn. The question of why the partners did not disavow Hoover's cause owes something to Morgan culture, which forbade open political involvement, and something to engrained Republican sentiment. While informed observers knew where the political sympathies of the Morgan partners lay, the firm itself adopted no partisan position. Hoover's rigidity was a source of despair at the Corner but was not enough to dispel the bank's dominant Republicanism. Writing the Morgan Grenfell partner Vivian Smith, Leffingwell reflected, "Most men of property in these parts are hereditary Republicans ... [and] the belief they suck in with their mother's milk [is] that the Republican party is the party of prosperity."[127] While the "rude shocks" since 1929 had shaken this inherited identification, they had not displaced it, he concluded. Anderson remarked, "[a] Republican by instinct, if not by conviction, I found it very difficult to stomach a good deal of the Republican doctrine as to what had been done and what ought to be done," before confessing that he had voted for Hoover.[128] Welding partner affinity to Republicanism was the shuddering of the old order under the impact of the Depression. Morgan Republicanism remained the liberal, international Republicanism of the 1920s before the deluge. Belief that the Depression could only be understood and mastered as

---

[124] Egan to Lamont, 14 July 1932, BL, TWL, Series II, Box 98, Folder 22, Hoover, Herbert C.

[125] Parker Gilbert and Leffingwell to Jack Morgan, 4 August 1932, TML, MBEP, Series 5, Gilbert, Parker S.

[126] Lamont to Hoover, 4 August 1932, BL, TWL, Series II, Box 98, Folder 21, Hoover, Herbert C., 1932.

[127] Leffingwell to Vivian Smith, 11 November 1932, YUL, RCL, Series I, Box 7, Folder 155.

[128] Anderson to de Sanchez, 23 November 1932, TML, MBEP, Box 25, Folder AMA.

an international phenomenon arising from World War I helped keep the majority of the Morgan partners Republican. The Morgan partners may have lost faith in Hoover but not in Republicanism.

Lamont worked behind the scenes to support the Republican cause, intervening where he could to bolster the campaign, lobbying, and partaking in last-minute fundraising efforts to push Hoover over the line. Personally, Lamont gave at least $7,000 to the Republican campaign, while the Morgan partners collectively donated $13,500 to the Republican National Committee, amounts that, while substantial, were much smaller than the $61,500 donated by bankers affiliated with Chase National or even the $28,500 donated by the partners of Kuhn, Loeb & Co.[129] Contrary to what has been suggested, Jack Morgan did not furnish the Republican campaign with $500,000. After a direct personal plea from Hoover in October, he guaranteed this sum against money to be raised later from donors.[130]

While Lamont was exerting his influence to secure Hoover's re-election, his partner Leffingwell was ruminating on his decision to support Roosevelt. In some ways this was not unexpected; Leffingwell was a Democrat. Just how unusual this was in the corridors of power on Wall Street was illustrated by a January 1933 *Fortune* article that identified only his partner Parker Gilbert and two other leading figures on the Street (Thatcher M. Brown of Brown Brothers Harriman and Charles H. Sabin of Guaranty Trust) as Democrats.[131] Leffingwell told Lippmann that his decision to back Roosevelt had been sudden, prompted by a combination of Roosevelt's embrace of cutting tariffs and Hoover's flirtation with leaving gold. "Hoover's lack of economic and social convictions, principles and foresight" and his "nervous irritability and political ineptitude" were, in Leffingwell's eyes, "a great peril to the state." Roosevelt, in contrast, "will have, I think, a sedative effect upon men's minds and souls for some time ... When the patient is dying a change of doctors

[129] William Ziegler Jr. to Lamont, 20 October 1932, 3 November 1932, BL, TWL, Series II, Box 123, Folder 17. Ziegler was the Republican New York State Committee Treasurer acknowledging donations of $2,000 and $5,000; Louise Overacker, "American Government and Politics: Campaign Funds in a Depression Year," *The American Political Science Review*, vol. 27, no. 5 (1933), p. 777.

[130] Lamont to John Markle, 26 October 1932, BL, TWL, Series II, Box 123, Folder 17. In this letter Lamont informed Markle that Seward Prosser of Bankers Trust was trying to drum up $500,000 for Hoover. In the same folder are various documents attesting to Lamont's and J.P. Morgan & Co. efforts to find attendees to a meeting in New York on 27 October 1932 with mixed success. As for Jack Morgan donating $500,000, see the mistaken claim in Jeansonne, *The Life of Herbert Hoover*, p. 414. Donald Ritchie, *Electing FDR: The New Deal Campaign of 1932*, Lawrence, KS: University Press of Kansas 2007, p. 154, sets the record straight.

[131] "Democrats in Big Business," *Fortune*, vol. 7, January 1933, no. 1, p. 18.

may arouse new hope and even that hope may help him to live."[132] Though Leffingwell and Parker Gilbert were in the minority of Morgan partners supporting Roosevelt, they were the Morgan economists and theirs was the counsel that J.P. Morgan & Co. endeavoured to follow in economic affairs. For the moment, they clung to familiar maxims, the pursuit of open-market operations by the Federal Reserve, adherence to the gold standard, the sanctity of balanced budgets, and an insistence on cutting tariffs, but the possibility of a new course beckoned.

*****

Roosevelt's electoral triumph was not viewed with alarm by the Morgan partners. Dean Jay, writing Carter on 10 November, told him that, while only Leffingwell and Parker Gilbert had voted for Roosevelt, "I could discover no enthusiasm among the others who voted Hoover." The result had been taken "philosophically." Perhaps, Jay ventured, the "tide has turned."[133] Some of this calmness derived from the fact that the senior Morgan partners knew Roosevelt; given the compact nature of the eastern American seaboard elite and the common paths that its denizens followed in their upbringing, education, and social milieu, how could they not? Roosevelt was part of "our crowd."[134] Lamont and Leffingwell addressed their letters to him, "Dear Frank." This did not mean that they were friends with the president-elect. Lamont and Leffingwell, like Jack Morgan and Whitney, were acquaintances of Roosevelt's, not his intimates.[135] Their view of Roosevelt was expressed by Leffingwell:

I look for better feeling and somewhat better times under Frank, who is a pleasant and well-meaning fellow, and who has shown no evidence of thinking that he is a superman. He is not. Though I always liked him I thought until a few months ago that Frank was hardly good enough for the job. Some friend of Frank's, Roland Norris I think, is quoted as saying that from college days on Frank has always been chosen for some job or other that his friends thought he was not good enough for. They have always said that Frank was a good fellow, but that he really was not up to the job. But each time he has gotten away with the job very well, whether it was editor of the Harvard Crimson, or State Senator, or Assistant Secretary of the Navy, or Governor of the State.[136]

[132] Leffingwell to Walter Lippmann, 27 October 1932, YUL, Walter Lippmann papers, Series III, Box 84, Folder 1313.
[133] Dean Jay to Carter, 10 November 1932, NDJ papers, Knox College.
[134] A borrowing from the title of Stephen Birmingham's classic, *Our Crowd: The Great Jewish Families of New York*, New York: Harper & Row, 1967.
[135] Contrary to the misguided assertion made in Nomi Prins, *All the Presidents' Bankers*, New York: Nation Books, 2014, which fails to consult the Morgan archival material.
[136] Leffingwell to Vivian Smith, 11 November 1932, YUL, RCL, Series I, Box 7, Folder 155.

This guarded praise incorporated the oft-expressed view that Roosevelt was a lightweight but, more penetratingly, the insight that Roosevelt had been serially successful in office, which suggested far greater capability.

Leffingwell's exchanges with Roosevelt prior to the election had extracted from the latter the admissions that he was in favour of the gold standard, a balanced budget, and tariff reform, all mainstays of the Morgan economic world view, acknowledgements that reassured. The sole divergence was on war debts, on which Roosevelt declined to budge, despite an impassioned plea from Leffingwell.[137] Roosevelt cited the Democratic Party platform that war debts must be paid in full and on time as justification for his implacability. What Leffingwell failed to realize was that Roosevelt, unlike Hoover and the Morgan partners, did not see the wellspring of the Depression in Europe. For Roosevelt, it lay in the United States. Disagreement on war debts was not enough to banish Morgan comfort with the president-elect. Warmth extended far enough in the dying days of 1932 that even Whitney, the senior partner most dubious about Roosevelt, thawed.[138] If Leffingwell fretted to Lippmann early in 1933 that Roosevelt was exhibiting no inclination to treat "with responsible leaders rather than closet advisers," a complaint that arose because Roosevelt had ignored Leffingwell's advice on how to aid the farming sector while remaining mute on war debts, the president-elect's cabinet choices placated.[139] Although Glass declined the post of secretary of the Treasury, the Morgan partners greeted the selection of William Woodin as the new secretary of the Treasury with approbation. Cordell Hull, the new secretary of state, was also deemed a sage choice. Unease about some of Roosevelt's advisors, such as Adolf Berle, Raymond Moley, and Rexford Tugwell, was offset by the installation of Lewis Douglas as Director of the Budget.[140] The latter's commitment to sound money was renowned. For the Morgan partners, the auspices as they read the entrails were favourable when they contemplated a Roosevelt future.

What did Roosevelt think of the Morgan partners? For many historians, Roosevelt's experimentation, malleability, and proclivity to agreement with whomever he was speaking betray a pragmatism that facilitated, rather than drove, the reconstruction of American capitalism. Scholars

---

[137] Leffingwell to Roosevelt, 6 October 1932, YUL, RCL, Series I, Box 7, Folder 146.
[138] Carter told Dean Jay in mid-December that "George Whitney in particular has become quite an admirer" of Roosevelt. Carter to Dean Jay, 15 December 1932, KC, NDJ.
[139] Leffingwell to Lippmann, 9 January 1933, YUL, RCL, Series I, Box 5/110.
[140] JPM & Co to MG; 23 February 1933, TML, CP, Box 19, Folder Morgan & Co. – MG & Co. Misc Private Telegs 2 September 1932 to March 1933; Leffingwell to Lamont, 23 February 1933, BL, TWL, Series V/211/12.

of this persuasion have tended to see the triumphs of the New Deal as owing a great deal to the Hoover administration and to congressional intervention rather than Roosevelt.[141] Portrayed this way, Roosevelt's relationship with Wall Street was responsive to transient political pressures. Roosevelt was willing to accommodate demands from his supporters to constrain the Street and, as part of it, J.P. Morgan & Co., but he harboured no particular animus toward 23 Wall Street nor any especial desire to clip its power. A different interpretation has been advanced by Eric Rauchway. He has argued that Roosevelt had a pre-existing liberal plan for economic recovery that contemporaries well understood. Historians have forgotten this reality, Rauchway suggests, their perception occluded by the influential yet misinformed writings of Frances Perkins, Roosevelt's secretary of labour, who sketched a Roosevelt bereft of strategic planning, the dictates of the Cold War which favoured portraits of Roosevelt that emphasized his reactiveness, and the inaccessibility of archival material to the great early historians of the New Deal, Arthur Schlesinger Jr. and William Leuchtenberg.[142] For Rauchway, Roosevelt meant to constrain business to save capitalism from itself. Credit for doing so was Roosevelt's, not Hoover's. Rauchway's Roosevelt was wary of Wall Street, determined to bring the Morgan bank, and the rest of the Street, to heel.

During the presidential campaign, emphatically in a speech on 21 August 1932 at Columbus, Ohio, Roosevelt had attacked "concentrated economic power," lamenting the "fewer than three dozen private banking houses, and stock-selling adjuncts of commercial banks, directing the flow of American capital," which constituted "an economic Government of the United States." He promised sweeping regulation of Wall Street should he be elected. The speech, with its Money Trust rhetoric, prompted Leffingwell to write Roosevelt. He opened by congratulating Roosevelt on the Democratic nomination, recalled their joint service under President Wilson, while confessing that he was "disappointed" in the "affirmative" elements of the speech, which Leffingwell thought smacked of Glass's more punitive declarations. The subsequent exchange between the two focused on banker conduct between 1927 and 1929. Leffingwell defended bankers on the ground that little was to be

---

[141] Patrick Maney, *The Roosevelt Presence*, Berkeley, CA: University of California Press, 1998, pp. 47–55 is an exemplar.

[142] Eric Rauchway, *Winter War: Hoover, Roosevelt and the First Clash Over the New Deal*, New York: Basic Books, 2018, pp. 14–17. Alan Lawson, in his *A Commonwealth of Hope*, Baltimore, MD: Johns Hopkins University Press, 2006, makes a broader argument for a Roosevelt who as president was committed to implementing a progressive agenda that predated his presidency.

gained by assigning blame for the past; what the American people wanted to hear was how deflation would be overcome today. This did not impress Roosevelt, whose riposte insisted that the bankers needed to admit their failings and demonstrate a willingness to reform. Leffingwell rejected this notion, dismissing any idea of a "false confession." Yet Leffingwell had admitted to Lippmann months earlier that introspection was needed, remarking "I do believe in reform and in heart-searching by bankers and brokers, and all of us, big and little."[143] Why Leffingwell was unwilling to concede this point to Roosevelt is uncertain, though he may have feared those around the president-elect whose ambition harkened back to the days of the Pujo Committee.

Roosevelt understood how tightly the Morgan bank was bound to the fallen gods of banking. This belief had in Frankfurter, an acolyte of Brandeis, an advocate close to Roosevelt. Late in 1931 Frankfurter had written a letter to the *New York Herald Tribune* arguing that banking needed to be segregated into its principal functions. Banking promiscuity, he suggested, had led to a conflation of savings banking, commercial banking, and investment banking, to the weakening of the economy, and the furthering of the Depression. It was a view with similarities to the conclusion Glass had reached about the necessity of severing commercial banking from investment banking. Frankfurter forwarded the letter to Roosevelt who agreed with it.[144] Lamont delivered an address in November 1932 calling for major changes to American banking but did not answer Frankfurter's criticism while only alluding to Roosevelt's Columbus speech. Lamont, while conceding that there had been isolated instances of malfeasance responsible for bank suspensions, argued that the combination of lax regulation by too many regulators married to the existence of too many banks was the decisive factor in the epidemic of banking failures. The way forward, in Lamont's view, was to force all banks to become members of the Federal Reserve system subject to one regulator. Advancing this idea, Lamont dismissed notions that the Federal Reserve was the embodiment of the Money Trust, which he claimed was a figment of overheated imaginations. Allowing branch banking on a regional basis, ideally congruent with the twelve Federal Reserve districts, would reduce the harmful profusion of existing banks

---

[143] The text of the Columbus speech may be found in the *New York Times*, 21 August 1932, p. 18. Leffingwell to Roosevelt, 23 August 1932, Roosevelt to Leffingwell, 14 September 1932, Leffingwell to Roosevelt, 6 October 1932, YUL, RCL, Series I, Box 7, Folder 146.

[144] Frankfurter to the *New York Herald Tribune*, 19 October 1931, Roosevelt to Frankfurter, 4 November 1931, in Max Freedman ed., *Roosevelt and Frankfurter: Their Correspondence, 1928–1945*, Boston: Little, Brown, 1967, pp. 58–60.

while propagating stronger, larger banking units. Privately, Leffingwell
bitingly laid the blame for the weakness induced by too many banks on
"the wicked cowardice of our politicians, and their subservience to the
views of the stupid and numerous, in preference to the few and intelligent,
that forced us into the great storm in a flotilla of canoes instead of a few 50
thousand ton liners."[145] Lamont's speech, publicized widely, drew praise
in quarters that typically harboured suspicions of the Morgan bank. *The
New Republic* thought it a welcome sign that the more enlightened elements in banking understood that tighter regulation was coming to the
banking sector.[146] Yet it did not address Frankfurter's desire for segrega-
tion, nor did it change his conviction that the Morgan bank wielded too
much authority.

Roosevelt was aware that many whose support he needed thought as
Frankfurter did. On 11 January 1933 Roosevelt met with Ed Coblentz,
a New York–based editor for the Hearst papers. Coblentz transmitted
Hearst's view that bankers, stingy with their loans, were crippling recovery. In reply, Roosevelt promised that his cabinet would be free of banking
influence: "There will be no one in it who knows the way to 23 Wall
Street."[147] Days later, meeting Hiram Johnson to offer him the position of
secretary of the interior, Roosevelt was treated to an outburst against J.P.
Morgan & Co. Johnson made the case to Roosevelt that, "[d]uring these
past twelve years, our foreign affairs have been manipulated, operated,
managed, directed and controlled by Morgan and Company." Mollifying
Johnson, Roosevelt pledged that his secretary of state would be free from
Morgan taint.[148] The same day that Roosevelt met Johnson, he urged
Glass to accept his offer of the position of secretary of the Treasury.
Raymond Moley, who was delegated by Roosevelt to handle the discussions with Glass, discovered that Glass wanted Leffingwell as his deputy,
a desire that he relayed to Roosevelt. Roosevelt responded, "Make it
perfectly clear to him that, so far as subordinates go, we simply can't tie
up with '23'."[149]

Veto of Leffingwell aside, there is little to suggest that Roosevelt was
preparing to tackle J.P. Morgan & Co., at least not before the explosive

[145] Leffingwell to Lamont, 4 January 1933, YUL, RCL, Series I, Box 4/95.
[146] "Banking Reform," Lamont speech to the Academy of Political Science,
18 November 1932. The speech was published in its entirety in the *New York Times*
on 19 November 1932; see the regular column, "Not on the Ticker Tape," *The New
Republic*, 7 December 1932.
[147] Rauchway, *The Winter War*, pp. 174–76.
[148] The meeting was 19 January 1933. Johnson wrote separate letters to his sons Archibald
and Hiram Johnson Jr. on 21 and 22 January 1933, respectively. Burke, *The Diary Letters
of Hiram Johnson*, vol. 5.
[149] Raymond Moley, *After Seven Years*, New York: Harper & Brothers, 1939, p. 119.

revelations accompanying the interrogation of Mitchell of National City Bank by Ferdinand Pecora in late February 1933 demonstrated the scale and scope of banking abuses to a fascinated and horrified American public.[150] Certainly, Moley and his fellow Brain Trusters, Berle and Tugwell, were not partisans of Brandeis or Frankfurter; their thinking about reform was varied, eschewing the tropes of the Money Trust in favour of projects devoted to rebalancing an American economy distorted by industrial capitalism.[151] Insofar as J.P. Morgan & Co. was concerned, Roosevelt was prepared to wait on events, which suggests that Rauchway's argument is too rigid.

Irrespective of his advisors' competing intents, or Roosevelt's desires, the Morgan partners did not see in him a threat to reform Wall Street. Much more pressing to the Corner than fears Roosevelt might be unsound were two issues. The first was the poisoned chalice of war debts. The Lausanne Conference had left unsettled whether Britain and France would meet their scheduled war debt payments to the United States. Lamont's efforts in November and December 1932 to broker a compromise – Britain and France were supposed to pay their outstanding amount due on 15 December to the United States – illustrated the fatigue in London, Paris, and Washington with both the question and Morgan engagement. Parker Gilbert and Lamont interlaced conversations with Norman and Morgan Grenfell in London with soundings with Hoover and Stimson on whether British payment of the 15 December instalment to the United States was necessary. Gently, Whigham made it clear to his New York counterparts that discussions were no longer a matter for the Treasury or the Bank of England. The Foreign Office was overseeing talks and was disinclined to listen to Morgan counsel. Hoover's attempts to draw Roosevelt on the matter failed signally, leaving all parties, in Lamont's words, "exhausted, erotic and embittered" with the struggle. Despite Lamont lobbying Roosevelt early in the new year, Leffingwell was more convinced than ever that nothing would be gained from continuing to talk about war debts. While the British had made their payment in December, France had not and Leffingwell thought the prospects of ever obtaining it dim.[152] Faced with Roosevelt's evident unwillingness to forgive war debts, the Morgan partners dropped the matter though it did not change their understanding that full economic recovery required a resolution. Roosevelt and the Brain Trust did not

---

[150] Michael Perino, *The Hellhound of Wall Street: How Ferdinand Pecora's Investigation of the Great Crash Forever Changed American Finance*, New York: Penguin Press, 2010.

[151] Leuchtenburg, *Franklin Roosevelt and the New Deal*, pp. 32–35.

[152] Lamont to Roosevelt, 3 January 1933, BL, TWL, Series II, Box 127, Folder 21; Leffingwell to Lamont, 10 January 1933, YUL, RCL, Series I, Box 4/95.

share the Morgan conviction that the Depression had arisen from World War I and the complications that ensued. Their outlook was fundamentally American, seeking American solutions to American Depression. The war debts question was, if not immaterial, of little import in the eyes of the president-elect.

The second question was the direction of the American economy. Leffingwell was cautious on how the economy might fare in 1933. Prompted by growing signs of a flagging economy post-election, he had written Harrison before Christmas, worried about the direction of Federal Reserve policy. He feared that Harrison's commitment to open-market operations was not whole-hearted. Leffingwell argued that the open-market policy followed in the spring had done "an immense amount of good," and now was not the time to forego it. Leffingwell pointed out that reserve bank credit had dropped about 10 per cent since July 1932 and the total money supply was roughly where it had been at the outset of 1932. He urged that there be no "weakening" in fighting deflation.[153] Lamont was more optimistic. He judged that deflation had reached its end, assuming that the Federal Reserve continued open-market operations. Lamont told Dawes he thought "we are finished with banking panics."[154] There was also confidence in the Corner that the firm was positioned to cope with whatever storms might blow. Jack Morgan told Grenfell in December 1932,

We are closing the year with a sigh of relief, and I have the most agreeable feeling that all of the houses now are in excellent condition, financially completely sound, and know where they stand. If among us we cannot, with sufficient capital, the intelligence we have among the partners, and our standing in the community, make a decent living, I shall be very much surprised.[155]

He was to be surprised. The gradual, then rapid, implosion of the American financial system in February and March 1933 caught J.P. Morgan & Co. flat-footed. Both Parker Gilbert, now "economic advisor" to the Treasury, and Leffingwell participated in meetings in January 1933 that canvassed policy, ranging from balancing the budget, to Treasury purchases of securities, to Federal Reserve open-market operations, and war debts. Little consideration was given to the idea of either devaluing the gold content of the dollar or leaving gold.[156] Leffingwell and Parker Gilbert continued to insist to the Morgan houses in London and Paris

---

[153] Leffingwell to Harrison, 19 December 1932, YUL, RCL, Series I, Box 3, Folder 73.
[154] Lamont to Dawes, 5 January 1933, BL, TWL, Series II, Box 91/11.
[155] Jack Morgan to Grenfell, 29 December 1932, TML, JPM, Box 25, Grenfell.
[156] Burgess to Mills, 19 January 1933, HHPL, HH, FRBNY papers, Box 2/2012.2 Mills, Ogden, 1932–33; FRBNY to Ogden Mills, 30 January 1933, LC, OLM papers, Box 11, Federal Reserve 1933 Folder.

well into February 1933 that the gold standard was indispensable, much to the relief of Morgan & Cie. where gold still ruled and the irritation of Morgan Grenfell where it did not. Both men were worried by the fragility of the economy, but until mid-February 1933 this concern was muted, superseded by the extraordinary effort that the partners were making in preparation for Lamont's scheduled appearance at the Senate Finance Committee hearings on the origins and course of the Depression. Though the partners produced a lengthy analysis which stressed the global nature of the Depression, the centrality of the world war in its origins, and the "intense and alarming nationalism" worldwide for its continuation, in the end their work did not see the light of day until June 1933. Lamont, following Leffingwell's advice, declined to appear before the committee, on the grounds that public confidence was at a low ebb and, with the Roosevelt administration days from taking office, presenting Morgan ideas to a new secretary of the Treasury made more sense than testifying to a lame-duck Senate Finance Committee.[157]

The banking crisis in Michigan in February 1933, which overlapped with Morgan preparations for the Senate hearing, was dismissed initially as a local phenomenon by J.P. Morgan & Co. Difficulties in Detroit were seen as occasioned by "incompetent" management in the two leading banks in the state, by the idiosyncratic nature of the Michigan economy, dominated by the automobile industry, and by the rivalry between Henry Ford and Couzens that had frustrated effective response. There was no need to panic, New York reassured the London and Paris houses, for Detroit "is not a great railroad and trading center like New York or Chicago." Such confidence was soon shown to be misplaced, as over the ensuing days twenty-five states declared a banking holiday. Leffingwell confessed to Carter in Paris on 1 March that "[t]he Detroit thing has spread as we had no notion it would from State to State, and it gives us grave concern."[158]

Belatedly, the partners realized the scope of the unfolding disaster. The last days of the Hoover administration saw Parker Gilbert, Leffingwell, and Lamont make frantic efforts. Over the weekend of 25–26 February, Parker Gilbert and Leffingwell met with Mills, Woodin, Harrison, and Meyer to discuss what might be done. It seems that Parker Gilbert and Leffingwell advanced the notion of direct Treasury or RFC deposits into banks to ensure their solidity. Mills, who had emerged as the most forceful administration exponent for action, raised this possibility with Senators Glass and Joe Robinson, the Democratic majority leader.

---

[157] Leffingwell to Lamont, 23 February 1933, BL, TWL, Series V, Box 211, Folder 12.
[158] Leffingwell to Carter, 1 March 1933, YUL, RCL, Series I, Box 1, Folder 17.

Neither man was prepared to agree to this or any other plan until Congress reconvened.[159] Lamont had by then implored Roosevelt to sanction direct RFC deposits as a part of a package of measures he recommended to the president-elect on 27 February. Lamont pressed Roosevelt to cooperate with Hoover to enable emergency legislation to end the moratoria, arguing that the spectre of societal breakdown arising from restless urban populations deprived of money was too ominous to countenance. He urged the president-elect to allow Federal Reserve banks to buy government securities without limit to provide needed credit. Lamont pointed out to Roosevelt that the federal government needed to raise $1 billion by 15 March, an onerous task unless confidence was restored.[160] Roosevelt had no intention of heeding Lamont's plea, as he refused to deal with Hoover, secure in the knowledge that the banking debacle was Hoover's in popular estimation with his own inauguration just days away.

Lamont's conversations with Woodin on 2–3 March tried anew to enlist Roosevelt, asking him to persuade Roosevelt to issue a statement condemning new moratoria. The partners blamed the spread of banking moratoria upon the action of Congress in publicizing the extent of assistance from the RFC to troubled banks. This, in association with the revelations emerging about the conduct of National City Bank, had undermined confidence. Customers had rushed to withdraw their money. While New York was sound, the strain was mounting. Insuring deposits, as had been proposed, was an idea that the Morgan partners rejected as unwise. Lamont conceded that given the current strain on the gold reserve of the Federal Reserve it might be necessary to suspend gold payments, which would be regrettable but not fatal. This acknowledgement, made on 2 March, was prompted by Leffingwell. Lamont, Leffingwell, and Whitney were among the assembled bankers gathered with Governor Herbert H. Lehman when he opted to declare a moratorium on the night of 3–4 March. To the end the Morgan partners were dissenters, arguing against this step before giving way.[161]

Their counsel was now less and less heard. The key figures in the discussions on saving the banking system were holdovers from the

---

[159] Memorandum by Ogden Mills, 2 March 1933, HHPL, HH, Subject Files, Box 185, Financial Matters Banking and Bankruptcy 1933.
[160] Lamont to Roosevelt, 27 February 1933, BL, TWL, Series II, Box 127, Folder 22. Lamont spoke on the phone with Roosevelt this day as well as writing him.
[161] Lamont to Woodin, 2 March 1933, 3 March 1933, BL, TWL, Series II, Box 138, Folder 5; JPM & Co. to Morgan Grenfell, 2 March 1933, TML, CP, Box 19, Folder Morgan & Co. – MG & Co. Misc Private Telegs 2 September 1932 to March 1933; JPM & Co. to Morgan & Cie, 5 March 1933, TML, MBEP, Box 16, Cables rec'd, 3 January to 31 March 1933.

Hoover administration – men such as Arthur Ballantine, the under-secretary of the Treasury, and Mills, intermixed with Harrison and Meyer of the Federal Reserve, while Berle and Woodin represented the Roosevelt administration. The New York banker most involved was George W. Davison of Central Hanover Trust. Francis Awalt, who as the Acting Comptroller of the Currency in the Hoover administration played an important role in the drafting of the Emergency Banking Act, recalled: "Conference continued on March 6. Mr. Mills was more in the background but in close touch; Parker Gilbert was still more in the background, and it became increasingly evident that a J.P. Morgan part-ner was not wanted around."[162]

*****

As the Depression unfolded, the Morgan partners were fearful, self-interested, and reactive, but they were neither cowed nor passive. They were not Agnes Meyer's small-minded New York banker. Their posture in confronting the Depression was conditioned by the bank's financial fortunes. J.P. Morgan & Co.'s balance sheet was riven by the events of 1931 and then savaged once more between January and March 1933. Would a stronger, more financially flexible J.P. Morgan & Co. have been more adventurous in confronting the Depression? Perhaps their effort to aid private banks would have lasted longer than 1930–31, but the partners knew that they had neither the influence nor the means that myth bestowed on them to check the Depression. Crucially, the Morgan part-ners did not feel that it was their responsibility to lead the struggle against the Depression. That was the duty of the Federal Reserve. It might be suggested that this abdication represented a form of irresponsibility endemic on the Street. A more nuanced perspective is that Wall Street itself was not of one mind, its denizens listening to more than one voice. J.P. Morgan & Co. was the leader of the Street, but its followers were scattered.

It did not help that Morgan remedies for the Depression managed to be both orthodox and incoherent. Leffingwell was insistent that deflation must be checked, but he shied away from any policy that might suggest inflation, favouring what he called a "middle of the road course." As the abyss yawned on 2 March 1933, J.P. Morgan & Co. worried about "federal action which it might be difficult later on to get rid of and the workings of which might lead to inflation upon a considerable scale." Plaintively, Leffingwell bemoaned to Lamont in April 1933 that J.P.

---

[162] Francis Gloyd Awalt, "Recollections of the Banking Crisis of 1933," *Business History Review*, vol. 43, no. 3 (1969), pp. 360–63.

Morgan & Co. were seen as "deflationists."[163] The failure to impress upon the Federal Reserve, upon the financial community, and upon the Hoover administration that the Morgan partners regarded deflation as the existential threat was in some degree the outcome of Leffingwell's insistence on a balanced budget, on government expenditure cuts, and on forcing American prices and wages downward to match lower world levels. He never appreciated that these remedies might contribute, rightly, to the impression that J.P. Morgan & Co. were "deflationists" even while his advocacy of arresting deflation was fierce and sincere.

Confusion over the genuineness of Morgan commitment to the struggle against deflation was exacerbated by the Morgan analysis of the origins and course of the Depression. The resolute insistence on its gestation in World War I and the consequent necessity of redressing war debts and reparations as preconditions to American recovery suited a banking house with associated firms in London and Paris. This insistence meant that the Morgan view of events in the United States was impaired. On 22 February 1933 Leffingwell discussed Michigan with Woodin prior to the metastasizing of the moratorium crisis. He told Lamont, "[t]he Detroit problem seems to be still very difficult, and the general situation in the provinces is I gather bothersome." Days later the Morgan partners cabled Morgan Grenfell that "we are wholly puzzled as to the immediate trend of things in the banking world outside of New York."[164] Beyond, they knew little of what was transpiring in the "provinces," a weakness the costs of which were demonstrated graphically in February and March 1933 when rolling bank moratoria stunned the partners. Morgan internationalism reinforced Morgan myopia in understanding the Depression at home.

Equally striking was the contentious relationship with the Hoover administration. The Morgan partners wanted the Hoover administration to master the Depression. Regrettably, Hoover was not up to the job in the eyes of the Corner. He needed Morgan guidance. Hubris was at work here, for plainly the Morgan regard for Hoover ignored his dedication, his intelligence, his willingness to experiment, while emphasizing the flaws in his character. Hoover's own suspicion of J.P. Morgan & Co. and more generally Wall Street grew under pressure in 1931–32 so that by the summer of 1932 tensions on issues such as short-selling had strained

---

[163] JPM & Co. to Morgan Grenfell, 2 March 1933, TML, CP, Box 19, Folder Morgan & Co. – MG & Co. Misc Private Telegs 2 September 1932 to March 1933; Leffingwell to Lamont, 14 April 1933, YUL, RCL, Series I, Box 4, Folder 95.
[164] Leffingwell to Lamont, 23 February 1933, BL, TWL, Series V, Box 211, Folder 12; JPM & Co. to Morgan Grenfell, 2 March 1933, TML, CP, Box 19, Folder Morgan & Co. – MG & Co. Misc Private Telegs 2 September 1932 to March 1933.

the tie between the White House and the Corner to near breaking. Hoover's defeat in the presidential election in November 1932 provided some relief but the prolonged interregnum required ongoing interaction. Tellingly, as 1933 progressed, the Morgan partners were more in contact with Mills and his officials than Hoover.

This helps explain why Hoover's defeat and Roosevelt's triumph were not an occasion for gloom at J.P. Morgan & Co. Parker Gilbert and Leffingwell, the Morgan economists, had decided that Roosevelt was preferable, while none of the Republican partners shed tears for Hoover's loss. The Morgan partners anticipated that Roosevelt would not differ markedly in his policy prescriptions from Hoover. What would be distinctive was the climate of the Roosevelt administration, which would be sunnier. They did not expect that their voices would receive any less of a hearing from the incoming Roosevelt administration. The events of February and March 1933 suggested otherwise. While J.P. Morgan & Co. beseeched Roosevelt to act in the week before his inauguration, he ignored these overtures. Similarly, the drafting of what became the Emergency Banking Act found Parker Gilbert shunted aside as the meaningful work was conducted by others.

Yet the Morgan bank had already taken a major stride toward Roosevelt before his inauguration, when Lamont told Woodin that the gold standard might have to be suspended. This concession demarcated the moment at which the Morgan bank deviated from the true religion of monetary orthodoxy. There had been hints before, notably in December 1931 when the Morgan partners feared sweeping defaults of governmental debts, that the partners would jettison the gold standard if the circumstances were dire enough. This was the case in March 1933. They were driven to this admission from fear that rippling banking moratoria threatened American capitalism. They could see the effects of deflation in the contraction of their own balance sheet. Unquestionably, the partners hoped that the gold standard would be restored quickly, but if it was not, they were prepared to move forward. If capitalism was to be saved from crisis, then the gold standard must be forfeited.

6   "In the Storm Cellar": J.P. Morgan & Co. and
the New Deal, 1933–1936

On 16 June 1933 Roosevelt signed the Banking Act of 1933. Glass–Steagall, as the act is better known, came at the end of the first Hundred Days of the New Deal. After a pause, there ensued a second round of legislation in 1935–36, labelled by historians the Second New Deal. Collectively the New Deal initiatives between 1933 and 1936 transformed the relationship between the American state and the American people.[1] For the Morgan partners, the consequences of the New Deal were likewise convulsive, remaking their bank and their world. Glass–Steagall was the fulcrum of their relationship with the New Deal. Other New Deal measures, such as the Securities Act of May 1933 and the Banking Act of 1935, were consequential, but it was Glass–Steagall that reconfigured J.P. Morgan & Co. The act stipulated that banks, including private banks like Morgan, could no longer be both a deposit-taking commercial bank and an investment bank – they must make a choice between the two. Grudgingly, the partners complied, announcing in June 1934 that henceforth J.P. Morgan & Co. would conduct a commercial banking business. Little more than a year later, in September 1935, they re-entered investment banking at arm's length, creating Morgan Stanley out of the partners and staff of J.P. Morgan & Co.

Before Glass–Steagall, in the early weeks and months of the Roosevelt administration, the central problem confronting the new president had not changed – ending the Depression and securing the future of American capitalism was the task. How this might be accomplished remained uncertain. Morgan imagining that they might participate in the

[1] The literature on the New Deal is massive. The classic accounts are Schlesinger, *The Coming of the New Deal*, and *The Politics of Upheaval*, Boston: Houghton Mifflin, 1960, and William E. Leuchtenberg, *Franklin D. Roosevelt and the New Deal, 1932–1940*, New York: Harper Torchbooks, 1963. Anthony Badger, *FDR: The First Hundred Days*, New York: Hill and Wang, 2008, is a very good short study. On bankers, see Helen Burns, *The American Banking Community and New Deal Banking Reforms 1933–1935*, Westport, CT: Greenwood Press, 1974.

conversation was less jejune than it appears. Roosevelt was committed to change but was not committed to the form of that change. The Morgan partners pressed an incremental course on the president, stressing the dangers of disrupting the capital markets, the indispensability of private investment, and the threat posed by ill-considered legislation that might throttle a nascent New Deal recovery. This counsel, whatever its attractions, was doomed by the publicity attendant on the investigation conducted by Ferdinand Pecora into J.P. Morgan & Co. in May and June 1933. Emblazoned on papers across the United States, Pecora's findings supercharged suspicions of Morgan power and influence with disclosures of taxes not paid, directorships held, and favourable stock deals for the powerful and well-connected on the so-called preferred lists. Pecora was political theatre, serving up "first-rate entertainment" to an entranced country.[2] If Pecora's findings had little influence on the legislative provisions of Glass–Steagall, this was immaterial. What mattered was that Pecora guaranteed the political toxicity of J.P. Morgan & Co.

After the passage of Glass–Steagall, the Morgan partners looked inward ever more. Feeding this change was the conservatism apparent in J.P. Morgan & Co.'s business practices since the 1931 crises, amplified by uncertainty surrounding whether their investment banking activity would be amputated. Instinctively the reaction was to conserve and curtail. As the economic recovery engendered by the New Deal continued, but became more fitful, the lingering Depression was ascribed to the malignant effects of Glass–Steagall and the Securities Act.[3] Throughout the Hoover years Leffingwell had insisted combatting deflation was the curative for an American capitalism reeling from the long-term structural damage of World War I. Slowly this insistence gave way to another, more parochial explanation in Morgan thinking: the impairment of the capital markets encompassed by Glass–Steagall and the Securities Act was contributing to ongoing economic sluggishness. The existential threat to J.P. Morgan & Co. encapsulated in Glass–Steagall was thus conflated with, and partially displaced, the previous Morgan understanding of why the Depression was occurring while darkening the Morgan assessment of the New Deal. Put differently, the Morgan partners became less concerned with the crisis of American capitalism and more preoccupied with the crisis of J.P. Morgan & Co.

The obsession with Glass–Steagall helps explain why the Morgan partners were "in the storm cellar" as Leffingwell remarked in 1934, as

---

[2] Eugene Lokey, "Along the Highways of Finance," *New York Times*, 28 May 1933, N 11.
[3] For a different view of the American economy in the 1930s, see Alexander J. Field, *A Great Leap Forward: 1930s Depression and U.S. Economic Growth*, New Haven, CT: Yale University Press, 2011.

American business and finance responded to the New Deal.[4] Historians have agreed that big business and finance, with few exceptions, tacked away from the New Deal as it aged even if detailed explorations are scarce. The most visible political manifestation of this phenomenon was the advent of the American Liberty League in 1934, populated by a roster of the who's who of the American business world.[5] Yet the Morgan partners were not in the van of the Liberty League. If most of the partners, including Jack Morgan, Lamont, and Whitney, were antipathetic to Roosevelt and the New Deal after 1934, Parker Gilbert and Leffingwell remained supportive. All the Morgan partners wanted revision of Glass–Steagall, to which end their energies were bent between June 1933 and September 1935. This preoccupation transcended the appeals of the business and financial community to confront the waywardness of the Roosevelt administration. While depicting J.P. Morgan & Co. as a shorthand for American banking, let alone American business, is far-fetched, the complexity of their relationship with the New Deal has not been understood. Certainly, the judgement reached by the standard survey, that bankers opposed the New Deal, "detested" many of Roosevelt's advisors, and worried that the complete nationalization of the banking system might be on the agenda, does not conform to J.P. Morgan & Co.[6]

Many Americans believed that the "Masters of Finance," led by the Corner, were preventing the redressment of economic and political ine-quality promised by the New Deal. Morgan recalcitrance was hindering the arrival of a better future. Father Coughlin and Huey Long – the tribunes of populism – voiced this anger and Roosevelt manipulated it. From his inaugural speech attacking "money changers" to his lambasting of "eco-nomic royalists" at the Democratic convention in Philadelphia in the summer of 1936, the appeal of J.P. Morgan & Co. as a political foil was apparent to the president. Rarely did Roosevelt voice the Morgan name. He did not need to – all in American life knew who he meant. The Morgan partners, unaccustomed to being villains, found this assault galling.

---

[4] Leffingwell to Lamont, 25 July 1934, YUL, RCL, Series 1, Box 4, Custom 96.
[5] Patrick Reagan has made the point on the lack of business studies. See Patrick Reagan, "Business." For an overview of the Du Ponts and the American Liberty League, see George Wolfskill, *The Revolt of the Conservatives: A History of American Liberty League, 1934–1940*, Boston: Houghton Mifflin, 1962; more recently, Kim Fein-Phillips, *Invisible Hands: The Making of the Conservative Movement from the New Deal to Reagan*, New York: W.W. Norton, 2009, pp. 3–25. For business support of the New Deal, Kim McQuaid, "Corporate Liberalism in the American Business Community, 1920–1940," *Business History Review*, 1978, vol. 52, pp. 342–68, and the biography of Young by Case and Case, *Owen D. Young*. Ellis Hawley, *The New Deal and the Problem of Monopoly*, Princeton, NJ: Princeton University Press, 1966 is the canonical overview.
[6] Burns, *The American Banking Community and New Deal Banking Reforms*, p. 182.

If by the summer of 1936 the Morgan relationship with the Roosevelt administration had frayed, what follows weighs the evolution of J.P. Morgan & Co. and its partners under the impact of the New Deal. The Hundred Days, the Pecora hearings, the Morgan effort to modify Glass–Steagall, the struggles of the Corner as a banking business, and the Banking Act of 1935 illustrate how the Morgan partners sought to adapt to a crisis environment that was altering the nature of capitalism as they understood it.

*****

Closed by the Emergency Banking Act, J.P. Morgan & Co. reopened in the first wave of banks on 13 March 1933. Stunned, the partners took stock. Their houses in London and Paris, as well as Fummi in Rome, were clamouring for information. They were eager for New York's assessment of Roosevelt. Unabashed praise was conveyed:

> The record of his accomplishments in just one week seems incredible because we have never experienced anything like it before. With his skill and tact he has harmonized all forces and everything that has been done is sound. He has shown great courage and qualities of leadership which were necessary in this emergency.[7]

Such gushing, which the New York partners admitted might be a "bit over-optimistic," was not uncommon in March 1933. Alexander Dana Noyes, the financial editor of the *New York Times*, later remarked that "[j]udged by the quite unanimous approval from all classes of the community, this action in the banking crisis was the greatest single achievement of the Roosevelt administration."[8]

Amidst the rejoicing at Roosevelt's success, there was disquiet at the Corner. How the new administration would proceed was uncertain. Lamont confessed to Fummi that his record as a prophet was abysmal, cautioning that his prognostications amounted to "drool."[9] Warning lights flashed. On 8 March 1933 Winthrop Aldrich, the chairman of the Chase National Bank, gave a speech that outlined a program for banking and securities reform. Aldrich welcomed the separation of security affiliates from commercial banks that had been embedded in the Glass bill,

---

[7] J.P. Morgan & Co. to Morgan Grenfell and Morgan & Cie., 15 March 1933, TML, CP, Box 19, Folder Morgan & Co. – MG & Co. Misc Private Telegs 2 September 1932 to March 1933. Lamont wrote Dean Jay on 16 March 1933 in a more restrained, albeit still positive, tone. Lamont to Dean Jay, 16 March 1933, NDJ, Knox College.

[8] Alexander Dana Noyes, *The Market Place*, Boston: Little, Brown and Company, 1938, p. 366.

[9] Lamont to Fummi, 17 March 1933, TML, CP, Box 9, Morgan & Co. – Banking Situation and Crisis, 1930–33, File 2.

which had stalled in the Senate in February 1933. He suggested, however, four additional restrictions: no corporation or partnership should be allowed to take deposits unless it was governed by the same regulations and disclosures that constrained commercial banks; no securities dealer should be allowed to take deposits; no officer or director dealing in securities should be allowed to be a director of a commercial bank and vice versa; and, finally, boards of directors should be limited to a more manageable number. Observers were quick to grasp the implications. The *New York Times* noted that Aldrich's reforms were aimed at private bankers. The latter would be deprived of financing from commercial banks to fund securities deals at the same time as the convenient outlet of the security affiliates for placing blocks of securities would be closed. Reducing the private bankers' presence on boards would hurt their influence and curtail access to insider information.[10]

The Morgan partners were mystified. Why had Aldrich made these proposals? Evidently, he was responding to the revelations emanating from Pecora's investigation of National City Bank which had concluded on 2 March. Yet Aldrich's conversion to the reform cause was unexpected. Aldrich was a substantial figure in the New York financial world. His accession to the leadership of Chase after Albert Wiggin stepped down in December 1932 was greeted warmly at J.P. Morgan & Co. Lamont told a correspondent in January 1933 that "Winthrop Aldrich is a grand fellow, and things will carry on in good shape."[11] For some, because Chase was perceived as a Rockefeller bank, Aldrich's reform proposals were deemed the opening salvo in a Rockefeller–Morgan clash. This idea bemused the Morgan partners.[12] Cabling Fummi on 15 March, the New York partners were blunt; despite what the papers were reporting, there was no divide between J.P. Morgan & Co. and Chase National – tales of Morgan–Rockefeller rivalry had no substance.[13] Aldrich's biographer thought that

[10] Coverage of Aldrich's comments was widespread. All of the leading New York papers featured his remarks prominently. The *New York Times* report was on p. 1 on 9 March 1933, with a follow-up article the next day, "Aldrich Proposal Stirs Private Banks," *New York Times*, 10 March 1933, p. 27.

[11] Lamont to Fleishacker, 24 January 1933, BL, TWL, Series II, Box 93, Folder 25.

[12] The *New York Times*, the *New York American*, and the *New York World Telegram* drew this inference, as did *The New Republic*, Vol. 74, no. 955, 22 March 1933, p. 142. One magazine, *Real America*, declared that what was at stake was a struggle between Rockefeller and Morgan interests for the control of the world's oil supply. Parker Gilbert to Lamont, 12 June 1933, BL, TWL, Series II, Box 96, Folder 4.

[13] J.P. Morgan & Co. to Fummi, 15 March 1933, TML, CP, Box 9, Morgan & Co. – Banking Situation and Crisis, 1930–1933, File 2; the argument made in Alexander Tabarrok, "The Separation of Commercial and Investment Banking: The Morgans vs. The Rockefellers," *The Quarterly Journal of Austrian Economics*, vol. 1, no. 1 (1998), pp. 1–16, is not credible. Tabarrok did not have access to the Morgan archives.

Aldrich believed genuinely in reform.[14] Pondering the matter, Leffingwell advanced the speculation that perhaps Aldrich was playing a deep game, seeking to cripple the private banks, rendering their inability to finance the capital markets apparent, and thus opening a way back into the bond business for commercial banks such as Chase once the blockage of the capital markets was demonstrated.[15]

Pecora's decision to investigate J.P. Morgan & Co. after National City complicated matters for the Morgan partners, who now faced three threats: Aldrich, Pecora, and a revived Glass bill. Between March and May 1933, the Morgan partners mounted an effort to persuade the White House of the pitfalls of overly zealous reform, by suggesting to the president the fragility of the capital markets, Morgan centrality to those markets, and the indispensability of J.P. Morgan & Co. to recovery. Banking and securities reform were not foremost in Roosevelt's mind, nor had J.P. Morgan & Co. been subjected to the opprobrium that had descended on National City Bank. Stirring Morgan hope was the assumption that Roosevelt and Woodin were fiscal conservatives. As the New York partners told Morgan Grenfell early in May 1933, they were confident that Roosevelt and Woodin were "on the side of sound money," would resist the "dangers of budgetary inflation," and could be trusted to put their faith in open market operations. There were reasons to think this was the case, among them the reassuring presence of Douglas as the Budget Director.[16]

Lamont laid the groundwork by lobbying Noyes, arguably the most influential figure in the financial press. The gist of Lamont's message was that the Aldrich proposals were entirely negative. His suggested reforms would, Lamont told Noyes, disrupt the capital markets through destroying the mechanism for marketing securities without having a suitable replacement in hand. This criticism was to be a constant refrain in Morgan attacks on the New Deal banking and securities legislation over the next two years. While Lamont thought that requiring all banks to

---

[14] Arthur M. Johnson, *Winthrop W. Aldrich: Lawyer, Banker, Diplomat*, Cambridge, MA: Harvard University Press, 1968, pp. 149–52.

[15] Leffingwell to Glass, 16 March 1933, UVA, Glass MS, Series I, Box 37, Russell C. Leffingwell to Carter Glass.

[16] J.P. Morgan & Co. to Morgan Grenfell, 6 May 1933, TML, CP, Box 19, Folder Morgan & Co. – MG & Co. Misc Private Telegs 10 April to 4 December 1933. For an argument that fiscal conservatism was integral to Roosevelt's New Deal, stressing the role of Lewis Douglas and Henry Morgenthau Jr., see Julian E. Zelizer, "The Forgotten Legacy of the New Deal: Fiscal Conservatism and the Roosevelt Administration, 1933–1938," *Presidential Studies Quarterly*, vol. 30, no. 2 (2000), pp. 331–58.

become members of the Federal Reserve system was reasonable, an unsurprising concession given that the Morgan partners favoured such a step, much of the criticism levied at the security affiliates of commercial banks was, in Lamont's estimation, unfounded. As for the question of directors, Lamont told Noyes that J.P. Morgan & Co. had six partners out of ninety-six directors on the boards of Guaranty Trust, Bankers Trust, and New York Trust, three of the strongest financial institutions in the country. It beggared belief to imagine, Lamont suggested, that so few directors could dictate the course of these institutions.[17] These arguments were repeated subsequently by Lamont in conversation with Woodin and Roosevelt.

Lamont's request for an interview with Roosevelt was ostensibly for a discussion of the perilous state of New York City's finances.[18] On 23 March Lamont met Woodin, prior to a talk with Roosevelt at the White House. The two discussed prospects for a government bond issue, the gold embargo and the looming Pecora investigation. Lamont told Woodin that now was not the moment for the government to embark on major funding, for the capital markets needed a period of recuperation after the recent upheaval. Too early a move might well lead to more deflation by siphoning money from the banks. He urged Woodin to stand firm on the gold embargo, despite murmurings that perhaps it should be abrogated. Returning to gold could wait, Lamont advised, until things had settled down. As for Pecora, Lamont informed Woodin that he had met with Pecora the previous day in New York. He warned that if J.P. Morgan & Co., which to this point had been the rock of the Street, was held up to "obloquy," then confidence would be eroded, imperilling stability. He asked the Treasury secretary to mention this danger to Roosevelt.[19]

The president wanted to discuss New York City. Morgan was acting as agent for the banking syndicate that was negotiating with the City on its looming debt renewal. Lamont had more in mind. He impressed on the president his thoughts on Aldrich, on banking reform, on the Glass bill, on Pecora, while stressing the importance of J.P. Morgan & Co. to the capital markets. Roosevelt opened the conversation by observing he had told James Perkins of National City Bank that in light of the Mitchell

---

[17] Lamont phoned Noyes and then forwarded to him a memorandum. Lamont to Noyes, 10 March 1933, BL, TWL, Series II, Box 80, Folder 13.

[18] Lamont to Roosevelt, 14 March 1933, 20 March 1933, BL, TWL, Series II, Box 127, Folder 21. Both of these messages on New York City went through Margaret (Missy) Lehand to the president. The second asked for an interview.

[19] Notes, Lamont visit to Washington, 23 March 1933, BL, TWL, Series V, Box 211, Folder 13, p. 337 states that John W. Davis accompanied Lamont to the meeting with Woodin.

revelations something must be done about security affiliates. Perkins had indicated (on 7 March) that he was willing to divorce his scandal-ridden affiliate. Could commercial banks shed their security affiliates within a year, the president asked? Lamont was dubious, replying that two years would be necessary to prevent unwanted disorder in the markets. The moment, Lamont told Roosevelt, was delicate. Exit from the Depression required private capital to lead, a function that historically J. P. Morgan & Co. had performed. Nothing should be done that might prohibit the Morgan bank from reprising this role. Lamont told Roosevelt that throughout the Hoover years the Corner had been working to salvage what it could from the wreckage. On two occasions, Lamont asserted, the Morgan bank had saved Chase from oblivion.[20] His broader point was that reform proposals, whether Aldrich's or Glass', would inflict damage if they were implemented too hastily. Lamont asked the president whether he would welcome Morgan memoranda on banking reform. It cost Roosevelt nothing to agree. How reform might be accomplished remained open. Roosevelt floated the idea of bifurcating the proposed Glass legislation into two bills, one to deal with penalties and prohibitions, the other to allow branch banking and other changes. Lamont was happy to endorse this suggestion. Lamont then raised the subject of Pecora's investigation, pledging that, while J.P. Morgan & Co. were committed to cooperation, he worried about its scope. Lamont urged Roosevelt to consider replacing Pecora, or at the least limiting his inquiry through introducing a more responsible associate to his team. Roosevelt, cagy and genial, told Lamont that he would have a word with Senator Duncan U. Fletcher, the chair of the Senate Banking and Currency Committee which had oversight of the Pecora investigation. He did not reveal that he had encouraged Pecora to inquire into J.P. Morgan & Co. via Fletcher. Lamont left his meeting with Roosevelt by promising he would send the memoranda and keep the president updated on New York City and complimenting him on the degree to which his enthusiasm and passion contrasted with Hoover.[21]

---

[20] Lamont claimed that J.P. Morgan & Co. had done this by "holding their foreign deposits." It is not clear what he meant by this reference; he may have been alluding to the strain that the Chase was under in the fall of 1931 when rumours were circulating on the Street and in Europe that leading New York banks were in danger. Wilson in his study of Chase, *The Chase: The Chase Manhattan Bank, 1945–1985,* admits that the bank was hit hard by the Depression but does not suggest that it came close to failing nor is there any indication in the Johnson biography of Aldrich of this peril.

[21] Lamont, *The Ambassador*, pp. 338–39, prints chunks of the Lamont notes on his talk with Roosevelt. The original notes, which are in Lamont's long hand, should be consulted for completeness. TWL visit to Washington, 23 March 1933, BL, TWL, Series V, Box 211, Folder 13.

Lamont sent the president the requested banking memoranda on 27 March. Written by Parker Gilbert and Leffingwell, the two memoranda were distinct. They represented a Morgan effort to shape the nascent New Deal's financial and securities legislation. The first memorandum questioned the English Companies Act as a model for American legislation, the second was a disquisition on banking reform. American banking travails, according to the latter, were due to "the terrible deflation, which is world-wide as well as domestic." Banks outside of New York had been struck particularly hard, where "frozen and shrunken real estate loans and farm mortgages" were the main culprits in bank failures. Unfortunately, due to "witness-stand disclosures," the public had formed the impression that the banking crisis was a product of chicanery by New York banks. Leffingwell and Parker Gilbert argued that this was not the case, for the New York banks were sound and liquid. Restoring function to banks beyond New York was critical, wracked as they were by deflation. Permitting branch banking would be a positive step, though the real problem might be the unwillingness of large, sound banks to take over small, imperilled banks. The practice of chartering state banks should be abolished in favour of mandating that all banks be part of the Federal Reserve system. Competition between state superintendents and the Federal comptroller had been "one of the main causes of the banking disaster." The memorandum was sceptical of bolstering government oversight on the banking sector, given that ten thousand banks had failed in the last decade with supervision in place. Turning to commercial banks, Leffingwell and Parker Gilbert argued that they should not be allowed to take savings deposits, nor to make loans on real estate, instead advancing loans only on stocks and bonds. The capital markets needed succour as they were fundamental to recovery, but contrary to what Aldrich was propounding, the memorandum recommended that commercial banks be stripped of their security affiliates in favour of "private bankers, issuing houses and dealers," though commercial banks would still be allowed to buy and sell bonds. Tellingly, the memorandum advocated fostering more private bankers via legislative changes that would encourage their formation. Regulation of the capital issues market should be based on the Martin Fraud Act used in New York rather than Blue Sky laws.[22] While there was much in the memoranda that was sound and had been discussed in reformed minded circles for some time, the advice to depend more heavily on private bankers was breath-taking in its political naiveté.

Supplementing the banking memoranda was a steady flow of information from Lamont to Roosevelt about New York City. Lamont was

---

[22] Lamont to Roosevelt, 27 March 1933, BL, TWL, Series II, Box 127, Folder 31.

assiduous in keeping the president abreast. Communications on 11 and 18 April, followed by another on 12 May, laid out the negotiation between the bankers and the City on refinancing the City's debt. The banking group and the City had been wrangling for more than year on the City's finances. With maturities of $126 million coming due in late April, the bankers were pushing Mayor John P. O'Brien, a veteran Tammany politician who had succeeded the colourful Jimmy Walker, to proceed with subway unification. Lamont warned Roosevelt that the New York Clearing House was reluctant to extend credit unless this transpired, pointing out that the City would need another $100 million over the course of the year. A week later Lamont told the president that the Clearing House banks had agreed to roll over $123 million of the outstanding debt to 10 June, an outcome that Lamont regarded as poor but better than default. Through Marvin McIntyre, the assistant press secretary, Lamont, relying on the views of Fraser, the new president of the BIS, voiced the fear that New York's continued troubles would lead to flight from the dollar. He reiterated the banking group's unhappiness with O'Brien in a phone call with Louis Howe in May.[23]

The closure of the Harriman National Bank in New York, which occurred while the New York City negotiations were ongoing, complicated Morgan efforts to craft their image of indispensability. The Harriman bank, with deposits of $24 million and no connection to Brown Brothers Harriman, had not reopened on 13 March with other New York City banks. A conservator was appointed. It soon emerged that the former head of the bank had misappropriated monies. Making the collapse of Harriman National awkward were various factors. Roosevelt had insisted publicly that banks would be reopened on a case-by-case basis, dependent on their soundness. This principle, the New York Clearing House argued, absolved them of responsibility for Harriman. Harriman, however, was a member of the Clearing House. Past assurances from the Clearing House had led to the widespread assumption that the Clearing House would stand behind the obligations of its members. Confronted with the possibility of having to make good on the Harriman's obligations, the Clearing House members split. Some, notably Guaranty Trust and National City, believed that they owed nothing to Harriman's depositors. The subsequent row involved Harrison of the FRBNY and reached directly into the Roosevelt administration. According to Jesse Jones, the RFC head, he called on Jack Morgan and asked him directly to put up the funds

---

[23] Lamont to Roosevelt, 11 April 1933, 18 April, 12 May, BL, TWL, Series II, Box 127, Folder 22. The issue was not settled until the fall when a comprehensive debt agreement was forged. The text of the agreement between the banking group and the City is reprinted in the *New York Times*, 1 November 1933, p. 40.

necessary ($5–6 million in the Jones telling) to bail out the Harriman depositors. Precisely why Jones thought Morgan – not a Clearing House member – would undertake to advance its own funds is uncertain though it may attest to a conviction that Morgan controlled the Clearing House. After a fruitless conversation with Jack Morgan and two other unnamed Morgan partners, likely Lamont and Whitney, Jones left after reminding the Morgan partners that the Clearing House had run an advertisement touting the soundness of its members. Jones enlisted Roosevelt to lobby Perkins of National City to stand behind the Harriman bank. The president did so, informing Perkins that he had already spoken about Harriman with Whitney.[24] Independently, Harrison recruited Lamont and Whitney to mediate the dispute. Harrison felt strongly that the Clearing House should honour its "moral obligation" to backstop the Harriman depositors. Harrison wanted to demonstrate that the New York financial community could resolve its own problems without the intervention of Washington. Harrison hoped that Lamont and Whitney might be able to broker a compromise. Guaranty and National City were intransigent. The solution reached owed more to the willingness of Manufacturers Trust, another Clearing House member, to shepherd payment to the Harriman depositors than to Lamont and Whitney.[25]

If their involvement in the Harriman affair had been more happenstance than design, the apogee of seeming communion between the Morgan partners and Roosevelt came with the president's announcement on 19 April that the United States was abandoning the gold standard. The following day Jack Morgan issued a press statement that congratulated the president warmly, shocking observers.[26] A nonplussed columnist in *The New Republic* observed that the Morgan comment was "in no way a spontaneous endorsement" but was "[c]arefully planned." *The New Republic* pointed out that, while Morgan sanction had undercut conservative Wall Street opposition prepared to shriek about the sanctity of the gold standard, it had also worried "progressive statesmen" who feared that there was a catch that they had not contemplated when advocating the suspension of the gold standard. *The New Republic* concluded that the Morgan announcement was written by Lamont whose contacts with the White House were close.[27] J.P. Morgan & Co. had played a part in Roosevelt's

---

[24] Jones, *Fifty Billion Dollars*, pp. 23–25.
[25] The Harriman case may be followed in the Harrison papers, 28 March 1933, 29 March 1933, 9 April 1933, 10 April 1933, FRBNY, Harrison papers, 2610.1. The *New York Times*, among other papers, followed the story closely. Harriman dragged on for years, with lawsuits threatened by aggrieved depositors.
[26] Schlesinger, *The Coming of the New Deal*, p. 202.
[27] "Washington Notes," *The New Republic*, vol. 74, no. 961, 3 May 1933, p. 333.

announcement, but Morgan influence was less determinant than *The New Republic* deemed. Leffingwell had persuaded Lippmann that leaving the gold standard was necessary because of its deflationary effects, citing the rebound in the British economy apparent after sterling's devaluation. Roosevelt, willing to experiment, had read Lippmann's *Today and Tomorrow* column of 18 April to this effect, though the president was unaware that Lippmann's arguments had been shaped by Leffingwell.[28]

Rexford Tugwell thought that Leffingwell was Roosevelt's closest touchstone on the Street. Roosevelt and Leffingwell shared a common worry – deflation – which explained their mutual apostasy on gold. Writing Dean Jay at the end of March 1933, Leffingwell expressed his unease. While praising Roosevelt for his "great courage" in handling the banking crisis and tackling the budget deficit, which was "splendid," Leffingwell observed that the president's policies "have been on the whole deflationary" wondering "[w]hether he and his advisors are going to be able to evolve constructive policies adequate to deal with the deflation." Leffingwell voiced the fear that "everything that is intended to stop the deflation is condemned as unsound and inflationary both here and abroad."[29] Leffingwell was guilty of the sin that he decried. He, like his partners, had welcomed the Economy Bill in March 1933 that slashed government expenditures at the expense of government workers and veterans.[30] Leffingwell was in the phalanx of sound-money men who savaged Senator Elbert Thomas' April 1933 amendment that envisaged boosting the money supply through recourse to printing money and silver purchases. Nevertheless, his assessment of the president's policies was not wide of the mark. Roosevelt, as Leuchtenberg has observed of his opening weeks in office, had "pursued a policy more ruthlessly deflationary than anything Hoover had dared."[31] Yet Roosevelt recognized that this was so in a way that Hoover never did; he understood that he needed to implement measures that would be inflationary to offset deflation. Squaring the circle was thought possible by departing from gold.

The gold standard announcement prompted contemporaries to think that the Morgan voice would be heard in Roosevelt's White House, as it had been in every presidency since the Wilson administration. There were, however, and continued to be, strong countervailing pressures. Roosevelt,

---

[28] Martin Horn, "J.P. Morgan & Co., the House of Morgan and Europe 1933–1939," *Contemporary European History*, 14, no. 4 (2005), pp. 524–25.

[29] Leffingwell to Dean Jay, 31 March 1933, YUL, RCL, Series I, Box 4, Folder 83.

[30] The Economy Bill was the work primarily of Lewis Douglas but had Roosevelt's backing. Among other measures it cut federal salaries by 15 per cent. Robert Paul Browder and Thomas G. Smith, *Independent: A Biography of Lewis Douglas*, New York: Alfred A. Knopf, 1986, pp. 86–87.

[31] Leuchtenburg, *Franklin D. Roosevelt and the New Deal*, p. 47.

as discussed in the previous chapter, was not ill-disposed personally to J.P. Morgan & Co. but he looked askance at its influence and shied away from being associated with the Corner. This had shone through in the inauguration speech. James P. Warburg, still in Roosevelt's good graces, labelled the Morgan firm "taboo" in the White House.[32] The Morgan partners were correct in identifying Roosevelt's basic financial orthodoxy but wrong to assume that this meant that J.P. Morgan & Co. would be sheltered. Men such as Jones, who shared Roosevelt's conservative financial disposition, were anti-Morgan and more generally anti–Wall Street. If neither Jones nor Roosevelt were willing to subscribe to the agitation of advisors such as Tugwell who hankered to nationalize the banking system, this did not mean that they viewed the Corner favourably. Roosevelt's sometime advisor, Frankfurter, told Lippmann on 11 March 1933 that:

It's absurd, tragically absurd, that the House of Morgan should be exercising the power it is exercising, not because they are wicked but because a long term of years, and particularly the last few years, has shown that they are singularly unknowing, and do not even understand the meaning of their own actions.[33]

Others outside the White House chimed in. No paper was more assertive than the *New York American*, Hearst's daily. In an intemperate and violent editorial on 13 March the *American* charged that "confidence men of big business" had done more to undermine the republic than all of the "bolshevists and anarchists in existence." J.P. Morgan & Co., the leader of this cabal, was accused of fostering inflation and speculation, for "pirating from the public and betraying the best interests of the nation," and for acting as a tool of foreign interests, specifically Britain and its empire. The editorial claimed that the Morgan bank had "dominated both political parties in the United States." Thankfully, it continued, Roosevelt was not Morgan's creature and was not beholden to the bank. Aldrich, depicted as the archangel Gabriel, was leading the way to banking reform.[34] Huey Long made it clear in interviews and speeches that the New Deal needed to redress the imbalance in power between the mass of Americans and those such as the Morgans. Long's blunt statement that Parker Gilbert and Leffingwell were among a group of bankers who were "running the thing," testified to his willingness to allege that, while presidents might have changed, Morgan control of the White

---

[32] Warburg interview, CUL, COHC, p. 87.
[33] Frankfurter to Lippmann, 11 March 1933, Max Freedman ed., *Roosevelt and Frankfurter: Their Correspondence, 1928–1945*, Boston: Little, Brown, 1967, pp. 116–17.
[34] Lamont, *The Ambassador*, pp. 336–37, reproduces a substantial chunk of the editorial. A copy may be found in Lamont to William Randolph Hearst, 13 March 1933, BL, TWL, Series II, Box 98, Folder 3.

House had not lapsed.[35] *Barron's* admitted in early May 1933 that "[a] mong the depression grievances common to the great mass of Americans probably none is more bitter than their sense of injury at the hands of investment bankers."[36] Leffingwell had conceded as much when he wrote Dean Jay: "you will have seen there is an anti-big-banker crusade on. There is so much hunger and distress that it is only too natural for the people to blame the bankers and to visit their wrath on the greatest name in American banking."[37]

*****

Crusading found expression in the public response to the announcement that Pecora intended to investigate J.P. Morgan & Co. Americans flooded Pecora's office with suggestions, tips, and recommendations usually baseless or far-fetched but occasionally accurate.[38] Pecora's handling of Mitchell had already won him plaudits, inspiring confidence, ensuring that his inquiry into Morgan would be taken seriously. Expectation ran high. What was Pecora seeking to accomplish? Marrinan wrote a personal and private letter to "Dear Ferd" shortly before the Morgan hearings opened urging that the goals should be to unmask the Morgan "virtual dictatorship" that characterized much of American business and financial life, with the aim being "to break that dictatorship."[39] Pecora's conception was not as far-reaching. Early in May Pecora had, in consultation with Senator Fletcher, rejected calls to expand the inquiry of the Morgan firm into questions such as the entrance of the United States into war in 1917 on the grounds that doing so might embarrass the Roosevelt administration.[40] Pecora, an experienced prosecutor, having reviewed the documents unearthed by his investigators, knew that they did not show that the Morgan partners headed a "dictatorship" commanding American business and finance. He admitted so years later in his 1939

---

[35] Schlesinger, *The Politics of Upheaval*, pp. 54–55.
[36] "Regulation and Recovery," *Barron's*, 8 May 1933, p. 10.
[37] Leffingwell to Dean Jay, 31 March 1933, YUL, RCL, Series I, Box 4, Folder 83.
[38] An example of a well-informed tip was an anonymous writer who suggested that Pecora's investigators look closely at the ties between J.P. Morgan & Co. and the Metropolitan Museum of Art and leading newspapers, particularly the *New York Herald Tribune*. No. 12, 23 March 1933, CLA, NARA, RG 46, Sen 73A-F3, Investigation of Stock Exchange Practices (Pecora Committee), Box 138, Remedies-General A-G.
[39] Marrinan to Pecora, 15 May 1933, CLA, NARA, Sen 73A-F3, Investigation of Stock Exchange Practices (Pecora Committee), Box 130, E.W. Marland.
[40] Fletcher to Ferdinand Pecora, 5 April 1933; Pecora to Fletcher, 6 April 1933, CLA, NARA, RG 46, Sen 73A-F3, Investigation of Stock Exchange Practices (Pecora Committee), Box 143, World War I. Marrinan had sent Fletcher a memorandum advancing the idea, arising from Untermyer and others.

book *Wall Street under Oath*. Pecora's aim was less to destroy a fictional control that the Corner exerted and more to paint J.P. Morgan & Co., the leader of the Street, as tarnished by questionable activity despite its sterling reputation.

Opening on 23 May 1933 and lasting until 9 June, there were twelve days of hearings. For eight of those days, Pecora quizzed the Morgan partners, principally Jack Morgan and Whitney, who consulted frequently with Lamont and John W. Davis, the lead Morgan lawyer and former Democratic presidential nominee in the 1924 election.[41] On specific questions, notably taxation, Keyes, the general manager of J.P. Morgan & Co., testified. The appearance of the Morgan partners before the Senate committee garnered tremendous interest. Media coverage was torrid, the hearing room and adjacent hall so jammed that senators complained about the noise generated by spectators, reporters, and photographers. Moving to the larger marble-floored caucus room on 25 May where the Teapot Dome inquiry was held did not solve matters; in some ways it made it worse for the scraping of chairs on the marble floor drowned out much of the testimony, difficulties that were overcome in the afternoon session by the hasty laying down of carpets and the provision of a loudspeaker (see Figure 6.1).[42] Amid the sweltering heat, *The New Republic* observed, "[s]o completely has the Senate probe into the great House of Morgan blanketed all other issues on the Washington stage that it is impossible at this time to arouse interest in any other topic."[43]

Jack Morgan was first to testify. With the preliminaries dispensed, he delivered a statement about the duties and responsibilities of the private banker that expressed not only his personal convictions but those of his partners. He aimed to shield J.P. Morgan & Co. by depicting private banking as an ethical, honourable profession with a venerable tradition running back to the Middle Ages. Private banking, he told the committee, rested on an appreciation that reputation was paramount: "I should state that at all times the idea of doing only first-class business, and that in a first-class way, has been in our minds." Private bankers, given that they were dependent on their own resources, had to be sure their financial position was sound, a stricture that mandated "disinterested advice" to clients. The uses of private bankers, he continued, were varied. Their

---

[41] The other four days were devoted to the testimony of O.P. van Sweringen, chiefly on Alleghany Corporation.

[42] The *Christian Science Monitor*, 23 May 1933, p. 1. remarked of the opening day, "A crowd unprecedented in the annals of such Senate committee investigations lined the outside corridors of the Senate Office Building and jammed the big committee room, as flashlight and motion picture cameras recorded the event." *The New York Times*, 26 May 1933, p. 14.

[43] "Washington Notes," *The New Republic*, vol. 75, no. 966, 7 June 1933, p. 98.

Figure 6.1 Jack Morgan and partners at the Pecora hearings in 1933 in
a photograph showing the oppressive heat. Bettmann/Getty Images.

freedom of action, Jack Morgan argued, was greater than incorporated
banks who had to answer to boards of directors and to shareholders.
Consequently, private bankers fulfilled a vital function in the allocation
of distribution of capital to industry. Contrary to what was often alleged,
there was a logic to private bankers serving as directors for companies with
whom they did business. Their position imparted confidence to the
market that the offerings made on behalf of the company bore the imprimatur of its bankers, while their financial expertise complemented the
expertise of the existing management. Acknowledging that, while the
Depression had diminished demand from industry for capital, Jack
Morgan affirmed that this was temporary. He warned against any changes
in the "machinery of distribution" of securities that would follow from
restricting the activities of private bankers on the grounds that doing so
would imperil recovery as industrial demand for capital revived. Limiting
the ability of private bankers to take deposits would reduce the flow of
capital to succour industry. On the issue of private bankers serving as
directors of other banks – hotly debated – Jack Morgan admitted that he

was not in favour of it as a policy but demurred to his partners. Banker directors assisted the financial community, situating the private banker as a mediator within the banking world. Robustly, he concluded that "I state without hesitation that I consider the private banker a national asset and not a national danger."[44]

Pecora pursued three themes in rebuttal. First, he sought to demystify the bank, to show how it was organized, to identify its partners, to document the business it conducted, while revealing J.P. Morgan & Co.'s financial condition. Second, Pecora made a case for the preponderance of Morgan influence in American economic and financial life. Morgan loans – to directors of other banks, to individuals with powerful business and political affiliations – were detailed. The directorships held by the partners were disclosed, while senators were encouraged to probe the issue of interlocking directorates. The crucial issue was the so-called preferred lists. The lists documented the preferential distribution of stock to individuals at below-market prices in the three Morgan-sponsored holding companies created in 1929 – Alleghany, United Corporation, and Standard Brands – ahead of the opening of the shares on the NYSE enabling the recipients to make an immediate profit. Third, Pecora endeavoured to demonstrate that the bank and its partners were less high-minded than Jack Morgan had portrayed in his opening statement. Taxes were central. Pecora sought to show that the Morgan partners had manipulated the tax code to their advantage. He pressed home the argument that Morgan behaviour skirted the law on the last day of the hearings when he targeted William Ewing, Thomas S. Lamont, and Harold Stanley for private transactions such as reaping tax losses by selling shares to their wives. He wanted this impression of the Morgan partners to be the lasting one in the public mind.

All three themes were introduced on the first day of the hearings. Laying out for Americans who the Morgan partners were, how the bank was constituted, and who banked with it was a calculated gambit. While doing so illustrated the involvement of J.P. Morgan & Co. with many of the most prominent corporations in American life, demonstrated the privileged place that the Corner had vis-à-vis regulators and the FRBNY, and detailed its connections in London and Paris, it also laid out starkly that J.P. Morgan & Co. was an elite institution with scant connection to the vast majority of Americans. Given that the Morgan bank did not accept deposits from the public, did not retail securities, and had eschewed stock offerings, concentrating almost entirely on issuing bonds since 1913, greater pressure fell on making the case that the scale of

[44] Pecora Committee, 23 May 1933, p. 11.

Morgan influence touched the daily lives of Americans. Disclosure of the Morgan balance sheet occasioned an additional difficulty. J.P. Morgan & Co., whether gauged by assets, deposits, or its capital (net worth), was far smaller than the leading trio of New York money-centre banks, Chase, National City, and Guaranty Trust, all of which had assets and deposits in excess of $1 billion. The Morgan bank was closest in size to Bank of the Manhattan and Chemical Bank & Trust, neither of which stood accused of dominating American economic and financial life. Acute newspaper analyses hinted at this; Pecora, whether he wanted to or not, had to follow the path blazed by Pujo in 1912 by arguing that Morgan influence far outpaced its resources.[45]

Pecora opened by asking Jack Morgan to read a list of the 167 director-ships his investigators had determined the partners held. It made, as Pecora hoped, an impression. The *Christian Science Monitor* reported, "Pipe lines, Alaskan mines, chain stores, transportation companies, great foundries, mail order houses, street car lines, all had their Morgan representatives on their board of directors."[46] However, the aggregate figures were misleading, a point that was driven home on the last day of the hearings in Lamont's exchange with Democratic Senator Edward P. Costigan of Colorado. Costigan, who relied on Corey's 1930 book on the House of Morgan, found his arguments about directorships dis-mantled as Lamont demonstrated that, while it was simple to identify directors, it was far harder to prove that control followed. Two and a half years later, Lawrence Brown, part of the investigative team preparing to question the Morgan partners in the hearings into the munition industry (the Nye hearings), reflected that Pecora had gained less than expected in probing directorships: "this method has been tried, I think, too many times with too questionable results to make me feel happy about proceed-ing with it again. Pecora tried it and Lamont and Whitney riddled it on the stand."[47]

Pecora was on sounder footing when it came to the preferential distri-bution of securities to individuals at below-market prices in Alleghany, United Corporation, and Standard Brands. Not all the committee mem-bers were swayed; Glass, who emerged at the hearings as Pecora's chief

[45] "Morgan assets, deposits compared with 10 banks," *Wall Street Journal*, 24 May 1933, p. 13. The header to the table remarked that it "shows the relation which the firm bears in size to the commercial banks of New York." "Morgan Holdings Surprise Wall St.," *New York Times*, 24 May 1933, p. 16, observed the severe fall in deposits.
[46] "Morgan Holds Private Banker fills Big Need," *Christian Science Monitor*, 23 May 1933, p. 1.
[47] Lawrence Brown to Stephen Raushenbush, 6 December 1935, CLA, NARA, RG 46, 74th Congress, Special Committee Investigating the Munitions Industry, Box 323, Brief 240.

Figure 6.2 Senator Carter Glass and Ferdinand Pecora during the Pecora hearings, 1933. Bettmann/Getty Images.

foe, signalled his opposition (see Figure 6.2). It was only following the retreat of the committee into closed executive session that Pecora prevailed and the lists were duly made public. The great and the good were revealed to have been proffered Morgan largesse. In the case of Alleghany, of a total of 3.5 million common stock shares issued, J.P. Morgan & Co. was earmarked a bloc of 1.25 million. From this bloc 500,000 shares were sold to Guaranty Trust. Of the remaining 750,000, the firm kept some 175,000 for its account, while 575,000 shares were allotted to the partners, business associates, family members, friends, and politicians at a price of $20, well below the market opening figure of $37.[48] Among the names on the Alleghany preferred list were luminaries such as Newton D. Baker, Wilson's secretary of war from 1916 to 1921 and a candidate for the Democratic presidential nomination at Chicago in 1932, Charles Lindbergh, and General John Pershing. Especially embarrassing in Democratic circles was the revelation that Woodin, now the

---

[48] Pecora Committee, 24 May 1933, pp. 138–46.

secretary of the Treasury, and William G. McAdoo, a member of the Senate committee inquiring into J.P. Morgan & Co., were named. More consternation accompanied the revelation of the preferred lists for United and Standard Brands, where other prominent citizens, such as the roving diplomat Norman Davis, featured. Whitney, interrogated by Pecora about whether the Morgan firm expected reciprocity from these favours, denied it. At perhaps the darkest moment in the hearings for the Morgan partners, Pecora then read into the record a response Whitney had received from John J. Raskob, the former Du Pont and General Motors executive, and ex-chairman of the Democratic National Committee from 1928–32: "I appreciate deeply the many courtesies shown me by you and your partners, and sincerely hope the future holds opportunities for me to reciprocate." Whitney's rejoinder that he thought that Raskob's letter was simply a polite acknowledgement did nothing to dispel the image of influence peddling.[49]

The preferred lists cast J.P. Morgan & Co. in a sinister light. Pecora sought to build on this success by delving into taxes as well as the private financial affairs of selected Morgan partners. Taxation was the more effective line of inquiry. It emerged that the Morgan partners paid no income taxes in 1931 and 1932 because of the losses suffered by the firm. When Jack Morgan admitted that he had paid taxes in Britain in the same period, the inequity appeared palpable. Whitney's observation the next day that in 1930 the Morgan partners had paid $11 million in taxes on their 1929 earnings did little to salve the wound. Pecora parlayed his opening by hammering at the question of when Parker Gilbert was admitted to the Morgan partnership. The entrance of any new partner meant reconstitution of the partnership. The decision to date Parker Gilbert's entrance to 2 January 1931 rather than 31 December 1930 allowed the partners to extend the carryover for tax losses an additional year, a point Pecora returned to repeatedly.[50] These attacks had their effect. The Washington Post, in an editorial, "Rich Men Pay No Taxes," acknowledged that, while what the partners had done did not constitute "fraud," it imposed "an unjust burden upon low-salaried citizens who are unable to escape through tax-exempt securities or manipulation of assets."[51] The implication was clear – legal or not, such behaviour transgressed acceptable standards.

If taxes besmirched the Morgan image, Pecora's attempt to extend doubts about Morgan propriety through querying their private

---

[49] Pecora Committee, 25 May 1933, pp. 174–75.
[50] See the jousting between Pecora and Keyes, Pecora Committee, 23 May 1933, pp. 77–87.
[51] "Rich Men Pay No Tax," Washington Post, 24 May 1933, p. 6.

transactions was less successful. The Morgan partners varied considerably in how they conducted their private financial affairs. Marrinan, summarizing the insider trading transactions of partners in stock of firms in which they were directors, observed that Bartow, Cochran, Stanley, Steele, and Whitney made substantial sums between 1928 and 1931, ranging from $200,000 to more than $1.3 million. Anderson and Parker Gilbert, though, did no trading, while Davison, Thomas S. Lamont, Harry Morgan, and Junius Morgan lost money on trading. Ewing, Thomas W. Lamont, and Jack Morgan made modest profits ranging from $15,000 to $60,000 in total across the four years.[52] Given that there was no consistent pattern of Morgan exploitation and that insider trading was not illegal, Pecora opted to underscore more dubious transactions. Pecora cornered Thomas S. Lamont, who had sold stocks to his wife in 1930 and then claimed tax losses associated with the sale, forcing him to admit that he had benefited far more than he claimed, revealing a shabbiness of spirit distant from Jack Morgan's encomium to Morgan principles. Ewing's behaviour was equally grubby. Under questioning from Pecora, Ewing conceded that he and his wife had sold short stocks on behalf of trusts in which they were the trustees. After extracting from Ewing the admission that firm policy prohibited short-selling, Ewing admitted that the stock concerned was Johns-Manville Corporation, on whose board Bartow and Whitney served as directors. Stanley too had sold stock to his wife which produced a tax loss for him.[53] While the blows were real, how damaging they were to the Morgan reputation is uncertain. Thomas S. Lamont, Ewing, and Stanley were not the partners whose names resonated. Of the senior partners, Whitney had engaged in questionable activity but Leffingwell, Jack Morgan, and Lamont were untainted.

When the hearings concluded, their import, despite the blaze of publicity that attended them, was equivocal. The partners were infuriated, railing in their private correspondence at the indignities that they had suffered and maligning Pecora for months thereafter in uncomplimentary, dismissive, insulting terms, attacking his appearance, ethnicity, and religion. Much of this carping was drawn from the wellspring of prejudice rather than any legitimate objection arising from how Pecora had conducted the hearings.[54] The most (in)famous moment, when Jack Morgan

---

[52] Marrinan to Pecora, 29 April 1933, CLA, NARA, RG 46, Sen 73A-F3, Investigation of Stock Exchange Practices (Pecora Committee), Box 141, United Corporation.

[53] Pecora Committee, 9 June 1933, pp. 799–822.

[54] A taste of this vitriol may be found in Jack Morgan's letter to his son Junius in October 1933 disparaging Pecora as a "dirty little wop." Jack Morgan to Junius S. Morgan, 9 October 1933, TML, MBEP, Box 23, Junius S. Morgan.

was photographed with the circus midget Lya Graf on his lap, was the product of the overzealous prompting of a press agent for Ringling Brothers circus. It had nothing to do with Pecora. Pecora's questioning was on occasion sharp, but there was little of the Spanish Inquisition that Lamont bemoaned to correspondents.[55] Though *The Nation*'s antipathy toward the Morgan firm was habitual, there was a ring of truth in its retelling of an observation from a Morgan familiar, "What I cannot stand about them is their smug sureness that they know better than anybody else how everybody else should act."[56] Pecora punctured certainty, which stung. Nevertheless, Morgan fulminations against Pecora dissipated as time passed, leaving a residue of bitterness but little of permanence.

The partners were concerned about the press refracting the hearings in a way that would bend public opinion. They had striven before the hearings to diminish this likelihood, circulating memoranda to selected journalists and papers laying out the Morgan case. Once ended, Lamont orchestrated the despatch of a reprint of Morgan statements made during the course of the testimony – Jack Morgan's opening remarks, Whitney's statement detailing the firm's public securities offerings since 1918, Jack Morgan's concluding comments, and Leffingwell's analysis of the origins, course, and development of US financial and economic matters postwar – to 265 journalists, businessmen, academics, civil servants, financiers, politicians, and diplomats in the United States and Europe.[57] Much of the Morgan worry was ill-founded: the revelations at Washington tended to reinforce pre-existing attitudes. Newspapers and journals that were hostile to J.P. Morgan & Co. before Pecora remained so, while those who were supportive were inclined to find in the testimony much to admire. Attitudes perhaps hardened and the force with which they were expressed heightened. The veteran muckraking journalist Paul Y. Anderson, whose writings had done much to publicize the Teapot Dome scandal in the 1920s, was an example. Working for *The Nation* since 1929, Anderson gave free rein to his contempt, referring to "those creatures, the bankers," whose actions were dominated by greed and self-centredness. What had emerged in Washington "was no shock to me, because I have devoted much study to this particular form of animal life."[58] Obscure tracts depicted Jack Morgan as a half-human, half-spider figure, preying on

[55] Lamont to Lord Reading, 5 June 1933, British Library, India Office Records, Lord Reading papers, f. 118/45. The same letter was sent to Sybil Colefax, 5 June 1933, BL, TWL, Series II, Box 87, Folder 21.
[56] O.G. Villard, "Issues and Men: They Will Never Learn," *The Nation*, vol. 137, no. 3557, 6 September 1933, p. 259.
[57] Lamont to E.T. Sanders, 1 April 1933, BL, TWL, Series V, Box 211, Folder 25; Lamont to Leffingwell, 14 June 1933, BL, TWL, Series V, Box 212, Folder 16.
[58] Paul Y. Anderson, 10 June 1933 and 21 June 1933, *The Nation*, vol. 136, no. 3546.

the American public, as a leering, violent ogre squeezing blood out of
a helpless American populace, or as a laughing, maniacal steam-roller
driver, puffing merrily on his cigar while crushing his fellow citizens.[59] If
neither Anderson nor the cartoons were typical, they attested to the
degree to which Depression and Pecora had interacted with legends of
Morgan power to produce a rhetoric emphasizing violence, suffering, and
redemption through the New Deal.

While the Morgan partners dismissed the cartoons as the ravings of
a "lunatic," two responses wounded: those of the *New York Times* and
Lippmann. The *Times* editorial of 27 May, "Why It Hurts," struck at the
Morgan sense of themselves, lamenting that the partners had foregone
their "fine consciousness of responsibility and trusteeship," sacrificing in
the process "something intangible, something imponderable, that has to
do with the very highest repute." The partners, the editorial continued,
had forgotten that they must not only be unassailable for their financial
integrity, which was not in question, but they must be seen to be unim-
peachable. Nothing could have been more calculated to cut Jack Morgan
to the quick. A disturbed Lamont fired off a rejoinder to Adolph Ochs,
protesting that when the shares were offered none of the men to whom the
privilege was extended were in office, nor were they expected to be in the
future.[60]

Lippmann's defection was graver. More than any single figure in the
print world Lippmann mattered to the Morgan partners. He had been
cultivated by Lamont, Leffingwell, and Parker Gilbert and had in turn
cultivated them. Lamont and Leffingwell regarded Lippmann as
a personal friend. His two columns on the hearings, published on 26
and 31 May, were thus unforeseen. The first, "The Investigation of the
Private Bankers," was upsetting, urging Pecora to ascertain whether
a Money Trust existed and, if it did, to recommend reform.
The second, "The Morgan Inquiry," was injurious. Lippmann was convinced that Pecora had demonstrated that a Money Trust existed, asserting that, "[t]he firm is the center of an immense network of power and
influence embracing the largest corporations in almost every line of
economic activity ... by its prestige and its connections it has exercised
a towering influence upon American corporate financing." Lippmann
argued that this concentration of power in private hands was

[59] Jack Morgan to William A. Otis, 12 June 1934, TML, JPM, Box 55, Folder O/3. Otis had
sent copies of the cartoons to Jack Morgan who had already seen them. Jack Morgan told
Otis that the last one had appeared "four or five months" earlier, suggesting that they
were circulating in the wake of Pecora. William Nulsen may have been the author.
[60] "Why This Hurts," *New York Times*, 27 May 1933. Lamont to Ochs, 27 May 1933, BL,
TWL, Series II, Box 112, Folder 3; Chernow, *The House of Morgan*, pp. 373–74.

incompatible with a healthy democratic state. Looking forward, he suggested, there must be changes, though those that he called for imagined regulating the securities markets to curtail private power, rather than fostering more expansive government control in Washington. The blow was more shocking because Lippmann wrote for the *New York Herald Tribune*, whose owners, the Reids, were beholden to the goodwill of the Corner. Lamont especially, and to a lesser degree Leffingwell and Parker Gilbert, was enraged.[61] While the relationship between Lamont and Lippmann never regained its former warmth, Lippmann's distancing from the New Deal, which accelerated after 1933, revived his engagement with the Morgan partners, though he no longer holidayed with them.

The political effects of the Morgan hearings were muted. The reserved attitude of committee members, especially Democratic senators, who were not inclined to maximize Morgan discomfort, struck observers.[62] Democratic reticence arose from more than McAdoo's embarrassment – the repercussions of the preferred lists reached into the White House. Harold Ickes, the secretary of the interior, recorded that at a Cabinet meeting on 26 May, the question of whether Woodin should resign was raised. Vice-president John Nance Garner was in favour, fearing that public opinion would draw the conclusion that Morgan interests dominated Roosevelt's administration, as they had Hoover's and Coolidge's. Garner's worry was not without foundation. Senator Arthur Robinson of Indiana had insisted the day before Cabinet met that Woodin must go. Robinson, a Republican, was of little moment to the White House. It was harder to overlook Huey Long, who in a speech to the Senate entitled "Our Constant Rulers" on 26 May echoed Garner's charge – administrations might come and go but Morgan power remained. Garner's view did not carry the day. Attorney-General Homer S. Cummings and, crucially, Roosevelt were opposed to asking for Woodin's resignation. Roosevelt may have deflected calls for changes in his administration but the price was acquiescence to Glass–Steagall. The Roosevelt administration did not have the bill as a priority and was opposed to its deposit insurance clauses. The form of Glass–Steagall owed little to Pecora's dramatic confrontation with the Morgan partners. Its legislative guts had been crafted before the Morgan hearing. Raymond Moley was right when he wrote that Glass–Steagall "can hardly be classed as a New Deal

---

[61] Steel, *Walter Lippmann and the American Century*, pp. 289–90; Lippmann, "The Morgan Inquiry," *New York Herald Tribune*, 31 May 1933, p. 17; Lamont's letter to Leffingwell, 10 July 1933, TML, CP, Box 6, Folder Morgan & Co. – Senate Stock Exchg. Hearings Misc. Notes, makes plain just how upset he was at Lippmann.

[62] Arthur Krock, "Democratic Senators Are Not Aggressive to Morgan," *New York Times*, 24 May 1933, p. 20. Krock was the Washington bureau chief of the *Times*.

measure."[63] Nevertheless, the effects of the dramatic testimony in Washington left no doubt that open association with J.P. Morgan & Co. was a liability for a Democratic administration.[64]

*****

As Carosso observed, the Morgan partners were slow to appreciate that politics had changed in Washington.[65] This myopia owed something to continued Morgan belief in Roosevelt and the New Deal. Admiration for the president remained intact. Leffingwell was supportive of Roosevelt's course at the World Economic Conference underway in London in June and July 1933. Unlike many commentators, then and subsequently, Leffingwell approved of the president's decision to scuttle the talks.[66] Though Leffingwell thought New Deal banking and security legislation unwise, he was confident that it could be modified: "[t]he Glass-Steagall Bill and the Securities Bill present the most difficult problems; of which we have not yet found the solution." Optimistically, Leffingwell continued, "I do not consider them insoluble; and I think the best way to solve them is to forget them for a month or two and come back fresh to them in the autumn."[67] It was advice his partners had already taken. With the hearings concluded, Jack Morgan and Lamont both headed to Britain where they found refuge, taking particular pleasure in an editorial published in *The Times* that characterized the Pecora investigation as a witch-hunt. The Morgan partners remaining in New York were encouraged by the direction of the New Deal. Writing his father on 1 August, Thomas S. Lamont chided him for being too "pessimistic," arguing that "the improvement is real, and that, with possible set-backs, it will continue," leading him to recommend purchasing stocks as a long-term investment. Days later Parker Gilbert, in a commentary to Dean Jay, commended the Treasury for its "good job with the public finances." Inflation was dormant, employment was on the mend, leading him to conclude that "[b]usiness is really a good deal better." A month on, in mid-September, a similar view was cabled to Paris, reiterating that we are "very cautiously optimistic."[68]

---

[63] Raymond Moley, *The First New Deal*, New York: Harcourt, Brace & World, 1966, p. 317.
[64] Donald Ritchie, "The Legislative Impact of the Pecora Investigation," *Capitol Studies*, vol. 5, no. 2 (1977), p. 91.
[65] Carosso, "The Morgan Houses," pp. 18–19.
[66] "The Dollar and the Conference," Leffingwell to Partners, 29 June 1933, YUL, RCL, Series I, Box 8, Folder 174.
[67] Leffingwell to Lamont, 30 June 1933, BL, TWL, Series VIII, Box 246, Folder 23.
[68] Thomas S. Lamont to Thomas W. Lamont, 1 August 1933, BL, TWL, Series VIII, Box 246, Folder 23; Parker Gilbert to Dean Jay, 4 August 1933, TML, MBEP, Box 16, Cables rec'd 1 June to 31 August 1933; J.P. Morgan & Co. to Morgan & Cie.,

Through the fall of 1933 the partners, like many, were perplexed by the president's monetary policy. They doubted the soundness of the counsel that Roosevelt was receiving from men such as the Cornell economist George F. Warren and were admittedly "cloudy" on what the president intended.[69] The administration's gold-purchasing program, the subject of acrimony in orthodox financial circles, bewildered. Nevertheless, while the partners were puzzled, they defended Roosevelt. Surveying developments at the year's end, Lamont told his frequent correspondent Sybil Colefax that "[t]he feeling on the whole is that President Roosevelt has, even with some inevitable errors, done a very good job." A month later Anderson repelled criticism from his former Morgan colleague, de Sanchez, describing the president's policies as "pretty intelligent" since entering office, noting that there was no question that the "vast majority" of Americans supported Roosevelt. Writing to the Paris partners at the end of January 1934, Lamont informed them that business was "better" and that "On the whole I should say that we are distinctly cheerful." Weeks later, Leffingwell echoed this sentiment, opining to Dean Jay that the United States is "now out of the depression of 1929 ... [w]e are well on our way out of the slough of despond." Leffingwell remarked that he doubted that there would be a relapse and was positive there would not be "if we can get the capital market open again."[70]

In this last comment lay the tendrils of doubt. Leffingwell, not Lamont, was the principal Morgan point of contact with the president after the passage of Glass–Steagall. Leffingwell's standing as a Democrat, a supporter of Roosevelt and the New Deal, coupled with his identification as one of the more flexible, imaginative thinkers on Wall Street afforded, the partners calculated, a greater chance of a hearing from the White House. Animated by worry that securing revision of Glass–Steagall and the Securities Act would be more difficult than anticipated, Leffingwell wrote Lamont early in the New Year. Reflecting on the passage of Glass–Steagall, Leffingwell dismissed stories that Aldrich had influenced the legislation, a view that explained why Leffingwell had accepted calmly Carter Glass's warning that it had been Aldrich who had concocted the specific clauses targeting the private

---

13 September 1933, TML, MBEP, Box 16, Cables received, 1 September to 29 November 1933.

[69] Jack Morgan to Stanley Baldwin, 23 October 1933, TML, JPM, Box 25, Stanley Baldwin; Lamont to Cochran, 25 October 1933, BL, TWL, Series II, Box 87, Folder 16.

[70] Lamont to Sybil Colefax, 26 December 1933, BL, TWL, Series II, Box 87, Folder 21; Anderson to de Sanchez, 24 January 1934, TML, MBEP, Box 25, Arthur M. Anderson; Lamont to Morgan & Cie, 31 January 1934, NDJ papers, Knox College; Leffingwell to Dean Jay, 17 February 1934, YUL, RCL, Series I, Box 4, Folder 83.

bankers in Glass–Steagall in concert with Roosevelt.[71] The real foes were old ones – Brandeis and Frankfurter.[72]

These views have been described as "rancid musings," redolent of Morgan anti-Semitism, hostility, and paranoia regarding the New Deal. Such a reading is mistaken. Anti-Semitism there was but Leffingwell's letter has been misunderstood because of the failure of historians to read it in its entirety.[73] Leffingwell was tracing Glass–Steagall and the Securities Act to the Pujo hearings, to *Other People's Money*, to Progressivism and the Money Trust, and was suggesting a policy of concessions to allow J.P. Morgan & Co. to preserve itself. Notable was his conviction that the banking side of J.P. Morgan & Co. was dependent on its investment side. Much of this prognosis was incorrect. Neither Brandeis nor Frankfurter had as much sway with the administration as Leffingwell believed, though scholars continue to debate how much influence they enjoyed. Glass–Steagall had many parents, not least of whom was Glass. Nor did Leffingwell's partners accept his suggestion

---

[71] Glass to Leffingwell, 12 July 1933, YUL, RCL, Series I, Box 3, Folder 67; Leffingwell to Glass, 18 July 1933, UVA, Glass MS, Series I, Box 27, Banking Correspondence Glass Steagall Act.

[72] Leffingwell to Lamont, 2 January 1934, YUL, RCL, Series I, Box 4, Folder 96. The complete passage: "It is because it never does to underestimate antagonistic forces that I suggest you reread Brandeis's 'Other People's Money,' ... I have no doubt – but no proof – that Brandeis and Frankfurter are responsible for the clauses in the Glass Bill directed against private bankers, as well as for the Securities Act. Though action on Brandeis's views was suspended by the war and the political reaction which followed the war, they are clearly and effectively expressed in this legislation. I have little doubt that he inspired it, or even drafted it. The Jews do not forget. They are relentless ... The reason why I make so much of this is that I think you underestimate the forces we are antagonizing; and that not any inherent weakness in those forces, but the war and the reaction which followed it held them in suspense. Because I believe that we are confronted with the profound politico-economic philosophy, matured in the wood for twenty years, of the finest brain and the most powerful personality in the Democratic party, who happens to be a Justice of the Supreme Court. I believe that we must give up our directorates, particularly our banking directorates, to save our securities business. I believe further that our securities business is a necessary feeder of our banking business, and that without it the banking business would in time dry up. I shall of course do my very best to present the arguments for the amendments that are necessary, but I am afraid that we are beaten before we start unless we are prepared to make a concession to Brandeis's views."

[73] See Fraser, *Every Man a Speculator*, p. 469, for "rancid musings." Fraser had drawn on Geisst's *Wall Street*, p. 431 as his source. Geisst in turn had adopted his rendition of Leffingwell's comments from Chernow, *The House of Morgan*, p. 379. Unfortunately, Chernow did not include the sentences after the words "Justice of the Supreme Court" reproduced in Note 72. Consequently, neither Chernow nor Fraser nor Geisst understood what Leffingwell was driving at. Perhaps because of this, Fraser indulged in an ill-founded bromide against Leffingwell, portraying his remarks as the expression of a threatened, dispossessed WASP who was anti–New Deal and anti-Roosevelt despite being a "family friend." Leffingwell was anti-Semitic – on that point Fraser is correct – but he was not a Roosevelt family friend, he remained a consistent supporter of the New Deal through the 1930s, and he defended Roosevelt within and without the firm.

J.P. Morgan & Co. and the Crisis of Capitalism

to sacrifice their banking directorships as the price that must be paid to secure revision. As it happened, Leffingwell's partners chose not to follow his counsel but opted rather to persuade a Roosevelt imagined to be amenable to Morgan diagnosis.

Couched within a framework of wide-ranging economic advice, Leffingwell marshalled his arguments, mixing a core message of the imperative of private investment driven by unshackled capital markets as fundamental to the long-term recovery of the American economy with observations on deflation, on gold, and on Federal Reserve policy. Too much intervention, he told the president, risked hobbling recovery. Roosevelt replied with short, genial missives, conceding little while basking in the warmth of Leffingwell's praise.[74] To others, such as Colonel House and Ickes, Roosevelt revealed a different mind, portraying himself as facing a hostile banking coterie that had controlled governments since Andrew Jackson.[75] Undeterred by the president's evasiveness, Leffingwell sent Roosevelt a flurry of letters and memoranda in January and February 1934. If Leffingwell's ideas stamped him as distant from a business community in thrall to the dogmas of "the old prescription of 1932" – chopping government expenditure, restoring a balanced budget, and returning to gold – his urgings were familiar.[76] The basic problem, Leffingwell thought, was that, while the Roosevelt administration had made the correct choices in leaving gold, in managing money, and in prodding the Federal Reserve to lend more freely, permanent recovery rested on a revival of private investment. American capitalism could not survive on a diet of loans originated by the RFC.[77] Changes, therefore, were required to Glass–Steagall and to the Securities Act, for they were damming the flow of capital. Leffingwell argued that raising and distributing capital was the province of those well-versed in fulfilling these functions, namely investment banks and investment bankers. Glass–Steagall

---

[74] Leffingwell to Roosevelt, 2 October 1933, FDR, PPF, 866, Leffingwell, Russell C., Roosevelt to Leffingwell, 12 October 1933, FDR, PPF, 866, Leffingwell, Russell C.; RCL to FDR, 12 October 1933, YUL, RCL, Series I, Box 7, Folder 146; Roosevelt to Leffingwell, 15 December 1933, FDR, PPF, 866, Leffingwell, Russell C.

[75] Schlesinger, *The Coming of the New Deal*, pp. 247–48; Leuchtenberg, *Franklin D. Roosevelt and the New Deal*, pp. 79–80; Harold LeClair, ed., *The Secret Diary of Harold Ickes*, New York: Simon & Schuster, 1953–54, vol. 1, pp. 108–09, 17 October 1933.

[76] Leffingwell to Roosevelt, 4 January 1934, 8 January 1934, 8 February 1934, YUL, RCL, I, Box 7, Folder 146; the correspondence is also in FDR, PPF, 866, Leffingwell, Russell C.; the phrase is Schlesinger's, *The Coming of the New Deal*, p. 478.

[77] Total outstanding Federal direct loans rose from $3.324 billion in 1932 to $4.303 billion in 1933, before jumping to $7.815 billion in 1934. These figures include RFC lending which constituted the bulk of loans but incorporate all Federal agency lending. *Historical Statistics of the United States from Colonial Times to 1957*, table X 389, p. 663.

had attainted experienced and capable borrowers. Making matters worse, the act's authors had failed to understand that investment banking was an intermittent activity. Banks like J.P. Morgan had overcome this problem with a complementary bread-and-butter banking business that underwrote investment banking in lean times. Glass–Steagall, with its stricture against mingling investment and commercial banking, imperilled this sensible arrangement rendering the edifice of capital origination and distribution far ricketier. The Securities Act, if less crimping, had nevertheless installed fear in the minds of those who contemplated lending and borrowing. The liability of directors and officers should be limited, plaintiffs should be required to post a bond for the costs of the litigation, and the registration statement and prospectus should be shortened.

Considering these ideas, Roosevelt redirected the conversation. Leffingwell had sent Harrison before the New Year a lengthy memorandum on "Gold, Money and Prices" that formed part of the package of material given to the president.[78] Though Roosevelt viewed Harrison as the instrument of Wall Street, Leffingwell's willingness to challenge those pining for a precipitous return to gold appealed. Meeting with Leffingwell in early February, Roosevelt solicited suggestions on how interest rates might be lowered. Leffingwell told Roosevelt that the right way, "the inflationary way," was to make the Federal Reserve Banks buy government securities and especially long maturities. Doing so would not only offer relief on the deficit front; it would produce a decline in interest rates which were linked to government bond rates. If this was done, it would allow business to refinance cheaply, especially when Glass–Steagall and the Securities Act were amended. The wrong way, Leffingwell informed Roosevelt, was to proceed "by standstill, moratorium, forced reduction, default, receivership, foreclosure, and all that ilk." Leffingwell warned that this would have a perverse effect, for "by frightening capital . . . and depreciating bonds and mortgages" it would move interest rates higher.[79] Rates – whether one- to five-year corporate bonds, federal governments, municipal bonds, United States Treasury bills, short-term commercial paper, or the FRBNY discount rate – fell sharply from 1934 to 1935 but this had little to do with Leffingwell's advice. Broad-based interest rate reduction rested on the struggling economy, which lost momentum after 1933. Leffingwell's embrace of lower rates went unreciprocated by Roosevelt. Leffingwell pushed the president to allow bankers and private bankers to continue to underwrite on the grounds that otherwise the

---

[78] The memorandum was dated 26 December 1933 and may be found in the 4 January 1934 missive to the president referenced in Note 76.
[79] Leffingwell to Roosevelt, 8 February 1934, YUL, RCL, Series I, Box 7, Folder 146.

government would have to supply needed capital via the printing press. An unimpressed Roosevelt rejoined that this would open the door for bankers to unload securities on captive trust accounts as well as gullible customers. Leffingwell's willingness to insert a proviso that bankers must sell securities through stock exchanges and recognized dealers did not sway the president. Nor did a direct appeal asking for a year's grace on the implementation of Glass–Steagall, postponing a decision until June 1935 rather than June 1934.

The steam went out of Leffingwell's efforts. Periodically he returned to the fray, but his letters to Roosevelt demonstrate that he had conceded, and his protests became less forceful with every sally.[80] Leffingwell did not renounce Roosevelt, defending the administration's policy at an Academy of Political Science public event late in March against the attacks of Mills. Forthrightly, Leffingwell insisted that an "orthodox cheap money" policy would overcome deflation, observing that "It is clearly premature as yet to count upon a balanced budget. The Government cannot and must not let people starve. Nor can it squeeze blood out of a stone or taxes out of losing business." Consistent with his views since 1931, Leffingwell dismissed inflation as a spectre, remarking that he was "whole-heartedly" behind Roosevelt's policy of monetary reconstruction.[81]

The ruction over the Securities Exchange Act early in 1934 displayed the divide between the Corner and the wider financial community on treating with the Roosevelt administration. The Morgan partners, though deploying their press contacts, preferred to try to influence the president directly. Insofar as the Securities Exchange Act was concerned, while the struggle mobilized much of the Street in opposition, J.P. Morgan & Co. was not one of the combatants, appearances notwithstanding. The visibility of Richard Whitney, perhaps the most prominent leader of the die-hard NYSE faction challenging the proposed legislation, and the brother of George Whitney, suggested Morgan involvement. It was assumed that Richard Whitney was voicing, in part, the view of the Corner. Yet the Morgan gaze was focused on Glass–Steagall and the Securities Act, not what became the Stock Exchange Act.[82] Lamont, forwarding to George

---

[80] Leffingwell to Roosevelt, 20 February 1934, 3 March 1934, YUL, RCL, Series I, Box 7, Folder 146; Leffingwell to Roosevelt, 15 May 1934, YUL, RCL, Series I, Box 7, Folder 146.

[81] "World Economists Weigh New Deal; Mills Leads Foes," *New York Times*, 22 March 1934, p. 1. Leffingwell's remarks, in his paper, "The Gold Problem and Currency Revaluation" are reproduced on p. 16 of the *Times* from the event on 21 March.

[82] Chernow, *The House of Morgan*, p. 379, suggests that J.P. Morgan & Co. was part of a "zealous lobbying effort." The most thorough study, Michael Parrish, *Securities Regulation and the New Deal*, New Haven, CT: Yale University Press, 1970, makes no such claim in his chapter, pp. 108–44. Parrish notes the deep involvement of Richard

Whitney information received from Herbert Bayard Swope, warned his partner in February 1934 that his brother was a poor choice if the NYSE hoped to obtain modification of the proposed legislation. Such a reference is rare in the Morgan correspondence. Months later Lamont told his long-time friend William North Duane that J.P. Morgan & Co. was not perturbed by the Stock Exchange Bill because "[o]ur business is not chiefly Stock Exchange business, and, therefore, we would be affected only as the general community is affected." He made it plain that the Corner had "no part" in the "furore" surrounding the bill.[83] Unspoken was acknowledgement that, while Leffingwell was lobbying Roosevelt on Glass–Steagall, J.P. Morgan & Co. could ill afford to alienate the White House with participation in the fight over Stock Exchange regulation. Time pressed; June 1934 loomed.

Late in May 1934 the Associated Press reported that J.P. Morgan & Co. had opted for commercial banking rather than investment banking. The *New York Times* ran a confirmatory article on its front page on 1 June. Analysing the decision, the piece paid attention to the existing state of the securities markets, described as dead or stagnant, while noting that "no definite decision" had been made at the Corner. Speculation was advanced that perhaps some partners might leave to form a new securities house, Drexel in Philadelphia might be hived off, or it was conceivable that the Morgan firm could halt participation in the investment banking business, make no formal choice, and then re-enter it at some future date.[84] Anderson laid matters out starkly to Cochran: "[t]here really is nothing going on outside of the ordinary banking business," observing that "[w]e have done no security business in this office."[85] Awareness that the bulk of the bank's employees, approximately 425, were occupied in routine banking was a potent consideration. Had the partners chosen investment banking J.P. Morgan & Co. would have been overstaffed, forcing large-scale redundancies, a course that was at odds both with the bank's culture and with any future dream of rebuilding the bank's business due to the shedding

Whitney, but the sole reference to Morgan engagement is a 1940 letter retelling a story that Richard Whitney claimed the Jews were out to get Morgan. See Parrish, *Securities Regulation and the New Deal*, p. 130n25. William Lasser's account, *Benjamin V. Cohen: Architect of the New Deal*, New Haven, CT: Yale University Press, 2002, is notable for its lack of reference to involvement by J.P. Morgan & Co. partners.

[83] Lamont to Whitney, 10 February 1934, BL, TWL, Series II, Box 137, Folder 12; TWL to William North Duane, 20 April 1934, BL, TWL, Series II, Box 92, Folder 11.

[84] Leffingwell to Walcott, 26 May 1934, BL, TWL, Series II, Box 104, Folder 13; Associated Press, "No Big Shakeups Now Anticipated in Wall Street," *Christian Science Monitor*, 25 May 1934, p. 10; Associated Press, "Morgan & Co. Plan to be Commercial, Not Security Bank," *New York Times*, 1 June 1934, p. 1.

[85] Anderson to Cochran, 21 May 1934, TML, MBEP, Box 25, Arthur M. Anderson.

of expert staff.[86] Writing Charles Steele months later, Lamont made plain the tactical nature of Morgan compliance:

We all feel, I think, that ways and means will be found to get us back into the security business, either through the amendment of the existing laws or through some separate corporate plan or otherwise. We are considering all these matters now, but have by no means accepted the idea that from June 7, last, we are to be eliminated from the security business.

These hopes intersected with a tentative rapprochement between the Roosevelt administration and the banking industry represented by the American Banking Association (ABA). The ABA had been more hostile toward the New Deal than J.P. Morgan & Co. Surveying the Hundred Days, an ABA editorial warned of the National Industrial Recovery Act, "the words are American but the thought is bearded and strongly Muscovitic." The same issue featured a column by the conservative journalist Mark Sullivan who detected a desire to implement a planned economy. Sullivan was convinced that Roosevelt's policies borrowed indiscriminately from European dictatorships: "We are for the time being, part American and part Russian-Italian-German."[87] Examining the credit markets in the spring of 1934, the title of an ABA article, "National Credit Control," proclaimed banker fears – the New Deal with its panoply of agencies and its reliance on the RFC was in the process of crowding out "private capital in the national credit system."[88] The Morgan partners kept their distance from the ABA, seeing little that was congenial. Leffingwell would later tell Parker Gilbert and Thomas S. Lamont that the ABA has "often been a bad influence in American banking" citing its strident opposition to branch banking as evidence.[89] Despite the recrudescence of business opposition to the New Deal and the resignation of Douglas as Budget Director at the end of August, Roosevelt's willingness to speak at the upcoming ABA convention in October hinted that the divide was not unbridgeable.

Lamont and Leffingwell participated in conversations amid press reports of corporate skulduggery undermining the New Deal, as the United States Chamber of Commerce warned that a "general state of

[86] Lamont, *The Ambassador*, p. 366.
[87] "The Words are American," *American Bankers Association Journal*, vol. 26, no. 1 (1933); Mark Sullivan, "Appraisal of the Revolution," *American Bankers Association Journal*, vol. 26, no. 1 (1933).
[88] George E. Anderson, "National Credit Control," *American Bankers Association Journal*, vol. 26, no. 10 (1934), p. 11.
[89] Leffingwell to Parker Gilbert and Thomas S. Lamont, 8 June 1936, YUL, RCL, Series I, Box 3, Folder 63.

apprehension" existed among businessmen.[90] Lamont was a guest at two dinners held in the second half of September which featured corporate heavyweights – James Perkins of National City Bank, Clarence Woolley of American Radiator, Gerard Swope of General Electric, Alfred Sloan of General Motors, Floyd Carlisle and Alfred Schoellkopf of Niagara Hudson, and Lewis Brown of Johns-Manville – convened to mull over business, unemployment, and the New Deal. Perkins, noted for his access to the White House, hosted the first dinner, while Carlisle took the chair at the second. Harry Hopkins attended the second gathering on behalf of the administration, which Swope was unable to make. Those meeting were men with a willingness to meditate on New Deal heresies. Lamont nevertheless felt compelled to justify the dinners to Roosevelt in the wake of rumblings that business was dictating to the White House, composing a memorandum dated 1 October 1934 sent to the president via Davis. Lamont took pains to assure Roosevelt that business was not seeking to call the tune, stressing that Perkins wanted to sound out the temper of business with the best interests of the administration in mind. Lamont's particular concern, unsurprisingly, was to defend the banking community and his New York brethren as doing what they could to support the president's agenda. Admitting that the banks were flush with cash, Lamont argued that good loans were unavailable. Hopkins attributed to Lamont the view that Roosevelt was "the only hope" in American politics for business.[91] Undoubtedly Lamont would have been delighted by this misleading description, for his allegiance remained Republican.

The day that Davis wrote Roosevelt enclosing Lamont's memorandum, Leffingwell met the president in Washington. There ensued an exchange of letters between the two men on economic recovery that overlapped with Roosevelt's appearance at the ABA convention. Roosevelt inquired what effects a large-scale program of public works designed to put five million to work would have. Leffingwell did not believe that such spending would accomplish its aims. Deficit spending did not perturb him; Leffingwell's fear was that inflation would follow without reigniting the fires of heavy industry. He raised a familiar spectre – such a course would shutter the capital markets permanently through shunting private capital to the margin. Leffingwell recommended loosening National Recovery Administration controls and reopening the capital

[90] "Denies War on New Deal," *New York Times*, 16 September 1934, p. 30; "Six Recovery Issues Raised by Business," *New York Times*, 25 September 1934, p. 10.
[91] Norman Davis to Roosevelt, 10 October 1934, FDRPL, FDR papers, PSF, Box 141, enclosing Lamont's memorandum of 1 October 1934. It is likely that the dinners took place on 16 September and 28 September 1934. Schlesinger, *The Coming of the New Deal*, pp. 497–98.

markets. At Roosevelt's request, Leffingwell expanded on these themes. He suggested steps to "hood the Blue Eagle, and ease up on the codes generally, and have few of them." On agriculture, Leffingwell argued that, while he agreed with Henry Wallace that America could not export its agricultural surplus without trade in manufactured goods, it made no sense to pay farmers to not produce, for it undercut private initiative. The railroad situation needed to be addressed by cutting subsidies to other modes of transportation. Broadening the tax base through the introduction of an income tax akin to that in England was also desirable. He concluded, "more important than any other thing, the market for investment capital must be opened up. Without that there can be no private enterprise, no initiative and no profit to business." Roosevelt was unimpressed. Forwarding the correspondence to Frankfurter, he remarked "somehow I feel strangely cold because I cannot see one constructive thought in either of his letters – do you?" Frankfurter agreed.[92] So ended Leffingwell's direct attempts to nudge the White House toward his prescription for economic recovery. Roosevelt's disenchantment with Leffingwell followed his admonishment to the ABA convention that bankers must follow government in the task of rebuilding the American economy. Scepticism about the genuineness of the ABA's willingness to cooperate permeated the White House. While the ABA might declaim that "[t]he banking and business situation in the United States in these mid-Autumn days may be considered the soundest it has been for the past three years ... There is less of a spirit of experimentation on the part of the Government and less of a spirit of intransigence on the part of business," reconciliation had already faded when these words were published.[93]

*****

At the Corner the confident expressions saluting the New Deal's handling of the Depression dissipated. Leffingwell remarked that things "have taken a turn for the worse."[94] Between March 1933 and September 1935, when Morgan Stanley was established, the salient characteristic of J.P. Morgan & Co.'s banking practice was stasis. Some of this arose from the private banker's ingrained caution; some of it followed from the battering, both financially and psychologically, the bank and its partners had taken in the years since 1930; some of it followed from the grip of the Depression. Some of it,

[92] Leffingwell to Roosevelt, 13 October 1934, Roosevelt to Leffingwell, 23 October 1934, Leffingwell to Roosevelt, 30 October 1934, YUL, RCL, Series I, Box 7, Folder 146; FDRPL, PPF, Box 866, Roosevelt to Frankfurter, 2 November 1934.
[93] Schlesinger, *The Coming of the New Deal*, pp. 499–503; "The Condition of Business," *American Banking Association Journal*, vol. 27, no. 5 (1934).
[94] Leffingwell to Lamont, 25 July 1934, YUL, RCL, Series 1, Box 4, Folder 96.

though, was by choice, brought on by uncertainty surrounding the future. What would the shape of J.P. Morgan be? That question, which was not resolved until September 1935, drove a policy of extreme prudence. Frederick Osborn, who had forged an impressive business career before moving on to the board of the Carnegie Foundation in the 1930s, discovered this when he attempted to contest Carnegie's investments, then directed by Leffingwell: "I didn't have a very high opinion of the imaginative ability of J. P. Morgan, as I said. They played everything very safe."[95] Shortly after Lamont had disputed the assertion that banks were unwilling to lend in his memorandum to Roosevelt, he wrote Edward A. Filene, of Filene department store fame. Filene had approached Lamont with a plan that he was working on to establish a cooperative department store chain. He wanted Morgan financing to underwrite the scheme. The financing costs would be discharged out of profits. Morgan staff thought that Filene's idea might work. Lamont informed Filene that J.P. Morgan & Co. would not extend financing, remarking "[t]hese are not like the old days when there were a great many men with money quite willing to undertake any enterprise because they felt that if such enterprises were successful they would reap an adequate profit."[96] Lamont's spurning of Filene was representative. Loans made by J.P. Morgan & Co., which stood at nearly $74 million on 31 March 1933, fell to just over $53 million on 1 June 1934, before sliding to under $35 million at year's end on 31 December 1934. Thereafter, while loans recovered somewhat, the total resting on the books of the Corner at the end of June 1935 was just over $42 million – 57 per cent of the figure at the end of Roosevelt's first month in office.[97]

It was not simply that the Corner was lending less. The bank was pinned to the fortune of industries limping under the impact of the Depression. Nowhere was this more apparent than the railroads. The latter was a "sick industry," that had seen freight volumes fall by 50 per cent from 1929 to 1933, employment rolls decline by 41 per cent, and bankruptcies surge, including the Missouri Pacific.[98] The Missouri Pacific had been placed in the hands of a trustee on 31 March 1933 after the Van Sweringens conceded they could no longer withstand the strain. At the Pecora hearings Morgan involvement with the Van Sweringens had absorbed four days of testimony. Consolidation of

[95] Frederick Osborn, CUL, COHC, 1967 interview, p. 29.
[96] Vernon Munroe to Lamont, 24 October 1934, Lamont to Filene, 19 November 1934, BL, TWL, Series II, Box 93, Folder 21.
[97] See Appendix 2 for details.
[98] Earl Latham, *The Politics of Railroad Coordination 1933–1936*, Cambridge, MA: Harvard University Press, 1959, p. 8; "Missouri-Pacific Put in Bankruptcy," *The New York Times*, 1 April 1933, p. 23.

the railroads was fraught with complications, chief among them the difficulties of dragging a fractious industry toward acceptance of a common plan, as Joseph Eastman, Roosevelt's federal coordinator of railroads, discovered.[99] With the Morgan balance sheet under pressure, the railroads preoccupied the partners. Their Van Sweringen exposure was an ulcer. Jack Morgan had sent Woodin two memoranda in March 1933 suggesting ways to improve Interstate Commerce Commission regulation of the industry, while advocating reducing wages. Neither attracted the support of the Roosevelt administration. During the halcyon days of the summer of 1933, the partners indulged in the fancy that the railroad sector was healing as the economy strengthened.[100] As this hope faded, the problem remained.

Morgan sensitivity to the Van Sweringen tie was illustrated by Lamont's intervention with Vincent Astor, the publisher of Raymond Moley's *Today* magazine, when the latter ran an article entitled "Cleveland Whirlpool" that alleged Morgan loans to the brothers had been saved through the expedient of coercing the Van Sweringens into furnishing more collateral. Lamont insisted on, and obtained, a printed correction. Frederick Lewis Allen experienced Morgan touchiness about the Van Sweringens firsthand. His account of the Morgan–Van Sweringens relationship in his upcoming book, *The Lords of Creation*, was challenged by a fifteen-page-long memorandum composed by Anderson.[101] Lamont referred to the "Van Sweringen pyramid" in a memorandum written for his partners, language that was not heard beyond the walls of the Corner.[102] When Charles A. Beard appeared before the Senate Interstate Commerce Committee on behalf of the Missouri Pacific independent bondholders to argue that "the Morgan banking syndicate ... [has] the power at any time to deprive the Van Sweringens of their seat at the table and to send them to the bread line," he misunderstood the Morgan relationship with the brothers.[103] The partners shackled

---

[99] See Latham's concluding remarks, where defence of Eastman rests in part on the intractability of the railroad problem. Latham, *The Politics of Railroad Coordination*, pp. 267–77.

[100] Jack Morgan to Woodin, 21 March 1933, TML, JPM, Box 25, William H. Woodin; Parker Gilbert to Dean Jay, 4 August 1933, TML, MBEP, Box 16, Cables rec'd, 1 June to 31 August 1933.

[101] Lamont to Vincent Astor, 6 February 1934, BL, TWL, Series II, Box 107, Folder 28. The corrective appeared on 17 February 1934. Frederick Lewis Allen to Hildegard Allen, 10 June 1935, LC, FLA papers, Box 2, correspondence 1935.

[102] Lamont, 1 June 1934, "J.P. Morgan & Co. and Their Relations to the Public," BL, TWL, Series V, Box 214, Folder 13. Years later Lamont was still defending the Van Sweringens to outsiders, as in a letter to William Allen White, 11 March 1939, BL, TWL, Series II, Box 137, Folder 5 in rebuttal of comments that White had made in his biography of Coolidge.

[103] Beard's comments are reported in "Asks Wide Inquiry in Rail Financing," *New York Times*, 21 March 1935, p. 37.

the Van Sweringens but were in turn cuffed to them. Unlocking these manacles became ever more desirable with the announcement by Eastman in July 1935 of an inquiry into the railroads, including the Missouri Pacific, to be conducted by Senator Burton Wheeler.[104] O.P. Van Sweringen's subsequent attempt to propose a reorganization of the Missouri Pacific, bruited as having the sanction of the Corner, attracted strong opposition. The Morgan partners decided that they could wait no longer – the time had come to end their association with the brothers, putting the Van Sweringen railroad empire, which the Morgan banking group had controlled since the default by Alleghany on loan payments due on 1 May 1935, up for auction. It was not coincidental that excising their most embarrassing affiliation was juxtaposed with the creation of Morgan Stanley. Held on the last day of September 1935, the Van Sweringens repurchased their lost empire at the auction with a bid of $3.121 million. The Morgan syndicate absorbed a loss of $43 million.[105]

As the Depression continued, J.P. Morgan & Co. found refuge in the harbour of US government securities. Lamont had pointed out in his October 1934 memorandum to the president that banks had made heavy purchases of US government bonds, observing that Morgan's holdings had surged by $25 million in the last four months. This understated what had happened and was in the process of happening. J.P. Morgan & Co. had slightly more than $146 million in US government securities on its books at 31 March 1933, a figure that rose to nearly $170 million at the end of June 1934 before surging to reach $242 million at the close of the year. A decline in the first quarter of 1935 was soon corrected, and on 29 June 1935 J.P. Morgan & Co. held more than $255 million of US governments. Cash, US government securities, and state and municipal bonds equalled 70 per cent of Morgan assets on 1 June 1934, a proportion that rose to 79 per cent a year later.[106] If a *Barron's* editorial, entitled "The Case for the Banks," observed that such defensiveness was a sectoral affliction, the *Wall Street Journal* pointed out just how much of an outlier the investment by the Corner in US government securities was, far outstripping any competitor.[107] Morgan propensity to invest in US government bonds was not a "capital strike," designed to pressurize the Roosevelt

---

[104] C.C. Colt, "Rail Probe Aims at Several Roads in Reorganization," *Wall Street Journal*, 6 July 1935, p. 1.
[105] "Bankers Hold Key in Missouri Pacific," *New York Times*, 4 August 1935, F 3; "Vast Rail Empire Re-Won at Auction by Van Sweringens," *New York Times*, 1 October 1935, p 1.
[106] Appendix II, J.P. Morgan & Co. Condensed Financial Statement.
[107] "The Case for the Banks," *Barron's*, 21 October 1935, p. 12; "Morgan & Co. Holdings of U.S. Governments Up $122,000,000," *Wall Street Journal*, 4 January 1936, p. 1. There were extenuating circumstances, namely the Italian invasion of Ethiopia and the

administration as has sometimes been charged.[108] Morgan was motivated by uncertainty regarding Glass–Steagall. With reticence guiding, J.P. Morgan & Co. was struggling for profitability. The arc of surplus and partners' balances (net worth) was downward: when Roosevelt entered office, they stood at nearly $45 million, itself a sharp fall from the lofty figure of almost $119 million at the end of 1929; as of 29 June 1935, they amounted to just over $30 million. Although deposits rose more or less steadily, climbing from nearly $239 million on 31 March 1933 to reach more than $360 million on 29 June 1935, this was of little comfort.[109]

Reflecting on the conundrum facing the firm, Lamont wrote his partner Charles Steele in November 1934. Lamont and Steele had the two largest capital positions in J.P. Morgan & Co. Reviewing, Lamont stated his conviction that a way out of the invidious choice forced by Glass–Steagall would be found. For the moment, he told Steele that Morgan business had been halved due to the New Deal legislation that exiled the firm from the securities business. Consequently "we shall, of course, have difficulty showing any substantial profit" despite Bartow's skill in managing matters. If the bank was to remain on an "even-steven" basis, expenditures had to be slashed. Salaries had been reduced – Bartow had economized to the tune of nearly $1 million. The firm's summer camp for employees and their families was shuttered for 1934.[110] Rather than paying 6 per cent on the capital balances, Lamont suggested that the firm should reduce it to 5 per cent, a change that would pain him and Steele most but would produce savings of approximately $550,000–$600,000 per year. Leffingwell, who had been consulted, proffered the view that partners' drawing accounts be reduced by another 25 per cent, which would reinforce the stricture "that personal expenditure must be curtailed." Jack Morgan had taken this to heart, aiming to cut his expenditures in the coming year by $60,000 while keeping his yacht *Corsair* in dock. The letter concluded, "Jack is on the ocean; due next Tuesday or Wednesday. He, of course, knows nothing of this suggestion."[111]

Despite the tone of the letter to Steele, Lamont's belief that J.P. Morgan & Co. need not accept Glass–Steagall's stringencies was buoyed by Roosevelt's nomination of Marriner Eccles to lead the Federal Reserve

subsequent flight of European capital seeking safe haven in the United States, where the Morgan name remained a beacon of stability.
[108] The phrase "A Strike of Capital" was the title of an article by Raymond Swing for *The Nation* where Swing made the connection between capital shortage and fascism. Raymond Swing, *Good Evening: A Professional Memoir*, New York: Harcourt, Brace & World, 1964, p. 173.
[109] Appendix 2.   [110] Lamont, *The Ambassador*, p. 373.
[111] Lamont to Steele, 15 November 1934, BL, TWL, Series II, Box 131, Folder 21.

Board. Eccles was a banker from Utah, who had guided his bank through the tumult of the Depression before coming to wider attention for his testimony to the Senate early in 1933. Following a brief sojourn in the Treasury – a perplexing deviation given the rancour between himself and Henry Morgenthau Jr. – he was put forward by the president to head the Federal Reserve Board.[112] Eccles, convinced that the Federal Reserve system had been dominated throughout its existence by the New York financial community, to its detriment, and to the lasting damage of the American economy, lusted after a transformative project. Expunging Wall Street's influence on the Federal Reserve while transferring power from New York to Washington was his aim. The memorandum that he submitted to Roosevelt as a condition of taking the job, which declared this objective, had been drafted by Lauchlin Currie with whom Eccles had worked at the Treasury and who was to become his assistant at the Federal Reserve.[113] The Eccles proposals, contained in what became the Banking Act of 1935, would consolidate authority over the Federal Reserve system in a revamped Federal Reserve Board at the expense of Wall Street and the FRBNY. Critics assailed the idea as the domination of credit by political partisanship.

The Eccles plan gave the Morgan partners renewed hope of overturning Glass–Steagall. While they were unsympathetic to Eccles' ideas, and were aghast at the idea that Washington should be the new locus of monetary authority, the struggle offered an opening. Glass, with his fearsome self-identification with the Federal Reserve, derided Eccles, "this damned ex-Mormon missionary," ceaselessly. Glass had long since left his sympathies for the New Deal behind, convinced that Roosevelt was constructing a personal dictatorship enabled by men of Eccles' ilk. Glass conceived of Eccles' ambitions as perverting the Federal Reserve system that he had fashioned. His power in the Senate was such that Glass could not be ignored. Glass found an ally in the apostate Warburg, who had left the Roosevelt administration and was now attacking its policies at every turn, publishing incendiary works excoriating the New Deal.[114] Glass and

---

[112] A capsule biography of Eccles may be found at Federal Reserve History: www.federalreservehistory.org/people/marriner_s_eccles. Eccles wrote an autobiography, Marriner S. Eccles, *Beckoning Frontiers*, New York: Knopf, 1951; the older biography by Sydney Hyman, *Marriner S. Eccles*, Palo Alto, CA: Stanford University Press, 1976, has now been supplanted for the New Deal years by Mark Wayne Nelson, *Jumping the Abyss: Marriner S. Eccles and the New Deal, 1933–1940*. Salt Lake City: University of Utah Press, 2017.
[113] Nelson, *Jumping the Abyss*, pp. 178–79.
[114] Irving S. Michelman, "A Banker in the New Deal: James P. Warburg," reprinted in Melvyn Dubofsky and Stephen Burwood, eds., *The American Economy during the Great Depression*, New York: Garland, 1990, pp. 181–205.

Warburg were willing to modify Glass–Steagall to Morgan advantage by either excising or weakening the clauses prohibiting private bankers from taking deposits while engaged in investment banking. This was a by-product of their desire to thwart Eccles and the Banking Act rather than a fundamental principle they believed in.

The Morgan partners chose to stay in the background, appreciating that Glass and Warburg would make the running. Warburg was aware that bankers were skittish about the prospect of confronting Eccles, telling Glass before testifying to his Senate committee that "so far as I can see, there are very few bankers who are going to take any kind of stand on the proposed legislation." Circumspection may have been warranted. The *New York Herald Tribune* reported that many bankers were staying on the sidelines because they worried that if the proposed legislation was defeated what would follow was the introduction of the so-called Chicago Plan backed by Senator Bronson Cutting that would mandate 100 per cent reserves for demand deposits.[115] This possibility was more than unpalatable; it was unimaginable given that its implementation would constrict dramatically banker freedom in lending. The ABA, in an editorial "Politics Out," warned against the "political control over banking" but feared that "selfish obstructionism" to the bill would be the excuse for some in Washington to propound more radical change.[116] The Morgan partners quietly urged Eccles' foes on. Jack Morgan, writing Rodd early in July 1935, referred obliquely to both Morgan optimism and Morgan activity: "it looks more hopeful for ourselves especially. Mr. Lamont will have told you of his telephone conversations regarding the Banking Bill."[117]

Others, however, were also aware of what was at stake. *The Nation* ran an article postulating that the legislation was the most important banking bill since the Civil War, arguing that it would correct Woodrow Wilson's failure to overcome the Money Trust. *The Nation* asserted that Eccles, in alliance with Giannini of Bank of America, was doing Roosevelt's work in bidding to end Morgan hegemony over "the credit policies of the nation."[118] Harold M. Fleming, in his weekly column on Wall Street

[115] "The Week in Finance," *New York Herald Tribune*, 25 February 1935, p. 23; Ronnie J. Phillips, "The Chicago Plan and New Deal Banking Reform," Working Paper No. 76, Levy Institute, June 1992, pp. 25–40, www.levyinstitute.org/pubs/wp/76.pdf.
[116] Warburg to Carter Glass, 8 April 1935, UVA, Glass MS, Series I, Box 35, Banking Act of 1935 Carter Glass and James P. Warburg; "Politics Out," *American Banking Association Journal*, vol. 27, no. 11 (1935).
[117] Jack Morgan to Rodd, 3 July 1935, TML, CP, Box 31, Morgan & Co. – Foreign Loans and Financing.
[118] Sassoon G. Ward, "Giannini Fights Morgan," *The Nation*, vol. 140, no. 3651, 26 June 1935, p. 737.

for the *Christian Science Monitor*, charted the ebbing of Morgan hopes. Noting that the ABA had shifted to a neutral stance on the bill, Fleming observed that the clause pertaining to letting deposit-taking banks underwrite remained contentious. He remarked, "there is considerable doubt that the president will pass the new feature. It is too favorable, among other things, to the firm of J.P. Morgan & Co. to be politically palatable in Washington." Two weeks later, Fleming signalled that, while the "prestige of Senator Glass" meant that the Senate version of the legislation would likely prevail, one aspect would be struck – ending the ban on letting commercial, deposit-taking banks underwrite.[119] The ABA acquiesced, telling its members after passage of the Banking Act that the "new law is basically sound and merits confidence on the part of the banks."[120] Though Warburg lauded Glass for his splendid fight, in truth Eccles had triumphed (see Figure 6.3). The bill that emerged accomplished what he wanted – the relocation to Washington of monetary sovereignty in a Federal Reserve system that bridled Harrison, the FRBNY, and by implication J.P. Morgan & Co.[121]

The Morgan partners knew defeat when they saw it. Writing his father, Junius Morgan told him the legislation had emerged from the Senate Finance Committee without the underwriting clause permitting J.P. Morgan & Co. to re-enter investment banking. He and Parker Gilbert were sailing on the *Europa* that evening to meet Jack Morgan at his Scottish retreat of Gannochy where they would iron out the last details ensuring that the formation of XYZ corporation (Morgan Stanley), would go ahead.[122] Announcement of Morgan Stanley was front-page news. Fleming remarked on the "degree of ceremony rare in the financial district" with which Lamont made the declaration to reporters. Jack Morgan was resigned in his letter to Montagu Norman:

> By doing this we hope to be able to continue to serve our old clients, and any suitable new ones … We are assured it is legally sound, and while it's most distasteful to me … it seems the only way to accomplish what we want at present … If and when a certain amount of freedom returns … we can undo this easily and go on as before.[123]

---

[119] Harold M. Fleming, "The Week in Wall Street," *Christian Science Monitor*, 15 July 1935, p. 9; Fleming, "Underwriting of New Securities by Commercial Banks Defended," *Christian Science Monitor*, 31 July 1935, p. 11.

[120] Editorial, *Banking* (the renamed *American Banking Association Journal*), vol. 28, no. 3 (1935), p. 37.

[121] Schlesinger, *The Politics of Upheaval*, pp. 300–1. Whether Eccles appreciated that his reformed Federal Reserve system would be subject to Treasury authority is another matter. Meltzer, *A History of the Federal Reserve*, p. 415.

[122] Junius Morgan to Jack Morgan, 24 August 1935, TML, MBEP, Box 23, File 6.

[123] Jack Morgan to Montagu Norman, 8 September 1935, BE, G1/143.

Figure 6.3 President Franklin D. Roosevelt signs the Banking Bill 1935.

From left: Senator Carter Glass; Comptroller of the Currency J.F.T. O'Connor; Senator Duncan U. Fletcher; Secretary of the Treasury Henry Morgenthau Jr.; Jesse Jones, Chair of the Reconstruction Finance Corporation; Representative Henry Steagall; and Governor Marriner Eccles of the Federal Reserve. Harris & Ewing Collection, Library of Congress, Prints & Photographs Division, LC-DIG-hec-47151 (digital file from original negative).

Morgan Stanley began life with Harold Stanley, Harry Morgan, and William Ewing as its guiding triumvirate, joined by two Drexel & Co. partners, Perry E. Hall and Edward H. York Jr. Two senior staff, John M. Young and A.N. Jones, respectively the managers of the bond and statistical departments, also transferred. Capitalized at $7.5 million, Morgan Stanley was private, its common and preferred shares held entirely by the officers of the new bank and by the senior J.P. Morgan & Co. partners, including Jack Morgan, Lamont, and Steele. If the appearance of Morgan Stanley was the most wrenching manifestation of imposed change, it was not singular. Earlier, the long-standing relationship with Morgan Grenfell in

London, heartfelt to Jack Morgan, was transformed in compliance with Glass–Steagall. Fearing that its existing partnership structure would enmesh J.P. Morgan & Co. in unwanted complications, from June 1934 Morgan Grenfell became a private limited company in which J.P. Morgan & Co. held shares. The New York partners were no longer partners in London. Only Jack Morgan was a director, with the remaining board consisting of the resident Morgan Grenfell partners. Though a similar change was mooted vis-à-vis Morgan & Cie. in Paris, this proved unnecessary, for unlike Morgan Grenfell, the Paris house did not issue securities.[124] A quiet revolution had also taken place in leadership. Jack Morgan's acknowledgement at the Pecora hearings that he was semi-retired was offset by his public prominence during the hearings; Lamont's letter to Steele revealed the reality of the firm's internal power dynamic. The J.P. Morgan & Co. that continued from September 1935 was distinct from the firm that had existed before Glass–Steagall even if the name and partnership continued. This transformation was not understood by outsiders, who continued to see the Morgan bank as unreconstructed. Nowhere was this more apparent than in politics.

******

Toward the end of March 1935 Jack Morgan received a letter from an unknown correspondent, F.W. Muth. Muth asked why J.P. Morgan & Co. had abdicated its responsibility to lead America out of the trough of Depression. He claimed that many of his acquaintances were as mystified as he by Morgan inaction. Muth's plaintive inquiry spoke to an abiding conviction that J.P. Morgan & Co. tapped out the rhythms of American economic life. Muth's puzzlement was genuine, fostered by certainty that the Morgan firm would set a positive beat. Others, while agreeing that J.P. Morgan & Co. was at the centre of things, reached very different conclusions. During the debate on the Banking Act of 1935 Glass was threatened:

You will die an early death if you block confirmation of Mr. Eccles as Governor for the Federal Reserve Board. You are also fighting the bill to create a gov't controlled Central Bank to take control of money matters out of the hands of Morgan. How much are you getting from Morgan to be his office boy and faithful stool pigeon?

The letter writer(s) accused Glass and J.P. Morgan & Co. of fomenting the Depression and of plotting to begin another world war as an escape from economic calamity. Glass was warned that he was being watched.

[124] Morgan Grenfell, 16 June 1934, TML, MBEP, Box 22/403 C/2. Capital was £5,000,000 of which £1.7 million was paid up; on Morgan & Cie., Lamont to Cochran, 15 August 1934, BL, TWL, Series II, Box 87, Folder 16.

The letter concluded, "<u>Down WITH ALL TYRANTS.</u>" It was signed "The GET RID OF MORGAN SOCIETY."[125]

There is no reason to think that any such society existed beyond the imaginings of the letter writer(s). Through the 1920s animosity toward J. P. Morgan & Co. had been tempered by economic prosperity. After 1929 the Hoover administration, though its relationship with the Corner was strained, had sheltered J.P. Morgan & Co. from the political winds. The advent of Roosevelt, followed by the Pecora hearings, tore away the protective presidential covering. Those like Muth who were well-disposed to the Morgan firm signalled their perturbation with polite, anxious letters. However, as the Get Rid of Morgan Society letter made plain, one retelling of American catastrophe assigned culpability to Wall Street in alliance with nefarious international bankers, as expounded by Father Coughlin and Huey Long. What made Coughlin and Long distinctive was less their message, which channelled long-standing grievances, albeit blended in a new way, but rather their skilful use of media as the means to disseminate that message to a much larger audience.[126] American populism reached every corner of the nation with radio. If neither man implied violence as openly as the Get Rid of Morgan Society author(s), Coughlin and Long wanted to see Wall Street bankers fettered.

Coughlin, whose radio audience burgeoned from the summer of 1930, and Long, who entered the Senate in 1931, targeted bankers in their addresses and speeches. The local community banker was not the object of complaint. Money-centre banks, New York banks, Wall Street banks, conflated and jumbled, were their butt. As Alan Brinkley has noted, this did not mean that the two thought identically. Coughlin focused his arrows on those who he believed controlled the financial system, a group consisting largely of bankers but also encompassing men such as Andrew Mellon and Ogden Mills. Long's shots spattered more widely, landing on the wealthy generally, such as the Rockefellers and Du Ponts. Long, as his subsequent National Share Our Wealth society showed, evinced a conception of American equality that was more far-reaching than Coughlin's, though neither Long nor Coughlin were systematic thinkers. Both charged that the Depression was due to the fecklessness of the elite, even if underlying it were the problems of modernity

---

[125] Anonymous, Undated, UVA, Glass MS, Series I, Box 37, 1935 Federal Reserve Board Appointment Marriner S. Eccles as Governor.

[126] Warren, *Radio Priest*, on Father Coughlin; T. Harry Williams, *Huey Long*, New York: Alfred A. Knopf, 1969 is still the standard; for an insightful comparison, Alan Brinkley, *Voices of Protest: Huey Long, Father Coughlin, and the Great Depression*, New York: Alfred A. Knopf, 1982.

associated with the transition to an industrialized society. Insidious forces headquartered in London, the "international bankers," working with Wall Street, had gulled the United States. American participation in the world war was due to their conniving. Nor had this malignant influence ended with peace; if Coughlin and Long supported Roosevelt in 1932, they soon came to see his administration as in thrall to the bankers.[127]

Before 1933 there is little to suggest that the Morgan partners perceived either Coughlin or Long as a threat. This changed. Late in November 1933 before an audience estimated at 6,000–7,000 in a packed New York Hippodrome, Coughlin charged that the "Wall Street and Morgan attack on the Administration" was designed to "ruin Mr. Roosevelt and build up Ogden Mills for president in 1936." He asked his listeners to boycott newspapers that supported Wall Street. Al Smith, Hoover's Democratic opponent in the 1928 presidential election and at odds with Roosevelt, was, Coughlin declared, complicit in this unholy alliance against the New Deal. Over the next two weeks Coughlin told his radio audience that he had "entered the lists against Morganism" with the aim of combatting "their financial imperialism" and resisting "their domination and dictatorship in the economic sphere." Slavish Morgan adherence to the gold standard, Coughlin alleged, was responsible for the Depression. Morgan, he went on, dictated the hours and wages paid in various industries. The Morgan bank was, Coughlin intoned, the "gold-standard capitalist."[128] The Morgan partners were unsure how to respond. "Poisonous" Coughlin might be but his massive audience required caution. Lamont and Leffingwell drafted a rebuttal to an earlier Coughlin address in which the radio priest had described the firm as opponents of New Deal monetary policies. At length the partners decided not to send it, fearing that to do so would only make matters worse. This pattern – provocation by Coughlin, dalliance with the temptation of responding, and then ultimately silence from the Corner – continued as Coughlin broadened his attacks, focusing increasingly on the intersection of domestic and foreign policy. Addressing a crowd of 18,000 at a sold-out Madison Square Garden on 22 May 1935, Coughlin labelled Jack Morgan "the fiscal agent of Great Britain, the master mind behind the Federal Reserve Bank."[129] Again the partners declined to reply. Morgan forbearance was motivated in part because, while the partners recognized

[127] Brinkley, *Voices of Protest*, pp. 145–53.
[128] "Priest Charges Morgan Seeks Roosevelt Ruin," *Washington Post*, 28 November 1933, p. 24; "Coughlin Assails Roosevelt Critics," *New York Times*, 4 December 1933, p. 8; "Coughlin hits Gold as Oppressing Men," *New York Times*, 11 December 1933, p. 2.
[129] Lamont to Whitney, 28 December 1933, Lamont to Leffingwell, 15 January 1935, BL, TWL, Series II, Box 89, Folder 16; "Text of Father Coughlin's Address Attacking Plutocracy and the Bonus Veto," *New York Times*, 23 May 1935, p. 18.

252 J.P. Morgan & Co. and the Crisis of Capitalism

the appeal of fighting fire with fire, there might be undesirable consequences. When another cleric, the Philadelphia Reverend John Clover Monsma, offered a countervailing set of sermons on radio if J.P. Morgan & Co. would fund him, he was declined.[130] Inciting a conflict between the Catholic Father Coughlin and the Presbyterian Reverend Monsma was perilous. Making such a choice easier was the Morgan understanding that the divide between Coughlin and the Roosevelt administration was widening with every passing month as the radio priest chafed at his lack of influence with the White House. Coughlin annoyed the partners; but Morgan hopes of overturning Glass–Steagall rested in Roosevelt.

Long's populism posed a greater menace in that his control of Louisiana politics buttressed by his senatorial position furnished a platform for a presidential bid in 1936. His establishment of the National Share Our Wealth society early in 1934 signalled a move in this direction, accompanied shortly thereafter by a definitive break from Roosevelt. Long did not hide his intention to tackle the "Masters of Finance," as the Morgan partners were labelled in his posthumously published tract, *My First Days in the White House*, rushed into print after his assassination in September 1935. The book imagined a confrontation between Long, the newly elected president, and a Wall Street overawed by his most implacable, obstinate foe – Jack Morgan. While most plutocrats soon fell into line, J.P. Morgan & Co. continued to oppose redistribution of American wealth. Aided by John D. Rockefeller Jr., whom Long had appointed as Chair of the National Share Our Wealth Committee and to whose side flocked Mellon, Young, Charles M. Schwab, Baruch, Aldrich, and even Henry Ford, Jack Morgan's defiance was overcome and the way opened to the creation of an American utopia.[131] Fanciful as it was, the tale drives home the moral that, for Long, J.P. Morgan & Co. was the bedrock of obdurate American capitalism. If in Coughlin's case the Morgan partners flirted with challenging his claims publicly, there was no idea of engaging with the Kingfish. The Morgan attitude toward Long was careful, for his interrogation of Lamont during the Pecora hearings had demonstrated Long's agility as a questioner. Yet Long was an outlier in the Senate with few allies and fewer friends. While there existed a substantial senatorial cohort chary of J.P. Morgan & Co., seeing the bank as the ruler of an exploitative eastern capitalism that was alternately hostile, indifferent, and ignorant to the United States beyond the

---

[130] Rev. John Clover Monsma to Lamont, 15 December 1934, Lamont to Thomas S. Lamont, 17 December 1934, BL, TWL, Series II, Box 89, Folder 16; Leffingwell to Lamont, 6 October 1934, YUL, RCL, Series I, Box 4, folder 96.
[131] Huey Pierce Long, *My First Days in the White House*, Harrisburg, PA: The Telegraph Press, 1935. Reprint: New York: Da Capo Press, 1972, pp. 67–115.

Mississippi, men such as William Borah of Idaho, Edward Costigan of Colorado, Hiram Johnson of California, Robert La Follette Jr. of Wisconsin, Gerald Nye of North Dakota, Elbert Thomas of Utah, and Burton Wheeler of Montana were not inclined to follow the Kingfish. The threat represented by Long's demagoguery, though it persisted in the shape of his acolyte Gerald K. Smith, rested on the possibility that Long might become president – and died with him.

Coughlin and Long, however, were material in shaping Roosevelt's political stance toward Wall Street. Writing in the *New York Times* in June 1935 Delbert Clark observed:

At the extreme left are the Pied Pipers, playing strange music that fascinates as it repels. By swinging definitely to what his conservative opponents term the left, Mr. Roosevelt is in a fair position to drown out the piping of Long, Coughlin and company. If the country really wants more liberalism, his advisers hold, the best opposition he can have is that of "Wall Street," and this opposition he can have and retain by such measures as the Banking Bill, the Wagner Labor Relations Bill, and the Holding Company Bill.[132]

Supplementing these bills were the Revenue Act of 1935, popularly known as the "Wealth Tax Act" or the "Soak the Rich" tax. The latter served Roosevelt well, masking the failure to make the American tax system more progressive and redistributive through a symbolic assault on "economic royalists." The top 1 per cent, including the Morgan partners, paid more, but few others did.[133] The ABA, its minuet with Roosevelt ended, in the fall of 1935 took up a more obstructive course, criticizing the president sharply. He in turn attacked "entrenched greed," referencing anew the "unscrupulous money-changers" in his annual message to Congress in January 1936.[134] As one historian has put it, the "mailed fist of open political warfare" was adopted by Roosevelt in his dealings with the business community in 1935–36.[135] His fiery renomination speech in Philadelphia with its savaging of the enduring power of "economic tyranny" stressed that the New Deal had not finished its tasks.[136] It was precisely this prospect that excited the animosity of much of the business and financial community who saw in a second Roosevelt triumph the destruction of American capitalism.

[132] Delbert Clark, "Roosevelt Recharts His Course," *New York Times*, 30 June 1935.
[133] Mark H. Leff, *The Limits of Symbolic Reform: The New Deal and Taxation, 1933–1939*, Cambridge: Cambridge University Press, 1984.
[134] Annual Message to Congress, 3 January 1936, *The American Presidency Project*, www.presidency.ucsb.edu/documents/annual-message-congress-2.
[135] Kennedy, *Freedom from Fear*, p. 278; Leuchtenburg, *Franklin D. Roosevelt and the New Deal*, pp. 183–84.
[136] *The American Presidency Project*, www.presidency.ucsb.edu/documents/acceptance-speech-for-the-renomination-for-the-presidency-philadelphia-pa.

254   J.P. Morgan & Co. and the Crisis of Capitalism

For J.P. Morgan & Co., what mattered was Glass–Steagall. Under its impact, the Morgan partners either had their faith shaken or lost faith in the New Deal, wondering if its aims were more far-reaching. Leffingwell ruminated: "This whole thing [the New Deal] is not an attack on J.P. Morgan & Co., but an attack on our social order and incidentally upon J. P. Morgan & Co."[137]

Leffingwell's remarks might be dismissed as little more than puffery save that some contemporaries thought similarly. The "Unofficial Observer" (John Franklin Carter), a fierce critic of the Corner, remarked in his 1934 book *The New Dealers*, "The bankers ... are the center of power of the Old Order which is being displaced by the New Deal. If Roosevelt can establish social control over the whole credit system, the victory of the New Deal is half won."[138] It was in this vein that Leffingwell wrote Lippmann in the spring of 1935 that

so long as the Administration lends the great weight of its authority to the doctrine that not merely the bankers but the business leaders in all fields are contemptible and untrustworthy ... then the average man will conclude that it is wrong in not proceeding further to the left, to Senator Huey Long and Father Coughlin.

He feared that Roosevelt's administration was "gradually undermining the capitalist system." Lippmann thought Leffingwell's apprehensions overwrought, though he agreed that the New Deal was showing itself to be less and less friendly to business.[139]

If Leffingwell worried, Morgan trepidations tumbled out in Jack Morgan's reply to Muth. Inquiries commissioned by the bank had revealed that Muth was a solid citizen from a good family and might well be a Republican. Jack Morgan told Muth that his missive had affected him "very deeply." He and his partners were filled with "pain and grief" at their "helplessness." The explanation for Morgan passivity, Jack Morgan explained, lay in the New Deal's legislation. Regrettably, "the active stand which you call for is ... utterly impossible," lamenting that J.P. Morgan & Co. was "the center of the attack."[140]

If this letter was crafted by various hands it rings true as an approximation of Jack Morgan's views. Between 1934 and 1935 Jack Morgan became a bitter critic of the New Deal, penning comments in his private correspondence that expressed his antipathies, as when he wrote a relative

---

[137] Leffingwell to Lamont, 6 October 1934, YUL, RCL, Series I, Box 4, Folder 96.
[138] The Unofficial Observer, *The New Dealers*, p. 389.
[139] Leffingwell to Lippmann, 7 March 1935, Lippmann to Leffingwell, 17 March 1935, YUL, Lippmann MS, Series III, Box 84, Folder 1314.
[140] Jack Morgan to F.W. Muth, 2 April 1935, TML, JPM, Box 108, Folder 382. Almost certainly Jack Morgan did not write this letter on his own. It was likely a product of various partners.

in June 1936 to complain about "Roosevelt and his Jew counsel" inhibiting recovery.[141] Increasingly he fulminated about what he saw as Roosevelt's predilection for dictatorship. When Childs remarked in May 1936 on "the fanatical hatred of the President which today obsesses thousands of men and women among the American upper class" he did not have Jack Morgan in mind specifically, but the description fit.[142] The most persuasive explanation for Jack Morgan's animosity is that the New Deal threatened J.P. Morgan & Co. – the bank of his father, his bank since 1913. Lamont, ever careful, was opposed to the New Deal and his partner Whitney was of like mind. Those close to both knew how deep their private feelings ran; ascertaining the attitudes of the other Morgan partners is more difficult.[143] Given that most were Republicans and Glass–Steagall threatened the breakup of J.P. Morgan & Co., why did the Morgan partners not move whole-heartedly into opposition against the New Deal if they believed they were the "center of the attack"?

The journalist George Sokolsky proffered one explanation. Writing in the *Washington Post*, he posited that the appeal of fascism was on the rise among capitalists disenchanted with the New Deal, unhappy with Republicanism, and fearing communism. Fundamentally, Sokolsky opined, capitalists like J.P. Morgan & Co. were "cowardly" and "paralyzed in the face of mass agitation." Wall Street welcomed fascism, because of "the success of industrialists and financiers in Italy and Germany in their control of Fascist governments."[144] Morgan inaction thus followed from the hope that fascism was on the march in the United States. Such a reading misunderstood the Morgan partners – they had no brief for fascism even if they had done business with Mussolini and were slow to distant themselves from his regime. Fascism's appeals fell on deaf ears at the Corner. The Morgan partners believed in American enterprise, American government, and American liberty as testified to by Lamont's contemptuous rejection of feelers from representatives of Oswald Mosely.

The curious affair involving Major General Smedley D. Butler, a marine accused of being complicit in a murky coup d'état against the Roosevelt administration in the fall of 1934, strengthens this interpretation. Lamont's name was advanced as one of the putative backers of a plot

---

[141] Jack Morgan to Mrs. William Cooper, 9 June 1936, TML, JPM, Box 112, Folder 455/6.
[142] Childs, "They Hate Roosevelt."
[143] Lamont, *A Life in Letters*, pp. 139–40, claimed that Thomas Lamont shared his wife Florence's views. The latter would "assemble a group of friends to join her at the Trans Lux theatre to boo the President on screen."
[144] George Sokolsky, "Fascists Seen Gaining Ground in American Politics," *Washington Post*, 24 December 1933, R2.

redolent with fascist echoes of the March on Rome in 1922.[145] Lost in the fog was that the stated desire of the plotters – to restore the gold standard to the United States, thus repairing the damage done by the Roosevelt administration to American economic well-being – was at odds with the Morgan embrace of Roosevelt's monetary policy. J.P. Morgan & Co. had been the first on Wall Street to congratulate Roosevelt on leaving gold in 1933 and in the years after did not waver from the conviction that this had been the correct step. The Morgan partners were hardly likely to finance a comic-opera coup devoted to restoration of a gold standard that they had repudiated publicly. There were those in American life in the 1930s who self-identified as fascist, or aspired to it, or sought to ape it, or wanted its triumph, but they were not located in the Corner.[146]

The American Liberty League might have been thought to have been a natural vehicle for the Morgan partners to express their discontent. Though the League's professed intent was non-partisan, it was apparent from the beginning that its architects conceived of its purpose as combatting the New Deal. While many of the corporate and political chieftains who flocked to the standard raised by the Du Ponts were well-known to the Morgan partners, it was Davis, a personal friend of Jack Morgan, Lamont, and Whitney, who became one of the driving forces of the League. Davis' biographer attributed to the latter an influence that "brought in about half the Morgan firm" to the League.[147] Yet tellingly, no Morgan partner played a substantive role within the Liberty League; none sat on its executive committee, assisted in policy development, propagandized on its behalf, or advanced large sums for its purposes. Some Morgan donations found their way to League's coffers, though the amounts were dwarfed by the largesse provided by the Du Ponts who were the organization's paymasters. During the 1936 campaign the Democratic National Committee issued a pamphlet, "Who's Who in the American Liberty League," that strained to make a connection between J.P. Morgan & Co., the Du Ponts, and the League. Unable to show direct Morgan engagement with the League, the pamphlet noted that Davis was the Morgan lawyer. While it is tempting to suggest that Morgan unwillingness to become involved meaningfully in the American Liberty League arose from a prescient appreciation of its elite nature and its consequent lack of appeal to Americans, this affords too much credit to

[145] Jules Archer, *The Plot to Seize the White House*, New York: Hawthorne Books, 1973; Sally Denton, *The Plots Against the President: FDR, A Nation in Crisis, and the Rise of the American Right*, New York: Bloomsbury Press, 2012, pp. 186–97.
[146] Diggins, *Mussolini and Fascism*. On the related theme of those who admired the Third Reich, Bradley W. Hart, *Hitler's American Friends*, New York: St. Martin's Press, 2018.
[147] Harbaugh, *Lawyer's Lawyer*, p. 346.

the Morgan partners. Fear of discarding the bank's cherished avoidance of affiliation with sectarian politics, despite the more or less open understanding that the partners skewed Republican, was at work. So too was fear of another kind – alienating unduly the White House until the last hope for revision of Glass–Steagall had been dashed.

Certainly, the Morgan partners were not skittish about making political contributions – Senator Hugo Black placed the giving of the wider J. P. Morgan & Co. firm in April 1936 at $68,226 to various groups, including the Sentinels of the Republic, a right-wing organization permeated by anti-Semitism that was opposed vociferously to the New Deal's expansion of government. E.T. Stotesbury, the senior Drexel partner in Philadelphia, was a principal benefactor of the Sentinels.[148] Of the New York partners, Jack Morgan was the chief contributor to the political foes of the New Deal. He gave $50,000 to the Republican effort in the 1936 presidential and congressional elections, distributed in parcels of $5,000 to various Republican committees from the local to the national level. This generosity was in spite of the Morgan distaste for Alf Landon, the Governor of Kansas, and the Republican presidential nominee in 1936, who during the Pecora hearings had referred dismissively to "[r]acketeers like Insull, Morgan and Van Sweringen."[149] Other Morgan partners, such as Steele, Whitney, Harry Morgan, and Ewing, donated lesser amounts to the Republican effort in 1936. Noteworthy was the absence of Lamont, whose name did not appear as contributing more than $1,000 to the Republican National Committee in 1936. Leffingwell and Parker Gilbert, the firm's resident Democrats, were never prepared to contribute to Republican causes.

*****

By 1936 the New Deal was three years old, old enough for disenchantment, frustration, and vituperation to supplant the enthusiastic welcome with which business had showered Roosevelt in March 1933. Writing as the 1936 presidential campaign was in full swing, Elliott Bell pondered the "wide rift" between Roosevelt and business. Its origins, he thought, went back to the inaugural address. Running through the years since

---

[148] "New Deal Foes Help Sentinels, Inquiry Is Told," *Washington Post*, 18 April 1936, p. 5.
[149] On Morgan contributions to Republican causes, *New York Times*, 11 September 1936, p. 10; 24 October 1936, p. 9; 2 December 1936, p. 10; as well as Jack Morgan to J.P. Morgan & Co., 1 October 1936, TML, JPM, Box 39, Cables (Personal) Sent 24 September 1935 to 30 December 1937, in which he remarked "H.P. Davison knows all I have done ... Remember, I gave no more than $5,000. to any one person." Leffingwell to Lamont, 27 August 1936, YUL, RCL, Series I, Box 4, Folder 96 for Morgan unhappiness with Landon.

1933, Wall Street believed, was a sustained assault designed to recast American capitalism in a new mould. The New Dealers for their part scoffed, countering that the Street resented the loss of its power. Roosevelt himself was seen negatively, his language toward the financial community animated by a "punitive spirit." Bell concluded that the chances of a rapprochement between Wall Street and the president were "remote."[150] Two weeks after Bell's analysis, Leffingwell called on Roosevelt to cease his attack on businessmen and bankers, observing that, while "scapegoats" were understandable in crisis in 1933, the continuance of a rhetoric of "money changers and economic royalists" was harmful.[151] Doing so threatened public harmony. Roosevelt was neither dissuaded nor perturbed by Leffingwell's complaint; he asked his secretary Marvin McIntyre to remind him to reply to Leffingwell at a future date. The Democratic presidential campaign continued in the same vein.

Swaying Roosevelt proved impossible for J.P. Morgan & Co. During the opening months of the New Deal, Lamont and Leffingwell had proved unable to cajole the president to their line of thinking. Roosevelt neither wanted nor needed J.P. Morgan & Co. as an ally, appreciating how deep-seated hostility toward the Corner was among Americans. He was not inclined to pursue the gradualist Morgan advice on how to remedy the Depression, even if the balance of his deflationary versus inflationary impulses accorded well with Leffingwell's thoughts. Pecora made it possible for Roosevelt to distance himself from the Morgan partners without severing the tie completely. Roosevelt continued to solicit and listen to the advice of Leffingwell for some months, a reflection of the president's willingness to receive advice from many quarters. At the Corner this receptiveness was misunderstood – it was not appreciated that Roosevelt was not interested in what mattered most to the partners, namely Glass–Steagall, but was interested in gleaning ideas. From late 1934 the attractiveness of Morgan wisdom palled, as Roosevelt distanced himself from an American business community that he deemed incorrigible. For the Morgan partners, this development was bracing. Scrambling to preserve J.P. Morgan & Co. intact, they became what they had never been, and what critics alleged – stewards of a parochial interest. Leffingwell and his partners did not forget the ongoing Depression and the crisis of capitalism; but they were overwhelmed by their fears for the future of J.P. Morgan & Co.

[150] Elliott V. Bell, "Roosevelt and Business: The Wide Rift," *New York Times*, 16 August 1936, SM 5.
[151] Leffingwell to Roosevelt, 1 September 1936, FDRPL, FDR, PPF, 866.

Feeding apprehension was the Morgan banking business. Since 1931 retrenchment had been the order of the day at the Corner. Hope of a rebound bloomed in 1933 with the advent of the New Deal and continued into 1934. Optimism, however, rested in part on the assumption that the Roosevelt administration would see the virtue in modifying Glass–Steagall. The Morgan partners believed doing otherwise was contrary to the restoration of American prosperity: what was good for the Morgan bank was good for the country. Restoring the capital markets as they had existed before Glass–Steagall and before the Securities Act would benefit both the nation and J.P. Morgan & Co. Until that occurred, having suffered grievously before March 1933, the partners were risk-averse, embraced conservatism in their investments, and were not willing to lend until a positive manifestation of change, defined as revision of Glass–Steagall, occurred. Waiting exacted a toll. J.P. Morgan & Co. was struggling – loans fell, partner net worth declined, and assets became more and more vested in US government securities. Morgan capital did not go on strike; it retreated until certainty over the future structure of the bank was clear.

The politics of Roosevelt's first term were wrenching for the Morgan partners. Used to being listened to in the halls of Washington, astounded that they were supplicants, the partners found themselves marginalized even as Pecora dramatized their influence while Coughlin, Long, and their imitators trumpeted the dangers of Morgan power. The Morgan reaction was not to embrace opposition of the kind championed by the American Liberty League. Days before he called on Roosevelt to modulate his remarks about business, Leffingwell wrote Lamont. Defending his continued support of Roosevelt, he declared:

Roosevelt's sayings and doings have distressed me beyond measure time and again. But he did follow the principal major monetary policy which I believed in and urged in every way I knew how. He did pull the country out of the slough. He did save our people. He did save capitalism.[152]

The letter exposed how crisis and the politics of the New Deal had shaken the Corner. Partnership as practised under Jack Morgan's leadership rested on consensus but the Morgan partners were not of one mind about the New Deal. Pecora bothered; Glass–Steagall was abhorrent; the Banking Act of 1935 was unwarranted. On these issues the partners were united. Yet this did not mean that in the Depression crisis J.P. Morgan & Co. was prepared to abandon

[152] Leffingwell to Lamont, 27 August 1936, YUL, RCL, Series I, Box 4, Folder 96.

capitalism because most of the partners disliked Roosevelt's New Deal. What mattered was that liberal, democratic capitalism had survived and so too had the Morgan bank even if adaptation meant division with the creation of Morgan Stanley. Accordingly, Roosevelt's re-election in 1936 produced resigned acceptance, not rejection, at the Corner.[153]

[153] Lamont, Junius Morgan, Whitney to Jack Morgan, Jack Morgan to Lamont, Junius Morgan, Whitney, 5 November 1936, TML, MBEP, Box 24, File 7.

7   J.P. Morgan & Co. and the Foreign Policy of the New Deal
Germany, Italy, Japan, and the Nye Committee, 1933–1937

The revisionist challenge of the 1930s arose in Tokyo, Berlin, and Rome. From 1931, Japan's course raised alarm; from 1933, Hitler embodied German dissatisfaction; from 1935, Italy made explicit its expansionism. Depression fuelled the challengers to the status quo, whose desire to create a new international order in their favour exacerbated the crisis of capitalism.[1] Confronted with the disintegration of the postwar order, one influential account of Roosevelt's foreign policy has depicted a president torn between the competing calls of internationalism and nationalism as domestic considerations pressed. Gradually, internationalism gave way – "Farewell to Internationalism" led to the "Internationalist as Isolationist" between 1935 and 1938.[2] If historians might disagree with this schema, few would contest the proposition that American foreign policy was secondary to restoring the health of the American polity during Roosevelt's first term.[3] While this was so, Roosevelt understood the interplay between the New Deal and the world. Roosevelt's oft-cited January 1936 message to Congress remarked, "Were I today to deliver an Inaugural Address to the people of the United States, I could not limit my comments on world affairs to one paragraph. With much regret,

---

[1] Chap. 4 of Mark Mazower, "The Crisis of Capitalism," in *Dark Continent: Europe's Twentieth Century*, New York: Alfred A. Knopf, 1999, pp. 104–37. The literature on the crisis of the 1930s is enormous. One survey must suffice: Zara Steiner, *The Triumph of the Dark: European International History 1933–1939*, Oxford: Oxford University Press, 2011.

[2] Robert Dallek, *Franklin D. Roosevelt and American Foreign Policy, 1932–1945*, New York: Oxford University Press, 1981. "Farewell to Internationalism" is the title of Dallek's chap. 4; "The Internationalist As Isolationist, 1935–38," is the title of part 2 of Dallek's history. Alonzo Hamby, *For the Survival of Democracy: Franklin Roosevelt and the World Crisis of the 1930s*, New York: The Free Press, 2004, is more critical. Brooke Blower has argued that the term "isolation" misconstrues the 1930s debate, "From Isolationism to Neutrality: A New Framework for Understanding American Political Culture, 1919–1941," *Diplomatic History*, vol. 38, no. 3 (2014), pp. 345–76.

[3] Richard Harrison, "A Neutralization Plan for the Pacific: Roosevelt and Anglo-American Cooperation, 1934–1937," *Pacific Historical Review*, vol. 57, no. 1 (1988), p. 48, takes exception, arguing that Roosevelt "vigorously tried to assert American influence in the world from his earliest months in office."

I should be compelled to devote the greater part to world affairs." We should recall this rueful musing, as Kiran Patel has reminded us, when considering the New Deal's opening stanza.[4] Depression at home devoured, but it did not consume utterly American relations with the world.

A broader question remains central: How do we explain the varying responses to the aggression of the revisionist states in London, Paris, and Washington? Understanding the Morgan response to developments sheds light on an answer in the United States. After all, as one journalist wrote late in July 1937, "The Morgan firm probably is better informed on national and international developments than any other concern in the country."[5] As revisionism gained strength, its traction alarmed the Morgan partners. Internationalist by conviction and heritage, J.P. Morgan & Co. had been standard-bearers for a reconstructed capitalism through the 1920s and had tried to shore up its rickety edifice from 1929 to 1932. *Mutatis mutandis*, the partners clung to the hope that the lineaments of the postwar peace would survive, an aspiration shared by many. Yet previous eminence haunted. If the Morgan houses in London and Paris bound the Corner to Britain and France and the courses those states pursued, J.P. Morgan & Co. was associated with Berlin, Rome, and Tokyo. The new Nazi regime halted payments on the Dawes and Young Plan loans in pursuit of Hitler's diktat of untrammelled rearmament. Worse was the reality that J.P. Morgan & Co. was the American banker for Japan and Italy. From Manchuria in 1931 to the Italian invasion of Ethiopia in 1935 and the outbreak of the Sino-Japanese War in the summer of 1937, J.P. Morgan & Co. shied away from criticizing Tokyo and Rome. The Corner's stance was neither admirable nor bold and its reticence was due to more than the discretionary culture of the private merchant banker. Misapprehension was at work. The Morgan partners, like many in the "low, dishonest decade," failed to discern how intense the cravings of Nazi radicalism were, while understating changed Italian and Japanese behaviour. Despite their experience, information, and knowledge, the Morgan partners misperceived the threat. They were not alone in making this error, but the Morgan inability to see supports interpretations that have stressed the difficulty of discerning through the fog intent in Berlin, Rome,

---

[4] Franklin D. Roosevelt, Annual Message to Congress, 3 January 1936, *The American Presidency Project*, www.presidency.ucsb.edu/documents/annual-message-congress-2; Kiran Klaus Patel, *The New Deal: A Global History*, Princeton, NJ: Princeton University Press, 2016, pp. 1–9.
[5] Ralph W. Henderson in his column, "Wall Street," 29 July 1937 in the *New York World-Telegram*. Henderson was the financial editor of *The World-Telegram*, a Hearst paper critical of J.P. Morgan & Co. The clipping is in BL, TWL, Series VI, Box 227, Folder 4.

and Tokyo. Roosevelt did little better. Certainly, the more bellicose German, Italian, and Japanese foreign policy became, the more J.P. Morgan & Co. mimicked the president's calibrated responses.

Common – if uncoordinated – cause between the bank and the White House was promoted by the spectre of another war. Inchoate as the 1930s began, but taking shape as the decade waned, sustenance for the growth of this alignment was drawn not only from the appetites of the revisionist states but also from the past. The high-profile Special Committee on Investigation of the Munitions Industry hearings, better known as the Nye Committee, explored the relationship between American munitions makers and American entry into World War I. It expanded its remit to explore whether bankers and financiers played a part in orchestrating American belligerency, leading to testimony by the Morgan partners in 1936. The Roosevelt administration resisted the Nye Committee's efforts to dragoon material on Morgan wartime dealings with London and Paris, fearful of the consequences for American foreign relations. As the American debate on neutrality heated, the events of 1917 and the Morgan role therein soaked public consciousness. It was a small step from belief in Morgan maleficence in 1917 to certainty that J.P. Morgan & Co. sought to entangle the United States anew in European conflict.

The effect of these considerations –imagined, exaggerated, real – was dual: first, they kept the Morgan name in the limelight. Morgan influence on New Deal foreign policy was limited, but perception suggested otherwise, prompting minds wooed by the "voices of protest" to ponder whether Morgan was un-American. The second development followed naturally. The Morgan partners sought surety in unsure times by hewing closely to the line advanced by the president, irrespective of the chasm between Roosevelt and them on the New Deal at home. This was demonstrated in October 1937 when Roosevelt delivered his "quarantine speech" in Chicago, warning his fellow Americans that an "epidemic of world lawlessness" was spreading, as evinced in the rearmament programs of aggressor states. Insistently the president told his listeners of his "determination to pursue a policy of peace." Seventeen days later, also speaking in Chicago, Lamont declaimed that "nobody wants war." Like Roosevelt, Lamont bemoaned armament expenditures while decrying "intense nationalism." The two speeches were cut from the same cloth.[6] Years later, Roosevelt would acknowledge Morgan faithfulness, describing Lamont to Vice-President Henry Wallace: "On all these

---

[6] The text of Roosevelt's Address at Chicago, 5 October 1937, may be found at *The American Presidency Project*, www.presidency.ucsb.edu/documents/address-chicago; Lamont's 22 October 1937 speech, given at the Commercial Club, was circulated widely, with front-page coverage in the *New York Times* (the latter printed the speech in its

foreign things he is, and always has been, one hundred per cent loyal."[7] The foundation of that encomium was laid between 1933 and 1937.

*****

Adolf Hitler's appointment as chancellor at the end of January 1933 prompted an immediate shift in German economic priorities. Days after entering office, he told assembled generals that he intended to expand and re-equip the armed forces with the aim of "the conquest of new living space in the East and its ruthless Germanization . . . only through political power and struggle can the present economic circumstances be changed."[8] Political opposition had to be overcome before this was realizable. The unsatisfactory Reichstag election result early in March that left the Nazi Party short of a majority was corrected by the passage of the Enabling Act later the same month, giving Hitler the means, subject to the aged President Paul von Hindenburg's consent, to rule without parliamentary interference. With this weapon in hand, the Nazis moved expeditiously. From the summer of 1933 Germany was a one-party state. With internal voices silenced, rearmament could proceed. Obstacles remained. The German economy was dependent on imports. Lacking foreign currency, Schacht scrambled to economize in light of the additional burden imposed by Hitlerian demands that the rearmament push not be sacrificed on the altar of domestic consumption. It was never a question of butter and guns; for Hitler, there was only guns and guns. Adam Tooze has demonstrated just how serious the ensuing economic-political crisis was in 1933–34 for the new regime, emphasizing that clearing away the difficulties facing the economy occasioned by Hitler's insistence on full-throttle rearmament was Schacht's task.[9]

Hitlerian ambitions had ramifications for J.P. Morgan & Co. One means Schacht settled on to meet Hitler's demands was squeezing the payments owed abroad on the Dawes and Young Plan loans. The two loans had not been affected by the Standstill agreements of August 1931 as their privileged status was enshrined by treaty. Brüning's government and its successors accepted that service on the two loans must continue.

entirety) and the *Wall Street Journal* on 23 October 1937, while *Banking* reprinted excepts in its December 1937 issue, vol. 30, no. 6, p. 86.
[7] Roosevelt to Henry Wallace, 26 April 1941, in Elliott Roosevelt, ed., *FDR: His Personal Letters*, 4 vols., New York: Duell, Sloan and Pearce, 1947–50, vol. 2.
[8] Notes taken by General Kurt Liebmann, 3 February 1933, cited in Jeremy J. Noakes and Geoffrey Pridham, eds., *Nazism, 1919–1945: A History in Documents and Eyewitness Accounts*, 2 vols., New York: Schocken Books, 1988, vol. 2, pp. 628–29; Ian Kershaw, *Hitler: 1889–1936*, 2 vols., London: Allen Lane, 1998, vol. 1., pp. 441–42.
[9] Adam Tooze, *The Wages of Destruction: The Making and Breaking of the Nazi Economy*, London: Allen Lane, 2006, pp. 49–96.

For his part, Schacht had never considered the Young loan legitimate. Prodded by Hitler, he moved steadily toward seeing the Dawes loan as illegitimate as well.[10] J.P. Morgan & Co. was not the specific target – Schacht was interested in reducing and, if possible, ending German payments on all loans. This approach, pursued with conviction and guile, exploited the divisions among bondholders as the possibility of default unsettled investors. Early efforts by Schacht in May and June 1933 to bludgeon American compliance into reducing or cancelling German obligations had drawn the attention of Hull and Roosevelt. The president instructed his new ambassador at Berlin, William E. Dodd, to thwart moves toward a moratorium.[11] Schacht, however, was not deterred. He returned to the idea, moving ahead with blandishments and threats.

As negotiations intensified in 1934 the Morgan posture was driven by two considerations. Fear that repudiation would damage Morgan prestige animated the Corner. During the Pecora hearings the Morgan defence had in part been predicated on the excellence of their record in bonds, especially those floated for foreign governments. Bonds placed by J.P. Morgan & Co. did not default. The Dawes and Young loans, identified so intimately with the firm, were trophy loans. Any caesura in their servicing would exact a reputational toll. To the partners, this mattered greatly. Prestige and reputation were important, but so too was the abiding Morgan conviction that maintaining the Dawes and Young loans was an indispensable precondition for international harmony. Lamont told Schacht in April 1934 that his plans would dash "all efforts for future economic cooperation on an international basis ... for a generation to come."[12]

Alone J.P. Morgan & Co. could not expect to make headway. Fortunately, Young, Harrison, and Fraser were allies. Young reminded Schacht of the damage that his course would do to international economic cooperation, reinforced by Harrison, while Fraser, as president of the BIS, met Schacht frequently to discuss central banking matters.[13] Information about these encounters was relayed faithfully to the Morgan partners, either directly or through the intermediary of Dean Jay. Jay was a trustee of the Dawes loan and enjoyed good contacts with the BIS. Amid

[10] Piet Clement, "'The Touchstone of German Credit': Nazi Germany and the Service of the Dawes and Young Loans," *Financial History Review*, vol. 11, no. 1 (2004), pp. 38–42.
[11] Avner Offner, "William E. Dodd: Romantic Historian and Diplomatic Cassandra," *The Historian*, vol. 24, no. 4 (1962), p. 454.
[12] Lamont to Schacht, 7 April 1934, BL, TWL, Series II, Box 129, Folder 22.
[13] Young to Schacht, 23 March 1934, CUL, Harrison papers, Box 45, Folder Germany Dawes and Young bonds. On Young, SLU, ODY, Box 414, Folder 826 documents his efforts and those of J.P. Morgan & Co. and the BIS to stop Schacht.

the "reams of cables," the Morgan partners stressed the "necessity of solidarity" among Paris, London, and Washington.[14] What ensued was a demonstration of the difficulty of maintaining a united front. Schacht was aided by the campaign that the Nazi regime had embarked on vis-à-vis non-protected loans (all loans other than Dawes and Young) extended to Germany. The Dutch and the Swiss, worried that their credits were in jeopardy, had agreed to clearing arrangements late in 1933. As for Britain and the United States, their trade balances with Germany were a factor – with Britain the Germans ran a trade surplus, whereas with the United States the German trade account was in deficit. Trade afforded Schacht opportunity. He claimed that restrictions on German exports imperilled the ability of the Reich to earn the foreign exchange necessary to meet the payments on outstanding loans abroad, thus connecting loan servicing with trade issues. Hull's desire to support American creditors against Schacht was complicated by discord in Washington. Roosevelt's willingness to explore the possibilities of expanding American trade with Germany, through offhand conversations with the German ambassador, Hans Luther, were seized on with alacrity by the ambitious George Peek, whose tenure as head of the Agricultural Adjustment Act had petered out ingloriously in December 1933. Peek soon rebounded, becoming the first president of the Export-Import Bank in February 1934, from which office he pursued schemes to exchange American cotton for German wine in the face of fierce opposition from Hull.[15] Internecine squabbling was harmful but the deeper problem was that any threat to retaliate against Germany would mean injuring American exporters, who might not be paid for their goods, leaving the American bargaining position weak in contradistinction to Britain who had at their disposal the weapon of seizing German balances in London built up by the German trade surplus.[16]

The frailty of "solidarity" was soon apparent. Norman signalled a willingness to broach a clearing arrangement with Germany, thus casting into doubt the inviolability of the Dawes and Young Plan loans. When Norman justified his action on the grounds that countries that were running a trade deficit with Germany might institute clearing arrangements to safeguard the integrity of their non-protected loans, the Morgan partners

[14] Lamont to de Sanchez, 23 April 1934, BL, TWL, Series II, Box 129, Folder 22; Dean Jay to J.P. Morgan & Co., 8 May 1934, TML, MBEP, Box 17, Cables rec'd, 1 May to 31 August 1934.

[15] Michael Butler's account in *Cautious Visionary: Cordell Hull and Trade Reform, 1933–37*, Kent, OH: Kent State University Press, 1998, pp. 97–112, is favourable to Hull and less so to either Peek or Roosevelt.

[16] Tooze, *The Wages of Destruction*, pp. 72–73, 86–89; Neil Forbes, "London Banks, the German Standstill Agreements, and 'Economic Appeasement' in the 1930s," *Economic History Review*, 2nd series, vol. 40, no. 4 (1987), p. 579.

bridled, observing that clearing arrangements were not incompatible with continuance of payments on the two loans and reminding Norman sharply that if he was forceful enough servicing of the Dawes and Young Plans loans would continue. Whigham, rushing to pour oil on troubled waters, drew attention to the "volume" of middle- and long-term loans creditors had made to Germany. He told the Morgan partners in New York that these lenders did not agree that the Dawes and Young Plan loans should be in a privileged category. Writing to Dean Jay, Whigham stressed the "extremely complicated and delicate nature of the situation." Schacht, Whigham thought, was genuine in his insistence that he lacked foreign exchange and that countries that had a favourable balance of trade with Germany would seek to deploy this leverage.[17] Such reassurances did not mollify. Lamont wrote Schacht early in April 1934 to press the Morgan case for continued service. Reviewing it, the Bank of England opined, "Good letter but useless."[18] And so it proved, for Schacht's rejoinder insisted that Germany had no means to make payments. Jack Morgan, whose standing with Norman was high, cabled Grenfell with a personal message for the governor urging Norman to remain committed to the "fight" because he was the only individual with influence over Schacht. Grenfell declined to present the cable, informing Jack Morgan that Norman might be "affronted" by it. Grenfell stressed that Norman was alive to the "sanctity" of the Dawes and Young loans. In his reply Grenfell warned that Schacht might implement a moratorium on all transfers after 1 July, driven by "real difficulties of transfer" and possibly "political pressure."[19]

Formal announcement in June 1934 that Germany was ceasing payment on the Dawes and Young loans was thus not a surprise to the Corner, even if Lamont had hoped that the Dawes payment might be preserved. Dean Jay was better apprised. Drawing on a cable from Fraser, Jay told J.P. Morgan & Co. in late April that Schacht would cease meeting German obligations on all outstanding loans.[20] Once public, there was little recourse for the Morgan partners. Ramsay MacDonald was pressed to intercede, but the limits of this approach were demonstrated when on

---

[17] Norman diary, 2 March 1934, BE, ADM 34/23; Morgan Grenfell to J.P. Morgan & Co., 28 February 1934, J.P. Morgan & Co. to Norman, 2 March 1934, Morgan Grenfell to J. P. Morgan & Co., 6 March 1934, J.P. Morgan & Co. to Morgan Grenfell, 16 March 1934, BE, G1/446. Whigham to Dean Jay, 6 March 1934, TML, CP, Box 31, Morgan & Co. – Foreign Financings Germany.

[18] Lamont to Schacht, 7 April 1934, BL, TWL, Series II, Box 129, Folder 22. A copy of the letter is in the Bank of England files, BE, G1/446 with the marginalia.

[19] Jack Morgan to Grenfell, 23 April 1934, Grenfell to Jack Morgan, 24 April 1934, Jack Morgan to Grenfell, 24 April 1934, TML, MBEP, Box 23, Folder 5.

[20] Dean Jay to J.P. Morgan & Co., 25 April 1934, TML, MBEP, Box 17, Cables sent, 16 February to 30 April 1934; Lamont to de Sanchez, 23 April 1934, BL, TWL, Series II, Box 129, Folder 22.

4 July Britain reached a separate arrangement with Germany that sheltered British creditors from the effects of the German declaration.[21]
A front-page article in the *New York Times* two weeks later drew the lesson
"that the pledge of a foreign government's revenues for loans can carry no
real guarantee if there is no way to collect from governments unable or
unwilling to pay – except by force."[22] The weakness of the Morgan
position was illustrated in their response to an offer made by Schacht in
October 1935 to purchase Dawes and Young Plan bonds at a discounted
price. While J.P. Morgan & Co. did not recommend publicly the deal,
privately they deemed it to be the best that investors would receive.
Schacht repeated the offer in 1936 and 1937.[23]

The quarrel over the Dawes and Young Plan loans was overlaid with
worries about American bankers sustaining the nascent Nazi regime.
Acting on material furnished by George S. Messersmith, the American
consul at Berlin until May 1934, and subsequently Minister at Vienna
from 1934 to 1938, Hamilton Fish Armstrong, the moving spirit on the
Council of Foreign Relations and managing editor of its journal *Foreign
Affairs*, wrote Hull that American bankers were mulling fresh loans to
Germany.[24] Messersmith, in his reports to Washington, had emphasized
the breakneck pace of rearmament and the seriousness of the political-
economic crisis enveloping Germany. Armstrong, drawing on
Messersmith, believed that the Nazi regime was teetering. Rumblings of
new credits that would rescue Hitler's government had surfaced in the
New York press. Frederick Birchall, in the *New York Times*, pointed to the
presence of James Perkins of National City Bank in Berlin, the supposed
willingness of Norman to consider credits, and Perkins' subsequent
meeting with Lamont in Paris as grist for his story, "American Bankers
Seek to Aid Reich: Hope to Avert a Sudden Crash by Temporary Credits
for Raw Materials."[25] Superficially plausible as a quid pro quo to prod
Schacht to continue payments on the Dawes and Young loans, Birchall's
report was inaccurate – the Morgan partners had no intention of lending
money to Germany. Nevertheless, Armstrong, after reading Birchall's

[21] J.P. Morgan & Co. to MacDonald, 20 June 1934, TML, CP, Box 31, Morgan & Co. –
Foreign Financings Germany.
[22] Otto D. Tolischus, "Germany Seizes Revenue Pledged for Dawes Loan," *New York
Times*, 18 July 1934, p. 1.
[23] Lamont to J.H. Brewster Jr., 14 October 1935, BL, TWL, Series IV/C, Box 182, Folder
13. Brewster Jr. was vice-president and treasurer of Aetna Life Insurance.
[24] Hamilton Fish Armstrong to Hull, 24 July 1934, Princeton, Mudd Library, HFA Papers,
Series 1, Box 36, Folder 7. Messersmith's reports, especially those in 1933–34, may be
read in his papers at the University of Delaware Library. Helpfully, the collection has
been digitized and is online.
[25] Frederick T. Birchall, "American Bankers Seek to Aid Reich: Hope to Avert a Sudden
Crash by Temporary Credits for Raw Materials," *New York Times*, 23 July 1934, p. 5.

story, phoned Leffingwell. As Leffingwell informed Lamont, Armstrong "was concerned lest we were going to save the Nazi regime with fresh credits. His information and hope was that they would fall within a month unless credits were extended ... I told him that there is nothing in it so far as we were concerned."[26] Lamont reinforced Leffingwell's denial, but Armstrong's doubts lingered, sustained by Messersmith.[27] How far these warnings were taken seriously in Washington is unclear. Herbert Feis, the economic advisor to the State department, thought highly of Messersmith's analyses, while Hull later lauded him as "one of our ablest officials."[28] While agreeing with the Messersmith thesis that Nazism was vulnerable and fresh American capital would offer succour at an inopportune moment, Roosevelt was not convinced that the Nazi regime teetered on the brink of economic collapse.[29]

The Night of the Long Knives (30 June to 2 July 1934), the murder of critics within the Nazi Party and opponents outside it, jolted the Corner. The Morgan partners thought events signalled Nazism's vulnerability. Walter Layton of *The Economist* and Robert Brand of Lazard Brothers speculated that the end was near for Hitler at lunch with Lamont, leading Lamont to record in his diary, "Is Hitler done for?"[30] Internal crisis may have been staved off by violence temporarily, but the Morgan partners believed that if the Third Reich was to survive in the long term its hopes rested on a Hitler–Schacht axis. Norman, who was visiting the United States, told Leffingwell that "Hitler and Schacht are the bulwarks of civilization in Germany and the only friends we have. They are fighting the war of our system of society against communism."[31] Though Leffingwell doubted this diagnosis, his partners were more accepting. Parker Gilbert wrote Fraser early in August 1934 in terms that portrayed Hitler and Schacht as coevals, a supposition echoed by Lamont two weeks later when he told Parker Gilbert that "Schacht-Hitler may execute a volte-face" on Nazism's more radical measures, before referring subsequently to "Hitler-Schacht" in the same letter. Early in January 1935 Dean Jay passed on to Leffingwell Fraser's assessment that Schacht was

---

[26] Leffingwell to Lamont, 25 July 1934, YUL, RCL, Series 1, Box 4, Custom 96.
[27] Lamont to Armstrong, 14 August 1934, Princeton, Mudd Library, HFA papers, Box 40, Folder 3; Armstrong to George S. Messersmith, 20 August 1934, Messersmith to Armstrong, 2 October 1934, Princeton, Mudd Library, HFA Papers, Series 1, Box 44, Folder 1.
[28] Hull, *Memoirs*, vol. 1, p. 235.
[29] Priscilla Roberts, "'The Council Has Been Your Creation': Hamilton Fish Armstrong, Paradigm of the American Foreign Policy Establishment?," *Journal of American Studies*, vol. 35, no. 1 (2001), pp. 75–76.
[30] Lamont diary, 9 July 1934, BL, TWL, Series IV B, Box 173, Folder 6. On this entry there is a later marginal note, "Haha." It is tempting to think Lamont, rereading, wrote it.
[31] Leffingwell to Lamont, 25 July 1934, YUL, RCL, Series 1, Box 4, Custom 96.

"now the Economic Dictator of Germany" and might even become vice-chancellor.[32] Later that year, at a dinner hosted by Armstrong for Heinrich Brüning, the ex-chancellor in exile, the attendees, including Leffingwell, heard Brüning dilate that the economic situation in Germany was "desperate" and that "Reichswehr /and allied conservative forces are in real control," leading Brüning to forecast that Hitler would only survive as "a figure-head."[33] Fanciful as this was, it sated the Morgan predilection to view Schacht as a key constituent in the conservative forces binding Hitler. When Francis Rodd, a Morgan Grenfell partner, returned from a trip to Germany early in 1936, his assessment was similar. Rodd's analysis described Schacht and the Army as the only calming elements inside a country where the economic situation remained alarming.[34] Until late 1937, when Leffingwell asked Lamont whether he knew that "the skids are said to be under Dr. Schacht?," J.P. Morgan & Co. believed Schacht wielded disproportionate power within the regime.[35]

This misreading drew on the history of Morgan dealings with Germany, wherein Schacht was the central figure. For the Morgan part-ners, Schacht had long been the *éminence grise* of German finance. Given the shortage of economic and financial experts within Nazi ranks, his reach appeared to be lengthening, extending beyond finance into politics. What this inference lacked was an appreciation of the internal dynamics of Nazism. The only J.P. Morgan & Co. partner in the 1930s who had working experience in Germany was Parker Gilbert. However, Parker Gilbert did not speak German and had cultivated few German friends. After the advent of Hitler, Parker Gilbert's informants in Germany dwindled. For more reliable intelligence, the Morgan partners relied on information collated by Dean Jay. Jay's base in Paris afforded him access to other well-informed bankers, such as Carel Eliza ter Meulen, the Dutch banker who headed Hope & Co. in Amsterdam. Such men had ties in Germany, but generally to well-established figures of the traditional

[32] Parker Gilbert to Fraser, 6 August 1934, BL, TWL, Series IV C/Box 182, Folder 6; Lamont to Parker Gilbert, 20 August 1934, BL, TWL, Series II, Box 96, Folder 4; Dean Jay to Leffingwell, 21 January 1935, NDJ papers, Knox College.
[33] Armstrong, 18 September 1935, Princeton, HFA papers, Series IV, Box 99. The dinner was held on 17 September and was not disclosed to the press. Present were the Dulles brothers, Stimson, Lippmann, and George Murnane (a partner in Lazard Freres New York).
[34] Lamont diary, 9 July 1934, BL, TWL, Series IV B, Box 173, Folder 6; Leffingwell to Lamont, 25 July 1934, YUL, RCL, Series 1, Box 4, Custom 96; Francis Rodd to Lamont, 6 February 1936, BL, TWL, Series IV C, Box 182, Folder 14.
[35] Leffingwell to Lamont, 19 October 1937, YUL, RCL, Series I, Box 4, Folder 97; Volker Ullrich, *Hitler, Vol. 1: Ascent*, London: Vintage, 2016, pp. 586–89, for comments on Schacht, Hitler, and his paladins.

conservative type, not the radicals that thronged the corridors of Nazism in power. Consequently, while Dean Jay was closer to developments than the Morgan partners in New York, he was nevertheless remote from Berlin. Nor did it help that the Morgan partners considered the American ambassador, Dodd, a naïve academic out of his depth. Writing Grenfell in 1935, Lamont derided Dodd as someone who "thinks that all the foreign loans ever made to Germany, including the Dawes and Young, were probably foisted on wronged and innocent people by greedy British and American bankers, and he has little sympathy with the attempt to get poor Germany to fulfill her obligations."[36] Dodd was ill-suited for the embassy, but this did not mean that all he learned was worthless. Messersmith's reports, which offered a more bracing assessment of Schacht, were not disseminated to J.P. Morgan & Co. Messersmith considered Schacht a paper tiger. He told William Phillips, the under-secretary of state, that "[o]ur own bankers ... place much more confidence in the man and his power than he deserves." Schacht, Messersmith went on, was mendacious, undependable, au fond a "servile instrument" of Hitler.[37] If the Morgan partners concurred that Schacht was duplicitous, understanding that he served at Hitler's beck and call eluded them.

*****

While the Morgan partners misconstrued German developments, Italy and Mussolini's dictatorship, long familiar to the Corner, should have been more accurately appraised. Since the 1920s J.P. Morgan & Co. had been the foreign banker to Italy. The Corner orchestrated three Italian loans in the 1920s after Mussolini consolidated his authority following the kidnapping and murder of Giacomo Matteotti in 1924: a $100 million 7 per cent bond issue in November 1925 to the Italian government, a $12 million bond placed in March 1927 bearing interest of 7 per cent again for the Italian government, and a week later a $30 million bond floated at the rate of 6.5 per cent for the municipality of Rome. Lamont was the principal Morgan interlocutor with Il Duce, aided by Fummi.[38] The latter's presence in Rome as the Morgan representative stamped Morgan knowledge of Fascism as qualitatively superior to their understanding of the new Nazi regime in Berlin. The Morgan relationship with Fascist Italy was strengthened by the 1929 Concordat between the Vatican and Mussolini's regime.

[36] Lamont to Grenfell, 23 May 1935, BL, TWL, Series IV C, Box 182, Folder 9. Offner, "William E. Dodd," pp. 451–69 is a defence of the ambassador.
[37] Messersmith to William Phillips, 18 August 1934, University of Delaware, George S. Messersmith papers, Series III, Box 4, F 25.
[38] Migone, The United States and Fascist Italy, pp. 90–165, is the best account of the Morgan relationship with Italy in the 1920s.

Bernardino Nogara, the banker appointed by Pope Pius XI in 1929 to head the *Amministrazione Speciale della Santa Sede* that oversaw the Vatican's investment funds arising from the Concordat, enjoyed close ties with the House of Morgan. Nogara spoke "excellent" English. He had been a member of the Italian delegation to the Paris Peace talks, was one of the Italian representatives on the reparation committee thereafter, and from 1924 to 1929 headed the industry section of the Inter-Allied Commission overseeing the Dawes Plan in Berlin. He had, in these capacities, interacted with Lamont. Nogara had close relationships with the men who mattered in Italian financial circles, such as Bonaldo Stringher, the dominant figure in the Bank of Italy until his death in 1930, and Alberto Pirelli of the eponymous Pirelli family, well known to the Morgan partners for his role as one of the Italian negotiators on both the Dawes and Young committees.[39]

Through Fummi, an account with Morgan Grenfell was opened on behalf of the Vatican in the summer of 1931. Vatican business with Morgan Grenfell took various forms. As Michael Herbert wrote Dean Jay in January 1932, the Vatican has "a substantial cash account with us in addition to which they have a big holding of British securities." Later that year, visiting London, Nogara met with Whigham for the express purpose of setting up a real-estate investment company in Britain, modelled on the example of existing Vatican vehicles on the continent. At that time – November 1932 – the Vatican had £328,000 on deposit with Morgan Grenfell along with a dollar deposit of $300,000. The following year, acting via Morgan Grenfell and J.P. Morgan & Co., Nogara applied to purchase $250,000 of US government securities, paying 4 per cent, while in the fall of 1934, deploying money received from Hope & Co. of Amsterdam, Morgan Grenfell purchased gold bars for Nogara.[40] These two transactions, conservative in character, were unsurprising given the Depression. The papacy's finances suffered in the Crash, with the collapse of Krueger & Toll exacting a hefty tithe. For this reason, Nogara displayed an aversion to buying US railroad securities.[41]

---

[39] On Nogara, see John F. Pollard, *Money and the Rise of the Modern Papacy: Financing the Vatican, 1850–1950*, Cambridge: Cambridge University Press, 2005, pp. 143–47.
[40] Vivian Smith to Fummi, 25 August 1931, Herbert to Dean Jay, 8 January 1932, Whigham to Fummi, 24 November 1934, Morgan Grenfell to Fummi, 13 March 1933, Rodd to *Amministrazione Speciale della Santa Sede*, 24 October 1934, TML, CP, Box 9, Folder Morgan & Co. – MG & Co. Vatican Business.
[41] John F. Pollard, "The Vatican and the Wall Street Crash: Bernardino Nogara and Papal Finances in the Early 1930s," *Historical Journal*, vol. 42, no. 4 (1999), pp. 1077–91; Fummi to Morgan & Cie, 2 May 1934, TML, MBEP, Box 17, Cables rec'd, 1 May to 31 August 1934.

While the Vatican sought stability for its external investments and hoped to find it in the refuge of the United States, Mussolini's ambitions were more expansive. Il Duce fretted, perceiving in Britain and France powers that checked his desire to establish Italian control over the Mediterranean. He wanted to "break the bars of the prison," to assail his British and French gaolers.[42] In the 1920s these dreams were not aired. Mussolini posed as a supporter of a newly stabilized European order. The symbol of his peaceful intent was Italy's accession to the Locarno Pact of 1925. Until the mid-1930s Mussolini operated in the shadows, for Italy was not strong enough to accomplish his desires. He concealed his hankering to wage war against Yugoslavia and his desire to expand the Italian imperium in Africa at the expense of Ethiopia. Sponsorship of terrorist groups such as the Internal Macedonian Revolutionary Organization (IMRO), the Macedonian revolutionary organization dedicated to the overthrow of Yugoslavia, which led to the assassination of the Yugoslav king Alexander I (and accidentally the French foreign minister Louis Barthou) at Marseilles in October 1934, had to suffice until Il Duce deemed the moment ripe for the assault on Ethiopia.

The Morgan partners were oblivious to this aggressive, dark Mussolini, despite warnings. Charles Rist, writing Leffingwell in February 1933 in a letter that was circulated to all the New York partners, commented "[a]s to Mussolini, I believe that he is at present sincerely pacifistic. In using the word 'sincerely' I would say that the necessity for peace is so strong to Mussolini as to make it impossible for him to get around it."[43] Rist's cautionary words were, seemingly, belied by events. Italian anxieties about Austrian independence, fears of German economic encroachment in the Danube basin, coupled with Mussolini's jaundiced appraisal of the new German strongman, led Rome to chart a cautious course in 1933 – Mussolini's proposal for a Four Power Pact in March 1933 (Britain, France, Germany, Italy) aimed under the guise of a mutual pledge of disarmament to restrain Germany. That summer, Dino Grandi, the Italian ambassador at London, asked Lamont to relay to Roosevelt the message that Mussolini, by restraining Germany from swallowing Austria, was doing more for American benefit than any debt repayment scheme.[44] A year later, the day after the Austrian Chancellor Engelbert

---

[42] Robert Mallett, *Mussolini and the Origins of the Second World War, 1933–1940*, London: Palgrave Macmillan, 2003, pp. 1–15, discusses the historiography.

[43] Rist to Leffingwell, 25 February 1933, YUL, RCL, Series I, Box 7/145.

[44] Christian Goeschel, *Mussolini and Hitler: The Forging of the Fascist Alliance*, New Haven, CT: Yale University Press, 2018, pp. 27–36; Lamont diary, 17 August 1933, BL, TWL, Series IV B/173/5.

Dollfuss was assassinated during a Nazi-inspired coup attempt in Austria, Lamont told Cochran that Barthou had made clear how pleased Paris was with Mussolini's vigorous response to this provocation, moving troops to the Brenner Pass.[45] Fortifying the impression that Mussolini was committed to a reasonable course were assessments that the Italian economy was struggling. Harrison, returned from his trip to Europe in the summer of 1934, sketched matters bleakly: "I was much struck by his adverse impression of conditions in Italy" Leffingwell remarked.[46] Signs that the Italian economy was encountering headwinds were apparent in the decision late in December 1934 to impose foreign exchange controls, a signal that Rome was seeking to husband its reserves. When the Italian Cabinet was reshuffled early in 1935, Fummi hastened to reassure that the changes would not produce any alteration, remarking on Mussolini's "extraordinary grasp" of financial policy.[47]

Through 1933 and 1934 the Roosevelt administration considered Mussolini a "moderating influence" in Europe.[48] If the clash between Italian and Ethiopian forces at Wal Wal in December 1934 suggested otherwise, the Stresa Front talks with Britain and France in April 1935 seemed proof of Mussolini's peaceable intent. The discussions, which promoted the notion of the three powers keeping a watchful eye on Berlin, were interpreted as reassuring for European stability. Unbeknownst to those outside Rome, Mussolini had months before ordered the invasion of Ethiopia, confirming the decision at the end of 1934.[49] His discussions with Pierre Laval, the French foreign minister, early in January 1935 in Rome were motivated by a desire to probe the likely French response to Italian action. Laval's reassurance that Paris would acquiesce was neither novel nor unexpected, given the French fixation with Germany, but gratified Mussolini.[50] Stresa was an effort by Rome to remind London and Paris of the threat from Berlin. The British attitude was crucial given the stranglehold occasioned by Italian dependence on imports for its energy needs. The Royal Navy, with its bases at Gibraltar, Malta, and Alexandria, was well-positioned to interdict Italian commerce should war

---

[45] Lamont to Cochran, 15 August 1934, BL, TWL, Series II, Box 87, Folder 16.
[46] Leffingwell to Lamont, 25 July 1934, YUL, RCL, Series 1, Box 4, Folder 96.
[47] Fummi to Morgan & Cie., 26 January 1935, TML, MBEP, Box 18, Cables received, 2 January to 31 May 1935. The cable was relayed to New York.
[48] David F. Schmitz, *The United States and Fascist Italy 1922–1940*, Chapel Hill, NC: University of North Carolina Press, 1988, pp. 135–52, "moderating influence," p. 141.
[49] John Gooch, *Mussolini and His Generals: The Armed Forces and Fascist Foreign Policy, 1922–1940*, Cambridge: Cambridge University Press, 2007, pp. 249–51.
[50] Martin Thomas, "France and the Ethiopian Crisis, 1935–1936: Security Dilemmas and Adjustable Interests," in G. Bruce Strang, ed., *Collision of Empires: Italy's Invasion of Ethiopia and Its International Impact*, London: Ashgate, 2013, pp. 111–14.

erupt. Yet trepidation in London at the possibility of an Italian war interacted with a desire to maintain the Stresa Front, with the threat from Japan and Germany, and with doubts about the reliability of the United States, discouraging Whitehall from confrontation.[51] Ignorant of London's strategic calculations, the Morgan partners could nevertheless read the tea leaves. J.P. Morgan & Co. began withdrawing from Italian commitments in June 1935 as Italian bellicosity waxed. Lamont cabled Fummi on 6 June that the bank had opted to reduce its credits by 25 per cent, limiting acceptances to a maximum of three months maturity, while exercising the right to cancel any credits with ninety days' notice. Lamont made plain Morgan displeasure: "public opinion in this country regards the African development with little sympathy." A month later, Lamont, after consulting with Whigham and Rodd, limited Morgan exposure further. The firm gave notice of the ninety-day cancellation clause in its lines of credits to Italian banks, meaning that, from 15 October, J.P. Morgan & Co. would be positioned to end its credits entirely. Fummi protested, informing New York that he feared that such steps would incite a negative reaction from Rome, suggesting a delay to 1 August on the grounds that arbitration might yet succeed in resolving Italo-Ethiopian differences, telling Lamont in confidence that a well-placed authority had intimated such an outcome was likely.[52] Ordinarily Lamont may have succumbed to the temptation of having privileged information but in this instance he was not seduced. While his partner Leffingwell remained impressed by Mussolini, arguing that it was the latter's skill that made possible the stability of the lira in the face of buffeting headwinds occasioned by deflation, admiration for Il Duce was distinct from willingness to continue doing business with Italy.[53] Morgan coolness was dictated by various considerations.

American legislation was one. Two acts were pertinent, the Johnson Act of April 1934 and the Neutrality Act of August 1935. The Johnson Act prohibited loans to European states that were in default on their war debts to the United States. Italy fell into this category. For J.P. Morgan & Co., the Johnson Act was too broad-brush; Lamont wrote Johnson pointing out that the act's provisions made possible discrimination against

---

[51] Steven Morewood, "'This Silly African Business': the Military Dimension of Britain's Response to the Abyssinia Crisis," in G. Bruce Strang, ed., *Collision of Empires: Italy's Invasion of Ethiopia and Its International Impact*, London: Ashgate, 2013, pp. 73–108; Michael L. Roi, "'A Completely Immoral and Cowardly Attitude': The British Foreign Office, American Neutrality and the Hoare-Laval Plan," *Canadian Journal of History*, vol. 29, no. 2 (1994), pp. 333–51.

[52] Lamont to Fummi, 6 June 1935, Lamont to J.P. Morgan & Co., 11 July 1935, Fummi to Lamont, 1 August 1935, BL, TWL, Series IV D, Box 191, Folder 4.

[53] Leffingwell to Lamont, BL, TWL, Series IV D, Box 191, Folder 4.

private loans that were not in default and in many instances had risen in price, an observation that was reiterated in separate communications to Noyes and Lippmann.[54] This protest had little effect but attested to the Morgan bank's sensitivity, which was demonstrated in July 1934 when the pleas of Morgan & Cie. that they might risk losing "our old European clientele" if the firm did not subscribe to a new French government loan were rejected by New York on the grounds that the Johnson Act forbade it.[55] The bracing effect of the Johnson Act was marked; fear of violating its stipulations reinforced Morgan conservatism through the remainder of the 1930s whenever European governments inquired about borrowing.

The Neutrality Act struck directly at American business links with Italy. Pressure had been building within Congress for statutory action that would address the complications that might arise from future conflicts. Belief that American economic and financial assistance between 1914 and 1917 to the Allies had tugged the United States into war underpinned this push. Roosevelt had asked Nye's committee investigating the munitions industry to explore legislation in a White House meeting in March 1935, a suggestion that Nye and his colleagues seized on with alacrity. From the outset it was apparent that Nye envisaged J.P. Morgan & Co. as a target. As he remarked, "if Morgans and other bankers must get into another war, let them do it by enlisting in the Foreign Legion."[56] Driving draft legislation forward was an amalgam of bitterness regarding World War I and growing European tensions. What ensued over the spring and summer of 1935 was a demonstration of how tangled neutrality was in American politics. Pittman's Foreign Relations Committee, angered at the intrusion of Nye on to their territory, sought to fend off the interloper, while Roosevelt, fortified by Hull, his State department officials, and Norman Davis, backtracked. The administration reverted to the traditional executive insistence that its prerogatives over foreign affairs not be infringed.[57] Once it became apparent, following the collapse of tripartite talks among Britain, France, and Italy on 19 August, that war was likely, under duress Roosevelt signed the Neutrality Act at the end of August. The act, of six months' duration, fashioned a general embargo on the shipment of war material to

---

[54] Lamont to Johnson, 11 May 1934, BL, TWL, Series II, Box 104, Folder 13, indicating that a copy of the memorandum was sent to Lippmann; Lamont to Noyes, 18 May 1934, BL, TWL, Series II, Box 120, Folder 23.

[55] The exchange may be followed in Morgan & Cie. to J.P. Morgan & Co. 9–13 July 1934, TML, MBEP, Box 17, Cables sent, 1 May to 31 July 1934.

[56] John E. Wiltz, *In Search of Peace: The Senate Munitions Inquiry, 1934–36*, Baton Rouge, LA: Louisiana State University Press, 1963, p. 176.

[57] Wayne S. Cole, *Roosevelt and the Isolationists, 1932–1945*, Lincoln, NE: University of Nebraska Press, 1983, is the classic account.

belligerents.[58] Its effect on Morgan communications with Fummi and, through him, Mussolini's regime was immediate.

Cabling Fummi on 23 August, after noting their credit line arrangements with Italian banks, specifically the Banco di Roma, the Banca Commerciale Italiana, and Credito Italiano, J.P. Morgan & Co. remarked: "in view of governmental attitude here as shown by recent resolution passed by the Senate and now pending before the House of Representatives any utilization by them of these lines might result in situations troublesome to them and of great embarrassment to the whole situation." Bluntly, New York told Fummi not to ask for new credits.[59] Making frankness simpler was the scale of Morgan business with Italy. As of late August 1935, there was no open line of credit or acceptances with the Banco di Roma, acceptances to the derisory amount of $1503.00 were on the books with the Banca Commerciale d'Italia, and only the Credito Italiano was drawing, with their line reaching $279,702.82 early in September 1935.[60] There was no reason for the Morgan partners to preserve a pittance. Despite repeated messages from Fummi emphasizing the commitment of the Italian people to Mussolini, to the Fascist regime, and to the Ethiopian affair, far from Rome the Morgan evaluation was that Italian readiness for war was questionable. Carter told his New York partners that, though Mussolini's regime had sequestered holdings of foreign securities in the amount of $120 million, he thought that this was a "surprisingly low figure" for a state girding for war. Carter's doubts extended to disparaging Fummi's prediction that a "strongly-armed" Italy might have to be rescued from its economic woes when a general settlement of monetary and financial questions occurred. Carter described such imaginings as "a pretty wobbly foundation on which to base a country's financial future."[61] The outrage expressed in the Morgan cable to Fummi, composed days after the Italian campaign opened, in the wake of reports in the American press of bombings of villages resulting in the killing and maiming of women and children, was genuine, but it risked little because there was little Morgan business with Fascism.[62]

[58] Dallek, *Franklin D. Roosevelt and American Foreign Policy*, pp. 101–8, and Wiltz, *In Search of Peace*, pp. 174–86, have accounts.
[59] J.P. Morgan & Co. to Fummi, 23 August 1935, TML, MBEP, Box 18, Cables received, 1 June to 31 October 1935.
[60] J.P. Morgan & Co. to Fummi, 6 September 1935, TML, MBEP, Box 18, Cables received, 1 June to 31 October 1935.
[61] Fummi to Morgan & Cie., 4 September 1935, Carter to Lamont, 4 September 1935, Fummi to Lamont, 11 September 1935, TML, MBEP, Box 25, Giovanni Fummi, File 3.
[62] J.P. Morgan & Co. to Morgan & Cie., 11 October 1935, TML, MBEP, Box 18, Cables rec'd, 1 June to 31 October 1935. New York asked Paris to relay this cable to Fummi, stating that they were "inexpressibly shocked" by the newspaper reports on atrocities in Ethiopia.

Mussolini's adventurism led to a re-evaluation of the Italian tie. The spike in demand deposits that J.P. Morgan & Co. experienced in the last quarter of 1935, from $356.6 million on 1 October 1935 to $446.7 million on 31 December 1935, bore witness to money fleeing Europe after the outbreak of Italo-Ethiopian hostilities.[63] Amid a New Deal economy that was becalmed, while tensions between Wall Street and the White House were mounting, capital flight was unwelcome. Fummi's role was under review in New York. Morgan Grenfell, coping with lowered levels of profitability, was seeking economies. Fummi was drawing a salary of $30,000 a year, supplemented by a special account of $10,000 and an expense account of $10,000. These expenses were divided. Morgan Grenfell covered 40–45 per cent, Morgan & Cie., 15–20 per cent, with J. P. Morgan & Co. meeting the balance. Baulking at what they estimated was an outlay of $20,000 a year for Fummi, Morgan Grenfell wanted a reduction. Fummi, informed that a cut of $10,000 in his salary was contemplated, lobbied for a smaller decrease of $5,000. Writing the Morgan Grenfell partner Vivian Harris Smith in December 1936, Lamont mused:

So far as Italian business is concerned, we have . . . done little or nothing in the last few years. We see little chance of doing any amount of such business for a considerable time in the future, if at all. Therefore, are we justified in continuing indefinitely what is a very considerable item of expense for the maintenance of what is in effect an all-round Continental ambassador?[64]

While Fummi's presence in Rome perhaps encouraged Italy to service its outstanding loans, Lamont was confident "that if he was hit by a bus, [the government] would still service."[65] Lamont acknowledged there was little to show from Fummi's efforts. The decision was made to retain Fummi's services but at a less lavishly provisioned level, in the hope that his future efforts would be more valuable to J.P. Morgan & Co.

Fummi had survived because of his perceived indispensability as an interlocutor. Even as Lamont claimed that the combination of a general war arising from Fascist aggression, compounded by the losses that J.P. Morgan & Co. had sustained since the onset of the Depression, ruled out new Morgan credits for Italy, he sought to soothe Fascist sensibilities.[66] Fummi played a role, telling all and sundry in Rome that Morgan

[63] DB Morgan Grenfell Papers, Box 50596681, J.P. Morgan & Co. Inc., Condensed Statement of Condition, 1 October 1935 and 31 December 1935.
[64] Thomas S. Lamont to Lamont, 8 December 1936, Lamont to Vivian Harris Smith, 18 December 1936, BL, TWL, Series II, Box 112, Folder 8.
[65] Lamont to Vivian Harris Smith, 18 December 1936, BL, TWL, Series II, Box 112, Folder 8.
[66] Migone, *The United States and Fascist Italy*, p. 375.

faithfulness to Fascism was intact, pointing to Morgan resistance to American legislative developments. Lamont, his fondness for face-to-face diplomacy undimmed, had signalled his willingness to travel to Italy early in 1936 despite the ongoing war. Discouraged by Fummi on the grounds a trip might fuel speculation about Morgan loans to Rome, the idea was revived in the spring of 1937 as new Italian feelers for credit were extended. Credito Italiano inquired about obtaining a $250,000 line of credit from J.P. Morgan & Co. in the spring of 1937 and were spurned, despite their argument that both Chase National ($800,000) and National City ($500,000) had extended credit.[67] Perhaps to soften the blow, Lamont issued guidance to T.H. Beck, the president of Crowell Publishing, in which Lamont had a substantial personal interest. Crowell published *Women's Home Companion*, *The American Magazine*, and critically *Collier's*, with its massive audience. Lamont told Beck that "[t]he Duce should be presented to the public not as a warrior or in warlike attitudes, but in pastoral, agricultural, friendly, domestic and peaceful attitudes."[68] This was matched by deed, as Lamont journeyed to Italy in April 1937, meeting among others Azzolini and Mussolini. His willingness to visit was seen as a benediction for Fascism. Detailing his half-hour meeting with Mussolini, Lamont told his partners that his impression was that Mussolini was not unduly upset about Morgan unwillingness to provide credits. He reported that Il Duce had insisted on his peaceful intent, which Lamont questioned. When asked by Mussolini what his advice was, Lamont counselled greater amity with Britain and the United States, particularly through closer economic cooperation. Recounting the interview, Lamont told his partners that he had informed the dictator that "many Americans" admired him but there were concerns in the United States about his policy course. Spain, he indicated, did not come up due to its delicacy and because he had been informed not to raise the subject. The foregoing, Lamont informed New York, had been passed to Phillips, from August 1936 the American ambassador at Rome, who had promised to cable Hull.[69] A memorandum, to assist Fummi in deciphering American public opinion for Italian audiences, followed.

Wooing Rome conformed to the broader Morgan wish to see prosperity and stability through international trade and economic cooperation. More crucial, however, was a pragmatic consideration: Vatican business.

---

[67] W.A. Mitchell to Fummi, 25 March 1937, BL, TWL, Series VIII, Box 247, Folder 20.
[68] Lamont to T.H. Beck, 31 March 1937, BL, TWL, Series II, Box 83, Folder 25.
[69] Lamont to Thomas S. Lamont and J.P. Morgan & Co. partners, 27 April 1937, BL, TWL, Series IV B, Box 191. The reference to Spain was to the Battle of Guadalajara, fought in March 1937, in which Italian forces had been routed by troops loyal to the Madrid government, including a contingent of Italian exiles from Fascism.

Lamont's diary for April 1937 recorded that he and Fummi visited the Vatican to discuss Nogara's investment plans: "Told him I thought $ still best currency. He will probably transfer some of his £3000 m from London." While this hope petered out by the early summer, Nogara's visit to the United States with Fummi in November 1937 resulted in substantial investments, with Nogara purchasing $3.5 million in stocks and treasury bonds guided by J.P. Morgan & Co.[70] Given the sharp contraction of the American economy in 1937–38 and the continued financial challenges the bank faced, there was greater importance attached to Vatican funds. Dealing with Nogara necessitated a modicum of goodwill toward Fascism. A second factor was non-financial, driven by the Morgan desire to follow Washington. Phillips did not disguise his sympathies for the Fascist regime. He enjoyed considerable influence with Hull from his past tenure and his conspicuous flattery of the secretary of state.[71] He was listened to as well by the president. Roosevelt had revoked his Neutrality Proclamations in June 1936 after months of American oil companies flouting with impunity limitations on trade to belligerents. Reluctant or not, the step signposted the administration attitude. More generally, Roosevelt's passivity regarding Mussolini from 1935 to 1937 sent a signal which J.P. Morgan & Co. could hardly fail to interpret.[72] Cordial relations with the Roosevelt administration on foreign policy were imperative, a salience motivated in part by the Nye investigation.

*****

Nye was the second of the series of Senate investigations during the 1930s in which J.P. Morgan & Co. played a starring role. Although the Nye Committee had been charged with exploring the American munitions industry and American involvement in World War I, those engaged appreciated that the politics of Nye were not exclusive to either munitions or to what had happened between 1914 and 1918. Contemporary preoccupations swirled, as the Italo-Ethiopian war loomed and was then realized, sparking fears of a greater conflagration to come. Neutrality was on all lips. Unlike Pecora, Nye was domestic and international in its

---

[70] Lamont diary, 19 April 1937, BL, TWL, Series IV B, Box 173, Folder 9; Pollard, *Money and the Rise of the Modern Papacy*, p. 180.

[71] Irwin F. Gellman, *Secret Affairs: Franklin Roosevelt, Cordell Hull and Sumner Welles*, Baltimore, MD: Johns Hopkins University Press, 1995, pp. 102–3.

[72] For criticism of Roosevelt's policy, see G. Bruce Strang, "'A Sad Commentary on World Ethics': Italy and the United States during the Ethiopian Crisis," in G. Bruce Strang, ed., *Collision of Empires: Italy's Invasion of Ethiopia and Its International Impact*, London: Ashgate, 2013, pp. 135–63, esp. pp. 161–63.

scope. Domestic concerns had ruled Pecora, amid the ravages of the Depression and the hope registered in the Hundred Days. Then Roosevelt had encouraged inquiry into J.P. Morgan. Now the president was arrayed against the Nye Committee exploration, as was the State department, as were the British and French governments. Roosevelt, Hull, and their counterparts in London and Paris feared that the revelations that might ensue from allowing Nye investigators to rummage unimpeded in the Morgan files would be embarrassing. The consequence, as a column by Raymond Gram Swing in *The Nation* observed on 1 May 1935, was that Roosevelt, Hull, Baldwin, Sir Ronald Lindsay (the British ambassador), and Senators Nye, Bennett Clark of Missouri, and James Pope of Idaho were negotiating what investigators might see. This was understandable, Swing thought, mixing his metaphors: "the banking aspect is the climax, and Morgan and Company is the heart of the problem."[73] Months of talks ensued. Agreement was reached at length in August. The British and French turned over sensitive files to the State department, who deposited them in a secure room where the Nye investigators were permitted to pore over the documents but were not allowed to remove them.

Throughout these discussions, J.P. Morgan & Co. was happy to let the Roosevelt administration and the British and French governments combat the Nye Committee. Occasionally the partners raised the investigation, as Lamont did when he visited Baldwin in July 1935, but they preferred to remain in the background.[74] They did not repeat the misstep of 1933 when Lamont had attempted to head off the Pecora investigation through a direct appeal to Roosevelt. Contrasting with the drawn-out negotiations on the international side, the partners skirmished only briefly with the Nye investigators, before retreating abruptly, granting Nye's nonplussed team more or less open access to their files. Lawrence Brown, who headed the New York financial investigative team for Nye, told Alger Hiss (in the Washington office of the Nye Committee team), on 3 May that:

For some reason which I have not yet completely fathomed, Morgans have suddenly and apparently completely reversed their attitude. After three weeks of trying to give us surface nonsense about their business, they turned around yesterday and coughed up their confidential correspondence and cables and a complete transcript of repayments on the famous overdraft ... What this change in attitude means, I don't know. Whether they have suddenly decided that they

---

[73] Raymond Gram Swing, "The Morgan Nerve Begins to Jump," *The Nation*, vol. 140, no. 3643, 1 May 1935, p. 504. Swing had joined *The Nation* after a long career as a European-based correspondent for various American newspapers. Swing, *Good Evening*, pp. 171–72.
[74] Lamont to Leffingwell, 9 July 1935, BL, TWL, Series II, Box 83, Folder 15.

must yield anyway and that the ultimate responsibility is the British Government's or whether they hope by being ninety-eight per cent frank it will be easier to conceal the other two per cent on the ground that we will be off our guard, I don't know. The problem I suppose is to wait and see.[75]

As Brown suspected, the Morgan partners had a plan.

The day that Brown wrote Hiss, Leffingwell wrote Carter Glass, to inquire whether he wished to stay with Leffingwell on his upcoming visit to New York. The invitation afforded Leffingwell opportunity to advance his purpose, namely informing Glass that Nye was planning to argue that the United States had entered the war to save Morgan loans, that the Treasury had lent Britain money to discharge the loans, and that Leffingwell, then in the Treasury, was instrumental in this process. Leffingwell disparaged these assertions, describing them as "grotesque," before remarking tartly that: "Surely there must be enough men living to remember the violation of Belgian neutrality, the sinking of the Lusitania and finally the unrestricted U-boat campaign, on the one hand, and the antagonism and even hostility between Wall Street and Wilson, Bryan, McAdoo, to make such a canard fall flat." Leffingwell continued that, while he did not know Nye, he found it impossible to believe that he would stoop so low. Responding the next day, Glass, politely declining Leffingwell's invitation, remarked: "I do not think you need give yourself any worry about Nye's investigation. He cuts very little figure in the Senate and should he make any attack on the Wilson Administration you may be sure that McAdoo and I will be prepared to meet the issue."[76] Glass had been secretary of the Treasury in the Wilson administration from 1918 to 1920, succeeding McAdoo, who had held the position from 1913 to 1918. The two Senators commanded first-hand knowledge of American finance and the American entry into war in 1917 that Nye could not match; both men revered Wilson and would, as Glass assured, be alert to any tarnishing of his legacy. Glass and McAdoo's posture joined with Roosevelt's opposition to ensure that the political calculus of the Nye hearings was much more favourable to J.P. Morgan & Co. than Pecora had been.

The partners had been caught unaware by Pecora, with the compression of the time frame between announcement of the investigation and the giving of their testimony in Washington working against them. Morgan efforts to portray the Pecora hearings as validating their integrity

---

[75] Brown to Alger Hiss, 3 May 1935, NARA, RG 46, 74th Congress, Special Committee Investigating the Munitions Industry, Box 323, Directive #240/240-#38.
[76] Leffingwell to Glass, 3 May 1935, Glass to Leffingwell, 4 May 1935, UVA, Glass MS, Series I, Box 38, Treasury of the United States Carter Glass and Russell C. Leffingwell.

were *ex post facto*, leaving the shaping of the narrative, for good or ill, to others. A determination not to let this happen again pervaded the Corner. Nye helped. Addressing a crowd of 2,500 at Carnegie Hall on 27 May 1935 in the company of Senator Clark, sharing the stage with representatives of the National Peace Conference and the National Council for Prevention of War, aware that Lamont was in the audience, Nye listed four classes of public enemies. Public enemy number two was the banker. J.P. Morgan & Co. was the only banking firm that Nye mentioned.[77] There could be no doubt who Nye intended to target. Several weeks after the Carnegie Hall event, Wasson who had replaced Egan as Lamont's principal aide on public relations questions, wrote Leffingwell. Wasson was direct – he argued that J.P. Morgan & Co. had to take the offensive against Nye, rather than letting Nye draw out what he wanted through sustained grilling of Morgan partners on the stand. Wasson warned:

All the innuendoes that a Senatorial inquisition delights in will thus be exploited to the full, and all the tricks of the stage setting will be used. Nye's thunder must be stolen from him in advance. We must take the edge off the figures by issuing them ourselves in a connected narrative, in their right setting. Furthermore, they will draw less newspaper attention in that way than if extracted, after all these years, from a Morgan partner, in the presence of the public, by St. Gerald the Evangel of Peace.[78]

There followed a campaign. Of the quality New York papers, the *New York Herald Tribune*, indebted to Morgan goodwill, could be counted on to be for the Corner, but its star columnist, Lippmann, was an unknown quantity. His writing had wounded the partners deeply during Pecora. Lippmann, however, was no longer a New Deal partisan, had no brief for Nye, and was dubious about neutrality. His sin against the Morgan firm overlooked, Lippmann was enlisted. He was the recipient of a memorandum from Lamont entitled "Neutrality and Munitions" defending Morgan conduct during American neutrality. Lippmann told Lamont that the memorandum was "very useful."[79] The *New York Times* was the other paper that mattered. Lamont passed on material to Bell that made its way via Arthur Krock to the publisher, Arthur Hays Sulzberger,

[77] Lamont to Wasson, 28 May 1935, BL, TWL, Series V, Box 214, Folder 14, with a memorandum by Lamont on Nye's speech. Press accounts in "Anti-War Rally Hears Plea to Forbid Profits," *New York Herald Tribune*, 28 May 1935, p. 4; "Nye and Clark Urge Peace Laws Here," *New York Times*, 28 May 1935, p. 27. Representative Maury Maverick, Democrat of Texas, was also on the stage.
[78] Wasson to Leffingwell, 20 June 1935, BL, TWL, Series V, Box 215, Folder 4.
[79] Lamont to Lippmann, 9 August 1935, Lippmann to Lamont, 12 August 1935, YUL, Walter Lippmann papers, III, Box 83, 1278.

284   J.P. Morgan & Co. and the Crisis of Capitalism

casting doubt on Nye's methods.[80] Leffingwell subsequently wrote Noyes, still with the *Times*, to praise its editorials in late October on why the United States entered the war. He took the opportunity, once more, to hammer home the Morgan argument: "When I read now that we went to war to collect the Morgan loans, or to make profits for munitions manufacturers, I pinch myself and wonder, can I be dreaming? . . . Morgan influence in the Democratic administration of President Wilson was considerably less than nothing."[81]

To support the Morgan case, Lamont looked for academic expertise to wield against the popularity of works such as Walter Millis' *Road to War, 1914–17* (1935). Millis had argued that economic self-interest had tied the United States irrevocably to the Allied cause, even if the American declaration of war was not attributable directly to the financiers. Lamont found what he wanted in Charles Seymour, a diplomatic historian at Yale and editor of the papers of Colonel House, whose 1934 book, *American Diplomacy during the World War*, was followed by *American Neutrality, 1914–17: Essays on the Causes of American Intervention* (1935). Seymour reviewed Millis in *Southwest Review* and *The Yale Review* in 1935. Seymour dismissed the Millis argument as an unfounded misreading of the evidence and, by implication, suggested that the Nye investigation was baseless.[82] Seymour tackled head-on the notion of economic causes for American belligerency, rubbishing the idea, particularly in his slim 1935 essay collection. Seymour's efforts extended beyond his reviews of Millis. He was commissioned by Lamont to write a series of memoranda, fourteen in all, that covered wartime American diplomacy. As a sweetener, Lamont subsidized the publication of Seymour's 1935 book, purchasing enough copies from Yale University Press to guarantee its viability. The bank assisted publication in another way – helping to draft the leaflet that accompanied the book on its publication.[83]

Lamont deployed Seymour's standing to suggest to John Foster Dulles, then at the New York law firm of Sullivan and Cromwell, that he might consider penning a "brief article" on Millis.[84] James T. Shotwell, of Columbia University and the director of research at the Carnegie

---

[80] Krock to Sulzberger, 26 September 1935, Princeton, Mudd Library, Arthur Krock papers, Box 56, Folder Arthur Hays Sulzberger 1927–1933; 1935–1949.
[81] Leffingwell to Noyes, 29 October 1935, YUL, RCL, Series I, Box 6, Folder 131.
[82] *The Southwest Review* piece is unusual for its length – more than five pages. *The Southwest Review*, vol. 20, no. 4 (July 1935), pp. 1–6.
[83] Lamont to Shotwell, 24 October 1935, 26 November 1935, 30 November 1935, Shotwell to Lamont, 25 October 1935, BL, TWL, Series V, Box 216, Folder 26. On Seymour and the commissioned memorandum, see BL, TWL, Series V, Box 215, Folder 1. Lamont tried to get Joseph Knapp of Crowell to publish the Seymour memoranda.
[84] Lamont to Dulles, 11 October 1935, BL, TWL, Series V, Box 216, Folder 26.

Endowment for International Peace, was recruited. Shotwell was an outspoken advocate of the League of Nations and had a dim view of Millis' bestseller. Shotwell believed that American entry to the League would help thwart Nye. Leffingwell was incredulous about this notion, but Shotwell's September 1935 article, "The Promise of the League," that appeared in the *New York Times* magazine, was sufficient proof of his good faith for such scepticism to remain buried.[85] The Morgan partners did not restrict themselves solely to intermediaries. When William Chenery of *Collier's* approached Lamont about writing an article on bankers and the war from 1914 to 1917, Lamont agreed, eventually working his way through eight drafts with the help of Leffingwell, Whitney, Stanley, and his son, Thomas S. Lamont. While the piece never appeared, the exercise proved useful to the partners, preparing them for the hearings to come. Communication between Lamont and Chenery demonstrated that Lamont, in tandem with Parker Gilbert, was influencing the editorial policy of *Collier's* as well as articles appearing under George Creel's byline.[86]

Once the hearings opened, the Morgan partners, as they had been during Pecora, were the star attraction. Once again, the partners decamped to Washington, on this occasion to the Shoreham hotel. Once again, the press coverage was overwhelming, the crush inside the hearing room making the atmosphere fetid. The bank had learned from Pecora about how to manage and to respond to senatorial investigations. The partners and their staff responded with alacrity to every line of questioning raised, circulating supporting material for the Morgan position, drawn from the preparatory work that the firm had undertaken, to grateful journalists. Adding to this was the personal touch, with the partners, led by Jack Morgan, making themselves available for interviews and comment to the media, an openness that charmed the assembled reporters. It helped that the Nye who had inveighed so lustily against J.P. Morgan & Co. at Carnegie Hall was scarcely in evidence during the hearings. His interjections were infrequent, his attitude cautious (see Figure 7.1). Less anti-business than he was made out to be, also less Progressive in his sympathies, and imbued with a strong sense of the gravity of his responsibility as chair, Nye let others lead.[87] Most of the

---

[85] A pencilled memo from Leffingwell to Lamont, undated, in BL, TWL, Series V, Box 216, Folder 27 makes it clear what the Morgan interest in cultivating Shotwell was: "But fighting Nye by an appeal for our entry into the League of Nations! Well really! Where has Shotwell been all these years?"

[86] Chenery to Lamont, 17 October 1935, Lamont to Chenery, 18 November 1935, Chenery to Lamont, 21 November 1935, BL, TWL, Series V, Box 215, Folder 17. On the decision to forego publication, Lamont to Whitney and Stanley, 23 December 1935, BL, TWL, Series V, Box 215, Folder 23.

[87] Wiltz, *In Search of Peace*, pp. 222–25.

Figure 7.1 Senator Gerald P. Nye in conference with Thomas
W. Lamont, Jack Morgan, and George Whitney during the Nye
hearings, 1936. Bettmann/Getty Images.

questioning of the Morgan partners – Jack Morgan, Lamont, and
Whitney principally – emanated from Clark.[88]

Jack Morgan, after being sworn in, as he had in 1933, read a short
statement. Unlike 1933, when Jack Morgan spoke in lofty terms about the
duties of the private merchant banker, his remarks to the Nye Committee
spoke directly to neutrality. Jack Morgan admitted that he and his partners had not been neutral either in thought or in deed from the moment
that Germany invaded Belgium in 1914. They had done all that they
could, within the confines of American law, to bring about Allied victory.
He concluded unapologetically: "The fact that the Allies found us useful
and valued our assistance in their task is the fact of which I am most proud
in all my business life of more than 45 years." Yet he denied that the
actions of J.P. Morgan & Co. had induced the Wilson administration to

[88] Matthew Ware Coulter, *The Senate Munitions Inquiry of the 1930s*, Westport, CT: Greenwood
Press, 1997, remarked that Clark "dominated the hearing room in 1936,", p. 114.

declare war in 1917, placing the blame for American intervention entirely on Germany.[89] This laid down an unwavering Morgan position, as became apparent during the days of testimony by the partners on 7–10 January, 13–16 January, and 4–5 February. Pecora in 1933 had played a strong hand skilfully; Clark and Nye, dealt a less powerful hand, played it less well.

To some extent the difficulties they faced arose from the material. The published record of the committee hearings illustrates the problem. For the crucial opening two days of the hearings the topics addressed were the structure and valuation of J.P. Morgan & Co.; financial operations at the outbreak of war; the change in government policy toward belligerent loans; the material given to the committee by J.P. Morgan & Co; the attempts of the National City Bank to establish a commercial agency; the early expansion of the rifle industry; the financial difficulties of the rifle manufacturers; the relation of British finance to the rifle situation; the settlement of the rifle difficulties; and the control of the Eddystone Ammunition Corporation. The evidentiary trail was intricate. One of the first witnesses was Frank Vanderlip, a former National City banker whose national renown was non-existent. The hearing then wandered into the thickets of rifle procurement and, crucially, did not show the culpability of J.P. Morgan & Co. in the American move to war. As the hearings moved deeper into the war years and neared 1917, the Morgan role in American intervention became murkier. Clark and Nye acknowledged as much in an exchange with Jack Morgan on 10 January:

SENATOR CLARK. This committee is not concerned with the relation between J.P. Morgan & Co. and the British or French Governments, or any other elements. What our committee is interested in is seeing the effect of certain economic issues on our neutrality policy.

MR. MORGAN. You have not adhered to that entirely, Senator, because in certain speeches by several members of the committee there have been direct accusations against the New York bankers having brought on the war, and that is one of the things with which I have not been particularly pleased, and one of the things which is not borne out.

THE CHAIRMAN. I want to deny, as one member of the committee, that you are right in concluding that the charge has been as direct as that.

MR. MORGAN. Well—.

THE CHAIRMAN. I am more convinced this morning than I have ever been at any stage heretofore, that it was the commercial activity as a whole, in which the bankers had a hand, which did finally break down completely our neutrality.[90]

---

[89] Jack Morgan, 7 January 1936, Nye Committee hearings, Part 25, pp. 7483–85.
[90] 10 January 1936, Nye Committee hearings, Part 26, p. 7893.

Here was the problem. Having placed J.P. Morgan & Co. at the heart of the investigation, Nye was forced to retreat to the vague formulation of "commercial activity as a whole" when Jack Morgan asserted that New York bankers had not been responsible for American belligerency. Nye's rejoinder was the Millis argument, but it did not fare well amid the glare of the hearing room. The Morgan partners told a simple story – they were following their beliefs in helping the Allies. Spurred by a conviction that the German course was evil, J.P. Morgan & Co. had taken a morally upstanding path. Pecora had had the advantage of the taint of moral opprobrium arising from the misdeeds of the Mitchells of the American banking world. Nye had no such crutch.[91]

When Nye injected morality the following week, he gave his opponents ammunition. On 15 February, in the morning session of the committee, without the Morgan partners present and only four out of seven senators attending, Clark and Nye built a case connecting Allied war aims, the secret treaties, and American belligerency. Nye charged that Wilson and his secretary of state, Robert Lansing, had "falsified" their knowledge of the so-called secret treaties binding the Allies at the Paris Peace Settlement talks in 1919. This statement fractured the committee. The next day Pope, who had been absent when Nye made his remark, read a statement repudiating Nye and the committee's investigation on the grounds that the committee had degenerated into mud-slinging against Wilson.[92] Pope was supported by Walter George of Georgia, another committee member who had also not been in attendance. The latter's co-signature exposed an emerging fault line in the Senate Democratic caucus: Southern Democratic senators whose politics were distant from Nye, Clark, and Vandenberg took umbrage. At the forefront was Glass. Indignant at the slur to Wilson's name and reputation, he lambasted Nye on the floor of the Senate "brutally and well."[93] Besieged within and without, the committee's inquiry foundered, its foes knew that its funds were exhausted, or nearly so.[94] For the Morgan partners, though they appeared again before the committee on 4 and 5 February, the hearings were over.

Nye was a triumph for J.P. Morgan & Co. Lamont told his former classmate and long-time friend and correspondent North Duane that

---

[91] Modern scholarship agrees that the Morgan bank did not push the United States into war. Burk, *Britain, America, and the Sinews of War*, is definitive.

[92] Nye, 15 January 1936, Nye Committee hearings, Part 28, p. 8512; Pope, 16 January 1936, Nye Committee hearings, Part 28, pp. 8534–35.

[93] The phrase was Hiram Johnson's. Johnson to Hiram Johnson Jr., 18 January 1936, in Burk, *The Diary Letters of Hiram Johnson*, vol. 6.

[94] Wiltz, *In Search of Peace*, pp. 202–8; Coulter, *The Senate Munitions Inquiry*, pp. 115–19.

"Washington went off better than we could have anticipated and what seemed at first like a hideous dream is fading into a hectic but not rancorous memory."[95] The tone in major media outlets was positive. Flattering commentaries appeared, complimenting the Morgan response to the queries lobbed at them and Jack Morgan's warmth in dealing with reporters and senators alike. The bemused headline in the *Christian Science Monitor*, "J.P. Morgan is now friend, not foe, of Newspapermen," captured the feeling. *Time* magazine featured Jack Morgan on the cover, declaring that the hearings had been bereft of scandal, while clearing J.P. Morgan & Co. of any suggestion that they had conspired to inveigle American belligerency.[96] There was a gratifying *New York Times* editorial:

Senator Nye himself had been so imprudent as to predict in public addresses the horrifying nature of the discoveries that had been made and would be revealed to the public ... the prolonged and searching investigation utterly failed to prove that there was any real foundation for these charges. With the utmost frankness, patience and good nature, Mr. Morgan and his partners answered every question, produced every relevant document and explained every transaction. No one can have read the record of the hearings without being convinced that all the attacks have been successfully met ... the firm under scrutiny was shown to have conducted its affairs honorably and generously, with high regard for its great responsibility, and to have taken no step in the delicate matter of war loans without the knowledge and consent of the American Government.[97]

With much of the American press chiming its accord, it was left to Millis to sound a dissonant note. Writing in *The Nation*, Millis decried the opinion manufactured by a "flood" of letters from Lamont, aided by the *New York Times* and others, that had concealed the truth, namely that economic considerations had driven the United States into war even if the bankers alone were not responsible. What mattered, Millis averred, was forging effective neutrality legislation, a reference to the ongoing tussle over the expiring 1935 Neutrality Act.[98]

Wrangling between Congress and the Roosevelt administration on neutrality, though concurrent with the Nye inquiry into J.P. Morgan & Co., was independent of what was transpiring in the Senate Caucus room. The successful Morgan defence repelled the charge that they had duped the Wilson administration into war, instead reinforcing their identification with the Allied cause. American public opinion, offended by

[95] Lamont to North Duane, 8 February 1936, BL, TWL, Series II, Box 92, Folder 12.
[96] Staff, *The Christian Science Monitor*, 14 January 1936, p. 2; *Time*, vol. 27, no. 3, 20 January 1936, pp. 12–16.
[97] "An Inquiry Ends Well," *New York Times*, 9 February 1936, E8.
[98] Millis penned two articles that appeared in *The Nation*, the first on 22 January 1936, "The Last War and the Next: Morgan, Money, and War," and the second on 29 January 1936, "The Last War and the Next: What Does Neutrality Mean?"

Mussolini's Ethiopian rapacity, could hardly fail to draw the lesson that J. P. Morgan & Co. continued to support London and Paris even as disclosure of the Hoare–Laval Pact demonstrated the extent to which Britain and France were determined to avoid a general war arising from Mussolini's ambitions.[99] If the 1936 Neutrality Act was a compromise between the Roosevelt administration on the one hand and congressional opponents on the other, its prohibition on loans and credits to warring states was an implicit rebuke of Morgan financial aid to the Allies from 1914 to 1917. More to the point, the legislation represented a fear that J. P. Morgan & Co. would be drawn once more to support Britain and France should a general war occur in Europe. This was tilting at windmills, for Morgan enthusiasm for European loans was non-existent – the cumulative effect of Nazi repudiation, Italian fecklessness, the Johnson Act, and straitened Morgan finances occasioned by the Depression had ended any desire of the partners for European credits. J.P. Morgan & Co. had no more wish to see war in Europe than any senator.

*****

Undeclared war had come to Asia years earlier. Officers of the Japanese Kwantung army conspired to manufacture an explosion on the South Manchurian railroad in September 1931. Blaming the Mukden Incident, as it became known, on the Chinese, the Kwantung army used the bombing as a pretext to overrun Manchuria. Manchuria proved the starting point rather than the conclusion of Japanese expansionism in China. A vicious struggle for control of Shanghai that engaged the Japanese army and navy against Jiang Jieshi's Nationalist troops early in 1932 was followed by a report from Lord Lytton's commission empowered by the League of Nations to investigate Japanese aggression in Manchuria. The Lytton report, made public on 1 October 1932, not only chastised Japan, placing the blame on Tokyo for aggression in Manchuria, it disavowed the existence of the puppet state of Manchukuo, which had been extended diplomatic recognition by Japan a month earlier. The rebuke was shrugged off; Japan moved to occupy the province of Jehol late in February 1933 and, subsequently, in the face of

---

[99] The Hoare–Laval Plan, named after Sir Samuel Hoare, the British foreign secretary and Pierre Laval, the French foreign minister, was concocted in December 1935 as a face-saving means of ending the Ethiopian war. It promised to buy Mussolini off by awarding Italy roughly two-thirds of pre-war Ethiopia in return for a cessation of the conflict. Leaked to the Parisian press a week after it was agreed, its details provoked howls of protest, leading to the resignation of Hoare, Laval's subsequent departure from office, and a reaffirmation of public opinion in favour of the League of Nations, while affronting Mussolini.

the General Assembly's adoption of the Lytton report, departed the League of Nations in March 1933.

Japan was unique in the Morgan firmament. Its singularity did not arise from either the scale or frequency of Morgan lending – between 1924 and 1930 J.P. Morgan & Co. made four loans to Japan, two (1924 and 1930) to the Japanese government and two more to the cities of Yokohama (1926) and Tokyo (1927) – which Morgan lending to Europe surpassed. Japan was distinctive because it was Lamont's special province. The difficulties arising from Nazi ambitions or Mussolini's expansionism engaged the Morgan houses in London and Paris as well as Fummi in Rome, while in New York multiple partners registered their views on what should be done. Tokyo, as Harry Morgan told Carosso, was Lamont's bailiwick.[100] Not all J.P. Morgan partners viewed the Japanese connection favourably. Thomas S. Lamont, for one, did not cloak his racial prejudices when writing his partner Harry Davison on the occasion of a looming social occasion with Japanese guests.[101] His father, however, was different. Lamont was a long-standing member of the Japan Society, acting as its honorary vice-president from 1931 to 1937. Along with Martin Egan, Lamont served on the Institute for Pacific Relations, established in 1925, which published the journal *Pacific Affairs*. Egan had been one of the original owners of *The Manila Times* and was an active member of the American Asiatic Association, serving as its vice-president in 1927 and then president from 1928 to 1929. Egan was convinced of Lamont's influence with Tokyo. Writing in December 1929, after a lunch Lamont and Egan had attended for the Japanese delegation heading to the upcoming London Naval Conference, Egan reminded Morrow, one of the American delegates, "I hope when you meet these men again you will recall to them that you are the intimate friend and former partner of T.W. Lamont. His influence is greater than that of any American with the powers that be in Japan."[102] Whether Lamont's writ extended as far as Egan believed is questionable, but there was no doubt that it was Lamont who was determinant in the evolution of Morgan policy vis-à-vis Tokyo in the 1930s.

Outside the bank several figures in the American diplomatic establishment molded Lamont's posture: Joseph Grew, from June 1932 to December 1941 the American ambassador at Tokyo, was well known to

---

[100] 4 December 1975, TML, CP, Box 8, Henry S. Morgan (interviews).
[101] Thomas S. Lamont to Davison, 15 February 1932, TML, CP, Box 19, Morgan & Co. – Misc. Notes 1930s.
[102] Egan to Morrow, 21 December 1929, AC, DWM I, Box 19, Folder 62. Egan was also a member of the China Society of America from 1920 to 1936 and a board member from 1926.

the Morgan partners, while Stanley Hornbeck, the chief of the Far Eastern division in the State department, was a frequent correspondent. Hornbeck doubted Tokyo more and more through the 1930s.[103] The most consequential outsider was Nelson T. Johnson, from February 1930 to 1935 the American minister to China and then ambassador to Jiang's Nationalist government from 1935 to 1941. Johnson was to be critical in prodding Lamont to shed long-standing convictions about China and Japan.

Lamont had first visited Japan in 1920. On his return, he wrote an article that appeared in *The Atlantic* in February 1921, entitled "The Two Japans." Lamont argued that there were two Japans: one that he labelled "liberal," drawn principally from "men of affairs," businessmen, merchants, and bankers who favoured trade and peaceful international development; and a second that he called "the militarists" who believed that the world was "ruled by force rather than by ideas" and who aspired to dominate Asia. The militarists were convinced that food supply was crucial and that Japan must secure it. Lamont thought that Americans did not understand Japan – they tended to think that it was a country of militarists, whereas in his judgement, it was "a nation loving peace and ardently desirous of peace with the United States."[104] Whatever the accuracy of the views that Lamont ascribed to his fellow Americans, the categorization that he made of "the two Japans," and the tension between the two, stayed with him for much of the 1930s and was apparent in his response to the Mukden Incident.

The day of the Mukden Incident was the day that the Morgan partners learned that Britain planned to abandon gold. The drama playing out in Britain fixed the Morgan gaze far from Manchuria. It was not until 1 October that Lamont sent Lippmann a memorandum placing responsibility for what had transpired in Manchuria on Chinese irresponsibility. Lippmann had doubts about this view, which Leffingwell hastened to reinforce, blaming "Chinese raiders and revolutionaries" for the violence, commending Japanese commitment to order in Manchuria, and assailing the idea of League or American support for China.[105] Several weeks later, a full-scale defence of Japanese actions in Manchuria, ostensibly written

[103] Waldo H. Heinrichs Jr. *American Ambassador: Joseph C. Grew and the Development of the United States Diplomatic Tradition*, New York: Oxford University Press, 1966, p.143; Sidney Pash, *The Currents of War: A New History of American-Japanese Relations, 1899–1941*, Lexington, KY: University Press of Kentucky, 2014, views Hornbeck as consistently anti-Japanese in the 1930s.

[104] Thomas W. Lamont, "The Two Japans," *The Atlantic Monthly*, vol. 112, no. 2900, 2 February 1921, pp. 172–73.

[105] Lamont to Lippmann, 1 October 1931, YUL, Lippmann MS, Box 83, Folder 1275; Leffingwell to Lippmann, 23 October 1931, YUL, RCL, Series 1, Box 5, Folder 108.

by Inoue Junnosuke, the minister of finance and a friend of Lamont's, appeared on the front page of the *New York Times*. It had, in fact, been ghostwritten by Lamont.[106] Historians have wondered if Lamont was duped by his Japanese friends, if prejudices against China and the Chinese were overriding, if it was a case of an amoral banker wishing to hold on to business in harsh times, or if all were at work in accounting for Lamont's acceptance of Tokyo's protestations.[107]

The fullest exposition of Lamont's thinking was decanted to Dean Jay in mid-November 1931:

Devoted as some of us are to the principles of the League of Nations, we think that in this particular matter, the members of the Council have been somewhat fooled by the Chinese. The Chinese are such a likeable people that they readily arouse public sympathy, especially because fifteen or twenty years ago the Japanese attitude towards them was certainly hardboiled. But we think that in the Manchurian situation the Chinese have been really the aggressors in that they have apparently had no interest in observing existing treaties and have not hesitated to encourage roving bands to beat up Japanese nationals both within and without the Railway zone. Of course, in a confused situation like this, no one can say that either side is without fault. But in our judgment, the Japanese have no imperialistic designs in Manchuria ... Four years ago when I was last in Japan, the Japanese Authorities were earnestly begging the Chinese to sit down with them in a friendly way to thrash out all questions in reference to Manchuria. This the Chinese have constantly refused to do, apparently thinking that by making a great public case, they could begin to force the Japanese out of Manchuria entirely. From the Press reports it would seem that the League Authorities gave rather complete credence to the Chinese view. If the League should insist that the Chinese should sit down and negotiate with the Japanese or else give the Japanese such assurances as could be relied upon, that Japanese nationals in the railway zone would not have their throats cut, the difficulties would be much lessened. Love from us all.[108]

Here was a potpourri – the League was gullible, the Chinese masterful propagandists playing on their status as victims, the Japanese selfless guardians of law and order immune from designs on empire, seeking only stability. Lamont was convinced that responsibility for what had ensued was due to Chinese provocation. He believed, genuinely, that Tokyo should be absolved.

The departure by Japan from the gold standard in December 1931, while a blow, was unsurprising, less traumatic than the shock of sterling leaving gold, and did little to shake Morgan faith in Tokyo. Stimson's

[106] Chernow, *The House of Morgan*, pp. 339–40.
[107] Lamont, *The Ambassador*, pp. 309–13; Chernow, *The House of Morgan*, pp. 337–45.
[108] Lamont to Dean Jay, 14 November 1931, KC, NDJ.

announcement that the United States would not recognize Japanese conquests in Manchuria was also absorbed with equanimity, given that Hoover had rejected the notion of levying economic sanctions, a step that the Corner regarded as ineffectual. The assassinations of Inoue (February 1932) and Baron Dan Takuma (March 1932) occurred as the fighting in Shanghai blossomed. Both men were known to Lamont and both were identified with the liberal cause. Political violence reached an apex in the murder of Prime Minister Inukai Tsuyoshi on 15 May 1932 at the hands of junior naval officers. The conspiracy had more far-reaching aims, including the denunciation of the 1930 London Naval Treaty, attacking the Bank of Japan, and targeting the Lord Privy Seal, Makino Nobuaki, a confidant of the emperor. The outcome was the breakdown of Japanese party politics. For Lamont, these events buttressed his understanding of what was transpiring – a struggle between liberals and militarists, in which the latter, enraged, were gaining the ascendancy through terror.

Throughout these chaotic months, Lamont charted a cautious diplomatic course with the Hoover administration and Japanese interlocutors. He told William Castle, the under-secretary of state, late in January 1932 that Japanese ability to borrow money in the United States had vanished, a message that may have been transmitted by Hoover to Tokyo.[109] In the wake of Dan's murder, Lamont reinforced this directly, writing the manager of the Yokohama Specie Bank in New York that it was impossible for Japan to raise money in the United States. The letter, as Lamont had undoubtedly expected, was passed on to Viscount Takahashi Korekiyo, the minister of finance and the true intended recipient of the missive. Takahashi had served before 1914 as president of the Yokohama Specie Bank and governor of the Bank of Japan. Fluent in English, he knew Lamont. Takahashi replied with a defence of the Japanese army, blaming Chinese provocateurs and the legitimate fears of the Japanese community in Shanghai as forcing a firm military response. This was dismissed as claptrap by Lamont when he forwarded it to Stimson. The contradiction between this reaction and what Lamont had asserted previously was stark. Simultaneously, Lamont was updating the secretary of state on Japanese efforts to borrow in Britain and the United States and their purchases of American cotton (which he reassured Stimson could not be used as gun cotton). When Lamont wrote Takahashi back, he did so with Stimson's sanction, couching his letter as the considered opinion of an American

---

[109] Memorandum of a Conversation by the Under Secretary of State with Mr. Thomas W. Lamont, 28 January 1932, *FRUS*, 1932, vol. 3, pp. 92–93; Heinrichs, *American Ambassador*, p. 412 n19, makes the suggestion that Hoover passed on the warning.

friend of Japan who wished to remain such, warning Takahashi that the Japanese image in the United States had suffered a severe blow. When no response was received, Lamont persisted, despatching two cables to Takahashi, with still no reply.[110] A month later, visiting Europe, Lamont met with Matsudaira Tsuneo, the former Japanese ambassador to the United States, the current ambassador at London, and the future head of the Imperial Household Agency. Coordinating with Norman Davis, then in Europe on the administration's behalf, Lamont urged Matsudaira to have a "frank" discussion with Stimson about the tensions in the relationship between Tokyo and Washington occasioned by Shanghai. Davis, who had separate discussions with Matsudaira, told Lamont that he had the impression that compromise might be possible, because the Japanese army was fearful of Soviet complications in Manchuria.[111] While this diplomatic activity suggested Lamont's uneasiness, his qualms were eased by Egan.

Returned from a recent trip to Japan, Egan composed a long memorandum for Lamont. Egan confessed that he travelled believing that the Japanese Army was responsible for the Shanghai paroxysm. He came home convinced otherwise: it was Japanese residents in Shanghai who had clamoured for protection and that the army demurred, but the Imperial Navy responded, "which bungled it tragically." As for the Manchurian intervention, it was, Egan conceded, "deliberately undertaken by the Army." Why? Because the policy of conciliation vis-à-vis China had failed, "[a]nd it may generally, but fairly, be said that it failed because China did not play the game. It failed so badly, too, that no Japanese Government could defend or survive it." According to Egan, the emperor had sanctioned the Manchurian intervention but kept it secret from the Japanese Foreign Office. Hirohito's room for manoeuvre was constrained by growing influence of the military faction, as evidenced by General Araki Sadao, the minister of war in the Inukai government, described by Egan as a "fanatic." Araki's sympathy for the ultranationalist Blood Brotherhood, responsible for the assassinations of Inoue and Dan, was open. Egan defended the officers and members of the patriotic societies involved: "One can understand much of the feeling against politicians held by the officers of the Army and by members of

[110] Lamont to Mr. S. Sonoda, 10 March 1932, Takahashi to Lamont, 17 March 1932, Lamont to Stimson, 18 March 1932, Stimson to Lamont, 22 March 1932, Lamont to Takahashi, 30 March 1932, BL, TWL, Series V, Box 209, Folder 23; "Japanese Matters," "Possible Japanese Boycott," Memoranda, Lamont to Partners, 15 April 1932, BL, TWL, Series II, Box 110, Folder 1.
[111] Lamont to Davis, 18 April 1932, LC, Norman H. Davis papers, Box 33, Folder Thomas W. Lamont 1928–1942; Davis to Lamont, 22 April 1932, BL, TWL, Series V, Box 209, Folder 23.

patriotic societies because there was a great deal of corruption and incompetence ... the party system has probably failed in Japan." Having justified terrorism dedicated to eradicating liberal Japan, Egan ventured that it was the emperor's influence that was responsible for the crackdown on the ultra-nationalist societies. None of the foregoing, Egan thought, implied a worsening of relations between the United States and Japan. Tokyo, he insisted, was committed to the open-door policy in Manchuria and desired good relations with Washington. The emperor, Egan remarked, had made known his aversion to any policy course that might lead to war with the United States, which was a contingency that must be avoided.[112] Here was an analysis that conformed to Lamont's two Japans, albeit with the wrinkle that it was the emperor whose engagement was restraining the militarists from outright triumph. Crucially, Japan wanted to stay on good terms with the United States and the other leading Western powers – at least in Egan's reading.

After 15 May an uneasy calm descended. Distressed at the savagery of the Depression in the United States, distracted by the looming presidential campaign, Japan receded from the Morgan outlook. Waiting – for the Lytton report – took centre stage. When it appeared in October 1932, Lamont wrote Stimson, suggesting that, despite the report's conclusions regarding Japanese behaviour, the appropriate tack was silence. Nothing, Lamont felt, would be gained through undue publicity.[113] It was thus no surprise to find Egan telling de Sanchez early in 1933, "I agree that the Japanese have gone way off the reservation but I am not prepared to go very far in the task of keeping them in order."[114] Morgan quiescence reflected the crushing weight of the Depression, the lame-duck status of the Hoover administration, and the hope for Roosevelt. Contributing was an ongoing belief that liberal authority in Japan would make a comeback. Grew, whose circle of Japanese friends and acquaintances overlapped with that of Lamont and Egan, thought this was occurring. Matsudaira, among others, had reassured him that the liberals would return to their ascendancy. Until the April 1934 announcement by a foreign ministry spokesman of the Amau Doctrine, which made plain Japan's desire to dominate the Far East, Grew listened. Thereafter, he became steadily more sceptical of the notion of liberal restraint. Lamont and Egan, like Grew, knew the same circles – the businessmen, the financiers, the diplomats, the older courtiers around the emperor, whose predisposition

---

[112] Egan to Lamont, 12 May 1932, TML, Martin Egan papers, Box 39, Folder Japan 3/1930–1937.
[113] Lamont to Stimson, 2 October 1932, BL, TWL, Series V, Box 209, Folder 24.
[114] Egan to de Sanchez, 23 January 1933, TML, Martin Egan papers, Box 64, Sanchez, J.A.M.

to the West was marked.[115] Neither Lamont nor Egan knew the army officers, whose dynamic radicalism powered military factionalism and drove the course of Japanese foreign policy and domestic politics in the 1930s. Consequently, Lamont's view of Japan was through a narrow aperture, often fuzzy, showing a liberal image.

Renewed Japanese expansionism, with the seizure of Jehol and their contemptuous departure from the League early in 1933, was insufficient to induce Morgan comment. Partisans of the League when it was first mooted, the Morgan partners, though they continued to contribute financially to the League of Nations Association, increasingly deemed the League a venue in which foolish calls for boycotts and economic sanctions were made. This had its roots in the Manchurian crisis, was to persist through the mid-1930s, and was given a tremendous fillip by the Ethiopian crisis and the outbreak of the Sino-Japanese War in 1937. Leffingwell, inclined to stridency, was the most ardent. Armstrong, after meeting Leffingwell in the company of Lippmann in November 1935, noted that both "expressed strong dislike and mistrust" of the sanctions advocated by the League.[116] Writing Lamont at the end of November 1935, Leffingwell put his objection to the League and what it stood for succinctly: "I don't believe in embargoes, boycotts, ostracism, political or social, sanctions, or any other form of so-called peaceful coercion. Far from tending to keep us out of war I think all these methods tend to involve us in war." During the war Leffingwell went further, charging that the League was in part responsible for the conflict: "I think it was as bad as opium, a habit-forming drug administered to the good countries which left them almost helpless at the mercy of the bad countries."[117] Such views led Leffingwell to question the idea of American interference in the affairs of Japan. Leffingwell criticized his partner's October 1937 Chicago speech on the grounds that the United States had no business telling other states how to order their affairs, something that he believed both Lamont and Roosevelt had indulged in.[118] If Lamont's views on the League were less antagonistic than Leffingwell's, there was little question that the two had moved a considerable distance from endorsement of the League.

[115] Heinrichs, *American Ambassador*, p. 169, on Matsudaira's assurances; pp. 193–204 on the persistence of belief in the liberals. Egan had mentioned Count Kabayama in his May 1932 memorandum to Lamont.

[116] Armstrong note, 13 November 1935, Princeton, Mudd Library, HFA, IV, Box 99/1935.

[117] Leffingwell to Lamont, 30 November 1935, YUL, RCL, Series I, Box 4, Folder 96; Leffingwell to Lamont, 19 May 1944, BL, TWL, Series II, Box 104, Folder 2.

[118] Leffingwell to Lamont, 19 October 1937, YUL, RCL, Series I, Box 4, Folder 97.

298   J.P. Morgan & Co. and the Crisis of Capitalism

Japan's withdrawal from the League was thus less unsettling than it may have been thought to the Corner. Home affairs, naturally, absorbed the bank. Amid multiple pressures, J.P. Morgan & Co., facing the upcoming Pecora hearings, coping with the New Deal, and fixated on Glass–Steagall, shunted Asian affairs to a siding. There they remained, rusting, until 1937. The absence of fresh violence in China, where an uneasy truce had descended, contributed to this state of affairs. So too did violence in Europe, where the Night of the Long Knives, the failed Nazi coup in Austria, the murder of Alexander of Yugoslavia, Mussolini's war against Ethiopia, and the outbreak of the Spanish Civil War marked a sanguinary trail that commanded attention. Lamont's involvement in Japanese and Chinese affairs in 1933–34 revolved principally around the hopes expressed initially by Jiang's minister of finance, T.V. Soong, of resurrecting the old China consortium of international banks as a vehicle to channel a substantial loan to the Nationalist government. There were many obstacles, not least of which was that Tokyo was opposed. Lamont, whose position as the chair of the China consortium made him critical, was non-committal. The past history of loans to China had not gone well from the point of view of the bankers, a tale that Lamont did not hesitate to recapitulate as Soong, and his successor H.H. Kung, pressed the scheme.[119] Setting aside the risks associated with lending money to the Nationalists, which Lamont regarded as high, there was the problem of Japan. As he wrote Johnson in October 1933, "I told Soong more than once that quite aside from the merits of the questions involved, there was no hope of getting fresh Western capital for China on any scale as long as practical warfare existed betwixt China and Japan." Wistfully, he commented that,

[t]he internal situation of Japan is by no means satisfactory. Of course it can be argued as to whether the attitude of the militarists is typical of that of Japan as a whole. But it is clear that for the time being the old and prudent element made up of your Count Makinos, Baron Dans, Inouyes, Shideharas, Uchidas, et al, are either killed off or blanketed.[120]

Loans, in such an environment, seemed foolhardy. The State department, in the persons of Hornbeck and Hull, was content to move slowly. With the enunciation of the Amau Doctrine, Lamont and State remained "relatively inactive."[121]

Avoidance of a Chinese loan did not mean greater closeness to Japan on the part of J.P. Morgan & Co. It became apparent that internal Japanese

[119] Dorothy Borg, *The United States and the Far Eastern Crisis of 1933–1938*, Cambridge, MA: Harvard University Press, 1964, pp. 63–87.
[120] Lamont to Johnson, 20 October 1933, BL, TWL, Series IV D, Box 184, Folder 8.
[121] Borg, *The United States and the Far Eastern Crisis*, pp. 86–88.

politics were dominated by competition among military factions, as the February 1936 mutiny in Tokyo illustrated, and holding on to Lamont's cherished "liberal" and "militarist" duality became less plausible. A shift in his interactions with Japan was evident from 1934 to 1935. This process was halting, framed by two developments. One was the retirement of Egan. Recurrent health problems forced his withdrawal from the Corner, taking with him a consistent pro-Japanese voice. The counsel that issued from Wasson, Egan's replacement as Lamont's principal aide on public relations, was very different. Asked by Lamont in May 1937 to supply a memorandum on talking points for discussion with a Japanese economic mission then touring the United States, an undiplomatic answer was returned:

We feel that really what the Japs need is some advice about the way they are behaving ... you might suggest to the Japs that they quit fascism and imperialism, quit the domination of Manchukuo, and the attempted domination of China, and treat these two countries as independent nations, with trade open to all on equal terms. We realize that this is a counsel of perfection.[122]

The other development was Johnson's waxing influence. The letters to Lamont – commenting copiously on Chinese affairs and packed with insight – were written with all the virtuosity that a veteran diplomat could command. Johnson warned Lamont in April 1935 that Japanese engagement with China was driven by a need to seize control of "China's major resources," which Japan was determined to exclude others from, though he expressed the view that this would not solve Tokyo's conundrum.[123] Lamont was unconvinced, remarking to Johnson after a further exchange of letters,

I am sorry to see China under the control of Japan, or any other power, but if she lacks the strength to protect herself from aggression and exploitation, she can not reasonably expect the other nations to do the job for her. Certainly America is not going to court trouble by any quixotic attempt to checkmate Japan in Asia.

These expressions were consistent with the cautious remonstration that Lamont had sent the previous fall to Fukai Eigo, the governor of the Bank of Japan, advising a reduction in Japanese military expenditures to reassure Western states that Japan was not bent on a policy of conquest in China.[124] Johnson was not deterred, telling Lamont that

[122] Wasson and Vernon Munroe, 1 June 1937, BL, TWL, Series IV D, Box 188, Folder 25. Munroe was Lamont's secretary.
[123] Lamont to New York partners, 15 April 1935, BL, TWL, Series IV D, Box 184, Folder 11.
[124] Lamont to Fukai, 13 September 1935, BL, TWL, Series IV D, Box 187, Folder 32.

the Japanese military now responsible for Japan's foreign policy had made up their minds eventually to eliminate all western influence of whatever kind from the Asiatic continent . . . I say to you that the Japanese are utterly contemptuous of the ability or willingness of the Western nations, singly or in combination, to make any effort to oppose by force Japanese force.[125]

Far-fetched as this might have seemed, 1937 gave a great deal more credibility to the ambassador's warnings. With the outbreak of the Sino-Japanese War in August 1937 following the Marco Polo Bridge Incident in July, the sack of Nanking laid bare the extent of Japanese ruthlessness. The subsequent attack on the USS *Panay*, in December 1937, accidental though it was, did little to diminish fears of looming confrontation.

Lamont was converted. His private communications with Japanese correspondents in September and October 1937 were markedly more critical of Japanese policy, even if responses to American interlocutors remained wary.[126] A lengthy reply to Johnson, self-justifying on Manchuria, which Lamont insisted was Japan's "life-line," retreated from his previous position. Professing that the Japanese diplomats whom he met in the United States were liberals opposed to the actions of their government, Lamont confided that he now had no truck for Japan or its military. The best thing, he remarked, would be if the Japanese islands would sink into the sea and a lightning bolt struck the army. Japanese military strength, Lamont thought, would allow Tokyo to rule metropolitan areas as well as the seaboard, but the bulk of China would escape Japanese control, leading to an endless guerrilla war. He told Johnson that American public opinion was virtually 100 per cent pro-China. The solution, however, was not a boycott, which Lamont rejected as unworkable. Circulating Johnson's letters to his partners, Lamont acknowledged their influence: "Here is what seems like a very interesting letter from my friend Johnson, the American Ambassador to China. It looks like it is really worth while perusing. The Ambassador has called the turn in his letters to me in quite a remarkable way." A personal aside to Johnson was admiring: "You have now such a long knowledge of, and

[125] Johnson to Lamont, 7 July 1936, BL, TWL, Series IV D, Box 184, Folder 13.
[126] See, for example, Lamont to K. Wakasugi, 17 September 1937, BL, TWL, Series IV D, Box 188, Folder 4. Wakasugi was the Consul-General in New York and Lamont to Chokyuro Kadono, 24 September 1937, BL, TWL, Series IV D, Box 188, Folder 4. Kadono was the president of the Chamber of Commerce and Industry of Tokyo and president of the Japanese-American Trade Council, chairman of Okura & Co., and executive director of the Japan Economic Federation. He had headed a Japanese economic mission to the United States in May and June 1937, meeting Lamont. Contrast these with Junius S. Morgan to Dr. E.J.M. Dickson, 8 October 1937, TML, JPM, Box 43, Folder 1. Dirksen had written asking the Morgan bank to condemn Japanese actions, a request that sent the partners into a lather, leading them to investigate Dirksen before replying with a carefully worded statement.

experience in, the Far East that it has given you, if I may say so, an almost uncanny gift of analysis and of prophecy."[127]

*****

Japanese aggression, Johnson's persuasiveness, and Egan's withdrawal from J.P. Morgan & Co. fostered a reappraisal of Lamont's understanding of Japan. It was, however, dogged by Lamont's abiding conviction in the existence of liberal, moderate voices as meaningful actors in Tokyo. If Japan was atypical in that Lamont's role was outsized within J.P. Morgan & Co., there was a shared commonality in the Morgan approach to the changes in Germany and Italy. Morgan reaction to the revisionist challengers was a mixture of dismay, misapprehension, and shock. Forced by previous engagement with all three states to cope, J.P. Morgan & Co. took refuge in closer ties with the Roosevelt administration. There was little more that the partners could do; for, despite the charges blaming Morgan for American belligerency in World War I, despite the continued reiteration of claims about their sway with the White House, Morgan say in American foreign policy was vanishing. The negotiations with Schacht showed the limitations the Corner faced confronted with a determined regime. Contributing to powerlessness was the private Morgan disavowal of the League of Nations as well as their cavilling on Italy and Japan. The Morgan partners never appreciated the imperatives driving Berlin, Rome, and Tokyo forward. Blinkered at the ideological underpinnings, unwilling to damn the revisionist challengers openly, the Corner contributed to the difficulty of descrying what Germany, Italy, and Japan sought. Heightening the impact was that, because the firm had played a significant role before 1933 in international relations, American observers thought that it must still have a part to play. Amplifying this was the narrative surrounding the Nye hearings, which encouraged belief in Morgan consequence. Lamont's October 1937 speech was public recognition of a private truth – now that the signal had been given by the White House, it was possible for J.P. Morgan & Co. to demonstrate their fealty by echoing the president's words.

Roosevelt's quarantine speech was months in the making. While his administration had pursued a policy of "inaction and nonprovocation" with regard to Tokyo, by the summer of 1937 doing nothing chafed.[128] War in China was matched by war in Spain, where the

---

[127] Lamont to Johnson, 26 February 1938, Johnson to Lamont, 21 April 1938, BL, TWL, Series IV D, Box 184, Folder 14; Lamont to Johnson, 1 July 1938, BL, TWL, Series IV D, Box 184, Folder 15.
[128] Dallek, *Franklin D. Roosevelt and American Foreign Policy*, p. 76.

flouting of non-intervention by Germany and Italy was undisguised. The speech, drafted with the input of Hull and Davis, targeted Germany, Italy, and Japan. However, it proposed little concrete, abjuring boycotts or sanctions as impracticable. Its aims were rhetorical rather than proscriptive, its audience less Berlin, Rome, and Tokyo and more Des Moines, Denver, and Los Angeles. There was no expectation within the White House that the speech would alter the behaviour of the aggressors, an anticipation soon borne out by Nanking. There was more than a dollop of distraction about the speech; Roosevelt had suffered serious political setbacks in the months preceding, notably in his failure to restructure the Supreme Court. There was, too, another cloud on the horizon – the economy was showing signs of slowing down. As Roosevelt made his speech in Chicago, the American economy was sliding into a vicious recession that threatened the recovery made since he had come into office.

8 The Coming of War and the End of the Partnership, 1937–1940

On 1 April 1940, when the doors at 23 Wall Street opened, visitors entered a new bank. What had been the essence of J.P. Morgan & Co. was gone – private merchant banking, as the Morgan partners had practised it since the nineteenth century, had ended. The partnership had been replaced by J.P. Morgan & Co. Inc. The officers of the new corporation were those of the old partnership – Jack Morgan was chairman of the board, Lamont was vice-chairman of the board and chair of the executive committee, Leffingwell was vice-chairman of the executive committee, and Whitney was the president. The other former partners were now vice-presidents.[1] The road to incorporation began with the creation of Morgan Stanley in 1935 when the Morgan partners had been confident that Glass–Steagall would either be scrapped or be watered down, allowing for the reintegration of investment banking at the Corner. Roosevelt's triumph in November 1936 removed the prospect of revision; what unfolded between 1937 and 1940 was, despite "the end of reform," the elimination of other possibilities.[2] The vicious recession of 1937–38 frightened both the White House and Congress, heightening the acrimony bred by Roosevelt's ill-fated attempt to restructure the Supreme Court, but it did not produce a groundswell to dismantle the New Deal economic changes *in toto*. American capitalism had surmounted crisis through the New Deal, not in spite of it, a verdict that most Americans accepted and that a chastened president and Congress recognized. Prosperity, however, remained elusive, with the struggles of the American economy stoking anxieties about the long-term fate of capitalism.

Seven months earlier, on 1 September 1939, Germany had invaded Poland, beginning World War II in Europe. The movement to war had been powered by Hitler's determination to have one. From the Hossbach

---

[1] Two long-time staff members, Keyes and John E. Meyer Jr., were also named vice-presidents. The bank had a complement of 33 executives and 623 staff. Lamont, *The Ambassador*, p. 450.

[2] Alan Brinkley, *The End of Reform: New Deal Liberalism in Recession and War*, New York: Vintage Books, 1996.

Conference in November 1937 to *Anschluss* in March 1938, to Munich that September, the occupation of Czechoslovakia in March 1939, and the Nazi-Soviet Non-Aggression Pact of August 1939, conquest was the hand-maid of the Nazi drive to create a purified racial community. Within days, Britain, France, and their empires were at war with the Nazi regime. Polish defeat was followed by tense months. The Soviets fought, and won, the Winter War with Finland in the fall and winter of 1939–40 while issuing ritualistic expressions of their faithfulness to the alliance with Berlin. Momentarily London and Paris contemplated coming to the aid of the Finns while the war with Germany was at a low ebb. They did not but nor did Germany attack in the West. The Phony War was due to repeated postponements of Hitler's invasion plans, delays occasioned principally by foul weather and the palpitations of his generals. The United States, neutral, watched while speculation about Roosevelt's candidacy for the November 1940 presidential election intensified.[3] There was little certainty about what might ensue after September 1939, save that war, on the heels of an enervating depression, represented another challenge for capitalism.

These twin developments – the end of the partnership and the coming of war – dominated the Morgan years from 1937 to 1940. The question of how a private bank shorn of its investment business could flourish pre-occupied the partners. Charles Steele's death in August 1939 forced a decision. Steele, though long inactive, had the largest capital stake in the partnership. Before Steele's death the partners had been contemplat-ing the way forward. Their ruminations were indivisible from the resusci-tation of the American economy. While much of the animating energy of the New Deal dissipated after 1936, this did not mean an end to discus-sion. How to propel a sluggish economy out of the doldrums remained a central question in American life. The Morgan partners were engaged in these conversations, sometimes as participants, sometimes as objects of suspicion, sometimes as imagined helpmates, sometimes in association with scandal. This was not a detached exercise for J.P Morgan & Co. After 1936 J.P. Morgan & Co. struggled as a bank, troubles that were exacer-bated by the downturn of 1937–38. Finding a way to cope with their business difficulties and the evolution of American capitalism was what mattered. Incorporation was the Morgan answer.

Survival amid a damaged American economy was complicated by the coming of war. The nightmare of a new war drew closer as the 1930s waned. As it did, the debate over American policy became more pressing. J.P. Morgan & Co. was bound to this discussion, though not, as this chapter

---

[3] Richard Moe, *Roosevelt's Second Act: The Election of 1940 and the Politics of War*, New York: Oxford University Press, 2013, is a recent treatment.

suggests, quite in the manner that contemporaries thought. Neville
Chamberlain replaced Jack Morgan's friend, Stanley Baldwin, as prime
minister in May 1937. Chamberlain was determined to pursue his appeasement policy, independent of American meddling.[4] French policy was more
nuanced, but Paris proceeded in tandem with London on appeasement
because it suited French interests. Shibboleths of the "English governess"
notwithstanding, the weaknesses of French rearmament meant seeking help
from the United States. Through Morgan & Cie., J.P. Morgan & Co. was
engaged with French procurement efforts. Conditioning Morgan thinking
on aiding France and Britain was not just their embrace of appeasement but
the imperative of avoiding American entry into a new European conflict.
However, many assumed that the Morgan partners sought to cajole the
United States into war. This was not so. The Morgan role in international
relations had long since foregone policymaking; at most the partners facilitated the actions of others. In the main they were observers. Roosevelt's
foreign policy, with its pursuit of peace, distant from the dictatorships, anti-
Soviet, but not violently so, aiming to keep the United States out of war,
suited J.P. Morgan & Co. The Morgan partners did not want an American
war even after war came in Europe, contrary to the suspicions that continued
to be articulated that, like 1917, J.P. Morgan & Co. was conspiring at
American belligerency. If, despite its intimate connections in London and
Paris, the Morgan firm preferred neutrality, this suggests that the ranks of
those who wished for belligerency in the United States were thin indeed.

*****

The persistence of the Depression in the second half of the 1930s flum-
moxed the Roosevelt administration. Mass unemployment oppressed,
heightening divisions among advisors to the White House about the
appropriate response. Some in the New Deal wished for what would be
called Keynesian measures, while others favoured a more conservative
course. If the former were grouped loosely around figures such as Currie
or Eccles, the latter found their stalwart in Morgenthau Jr. Roosevelt, as
was his proclivity, yawed.[5] Monetary policy was muddled. The shift of
power accompanying the Banking Act of 1935 to Washington had been
undertaken to diminish the perceived dominance of Wall Street, and
specifically Morgan influence, on the Federal Reserve. It was assumed
that, freed of the shackles of Wall Street, monetary policy would be more

[4] R.A.C. Parker, *Chamberlain and Appeasement: British policy and the Coming of the Second World War*, New York: St. Martin's Press, 1993, pp. 115–18; C.A. Macdonald, *The United States, Britain and Appeasement 1936–1939*, New York: St. Martin's Press, 1981, pp. 74–75.
[5] Brinkley, *The End of Reform*, pp. 23–105, is the best account.

supportive of American interests rather than those of the Corner. What transpired was unexpected. As fears that inflation was stirring revived, J. P. Morgan & Co. was distinguished in its insistence that the financial community, the Federal Reserve, and the Treasury were wrong. Inflation was not the threat – it was deflation that was the enemy to renewed American prosperity.

At issue was a dispute over the question of bank reserves, which had ballooned as gold flowed in from abroad. Memoranda written by Federal Reserve staff had been non-committal on the question of whether inflation would follow, but as reserves increased – by October 1935 banks were believed to hold nearly $3 billion more reserves than needed – worry mounted that such excess, left untended, would fuel inflation. Discussion on whether to curb reserves by requiring banks to boost their reserve requirements ensued among the Treasury, the Federal Reserve, and the banking community. Parker Gilbert was drawn into this debate by Morgenthau. Late in October 1935 Parker Gilbert, Jacob Viner of the University of Chicago, and Walter Stewart of Case, Pomeroy & Co. were asked by Morgenthau whether anything should be done about excess reserves. All three thought not, advising that it was premature to take any step that might hobble lending.[6] Parker Gilbert discussed the issue with Leffingwell. As was his wont, Leffingwell was unequivocal. Worry about a speculative boom was "wicked," given the "5 or 10 millions unemployed." Excess reserves, Leffingwell pointed out, were not distributed evenly in banks across the country. He feared that increasing reserve requirements would force large numbers of banks outside the money-centres to borrow from either correspondent banks or the Federal Reserve, driving up the cost of money. He raged, "[i]n all the history of central banking theory I have never heard of any suggestion so idiotic or so nearly criminal." The dangers for the Roosevelt administration, Leffingwell thought, were acute, amounting to "political and social suicide" should deflation revive. Leffingwell was sure as to where blame lay – with Benjamin Anderson of Chase National, whom he described witheringly as a "deflationist in season and out of season."[7]

Leffingwell was correct. Anderson, and more importantly his boss Winthrop Aldrich at Chase, were leading exponents of what emerged as a majoritarian view in banking circles. Reserves were too high. This was the message of Aldrich's speech to the Houston Chamber of Commerce on 11 December 1935. Telling his audience that the $3 billion in excess reserves was an unchecked threat that must be reduced, Aldrich attacked

[6] Meltzer, *History of the Federal Reserve*, pp. 492–95; Blum, *From the Morgenthau Diaries*, pp. 354–55.
[7] Leffingwell to Parker Gilbert, 6 November 1935, YUL, RCL, Series I, Box 3, Folder 63.

Eccles, arguing that his public utterances that there was little risk in reserves held by banks was not a view shared by the banking community, which, Aldrich asserted, was alive to the dangers of swollen reserves.[8] The Morgan partners, worried about the publicity attendant on Aldrich's speech – it had been carried on page one of the *Wall Street Journal* – decided on an atypical step. The day that the newspaper reports of Aldrich's speech appeared, Parker Gilbert phoned Morgenthau. He told the secretary that he intended to write a letter on excess reserves because the discussion in the media was "one sided." Morgenthau encouraged Parker Gilbert to proceed.[9] The letter, printed in the *New York Times*, duly appeared on 18 December 1935. It attracted attention immediately, with the *Wall Street Journal* and the *Times* running articles on the controversy the following day. Parker Gilbert argued that, while excess reserves now stood at 3.3 billion, there was no indication that these reserves were having an effect on credit expansion. He suggested that credit expansion was non-existent or negligible, the recovery was newborn, and raising the reserve requirement might strangle it. Much of the growth in reserves, he observed, was due to gold imports which he estimated at $1.1 billion in 1934 and $1.5 billion in 1935. Foreign balances in the United States had also increased through direct investment. There was, in Parker Gilbert's view, no need to freeze this money through raising reserve requirements, for it would shrink naturally as Europeans repatriated their assets, observing that "the present high figure is in a very real sense a protection against unnecessary deflation if, for example, there should be a large outflow of gold." Changing reserve requirements was a bad means of exerting credit control, he opined. Better tools existed to cope with the money supply, namely Federal Reserve open-market operations if liquidity needed sopping up. The core of the matter was simple – if the cheap money policy was abandoned, recovery might suffer.

Eccles and the Federal Reserve Board agreed, leaving excess reserve requirements alone. James McMullen of the *Oakland Tribune* expressed the amazement that Eccles and Parker Gilbert were of like mind: "After all, you can hardly expect a Morgan partner of being in cahoots with Stalin."[10] Commonality proved fleeting. It was Eccles who diverged. For reasons that remain contested, Eccles agreed to a progressive tightening of the excess reserve requirements, boosting them in two steps, each of 50 per cent, in August and December 1936. In his memoirs, Eccles betrayed his sensitivity that in so doing the Federal Reserve had hatched

[8] "Grave Problem Seen by Aldrich in Huge Reserves," *Wall Street Journal*, 12 December 1935, p. 1.
[9] Henry Morgenthau Jr., 12 December 1935, FDRPL, Henry Morgenthau Diaries, 13/295.
[10] Quoted in Nelson, *Jumping the Abyss*, p. 277.

the recession of 1937–38. Despite describing Parker Gilbert as "one of the most enlightened bankers in America" and the Morgan partners as among those "most sympathetic to Administration policy," Eccles wrote that Parker Gilbert had tendered "outdated" advice. Eccles insisted that he had been alive to the danger of altering the excess reserve requirement, documenting a meeting with Roosevelt at the White House in July 1936 in which he warned about ratcheting up requirements. Eccles argued that the 1937–38 recession was due to overly rapid expansion of business inventories coupled with reduced consumer demand. Contraction in private credit followed the recession rather than inducing it.[11]

Complementary to tightening excess reserve requirements was another step taken by the Federal Reserve – gold sterilization. Sterilization involved sequestering gold in the Federal Reserve, thus divorcing growing gold holdings from the money supply. Begun in December 1936, as gold flowed to the United States from Europe, fears that unrestrained inflows would, among other concerns, drive inflation were aired. Morgenthau championed sterilization, pushing through adoption of this course against the initial reluctance of Eccles. Morgenthau persuaded Roosevelt that sterilization was appropriate. Leffingwell and Parker Gilbert, however, believed that gold sterilization was unwise. Dining at Morgenthau's house in May 1937, Parker Gilbert argued that the means to check the inflow of gold was through boosting prices in the United States, which could be better accomplished by letting gold into the Federal Reserve System.[12] Sterilization was not discontinued until early in 1938. Parker Gilbert and Leffingwell remained convinced that inflation was not a danger, that liquidity was necessary, and that the true threat was a return to deflation. There was, in their judgement, no need to worry about either excess reserves or sterilizing gold. Retrospectively this insistence was correct

---

[11] Eccles, *Beckoning Frontiers*, pp. 287–95. Economists have not reached a consensus on monetary policy, the change in excess reserve requirements, and the origins of the 1937–38 recession. The most detailed reconstruction, by Kenneth Roose, is cautious. He acknowledges the difficulty of establishing a causal link, before concluding that increasing reserve requirements was a factor albeit not the most important. Kenneth D. Roose, *The Economics of Recession and Revival: An Interpretation of 1937–38*, New Haven, CT: Yale University Press, 1954, p. 7 and pp. 238–39. François R. Velde, "The Recession of 1937: A cautionary tale," *Economic Perspectives (Federal Reserve Bank of Chicago)*, vol. 33, no. 4 (2009), p. 23, lists economists who have argued that increasing excess reserves had no causal effect on 1937–38, before concluding, on p. 33, that it did in conjunction with gold sterilization.

[12] Henry Morgenthau Jr., 21 May 1937, FDRPL, Henry Morgenthau Diaries, 69/187, recording dinner on 20 May 1937 with Leffingwell and Parker Gilbert during which the Morgan partners urged ending sterilization. On sterilization's adoption, see Meltzer, *A History of the Federal Reserve*, pp. 504–7.

even if allowances are made for the uncertainty surrounding the precise influence of monetary policy on the coming of recession in 1937–38.

The broader argument over whether the New Deal had not gone far enough, or had gone too far, in restructuring American capitalism rumbled. Within a business community where the majority bemoaned the intrusion of the state as emblematic of the New Deal's Faustian bargain with *dirigiste* economic schemes, resistance to what was construed as the burden of regulation was fierce. Critics, searching, pointed to fiscal policy as another culprit. Reducing taxation, reining in expenditures, and restoring a balanced budget were championed as palliatives to restore economic health.[13] Unlike their stance on monetary policy, the Morgan partners were orthodox when it came to fiscal policy. During the Nye Committee hearings Jack Morgan had ventured that taxation had reached its maximum practical limit and what was needed was a broadening of the tax rolls, a sally that was overlooked in the rush to publicize his ill-conceived comments on the destruction of the American leisure class. That spring, Leffingwell, assailing the undistributed profits tax, grouched that, having ruined the railroads and the banks, government was on the road to bankrupting the utilities and now proposed to despoil the industrial sector: "Then the Government will own everything at the end of the next depression." As the presidential campaign intensified, Leffingwell appealed to Roosevelt to reduce taxes, arguing that misguided tax policies "may kill the goose that has been laying the golden eggs the Treasury gathers."[14] Roosevelt's victory at the polls did not change the Morgan view that New Deal fiscal policy needed modification.

This was apparent late in 1937, by which time contraction was biting and the president fearful. His counsellors were split. On 10 November 1937, the day when Roosevelt approved a memorandum calling for greater government spending to combat the recession, the Academy of Political Science met at the Hotel Astor in New York.[15] The featured speakers were Morgenthau, Senator Harry Byrd of Virginia, and Parker Gilbert. An audience of more than 1,000 heard a debate on taxation, the budget, and the deficit. Byrd and Parker Gilbert had the inestimable advantage of receptive listeners. Roosevelt had vetted Morgenthau's speech scrupulously. When Morgenthau suggested that the government was transitioning from an

---

[13] Decades ago, E. Cary Brown, "Fiscal Policy in the Thirties: A Reappraisal," *American Economic Review*, vol. 46 (1956), pointed out the modesty of New Deal fiscal action.
[14] The *New York Times* carried Jack Morgan's remarks on 5 February 1936, p. 12, under the heading "Morgan Calls Our Leisure Class Vital; They Are Those Who Can Afford a Maid"; Leffingwell to Lippmann, 9 March 1936, YUL, RCL, Series I, Box 5/111; Leffingwell to Roosevelt, 1 September 1936, FDRPL, FDR papers, PPF, 866.
[15] Kennedy, *Freedom from Fear*, pp. 355–56.

unbalanced budget to a balanced budget, a prescription at odds with larger-scale government expenditures, Parker Gilbert took care to pay tribute to Treasury leadership before declaring that the United States likely had "the worst tax system of any civilized country," a remark that drew sustained applause. He was aware that in the struggle within the administration Morgenthau stood closest to Morgan views, but closeness was one thing, concurrence another. Parker Gilbert advised that the way to reduce the deficit was by cutting expenditure and refraining from new taxation. Tax revision was needed, for the country was "already too heavily taxed." The current system was "unscientific ... hypocritical, un-democratic, and un-American." He called for the repeal of the undistributed profits tax and the removal of income tax on those with low incomes. Business was plodding; the way forward was to embrace free enterprise which Parker Gilbert couched in terms of the "old-time religion," "working and saving and living within our income."[16] Two days later Whitney, in conversation with Harrison, emphasized the heavy hand of regulation as well as the perception in the business community that the Roosevelt administration was hostile to profit-making as factors crimping the economy. Leffingwell wrote Morgenthau warning that, if a change of course was not in the offing, a return to full-blown depression was conceivable. Leffingwell urged that Morgenthau recommend to Roosevelt a reduction in taxation and the removal of regulation to "take the brakes off the hope of profit," which alone could bring the economy back from the brink.[17] While this counsel was ignored, the partners remained in Morgenthau's confidence despite the Hotel Astor meeting, with the secretary calling on Leffingwell and Harold Stanley in December 1937 for thoughts on the $450 million in obligations the government had coming due on 15 December.[18]

The blend of the conformist and the idiosyncratic represented by the Morgan stance on fiscal and monetary policy made it possible to cast the Morgan partners as stalwarts of unreconstructed capitalism and as flexible proponents of government action. Roosevelt, presiding over a divided administration, and realizing that this was so, zig-zagged in 1937–38 between assailing the Corner and enlisting its aid.

---

[16] Blum, *From the Morgenthau Diaries*, p. 395; the *New York Times* ran its report on the meeting on page one. "Tax Aid Is Pledged," *The New York Times*, 11 November 1937, p. 1.

[17] George Harrison, 12 November 1937, FRBNY, Harrison papers, 2610.1, Conversations with partners of J.P. Morgan & Co; Leffingwell to Morgenthau, 22 November 1937, YUL, RCL, Series I, Box 6, Folder 128.

[18] Morgenthau had broached the issue of government financing with Parker Gilbert in September 1937. Henry Morgenthau Jr., 30 September 1937, FDRPL, Henry Morgenthau diaries, 90/195; Henry Morgenthau Jr., 1 December 1937, FDRPL, Henry Morgenthau diaries, 100/110.

The hearings helmed by Senator Burton Wheeler of Montana in 1937 demonstrated this fluidity. Wheeler, chairing a sub-committee of the Senate Committee on Interstate Commerce, had received authorization for an investigation into interstate railroads, holding companies, their affiliates, and the financing of those concerns. Prompted in large degree by the Van Sweringen brothers, the Alleghany Corporation, and the mismanagement of the Missouri Pacific Railroad, the investigation looked to be another headline-grabbing affair. The railroads, confronted with the Depression and competition from the trucking industry, were struggling. With Max Lowenthal, a protégé of Frankfurter's, as committee counsel and the redoubtable Charles Beard advising the Missouri Pacific bondholders, the Corner might be embarrassed. Wheeler signalled his approach early in 1936. The clerk of the House of Representatives, South Trimble, released a letter to the United States Chamber of Commerce and the American Banking Association that Wheeler read on the floor of the Senate. Trimble's letter blamed a familiar bogeyman, "international bankers ... operating in this country through emissaries and their satellites," for the Depression.[19] If the politics were transparent, tarring of this sort, associating J.P. Morgan & Co. in a noxiously anti-Semitic manner, was ironic given deep-seated Morgan anti-Semitism. Junius Morgan told his father that the firm expected that the Wheeler hearings would be another production of "investigating Jews."[20] A more thoughtful appraisal was furnished by Anderson who informed Lamont in the summer of 1936 that, to "our surprise," the Wheeler investigators had opted to subpoena O. P. Van Sweringen and four of his lieutenants. Obstruction was the reason; Lowenthal, in Anderson's judgement the driving force on the committee, believed that he was not receiving cooperation from O.P. Van Sweringen.[21] The Morgan partners, by now well versed in congressional investigations, decided that the wisest approach was adopting a low-profile in the hopes of having the investigation focus on the Van Sweringen brothers. The partners were determined to keep Jack Morgan and Lamont off the stand.[22]

The death of O.P. Van Sweringen on 22 November 1936 was fortuitous for the Corner. M.P. Van Sweringen had died in December 1935. While it might be thought that the absence of the Van Sweringens would permit the investigators to concentrate on the Morgan partners, in practice this was not so. The hearings did not open until December 1936.

---

[19] "Trimble lays U.S. Depression to Bank Clique," *The Washington Post*, 21 February 1936, p. 6.

[20] Junius Morgan to Jack Morgan, 25 September 1936, TML, JPM, Box 100, Folder 260.

[21] Anderson to Lamont, 23 June 1936, TML, MBEP, Box 25, Arthur M. Anderson.

[22] Junius Morgan to Jack Morgan, 25 September 1936, TML, JPM, Box 100, Folder 260; Lamont to Leffingwell, 14 October 1936, BL, TWL, Series II, Box 103, Folder 20.

When they did, the first topics of inquiry were Alleghany Corporation, the MidAmerica Corporation, and the role of Guaranty Trust. Anderson and Whitney testified, but not until 17–18 December, the week before Christmas, by which time two weeks of hearings had passed. Anderson was not Jack Morgan nor was he Lamont. What he had to say was of less interest to reporters. Anderson's testimony was not front-page news. It was buried in the *Wall Street Journal* on page six, in a slight column on the regular page devoted to Bonds and Investment Comment.[23] The front page of the *Journal* that day featured, among other articles, a piece on bankers preparing for the rise in excess reserve requirements. This was not the reception for which Wheeler had hoped. Though the committee held hearings in January 1937, it was not until early March 1937 that the Morgan partners returned. On 3–5 March Lamont testified, as did Whitney.[24] Lamont's presence generated more interest, his testimony appearing on the front page of the *Wall Street Journal* on 4 March; but now the Supreme Court packing affair dominated politics and the head-lines. Roosevelt's bill to reform the Court had been introduced on 5 February 1937, whipping up a storm, leading the president on 9 March 1937 to devote a fireside chat to explain and to persuade his fellow citizens. Against this backdrop, the intricacies of railroad financing years earlier, in what seemed another era, palled. While Lamont, Whitney, and Harold Stanley jousted with Wheeler and Lowenthal about Alleghany, about the Missouri Pacific, there was little drive behind the questioning. Wheeler had shed his loyalty to the White House, to become the administration's principal critic in the Senate about the Supreme Court affair. That was his fixation. Lamont, writing to North Duane, summed up: "It wasn't as bad as I feared it would be. In fact, we got off pretty lightly. Senator Wheeler was very much occupied all about the Supreme Court, and while some of the usual bulldozing tactics were employed, they didn't get very far."[25] The White House, which ordinarily would have seized on the Wheeler hearings to bludgeon J.P. Morgan & Co., did not do so.[26]

While the Roosevelt administration might look askance at Wheeler, the eruption in June 1937 of a high-profile contretemps flagged the dangers of any tie to the Corner. Jack Morgan, returning from Europe, gave an

[23] "MOP and Morgan Relations Studied," *Wall Street Journal*, 19 December 1936, p. 6.
[24] Wheeler Committee, 17 and 18 December 1936 and Part 6, March 3, 4 and 5, 1937. The Hathi Digital Trust library has the full hearings: https://babel.hathitrust.org/cgi/pt?id=u mn.31951d03505331k&view=1up&seq=4&skin=2021.
[25] Kennedy, *Freedom from Fear*, pp. 333–34; Lamont to North Duane, 11 March 1937, BL, TWL, Series II, Box 92, Folder 12.
[26] Frank R. Kent, "The Great Game of Politics," *Wall Street Journal*, 18 March 1937, p. 4.

interview to reporters that suggested he condoned tax evasion. His comments were out of step with the efforts that the Roosevelt administration was making to crack down on wealthy scofflaws. Dovetailing with an investigation launched by the Internal Revenue Service, and the subsequent disclosure by Guy T. Helvering, the Internal Revenue Commissioner, that identified Lamont and his wife Florence among others as tax evaders, these incidents were sufficient to prod the Morgan partners into damage control efforts, which included a clarification by Jack Morgan of his remarks.[27] Leffingwell wrote Morgenthau in apologetic terms:

I am sorry for Mr. Morgan's remarks about taxes to the ship news reporters in the fog down by the bay yesterday. They do not reflect the views of the active partners, and I cannot believe that they are Mr. Morgan's considered views. Rather they seemed to be just the hasty and irritable expressions of a sick man.[28]

Writing to Lippmann, Leffingwell, while acknowledging that Jack Morgan's comments were "foolish," defended the comments as understandable, because "the income tax law and the income tax amendment did not authorize the government to tax deficits, and we are getting fed up with being scolded for not paying income taxes on our real deficits in the deficit years."[29] Leffingwell knew that Lippmann was sceptical about the White House's championing of the tax crackdown. Lippmann's column on 5 June, "Government by Indignation," had assailed the tax evader drive: "Is it surprising that throughout the country there exists already a deep suspicion that the objective is not law enforcement and revenue but political propaganda designed to create popular prejudice and strengthen the Administration's weakened political position?"[30] Writing in the *Washington Post*, Franklyn Waltman dismissed the upcoming congressional investigation into tax dodging as "witch-hunting" for the purpose of "Committee glorification." Waltman wondered whether there would be "another Roman circus on Capitol Hill, with a sweating, cowering economic royalist in the witness chair," a spectacle which Waltman thought that the administration wanted. Explicitly he contrasted Jack Morgan with Andrew Mellon, whose misdeeds on taxation were greater

[27] The *Christian Science Monitor*, for example, ran the headline, "Morgan Defends Tax Dodging on Legal Grounds," 8 June 1937, p. 1. Felix Frankfurter drew Roosevelt's attention directly to Jack Morgan's remarks, Freedman, *Roosevelt and Frankfurter*, p. 425. Helvering's testimony before Congress was reported on the front page of the *New York Times* on 25 June 1937, under the byline "Tax Carved for 67 By Company Device and It's All Legal."
[28] Leffingwell to Morgenthau, 8 June 1937, FDRPL, Henry Morgenthau diaries, v. 72/237.
[29] Leffingwell to Lippmann, 10 June 1937, YUL, RCL, Series I, Box 5, Folder 111.
[30] Walter Lippmann, "Government by Indignation," *New York Herald Tribune*, 5 June 1937, p. 13 A.

but less remarked on because Mellon had not appeared before a congressional committee.[31]

While "economic royalists" were hardly the American businessman on Main Street, the onset of the recession in 1937–38 deepened the cleavages within the Roosevelt administration and between the administration and business. Suspicions that the contraction had been engineered by a business world bent on suborning the White House circulated. The American ambassador at the Court of St. James, Robert Bingham, gave an interview in which he stated that Wall Street bankers were responsible for the slump, forcing Jack Morgan to seek a correction in a personal interview.[32] Such notions were lampooned by Lamont. Writing Dawes, Lamont noted that within the administration he detected receptivity to the phantasm of a plot by business to drive the stock market down at the expense of Roosevelt. "Nothing," Lamont told Dawes, "more fantastic could ever be imagined."[33] Nevertheless, there was no gainsaying that there was a recrudescence of literature depicting capitalism, particularly big business, in bleak terms. Early in 1936 Anna Rochester published *Rulers of Empire: A Study of Finance Capital*. Explicitly Marxist, following the model of Lenin's *Imperialism*, Rochester devoted considerable space to J.P. Morgan & Co. Several years before Rochester had penned a three-part series entitled "The Morgan Empire" in *The Daily Worker*, the house organ of the Communist Party of the United States of America (CPUSA). While Rochester embraced the Depression as evidence of the "crisis of capitalism" which might result in war – the "chronic disease of capitalism" – her analysis was not likely to persuade many beyond the ranks of the CPUSA and certainly not in the White House, for Rochester depicted Roosevelt as the stooge of late-stage capitalism.[34] Less proletarian were Herbert Agar and Allen Tate, whose edited collection of essays, *Who Owns America? A New Declaration of Independence* (1936), attacked "monopoly capitalism" as "evil and self-destructive," inimical to "true democracy."[35] Big business, of which J.P. Morgan & Co. was a part, was hand in glove with "monopoly capitalism." However, it was Ferdinand Lundberg's *America's Sixty*

[31] Franklyn Waltman, "Politics and People," *Washington Post*, 12 June 1937, p. 2. Waltman was a Republican and not impartial.

[32] Jack Morgan to J.P. Morgan & Co., 26 October 1937, Parker Gilbert to Jack Morgan, 26 October 1937, Jack Morgan to Morgan partners, 27 October 1937, TML, MBEP, Box 24, Folder 8.

[33] Lamont to Dawes, 27 October 1937, BL, TWL, Series II, Box 90, Folder 12.

[34] Anna Rochester, *Rulers of America: A Study of Finance Capital*, New York: International Publishers, 1936. On Rochester, Julia M. Allen, *Passionate Commitments: The Lives of Anna Rochester and Grace Hutchins*, Albany: State University of New York Press, 2013. The comparison to Lenin's *Imperialism* is on pp. 182–83.

[35] Herbert Agar and Allen Tate, *Who Owns America? A New Declaration of Independence*, New York: Houghton Mifflin, 1936, p. ix.

Families (1937) that had the greatest potency. With household names as the malefactors, including Jack Morgan and Lamont, Lundberg's book restated the view of an America controlled by a cabal. He argued that the Depression between 1929 and 1933 had strengthened the control of the sixty families.[36] The book was given a boost through public approbation by Ickes and Assistant Attorney General Robert Jackson as 1937 closed.[37] The Morgan partners were not quiescent as these charges aired; speaking at the University of Pennsylvania, Lamont addressed the "campaign against business men and bankers" apparent in books peddling "utterly fantastic theses … drawn chiefly from imagination." Such tracts, he continued, "without a vestige of supporting proof … spin … 'spider-webs' of capitalist ownership, control or influence."[38]

Roosevelt was not pinned to either side. Concern, hope, and suspicion intermingled at the White House. The president fastened on raising the national income as remedial for the devastation wrought by the rapidity and severity of downturn that had begun. Estimating national income at approximately $68 billion, in his public pronouncements he called for an increase to between $90 billion and $100 billion to restore prosperity.[39] He did not trust Wall Street, nor J.P. Morgan & Co., and resented being forced toward accommodation with business. Yet accommodate he did, notably in his first press conference in January 1938, where he declined to back Ickes and Jackson, a contradiction noted drily by Lippmann in his "Today and Tomorrow" column.[40] Roosevelt had good reason to tread carefully, both because of the frightening swiftness of the recession and because, with his blessing, Adolf Berle had opened conversations with leading financial, industrial, and labour figures, including Lamont. Berle, part of the Brain Trust, and known for his study with Gardiner Means, *The Modern Corporation and Private Property* (1932), served as Chamberlain of New York City from 1934 to 1938. He was to return to the Roosevelt administration to serve as assistant secretary of state in February 1938. Berle did not subscribe to the Money Trust trope. He

---

[36] Ferdinand Lundberg, *America's Sixty Families*, New York: The Vanguard Press, 1937. Among others Lundberg thanked Rochester in the acknowledgements, p. vii. See pp. 4–5 for the argument regarding 1929–33.

[37] Jackson spoke on radio on the Mutual Broadcasting System on 26 December 1937 and then to the American Political Science Association at Philadelphia on 29 December. Ickes delivered a radio address on NBC radio on 30 December 1937. Both men referenced Lundberg positively.

[38] "Lamont Denies Capital Strike, Sees 'Lock-Out'", *New York Herald Tribune*, 18 January 1938, p. 1, which reprints the text of Lamont's address.

[39] "Leaders with a Program for National Recovery to See Roosevelt Today," *New York Times*, 14 January 1938, p. 1.

[40] Lippmann, "Today and Tomorrow," *New York Herald Tribune*, 6 January 1938, p. 17.

316 J.P. Morgan & Co. and the Crisis of Capitalism

was not a naïf; like the president, he had his doubts about the genuineness of the business commitment. After a meeting with Lamont in mid-December 1937, at which Lamont pledged support for relief and an unbalanced budget but insisted on repealing the undistributed profits tax, altering the capital gains tax, reaching a deal with the utilities, and reducing animosity with business, Berle recorded in his diary: "making peace with business all too frequently involves whitewashing a lot of things that ought not to be allowed anyway."[41]

Berle's talks, which involved John L. Lewis, the president of the United Mine Workers of America; his ally Philip Murray, the vice-president of Lewis' Committee for Industrial Organization and the chair of the Steel Workers of America; their legal counsel Lee Pressman; along with Lamont; Owen Young; Charles Taussig, president of the American Molasses Corporation; and Tugwell, now a vice-president at American Molasses, took place on 22–23 December 1937 at the Century Club and in Taussig's Wall Street office. The conferees embodied the hope that a combine of finance, industry, and labour blessed with government patronage could overcome depression. Morgan willingness to participate reflected Lamont's habitual engagement, coupled with a desire to nudge the Roosevelt administration toward solutions to economic distress deemed more palatable by the Corner. From Berle's perspective, the Morgan presence served the purposes of representing finance and also heavy industry and transport. Before the talks opened, the Pennsylvania Anthracite Coal Industry Commission had issued a report charging that J.P. Morgan & Co. controlled eight out of the ten leading mining companies as well as seven of the nine leading railroads hauling coal. The chair of the commission inveighed, "There's no doubt in my mind as to the Morgan control of the industry, and if Morgan & Co. would cooperate we would soon solve the anthracite problems without Federal and State action. They were responsible for the breakdown, and ought to do something constructive for its revival."[42] All were mindful of the Morgan role in U.S. Steel, the bellwether of the American steel industry. Lewis for one was open in his belief that grappling with the Corner was necessary if labour was to make organizational inroads in steel.[43] The Berle group agreed on an ambitious program to end the acrimony among business, labour, and government;

---

[41] Berle, 16 December 1937, in Beatrice Bishop Berle and Travis Beal Jacobs, eds., *Navigating the Rapids, 1918–1971: From the Papers of Adolf A. Berle*, New York: Harcourt Brace Jovanovich, 1973, p. 153.

[42] "Anthracite Coal Rule Laid to Morgan and Bank Allies," *New York Times*, 25 October 1937, p. 1; W. Jett Lauck, "Morgan Aid is Demanded," *New York Times*, 29 October 1937, p. 7.

[43] Louis Stark, "Lewis Opens Union Fight to Organize Steel Men; Ready for Long Warfare," *New York Times*, 7 July 1936, p. 1.

increase relief even if it meant an unbalanced budget; encourage the Federal Reserve to furnish more credit while fixing the gold price of the dollar; repeal the undistributed profits tax as well as modifying the capital gains tax; foster the means, via government intervention, to allow utilities to expand; establish an expansive housing program to bolster the country's housing stock, perhaps through an agency akin to the RFC; mandate railroad consolidation; maintain the National Labor Relations Act and pass a wages and hours bill; limit attacks on monopolies as fruitless; and halt any movement toward war through a vigorous public opinion campaign. Taussig, Tugwell, and Berle undertook to present it to Roosevelt.

Appealing in boldness and vaulting in conception, the impossibility of this blueprint was understood from the outset. Obstacles of various kinds existed, not least of which was Roosevelt himself, who shied away from an organization of the American economy that smacked too much of dictatorships. His Jackson Day speech on 8 January 1938 referred explicitly to the utility companies, cautioned against the dangers of vesting power in a small minority, and sounded the tocsin that "there will be a few – a mere handful of the total of business men and bankers and industrialists – who will fight to the last ditch to retain such autocratic control over the industry and the finances of the country as they now possess."[44] While the Berle group, without Tugwell, met with Roosevelt at the White House on 14 January, following which Lewis acted as spokesman to the assembled reporters, the president was non-committal (see Figure 8.1). Some of his advisors, such as Corcoran and Cohen, were either opposed or entertained doubts about what they construed as steps on the path to collectivism, while the Berle group could pledge little more than their acquiescence. They were only in a limited sense representative of the sectors that they purported to speak for. A glum Berle blamed the loss of traction on the egos of Corcoran and Cohen, recording that Lamont and Young were displeased: "They planned a real attempt to reach an understanding with the Government and apparently it had been used to make third rate politics. Young is pretty well off the boat; so is Lamont, though he still would like to help it if he could see a way."[45] Jack Morgan concurred with Berle, writing Grenfell that "the whole administrative branch of Government is at loggerheads within itself."[46] Berle's later gloss that the talks were "productive" because they demonstrated that labour, capital, and government could get together was a fig leaf to cover how little was accomplished.

[44] Franklin D. Roosevelt, "Address at the Jackson Day Dinner, Washington D.C.," 8 January 1938, *The American Presidency Project*, www.presidency.ucsb.edu/documents/address-the-jackson-day-dinner-washington-dc.
[45] Berle, 31 January 1938, in Berle and Jacobs, *Navigating the Rapids*, pp. 161–62.
[46] Jack Morgan to Grenfell, 28 January 1938, TML, JPM, Box 26.

Figure 8.1   Business and labour leaders leaving the White House in January 1938 after conferring with Roosevelt on the plan sponsored by Adolf A. Berle to end the 1937–38 recession. Keystone-France /Gamma-Rapho/Getty Images.

From left to right: Adolf A. Berle, Philip Murray, John L. Lewis, Owen Young, and Thomas W. Lamont.

This did not mean that Lamont was prepared to concede. His combative speech at the University of Pennsylvania, which attacked as fallacious notions of a capital strike as responsible for the downturn and insisted on the loss of confidence endemic to the business community since the advent of the New Deal as causing ongoing American economic difficulties, left open the door. Lamont told a steel industry critic that he was "impressed" by Lewis and "his realistic views" as well as "the understanding he seemed to have of the difficulties of industry as well as of labor."[47] Moreover, the Morgan partners thought that Roosevelt was "capable of rapid and swift and full reversals of policy. He is like Lloyd George in this respect. He might just reverse himself quickly enough and completely enough to deal with the situation before it gets out of hand."[48] Visiting the White House on

---

[47] Lamont to Thomas R. Akin, 1 February 1938, BL, TWL, Series II, Box 80, Folder 5. Akin was president of the Laclede Steel Company of St. Louis. He complained about Lamont's willingness to be involved with Lewis.

[48] Leffingwell to Parker Gilbert and Lamont, 27 October 1937, YUL, RCL, Series I, Box 3, Folder 63.

14 February 1938 for the first time since 1934, Lamont met with Roosevelt. Notable was the extent to which Lamont retreated from the panaceas advanced by the Berle group. His preoccupations were familiar – freeing the capital market through axing both the undistributed profits and capital gains taxes, brokering peace between the government and the utilities, and reversing the deflationary policies of the Federal Reserve. These suggestions were incorporated into the memorandum that Lamont gave to the president. Roosevelt's concerns were wider – he worried about the railroads, which Lamont acknowledged was legitimate but whose solutions were long-term. Lamont told Jack Morgan after his meeting with the president that, "I don't think I got anywhere, but I came away with not quite the complete sense of futility that I did last time." Two days later Lamont wrote Roosevelt, arguing that the government was so indebted that any notion of Keynesian pump-priming was impossible. He rested this argument in part on a breakdown of capital investment between 1931 and 1937, demonstrating that net corporate financing constituted only 15.2 per cent of the total, whereas government investment issues (federal, state, municipal) constituted 84.8 per cent. If this was meant to buttress Morgenthau, it failed. At Roosevelt's behest Lamont met with Eccles. It went badly, with Lamont's insistence on the Federal Reserve changing course falling on deaf ears. As Lamont told Roosevelt, Eccles "seems quite philosophic about keeping the Reserve brakes jammed down tight as they are now." He asked Roosevelt to intercede personally with Eccles. Roosevelt had no intention of acting on any of Lamont's wishes, he limited his engagement to furnishing Morgenthau with Lamont's memorandum, asking him to pass it on to Under-Secretary of the Treasury Ross Magill, but no more. For his part, Lamont fed these interchanges with Roosevelt to Krock and Noyes of the *New York Times* in the hope of pressurizing the president.[49]

The Richard Whitney affair intruded as it became apparent that the discussions with Roosevelt had run their course. Whitney, George Whitney's brother, and the embodiment of the old guard on the NYSE resistant to reforms, was revealed as an embezzler and fraudster following the announcement of the failure of his eponymous firm in March 1938. The hearings into what had occurred, driven by the Securities and Exchange Commission (SEC) chair William O. Douglas, demonstrated that Whitney had been looting accounts held in trust by his firm,

[49] Lamont to Jack Morgan, 15 February 1938, BL, TWL, Series II, Box 108, Folder 16; Lamont, Memorandum; Lamont to Roosevelt, 16 February 1938, BL, TWL, Series II, Box 128, Folder 2; Lamont to Roosevelt, 25 February 1938, BL, TWL, Series II, Box 127, Folder 43; Roosevelt to Morgenthau, FDRPL, PSF, Box 141, Lamont, Thomas W; Lamont to Krock, 18 March 1938, Lamont to Noyes, 16 May 1938, BL, TWL, Series II, Box 128, Folder 3.

importuning acquaintances on Wall Street for funds to replace his thefts, and had been doing so for years. Worse, from the perspective of the Corner, was that Lamont and George Whitney were implicated. George Whitney's support of his brother was long-standing. Early in 1937 he loaned his brother money to alleviate his latest difficulties. More troubling was his next loan to his brother – totalling $1.082 million in November 1937. Richard Whitney had "borrowed" securities from a fund that he controlled and was now asked to replace them. He could not do so and went to his brother for help. George Whitney did not have the liquidity to loan the funds. He approached Lamont, telling him that Richard Whitney had gotten involved in a "serious jam." Lamont agreed to advance George Whitney the money. Subsequently, in December 1937, George Whitney asked Jack Morgan if he could tap his capital in the bank to discharge his obligation to Lamont. Jack Morgan agreed. Revelation of Whitney's peculation followed from internal NYSE probing of the Whitney firm's accounts that demonstrated not only the disarray of the books but irregularities. The NYSE sent in the accountants, leading Charles R. Gay, the NYSE president, to inform Douglas on 7 March of the findings.[50]

Overlapping was Richard Whitney's effort to extricate himself, including seeking assistance from the Morgan partners. On 5 March 1938 Whitney had two conversations with Bartow. Bartow ran J.P. Morgan & Co.'s Loan department and was responsible for the bank's investment portfolio. With George Whitney in Florida and Lamont in France, it made sense for Richard Whitney to approach Bartow. At the first meeting, Whitney told Bartow that he was in trouble, without providing specifics. At the second meeting, he confessed, spelling out what he had been doing – borrowing securities from accounts in his firm's control and pledging the securities as collateral for his personal borrowings. Whitney asked Bartow for an immediate loan of $280,000. Bartow demurred and met with John W. Davis and Gay later that day. The following day Bartow went to Jack Morgan's Long Island estate at noon, where he disclosed Whitney's fraud. Jack Morgan agreed that lending Richard Whitney money was unthinkable. On Monday 7 March Bartow called George Whitney to tell him of these developments.[51]

---

[50] Volume 2 of the SEC hearings, which contains the complete transcript of the Richard Whitney affair, may be found at: https://babel.hathitrust.org/cgi/pt?id=osu.32435021601497&view=1up&seq=825&q1=841. George Whitney's testimony on 19 April 1938, pp. 521–27, lays out his lending to his brother and borrowing from Lamont; George Harrison, memorandum of conversation with Charles R. Gay, 9 March 1938, FRBNY, Harrison papers, 2680.0.

[51] Bartow, 20 April 1938, pp. 591–93, of the SEC hearings: https://babel.hathitrust.org/cgi/pt?id=osu.32435021601497&view=1up&seq=825&q1=841.

The SEC hearings that unfolded from April to June 1938 featured the testimony of multiple Morgan partners. By the time that Anderson, Davison, Bartow, Lamont, Jack Morgan, and George Whitney appeared, there was no question about what Richard Whitney had done. He had confessed and had been convicted. At stake was not Richard Whitney's guilt but rather the reform of the stock exchange. Linked to this was J.P. Morgan & Co. and their influence over the NYSE. Historians have tended to see the Whitney affair as a critical moment in a contest between New Deal reformers and traditionalists over securities regulation, with the reformers, led by Douglas, triumphing, sweeping away Morgan influence.[52] The impact of the Whitney failure on J.P. Morgan & Co. has been misunderstood. It was of little import with regard to their putative sway over the NYSE. This was imaginary rather than real by 1937–38. As Thomas S. Lamont wrote his father, J.P. Morgan & Co. had not been "active" in NYSE affairs for years. We must counter this misperception, he recommended, pointing out that Richard Whitney "was never 'our candidate'. This view is so widely held by members of the N.Y. S.E. and by the public. We have never done anything to counter this erroneous opinion." Lamont's memorandum concluded that "From information that we have received, it is clear that there is a drive on to drive us off the New York Stock Exchange."[53] However, the partners did little. Lamont insisted at the SEC hearings that Morgan business on the NYSE was smaller than public opinion held and that the firm itself was "by a very large margin" a banking concern, not an exchange business, but this was half-hearted. Lethargy was motivated by overconfidence. Wasson, writing Lamont, laid out his survey of the media: "From the beginning we have obtained complete transcripts of what the radio commentators have had to say, and I have now perused upwards of 100 editorials that appeared in New England, the east, the south and the middle west." He informed Lamont that radio commentary had been "extraordinarily generous" to Richard Whitney. Just two editorials had mentioned George Whitney "and both of them interpreted it in a highly favourable way to George Whitney. He had stood loyally by his brother at great personal sacrifice." As for the press, "In the editorial comment I have been astonished to see how seldom the firm's name is mentioned.

---

[52] Brooks, *Once in Golconda*; Malcolm MacKay, *Impeccable Connections: The Rise and Fall of Richard Whitney*, New York: Brick Tower Press, 2011, is much slighter. John Steele Gordon, *The Great Game: The Emergence of Wall Street As a World Power, 1653–2000*, New York: Touchstone, 2000, p. 248 is an example. The most serious academic account is Joel Seligman, *The Transformation of Wall Street: A History of the Securities and Exchange Commission and Modern Corporate Finance*, Boston, Houghton Mifflin, 1982, pp. 167–79.

[53] Thomas S. Lamont to Lamont, 28 April 1938, BL, TWL, Series II, Box 103, Folder 21.

Most of them omit us altogether. Others mention us only incidentally, and not one of them with any suggestion of blame attached to us." Nor, Wasson went on, did the editorials think that the Whitney case is symptomatic of broader corruption on Wall Street – it is an "exceptional occurrence" and "several say that it will unfortunately blacken Wall Street as a whole for people who do not distinguish between the misdeeds of an individual and those of a class."[54] No wonder there was no sustained push by the firm with this optimistic analysis of public opinion. Wasson, alas, neglected Douglas. His ambitions were greater than chair of the SEC. The Whitney affair was tailormade for displaying his bona fides as a possible name on the Democratic ticket in 1940.

The Richard Whitney scandal mattered to the partners but not in a regulatory sense. They were indifferent on this count; the damage had long been done during the opening stanza of the New Deal with the Securities Act of 1934. The threat in 1938 was to Lamont and George Whitney. They knew about Richard Whitney's frauds, perhaps not every detail but more than enough to appreciate his guilt. From Florence Corliss Lamont, we know the toll exacted on Lamont. Writing her son from France, where she was holidaying with Lamont, she observed, "When all this Whitney thing came up, he was greatly troubled about it, & after those long telephone calls every night he could not sleep & his heart began to 'thump' (he calls it) & make a singing in his ears..[he] ..is worried all the time."[55] He was worried for good reason, as the hearings were to demonstrate. In not disclosing what they knew, Lamont and Whitney were guilty of misprision. They knew that Richard Whitney had committed crimes and they did not make that knowledge public. It was the possibility of charges against two of the most important Morgan partners, with the attendant reputational damage, that preoccupied the firm. The Justice Department opted not to proceed with charges against Lamont or Whitney in the fall of 1938, undoubtedly to the relief of the partners and to the chagrin of Douglas.[56]

Roosevelt was not deterred by the Whitney scandal from approaching J. P. Morgan & Co., though by this juncture Lamont was less and less discreet in his hostility to the president's domestic agenda. Lamont told Lord Robert Cecil for one that, "Hitler is menacing the peace of Europe, Franklin Roosevelt has menaced and is continuing to menace the progress of all enterprise and industry in this country. And the war that he is waging on business is far more devastating so far as this country is

[54] Wasson to Lamont, 24 March 1938, BL, TWL, Series II, Box 136, Folder 19.
[55] Florence Corliss Lamont to Thomas S. Lamont, undated, Smith College, Lamont-Corliss Family Papers, Box 5, Folder 7, March 1938.
[56] Seligman, *The Transformation of Wall Street*, pp. 171–73.

concerned than the threats that Hitler is throwing at you people."[57] Through Joseph Kennedy, the president sought a deal with the Morgan partners over U.S. Steel. Roosevelt's motivations were transparent. With the economy limping – the 1937–38 contraction did not end until June 1938 and thereafter improvement was sluggish – he wanted to forestall the possibility of wage cuts in the steel industry. His eyes were fixed on the upcoming November elections. He feared that labour unrest might make his political task ahead more daunting. This led to Roosevelt contacting Lamont late in June 1938.[58] Unlike many of the other companies that were assumed, incorrectly, to be controlled by the Corner, such as General Motors or Johns-Manville, at U.S. Steel the Morgan presence was real. Throughout the 1930s Jack Morgan and Lamont were consulted on major strategic decisions made by U.S. Steel.[59] Questions such as the dividends, strikes, and wages were referred to both men for comment. U.S. Steel was the largest company in the sector, with the highest number of employees, and its association with J.P. Morgan & Co. was indelible. Myron Taylor, the guiding force at U.S. Steel as chair of the board and chief executive officer from 1932 to 1938, had been chosen for the job by the Morgan partners, as was his successor, Frank Fairless.[60] It was with good reason that *Fortune* magazine observed in 1936, "The Corporation is the leading example of what is known as 'a Morgan company'. Indeed, considering its size and the fact that the elder Morgan created it, the Corporation may well be called *the* Morgan company." As *Fortune* noted, after downplaying the influence of directors on modern management, "If there ever was a case for banker influence on management, for good or evil, the Steel Corporation is it."[61]

Roosevelt knew the power of the Morgan voice at U.S. Steel. His choice of Kennedy was considered. Kennedy, who revelled in the shadows, was now the US ambassador at the Court of St. James and, while not an intimate of the Morgan partners, was familiar with them. Kennedy believed in appeasement as did the Morgan partners.[62] Arthur Krock of the *New York Times* served as the intermediary. His participation was

---

[57] Lamont to Lord Cecil, 31 May 1938, BL, TWL, Series II, Box 87, Folder 3.

[58] Roosevelt to Lamont, 25 June 1938, BL, TWL, Series II, Box 127, Folder 22.

[59] Some indication of Morgan involvement in U.S. Steel is furnished by an unusual internal memorandum composed by Lamont. It discusses a range of issues revealing deep familiarity with the company. Lamont memorandum, 25 September 1935, BL, TWL, Series VI, Box 226, Folder 32.

[60] Lamont to George Whitney, 27 October 1937, BL, TWL, Series II, Box 137, Folder 13.

[61] "The Corporation," *Fortune*, vol. 13, no. 3, March 1936, pp. 59, 63.

[62] Jane Karoline Veith, "Joseph P. Kennedy and British Appeasement: The Diplomacy of a Boston Irishman," in Kenneth Paul Jones, ed., *U.S. Diplomats in Europe, 1919–1941*, Santa Barbara, CA: ABC-CLIO, 1983.

more surprising. Krock had a social relationship with Thomas S. Lamont, was fed information by Thomas W. Lamont, and possessed an apartment where Kennedy and Lamont could meet discreetly. Yet Krock was not a friend of the New Deal nor of Roosevelt, though he was on Kennedy's payroll.[63] The proposal that was sketched out to Lamont by Kennedy was breathtaking. Roosevelt had welcomed in his fireside chat of 24 June the announcement by U.S. Steel that it was cutting steel prices while not reducing wages. The following day Edward R. Stettinius Jr., the chair of U.S. Steel, demurred, authorizing a press release that wage cuts were still under consideration. Kennedy brought Lamont a deal from Roosevelt – he suggested that U.S. Steel implement the reduction in steel prices for ninety days without a corresponding wage decrease. If at the end of that time U.S. Steel was still losing money, then negotiations could be opened with Lewis and the Congress of Industrial Organizations (CIO) about wages. Carrot and stick were proffered by Kennedy, who tabled two memoranda, one written by Corcoran, the other by Ickes, both sanctioned by Roosevelt, that promised that government steel contracts would be channelled to those firms "playing ball." According to Krock, the president had, acting on a suggestion from Corcoran, instructed the chair of the Tariff Commission to find a way to raise the tariff on iron ore as a means of striking at Bethlehem Steel, U.S. Steel's competitor, which was vulnerable because its iron ore was imported from Canada. Krock recorded that Lamont "turned pale" on hearing these words.[64] There ensued several days of jockeying among Lamont, Stettinius, and the White House, before the scheme was interred. Lamont, writing the president on 30 June 1938, told him that U.S. Steel was losing $4.2 million a month, suggesting that, since U.S. Steel was operating at less than 30 per cent capacity, Fairless and Lewis had to agree on a revision of wages, with Roosevelt as the broker. The administration concluded the talks were imprudent, while the U.S. Steel executive consulted Jack Morgan.[65] Through Junius Morgan cables were exchanged

[63] Nicholas Wapshott, *The Sphinx: Franklin Roosevelt, the Isolationists, and the Road to World War II*, New York: W.W. Norton, 2015, p. 34.

[64] Krock laid out this conversation in his *Memoirs*, New York: Funk & Wagnalls, 1968, pp. 187–88. The version in the Krock papers at Princeton is fuller. Arthur Krock, memorandum, 27 June 1938, Princeton, Arthur Krock papers, Appendix, Book I 1928–1948. The question, of course, is Krock reliable given his animus toward Roosevelt? Roosevelt wrote Lamont; Lamont did meet with Kennedy, as Krock describes, and the subject was U.S. Steel. From letters that Lamont wrote subsequently to Jan Christian Smuts and to Rodd of Morgan Grenfell, his unease with the Kennedy conversations is manifest. On balance I am inclined to think that Krock is conveying the Lamont–Kennedy talks accurately.

[65] Lamont to Roosevelt, 30 June 1938, BL, TWL, Series II, Box 127, Folder 22; Lamont to Jan Christian Smuts, 29 June 1938, BL, TWL, Series II, Box 131, Folder 2; Lamont to Joseph Kennedy, 30 June 1938, BL, TWL, Series II, Box 101, Folder 9.

with Jack Morgan, then in London, about the dividend and a wage cut. This was supplemented by a personal visit from Taylor to Jack Morgan in July. Roosevelt had not abandoned his hopes entirely, for in August he resurrected the matter, approaching the U.S. Steel leadership directly, stressing that he did not wish to see any wage cut by U.S. Steel until after the election.[66]

A characteristically Rooseveltian subterfuge – acting through emissaries endowed with vague authority in secretive ways – the episode confirmed Lamont's fears. Writing Jan Christian Smuts as he was being wooed, Lamont fulminated, lambasting Roosevelt and his advisors for their embrace of "perfectly fantastic economic and financial policies" that were "a dead weight on individual enterprise."[67] Recounting the U.S. Steel incident to Rodd, Lamont argued that what it demonstrated was the extent of the administration's control over industry. He forecast that the Temporary National Economic Commission (TNEC), with its stated objective of investigating monopoly concentration, was a device to sway the gullible at the polls.[68] The U.S. Steel episode did not create Morgan animosity toward Roosevelt – that was long-standing, arising from the repercussions of Glass–Steagall. Jack Morgan had converted early to hatred of the president. George Whitney was never fond of Roosevelt nor found his policies congenial. Lamont had been less sceptical of Roosevelt, less certain of his waywardness. The year 1938 converted Lamont wholly to the view that Roosevelt was inimical to American capitalism. Only Leffingwell among the Morgan partners remained a qualified supporter of the president's domestic policies.

*****

By 1939 the Morgan partners faced an unpleasant truth: J.P. Morgan & Co. was treading water as a commercial, deposit bank. The severity of the 1937–38 recession alone could not be blamed for indifferent results. Assets, which had stood at $550 million at the end of 1936, after falling in 1937, reached $582 million at the close of 1938. A spike took them higher to $671 million a year later. Assets had last been at this level at the beginning of 1931. Deposits, too, surged, rising from 1937's recession low of nearly $395 million to $521 million at the end of 1938 and almost $672 million in December 1939. These trends, dictated to a significant degree by inflows of money from Europe seeking security, were not unique to the Corner.

---

[66] Junius Morgan to Jack Morgan, 7 July 1938, Jack Morgan to Junius Morgan, 8 July 1938, Stettinius to Jack Morgan, 27 July 1938, TML, JPM, Box 40.
[67] Lamont to Smuts, 29 June 1938, BL, TWL, Series II, Box 131/2.
[68] Lamont to Rodd, 14 September 1938, BL, TWL, Series II, Box 112, Folder 10.

Chase, whose deposits by 1940 stood at a staggering $3.8 billion, was a conspicuous example of the phenomenon of European inflows.[69] Neither assets nor deposits revealed the cul-de-sac that the Corner found itself in. The J.P. Morgan & Co. balance sheet was distorted. It was dominated on the asset side by cash and government bonds, federal, state, and municipal. At the end of 1937, 81 per cent of Morgan assets were in cash and government securities, which was not out of line with past practice. Assets in these categories then rose to 88 per cent at the end of 1938, reaching the astonishing figure of 92 per cent when 1939 closed. As had been true since 1931, the Morgan preference for liquidity was not dissimilar to that of other American financial institutions. What stood out was just how far the Morgan partners went in seeking refuge. Loans and bills purchased at the close of 1937 constituted 11 per cent of assets, tumbling to 5 per cent in 1938, before reaching the miserly figure of 3.5 per cent as 1939 ended. Some sense of how extraordinary this disavowal of lending was may be gained by comparing the results of the Bank of Manhattan. The latter was of similar size to the Corner, with assets at the end of 1939 of $667 million. Its loans and discounts stood at just over $162 million, or 24 per cent of assets, when the Morgan bank's outstanding loans and bills purchased amounted to slightly more than $23 million.[70] This raises the question: What was J.P. Morgan & Co. doing? Foreign government lending, between 1918 and 1930, one of the chief activities of the Corner, did not return in the late 1930s as the partners refused to entertain any loan that might infringe on the Johnson Act. The firm continued to buy and sell stocks and bonds for its account and for clients. In 1937 the firm handled $849 million of US government notes and bonds, of which $709 million was for the firm account and $139 million for customer accounts. Other bonds (unspecified) showed a different distribution. Of the total, $32 million were for the firm and $162 million for clients. Stock transactions demonstrated the same pattern – of the 2.738 million shares that the bank bought and sold, 2.597 million were for clients and only 140,000 for the firm. This business was not lucrative. Jack Morgan testified that in executing purchases and sales the firm received 1/16 of 1 per cent as its share of the commission.[71] Extreme prudence notwithstanding, the bank suffered losses in both 1937 and 1938. Persistent low interest rates exerted pressure on margins, a point

---

[69] Wilson, *The Chase*, p. 17.

[70] For the results for the Bank of Manhattan, see "Year End Reports," *New York Times*, 3 January 1940, p. 27.

[71] In testimony to the SEC in May 1938, Junius Morgan detailed the figures associated with Morgan buying and selling, pp. 848–49, while Jack Morgan laid out the commission structure, p. 849. Lamont's remarks were made on 26 April 1938, p. 726. See note 50 in this chapter for bibliographic details to the hearing transcript.

Lamont acknowledged, commenting on how "meagre" Morgan returns were.[72] The surplus and partners' balances sagged to just under $19 million in December 1938.[73] While the comparison is inexact, at the high-water mark of December 1929 J.P. Morgan & Co.'s net worth was close to $119 million. It had been a long fall.

J.P. Morgan & Co. was in stasis. Jack Morgan understood this. He told Grenfell in January 1938 that "Business of course, in the way of enterprise, has ceased to exist for us," remarking that the firm was in a "comatose condition." A year later, Lamont echoed these comments in a pessimistic letter to Taylor.[74] Decisions made by the partners contributed to Morgan stagnation. Circumventing Glass–Steagall through the establishment of Morgan Stanley was predicated on a Democratic defeat in November 1936. When that failed to transpire, the partners were left bereft, for they had not thought about what might happen if Roosevelt was re-elected. Once he was, what could J.P. Morgan & Co. do? Should the partners wait for 1940 and a hoped-for Republican victory to reintegrate Morgan Stanley? If so, what did this mean for the bank in the interim? The partners had no immediate answers to these questions, preferring to wait and see. The rapid onset of the 1937–38 contraction fostered inactivity even while Lamont, Leffingwell, and Parker Gilbert pushed for action in Washington. While J.P. Morgan & Co. remained a partnership after 1935, it was a partnership that had lost much of its *raison d'être*. J.P. Morgan & Co. had fostered and pursued relationships with its clients. Those traits served the partners well when they catered to elites, to a selected corporate roster, and to foreign governments. Advising, investing capital, pooling funds, orchestrating loans, syndicating bond issues, had been what the Morgan partners did, complemented by their basic banking business of taking deposits, arranging foreign exchange purchases, and lending money. The Great Contraction between 1929 and 1933 diminished the elite and reduced their capital.[75] After 1935 the Morgan partners were private merchant bankers no longer in the private merchant banking business. Instead, they were commercial deposit bankers, a business in which most of the partners had neither expertise nor interest. According to Mitchell, Bartow was the "[o]nly partner who really understood commercial banking and was really willing to take an interest in it."[76]

[72] Lamont to Dean Jay, 26 December 1939, NDJ papers, Knox College.
[73] See Appendix 3.
[74] Jack Morgan to Grenfell, 28 January 1938, TML, JPM, Box 26; Lamont to Taylor, 20 January 1939, BL, TWL, Series II, Box 133, Folder 7.
[75] The phrase "Great Contraction" was a chapter title of Friedman and Schwartz's *Monetary History of the United States*.
[76] TML, CP, Box 13, Bartow, Francis D.

Long leery of pursuing commercial banking business, J.P. Morgan & Co. found itself competing against institutions who were whole-heartedly committed to that business.

Worrying too was the state of the House of Morgan. Morgan & Cie. in Paris was healthy, with a solid core of partners, but it was the lesser of the Morgan firms abroad. Looking at Morgan Grenfell in the spring of 1936, Jack Morgan and Lamont were concerned. A disinterested, elderly, and inexperienced group of partners staffed a London firm slouching toward insignificance. New York's situation was stronger. Faith was expressed in the composition and number of the rota of Morgan partners.[77] That faith was confounded by a series of deaths and illnesses. Jack Morgan had a stroke in the early summer of 1936, followed by Cochran's death in the fall. If Cochran had been inactive for years, his death necessitated a reformation of the partnership as his estate's share was discharged. Both Leffingwell and Whitney suffered serious ailments that forced their absence for substantial amounts of time in 1937–38. Short of man-power, Charles D. Dickey was shifted from Drexel & Co. in Philadelphia to New York in 1937. Then Parker Gilbert died. His death in February 1938 at the age of forty-five robbed the Corner of one of its hardest-working younger partners. Lamont's subsequent health issues prompted Florence Lamont to urge her son Thomas S. Lamont, "You must get more people in the firm & quickly."[78]

Discussions had been underway for some time. During Lamont's April 1937 visit to Europe, Carter of Morgan & Cie. voiced his desire to become a Morgan partner in New York. Dean Jay, on the other hand, "waived all claim to preference in New York firm."[79] Carter's ambition was not met – he stayed in Paris. It is not clear why the New York partners vetoed Carter's wish. It may have been motivated by unwillingness to weaken the French firm, for Carter was one of the two senior partners. After the war, Leffingwell observed "on the whole, the partners and directors have been chosen for personality and judgement and for busi-ness ability and business associations, because we thought we needed them for business reasons."[80] Carter had been in France for many years. His appointment to New York would do little to strengthen the firm's associations in the United States. The decision was made late in 1938 to add three new partners, the first since Parker Gilbert in 1931. Henry

---

[77] Lamont to George Whitney, 12 May 1936, TML, Pierpont Morgan papers, Box 3, Folder 2.

[78] Florence Lamont to Thomas S. Lamont, 7 March 1938, Smith College, Lamont-Corliss Family Papers, Box 5, Folder 7.

[79] Lamont diary, 24 April 1937, BL, TWL, Series IV B, Box 173, Folder 9.

[80] Leffingwell to Ernst, 26 December 1946, YUL, RCL, Series I, Box 2, Folder 36.

C. Alexander, Isaac C. Atkin, and William A. Mitchell were named partners in February 1939. Of the three, two – Atkin and Mitchell – were specialists who had come through the ranks of J.P. Morgan & Co. Atkin had joined the firm from the Royal Bank of Canada in 1925. From 1927 he headed J.P. Morgan & Co.'s foreign exchange department. His expertise was valuable in a world where currency blocs, restrictions, and capital flight were endemic. Mitchell, like Atkin, was another internationally orientated banker, though in his case he specialized in letters of credit. Like Atkin, he had begun working for J.P. Morgan & Co. in 1925. The third new partner, Alexander, was different. Alexander was a lawyer who made a favourable impression on Jack Morgan at the Nye Committee hearings. Alexander knew little about banking, but he was bright, young (thirty-six when he became a partner), and dynamic. Jack Morgan described Alexander as "very high quality" with his legal training adding to his appeal, for Parker Gilbert's death had left only Leffingwell among the partners whose judgements were infused by a legal sensibility.[81] These choices suggest the firm was battening the hatches with war in sight. Evidently, as of late 1938, the partners had decided not to abandon the idea of a partnership. Within months, they reversed course. Why?

The excuse was the death of Charles Steele on 5 August 1939. When he died he held more than 36 per cent of the firm's capital, the largest share in the partnership. Lamont held 34 per cent and he was sixty-nine years old with recent heart trouble. Jack Morgan, who held 9 per cent of the firm, was seventy-two. To pay out Steele's estate, the partners were forced to reduce their capital by $5 million, dropping the bank's capital to $20 million. Should Lamont die soon thereafter, the firm would find it hard to survive. The likelihood of Steele's death had hovered for some time, a contingency that the partners well understood. The critical issue was not Steele – it was the nature of the J.P. Morgan & Co. banking business. As Lamont confessed to Dean Jay, "[i]t has for a long time been clear that ... our banking business was being cramped by the manifest necessity of keeping overliquid. Any definite plans, however, to meet this situation were postponed – and perhaps I was the chief postponer – until the C.S. matter made it clear that action was necessary." Earlier, Lamont had told Dean Jay that it was the cumulative impact of the New Deal changes to the banking and security laws that spurred incorporation, for those changes had reduced J.P. Morgan & Co. to an "almost purely banking business" earning far less. This in turn had made recruiting new partners more difficult. Those of the requisite "timber" – with "large substance and capital" – were not "readily available." Worse, should new partners be admitted, then the fundamental

---

[81] Jack Morgan to Grenfell, (Lord St. Just), 2 February 1939, TML, JPM, Box 27.

problem would recur, for it was likely that deaths would not be "spaced out" given the ages of Lamont and Jack Morgan. New partners earned much less, were less able to amass capital, and were hard-pressed to sustain losses. Incorporation had the benefit of allowing J.P. Morgan & Co. to make its trust department operational, thus offering clients an in-house service, while capturing the associated fees. Steele's death concentrated Morgan minds: J.P. Morgan & Co. was faring poorly as a partnership in a modified American capitalism. That had to change if the bank was to prosper. The timing of what Jack Morgan told Grenfell and V.H. Smith was an "obviously essential" step was dictated by the difficulties of banking writ large as well as the war. With earnings as low as they were, any improvement in business irrespective of whether Roosevelt was re-elected for a third term would help. War made it possible to make the change quietly.[82] The capital pledges the partners made and the shares that they received varied. Lamont, with his 70,000 shares and $14.125 million pledged, took pride of place. Jack Morgan subscribed to 20,000 shares or $4 million, with Leffingwell comfortably in third with 17,500 shares and $3.5 million pledged. At the other extreme were the new partners. Atkin was allotted no shares, Mitchell 65, and Alexander 500.[83] With incorporation, the partners made the strategic decision that they had not been willing to make in 1935.

*****

After Hitler's remilitarization of the Rhineland in 1936 and the outbreak of the Spanish Civil War, the shadow of war grew. Its penumbra was uneven. Germany was the preeminent French concern. While the Alps and Italy irritated, the Rhine and Germany obsessed Paris. Britain looked to empire, where the Channel, the Mediterranean, and the Far East were all threatened in the eyes of Whitehall. Domestic politics complicated matters. A powerful strand of opinion in both Britain and France doubted the Soviet Union, despising communism, fearful of its stated intent, imagining the extirpation of capitalism in a sanguinary proletarian rising that would accompany war. If anti-Bolshevism anchored trepidation, it was given added impetus by the Show Trials, the onset of purges in the Red Army, and the consequent downgrading of Soviet military effectiveness by Western military observers. Hostility to the Soviet experiment was most apparent on the right but was not confined to it. Linked, though not identic, were voices that hankered for

---

[82] Lamont to Dean Jay, 26 December 1939, KC, NDJ; Lamont to Dean Jay, 1 February 1940, KC, NDJ; Jack Morgan to Grenfell and V.H. Smith, 19 March 1940, TML, JPM, Box 27; on the Trust department, Hinton and Longstreet, "Some Comments," pp. 46–54.
[83] See Appendix 4.

a revised postwar settlement that would accommodate German and, to a lesser degree, Italian grievances. Open partisans of Nazism or Fascism as the wave of the future in Britain and France were few, though more numerous in the latter if groups such as Colonel de la Rocque's *Parti Social Français* are deemed fascist. The moderate conservatism that dominated the National government in Britain and the Radical ministries that followed the Popular Front in France pursued appeasement to resolve the security problems each state faced. The architects of appeasement saw it as offering an acceptable solution but also a means of solidifying domestic political control at the expense of rivals, within and without their governing coalitions. Domestic and foreign calculations were linked indissolubly.[84]

Appeasement promised to induce harmony, through economic concessions and political settlement that would revive the liberal international trading order that J.P. Morgan & Co. believed in. Seeing the travails of the 1930s as provoked by the unsatisfactory postwar settlement, by the late 1930s the Morgan partners had embraced the conviction that it had been botched irrevocably. The disappearance of the Austro-Hungarian Empire was a tragedy, the League of Nations a toothless failure, the Soviet Union an ongoing threat. German resentments were legitimate and could be treated through application of the appeasement curative. As appeasement developed, the Morgan partners were bystanders, contributing little to it. This did not mean an absence of interaction; French vulnerability led Paris to seek the help of the Corner.

The Popular Front, led by Léon Blum, having kick-started French rearmament in their 1936 spending program at the cost of alienating domestic political support, found themselves mired in economic weakness and foreign threat.[85] The former was addressed with devaluation of the franc in September 1936, assisted by London and Washington, while the latter, in the shape of the Spanish Civil War, had to be fobbed off through the Non-Intervention Committee. Yet the French economy continued to limp. French weakness – economic and military –in the face of the growing German threat impelled resort to the United States. With a French National Defence Loan contemplated, Georges Bonnet, then the ambassador at Washington, was charged with exploring whether J.P. Morgan & Co. would act as the French paying agent for the coupon in

---

[84] Robert Crowcroft, *The End Is Nigh: British Politics, Power and the Road of the Second World War*, Oxford: Oxford University Press, 2019, is a recent addition to a crowded field; on France, see Philip Nord, *France 1940: Defending the Republic*, New Haven, CT: Yale University Press, 2015, pp. 3–57; Talbot C. Imlay, *Facing the Second World War: Strategy, Politics and Economics in Britain and France 1938–1940*, Oxford: Oxford University Press, 2003, is a comparative study.

[85] The classic account is Robert Frankenstein, *Le Prix du réarmement français (1935–1939)*, Paris: Publications de la Sorbonne, 1982.

the United States. As an expression of the perpetual French hope that assistance would be found from America, it was more than a touch illusory.[86] The French approach was not a shock to the Corner, as cables early in 1937 had raised the possibility. Lamont and Leffingwell, who were the principals on the Morgan side, were anxious. Neither man wished to violate the Johnson Act. They rushed to consult with Harrison and, through him, sought Morgenthau's views. Morgenthau was affronted, judging the idea premature. His annoyance was reflected in his diary: "[t]he nice thing about the French is, they never wait for your answer. They are sweet people."[87] When the answer returned that Morgenthau was opposed, the Morgan partners hastened to tell Morgan & Cie. that any notion that they might act on behalf of Paris was inconceivable, going so far as to stress that there was no confidence whatsoever on Wall Street in French finances.[88]

The French overture leaked. *The Washington Post* in its front-page article remarked the matter demonstrated the "near desperate" French need for funds to meet the German threat. Press reports stated that Morgan & Cie. had been appointed the fiscal agent of France, while the *New York Times* ran a story citing the French newspaper *L'Oeuvre* that Morgan & Cie. had subscribed to 1 billion francs of the loan in France. Neither assertion was true. Leffingwell reassured Morgenthau that much of what had been reported was a concoction, but the stories touched a political nerve. A high-powered congressional delegation, consisting of Senator Joseph Robinson, the Democratic Senate majority leader, Pittman, the Democratic chair of the Senate Foreign Relations Committee, William B. Bankhead, the Democratic Speaker of the House, and Sam D. McReynolds, the Democratic chair of the House Foreign Affairs Committee, visited Morgenthau to voice their opposition to any Morgan participation in a French placement. Another Democrat, Senator J. Hamilton Lewis of Illinois, threatened legislation that would empower Congress to seize any funds arising from an "illegal" loan. Borah, condemning a "miserable evasion of law," charged on the Senate floor that it was an "apparent conspiracy of American and French bankers."[89] The Morgan partners were aghast. They had made plain they would comply with the Johnson

[86] Blumenthal, *Illusion and Reality*, pp. 222–52; William Keylor, "France and the Illusion of American Support, 1919–1940," in Joel Blatt ed., *The French Defeat of 1940: Reassessments*, Providence, RI: Berghahn Books, 1998, pp. 222–44.

[87] Henry Morgenthau Jr., 6 March 1937, FDRPL, Henry Morgenthau Diaries, 58/157-8.

[88] Horn, "J.P. Morgan & Co., the House of Morgan," p. 534.

[89] "Failure of French to Finance Loan in U.S. Proves Bomb," *Christian Science Monitor*, 9 March 1937, p. 2; "House of Morgan Is Barred from Floating French Loan," *The Washington Post*, 9 March 1937, p. 1; "Treasury Objects to Naming French Fiscal Agent Here," *Wall Street Journal*, 9 March 1937; "New York Agency Dropped," *New York*

Act, but the damage was done. The perception of the Morgan bank working on behalf of France in contravention of American legislation had been established.

In 1938–39 Paris turned again to the Corner, motivated by French deficiencies in airpower. A combination of fears about the steadfastness of civil society under the threat of air warfare, a conviction that German air strength had lapped theirs, and the reality that efforts to ramp up aircraft production were encountering difficulties shaped the French national security outlook. Daladier's grudging acquiescence at Munich to a settlement he was dismayed by privately was conditioned by negative assessments of the French air force vis-à-vis the Luftwaffe, with predictions that the latter would sweep the French air force from the skies within days featuring in French thinking.[90] What unfolded as the French sought to redress their airpower weakness in part through American purchases was a demonstration of how risk-averse the Morgan firm had become, a realization that dawned slowly on French policymakers.

In May 1938 Morgan & Cie. cabled New York that the French were in talks with the Curtiss-Wright Corporation. Paris wanted to place an order for 100 of the newly developed Curtiss P-36 Hawk fighters that had been selected by the American Army Air Force. J.P. Morgan & Co. were asked to handle the financing end of the purchase. The Morgan partners were willing and, after consulting their lawyers and the State Department to ensure that there was no conflict with the Johnson Act, brokered the contract on the basis of a commission of 1.25 per cent. The engines for the P-36 planes were being furnished by United Aircraft. United had wanted to use National City Bank but the French Treasury insisted on J. P. Morgan & Co. By the end of June 1938 the package – planes, engines, propellers, spare parts – had been signed. That fall a smaller order was negotiated through the Corner between France and Lockheed Corporation. Other contracts, for hydraulic presses and locomotives, followed.[91]

Times, 10 March 1937, p. 9; Leffingwell to Morgenthau, 10 March 1937, BL, TWL, Series II, Box 103, Folder 20.
[90] Herrick Chapman, *State Capitalism and Working Class Radicalism in the French Aircraft Industry*, Berkeley: University of California Press, 1991; Peter Jackson, *France and the Nazi Menace: Intelligence and Policy Making, 1933–1939*, Oxford: Oxford University Press, 2000; Martin Thomas, "France and the Czechoslovak Crisis," *Diplomacy and Statecraft*, vol. 10, no. 2 (1999), pp. 122–59.
[91] The negotiations, with the cables between Morgan & Cie. and J.P. Morgan & Co., may be tracked in TML, MBEP, Box 19, Cables sent, 2 May to 30 September 1938. They open on 11 May 1938 and are wrapped up on 24 June 1938. The orders for the presses and locomotives follow in September and October.

Late in 1938 the French returned to the question of additional aircraft orders in the United States. This complemented Roosevelt's determination to bolster American airpower while assisting French efforts to improve their air strength. Like many, the president had been impressed by airpower as an element in German aggressiveness. Roosevelt's willingness, despite Morgenthau's initial fears that the French foreign exchange position was so fragile that it would be endangered by unrestrained buying, led the French to explore the possibility in December 1938 of placing an order for 1,000 planes in the United States.[92] One irritant was French resistance to payments being made through an American bank in dollars. Paris preferred direct payment, desiring to pay for orders with francs in whole or in part. Recognizing the importance of this proviso to the French, Morgan & Cie. cabled New York late in January 1939, suggesting a more flexible approach to payments. Their plan, which involved the French government, J.P. Morgan & Co., and Morgan & Cie. collaborating in a scheme designed to utilize francs on a large scale, was vetoed by New York on the grounds that both the size of the commitment conceived (a maximum of $20 million) and the Johnson Act ruled it out. While a solution was found subsequently in using the FRBNY as an intermediary, it owed nothing to the Corner.[93] As the Morgan partners mulled over the proposition advanced by Morgan & Cie., the crash of a Douglas bomber in California carrying a French military observer forced Roosevelt into a testy confrontation with a Senate delegation, raising doubts about how far the president was willing to go to accede to French pleas. Morgan enthusiasm about aiding France cooled as a proposed French order for 50,000 tons of copper illustrated. Approached to arrange the financing, the Morgan partners demurred, citing the Johnson Act, stressing that any operation would have to be either by cash or through the credit standing of French corporations. These views, communicated to the French Treasury and the Bank of France, elicited a fierce response. Fed up with Morgan foot-dragging, the French turned to others. Payment arrangements for the copper were struck with Chase National, National City Bank, and Bankers Trust, all of whom were willing. Lamely, Lamont sought to regain lost ground, assuring Paris that the Morgan attitude had been dictated by a desire to ensure that larger operations not be spoiled.[94]

[92] Dallek, *Franklin D. Roosevelt and American Foreign Policy*, pp. 172–75. John McVicar Haight Jr., *American Aid to France 1938–40*, New York: Atheneum, 1970, is the best study.
[93] J.P. Morgan & Co. to Morgan & Cie., 6 February 1939, TML, MBEP, Box 20, cables received 3 October 1938 to 31 March 1939.
[94] J.P. Morgan & Co. to Morgan & Cie. and Lamont, 24 June 1939, Morgan & Cie. to J.P. Morgan & Co., 26 June 1939, J.P. Morgan & Co. to Morgan & Cie., 28 June 1939,

If the French hoped to find material assistance in the United States using J.P. Morgan & Co., Chamberlain's government counted less on aid from America. Should war come and should it be lengthy, as was expected, then America would be required as a source of foodstuffs and goods.[95] Yet the British position was stronger than France's. Having recovered more rapidly from the Depression than France, blessed with a larger industrial base, able to draw on the greater resources of their empire, the British rearmament effort was proceeding more smoothly. Britain did not need to place orders for aircraft in the United States. There was guarded confidence in British financial assets and J.P. Morgan & Co.'s help was not sought. Tortuous discussions on an Anglo-American trade pact had resulted at length in an agreement in November 1938, an outcome in which Lamont had played a small part. Though Hull was pleased, for Chamberlain the pact was ancillary to his chief project of appeasement. Chamberlain would not brook dissent with regard to foreign policy. His sacking of Anthony Eden, the foreign secretary, in February 1938 over disagreements on Italy had made this evident. The Morgan partners applauded Chamberlain's rigour, seeing in his doggedness the best hope for amity and stability in international relations. Morgan approval of Chamberlain's course was one thing; shaping that policy quite another. The City of London was solidly pro-appeasement, and so too the Bank of England, but the influence of the Corner was at a low ebb as Morgan Grenfell sagged. Norman's jotting on a meeting with Lamont in July 1939, "Lunch + 10 mins hot-air," signalled where matters stood.[96]

Commending a foreign policy over which they had no say, but in which they believed, Lamont, Leffingwell, and Jack Morgan told their correspondents at home and abroad their conviction that Chamberlain had it right. They wrote Lippmann, pressed the columnist Dorothy Thompson, contacted Waldorf Astor, clashed with Lord Robert Cecil, promoted the wisdom of appeasement through Fummi in the hopes Mussolini would listen, and defended the Munich agreement to Smuts.[97] Munich was

---

Morgan & Cie. to J.P. Morgan & Co., 30 June 1939, TML, MBEP, Box 20, Cables rec'd, 1 April to 28 September 1939.

[95] David Reynolds, *The Creation of the Anglo-American Alliance, 1937–1941: A Study in Competitive Cooperation*, Chapel Hill, NC: University of North Carolina, 1981, is fundamental.

[96] Norman diary, 26 July 1939, BE, ADM 34/28.

[97] Lamont to Dorothy Thompson, 3 March 1938, BL, TWL, Series II, Box 133, Folder 18; Waldorf Astor to TWL, 5 April 1938, BL, TWL, Series II, Box 82, Folder 5; Lamont to Lord Cecil, 31 May 1938, BL, TWL, Series II, Box 87, Folder 3; Lamont to Fummi, 28 March 1938, BL, TWL, Series IV D, Box 191, Folder 7; Lamont to Jan Christian Smuts, 26 November 1938, BL, TWL, Series II, Box 131, Folder 2.

a triumph, the apotheosis of Chamberlain's endeavours. Jack Morgan despatched a congratulatory cable to Chamberlain expressing the relief that the partners felt.[98] The same day, Leffingwell wrote Lamont, relieved because war would "have imperiled the very existence of England as a great power, and have led to the spread of communism and the destruction of all the things we care about." Leffingwell was unsparing in his contempt for those who hoped for war in Europe – the Jews, the Communists, the adherents of the League of Nations, those who followed "Pretty Boy Eden," all of whom, in Leffingwell's judgement, had been thwarted by Chamberlain's resoluteness. Much of Leffingwell's vitriol had its wellspring in a melding of anti-communism and anti-Semitism. His warnings that war would benefit only the Bolsheviks, who would laugh "cacophonously" as Britain, France, and Germany warred, echoed standard tropes of the European right in the 1930s.[99]

Post-Munich, a cautionary note crept into Morgan evaluations. Lamont remained a true believer; his faith in appeasement never flagged. His colleagues were less sure. Jack Morgan wrote Lamont: "the whole question of peace depends entirely on keeping an honourable understanding; and whether you are safe to expect the Germans to keep one, or not, seems to me to be a very vital question, and one to which there is probably only one answer."[100] Jack Morgan's hostility to the Germans, his tendency to think in national, stereotypical terms, powered his uncertainty. Leffingwell's doubts, aired in April 1939, following Hitler's seizure of post-Munich Czechoslovakia, were predicated on different notions. Britain had issued a guarantee of territorial integrity to Poland in reaction, then extended to Romania and Greece. Talks were in train among Britain, France, and the Soviet Union on a wider pact. Leffingwell now wondered about Chamberlain. He opined that the guarantees seemed the product of "haste, fright and domestic politics." More damningly, "I begin to think that Chamberlain is not the great man he seemed at Munich, but just an elderly politician who wanted peace badly enough to give up Czecho-Slovakia to keep the peace, but who did not want peace badly enough to drink the cup of humiliation to the dregs."[101] For Leffingwell, the attraction of Roosevelt's foreign policy was that it

[98] Jack Morgan to Chamberlain, 30 September 1938, TML, JPM, Box 30, Neville Chamberlain.
[99] Leffingwell to Lamont, 30 September 1938, YUL, RCL, Series I, Box 4, Folder 97; Leffingwell to Lamont, 3 October 1938, BL, TWL, Series IV B, Box 173, Folder 36. The Maisky diaries are illuminating. Gabriel Gorodetsky, ed., *The Maisky Diaries: Red Ambassador to the Court of St. James, 1932–1943*, New Haven, CT: Yale University Press, 2015.
[100] Jack Morgan to Lamont, 5 October 1938, BL, TWL, Series II, Box 108, Folder 16.
[101] Leffingwell to Lamont, 7 April 1939, YUL, RCL, Series I, Box 4, Folder 97.

promised to salvage American capitalism from the looming wreck of war; what mattered was that the nightmare of the civilized world destroying itself be averted. There was a paradox evident: if at home the Morgan partners feared Roosevelt's policies were endangering capitalism, his foreign policy held out the lure of salvation for what they held most dear.

Roosevelt's interaction with Chamberlain was freighted with coolness, incomprehension, and suspicion. The president was content to allow the prime minister to blaze appeasement's trail, especially after the rejection of his January 1938 proposal suggesting an international conference to discuss European disputes.[102] D.C. Watt's "unreliable windbag" perhaps goes too far in describing Chamberlain's assessment of Roosevelt, but his broader point that the president moved to "following and supporting the same line – 'appeasement' – as the leaders of Britain and France" is on the mark.[103] Roosevelt, bruised by the domestic political events of 1937 and 1938, aware of opposition to any step that might be interpreted as leading the United States toward belligerency, proceeded deliberatively. Roosevelt's endorsement of appeasement was seized on by the Morgan partners, thus Lamont's remark to a British correspondent that he was "warmly in sympathy" with Roosevelt's foreign policy.[104] Lamont was gushing in his praise for Roosevelt's efforts in September 1938 to avert war.[105]

There is nothing that suggests that Roosevelt consulted the Morgan partners about his foreign policy in 1938–39.[106] The Corner followed the president. J.P. Morgan & Co. agreed with the means Roosevelt advanced to help Britain and France. The White House hoped to do so through the provision of economic and financial aid, a prescription that Lamont and his partners thought sensible, even if, as the French case showed, Morgan praxis was timid. The president wanted revision of the Neutrality legislation, another point of commonality with the Morgan partners. The Morgan perspective was straightforward: the Neutrality Laws were anything but neutral. Their insistence on prohibiting commerce was aiding the dictators by robbing those who would stand up to them of the means

[102] William R. Rock, *Chamberlain and Roosevelt: British Foreign Policy and the United States, 1937–1940*, Columbus, OH: Ohio State University Press, 1988.

[103] Donald Watt, "Roosevelt and Chamberlain: Two Appeasers," *International Journal*, vol. 28, no. 2 (1973), pp. 185, 187.

[104] Lamont to Sybil Colefax, 3 February 1938, BL, TWL, Series II, Box 88, Folder 2.

[105] Henry M. Kannee to Roosevelt, 28 September 1938, FDRPL, FDR papers, PPF/70, relaying a note from Lamont. Barbara Rearden Farnham, *Roosevelt and the Munich Crisis*, Princeton, NJ: Princeton University Press, 1997, is the most detailed study.

[106] Justus D. Doenecke, "U.S. Policy and the European War, 1939–41," *Diplomatic History*, vol. 19, no. 4 (1995), is a historiographical treatment. More recent work from different perspectives include Blower, "From Isolationism to Neutrality" and David Kaiser, *No End Save Victory*, New York: Basic Books, 2014, pp. 19–56.

to confront aggression. The Neutrality Laws made war more likely rather than less.[107] Such views were not singular, aligning with those inclined to portray the Neutrality legislation as an error, not least of whom was Lippmann.

Perceptions that J.P. Morgan & Co. was more than another fellow traveller persisted. Some of this was historical – the Morgan partners and their firm had been consequential in the postwar peace settlement, in its teething through the 1920s, in the effort to shore it up from 1929–33, and in contacts with the revisionist states of Germany, Italy, and Japan. Some of it was structural, with Morgan Grenfell in London and Morgan & Cie. in Paris prompting the conclusion that the Morgan firm was acting as a conduit among like-minded, democratic, capitalist powers. Some of it was due to Morgan activity, principally Lamont's indefatigability. During Lamont's summer 1939 trip to Europe, he met with Paul Reynaud, the French minister of finance, lunched with the American ambassador at Brussels after conferring with a senior official of the Reichsbank, then crossed the Channel to lunch with Chamberlain, visited Sir Edward Halifax, the foreign secretary, found time to see Norman, before journeying to Cliveden to stay with the Astors.[108] Less frenetically, Jack Morgan had Chamberlain to shoot at Gannochy (his Scottish estate) in 1938, was consulted by Baron Hardinge, the private secretary to George VI, on whether a tour of the United States by the royal couple would be welcomed, and hosted the king and queen at Gannochy before the outbreak of war.[109] Lamont's identification with the Cliveden set and in particular his ties to Philip Kerr, Lord Lothian, from September 1939 the British ambassador at Washington, noted for his appeasement ardour and his anti-communism, strengthened the impression that the Morgan partners still walked the corridors of power. Duly reported, observers could be forgiven for concluding that Morgan influence remained. The Cleveland-based industrialist Cyrus Eaton, in apoplectic cables to Hoover on the eve of the European war, cited Jack Morgan's hosting of the archbishop of Canterbury and the king and queen as evidence of his contention that the membership of the newly established War Resources Board, an outgrowth of the Army and Navy Munitions Board charged with implementing economic mobilization, was "selected in the Morgan office." His conviction was strengthened when the FRBNY announced a financial advisory committee that

[107] Leffingwell to Partners, 28 April 1939, YUL, RCL, Series I, Box 8, Folder 176, a seven-page memorandum on the Neutrality Acts and Johnston Act is a pithy statement of the Morgan view.
[108] Lamont to North Duane, 3 August 1939, BL, TWL, Series II, Box 92, Folder 13.
[109] Jack Morgan to John W. Davis, 2 November 1938, TML, JPM, Box 40.

featured, among others, Henry S. Morgan. Eaton pleaded with Hoover to intercede publicly, arguing that J.P. Morgan & Co. was reprising its role of 1914. Eaton was shocked that the White House "should countenance such a complete domination of the American economy."[110] Hoover did nothing, but Roosevelt was not oblivious to the political dangers, consulting with Morgenthau about the presence of men connected to J.P. Morgan & Co.[111] As it transpired, like many Roosevelt-era constructions, both the War Resources Board and the FRBNY advisory committee were more impressive in the announcement than in the operation.

War in Europe changed the relationship between the Morgan partners and Britain and France, but not as critics like Eaton dreaded. While Jack Morgan assured Chamberlain personally that the firm would do all that it could to aid Britain, a message that was communicated in different form to France, the partners set bounds. A cable to Morgan & Cie. on 1 September 1939, prior to the French or British declaration of war, professed that J.P. Morgan & Co. would do all that they could, "subject always of course to strict compliance with American laws." A more explicit treatment of what the Corner would do, would not do, and might consider was advanced several days later to Dean Jay. The Morgan partners were willing to help the French government undertake "mechanical financial transactions" of specific kinds, such as acting as paying agents for the French government on purchases made, including keeping the books on these transactions; if Paris decided to requisition French citizens' holdings of US securities, the Morgan firm would bundle them together and would conduct the sale; the partners were willing to assist France in vetting American business that they might be contemplating. Functionally this meant providing credit reports on American companies. Noteworthy was what the Corner would not do: J.P. Morgan & Co. would not handle foreign exchange as the respective treasuries – American, British, French – "are happily cooperating in complete harmony"; nor would they act as purchasing agents, a major distinction from 1914–17 practice. The Morgan advice was that it would be wiser if the French government set up its own purchasing commission. If, however, Paris decided against this advice, the partners confirmed they would be prepared to discuss acting as purchasing agents but wanted this possibility kept secret. The past, mixed with the controversies of the 1930s and an understanding of the political climate, was at work. The partners did not wish to be at the forefront of a concerted Allied economic effort in the

[110] Cyrus S. Eaton to Hoover, 30 August 1939, 1 September 1939, HHPL, PPICF, Box 52, Eaton, Cyrus S. Correspondence 1938–43.
[111] Roosevelt to Morgenthau, 7 September 1939, FDRPL, Henry Morgenthau diaries, 210/11-12.

United States. As the Morgan partners told Jay, "our own attitude is bound to be one that considers primarily the interests of our own country, those interests we believe lying first in complete access to the American markets on the part of the Allied Governments which are both cash purchasers." This was an accurate, if parochial, statement of Morgan intent. While there was never any desire on the part of the partners to hide their sympathies – this was impossible given J.P. Morgan & Co.'s identification with Britain and France – and the partners flocked to organizations that sponsored Anglo-French assistance, much had changed.[112] It was men such as Eaton who worried about the clock turning back twenty-five years; the Morgan partners knew that time had moved on.

This was apparent in Lamont's November 1939 speech to the Academy of Political Science, "American Business in War and Peace." Speaking once more at the Hotel Astor, Lamont argued that American business had three objectives: to stay out of "armed conflict"; to help the democracies to buy what they needed in the United States; and "to make our country's economic and financial strength impregnable, so that finally America may be in a position to render sound and wise co-operation towards an enduring Peace." This, he asserted, was the program of 95 per cent of American business. It was the Morgan program, but whether it was the program of American business was less certain. *Barron's* had editorialized on 4 September 1939, "Why and How We Can Stay Out of War," a pithy statement that was perhaps a more accurate reflection of where the business community stood. Appropriating the mantle of spokesman for American business was audacious, for the Morgan voice was not what it had been. A variety of observers had noted this development. Not all were hostile to J.P. Morgan & Co. Some, such as Randolph Phillips in *The Nation* or Stuart Chase in *Harpers*, were antagonists. Allen, whose appreciation of the Corner was agnostic, wondered in *Since Yesterday*, his retrospective look at the 1930s, if "perhaps the palmy days of the Wall Street bankers were over." Morgan admirers admitted that the firm's standing was not what it had been. Bell's 1938 essay, "The Decline of the Money Barons," made this plain. *Forbes* remarked that the days when a partnership in J.P. Morgan & Co. was the "blue ribbon" the Street aspired to had passed, while *Fortune* confided that, though respect remained, the firm's influence had "waned."[113] Business opinion on war was in truth fractured,

---

[112] Nicholas Cull, *Selling War: The British Propaganda Campaign Against American "Neutrality" in World War II*, New York: Oxford University Press, 1995, pp. 62–63.

[113] Chase, "Capital Not Wanted" and "Shadow over Wall Street," in *Harpers Magazine*, vol. 180, February 1940, pp. 228–34 and March 1940, pp. 367–74; Randolph Phillips, *The Nation*, vol. 148, nos. 24 and 25, 10 June and 17 June 1939, pp. 663–67 and pp. 696–700; "A Baedeker of Business," *Fortune*, vol. 20, no. 1, July 1939, p. 187; the

running the gamut from interventionists to the America First Committee in the shape of men such as General Robert E. Wood of Sears Roebuck. Lamont may have overreached in claiming to speak for American business, but he described where the Morgan partners stood in relation to the Roosevelt administration's foreign policy. As the president manoeuvred to defang the Neutrality Act, the Morgan partners were with him. Not all in the administration welcomed their presence. Berle, whose mistrust of Britain ran deep, recorded on 30 September that:

Steve Early, through T.W. Lamont, arranged to get Alfred E. Smith to make a campaign speech in favor of revision of the Neutrality Act. I finished up the negotiations with Lamont, and Al Smith goes forward. Lamont was likewise working to get President Conant, of Harvard, to make a similar speech. This is all very well as far as it goes, but it has a terribly suspicious ring about it. It was the Morgans, the Harvard New Englanders and the like who really influenced our entry into war in 1917; and now, in an endeavor to get our Neutrality Act in shape, we suddenly find ourselves relying on the same group. I am not too happy about this. Our policy is not to get into this, but to stay out; to have a true neutrality.[114]

Working primarily through General Edwin "Pa" Watson at the White House, Lamont threw himself into the Roosevelt cause. He suggested the names of individuals whose stature might help, he prompted men such as Stimson to weigh in on the public debate, and he lobbied senators. Early in 1940 Lamont and Roosevelt discussed which members of Congress might be persuaded to back the president and whether or not a committee should be constituted to aid the Finns or whether White should be approached to head a committee to aid the Allies.[115] Lamont became, as Langer and Gleason remarked long ago, "one of the most loyal supporters of the President's foreign policy." This was genuine but was not always congruent with Roosevelt's intentions. A good example was the Neutrality legislation. Lamont wanted immediate repeal of the Neutrality Act *in toto*, but Roosevelt understood that this was impractical after his embarrassing political setback in the spring of 1939 to expand the notion of cash and carry to arms sales was rebuffed by Congress. The modification of the Neutrality Act that the president secured in November 1939, permitting cash and carry to include arms sales, was as far as the politics allowed. Lamont and his partners hoped that the Johnson Act would be

comment is in the regular column, "Close Ups of High Ups," *Forbes*, vol. 43, no. 4, 15 February 1939, p. 32; Frederick Lewis Allen, *Since Yesterday*, New York: Harper and Brothers, 1940, p. 337.
[114] Berle diary, 30 September 1939, Berle and Jacobs, *Navigating the Rapids*, p. 259.
[115] E.T. Sanders to Lamont, 14 September 1939, BL, TWL, Series II, Box 127, Folder 23; Folder 24 in the same series and box contains the back and forth between the White House and Lamont in early 1940.

cast aside, another goal that the president shared but that he knew could not be achieved.[116]

*****

The Morgan rapprochement with Roosevelt should not be misinterpreted. In the debate that was underway in the United States that lasted until Pearl Harbor, the Morgan partners were "conservative internationalists," seeking the maximum American aid to Britain and France, after June 1940 to Britain alone, but no more.[117] Although they supported the president's foreign policy, this did not mean they wished to see him serve a third term. His domestic policies continued to be a source of consternation, albeit from September 1939 Morgan commentary shifted to a less hostile tone. Leffingwell forwarded suggestions for an overhaul of tax policy to John W. Hanes, a Morgan friend, at the Treasury in the fall of 1939 that conceded the legitimacy of some of the New Deal changes.[118] The Morgan appearance before the TNEC in December 1939 was unremarked, its most notable quality being Leffingwell's assured testimony that charmed his interlocutors. Behind the artificial bonhomie of the late New Deal in decline was not just the war but a conflicted J.P. Morgan & Co. The partners – save Leffingwell – were steadfast that Roosevelt's presidency had damaged American capitalism, if not irreparably, then enough to raise the prospect of a bastardized capitalism with a dictator at the helm. With Hitler and Stalin in view, this was less of a mirage than it appears today. War amplified Morgan uneasiness. Its advent might result in greater power in Roosevelt's hands, as Lamont told Smuts in February 1940. War might end in "Hitlerizing America."[119] From the vantage of the Corner, this was an appalling prospect whose possibility had been glimpsed in the queasy White House response to the 1937–38 recession. The Morgan partners did not have to look far to see the damage that had been done – all they had to do was to scan their balance sheet. Safety from what they thought was likely to be buffeting in the years to come was to be found in incorporation. The price was forfeiture of their culture as private merchant bankers.

---

[116] William L. Langer and S. Everett Gleason, *The Challenge to Isolation, 1937–1940*, New York: Harper Brothers, 1952, pp. 221–22. The Johnson Act was never repealed.

[117] Lise A. Namikas, "The Committee to Defend America and the Debate between Internationalists and Interventionists, 1939–1941," *The Historian*, vol. 61, no. 4 (1999), p. 847.

[118] Leffingwell to John W. Hanes, 11 October 1939, Hanes to Leffingwell, 13 October 1939, Leffingwell to Hanes, 31 October 1939, YUL, RCL, Series I, Box 1, Folder 1.

[119] Lamont to Smuts, 16 February 1940, BL, TWL, Series II, Box 131, Folder 3.

Conclusion

Eight days after J.P. Morgan & Co. Inc. began business, the Phony War in Europe ended. On 9 April 1940 the Wehrmacht invaded Denmark and Norway, setting in train a series of events that culminated with an assault on the Low Countries and France. The Fall of France in May and June altered the nature of World War II, leading Hitler, convinced more than ever of his own genius, to order planning to begin for the invasion of the Soviet Union while a recalcitrant Britain was attacked from the air.[1] The repercussions of French defeat were apparent in the United States. Whether Roosevelt had already made the decision to stand for a third term or not, his choice to do so was justified by the Allied catastrophe in 1940. Roosevelt forwarded plans for a massive expansion of American military capabilities, an action that intensified the debate in the United States over the war. For J.P. Morgan & Co., the French capitulation weighed heavily. Worries about the fate of their partners and staff in France preoccupied them and the New York firm made frantic efforts to determine the whereabouts of those who had been displaced. Once the armistice was signed and it became apparent that the war would be ongoing, Morgan & Cie. continued to operate, albeit in a much-modified fashion. The French collapse strengthened Morgan sympathies for a beleaguered Britain. Fundamentally, though, the Morgan attitude toward the war did not change. Even after June 1940 J.P. Morgan & Co. was not in favour of American belligerency on behalf of an isolated British Empire.

As had been the case for months, this reticence was not recognized beyond the Corner. Instead, the emergence of Wendell Willkie as the Republican nominee and the Morgan role therein attracted attention, with commentators drawing connections between Willkie's experience as a utility executive with Commonwealth & Southern and J.P. Morgan & Co. Lamont was active in raising support for Willkie, but much of

---

[1] David Reynolds, "1940: Fulcrum of the Twentieth Century?," *International Affairs*, vol. 66, no. 2 (1990), pp. 325–50.

Willkie's attraction for the Morgan partners lay in the similarity of his foreign policy to the president's, in contradistinction to the views articulated by other Republican contenders, such as Senator Robert A. Taft of Ohio and Thomas E. Dewey of New York. Roosevelt's re-election did not dampen disquiet about Morgan influence or suspicion that the Corner was inveigling American participation. Hugh S. Johnson, one of Roosevelt's collaborators in the early days of the New Deal, now a columnist for the Hearst newspaper chain where his isolationist inclinations were allowed full rein, wrote in January 1941, "The House of Morgan – at least as represented by Mr. Thomas W. Lamont – and other great international bankers are as active in guiding and propelling our steps toward involvement in this war as they were in 1917." An editorial in Colonel Robert McCormick's *Chicago Tribune*, the standard-bearer of isolationism in the Midwest, evoked familiar demons: "Mr. Roosevelt and his Royalists," decrying William Allen White's Committee to Defend America by Aiding the Allies. The editorial targeted J.P. Morgan & Co. specifically, leading to agitated letters addressed to Jack Morgan. Others, less alarmed, were dismissive. Hamilton Fish Armstrong recorded a conversation with Willkie at a dinner party early in 1941. Present was Roy Howard of the Scripps-Howard newspaper chain: "Howard said to Willkie that he was going to show up his 'Morgan friends,' which Willkie said was silly, as he wasn't under any obligations to the Morgan people, and as they had practically no influence in the country any more anyway."[2]

Willkie was disingenuous, but such a judgement would have been inconceivable in 1929. J.P. Morgan & Co. was of less import in 1941, though more than Willkie credited. Some of the decline in Morgan influence was due to the changes that had occurred to American finance in the 1930s. The peculiarities of the American financial system, with its myriad undercapitalized banks and dual charters, mixed with the vulnerabilities of the Federal Reserve system, combined with the Depression to plunge American banking into a near existential crisis. The whirlwind swept through American banking between 1929 and 1933. After 1933 American banking stabilized, as the New Deal managed to preserve the banking system through judicious reforms, aided by the infusion of cash via the RFC that allowed a chastened, more regulated sector to survive. J. P. Morgan & Co. was not immune to the Depression's havoc – the effect of two compressed blows to the Morgan balance sheet in the last quarter

---

[2] Lamont to Hugh S. Johnson, 22 January 1941, BL, TWL, Series II, Box 100, Folder 24; Mrs. Evelyn Phinney to Jack Morgan, 25 February 1941, BL, TWL, Series II, Box 107, Folder 5; Hamilton Fish Armstrong, 16 January 1941, Princeton, Mudd Library, HFA papers, Series IV, Box 100/1941.

of 1931 and the first quarter of 1933 inflicted permanent damage on the Morgan bank. Well before Glass–Steagall, the investment side of J.P. Morgan & Co.'s business had been crippled. Private merchant bankers are conservative by nature, protecting their unlimited liability. J.P. Morgan & Co. retreated into indecision. Forming Morgan Stanley was not a decision; it was a stopgap driven by the hope for a change in the government that did not occur. From 1936 onward the J.P. Morgan & Co. banking business was sclerotic as its senior partners recognized. Steele's death in 1939 was the excuse to discard a business model that was no longer functioning, rather than the reason for it. Roosevelt's victory in the 1940 presidential election was, if not unexpected, definitive. J.P. Morgan & Co. divorced itself formally from Morgan Stanley, selling off its shares and leaving the partners to do as they wished with their individual holdings. There would be no return – at least not for decades – to investment banking for J.P. Morgan & Co. Grenfell wrote an elegiacal letter to Lamont mourning the ending of the *ancien régime* with the abandonment of the partnership: "the days of private banking houses do seem to be passing as senior partners pass away from natural causes."[3] In 1940, after the Morgan conversion, no private bank of consequence remained in the United States. Longer term, Grenfell was wrong. Private banking made a comeback but did so in a different context in the decades after the 1960s. Not even Glass–Steagall lasted, to the regret of many and the rejoicing of others.

Between 1929 and 1940, while Morgan influence eroded, the Morgan partners were active in confronting the crisis of capitalism. Born of their past history, their ties to London and Paris, and their prominence, the Morgan bank was looked to for guidance. The partners did not realize what was happening until well into 1930, focused as they were on the Young Plan and the BIS. The Crash was in their estimation a transitory phenomenon. Leffingwell appreciated sooner than his partners the danger. In 1930–31 J.P. Morgan & Co. attempted to act as a lender of last resort for private firms, understanding that the wider responsibility for the health of the American financial system lay with the Federal Reserve. That Morgan effort was modest, selective, and short-lived. It came to a close as the year 1931 ended. The Morgan partners, led by Leffingwell, Parker Gilbert, and Lamont, tried to turn Hoover to a course that they thought wise. Affinity existed between the partners and the president as Hoover came increasingly to see the Depression as in international phenomenon imported to the United States. With their shared conviction that the debacle was an outgrowth of World War I and the

---

[3] Grenfell to Lamont, 11 February 1940, BL, TWL, Series II, Box 112, Folder 1.

internationalist orientation, it might be thought that the White House and the Corner would work together. They did not. Leffingwell and Parker Gilbert were contemptuous of Hoover, insistent that he needed to do more to combat deflation; for his part, the president resented what he perceived as the tone-deaf urgings of Wall Street bankers, chief among them J.P. Morgan & Co. Neither had a remedy for the Depression. Nevertheless, in searching for reasons as to why the American response to the Depression was so unsatisfactory between 1929 and 1933, attention should be paid to how conflict between Hoover and the Corner contributed to the incoherence.

After March 1933 and the advent of the New Deal, the American landscape was transformed, less in truth economically than politically. The partners welcomed the new president and signalled clearly that they did so with their emphatic public support of his repudiation of the gold standard, a position that the partners had moved to quietly earlier. Leffingwell and Parker Gilbert had come to the view that the gold standard was inimical to American capitalism and must be jettisoned. Unlike many in the American financial and business worlds, the Morgan partners did not distance themselves from Roosevelt's White House as the New Deal progressed between 1933 and 1936. Pecora and Glass–Steagall were resented bitterly, and the Morgan partners bent their energies to obtaining modification or repeal of the latter, in the process becoming fixated on their business crisis at the cost of seeking solutions to the crisis of capitalism. Undoubtedly Glass–Steagall engendered in Jack Morgan, Whitney, and other partners a dislike of Roosevelt that once established was never removed. The growth of this disdain did not embody Morgan attitude *in toto*. Lamont, whose diplomatic temperament meant he concealed his doubts about the president, favoured a discreet course. More consequential were Leffingwell and Parker Gilbert, the bank's economists, both of whom were partisans of Roosevelt. They backed the New Deal and maintained links to men such as Morgenthau. If scholars have wondered why J.P. Morgan & Co. did not side with those attacking the Roosevelt administration, it had as much to do with the internal division among the partners on the New Deal as it did with their aversion to open political identification. Morgan efforts to cooperate with the administration on the domestic economic front were arguably most salient in 1937–38 when the weakness of the Roosevelt administration engendered by the self-inflicted political damage of the Supreme Court packing case overlapped with economic contraction to render the White House vulnerable. The outcome was nugatory, for Roosevelt's interest in accommodation with J.P. Morgan & Co. receded as the 1938 elections neared and international tensions grew.

From the mid-1930s onward, as the threat arising from Berlin, Rome, and Tokyo became more exposed, there emerged a rapprochement between J.P. Morgan & Co. and the Roosevelt administration. This was not a coming together of equals; the White House led and the Morgan partners followed. However, the mistaken Morgan analysis of what was driving the revisionist challengers did not help Roosevelt and the State department see with clarity. This criticism, of course, has been made much more generally. A failure to realize the radicalism inherent in Berlin in particular was one of the mistakes many made when contemplating the Nazi regime. It was the discontented, the extremists in the United States and elsewhere, who best understood the true nature of Nazism in power. For the Morgan partners, their certainty that Schacht was a major player proved illusory, rendering more difficult their efforts to maintain loan payments on the Dawes and Young Plan loans. More serious because of the greater Morgan heft with Italy and Japan was the manner in which the Corner downplayed Rome's ambitions and Tokyo's desires. The Morgan view of Italy conformed to Washington's, at least before 1935 and Ethiopia, but even thereafter Morgan policy was animated by a willingness to exculpate Rome's actions. It was only somewhat a question of finance; money mattered but the business the bank did was more considerable with the Vatican than Mussolini's regime. Fummi's representations were at work and there was the hope that longer-term more meaningful business might be done. It helped too that London wished to avoid alienating Il Duce. Japan was different. Lamont made Morgan policy, aided by Egan. His perception, framed by a reliance on a conception of Two Japans birthed in the immediate postwar years, was occluded from 1931 by a mixture of prejudice against China and the murmurings of well-connected liberal-minded friends in Japanese business and political circles. Lamont's gradual turn-away from a rote defence of Japanese actions was actuated by mounting evidence of their aggression, the retirement of Egan, and the influence of Nelson Johnson. On Japan, Lamont was ill-informed but his assessment was not distant from that of the Roosevelt administration, as the similarities between their October 1937 speeches demonstrated.

This theme – growing closeness between the Roosevelt administration and J.P. Morgan & Co. on foreign policy – was amplified through the Neutrality legislation, the Nye hearings, and the recourse in London and Paris to appeasement. War frightened. It frightened the American people, the Morgan partners, and the White House. Associated with the American entry into World War I, proudly so, as Jack Morgan acknowledged, J.P. Morgan laboured under the misapprehension that not only had it conspired to take the United States into war in 1917 but it was manoeuvring to do so again. This charge was baseless. That did not matter. What mattered was that it was believed, at least by enough Americans for it to have traction. What was not realized, save for those who were well informed, was that by 1938 any Morgan influence on the making of American foreign policy was residual. In truth neither London nor Washington paid attention to the Corner in 1938–39. Paris did, at least until the limitations of Morgan willingness to assist it were illustrated graphically in the summer of 1939. After the outbreak of the European war in 1939, war brought the Morgan partners, especially Lamont, even closer to Roosevelt. They helped him when they could and supported his foreign policy loyally.

It has often been remarked how victory in World War II conveyed legitimacy on the Soviet Union, enabling its continuation for decades after 1945. Wartime triumph also aided capitalism, in particular American capitalism. Its triumph against Nazism, against Fascism, and against Japanese imperialism was a massive boost to its prestige. Capitalism and communism, endorsed by war, were able to wage their Cold War in part because of what had transpired between 1939 and 1945. The war gave each renewed strength. Its effects on J.P. Morgan & Co. were perhaps less than might be expected. Jack Morgan died in April 1943. When he did, with the war all-consuming, little notice was taken. This in itself was a verdict on what had befallen the bank. War confirmed the Corner's relative diminution, but this was not exceptional – the growth of the state to prosecute the greatest total war of the twentieth century diminished all else.

However, well before the arrival of the vaunted "dollar year men" embodied the World War II marriage of state power and capitalist pro-ductivity in the United States, a reckoning had transpired. The capitalist crisis of the 1930s had impelled change, especially for the avatars of a discredited order. J.P. Morgan & Co. was not responsible for the Depression but that mattered little; they were believed to be culpable, and consequently were at fault. The Corner in 1940 was emblematic of how American capitalism changed. Financial capitalism of Money Trust legend had passed into the mist. If 23 Wall Street was not the "heart of contemporary capitalism" any longer, both capitalism and the Corner had survived.

Among the many reasons for this mutual survival, one was articulated by Leffingwell:

I believe that J.P. Morgan & Co. have stood for the best things in American life, that they have been a constructive force, and that the reason why they have had such influence as they have had is that people believe in them. I think that that belief has been justified on the whole, and that though J.P. Morgan & Co. are not infallible their influence by and large has been for good in a world of free men.[4]

He went on to attack despotism in its Hitlerian and Stalinist forms. If the hubris is palpable, the assumption of centrality to the American dream off-putting in its arrogance, striking is the deep-seated approbation of American capitalism. It might be thought that elites – and few were more elite than the Morgan partners – should fight for the system that benefits them and nurtures them. That was not always so in the interwar years. Morgan failings were real; their advice often self-interested; their utterances too fixated on the health of the Corner. Yet J.P. Morgan & Co. was faithful to an image of liberal, democratic capitalism. This commitment to American capitalism through crisis was real and was more than could be said of other capitalist elites in other countries during the Depression decade. Unlike some, the Morgan partners did not lift their eyes worshipfully to the rising star of authoritarianism.

[4] Leffingwell to Ernst, 29 February 1940, YUL, RCL, Series I, Box 2, Folder 36.

Appendices

Appendix I J.P. Morgan & Co. & Drexel & Co. Consolidated Statement of Condition, 1927–32.

Consolidated statement of condition J.P. Morgan & Co. and Drexel & Co.

	Dec. 31, 1927	Dec. 31, 1928	Dec. 31, 1929	Jan. 2, 1931	Jan. 2, 1932	Dec. 31, 1932
ASSETS						
Cash on hand and in banks	$44,502,403.03	$42,031,527.67	$59,476,918.24	$67,461,469.73	$44,531,897.66	$33,857,665.95
Call loans	54,320,000.00	109,935,000.00	79,050,000.00	8,425,000.00	21,075,000.00	7,325,000.00
U.S. Government securities	178,152,075.89	113,397,933.76	165,667,994.49	190,739,957.32	110,821,189.69	224,580,150.03
Acceptances of other banks and bankers		14,365,263.59			15,671.20	
State and municipal bonds	163,340,854.03	103,981,950.65	64,577,005.43	82,752,582.41	12,173,741.20	6,745,299.56
Corporate bonds	26,019,843.93	15,789,649.59	7,072,801.18	21,403,738.52	10,031,368.25	15,073,885.29
Corporate stocks	40,989,357.21	68,546,325.22	64,281,479.74	57,822,593.90	22,607,957.56	13,875,028.21
Other investments	9,327,470.73	12,643,341.24	27,631,636.97	124,841.69	471,174.85	810,925.91
Loans:						
Time	86,895,651.70	43,329,916.96	62,771,917.34	66,384,784.73	86,489,535.77	34,836,442.07
Demand	34,671,119.98	39,001,772.81	69,553,613.15	92,232,402.18	55,419,267.26	47,869,164.93
Banking houses	8,309,504.47	8,593,304.12	9,471,304.12	9,471,637.45	9,661,470.78	9,691,304.12
Accrued interest receivable	1,806,637.51	1,698,277.57	1,668,065.44		8,947.60	
Acceptances sold under our guarantee per contra	3,558,751.23	20,681,366.33	18,466,338.56	45,092,618.78		
Customers liability account of acceptances per contra			20,061,175.65	21,854,208.09	21,684,166.75	11,397,271.20
Foreign exchange, per contra	12,398,937.19	35,779,192.53	30,631,698.32	40,143,568.89	37,575,400.15	10,645,958.29
Total	664,292,606.90	629,773,822.06	680,381,938.63	703,909,403.69	432,566,788.70	424,708,095.56
LIABILITIES						
New worth	71,638,314.32	91,555,934.99	118,604,183.75	91,843,140.28	52,959,772.70	53,194,076.80
Deposits	562,406,896.60	481,188,646.91	492,292,666.39	503,898,014.82	319,045,848.57	340,047,701.88
Bills payable	14,000,000.00					
Accrued interest payable	53,965.61	310,989.45	192,027.06	409,639.87	236,842.07	
Acceptances sold under our guarantee, per contra			18,466,338.56	45,092,618.78		
Acceptances payable, per contra	3,800,493.18	20,939,058.18	20,195,024.55	22,522,421.05	22,390,925.23	12,820,358.59
Foreign exchange, per contra	12,398,937.19	35,779,192.53	30,631,698.32	40,143,568.89	37,575,400.13	18,645,958.29
Total	664,292,606.90	629,773,822.06	680,381,938.63	703,909,403.69	432,566,788.70	424,708,095.56

Source: Stock Exchange Practices Hearing, Part I, 23 May 1933. All figures are in dollars.

Appendix II J.P. Morgan & Co. & Drexel & Co. Condensed Statement of Condition, Selected items, 1933–35.

	1 June 1934	31 December 1934	29 June 1935	1 October 1935
Assets				
Cash	59,957,872.67	65,811,081.99	50,340,997.67	135,343,997.68
U.S. Govt. Securities	169,509,469.58	242,117,585.48	255,543,401.89	195,406,676.44
State/Mun. Bonds	10,674,474.58	14,652,403.16	32,449,767.90	19,909,366.06
Stocks & Bonds	20,831,079.84	16,493,376.49	15,690,384.61	17,788,299.65
Loans & Advances	53,280,660.38	34,623,217,57	42,296,537.55	40,698,580.04
Total Assets	344,251,626.53	414,685,768.48	430,366,319.56	447,342,056.00
Liabilities				
Deposits: Demand	224,128,079,22	291,360,914.12	328,663,965.37	356,643,998.29
Deposits: Time	47,695,285.44	46,665,775.69	31,816,346.73	28,920,301.62
Acceptances & Letters	13,591,893.20	20,700,035.46	13,562,833.49	15,193,868.92
Special Reserve Fund	1,000,000	1,000,000	1,000,000	1,000,000
Capital	25,000,000	25,000,000	25,000,000	25,000,000
Surplus & Partners' Balances	32,607,114.90	29,934,133.20	30,268,608.38	20,498,914.98
Liabilities	344,251,626.53	414,685,768.48	430,366,319.56	447,342,056.00

Source: Deutsche Bank Morgan Grenfell Archives, Box 50596681, Folder J.P. Morgan & Co. Inc. Morgan & Cie. balance sheets. All figures are in dollars.

Appendix III J.P. Morgan & Co. & Drexel & Co. Condensed Statement of Condition, Selected items, 1935–39.

	31 December 1935	31 December 1936	31 December 1937	31 December 1938	31 December 1939
Assets					
Cash	105,581,281.60	89,657,159	91,709,065.53	164,137,704	168,631,768.87
US Govt. Securities	317,406,917.97	297,243,312	260,597,362.50	298,529,130	413,891,061.25
State/Mun. Bonds	25,330,933.11	63,318,110	18,724,210.03	53,310,495	37,795,080.57
Stocks & Bonds	15,306,138	14,666,050	11,504,453.13	n/a	6,894,414.74
Loans & Bills	44,300,994.40	50,854,643	48,739,540.38	29,206,993	23,187,065.90
Total Assets	537,943,911.18	550,338,618	457,111,631.96	582,343,544	671,578,699.22
Liabilities					
Deposits: Demand	446,688,151.16	478,922,407	394,997,148.49	521,164,653	619,512,616.65
Deposits: Time*	26,068,725.88				
Accepts. & Letters	16,675,352.39	20,763,467	13,880,909.67	n/a	11,957,194.18
Special Reserve	1,000,000	1,000,000	1,000,000	1,000,000	856,796.42
Capital	25,000,000	25,000,000	25,000,000	25,000,000	20,000,000
Surplus & Partners Balances	22,312,991.08	24,547,588	21,792,980.94	18,988,127	19,156,140.27
Liabilities	537,943,911.18	550,338,618	457,111,631.96	582,343,544	671,578,699.22

Source: Deutsche Bank Morgan Grenfell Archives, Box 50596681, Folder J.P. Morgan & Co. Inc. Morgan & Co. balance sheets. All figures are in dollars.

Appendix IV Distribution of partner shares in J.P. Morgan & Co. Inc.,
29 March 1940.

Partner	Shares	Sum ($)
Jack Morgan	20,000	4.0 million
Thomas W. Lamont	70,625	14.125 million
Junius Morgan	9,750	1.95 million
Whitney	9,500	1.9 million
Leffingwell	17,500	3.5 million
Bartow	5,000	1.0 million
Anderson	6,250	1.25 million
Thomas S. Lamont	2,000	0.4 million
Davison	2,500	0.5 million
Dickey	2,000	0.4 million
Alexander	500	0.1 million
Mitchell	65	$13,000

Source: J. P. Morgan & Co., 29 March 1940, TML, Pierpont Morgan papers, Box 6, Folder 3.

Bibliography

Archival Sources

Arthur Krock papers, Princeton University Library
Bank of England Archives, Bank of England
Carter Glass MSS, University of Virginia Library
Center for Legislative Archives, National Archives, Washington, DC
Columbia Oral History Collection, Columbia University Library
Deutsche Bank Morgan Grenfell papers, Deutsche Bank Morgan Grenfell London
Dwight W. Morrow MSS, Amherst College
Eugene E. Agger papers, Rutgers Special Collections and University Archives
Foreign Office papers, The National Archives UK
Franklin D. Roosevelt papers, Franklin D. Roosevelt Presidential Library
Frederick Lewis Allen papers, Library of Congress
George S. Messersmith papers, University of Delaware Library
Hamilton Fish Armstrong papers, Princeton University Library
Henry Morgenthau Jr. diaries, Franklin D. Roosevelt Presidential Library
Herbert Feis papers, Library of Congress
Herbert Hoover papers, Herbert Hoover Presidential Library
J.P. Morgan Jr. papers, The Morgan Library
Lamont-Corliss Family papers, Smith College
Lord Reading papers, India Office Records, British Library
Lord Rennell of Rodd papers, Bodleian Library, Oxford University
Marriner S. Eccles papers, http://fraser.stlouisfed.org
Morgan Bank European and Argentinian papers, The Morgan Library
Morgan Grenfell MSS, Guildhall Library
Nelson Dean Jay papers, Knox College
Norman H. Davis papers, Library of Congress
Ogden L. Mills papers, Library of Congress
Owen D. Young MSS, St. Lawrence University Library
Pierpont Morgan papers, The Morgan Library
Russell C. Leffingwell MSS, Yale University Library
Stuart M. Crocker papers, Library of Congress

Thomas W. Lamont papers, Baker Library, Harvard University
Vincent Carosso papers, The Morgan Library
Walter Lippmann papers, Yale University Library

Published Documents

Banking and Monetary Statistics, 1914–1941. New York: Board of Governors of the Federal Reserve System, 1943. https://fraser.stlouisfed.org
Budget of the United States Government. Washington, DC: Government Printing Office 2020.
Bureau of the Census. *Historical Statistics of the United States, Vol. 2: Colonial Times to 1970.* Washington, DC: Government Printing Office, 1975. https://fraser.stlouisfed.org/author/united-states-bureau-census#237
Office of the Historian. *Foreign Relations of the United States.* Washington, DC: Government Printing Office. https://history.state.gov/historicaldocuments
Historical Statistics of the United States, Vol. 2: Colonial Times to 1970. United States Bureau of the Census, Series X 510–15, p. 1006, https://fraser.stlouisfed.org/title/historical-statistics-united-states-237/volume-2-5808.
Investigation of Railroads, Holding Companies, and Affiliated Companies [Wheeler Committee]. Subcommittee of the United States Senate Committee on Interstate Commerce, 75th Congress, 1st session, Part 3, 17–18 December 1936, and Part 6, 3–5 March 1937. United States. Washington, DC: Government Printing Office, 1938. https://babel.hathitrust.org/cgi/pt?id=umn.31951d03505331k&view=1up&seq=4&skin=2021
Money Trust Investigation of Financial and Monetary Conditions in the United States [Pujo Committee]. Subcommittee of the Committee on Banking and Currency. United States. Washington, DC: Government Printing Office 1913. https://fraser.stlouisfed.org/title/money-trust-investigation-80?browse=1910s
Monthly Review of Credit and Business Conditions. New York: Federal Reserve Bank of New York.
The Public Papers of Presidents of the United States: Herbert Hoover, 4 vols. 1930. Washington, DC: Government Printing Office, 1974–77.
The Report of the Committee to Investigate the Concentration of Control of Money and Credit. House of Representatives. 62nd Congress, 3rd session. United States. Washington, DC: Government Printing Office, 1913. https://fraser.stlouisfed.org/title/report-committee-appointed-pursuant-house-resolutions-429-504-investigate-concentration-control-money-credit-1329
Sale of Foreign Bonds or Securities in the United States. Hearings before the United States Senate Committee on Finance, 72nd Congress, Part 1, 18–19 and 21 December 1931. United States. Washington, DC: Government Printing Office, 1932. https://fraser.stlouisfed.org/title/sale-foreign-bonds-securities-united-states-398?browse=1930s
Special Committee Investigating the Munitions Industry [Nye Committee]. United States Senate. 74th Congress, 2nd session, Parts 25–29, 7–8, 9–10, 13–14, and 15–16 January 1936, 4–5 February 1936. United States. Washington, DC:

Government Printing Office, 1937. https://catalog.hathitrust.org/Record/000964105

Stock Exchange Practices [Pecora Committee]. Hearings before the Sub-Committee of the United States Senate Committee on Banking and Currency, 73rd Congress, 1st session, Part 1, 23–25 May 1933, Part II, 26 and 31 May 1933, 1–2 and 5–9 June 1933. United States. Washington, DC: Government Printing Office, 1933. https://fraser.stlouisfed.org/title/stock-exchange-practices-87?browse=1930s

Temporary National Economic Committee. 76th Congress, 2nd session, Part 23, 15, 18–19, and 20 December 1939. United States. Washington, DC: Government Printing Office, 1940. https://babel.hathitrust.org/cgi/pt?id=hvd.32044032276537&view=1up&seq=4&skin=2021

United States of America before the Securities and Exchange Commission in the Matter of Richard Whitney, et al. United States. Vols. 1–3. Washington, DC: Government Printing Office, 1938. https://babel.hathitrust.org/cgi/pt?id=uiug.30112059644259&view=1up&seq=7&skin=2021

Newspapers and Journals

American Bankers Association Journal
Christian Science Monitor
Commercial & Financial Chronicle
Forbes
Foreign Affairs
Fortune
Harper's Magazine
The Nation
The New Republic
New York Herald Tribune
New York Times
Saturday Evening Post
Wall Street Journal
Washington Post

Diaries, Memoirs, and Secondary Sources

Accominitti, Olivier. "International Banking and Transmission of the 1931 Financial Crisis." London School of Economics and CEPR, November 2016. https://cepr.org/active/publications/discussion_papers/dp.php?dpno=11651

Agar, Herbert and Allen Tate. *Who Owns America? A New Declaration of Independence*. New York: Houghton Mifflin, 1936.

Aguado, Iago Gil. "The Creditanstalt Crisis of 1931 and the Failure of the Austro-German Customs Union Project." *Historical Journal*, vol. 44, no. 1 (2001), pp. 199–221.

Ahamed, Liaquat. *Lords of Finance: The Bankers Who Broke the World*. New York: Penguin Press, 2009.

Allen, Frederick Lewis. *The Lords of Creation.* New York: Harper Brothers, 1935. [Reprint: Quandrangle Books, 1966.]

Allen, Frederick Lewis. *Only Yesterday.* New York: Harper and Brothers, 1931.

Allen, Frederick Lewis. *Since Yesterday.* New York: Harper and Brothers, 1940.

Allen, Julia M. *Passionate Commitments: The Lives of Anna Rochester and Grace Hutchins.* Albany: State University of New York Press, 2013.

Allen, Robert S. *More Merry-Go-Round, by the Authors of Washington Merry-Go-Round.* New York: Liveright Press, 1932.

Anonymous. *The Mirrors of Wall Street.* New York: G.P. Putnam's & Sons, 1933.

Archer, Jules. *The Plot to Seize the White House.* New York: Hawthorne Books, 1973.

Artaud, Denise. "Reparations and War Debts: The Restoration of French Financial Power, 1919–1929," in Robert Boyce ed. *French Foreign and Defence Policy, 1918–1940.* London: Routledge, 1998, pp. 88–105.

Attack, Jeremy and Peter Passell. *A New Economic View of American History,* 2nd ed. New York: W.W. Norton, 1994.

Awalt, Francis Gloyd. "Recollections of the Banking Crisis of 1933." *Business History Review,* vol. 43, no. 3 (1969), pp. 347–71.

Badger, Anthony. *FDR: The First Hundred Days.* New York: Hill and Wang, 2008.

Barber, William. *From New Era to New Deal: Herbert Hoover, the Economists, and American Economic Policy, 1921–1933.* Cambridge: Cambridge University Press, 1985.

Beckert, Sven. *Empire of Cotton: A Global History.* New York: Alfred A. Knopf, 2014.

Beckhart, Benjamin Haggott. *The New York Money Market,* Vol. 3, ed. Benjamin Haggott Beckhart. New York: Columbia University Press, 1931–32. [Reprint: New York: AMS Press, 1971.]

Beckhart, Benjamin Haggott and James G. Smith. *The New York Money Market,* Vol. 2, ed. Benjamin Haggott Beckhart. New York: Columbia University Press, 1931–32. [Reprint: New York: AMS Press, 1971.]

Bell, Elliott V. "The Decline of the Money Barons," in Hanson W. Baldwin and Shepard Stone eds. *We Saw It Happen: The News behind the News That's Fit to Print.* New York: Simon and Schuster, 1938, pp. 135–67.

Bell, P.M.H. *The Origins of the Second World War in Europe,* 2nd ed. Harlow: Longman, 1997.

Bennett, Edward W. *Germany and the Diplomacy of the Financial Crisis, 1931.* Cambridge, MA: Harvard University Press, 1962.

Benston, George J. *The Separation of Commercial and Investment Banking: The Glass-Steagall Act Revisited and Reconsidered – A Retrospective of the Pecora Committee.* Oxford: Oxford University Press, 1990.

Berle, Beatrice Bishop and Travis Beal Jacobs, eds. *Navigating the Rapids, 1918–1971: From the Papers of Adolf A. Berle.* New York: Harcourt Brace Jovanovich, 1973.

Birmingham, Stephen. *Our Crowd: The Great Jewish Families of New York.* New York: Harper & Row, 1967.

Black, Conrad. *Franklin Delano Roosevelt: Champion of Freedom.* New York: Public Affairs, 2003.

Blower, Brooke. *Becoming Americans in Paris: Transatlantic Politics and Culture between the World Wars.* New York: Oxford University Press, 2011.

Blower, Brooke L. "From Isolationism to Neutrality: A New Framework for Understanding American Political Culture, 1919–1941." *Diplomatic History,* vol. 38, no. 3 (2014), pp. 345–76.

Blumenthal, Henry. *Illusion and Reality in Franco-American Diplomacy 1914–1945.* Baton Rouge, LA: Louisiana State University Press, 1986.

Boemeke, Manfed F., Gerald D. Feldman, and Elisabeth Glaser eds. *The Treaty of Versailles: A Reassessment after 75 Years.* Cambridge: Cambridge University Press, 1998.

Bonin, Hubert and Ferry de Goey, eds. *American Firms in Europe 1880–1980.* Geneva: Librairie Droz, 2009.

Bordo, Michael and John Landon-Lane. "The Banking Panics in the United States in the 1930s: Some Lessons for Today," in Nicholas Crafts and Peter Fearon, eds. *The Great Depression of the 1930s: Lessons for Today.* New York: Oxford University Press, 2013, pp. 188–211.

Borg, Dorothy. *The United States and the Far Eastern Crisis of 1933–1938.* Cambridge, MA: Harvard University Press, 1964.

Boulanger, Renaud. "La question de rapprochement financier et banquier entre la France et les États-Unis a la fin des années 1920. L'entremise de Pierre Quesnay." *Histoire@Politique,* no. 19 (2013).

Boyce, Robert. *British Capitalism at the Crossroads 1919–1932.* Cambridge: Cambridge University Press, 1987.

Boyce, Robert. *The Great Interwar Crisis and the Collapse of Globalization.* London: Palgrave Macmillan, 2009.

Brinkley, Alan. *The End of Reform: New Deal Liberalism in Recession and War.* New York: Vintage Books, 1996.

Brinkley, Alan. *Voices of Protest, Huey Long, Father Coughlin and the Great Depression.* New York: Alfred A. Knopf, 1982.

Brooks, John. *Once in Golconda.* New York: Harper & Row, 1969. [Reprint: New York: John Wiley & Sons 1999.]

Browder, Robert Paul and Thomas G. Smith. *Independent: A Biography of Lewis Douglas.* New York: Alfred A. Knopf, 1986.

Brown, E. Cary. "Fiscal Policy in the Thirties: A Reappraisal." *American Economic Review,* Vol. 46 (1956), pp. 857–79.

Brownlee, W. Elliott. "Russell Cornell Leffingwell," in Larry Schweikart ed. *Encyclopedia of American Business History and Biography, Banking and Finance.* New York: Facts on File, 1990.

Broz, J. Lawrence. *The International Origins of the Federal Reserve System.* Ithaca, NY: Cornell University Press, 1997.

Burk, Kathleen. *Britain, America and the Sinews of War.* London: Allen & Unwin, 1985.

Burk, Kathleen. "The House of Morgan in Financial Diplomacy, 1920–1930," in B.J.C. McKercher ed. *Anglo-American Relations in the 1920s.* Edmonton: University of Alberta Press, 1990, pp. 125–57.

Burk, Kathleen. "A Merchant Bank at War: The House of Morgan 1914–1918," in P.L Cottrell and D.E. Moggridge eds. *Money and Power*. London: Macmillan, 1988, pp. 155–72.

Burk, Kathleen. *Morgan Grenfell 1838–1988*. Oxford: Oxford University Press, 1989.

Burk, Robert E., ed. *The Diary Letters of Hiram Johnson, 1917–1945*, 7 vols. New York: Garland Publishing, 1983.

Burns, Helen. *The American Banking Community and New Deal Banking Reforms 1933–1935*. Westport, CT: Greenwood Press, 1974.

Butler, Michael A. *Cautious Visionary: Cordell Hull and Trade Reform, 1933–1937*. Kent, OH: Kent State University Press, 1998.

Cain, Peter J. and Anthony G. Hopkins. *British Imperialism, 1688–2000*. 2nd ed. Harlow: Longman, 2001.

Cairncross, Alec and Barry Eichengreen. *Sterling in Decline*. Oxford: Basil Blackwell, 1983.

Calomiris, Charles W. and Barry Wilson. "Bank Capital and Portfolio Management: The 1930's Capital Crunch and the Scramble to Shed Risk." *The Journal of Business*, vol. 77, no. 3 (2004), pp. 421–55.

Cannadine, David. *Mellon: An American Life*. New York: Vintage Books, 2008.

Carosso, Vincent P. *Investment Banking in America*. Cambridge, MA: Harvard University Press, 1970.

Carosso, Vincent P. *The Morgans: Private International Bankers 1854–1913*. Cambridge, MA: Harvard University Press, 1987.

Carosso, Vincent P. "The Morgan Houses: The Seniors, Their Partners, and Their Aides," in Joseph R. Frese and Jacob Judd, eds. *American Industrialization, Economic Expansion and the Law*. Tarrytown, NY: Sleepy Hollow Press, 1981, pp. 1–36.

Carosso, Vincent P. "The Wall Street Money Trust from Pujo through Medina." *Business History Review*, vol. 47, no. 4 (1973), pp. 421–37.

Carroll, John W. "Owen D. Young and German Reparations: The Diplomacy of an Enlightened Businessman," in Kenneth Paul Jones ed. *U.S. Diplomats in Europe, 1919–1941*. Santa Barbara, CA: ABC-Clio, 1983, pp. 43–62.

Case, Josephine Young and Everett Needham Case. *Owen D. Young and American Enterprise*. Boston: David R. Godine, 1982.

Cassis, Youssef and Eric Bussières, eds. *London and Paris As International Financial Centres in the Twentieth Century*. Oxford: Oxford University Press, 2005.

Cassis, Youssef and P.L. Cottrell, eds. *Private Banking in Europe: Rise, Retreat and Resurgence*. Oxford: Oxford University Press, 2015.

Chandler, Lester V. *America's Greatest Depression, 1929–1941*. New York: Harper & Row, 1970.

Chandler, Lester V. *Benjamin Strong: Central Banker*. Washington: Brookings Institution, 1958.

Chapman, Herrick. *State Capitalism and Working Class Radicalism in the French Aircraft Industry*. Berkeley, CA: University of California Press, 1991.

Chapman, Stanley. *The Rise of Merchant Banking*. London: George Allen & Unwin, 1984.

Chase, Stuart. "Capital Not Wanted." *Harper's Magazine*, vol. 180 (February 1940).

Chase, Stuart. "Shadow over Wall Street." *Harper's Magazine*, vol. 180 (March 1940).

Chernow, Ron. *The House of Morgan*. New York: Atlantic Monthly Press, 1990.

Childs, Marquis. "They Hate Roosevelt", in Frank Friedel ed. *The New Deal and the American People*. Englewood Cliffs, NJ: Prentice-Hall, 1964, pp. 98–104.

Clarke, Stephen V.O. *Central Bank Cooperation 1924–1931*. New York: Federal Reserve Bank of New York, 1967.

Clavin, Patricia. *The Failure of Economic Diplomacy: Britain, Germany, France, and the United States, 1931–36*. London: Macmillan, 1996.

Clavin, Patricia. "Reparations in the Long Run." *Diplomacy and Statecraft*, vol. 16, no. 3 (2005), pp. 515–30.

Clavin, Patricia. *Securing the World Economy: The Reinvention of the League of Nations, 1920–1946*. Oxford: Oxford University Press, 2013.

Clay, Sir Henry. *Lord Norman*. London: MacMillan & Co., 1957.

Clement, Piet. "'The Touchstone of German Credit': Nazi Germany and the Service of the Dawes and Young Loans." *Financial History Review*, vol. 11, no. 1 (2004), pp. 33–50.

Clements, Kendrick A. *The Life of Herbert Hoover: Imperfect Visionary, 1918–1928*. London: Palgrave Macmillan, 2010.

Cleveland, Harold van B. and Thomas F. Huertas. *Citibank, 1812–1970*. Cambridge, MA: Harvard University Press, 1985.

Cohrs, Patrick. *The Unfinished Peace after World War I*. New York: Cambridge University Press, 2006.

Cole, Wayne S. *Roosevelt and the Isolationists, 1932–1945*. Lincoln, NE: University of Nebraska Press, 1983.

Corey, Lewis. *The House of Morgan*. New York: G. Howard Watt, 1930. [Reprint: New York: AMS, 1969.]

Costigliola, Frank. *Awkward Dominion: American Political, Economic, and Cultural Relations with Europe, 1919–1933*. Ithaca, NY: Cornell University Press, 1984.

Costigliola, Frank C. "Anglo-American Financial Rivalry in the 1920s." *Journal of Economic History*, vol. 37, no. 4 (1977), pp. 911–34.

Coulter, Matthew Ware. *The Senate Munitions Inquiry of the 1930s*. Westport, CT: Greenwood Press, 1997.

Cross, Colin. *Philip Snowden*. London: Barrie and Rockliff, 1966.

Crowcroft, Robert. *The End Is Nigh: British Politics, Power and the Road of the Second World War*. Oxford: Oxford University Press, 2019.

Cull, Nicholas. *Selling War: The British Propaganda Campaign Against American "Neutrality" in World War II*. New York: Oxford University Press, 1995.

Dallek, Robert. *Franklin D. Roosevelt and American Foreign Policy, 1932–1945*. New York: Oxford University Press, 1981.

Davis, Kenneth S. *FDR: The New York Years 1928–1933*. New York: Random House, 1985.

Dawley, Alan. *Changing the World: American Progressives in War and Revolution*. Princeton, NJ: Princeton University Press, 2003.

Dayer, Roberta Allbert. *Finance and Empire: Sir Charles Addis, 1861–1945*. London: Macmillan, 1988.

De Grazia, Victoria. *Irresistible Empire: America's Advance Through Twentieth-Century Europe.* Cambridge, MA: Harvard University Press, 2005.

Dennis, Lawrence. *Is Capitalism Doomed?* New York: Harper Brothers, 1932.

Denton, Sally. *The Plots Against the President: FDR, A Nation in Crisis, and the Rise of the American Right.* New York: Bloomsbury Press, 2012.

Diggins, John P. *Mussolini and Fascism: The View from America.* Princeton, NJ: Princeton University Press, 1972.

Doenecke, Justus D. "U.S. Policy and the European War, 1939–41." *Diplomatic History,* vol. 19, no. 4 (1995), pp. 669–98.

Dulles, John Foster. "Our Foreign Loan Policy." *Foreign Affairs,* vol. 5, no. 1 (1926), pp. 33–48.

Dunlap, Annette B. *Charles Gates Dawes: A Life.* Evanston, IL: Northwestern University Press, 2016.

Eccles, Marriner S. *Beckoning Frontiers.* New York: Knopf, 1951.

Eichengreen, Barry. *Golden Fetters: The Gold Standard and the Great Depression, 1919–1939.* New York: Oxford University Press, 1992.

Eichengreen, Barry. "The Political Economy of the Smoot-Hawley Tariff." NBER Working Paper Series, No. 2001, August 1986.

Eichengreen, Barry. "U.S. Foreign Financial Relations in the Twentieth Century," in Stanley L. Engerman and Robert E. Gallman eds. *The Cambridge Economic History of the United States, Vol. 3: The Twentieth Century.* Cambridge: Cambridge University Press, 2000, pp. 463–504.

Ellwood, David. *The Shock of America: Europe and the Challenge of the Century.* Oxford: Oxford University Press, 2012.

Farley, James A. *Jim Farley's Story: The Roosevelt Years.* New York: Whittlesey House, 1948.

Farnham, Barbara Rearden. *Roosevelt and the Munich Crisis.* Princeton, NJ: Princeton University Press, 1997.

Fearon, Peter. *War, Prosperity and Depression: The U.S. Economy 1917–45.* Lawrence, KS: University Press of Kansas, 1987.

Feiertag, Olivier. "Pierre Quesnay et les réseaux de l'internationisme monétaire en Europe (1919–1937)," in Michel Dumoulin ed. *Les réseaux économiques de la construction européene au XXᵉ siècle.* Bern: Peter Lang, 2004, pp. 331–49.

Fein-Phillips, Kim. *Invisible Hands: The Making of the Conservative Movement from the New Deal to Reagan.* New York: W.W. Norton, 2009.

Feis, Herbert. *Europe: The World's Banker, 1870–1914.* New Haven, CT: Yale University Press, 1930. [Reprint: New York: W.W. Norton, 1965.]

Feldman, Gerald D. "The Reparations Debate." *Diplomacy and Statecraft,* vol. 16, no. 3 (2005), pp. 487–98.

Ferguson, Thomas. "From Normalcy to New Deal." *International Organization,* vol. 38, no. 1 (1984), pp. 41–94.

Ferrell, Robert H. *American Diplomacy in the Great Depression: Hoover-Stimson Foreign Policy, 1929–1933.* New Haven, CT: Yale University Press, 1957.

Field, Alexander J. *A Great Leap Forward: 1930s Depression and U.S. Economic Growth.* New Haven, CT: Yale University Press, 2011.

Findlay, Ronald and Kevin O'Rourke. *Power and Plenty: Trade, War, and the World Economy in the Second Millennium.* Princeton, NJ: Princeton University Press, 2007.

Fischer, Conan. "The Human Price of Reparations." *Diplomacy and Statecraft,* vol. 16, no. 3 (2005), pp. 499–514.

Fischer, Conan. *A Vision of Europe: Franco-German Relations during the Great Depression 1929–1932.* Oxford: Oxford University Press, 2017.

Flandreau, Marc, ed. *Money Doctors: The Experience of International Financial Advising, 1850–2000.* London: Routledge 2003.

Flandreau, Marc, Norbert J. Gaillard, and Ugo Panizza. "Conflicts of Interest, Reputation and the Interwar Debt Crisis: Banksters or Bad Luck." CEPR Discussion Paper Series, No. 7705, 2010.

Forbes, Bertie C. *Men Who Are Making America.* New York: B.C. Forbes Publishing Co., 1917.

Forbes, John Douglas. *J.P. Morgan, Jr. 1867–1943.* Charlottesville, VA: University of Virginia Press, 1981.

Forbes, Neil. "London Banks, the German Standstill Agreements, and 'Economic Appeasement' in the 1930s." *Economic History Review,* 2nd series, vol. 40, no. 4 (1987), pp. 571–87.

Frankenstein, Robert. *Le Prix du réarmement français (1935–1939).* Paris: Publications de la Sorbonne, 1982.

Fraser, Monika Pohle. "Personal and Impersonal Exchange. The Role of Reputation in Banking: Some Evidence from Nineteenth and Early Twentieth Century Banks' Archives," in Philip L. Cottrell, Evan Lange, and Ulf Olsson, eds. *Centres and Peripheries in Banking: The Historical Development of Financial Markets.* Ashgate: Aldershot, 2007, pp. 177–210.

Fraser, Steve. *Every Man a Speculator: A History of Wall Street in American Life.* New York: Harper Perennial Edition, 2006.

Fraser, Steve and Gary Gerstle, eds. *Ruling America: A History of Wealth and Power in a Democracy.* Cambridge, MA: Harvard University Press, 2005.

Freedman, Max, ed. *Roosevelt and Frankfurter: Their Correspondence, 1928–1945.* Boston: Little, Brown, 1967.

Friedel, Frank, ed. *The New Deal and the American People.* Englewood Cliffs, NJ: Prentice Hall, 1964.

Friedman, Milton F. and Anna Jacobson Schwartz. "The Failure of the Bank of the United States: A Reappraisal. A Reply." *Explorations in Economic History,* vol. 23 (1986), pp. 199–204.

Friedman, Milton F. and Anna Jacobson Schwartz. *The Monetary History of the United States 1867–1960.* Princeton, NJ: Princeton University Press, 1963.

Gage, Beverly. *The Day That Wall Street Exploded.* New York: Oxford University Press, 2009.

Galbraith, John Kenneth. *The Great Crash 1929,* 3rd ed. Boston: Houghton Mifflin, 1972.

Gardner, Lloyd C. *Economic Aspects of New Deal Diplomacy.* Madison, WI: University of Wisconsin Press, 1964.

Gay, Edwin F. "The Great Depression." *Foreign Affairs,* vol. 10, no. 4 (1932), pp. 529–40.

Geisst, Charles R. *Deals of the Century: Wall Street, Mergers, and the Making of Modern America.* Hoboken, NJ: John Wiley & Sons, 2004.

Geisst, Charles R. *Undue Influence: How the Wall Street Elite Put the Financial System at Risk.* Hoboken, NJ: John Wiley & Sons, 2005.

Geisst, Charles R. *Wall Street: A History.* New York: Oxford University Press, 1997.

Gellman, Irwin F. *Secret Affairs: Franklin Roosevelt, Cordell Hull and Sumner Welles.* Baltimore, MD: Johns Hopkins University Press, 1995.

Girault, René. *Emprunts russes et investissements français en Russie 1887–1914.* Paris: Librairie Armand Colin, 1973.

Glaser, Elisabeth. "The Making of the Economic Peace," in Manfred F. Boemeke, Gerald D. Feldman, and Elisabeth Glaser eds. *The Treaty of Versailles: A Reassessment after 75 Years.* Washington: German Historical Institute, 1998, pp. 371–400.

Goeschel, Christian. *Mussolini and Hitler: The Forging of the Fascist Alliance.* New Haven, CT: Yale University Press, 2018.

Gomes, Leonard. *German Reparations 1919–1932.* London: Palgrave Macmillan, 2010.

Gooch, John. *Mussolini and His Generals: The Armed Forces and Fascist Foreign Policy, 1922–1940.* Cambridge: Cambridge University Press, 2007.

Goodall, Alex. "U.S. Foreign Relations under Harding, Coolidge, and Hoover: Power and Constraint," in Katherine A.S. Sibley ed. *A Companion to Warren G. Harding, Calvin Coolidge, and Herbert Hoover.* Chichester: John Wiley & Sons, 2014, pp. 53–76.

Gordon, John Steele. *The Great Game: The Emergence of Wall Street As a World Power, 1653–2000.* New York: Touchstone, 2000.

Gorodetsky, Gabriel. *The Maisky Diaries: Red Ambassador to the Court of St. James, 1932–1943.* New Haven, CT: Yale University Press, 2015.

Haight Jr., John McVicar. *American Aid to France 1938–40.* New York: Atheneum, 1970.

Hall, Peter A. and David Soskice, eds. *The Varieties of Capitalism: The Institutional Foundations of Comparative Advantage.* Oxford: Oxford University Press, 2001.

Hamby, Alonzo. *For the Survival of Democracy: Franklin Roosevelt and the World Crisis of the 1930s.* New York: The Free Press, 2004.

Harbaugh, William H. *Lawyer's Lawyer: The Life of John W. Davis.* New York: Oxford University Press, 1973.

Harrison, Richard. "A Neutralization Plan for the Pacific: Roosevelt and Anglo-American Cooperation, 1934–1937." *Pacific Historical Review,* vol. 57, no. 1 (1988), pp. 47–72.

Harwood, Herbert H. *Invisible Giants: The Empires of Cleveland's Van Sweringen Brothers.* Bloomington, IN: Indiana University Press, 2003.

Hart, Bradley W. *Hitler's American Friends.* New York: St. Martin's Press, 2018.

Hawley, Ellis. *The Great War and the Search for a Modern Order: A History of the American People and Their Institutions, 1917–1933.* New York: St. Martin's Press, 1979.

Hawley, Ellis. *The New Deal and the Problem of Monopoly.* Princeton, NJ: Princeton University Press, 1966.

Heinrichs, Waldo H., Jr. *American Ambassador: Joseph C. Grew and the Development of the United States Diplomatic Tradition.* New York: Oxford University Press, 1966.

Herring, George C. *From Colony to Superpower: U.S. Foreign Relations since 1776.* New York: Oxford University Press, 2008.

"High Finance in the 'Twenties: The United Corporation (I)." *Columbia Law Review*, vol. 37, no. 5 (1937), pp. 785–816.

Hinton, Longstreet, John E. Meyer Jr., and Thomas Rodd. *Some Comments about the Morgan Bank.* New York: Morgan Guaranty Trust Company, 1979. [Reprinted 1985.]

Hogan, Michael. *Informal Entente: The Private Structure of Cooperation in Anglo-American Economic Diplomacy, 1918–1928.* Columbia, MO: University of Missouri Press, 1978.

Hogan, Michael. "Thomas W. Lamont and European Recovery: The Diplomacy of Privatism in a Corporatist Age," in Kenneth Paul Jones ed. *U.S. Diplomats in Europe, 1919–1941.* Santa Barbara, CA: ABC-Clio, 1983, pp. 5–24.

Hoover, Herbert. *The Memoirs of Herbert Hoover: The Great Depression, 1929–1941.* New York: Macmillan, 1952.

Horn, Martin. *Britain, France and the Financing of the First World War.* Montreal: McGill-Queen's University Press, 2002.

Horn, Martin. "J.P. Morgan & Co., the House of Morgan and Europe 1933–1939." *Contemporary European History*, 14, no. 4 (2005), pp. 519–38.

Huddleston, Sisley. *In My Time.* New York: E.P. Dutton & Co., 1938.

Hull, Cordell. *The Memoirs of Cordell Hull.* 2 vols. New York: The Macmillan Company, 1948.

Hyman, Sidney. *Marriner S. Eccles.* Palo Alto, CA: Stanford University Press, 1976.

Imlay, Talbot C. *Facing the Second World War: Strategy, Politics and Economics in Britain and France 1938–1940.* Oxford: Oxford University Press, 2003.

Irwin, Douglas A. "From Smoot-Hawley to Reciprocal Trade Agreements: Changing the Course of U.S. Trade Policy in the 1930s," in Michael D. Bordo, Claudia Goldin, and Eugene N. White eds. *The Defining Moment: The Great Depression and the American Economy in the Twentieth Century.* Chicago: University of Chicago Press, 1998, pp. 325–52.

Jackson, Peter. *France and the Nazi Menace: Intelligence and Policy Making, 1933–1939.* Oxford: Oxford University Press, 2000.

Jacobson, Jon. *Locarno Diplomacy, Germany and the West, 1925–29.* Princeton, NJ: Princeton University Press, 1972.

James, Harold. *The End of Globalization: Lessons from the Great Depression.* Cambridge, MA: Harvard University Press, 2001.

Jeansonne, Glen. *The Life of Herbert Hoover: Fighting Quaker 1928–1933.* New York: Palgrave Macmillan, 2012.

Johnson, Arthur M. *Winthrop W. Aldrich: Lawyer, Banker, Diplomat.* Cambridge, MA: Harvard University Press, 1968.

Jones, Jesse. *Fifty Billion Dollars: My Thirteen Years with the RFC 1932–1945.* New York: The Chronicle Company, 1951. [Reprint: New York: De Capo Press, 1975.]

Josephson, Matthew. *The Robber Barons*. New York: Harcourt Brace, 1934.
Joslin, Theodore. *Hoover off the Record*. Garden City, NY: Doubleday, Doran and Company, 1934. [Reprint: Freeport, NY: Books for Libraries Press, 1971.]
Kaiser, David. *No End Save Victory*. New York: Basic Books, 2014.
Kennedy, David. *Freedom from Fear: The American People in Depression and War*. New York: Oxford University Press, 1999.
Kennedy, Susan Estabrook. *The Banking Crisis of 1933*. Lexington, KY: University of Kentucky Press, 1973.
Kershaw, Ian. *Hitler*. 2 vols. London: Allen Lane, 1998–2000.
Keylor, William. "France and the Illusion of American Support, 1919–1940," in Joel Blatt ed. *The French Defeat of 1940: Reassessments*. Providence, RI: Berghahn Books, 1998, pp. 222–44.
Kindleberger, Charles. *The World in Depression*. Rev. ed. Berkeley, CA: University of California Press, 1986.
Klein, Maury. *Rainbow's End: The Crash of 1929*. New York: Oxford University Press, 2001.
Kotz, David M. *Bank Control of Large Corporations in the United States*, Berkeley, CA: University of California Press, 1980.
Kouwenhoven, John A. *Partners in Banking: An Historical Portrait of a Great Private Bank Brown Brothers Harriman & Co. 1818–1968*. New York: Privately Printed, 1968.
Krock, Arthur. *Memoirs*. New York: Funk & Wagnalls, 1968.
Kuisel, Richard. *Seducing the French: The Dilemma of Americanization*. Berkeley, CA: University of California Press, 1993.
Kunz, Diane B. *The Battle for Britain's Gold Standard in 1931*. London: Croom Helm, 1987.
Kynaston, David. *The City of London, Vol. 1: A World of Its Own 1815–1890*. London: Pimlico, 1995.
Kynaston, David. *The City of London, Vol. 2: Golden Years, 1890–1914*. London: Pimlico, 1995.
Lamont, Edward M. *The Ambassador from Wall Street*. Lanham, MD: Madison Books, 1994.
Lamont, Lansing. *A Life in Letters*. New York: Strawtown Press, 1999.
Lamont, Thomas W. *Across World Frontiers*. New York: Harcourt Brace & Co., 1951.
Lamont, Thomas. "The Final Reparations Settlement." *Foreign Affairs*, vol. 8, no. 3 (1930), pp. 336–63.
Lamont, Thomas W. *Henry P. Davison: The Record of a Useful Life*. New York: Harper & Brothers, 1933.
Lamont, Thomas W. *My Boyhood in a Parsonage*. New York: Harper Brothers, 1946.
Langer, William L. and S. Everett Gleason. *The Challenge to Isolation, 1937–1940*. New York: Harper Brothers, 1952
Lasser, William. *Benjamin V. Cohen: Architect of the New Deal*. New Haven, CT: Yale University Press, 2002.
Latham, Earl. *The Politics of Railroad Coordination 1933–1936*. Cambridge, MA: Harvard University Press, 1959.

Lawson, Alan. *A Commonwealth of Hope*. Baltimore, MD: Johns Hopkins University Press, 2006.

Laybourn, Kenneth. *Philip Snowden: A Biography, 1864–1937*. Aldershot: Temple Smith, 1988.

LeClair, Harold, ed. *The Secret Diary of Harold Ickes*. 3 vols. New York: Simon & Schuster, 1953–54.

Leff, Mark H. *The Limits of Symbolic Reform: The New Deal and Taxation, 1933–1939*. Cambridge: Cambridge University Press, 1984.

Leffler, Melvyn P. Leffler. *The Elusive Quest: America's Pursuit of European Stability and French Security, 1919–1933*. Chapel Hill, NC: University of North Carolina Press, 1979.

Leith-Ross, Sir Frederick. *Money Talks: Fifty Years of International Finance*. London: Hutchinson & Co., 1968.

Leuchtenberg, William E. *Franklin D. Roosevelt and the New Deal*. New York: Harper Torchbooks, 1963.

Leuchtenburg, William E. *The Perils of Prosperity*. 2nd ed. Chicago: University of Chicago Press, 1993.

Levy-Leboyer, Maurice. "La capacité financière de la France au début du vingtième siècle," in Maurice Levy-Leboyer ed. *La position internationale de la France*. Paris: École des hautes études en sciences sociales, 1977.

Lewis, Cleona. *America's Stake in International Investments*. Washington, DC: Brookings Institution, 1938.

Long, Huey Pierce. *My First Days in the White House*. Harrisburg, PA: The Telegraph Press, 1935. [Reprint: New York: Da Capo Press, 1972.]

Loucks, Henry. *The Great Conspiracy of the House of Morgan and How to Defeat It*. Watertown, SD: n.p., 1916.

Louria, Margot. *Triumph and Downfall: America's Pursuit of Peace and Prosperity, 1921–1933*. Westport, CT: Greenwood Press, 2001.

Lucia, Joseph L. "The Failure of the Bank of the United States: A Reappraisal." *Explorations in Economic History*, vol. 22 (1985), pp. 402–16.

Lundberg, Ferdinand. *America's Sixty Families*. New York: The Vanguard Press, 1937.

Macdonald, C.A. *The United States, Britain and Appeasement 1936–1939*. New York: St Martin's Press, 1981.

Macher, Flora. "The Austrian Banking Crisis of 1931: A Reassessment." *Financial History Review*, vol. 25, no. 3 (2018), pp. 297–321.

MacKay, Malcolm. *Impeccable Connections: The Rise and Fall of Richard Whitney*. New York: Brick Tower Press, 2011.

MacMillan, Margaret. *Paris 1919*. New York: Random House, 2001.

Mallett, Robert. *Mussolini and the Origins of the Second World War, 1933–1940*. London: Palgrave Macmillan, 2003.

Maney, Patrick. *The Roosevelt Presence*. Berkeley, CA: University of California Press, 1998.

Marcus, Nathan. *Austrian Reconstruction and the Collapse of Global Finance, 1921–1931*. Cambridge, MA: Harvard University Press, 2018.

Marks, Sally. *The Illusion of Peace: International Relations in Europe*. London: Macmillan Press, 1976.

Marks, Sally. "Mistakes and Myths: The Allies, Germany, and the Versailles Treaty, 1918–1921." *Journal of Modern History*, vol. 85, no. 3 (2013), pp. 632–59.

Marks, Sally. "The Myths of Reparation." *Central European History*, vol. 11, no. 3 (1978), pp. 231–55.

Martel, Gordon, ed. *The Origins of the Second World War Reconsidered: The A.J.P. Taylor Debate After Twenty-Five Years*. London: Unwin Hyman, 1986.

Mazower, Mark. *Dark Continent: Europe's Twentieth Century*. New York: Alfred A. Knopf, 1999.

McKercher, B.J.C., ed. *Anglo-American Relations in the 1920s*. Edmonton: University of Alberta Press, 1990.

McNeill, William C. *American Money and the Weimar Republic*. New York: Columbia University Press, 1986.

McQuaid, Kim. "Corporate Liberalism in the American Business Community, 1920–1940." *Business History Review*, vol. 52 (1978), pp. 342–68.

Mehrotra, Ajay K. "Lawyers, Guns and Public Monies: The U.S. Treasury, World War One, and the Administration of the Modern Fiscal State." *Law and History Review*, vol. 28, no. 1 (2010), pp. 173–225.

Meltzer, Allan H. *A History of the Federal Reserve, Vol. 1: 1913–1951*. Chicago: University of Chicago Press, 2003.

Michelman, Irving S. "A Banker in the New Deal: James P. Warburg," [reprinted] in Melvyn Dubofsky and Stephen Burwood eds. *The American Economy during the Great Depression*. New York: Garland, 1990, pp. 181–205.

Michie, Ranald C. "The City of London As a Global Financial Centre, 1880–1939: Finance, Foreign Exchange, and the First World War," in Philip L. Cottrell, Evan Lange, and Ulf Olsson eds. *Centres and Peripheries in Banking: The Historical Development of Financial Markets*. Ashgate: Aldershot, 2007, pp. 41–80.

Migone, Gian Giacomo. *The United States and Fascist Italy: The Rise of American Finance in Europe*, trans. Molly Tambor. New York: Cambridge University Press, 2015.

Moe, Richard. *Roosevelt's Second Act: The Election of 1940 and the Politics of War*. New York: Oxford University Press, 2013.

Moley, Raymond. *After Seven Years*. New York: Harper & Brothers, 1939.

Moley, Raymond. *The First New Deal*. New York: Harcourt, Brace & World, 1966.

Morewood, Steven. "'This Silly African Business': The Military Dimension of Britain's Response to the Abyssinia Crisis," in G. Bruce Strang ed. *Collision of Empires: Italy's Invasion of Ethiopia and Its International Impact*. London: Ashgate, 2013, pp. 73–108.

Morris, Charles R. *A Rabble of Dead Money: The Great Crash and the Global Depression, 1929–1939*. New York: Public Affairs, 2017.

Morrow, Dwight. "Who Buys Foreign Bonds." *Foreign Affairs*, vol. 5, no. 2 (1927), pp. 219–32.

Moser, John E. *Right Turn: John T. Flynn and the Transformation of American Liberalism*. New York: New York University Press, 2005.

Myers, Margaret. *The New York Money Market*, Vol. 1, ed. Benjamin Haggott Beckhart. New York: Columbia University Press, 1931–32. [Reprint New York: AMS Press, 1971.]

Namikas, Lise A. "The Committee to Defend America and the Debate between Internationalists and Interventionists, 1939–1941." *The Historian*, vol. 61, no. 4 (1999).

Nelson, Mark Wayne. *Jumping the Abyss: Marriner S. Eccles and the New Deal, 1933–1940*. Salt Lake City, UT: University of Utah Press, 2017.

Nicolson, Harold. *Diaries and Letters, 1930–1939*, ed. Nigel Nicolson. London: Collins, 1966.

Nicolson, Harold. *Dwight Morrow*. New York: Harcourt, Brace, 1935.

Noakes, Jeremy J. and Geoffrey Pridham eds. *Nazism, 1919–1945: A History in Documents and Eyewitness Accounts*. 2 vols. New York: Schocken Books, 1988.

Nolan, Mary. *Visions of Modernity: American Business and the Modernization of Germany*. New York: Oxford University Press, 1994.

Nord, Philip. *France 1940: Defending the Republic*. New Haven, CT: Yale University Press, 2015.

Nouailhat, Yves-Henri. *France et États-Unis: août 1914–avril 1917*. Paris: Sorbonne, 1979.

Noyes, Alexander Dana. *The Market Place*. Boston: Little, Brown and Company, 1938.

Obstfeld, Michael and Alan M. Taylor. *Global Capital Markets: Integration, Crisis, and Growth*. Cambridge: Cambridge University Press, 2004.

O'Brien, Anthony Patrick. "The Failure of the Bank of the United States: A Defense of Joseph Lucia." *Journal of Money, Credit, and Banking*, vol. 24, no. 3 (1992), pp. 374–84.

O'Connor, J.F.T. *The Banking Crisis and Recovery under the Roosevelt Administration*. Chicago: 1938. [Reprint: New York: Da Capo, 1971.]

Offner, Avner. "William E. Dodd: Romantic Historian and Diplomatic Cassandra." *The Historian*, vol. 24, no. 4 (1962), pp. 451–69.

Olson, James Stuart. *Herbert Hoover and the Reconstruction Finance Corporation, 1931–1933*. Ames, IA: Iowa State University Press, 1977.

Overacker, Louise. "American Government and Politics: Campaign Funds in a Depression Year." *The American Political Science Review*, vol. 27, no. 5 (1933), pp. 769–83.

Pak, Susie J. *Gentleman Bankers: The World of J.P. Morgan*. Cambridge, MA: Harvard University Press, 2013.

Parker, R.A.C. *Chamberlain and Appeasement: British Policy and the Coming of the Second World War*. New York: St. Martin's Press, 1993.

Parrini, Carl. *Heir to Empire: United States Economic Diplomacy 1916–1923*. Pittsburgh, PA: University of Pittsburgh Press, 1969.

Parrish, Michael. *Securities Regulation and the New Deal*. New Haven, CT: Yale University Press, 1970.

Pash, Sidney. *The Currents of War: A New History of American-Japanese Relations, 1899–1941*. Lexington, KY: University Press of Kentucky, 2014.

Patel, Kiran Klaus. *The New Deal: A Global History*. Princeton, NJ: Princeton University Press, 2016.

Pautz, Michelle. "The Decline in Weekly Cinema Attendance." *Issues in Political Economy*, vol. 11 (2002), pp. 54–65.

Pecora, Ferdinand. *Wall Street Under Oath*. New York: Simon & Schuster, 1939.

Pensiero, Luca and Romain Restout. "The Gold Standard and the Great Depression: A Dynamic General Equilibrium Model." *Institut de Recherches Économiques et Sociales de l'Université catholique de Louvain*, Discussion paper, 3 December 2018.

Perino, Michael. *The Hellhound of Wall Street: How Ferdinand Pecora's Investigation of the Great Crash Forever Changed American Finance*. New York: Penguin Press, 2010.

Peterecz, Zoltán. *Jeremiah Smith Jr. and Hungary, 1924–1926: The United States, the League of Nations, and the Financial Reconstruction of Hungary*. London: Versita, 2013.

Phillips, Randolph. "The House of Morgan: The Price of Its War and Post-War Policies." *The Nation*, vol. 148, no. 24, 25 (10 and 17 June 1939)

Phillips, Ronnie J. "The Chicago Plan and New Deal Banking Reform." Levy Institute, Working Paper No. 76, June 1992. www.levyinstitute.org/pubs/wp/76.pdf.

Pollard, John F. *Money and the Rise of the Modern Papacy: Financing the Vatican, 1850–1950*. Cambridge: Cambridge University Press, 2005.

Pollard, John F. "The Vatican and the Wall Street Crash: Bernardino Nogara and Papal Finances in the Early 1930s." *Historical Journal*, vol. 42, no. 4 (1999), pp. 1077–91.

Pound, Arthur and Samuel Taylor Moore, eds. *They Told Barron*. New York: Harper Brothers, 1930.

Prins, Nomi. *All the Presidents' Bankers*. New York: Nation Books, 2014.

Pulling, Edward ed. *Selected Letters of R.C. Leffingwell*. Oyster Bay, NY: Privately Printed, 1979.

Rauchway, Eric. *Winter War: Hoover, Roosevelt and the First Clash over the New Deal*. New York: Basic Books, 2018.

Reagan, Patrick. "Business," in William D. Pederson ed. *A Companion to Franklin D. Roosevelt*. Oxford: Wiley-Blackwell, 2011, pp. 186–205.

Reynolds, David. "1940: Fulcrum of the Twentieth Century?" *International Affairs*, vol. 66, no. 2 (1990), pp. 325–50.

Reynolds, David. *The Creation of the Anglo-American Alliance, 1937–1941: A Study in Competitive Cooperation*. Chapel Hill, NC: University of North Carolina, 1981.

Rhodes, Benjamin D. "Reassessing Uncle Shylock: The United States and the French War Debt, 1917–1929." *The Journal of American History*, vol. 55, no. 4 (1969), pp. 787–803.

Richardson, Gary and Patrick Van Horn. "Intensified Regulatory Scrutiny and Bank Distress in New York City During the Great Depression." *Journal of Economic History*, vol. 69, no. 2 (2009), pp. 446–65.

Richardson, Gary and Patrick Van Horn. "When the Music Stopped: Transatlantic Contagion During the Financial Crisis of 1931." NBER, Working Paper No. 17437, September 2011.

Ritchie, Donald. *Electing FDR: The New Deal Campaign of 1932*. Lawrence, KS: University Press of Kansas, 2007.

Ritchie, Donald. "The Legislative Impact of the Pecora Investigation." *Capitol Studies*, vol. 5, no. 2 (1977), pp. 87–101.

Roberts, Priscilla. "'The Council Has Been Your Creation': Hamilton Fish Armstrong, Paradigm of the American Foreign Policy Establishment?" *Journal of American Studies*, vol. 35, no. 1 (2001), pp. 65–94.

Roberts, Priscilla. "The Anglo-American Theme: American Visions of an Atlantic Alliance 1914–1933." *Diplomatic History*, vol. 21, no. 3 (1997), pp. 333–64.

Robinson, Henry M. "Are American Loans Abroad Safe?" *Foreign Affairs*, vol. 5, no. 1 (1926), pp. 49–56.

Rochester, Anna. *Rulers of America: A Study of Finance Capital.* New York: International Publishers, 1936.

Rock, William R. *Chamberlain and Roosevelt: British Foreign Policy and the United States, 1937–1940.* Columbus, OH: Ohio State University Press, 1988.

Roi, Michael L. "'A Completely Immoral and Cowardly Attitude': The British Foreign Office, American Neutrality and the Hoare-Laval Plan." *Canadian Journal of History*, vol. 29, no. 2 (1994), pp. 333–51.

Romasco, Albert U. *The Poverty of Abundance: Hoover, the Nation and the Great Depression.* New York: Oxford University Press, 1965.

Roose, Kenneth D. *The Economics of Recession and Revival: An Interpretation of 1937–38.* New Haven, CT: Yale University Press, 1954.

Roosevelt, Elliott, ed. *FDR: His Personal Letters.* 4 vols. New York: Duell, Sloan and Pearce, 1947–50.

Rosen, Elliot A. *Hoover, Roosevelt and the Brains Trust.* New York: Columbia University Press, 1977.

Rosen, Elliot A. *The Republican Party in the Age of Roosevelt.* Charlottesville, VA: University of Virginia Press, 2014.

Rosenberg, Emily S. *Financial Missionaries to the World: The Politics and Culture of Dollar Diplomacy,* Cambridge, MA: Harvard University Press, 1999.

Rottenberg, Dan. *The Man Who Made Wall Street: Anthony Drexel and the Rise of Modern Finance.* Philadelphia, PA: University of Pennsylvania Press, 2001.

Rudolph, Frederick. "The American Liberty League, 1934–1940." *The American Historical Review*, vol. 56, no. 1 (1950).

Sayers, R.S. *The Bank of England 1891–1944,* 3 vols. Cambridge: Cambridge University Press, 1976.

Schlesinger, Arthur M., Jr. *The Coming of the New Deal, 1919–1933.* Boston: Houghton Mifflin Company, 1959.

Schlesinger, Arthur M., Jr. *The Crisis of the Old Order, 1919–1939.* Boston: Houghton Mifflin Company, 1957.

Schlesinger, Arthur M., Jr. *The Politics of Upheaval.* Boston: Houghton Mifflin Company, 1960.

Schmitz, David F. *The United States and Fascist Italy 1922–1940.* Chapel Hill, NC: University of North Carolina Press, 1988.

Schuker, Stephen. "American Foreign Policy and the Young Plan, 1929," in Gustav Schmidt ed., *Konstellationen Internationaler Politik 1924–1932.* Bochum: N. Brockmeyer, 1983, pp. 122–30.

Schuker, Stephen. *American Reparations to Germany: Implications for the Third-World Debt Crisis.* Princeton, NJ: Princeton University Press, 1988.

Schuker, Stephen. *The End of French Predominance in Europe.* Chapel Hill, NC: University of North Carolina Press, 1976.

Schuker, Stephen. "Leffingwell, Russell Cornell," in John A. Garraty ed. *Dictionary of American Biography,* supplement 6, 1956–60. New York: Charles Scribner's & Sons, 1990.

Schwartz, Jordan A. *The Interregnum of Despair, Hoover, Congress and the Depression.* Urbana: University of Illinois Press, 1970.

Schwartz, Jordan A. *The Speculator: Bernard M. Baruch in Washington.* Chapel Hill, NC: University of North Carolina Press, 1981.

Self, Robert. *Britain, America and the War Debt Controversy: The Economic Diplomacy of an Unspecial Relationship, 1917–1941.* London: Routledge, 1988.

Seligman, Joel. *The Transformation of Wall Street: A History of the Securities and Exchange Commission and Modern Corporate Finance.* Boston: Houghton Mifflin, 1982.

Sharp, Alan. *The Versailles Settlement: Peacemaking After the First World War,* 2nd ed. London: Palgrave Macmillan, 2008.

Siegel, Jennifer. *For Peace and Money: French and British Finance in the Service of Tsars and Commissars.* Oxford: Oxford University Press, 2014.

Silverman, Daniel P. *Reconstructing Europe after the Great War.* Cambridge, MA: Harvard University Press, 1982.

Simmons, Beth A. "Why Innovate? Founding the Bank for International Settlements." *World Politics,* vol. 45, no. 3 (1993), pp. 361–405.

Skidelsky, Robert. *John Maynard Keynes, Vol. 2: The Economist As Saviour.* London: Macmillan, 1992.

Skidelsky, Robert. *Politicians and the Slump.* London: MacMillan, 1967.

Smith, Rixey and Norman Beasley. *Carter Glass: A Biography.* New York: Longmans, Green and Co., 1939.

Smith, Robert Freeman. "Thomas Lamont: International Banker As Diplomat," in Thomas J. McCormack and Walter LaFeber eds. *Behind the Throne: Servants of Power to Imperial Presidents, 1898–1968.* Madison, WI: University of Wisconsin Press, 1993, pp. 101–25.

Sobel, Robert. *The Big Board: A History of the New York Stock Market.* New York: The Free Press, 1965.

Sobel, Robert. *The Great Bull Market: Wall Street in the 1920's.* New York: Norton, 1968.

Steiner, Zara. *The Lights That Failed: European International Relations 1919–1933.* Oxford: Oxford University Press, 2005.

Steiner, Zara. *The Triumph of the Dark: European International History 1933–1939.* Oxford: Oxford University Press, 2011.

Steel, Ronald. *Walter Lippmann and the American Century.* New Brunswick, NJ: Transaction Publishers, 1999.

Strang, G. Bruce. "'A Sad Commentary on World Ethics': Italy and the United States during the Ethiopian Crisis," in G. Bruce Strang ed. *Collision of Empires: Italy's Invasion of Ethiopia and Its International Impact.* London: Ashgate, 2013, pp. 135–63.

Strouse, Jean. *Morgan: American Financier.* New York: Random House, 1999.

Swaine, Robert T. *The Cravath Firm and Its Predecessors, 1819–1948*, 3 vols. New York: Privately Printed, 1948.

Swing, Raymond. *Good Evening: A Professional Memoir*. New York: Harcourt, Brace & World, 1964.

Tabarrok, Alexander. "The Separation of Commercial and Investment Banking: The Morgans vs. The Rockefellers." *The Quarterly Journal of Austrian Economics*, vol. 1, no. 1 (1998), pp. 1–16.

Temin, Peter. "The Great Depression," in Stanley L. Engerman and Robert E. Gallman eds. *The Cambridge Economic History of the United States, Vol. 3: The Twentieth Century*. Cambridge: Cambridge University Press, 2000, pp. 301–28.

Temin, Peter. *Lessons from the Great Depression*. Cambridge, MA: MIT Press, 1989.

Thomas, Martin. "France and the Czechoslovak Crisis." *Diplomacy and Statecraft*, vol. 10, no. 2 (1999), pp. 122–59.

Thomas, Martin. "France and the Ethiopian Crisis, 1935–1936: Security Dilemmas and Adjustable Interests," in G. Bruce Strang ed. *Collision of Empires: Italy's Invasion of Ethiopia and Its International Impact*. London: Ashgate, 2013, pp. 109–34.

Tomita, Toshiki. "Direct Underwriting of Government Bonds by the Bank of Japan in the 1930s." NRI Research Papers, No. 94, September 2005.

Toniolo, Giovanni. *Central Bank Cooperation at the Bank for International Settlements, 1930–1973*. Cambridge: Cambridge University Press, 2005.

Tooze, Adam. *The Deluge: The Great War and the Remaking of Global Order, 1916–1931*. London: Allen Lane, 2014.

Tooze, Adam. *The Wages of Destruction: The Making and Breaking of the Nazi Economy*. London: Allen Lane, 2006.

Trachtenberg, Marc. *Reparation in World Politics: France and European Economic Diplomacy, 1916–1923*. New York: Columbia University Press, 1980.

Trescott, Paul B. "The Failure of the Bank of the United States, 1930: A Rejoinder to Anthony Patrick O'Brien." *Journal of Money, Credit, and Banking*, vol. 24, no. 3 (1992), pp. 384–99.

Ullrich, Volker. *Hitler, Vol. 1: Ascent*. London: Vintage, 2016.

Velde, François R. "The Recession of 1937: A Cautionary Tale." *Economic Perspectives (Federal Reserve Bank of Chicago)*, vol. 33, no. 4 (2009), pp. 16–37.

Vieth, Jane Karoline. "Joseph P. Kennedy and British Appeasement: The Diplomacy of a Boston Irishman," in Kenneth Paul Jones ed. *U.S. Diplomats in Europe, 1919–1941*. Santa Barbara, CA: ABC-CLIO, 1983, pp. 165–82.

Walker, W.M. "J.P. The Younger." *American Mercury*, vol. 40, no. 42 (1927).

Wapshott, Nicholas. *The Sphinx: Franklin Roosevelt, the Isolationists, and the Road to World War II*. New York: W.W. Norton, 2015.

Warren, Donald. *Radio Priest: Charles Coughlin, the Father of Hate Radio*. New York: The Free Press, 1996.

Warren, Harris Gaylord. *Herbert Hoover and the Great Depression*. New York: Oxford University Press, 1959. [Reprint: Westport, CT: Greenwood Press 1980.]

Warren, Kenneth. *Big Steel: The First Century of the United States Steel Corporation.* Pittsburgh, PA: University of Pittsburgh Press, 2001.

Watt, Donald. "Roosevelt and Chamberlain: Two Appeasers." *International Journal,* vol. 28, no. 2 (1973).

Weed, Clyde P. *The Nemesis of Reform: The Republican Party during the New Deal.* New York: Columbia University Press, 1994.

Weed, Clyde P. *The Transformation of the Republican Party, 1912–1936: From Reform to Resistance.* Boulder, CO: Lynne Rienner Publishers, 2011.

Weems, F. Carrington. *America and Munitions: The Work of Messrs. J.P. Morgan & Co. in the World War,* 2 vols. New York: Privately Printed, 1923.

White, Eugene N. "Banking and Finance in the Twentieth Century," in Stanley L. Engerman and Robert E. Gallman eds. *The Cambridge Economic History of the United States, Vol. 3: The Twentieth Century.* Cambridge: Cambridge University Press, 2000, pp. 743–802.

White, Eugene Nelson. *The Regulation and Reform of the American Banking System, 1900–1929.* Princeton, NJ: Princeton University Press, 1983.

Wicker, Elmus. *The Banking Panics of the Great Depression.* New York: Cambridge University Press, 1996.

Wicker, Elmus. *The Great Debate on Banking Reform: Nelson Aldrich and the Origins of the Fed.* Columbus, OH: Ohio State University Press, 2005.

Wigmore, Barry. *The Crash and Its Aftermath: A History of Securities Markets in the United States, 1929–1933.* Westport, CT: Greenwood Press, 1985.

Williams, T. Harry. *Huey Long.* New York: Alfred A. Knopf, 1969.

Williams, William Appleman. "The Legend of Isolationism in the 1920s." *Science and Society,* vol. 18, no. 1 (1954), pp. 1–20.

Williams, William Appleman. *The Tragedy of American Diplomacy,* 2nd ed. New York: Delta, 1962.

Williamson, Philip. "'A Banker's Ramp'? Financiers and the British Political Crisis of August 1931." *English Historical Review,* vol. 49 (1984), pp. 770–806.

Williamson, Philip. *National Crisis and National Government.* Cambridge: Cambridge University Press, 1992.

Wilkins, Mira. *The Maturing of Multinational Enterprise: American Business Abroad, 1914–1970.* Cambridge, MA: Harvard University Press, 1974.

Wilson, John Donald. *The Chase: The Chase Manhattan Bank, 1945–1985.* Cambridge, MA: Harvard Business School Press, 1986.

Wilson, Joan Hoff. *American Business and Foreign Policy 1920–1933.* Lexington, KY: University Press of Kentucky, 1971.

Wiltz, John E. *In Search of Peace: The Senate Munitions Inquiry, 1934–36.* Baton Rouge, LA: Louisiana State University Press, 1963.

Wolfskill, George. *The Revolt of the Conservatives: A History of American Liberty League, 1934–1940.* Boston: Houghton Mifflin, 1962.

Zelizer, Julian E. "The Forgotten Legacy of the New Deal: Fiscal Conservatism and the Roosevelt Administration, 1933–1938." *Presidential Studies Quarterly,* vol. 30, no. 2 (2000), pp. 331–58.

Index